More than Blood
Today's Reality and Tomorrow's Vision of Family

SHERILYN R. MARROW   DENNIS A. V. LEOUTSAKAS

Cover image © Shutterstock, Inc.

Kendall Hunt
publishing company

www.kendallhunt.com
Send all inquiries to:
4050 Westmark Drive
Dubuque, IA 52004-1840

Copyright © 2013 by Sherilyn R. Marrow and Dennis A.V. Leoutsakas

ISBN 978-0-7575-9796-1

Kendall Hunt Publishing Company has the exclusive rights to reproduce this work,
to prepare derivative works from this work, to publicly distribute this work,
to publicly perform this work and to publicly display this work.

All rights reserved. No part of this publication may be reproduced,
stored in a retrieval system, or transmitted, in any form or by any means,
electronic, mechanical, photocopying, recording, or otherwise,
without the prior written permission of the copyright owner.

Printed in the United States of America
10 9 8 7 6 5 4 3 2 1

Contents

Preface ix

Contributors xiii

About the Authors xxiii

Part 1. The Foundation 1

Chapter 1 On the Threshold: Evotypical Families Talk Themselves Into Being 2

Kathleen M. Galvin, *Northwestern University*

Chapter 2 More Than Blood: Rethinking Identities, Interactions, and the Future of Contemporary Families 6

Sherilyn Marrow, *University of Northern Colorado*
Dennis Leoutsakas, *Salisbury University*

Part 2. Communication Perspectives 25

Chapter 3 Family Stories: Communicative Values, Interactions, and Burdens 26

Dennis Leoutsakas, *Salisbury University*

Chapter 4 The Family that Inks Together, Links Together: Tattoos as Family Identifiers 36

Thomas G. Endres, *University of Northern Colorado*

Chapter 5 Appreciative Inquiry as a Model for Strengths-Based Decision Making in Couples and Families 49

Deborah Ballard-Reisch, *Wichita State University*

Chapter 6 Forgiveness and Reconciliation: Infidelity as a Case Study   60

Douglas Kelley, *Arizona State University*

Chapter 7 Decision Making in Dual-Career Couples: A Replication and Extension   70

Douglas C. Pennington, *Lynn Haven United Methodist Church, Panama City, Florida*
Lynne M. Webb, *University of Arkansas*

Part 3. Emergence of Evotypical Families   83

Chapter 8 The Communicative Effort of Negotiating Unmarried Family Life: Friction and Flexibility   84

Jay Baglia, *DePaul University*
Elissa Foster, *DePaul University*

Chapter 9 Living with a Ghost: Managing Memory in Postbereaved Families   95

Christine E. Kiesinger, *George Washington University*

Chapter 10 State Disciplinary Practices and the Emergence of Coparenting Families   104

Lynn Comerford, *California State University, East Bay*

Chapter 11 Single Family: Expanding Our Understanding   114

Tiffani Baldwin, *University of Denver*

Chapter 12 Speaking About Coupleness: Relational Roles in the Conversations of Gay and Lesbians   123

Brian L. Heisterkamp, *California State University, San Bernardino*

Chapter 13 "Not 16 Anymore": Identification Challenges of Teen Parents   133

Karen E. Cirulis, *University of Nebraska at Omaha, Omaha Public Schools*

Chapter 14 Interracial and Interethnic Families   141

Francis Wardle, *Red Rocks Community College*

Chapter 15 (Not) Talking About Race and Difference in Visibly Adoptive Families   152

Sara Docan-Morgan, *University of Wisconsin–La Crosse*

Part 4. Family Experiences from a Distance 163

Chapter 16 On the Evolution of Togetherness and Living with Two Hearts 164

Vinita Agarwal, *Salisbury University*
Suchitra Shenoy, *De Paul University*

Chapter 17 Family Relationships as More Than Blood: Military Families as Dialectics and Discourses 174

Erin Sahlstein, *University of Nevada–Las Vegas*
Katheryn C. Maguire, *Wayne State University*

Chapter 18 Ex-Prisoners Are Coming Home: A Reentry Court's Family Focus 183

Jeralyn Faris, *Purdue University*

Chapter 19 Family as an Academic Motivator for African American and Ghanaian Students' University Attendance 192

Eletra S. Gilchrist, *University of Alabama*

Part 5. Families in Grief and Loss 213

Chapter 20 The Boundary Management and Family Identity Issues in Postbereavement Remarried Families 214

Carrie L. West, *University of Denver*

Chapter 21 The Life of a "Twinkie": Performing Race as a Korean Adoptee 224

Gina Bacon, *University of Utah*

Chapter 22 Obstacle or Opportunity? Reflections on Rhetorical Resilience Following Family Crises 234

Sherilyn Marrow, *University of Northern Colorado*
Nancy J. Karlin, *University of Northern Colorado*
Betty Burdorff Brown, *University of Northern Colorado*

Part 6. Physical and Mental Health Considerations in the Family   255

Chapter 23 Reframing Addiction   256
Nicholas Fittante, *A.C.T. Family Counseling, Ontario, California*
Dennis Leoutsakas, *Salisbury University*

Chapter 24 When Family Blood Kills: Reflections on the Criminal Dangers of Confused Family Allegiances   264
Brad Goldschmidt, *University of Northern Colorado/Greeley, Colorado, Police Department*

Chapter 25 Intimacy and Connection: Parents Being Challenged from a Child's Disability   271
Stacy L. Carter, *Texas Tech University*
Narissra Maria Punyanunt-Carter, *Texas Tech University*

Chapter 26 A "Sounding Board and a Safety Net:" Privacy Boundary Management between Adolescents with Insulin-Dependent Diabetes and Their Parents   278
Jeanette Valenti, *University of Denver*

Chapter 27 Defining Caregiving Relationships: Using Intergenerational Ambivalence Theory to Explore Burden Among Racial and Ethnic Groups   289
Angela C. Henderson, *University of Northern Colorado*

Chapter 28 Implications of Family Communication on Nutritional Health and Obesity of Children   304
Wanda Koszewski, *University of North Dakota*

Part 7. Family Ties and Influences   313

Chapter 29 The Impact of Communication Technology on the Family   314
Cheryl Pawlowski, *University of Northern Colorado*

Chapter 30 The "Plugged-In" Family: The Dialectics of Digital Technology in the Everyday Life of Families   322
Charles Soukup, *University of Northern Colorado*

Chapter 31 Pathways to Marital Satisfaction in Interfaith and Interracial Marriages   332

Patrick C. Hughes, *Texas Tech University*
John R. Baldwin, *Illinois State University*
Bolanle Olaniran, *Texas Tech University*

Chapter 32 Mother and Daughter-in-Law Relationships: For Better or for Worse?   341

Paul Yelsma, *Western Michigan University*

Chapter 33 "I Want to Be a Marcks": Generativity in Relationships between Uncles and Nephews   353

David E. Weber, *University of North Carolina–Wilmington*

Chapter 34 Navigating a Mother–Daughter Relationship   366

K. T. Aldridge, *University of Northern Colorado*

Chapter 35 Media Depictions of Adoption Narratives   372

Beth M. Waggenspack, *Virginia Tech University*

Chapter 36 From Isolation to Connection: Former Sex Workers Conceptualize Family and Familial Interactions   386

Jennifer Mayer, *University of North Texas*
Brian K. Richardson, *University of North Texas*

Chapter 37 Mothering at the Boundaries: When Relative Being is More Important Than Being a Relative   398

Deborah Eicher-Catt, *Pennsylvania State University–York*

Epilogue   408

Preface

We appreciate your curiosity about the "More Than Blood" family. As your editors, we share that curiosity, leading to a book of readings that collectively showcases some of the many fascinating aspects of the "new," or what we call the "evotypical," family. We consider ourselves passionate scholars of family interaction and have both enjoyed several decades of hard work and rewards that accompany such roles. We feel honored to have written and compiled many interesting chapters for you to read, reread, and reflect on long after the last page is turned.

The research represented on the following pages has been crafted by excellent and well-respected authors from numerous fields of study (i.e. communication, family science, psychology, social work, counseling, mental health, law enforcement, and sociology). Their works are professionally solid and personally heartfelt, reflecting a genuine standard of excellence about what they do.

Please know that this reader, as with evotypical family research, is in its infancy. The parts and chapters within the book attempt to capture some of the research related to family dynamics at work within U.S. society today. We are under no illusion, thinking that we have captured all the research for every form of evotypical family, nor do we expect the content of this book to remain static. Family expectations and dynamics are changing and will continue to do so at a rapid pace; we capture only a moment in time. This does not mean that sometime in the distant future, family conceptualizations and standards once adhered to will not resurface, but they do not hold true for now and may never again.

Even though your editors did not know each other before taking on this project more than two years ago, we are proof that, through technology and patience, productivity and relationships can happen. Not surprisingly, the book took longer to write than expected. Much like families, unforeseen life situations and circumstances occurred that kept us "loose" with our publisher, Kendall/Hunt. Broken bones, relocations, promotions, marriages, births, deaths, divorces, chemotherapy, murder conviction of a guilty party, and global travel, to name a few situations, all took place during the book's production. But neither our publishers nor our contributing authors ever gave up in believing in the value of this reader. Kind of like within the family, a "stick-to-it" mentality eventually triumphed.

The basic underlying philosophy we hold true in this reader is that the family is perpetuated in "expression." It is our sincere hope that the findings in these chapters spark provocative discussions among readers. We ask that you invite conversation, dialogue, debate, comment, or, at the very least, a brief "nod" of understanding. In doing so, you will provide new energy to the overall family system conversations through your opinions, validations, or disagreements.

Organizational Design

Rationale

More Than Blood: Today's Reality and Tomorrow's Vision of Family is a research-driven, dynamic reader that features current family communication research about interpersonal behaviors and practices of understudied contemporary families. Evolving relational patterns and interactions in families that are now considered "common" are discussed throughout this edited volume. Each chapter features a specific family constellation and its defining interactions that have arisen to prevalence in contemporary Western society Following each chapter are discussion questions designed to provoke conversation and highlight the inherent challenges and possibilities experienced by the current everyday family.

Our rationale for this effort is to present a text that focuses on underrepresented family experiences and to provide a platform for researchers to give meaning to the editors' concept captured in the title, *More Than Blood: Today's Reality and Tomorrow's Vision of Family*. This concept represents a new paradigm that shifts families, once considered anomalies, into common constellations. Collectively, the articles in the text offer a perceptual framework for regarding all families as evolutionary systems that are no longer static. Families that were once considered atypical are now rapidly moving toward the center, or *core*, of the familial spectrum. This core, however, is fluid and arbitrary; its lines of demarcation are unclear, leaving speculation as to which family systems are "inside" or "outside" the core. Consequently, the contemporary Western family is in a constant state of flux and uniquely positioned to redefine itself via socially acceptable evolving norms of family interaction. The resulting family constellation, when the anomaly (atypical) evolves into the common (typical), is newly coined the evotypical family and is referenced often in this text when examining family norms in states of transition.

Furthermore, the text examines the manner in which contemporary family dynamics challenge societal norms, traditional family research, and the construction of domestic reality. Collectively, the chapters portray a broader, more forgiving definition of family and progress toward a better understanding of the ways in which contemporary family members enact their new roles and responsibilities.

The research presented in this book focuses on the ever-expanding but often overlooked family experiences and communicative practices that exist within the families. The concept of evotypical families is a paradigm that expands (and often contradicts) the married two-parent, male-female, 2.2 children, traditional treatment of family research that emerged in the 1900s. The new paradigm presented in this book mainstreams a wide spectrum of family contexts and their surrounding issues. Norms that once guided family configurations, identities, and feelings of self-esteem are being challenged. Extraordinary issues that historically placed families outside the traditional two-parent system are now common. As a reader, this book reframes dynamics that once marked families as abnormal or atypical, as ordinary phenomena encountered by modern families.

Goals

The overall goal of this reader is to foster a deeper appreciation and respect for the ever-changing contemporary family; specifically, other goals include the following:

- Expand conceptualization of contemporary families
- Enlighten self on communication power in families
- Recognize self and role(s) played in families
- Heighten awareness of the breadth of family experiences

- Counteract prejudicial assumptions about families
- Confirm uniqueness of own families
- Consider own family situations from a different perspective
- Become more accepting of peoples' differences
- Foster attempts toward understanding differences in families
- Appreciate the value of communication in families

Structure

Based on the evolution of families to date, this book is designed to reflect what we the editors see as logical subgroupings of common contemporary families. This is possible because as the more loosely defined evotypical family emerges, certain family configurations and interactions are repeated. There are seven parts in this reader. The first and second parts address the foundations of families and the importance of communication to family members. We then present the evotypical families under five general categories: Emergence of Evotypical Families, Family Experiences from a Distance, Grief and Loss, Physical and Mental Health Considerations with Families, and Family Ties and Influences.

In part 1, "The Foundation," Kathleen Galvin, Sherilyn Marrow, and Dennis Leoutsakas discuss recent family developments showing how evotypical families have emerged as the norm in U.S. society. These chapters remind readers of the evolutionary changes in families and describe, at length, the new perceptions of families during the last half of the 20th century. The part concludes with a discussion by the editors about the future possibilities of U.S. families.

In part 2, "Communication Perspectives," Dennis Leoutsakas, Thomas G. Endres, Deborah Ballard-Reisch, Doug Kelley, Douglas C. Pennington, and Lynne M. Webb discuss various forms of interactions showing how communication is vital to functional families regardless of their configurations. The discipline of communication is rich with family-related research, and the chapters in this part review some of the more recent research addressing family communication.

Part 3, "Emergence of Evotypical Families," is the first of the five family groupings conceptualized by the editors. Jay Baglia, Elissa Foster, Chrstine E. Kiesinger, Lynn Comerford, Tiffani Baldwin, Brian L. Heisterkamp, Karen Cirulis, Francis Wardle, and Sara Docan-Morgan contribute chapters that discuss family dynamics often taken for granted. While issues such as unmarried couples, adopted children, teen parents, and blended families are commonly mentioned in the literature, family research into such areas is incomplete. The authors' research provides readers with an enlightened view of such families.

In part 4, "Family Experiences from a Distance," Vinita Agarwal, Suchitra Shenoy, Erin Sahlstein, Katheryn Maguire, Jeralyn Faris, and Eletra Gilchrist provide us with insights into long-distance familial relationships. Clearly, the chapters in this part are not all-encompassing, but they provide readers with an appreciation for the family bonds that withstand the threat of long-distance separation. From this platform, readers can conceptually make the leap to other long-distance relationships, such as families supported by high technology, traveling family members, and families dealing with distant relatives.

Part 5, "Families in Grief and Loss," includes chapters by Carrie West, Gina Bacon, Sherilyn Marrow, Nancy Karlin, and Betty Burdorff Brown. Losses to families can occur at any moment and often under tragic circumstances. Remaining family members must seek ways to adapt and cope with the impact on their families. The chapters in this part address the manner in which families and family members adapt to tragic circumstances. The topics discussed range from death and identity development to family resilience following natural disasters.

Part 6, "Physical and Mental Health Considerations in the Family," with authors Nicholas Fittante, Brad Goldschmidt, Stacy L. Carter, Narissra Maria Punyanunt-Carter, Jeanette Valenti, Angela C. Henderson, and Wanda Koszewski, reminds us that all families are not created equally. Families coping with mental illnesses, alcoholism, abuses, and illnesses must compensate for the needs of the affected family members. At the same time, coping families often have a much greater need for support. The chapters in this part provide readers with a range of health circumstances faced by some families. Because such families and family members are often stigmatized, we expect many readers to actively identify with many issues presented in this part.

Finally, part 7, "Family Ties and Influences," includes chapters by Cheryl Pawlowski, Charles Soukup, Patrick C. Hughes, John R. Baldwin, Bolanle Olaniran, Paul Yelsma, David E. Weber, K. T. Aldridge, Beth Waggenspack, Jennifer Mayer, Brian Richardson, and Deborah Eicher-Catt. This part addresses some of the many outside influences asserting pressure on contemporary families. Often these outside influences receive mixed responses, being perceived as either positive or negative. Probably the most active instrument of family influence is modern technology. Adults must adapt to technology as it changes and families must evaluate the worth of modern influences to the family system. The chapters in this part provide the base for discussions addressing the effects of outside influences on the bonding process within families.

Conclusion

The family is as integral to life in society as the heart is to individual survival. Treating the family as if it were a loved one or a self-established organization struggling against a takeover means giving it our time, our tears, and, often, our blood. While actual blood relations play an important role in defining family for many, the prevalence of today's diverse families suggests that families are "more than blood" and have evolved into a new identity—one more broadly defined with evolving norms constantly under revision.

We the editors feel strongly about the need for conversations related to family. Conversations about family give life to the notion of family—rich with pulse and energy.

May this volume serve as a stimulant for meaningful discussions. We hope that readers' exchanges lead to a better understanding and deeper appreciation of this complex unit known as "family" during these interesting contemporary times.

Best Wishes,
Sherilyn Marrow and Dennis Leoutsakas

Contributors

Agarwal, Vinita

Vinita Agarwal (Ph.D., Purdue University) is an assistant professor at the Department of Communication Arts in Salisbury University, Maryland, where she lives with her husband, son, and 2-year-old chocolate lab. Her research agenda focuses on psychosocial factors in health behaviors with a special interest in women's issues. Her research has been published in the *Western Journal of Communication, Communication Research Reports*, and *Intercultural Communication Studies*. She was recently a recipient of a top three paper award in health communication from the Eastern Communication Association and the University System of Maryland Women's Foundation Faculty Research Award and is currently principal investigator on a university research mini-grant. She is serving on the Salisbury University Student Research Conference committee and is faculty co-adviser of the Delta Theta chapter of Lambda Pi Eta.

Aldridge, KT

KT Aldridge (B.A., University of Northern Colorado) graduated summa cum laude from the University of Northern Colorado in 2011 with a double degree in communication studies and French liberal arts. Currently, she is working toward a master's degree in Communication and Environmental Science at Evergreen State University in Olympia, Washington.

Bacon, Gina

Gina Bacon (M.A., University of Utah) won "Top Student Paper" in the Performance Studies Interest Group at the 2010 Western States Communication Association conference with "The Life of a Twinkie," and is proud that this is her first publication. She would not be where she is today without the bravery of Noh Eun Joo or the unconditional love and support of Theresa and Richard Bacon. To the three people who made her a "twinkie," she is forever grateful.

Baglia, Jay

Jay Baglia is an assistant professor in the College of Communication at DePaul University with a focus on gender, performance studies, and health communication. He is the 2011 recipient of the Sharadin Medal for Outstanding Faculty Member awarded by the College of Visual and Performing Arts. He also received the 2006 Book of the Year Award from the Organization for the Study of Communication, Language, and Gender. He is the oldest of five sons born to Lynn and Joe Baglia (1932–1992) of New Milford, Connecticut. He is in a long-term committed partnership with Elissa Foster, and together they are the parents of Aria Joy.

Baldwin, R. John

John R. Baldwin (Ph.D., Arizona State University) is professor of communication at Illinois State University. His research and teaching interests include domestic and international diversity (e.g., interethnic and intercultural communication), especially issues of group difference and intolerance (racism, sexism, and so on). He tends to take a cross-disciplinary and multiple-method perspective, as seen in his coedited book analyzing the notion of "culture" from several different disciplinary perspectives (*Redefining Culture*). He has recently turned his attention to issues of national, racial, and global identities in Brazilian popular music. He has been married for 24 years to Kim Baldwin, a professor of psychology at Lincoln Christian Seminary, and they have two children, a 20-year-old son and a 16-year-old daughter.

Baldwin, Tiffani

Tiffani Baldwin (Ph.D.candidate, University of Denver. Her area of emphasis is family communication with special interests in gender, aging, and identity. As an only child and always-single adult well into her 30s, she has spent her lifetime cultivating familial relationships with nonkin.

Ballard-Reisch, Deborah

Deborah Ballard-Reisch, Ph.D. (Bowling Green State University), holds the Kansas Health Foundation Distinguished Chair in Strategic Communication and is a professor at the Elliott School of Communication, Wichita State University. Her research interests include family and couple communication, strategic health and risk communication, and international women's health and narrative theory. Dr. Ballard-Reisch co-edited a volume on *Communication and Sex Role Socialization*, as well as special issues of the *Journal of Family Communication* (on family research methodology) and *Women and Language* (on globalization and feminism). She is the author of over 40 referred international, national and regional journal articles and book chapters and more than 20 public health and population reports. In her free time, Deborah loves to travel with her children, Stefan and Alyssa. She also enjoys horseback riding, tennis, hiking, reading, good food, music, movies and theater.

Bolanle A. Olaniran

Bolanle A. Olaniran (Ph. D, University of Oklahoma) is a professor in the Department of Communication studies at Texas Tech University, Lubbock. Bolanle's areas of research include technology in organization, small group and decision making process, intercultural communication and conflict management. His works have appeared in national and international journals. He is also a consultant to organizations and non-government organizations. He has served as keynote speaker in conferences and organized lecture series in the following countries: China, Hong-Kong, Taiwan, Russia, just to name a few. His work has gained recognition including outstanding Scholar from the American Communication Association and Gold Medal Award from "Women in Communication."

Brown, Betty Burdorff

Betty Burdorff Brown (M.A., University of Northern Colorado) holds both undergraduate and master's degrees from the University of Northern Colorado's Department of Human Communication. While not working formally in the discipline, she believes in the concept that "you cannot not communicate" and actively serves as secretary of the Colorado Chapter of the Partners of the Americas. She travels to Latin America frequently with her husband Roger to help with active projects or to connect with other Partners. In this volunteer work, she sees other families struggling to communicate through difficulties and changes, much the same as observed in her own family. A shrub rather than a tree is how she views her nontraditional family, consisting of four children, six grandchildren, and even three great-grandchildren.

Cheryl Pawlowski

Cheryl Pawlowski (Ph.D., New York University) is a professor at the University of Northern Colorado. She has published numerous articles on the effects of media on culture and published the book *Glued to the Tube*. She has also been a guest speaker on many radio programs discussing the effects of television.

Cirulis, Karen

Karen Cirulis (M.A., University of Nebraska, Omaha), a native Omahan, received dual B.S. degrees in education and speech pathology (B–12); and in secondary English (7–12) from the University of Nebraska, Omaha. Appreciating the interrelatedness of these fields, she later returned to UNO to earn a master's degree in counseling. She has counseled for over 20 years in the Omaha Public Schools, having received the Alice Buffett Outstanding Teaching Award in 2003. Her professional affiliations include UNO's Chi Sigma Iota Honorary, Nebraska School Counselor Association, American School Counselor Association. She also serves on the Omaha's Catholic Charities Behavioral Health Board. Parenting, time with family, travel, reading, writing, and "making a positive difference" in the lives of others (especially adolescents) are just some of her many passions.

Comerford, Lynn

Lynn Comerford (Ph.D., State University of New York, Albany) is director of the Women's Studies Program and associate professor of women's studies and human development at California State University, East Bay. Her research has explored how formal legal equality devalues gendered lives, the reconstitution of parental rights via child custody policy, and mother reproduction. She is currently completing a book on the sexual politics of child custody policy.

Docan-Morgan, Sara

Sara Docan-Morgan (Ph.D., University of Washington) is an assistant professor of communication at the University of Wisconsin–La Crosse. Her work has been published in the *Journal of Social and Personal Relationships*, the *Journal of Family Communication*, and the *Journal of Korean Adoption Studies*. She is an adult Korean adoptee and a mother of twins.

Eicher-Catt, Deborah

Deborah Eicher-Catt (Ph.D., Southern Illinois University, Carbondale) is associate professor of communication arts and sciences at Pennsylvania State University, York. She is currently the chair of the Philosophy of Communication Interest Group for the National Communication Association. She has published widely on the intersection of semiotics and communication, guest editing a special issue of the *American Journal of Semiotics*, commemorating communication theorist Gregory Bateson. She is currently working on a book project titled "The Sign of the Sacred in Bateson and Peirce."

Endres, Thomas G.

Thomas G. Endres (Ph.D., University of Minnesota) is professor of communication studies and served 10 years as founding director of the School of Communication at the University of Northern Colorado. He has delivered over 150 presentations and keynotes nationally and internationally; has published numerous articles and several book chapters in the areas of popular culture, family communication, and pedagogy; and is author of the 2002 book *Sturgis Stories: Celebrating the People of the World's Largest Motorcycle Rally*. While he is pleased with the fact that he has multiple family-related tattoos, he is more pleased with the fact that he has family.

Foster, Elissa

Elissa Foster (Ph.D., University of South Florida) is an associate professor in the College of Communication at DePaul University and the Director of the M.A. Health Communication Program. She is also a contractual educator for the Department of Family Medicine at Lehigh Valley Health Network. She is the winner of the 2011 Best Book Chapter Award from the Ethnography Division of the National Communication Association (NCA). She received the best book award from the Applied Division of the NCA in 2009 and the Janice Hocker Rushing Early Career Research Award in 2007 from the Southern States Communication Association. Elissa Foster is the middle child of Bill and Barbara Foster (Brisbane, Australia), proud partner of Jay Baglia, and proud mother of Aria Joy.

Galvin, Kathleen M.

Kathleen M. Galvin (Ph.D., Northwestern University) is a professor of communication studies at Northwestern University. She is the senior author of the first textbook in family communication titled *Family Communication: Cohesion and Change*, now in its eighth edition. Because of her strong interest in family diversity and communication, she developed the concept of discourse-dependent families and has published articles and book chapters related to communicative processes in families formed through stepparenting, adoption and same-sex parenting.

Gilchrist, Eletra S.

Eletra S. Gilchrist (Ph.D., University of Memphis) received her M.A. and B.A. degrees from the University of Alabama. She is an assistant professor in the Department of Communication Arts at the University of Alabama, Huntsville. Her research focuses on communication pedagogy, interpersonal communication, and cultural studies from both quantitative and qualitative perspectives. She is the editor of *Experiences of Single African-American Women Professors: With This Ph.D., I Thee Wed* and has published book chapters and journal articles in several national and regional publications, including the *Journal of Intercultural Communication Research*, the *National Academic Advising Journal, Basic Communication Course Best Practices: A Training Manual for Instructors, Communication Research, Communication Teacher*, and the *NIDA Journal of Language and Communication.*

Goldschmidt, Brad

Brad Goldschmidt (M.A., University of Northern Colorado) is a 30-year veteran of the Greeley, Colorado, Police Department. He has worked in all areas of the department and specialized in investigating homicide cases. He has been the lead investigator or supervised the investigations of approximately 50 murders. He was promoted to sergeant in 1999 and to lieutenant in 2005. He obtained a bachelor's degree from the University of Northern Colorado in 2004 and a master's degree in communication in 2007.

Heisterkamp, Brian

Brian L. Heisterkamp (Ph.D., Arizona State University) is an associate professor in the Department of Communication Studies at California State University, San Bernardino. His research interests involve the relationship between social action and social structures and the manner in which conversation can be examined to understand mediator behavior, conflict, and interpersonal relationships, particularly gay and lesbian relationships. He teaches courses in conflict and mediation, relational communication, nonverbal communication, and research methods and various graduate seminars.

Henderson, Angela C.

Angela C. Henderson (Ph.D., Purdue University). Her dissertation focused on comparing the role strain and role enhancement perspectives within the context of women caring for an older adult. She is currently an assistant professor of sociology at the University of Northern Colorado and teaches courses on sociological theory and family. Her most recent work focuses on mothers' Foucauldian surveillance of themselves and other moms as well as the effects of such behavior on well-being.

Hughes, Patrick C.

Patrick C. Hughes (Ph.D., University of Denver) is associate professor of communication studies and associate vice provost for undergraduate education at Texas Tech University, Lubbock. He teaches courses in communication research methods, interpersonal communication, and communication theory. His research centers around the influence of and experiences with religion and culture in interpersonal communication contexts, such as interfaith marriage and intercultural health dynamics.

Jennifer Mayer

Jennifer Mayer received her Master of Arts in Communication Studies from the University of North Texas. Her work there focused on the family dynamics of drug and alcohol dependent women and the need for further research into women's reasons for entering recovery programs. She credits her father for instilling in her the compassion and drive to complete this study, and will forever be humbled by the strength of the women who participated. Not only are they continuing to change their lives and those of their children, they graciously share their stories in the hope that they will benefit others.

Jeralyn Faris

Jeralyn Faris (Ph.D. Purdue University) is a continuing lecturer in the Brian Lamb School of Communication at Purdue University in West Lafayette, IN, where she is the director for the interviewing course and assistant director for the basic communication course. Her dissertation is the culmination of a 4-year qualitative study of a reentry Problem Solving Court in which she served as a volunteer for five years. Faris continues to volunteer as a member of the chaplain's team for a large county jail, serving for 18 years. Her essays have been published in *Prison Journal* and two books, *Problem Solving Courts: New Approaches to Criminal Justice* and *Working for Justice: A Handbook of Prison Education and Activism*.

Karlin, Nancy J.

Nancy J. Karlin (Ph.D., Colorado State University). For more than 25 years, Nancy Karlin has conducted a program of research devoted to understanding both the familial caregiver and issues relating to care of the chronically ill. She has traveled extensively gathering cross-cultural data related to both the aging process and recovery from natural disasters. She has served as both the past president and the secretary of the Rocky Mountain Psychological Association and currently serves as the convention coordinator.

Kelley, Douglas

Douglas Kelley (Ph.D., University of Arizona) studies interpersonal communication processes. Specifically, his research focuses on how couples negotiate relational expectations and transgressions within marriage. His three books, *Marital Communication*, *Communicating Forgiveness*, and *Marriage at Midlife*, focus on relational and life span challenges and transitions for couples. His most recent release, *Marital Communication*, examines how the long-term, committed, romantic nature of marriage creates a unique context for the development and management of intimacy, love, and conflict. He has served on the editorial board for the *Journal of Family Communication* and has published in such outlets as the *Journal of Social and Personal Relationships*, the *Journal of Applied Gerontology*, and *Human Communication Research*. He teaches relationship-based courses in family communication, conflict and negotiation, relational communication, forgiveness and reconciliation, and inner-city families. He is a frequent speaker at various community organizations regarding marriage and family communication. He has been doing the "marriage thing" with Ann for 30 years, has two grown boys and two dogs, and lives near the mountain preserve in Phoenix, Arizona, with four kayaks.

Kiesinger, Christine E.

Christine E. Kiesinger (Ph.D., University of South Florida) has been teaching in the area of family and relational communication since1995. Christine's scholarship has focused extensively on the emotional worlds of anorexic and bulimic women—particularly exploring the nature of their challenges as they relate to their closest relationships. More recently, Christine studies the complex communicative worlds of post-bereaved family systems as this relates to the death of a parent. Her own personal journey informs all of her teaching, scholarship and writing.

Koszewski, Wanda M.

Wanda M. Koszewski (Ph.D., Kansas State University) is a Clinical Associate Professor and Department Chair for the Nutrition and Dietetics Department at the University of North Dakota. Her research focus is in the area of nutrition education. She formerly directed two large nutrition education programs for the state of Nebraska: EFNEP and SNAP-ED. Under her leadership, the Nebraska SNAP-ED program has been recognized nationally for its excellence in partnerships, program delivery, and evaluation. She has previously been Principal and Co-Principal Investigator on two U.S. Department of Agriculture AFRI grants focused on the prevention of childhood obesity.

Maguire, Katheryn C.

Katheryn Maguire (Ph.D., University of Texas, Austin) is an assistant professor in the Department of Communication at Wayne State University. Her research centers on how individuals and families use communication to maintain relationships and cope with stressful situations in several contexts, including military deployments, long-distance romances, and hurtful family environments. She has a forthcoming book titled *Stress and Coping in Families* and has published in journals including *Communication Monographs*, *Journal of Applied Communication Research*, *Communication Education*, and *Communication Quarterly*.

Nicholas Fittante

Nicholas Fittante (MA, MFT, DCHt) is a licensed marriage and family clinical therapist in private practice since 1990. He is the director of ACT Family Counseling Services and Abraxas Hypnosis Center. He is a graduate of National University (1988, cum laude) and the Hypnosis and Motivation Institute (1996). He is a certified diplomate in clinical hypnosis by the National Board of Certified Clinical Hypnotherapists and is a member of the American Hypnosis Association. Blending the foundations of conventional and alternative approaches to counseling, he assists clients to find solutions to a wide range of life challenges and psychological issues.

Pennington, Douglas C.

Douglas C. Pennington (D. Ministry, Carolina Ministry of Theology) is senior pastor, Lynn Haven United Methodist Church, Panama City, Florida. He was ordained a Methodist minister in 1982 and appointed to serve his current congregation in June 1993. He has been married for over 30 years to his wife Sandy; they have two children and two grandchildren.

Punyanunt-Carter, Narissra Maria

Narissra Maria Punyanunt-Carter (Ph.D., Kent State University) is an associate professor of communication studies at Texas Tech University, Lubbock, where she teaches the undergraduate courses in interpersonal communication. Her research areas include mass media effects, father–daughter communication, mentoring, adviser–advisee relationships, family studies, religious communication, humor, and interpersonal communication. She has published over 30 articles that have appeared in several peer-reviewed journals, such as *Communication Research Reports*, the *Southern Journal of Communication*, and the *Journal of Intercultural Communication Research*.

Richardson, Brian K.

Brian K. Richardson (Ph.D., University of Texas, Austin) is an associate professor of communication studies at the University of North Texas. His research interests include whistle-blowing, sexual harassment, and crisis/disaster communication. His research has been published in *Management Communication Quarterly*, the *Western Journal of Communication*, the *Journal of Communication and Religion*, and *Communication Studies*. He and his wife Cheryl have two children: Keith, age 9, and Ella, age 7.

Sahlstein, Erin

Erin Sahlstein (Ph.D., University of Iowa) is an associate professor of communication studies at the University of Nevada–Las Vegas. Her research focuses on communicative activity within and about geographically separated relationships. Publications of her work may be found in journals such as the *Journal of Social and Personal Relationships*, *Communication Monographs*, and the *Journal of Applied Communication Research*. Growing up in a military household and community informed her more recent interests in familial communication and deployment. She is currently working on a project involving military couples as well as children regarding deployment and disclosure.

Shenoy, Suchitra

Suchitra Shenoy (Ph.D., Purdue University) is an assistant professor of communication at the College of Communication at DePaul University. In addition to pursuing her research interests in organizational assimilation, anticipatory socialization, and the construction of career discourses in contested work spaces, she wears the badge of a "cultural nomad" with pride and continues to live with two hearts.

Soukup, Charles

Charles Soukop (Ph.D., University of Nebraska) is an associate professor of communication studies at the University of Northern Colorado. His research and teaching emphasize the role of technology and media in the formation of culture and community. His research has examined virtual communities on the World Wide Web, the discourses of film and television, dialogue in interfaith communities, and digital popular culture texts. His work has appeared in a wide range of academic journals, such as the *Journal of Computer-Mediated Communication*, *New Media and Society*, *Critical Studies in Media Communication*, the *Journal of International and Intercultural Communication*, the *Western Journal of Communication*, and the *Southern Communication Journal*. He is currently exploring the experience of mobile technologies in the individual's everyday life.

Stacy L. Carter

Stacy L. Carter (Ph.D., Mississippi State University, NCSP, BCBA-D) is an Associate Professor at Texas Tech University in the Department of Educational Psychology and Leadership. His research focus includes evaluation of educational and behavioral interventions for children and adults with disabilities.

Valenti, Jeanette

Jeanette Valenti (Ph.D., University of Denver) is the youngest of three siblings and is married with two children. Although she is from Colorado, she is currently living in San Diego and is teaching communication courses online through the Metropolitan State College of Denver and Brigham Young University–Idaho. She is passionate about scuba diving, seashell collecting, kayaking, photography, diabetes education, and learning more about interpersonal relationships.

Waggenspack, Beth M.

Beth M. Waggenspack (Ph.D., The Ohio State University) is associate professor and director of the Communication Graduate Program at Virginia Tech. Her academic scholarship involves women and their rhetorical efforts as well as adoption and the media. Recent critical essays include analysis of the persuasive communication of American First Ladies (Helen Herron Taft and Eleanor Roosevelt) to women who argue for social change, such as children's rights activist Marian Wright Edelman and women's rights advocates Elizabeth Cady Stanton, Lucy Stone, and Lucretia Mott. As an adoptive parent involved in the first wave of adoptions from Russia and Ukraine, she was instrumental in establishing several of the initial listservs for those pursuing Eastern European adoption, and she has published in the area of adoption's symbolic crisis, particularly in terms of media narratives and representations.

Wardle, Francis

Francis Wardle (Ph.D., University of Kansas) has a Ph.D. in curriculum and instruction; a master's degree in the cultural foundations of education from the University of Wisconsin–Madison, and a B.S. in art education from Pennsylvania State University. He has taught in K–12 schools for 6 years in Taos, New Mexico; Kansas City, Missouri; and Pennsylvania. He has been involved with the federal Head Start program (a free program for 3- to 5-year-olds) since 1973 as a volunteer, educational manager, grant reviewer, program evaluator, and director. He has taught a variety of curriculum classes and life span development at the University of Phoenix and at a local community college in Colorado. He has also written educational textbooks and articles for many journals and magazines. Currently, he is an active member of Partners of the Americas, which has taken him to Brazil to conduct research on schools, race, and ethnicity. Married to Ruth and with four wonderful children, he enjoys photography, hiking, and travel.

Webb, Lynne M.

Lynne M. Webb (Ph.D., University of Oregon) is professor of communication at the University of Arkansas. She is an applied scholar and groundbreaking researcher in three areas: social media, family communication, and communication and aging. She has published two scholarly readers and over 50 essays, including multiple theories, research reports, and pedagogical essays. She has received numerous service and teaching awards during her 30 years as a college professor. She is a past president of the Southern States Communication Association and has served on the governing board of the National Communication Association.

Weber, David E.

David E. Weber (Ph.D., University of Denver) is an associate professor of communication studies at University of North Carolina Wilmington, where he designed and stewards the organizational communication concentration. His specialty areas are applied organizational communication (e.g., communication training and development, communication consulting skills, and interviewing skills), ethnographic methods, and international organizational communication. Prior to entering the academic world, he had a two-decade career in organizational development, including several years' work as an expatriate in the Middle East and Asia. His area of focus in research is the social construction of identity in organizational settings, and he has (as in the selection in this reader) explored the construction of identity autoethnographically.

West, Carrie

Carrie West (Ph.D., University of Denver) is an assistant professor of Communication Studies at Schreiner University in Kerrville, Texas. Carrie earned her bachelor's and master's degrees in Speech Communication from the University of Northern Colorado. Her area of concentration for research and teaching is Interpersonal and Family Communication. As part of her research and service, she works with an international widows group. Her research in this area investigates how communication and privacy management influence resilience and relationships in bereaved families and on health and well-being. Carrie lives in Kerrville, Texas with her husband, two sons, and three dogs.

Yelsma, Paul

Paul Yelsma (Ph.D., University of Michigan) began his education in a one-room country schoolhouse and after graduating from high school enlisted in the U.S. Army, where he became a helicopter electrician. His demonstrative awakening occurred traveling on a motorcycle for a year through 21 European countries. On returning to the United States, he married Julie and had two sons. He earned a bachelor's and a master's degree at the University of Denver, and then obtained a Ph.D. in communication research at the University of Michigan. He taught small-group communication courses and conducted research at Western Michigan University for 32 years. He is now retired and continues to be involved in writing books, growing walnut trees, biking, traveling, scuba diving, hiking, and skiing.

About the Authors

Sherilyn Marrow

Sherilyn Marrow (Ph.D., University of Denver) is a family enthusiast specializing in the study of resilience in families and how emotional expressiveness can transform lives. She holds education and communication degrees from the University of Nebraska, and a Ph.D. in human communication and family counseling from the University of Denver. She is a professor at the University of Northern Colorado in the School of Communication, where she has achieved numerous teaching awards, including "Outstanding Woman of the Year." She is founder/creator of the *TalkShareCare Wellness Program*—a communication teaching system for both children and adults. The program has outreached to several national and international communities including New Orleans following Hurricane Katrina, and Vina Vieja, Peru following devastating earthquakes. She has been a radio talk show host across Colorado and California, allowing her message on family communication topics to reach larger audiences. Her passions include her family (especially grandsons Luke and James), biking, spirituality, music, creating, and, always, having great conversations with interesting people.

Dennis Leoutsakas

Dennis Leoutsakas (Ph.D., University of South Florida) is an interdisciplinary associate professor at Salisbury University, a state university in the Maryland system of higher education. He was born in New York City and spent his childhood and youth in and around the New York City region. In addition, he has lived in Alaska, Florida, and now Maryland. Prior to becoming a university professor, he was an HIV counselor, a juvenile probation officer, a mental health clinician, and a single foster parent for emotionally struggling youth. His current interest is conducting international narrative research with a focus on the development of adults who were displaced from their birth parents as infants, children, youth, or adolescents.

PART 1
The Foundation

Chapter 1
On the Threshold: Evotypical Families Talk Themselves Into Being 2
Kathleen M. Galvin, *Northwestern University*

Chapter 2
More Than Blood: Rethinking Identities, Interactions, and the Future of Contemporary Families 6
Sherilyn Marrow, *University of Northern Colorado*
Dennis Leoutsakas, *Salisbury University*

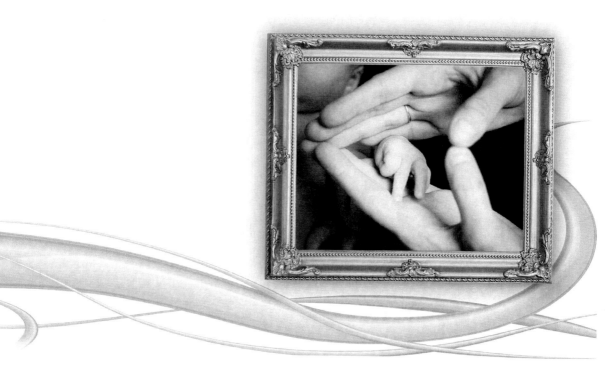

Chapter 1

On the Threshold: Evotypical Families Talk Themselves Into Being

Kathleen M. Galvin

We live in exponential times. Transformative changes situate us in a world of rapidly evolving contemporary families Advances, such as those driven by technology, globalization, medicine, and educational access, provide family members with previously unimagined ways to envision and enact their relational lives. Evotypical families, the evolving family forms that represent the cutting edge of family identity at any given point in time, emerge at the point when imagination, commitment, or need overrides norms and traditions. As newer family forms appear on the horizon, previously considered evotypical family forms lose their position.

Throughout much of the 20th century, family scholars focused extensively on marriage and two-parent biological families, but by its final quarter, divorce and remarriage, stepfamilies, teenage pregnancy, and working mothers dominated many academic discussions. Today, emerging and challenging family lifestyle concerns exemplify evotypical family issues. These include families formed, in part, through transracial adoption, same-sex parenting, anonymous or known sperm donors, third and fourth remarriages, child-free marriage, lifetime cohabitation, noncustodial mothers, and singles by choice. Radical changes abound. Heterosexual married couples no longer represent the majority partnership form; only 20% of American families fall into the category of traditional families—married couples with children—down from 43% in 1950 (Tavernise, 2011). Such familial evolution necessitates an ongoing redefinition of the "typical" family or forces the recognition that such a term has lost its meaning. Newly evolving family types face some of the predictable and unpredictable stresses encountered by previously evotypical families, now considered to normative, while enacting new possibilities.

Although certain concerns have remained salient to family life across generations, conversations within contemporary families address issues that could not have been imagined or addressed openly even 25 years ago. Some of those issues involve the actual family form and its structure and characteristics. Reflecting the lifestyle choices of one or more specific members, other issues reflect how societal changes affect family forms.

In our world of extraordinarily rapid change, language must be considered, along with blood and law, as a significant indicator of familial identity. Family communication scholars argue that language plays a constitutive role in family formation. At the turn of the century, Whitchurch and Dickson (1999) asserted that families will define themselves increasingly through their interactions with the result that, over time, communicative definitions of family will be privileged over structural definitions. From this perspective, language emerges as critical to the development and acceptance of a family form; members talk their family into being as they converse with themselves and with others about their familial self-conception. The more nontraditional the family form, the more critical the linguistic component of the family development process. In other words, "As families become increasingly diverse, their definitional processes expand exponentially, rendering their identity highly discourse dependent" (Galvin, 2006, p. 3). Such a reality necessitates the members engage in ongoing two ongoing discourses. The first involves managing their external family boundary in order to label, explain, legitimize, and, when necessary, defend their family form; the second requires members to maintain an internal sense of familyness through naming, discussing, narrating, and enacting rituals in order to confirm their identity (Galvin, in press).

Living in a world of fluctuations and possibilities requires extensive communication and metacommunication, or talking about how we talk, as couples struggle to create a viable partnership after a relational betrayal or ex-partners confront joint-parenting practices, such as talking about the other in front of the children. Communication complexities remain inherent in many extended family roles, biological or fictive, such as in-laws, aunt/uncles, or great grandparents, which remain understudied (Floyd & Morman, 2006). Increasing longevity provides opportunities to experience multiple family forms during a lifetime, many of which necessitate extensive identity-related negotiations among members of various generations. Language also affects the rejection of an ascribed family tie. One can reject a stepmother because she never married one's parent or a cousin because he is informally adopted.

Not all families choose to recognize or embrace major or minor societal changes, leaving them entrenched in a traditional form. In some cases, members who reject the family of origin's life may no longer find themselves included in ongoing family interactions. Witness the experiences of many who choose not to continue to live as Amish or Mormons or who choose to marry or partner across certain ethnic or religious lines.

Societal forces significantly impact the evolution of family life, whatever the familial structure (Socha & Stamp, 2009). Economic concerns trigger frustrating conversations as family members change their lifestyles in order to survive or renegotiate familial living arrangements for financial reasons. Health concerns create challenging interactions; a child's cancer or a father's heart failure may necessitate extensive interactions with medical professionals and negotiations among members regarding caretaking or finances. Similarly, a member's disability may require an adult child to negotiate his or her responsibilities to parents, children, and colleagues. New media may

trigger generational reversals as children gain power and influence because of their technological sophistication and parents lose their ability to monitor and discuss their offspring's online life. Career choices influence familial dynamics: dual career partners live a continuously negotiated existence, whereas dual career military couples experience long separations and ongoing negotiations of family roles.

Individual characteristics and family identity characteristics require discussion and negotiation. Although ethnicity and culture have received limited attention, the increasingly multicultural nature of society requires far more attention (Soliz, Thorson, & Rittenour, 2009); sustaining the dialogue regarding new immigration patterns remains critical (Turner & West, 2011). Additionally, the interface of religion and race impact family dynamics.

The exponential pace of change challenges family members to discursively negotiate evolving family forms and their accompanying social and technological advances. As the families currently viewed as evotypical are replaced by unforeseen possibilities, our language must expand to encompass these choices, and our hearts must do the same.

References

Floyd, K., & Morman, M. T. (2006). Introduction: On the breadth of the family experience. In K. Floyd and M. T. Morman (Eds.), *Widening the family circle: New research on family communication* (pp. ix-xvi). Thousand Oaks, CA: Sage.

Galvin, K. M. (2006). Diversity's impact on defining the family." In L. H. Turner & R. West (Eds.), *The family communication sourcebook* (pp. 3-19). Thousand Oaks, CA: Sage.

Galvin, K. M. (in press). The family of the future: What do we face? In A. Vangelisti (Ed.), *Handbook of family communication* (2nd ed.). New York: Routledge.

Socha, T. J., & Stamp, G. H. (2009). *Parents and children communicating with society: Managing relationships outside the home.* New York: Routledge.

Soliz, J., Thorson, A., & Rittenour, C.E. (2009). Communication correlates of satisfaction, family identity and group salience in multiracial/ethnic families. *Journal of Marriage and Family, 71,* 819-832.

Tavernise, S. (2011, May 26). Married couples are no longer a majority, Census finds. *New York Times,* p. A22.

Turner, L. H., & West, R. (2011). "Sustaining the dialogue": National culture and family communication. *Journal of Family Communication, 11,* 67-68.

Whitchurch, G. D., & Dickson, F. C. (1999). Family communication. In M. Sussman, S. K. Steinmetz, & G. W. Peterson (Eds.), *Handbook of marriage and the family* (2nd ed., pp. 687-704). New York: Plenum.

Chapter 2

More Than Blood: Rethinking Identities, Interactions, and the Future of Contemporary Families

Sherilyn Marrow
Dennis Leoutsakas

The bamboo that bends is stronger than the oak that resists (Japanese proverb)
A family . . . is a little kingdom, torn with factions and exposed to revolutions. (Samuel Johnson)

Change, as we know it, is constant. It occurs in most living things, including a unique mercurial system known as the "family." In general, the American family is an adaptive lot; it is a system that acts and reacts, it predictably moves in cycles, and it optimally acts as a safe haven to all or most of its members. Usually, the family accepts obvious and subtle emerging changes and consents to evolving norms with little resistance or fanfare. We as family members prevail and persevere, for family is from whence we came; it is what we know.

Changes in the modern family are real and undeniable. Intuitively, we realize that contemporary family constellations *look* and *feel* differently than they did in the days of our parents and ancestors. Cognitively, we acknowledge that a family is more than a human institution with collective behaviors— it is more than its biological inheritance, blood relatives, laws, and social networks. Emotionally, despite the blurred and often complicated familial systems to which we belong, we relentlessly strive for acceptance and inclusion, mindful that being a member of the family is usually more comforting than painful exclusion.

Considering the obvious changes, it is clear that the typical American family no longer exists. From ancient clans, tribes, colonialists, pioneers, agricultural families, and industrialized families to modern families of the 21st century, there were rules or characteristics that marked the typical westernized family. Previously, regions, religions, race, gender, blood, and birth rights set standards that helped define kinship, and any family that deviated from the established norms were considered atypical. For example, in the instance of alleged unfaithfulness, women, wives, or mothers were burned at the stake or forced to wear blazened symbols that publically communicated their assumed guilt and sinful or wicked ways. In a more recent case, *Loving v. Virginia* (1958, 1967), a Virginia couple found themselves arrested, jailed, and exiled from the state because they decided to interracially marry. This occurred in 1958 when "interracial unions were still illegal in the Commonwealth of Virginia as well as in fifteen other American states" (Gilbert, 2010). These ruthless sanctions signaled to society that certain behaviors threatened the status of the family unit and denigrated its relationships to such an extent that banishment, imprisonment, and even death were suitable punishments following the controversially aggrieved "wrongdoings."

Today, in the new millennium, our perceptions of familial systems are different. Those rigid rules, characteristics, and standards that once influenced our understanding of family no longer apply. Adjectives like "typical" or "normal," once used to modify the term "family," are obscure, if not obsolete. Because of the advancements of globalization, civil rights, and family planning (or lack thereof), along with a continuing separation of evolving political policies from religious rigidity and inflexible laws, the conceptual framework of the at one time "typical family" is disappearing and being relegated to memory.

Prevalent Theoretical Approaches to Studying Families

When examining identities and interactions of family, it is first necessary to review, epistemologically, how we know what we know about families. Certainly, we learn about families from *being* a part of them by experiencing the relationships, nodal events, values, rituals, roles, perspectives, and so on that accompany our interactions within our own foundational systems. We attach meanings to ongoing behaviors and eventually regard them as expected conduct, patterns, or enduring coincidences. These meanings (or at least our perceptions of them) often extend to multiple generations of our families and tend to impact the values we place on our family systems.

In addition, while every family has its own uniqueness or identity to some degree, most families in a society parallel each other in some way because of similar ethnicities, interests, and interactional patterns. In essence, family members perceive the status of their family in relationship to other families' behaviors. As a result, family members evaluate or regard their family as functional or dysfunctional based on the admired or frowned-on behaviors and characteristics of families with perceived cultural similarities.

Furthermore, we learn about families through research and those select theories or frameworks that help shape, support, or contradict our basic understandings. Family researchers discuss the meanings of family and its subsequent interactions from several perspectives. Family communication scholar Glen H. Stamp conducted a comprehensive review of the most common family theory articles published in research journals from 1990 to 2001 from both a methodological perspective'and their predominant supportive theories. He reported that over 90% (1,152 articles) of the total 1,254 articles discovered were empirically based, incorporating quantitative, experimental, survey, and behavioral coding methods; 6.46% (81 articles) of the articles were interpretive based, consisting of ethnographic and fieldwork studies, interviewing, and personal experiences approaches; and 1.67% (21 articles) adopted a critical approach revealing critical analyses and advocating social change (Stamp, 2004, pp. 4–5).

Additionally, Stamp identified 16 theories with the number of articles related to each that occurred most frequently in the data: attachment theory (61), family life course theory (54), family systems theory (50), role theory (38), exchange theory (34), network theory (28), theory of marital types (24), feminist theory (18), social learning theory (18), attribution/accounts theory (15), narrative theory (14), dialectical theory (14), social construction theory (10), symbolic interactionism (9), equity theory (9), and interdependence theory (9). Explaining these theories is beyond the scope of this chapter, but addressing some select theoretical frameworks that influence our perspectives of modern families do occur here.

The Changing Look of Family

As families have changed, so have their structures and demographics on both individual and collective levels. Today, families no longer need to be blood relations, nor do they need to share common cultural characteristics. All a small group needs to be designated a family in the United States is to want to be together and to be identified as a family. Such families have always existed throughout history—such as the single-parent neighbor who cares for a child whose parent has died or whose guardian is afflicted by addictions or other social issues—but it is only now that we willingly recognize such supportive groupings as families. When discussing changing families, there is a strong urge to compare contemporary families to model modern families of the mid-20th century that were comprised of a man, a woman, and 2.2 children. In the 21st century, however, families with those statistics are no longer the majority. Once-model 20th-century families must now take their place alongside all other socially acceptable families as just one family structure among a constellation of familial dynamics.

According to family researcher Andrew J. Cherlin (2010), demographers are challenged by categorizing and measuring the new family. He writes,

> Demographic trends in the 2000s showed the continuing separation of family and household due to childbearing among single parents, dissolution of cohabiting partners, divorce, repartnering, and remarriage; that trends such as marriage and divorce were diverging according to education; the elder population will largely increase, and that overall, demographic trends produced an increased complexity of family life and a more ambiguous and fluid set of categories than demographers are accustomed to measuring. (p. 403)

Radical changes in families are reflected by select demographics reported in Cherlin's (2010) research titled "Demographic Trends in the United States: A Review of Research in the 2000s." Heterosexual couples are waiting longer to marry, with the median age at first marriage rising to 27.4 for men and 25.6 for women in 2008 (U.S. Bureau of the Census, 2009b). This is especially prominent for those pursuing education since most do not marry before the age of 25 (Martin, 2004). Heterosexual *married* couples no longer represent the majority partnership form. Only 20% of American families fall into the category of traditional families—married couples with children—down from 43% in 1950 (Tavernise, 2011). The risk of divorce is declining from its high in 1980, yet nearly all studies report the divorce probability lying between 40% and 50% (U.S. Bureau of the Census, 2005). Cherlin's (1992) early studies initially stated that the probability of a marriage dissolving rose sharply for all groups, but since then, he notes that divorce has actually declined among married couples in which spouses are college educated (Cherlin, 2010; Martin, 2006). Over 20% of married couples dissolve their unions by separation or divorce within the first 5 years, and of cohabiting couples, over 50% close their unions within 5 years, whether they marry or not (Anderson & Philipov, 2002). Fertility rates in the United States during 2006 for women overall revealed an average birthrate per woman of 2.1, a number required to regenerate our population (National Center for Health Statistics, 2009a). The American overall fertility rate, however, was elevated by Hispanic women (mostly of Mexican origin), whose total rate was 2.89. In 2007, 39.75% of all children were born outside of marriage, dramatically up from only 4% in 1950 (National Center for Health Statistics, 2009b). Living arrangements within families have changed because of high levels of divorce and the increase in childbearing among cohabiting couples and unpartnered adults. This results in children experiencing multiple partnerships, parent figures, and family communication dynamics. For example, children born to cohabiting adults are at least twice as likely to see their parents separate as are children whose parents are married at the time of their birth (Cherlin, 2010; Heuveline, Timberlake, & Furstenberg, 2003). The most recent census data report that 13.6 million single-parents households exist, comprising approximately 29% of households (U.S. Bureau of the Census, 2009a). Immigration continues to impact families so that, by 2006, the foreign-born population comprised 12.1% of the American population (U.S. Bureau of the Census, 2008). First-generation families are the highest since the early 20th century (Brown & Bean, 2005). During the past decade, Hispanics grew in numbers, outnumbering African Americans as the largest minority group in the United States. Many families also consider themselves couples or a family but live in separate households. These family arrangements are identified as "living apart together" (Cherlin, 2010, p. 410). The American population 65 years or older makes up 12% of the population (U.S. Bureau of the Census, 2008) and is expected to increase to 16% by 2020 because of the baby-boomer life cycle. Support from grandparents providing partial or full responsibility for caring for grandchildren is substantial, with 5.8 million grandparents (42%) being responsible for most of the basic needs of one or more grandchildren. In late 2011, it was reported that 4.6 million parents were living with an adult child, up 13.7% from 4.05 million parents in 2008 (Quinn, 2012).

The latest demographics highlight the changes in contemporary family structures. Such familial evolution necessitates an ongoing redefinition of the "typical" family or forces the recognition that such a term has lost its meaning. Evolving family types face similar stresses encountered previously by families once considered outliers but now viewed as normative while engaging with new possibilities. As such, we contend that the American family has changed in its structure, commitment, enactment, communication, external influences, and expectations.

Emergence of "Evotypical" Families

Demographics and emerging family forms make rejecting past definitions of family a relatively easy task compared to the greater task of explaining the current state of families in contemporary U.S. society. The kinship relationships for each person is individualized and in a constant state of flux or change. Families are no longer static, and there is no longer an ideal family configuration. Galvin (2004) writes, "Families can no longer be usefully categorized in unitary terms, such as step-families, lesbian partners, single-parent families, or adoptive families, due to overlapping complexities of connection" (p. 677).

Since there is no typical family or unitary terms, we advance the term "evotypical" as a more accurate word for conceptualizing westernized families. We contend that evotypical families are different from past family units in terms of their identity, commitment, enactment, communication, external influences, expectations, inspiration, and flexibility. The following sections discuss what we call the basic tenets of the evotypical family system.

The Evotypical Family Is the Prevalent Family System (Identity)

Defined, evotypical families are "kinship ties bound together by the desire of caring for one another with the common goal of surviving as a single small group unit." Note the positivity in this definition, as we contend that the evotypical family is both uplifted and challenged by its new identity. There are definite signs of hopefulness and a sense of rekindled spirit, noncontingent on its previous responsibilities to its biological members or its fixed place in society. Evotypical families embrace a nonstatic, unstable system that allows for its members to cocreate precisely what they want or do not want in their family identities and interactions. The family structures can consist of both relatives and "more than blood" nonrelatives as their core membership and influential network. They look both inside and outside the family photo frame for their collective meanings and identities.

This evotypical family tenet particularly reflects social constructivism theory based on beliefs about reality, knowledge, and learning. It assumes that reality is created through human interaction and that family members, together, coconstruct their worlds' meaning (Kukla, 2000). For the social constructivist, reality is created only after its social invention. Further, culture and context influence a family member's understanding of their conflated interactions (Derry, 1999; McMahon, 1997).

To social constructivists, meaningful learning occurs when individuals are engaged in social environments and committed to human interaction and activities (McMahon, 1997). From this theory's perspective, the meaning attached to one's family identity is construed in relationship to other family systems that have been known, experienced, or indirectly engaged, such as in media portrayal or other vicarious influences. How one regards the viability or functionality of an evotypical family hinges largely on that individual's own experiences.

The Contemporary Family Is Dependent on Commitment by Its Members, Not Obligation (Commitment)

A sense of loyalty to family members, simply for the sake of family association, is much less prevalent in evotypical families. There appears to be more of a perceptual freedom from family members as to how much or how often "acts of doing family" *need* or *should* occur. Additionally, there seems to be a reduction of the hold that a family has on its members. No generativity is required, whereas, in the past, there were expectations to teach future generations the traditions that contributed to a family's uniqueness. In contrast to Confucianism, in which family duties are performed out of respect, obedience, and expectation, members of the evotypical family will be a family because they want to be a family. Family members can make a choice of whether they want to be active parts of a particular system without experiencing as many repercussions as in generations prior.

Galvin (2006) discusses these families as choice by using descriptions such as "intentional," "fictive," or "self-ascribed kin" (p. 6). These families are formed without the blood or legal connection and are maintained by members' self-definition while performing family functions for one another. In many ways, this voluntary commitment may be more genuine and healthy to the satisfaction of the system as a whole yet may run the risk of diminishing the initial family's existence and legacy.

Pursuant to Thibaut and Kelley's (1959) exchange theory, this tenet is monitored by the exchange of resources and assessment of rewards and costs within family relationships. Thibaut and Kelley's contention is that relationships continue when they are relatively rewarding and deteriorate when they are relatively costly. Family members often make conscious decisions of their costs and rewards when assessing family interactions, dynamics, and relationships. Should members feel that their efforts are not being rewarded, they may turn away from their families; if members perceive their family relationships as satisfying and worthwhile, most likely the family unit will continue to dialogue and exchange behaviors, thus preserving its interactive system.

Evotypical Families "Perform" the Institution of Family through Diverse and Complex Interactions, Rituals, and Roles (Enactment)

As in performance, evotypical family members can choose whether to participate, attend, stay, or leave the metaphorical "show" called family. Adult and adolescent members have the ability, most often, to make conscious choices to play roles or perform sets of behaviors within families. It is virtually impossible to define or determine familial enactments, as ideally each family arbitrarily directs its own performance; however, once scripted, balancing diverse and complex interactions, rituals, and roles is part and parcel of "doing" family. The crucial factor in this evotypical tenet is that family members interact like actors. They actually *do* things that resemble the roles and behaviors that have been previously set as functional to their families. Performances of these interactions, rituals, roles, and duties in families are paramount in modern times, as many evotypical families do not share the same name, blood, ZIP code or other diverse factors that once served to define and unify families.

This tenet reflects the work of Pacanowsky and O'Donnell-Trujillo (1983) in their performance theory in organizational culture. Collective performances are discussed via the meanings of culture that performances are (a) interactional—more like dialogues than soliloquies, (b) contextual and cannot be viewed as independent acts, (c) episodic, with beginnings and ends, and (d) improvised— never repeated the same way. Additionally, they present organizational communication performance categories, such as ritual, passion, sociality, and organizational politics, that focus on the outcomes of social interactions in organizations. This framework of performance enactment also exists within the family system as the performances within a family are demonstrated through its dialogue, collective acts (such as rituals), multiple episodes, and improvisation. These social interactions and performances contribute to the evotypical family culture and assist with understanding relationships within family systems.

The Functionality of the Evotypical Family Relies on the Ability and Action of Its Members to Communicate with Each Other and Includes the Use of Technology (Communication)

Galvin discusses family relationships being discourse dependent and how language must be considered, along with blood and law, as a significant indicator of familial identity; it plays a constitutive role. She eloquently frames this volume with her introductory chapter by writing, "Evotypical families, the evolving family forms that represent the cutting edge of family identity at any given point in time, emerge at the point when imagination, commitment, or need overrides norms and traditions."

Furthermore, Marrow's (2009) fundamental contention that "your talk is your family" corroborates this belief; one must communicate with the family to sustain its state of being. In essence, families' silence will take them out of being. Candidly speaking, if we *want* to dissolve our families and cease the potential for ongoing dynamics and generational influences, simply break off communication between family members. Positive and reliable family systems thrive on communication established with open and honest talk that provides its collective members with family life skills, including boundary setting, priority identification, emotional expression, decision making, values clarification, and behavioral management.

Evotypical families are sustained by their communicative dialogue, including technological support systems. This notion is supported with Steier's (1989) belief that families are constituted by the very communication processes that are thought of as being "within a family." While Galvin (2006) purports that "discourse dependency is not new, what is new is that discourse dependent families are becoming the norm" (p. 9). In addition, Galvin theorizes that "the greater the ambiguity of family form, the more elaborate the communicative processes needed to establish and maintain identity" (p. 4). Perhaps more now than ever, a family's discourse impacts and shapes family identity—even more than biological, geographical, or legal ties.

Contrivances that can either assist or challenge discourse-dependent family are often technology related. While distant family members are connected by technology, according to a study by the Kaiser Family Foundation (2010), the average child, ages 8 to 18, spends over 7.5 hours a day using technology gadgets equaling 2.5 hours of music, almost 5 hours of television and movies, and 3 hours of Internet and video games. If you count the content streams separately—many people multitask, such as texting while watching television—our youth are logging almost 11 hours of media usage a day, which adds up to 75 hours a week (Rideout, Foehr, & Roberts, 2010). Along with extensive media usage in families, researchers conducting a bleak study at California State University, Northridge (2012), found that the number of minutes per week that parents spend in meaningful conversation with their children averages only 3.5.

It is strikingly apparent that technology and family cannot be treated as two mutually exclusive spheres in the Internet age. Today, as families experience the norm of being discourse dependent on one another, it is crucial for family members to find better ways to incorporate technology into familial structures and generate more child–adult daily interactions so as not to jeopardize their very existence.

Chapter 2   More Than Blood: Rethinking Identities, Interactions, and the Future of Contemporary Families

Societal Influences Significantly Impact Evotypical Families, Regardless of Life Stage, Membership, or Living Arrangement (External Influences)

Popular culture portrays contemporary families as flexible and provocative systems, and many scholars advance the power of the popular culture in shaping our lives. Thomas G. Endres (2011) conducted a content analysis of a 1-day snapshot of pop culture, "Top in Pop," via *Billboard*, movie attendance and *TV Guide* ratings, to examine how much or how little relationships and families are attended to in popular media.

The following chart includes the top 20 *Billboard* hits, the top 20 rated television shows, and the top 10 box office hits for October 20, 2011. This represents a 1-day snapshot of pop culture to examine how much or how little relationships and families are attended to by the popular media.

Music—*Billboard*

1. "Someone Like You," Adele—"Sometimes it lasts in love but sometimes it hurts instead"
2. "Moves Like Jagger," Maroon 5—"Take control, own me just for the night"
3. "Pumped Up Kicks," Foster the People—"you'd better run, better run, faster than my bullet"
4. "Sexy and I Know It," LMFAO—"I got passion in my pants and I ain't afraid to show it"
5. "Stereo Hearts," Gym Class Heroes—"And know my heart's a stereo that only plays for you"
6. "We Found Love," Rhianna—"It's the way I'm feeling I just can't deny, But I've gotta let it go"
7. "Without You," David Guetta and Usher—"I can't take one more sleepless night without you"
8. "You Make Me Feel . . . ,: Cobra Starship—"And if you listen you can hear me through the radio"
9. "Party Rock Anthem," LMFAO—"Step up fast and be the first girl to make me throw this cash"
10. "Young, Wild & Free," Snoop Dog & Wiz Khalifa—. . . "so what we get drunk, so what we smoke weed"
11. "You and I," Lady Gaga—". . . a long time but I'm back in town, This time I'm not leaving without you"
12. "In the Dark," Dev—"I wanna see who you are, I got a sex drive just push to start"
13. "Super Bass," Nicki Minaj—"I said, excuse me you're a hell of a guy"
14. "Give Me Everything," Pitbull—"Make you feel so good tonite, cuz we might not get tomorrow"
15. "Headlines," Drake—"I guess it really is just me, myself and all my millions"
16. "Lighters," Bad Meets Evil—"I wanna just say thanks cuz your hate is what gave me the strength"
17. "It Girl," Jason Derulo—"This is it girl, Give me 25 to life, You could "
18. "Good Life," One Republic—"New names and numbers that I don't know"
19. "She Will," Lil Wayne—"Karma is a bitch? Well just make sure that bitch is beautiful"
20. "How to Love," Lil Wayne—"See you had a lot of moments that didn't last forever"

Television—*TV Guide*

1. *Dancing with the Stars*—Reality show where celebrities partner up with professional dancers
2. *Modern Family*—Satirical look at three different families and the comedic trials they face
3. *X Factor*—Simon Cowell and his fellow judges search for a singer who has the "X factor"
4. *Grey's Anatomy*—Drama on the personal and professional lives of five surgical interns
5. *New Girl*—After a bad breakup, a quirky young woman moves into an apartment with three men
6. *Two and a Half Men*—The naked truth about breakups, hookups, and everything in between
7. *Criminal Minds*—An elite group of profilers analyze the nation's most dangerous criminal minds
8. *Breaking Bad*—Informed he has cancer, a chemistry genius produces crystal meth

9. *True Blood*—Vampires walk the earth using synthetic blood
10. *Big Brother*—Contestants compete in a house wired with cameras and microphones
11. *So You Think You Can Dance*—Searching for America's favorite dancer
12. *The Closer*—Chief Brenda Johnson runs the LAPD Homicide Division with an unorthodox style
13. *The Bachelorette*—A spin-off of the American competitive reality dating game show
14. *Weeds*—Comedy about a suburban mother turned marijuana dealer
15. *Jersey Shore*—A reality-based look at the vapid lives of several New Jersey 20-somethings
16. *The Voice*—Four famous musicians search for the best voices in America
17. *America's Got Talent*—Talent competition where an array of performers vie for a $1 million prize
18. *American Idol*—Future singers who were selected from America compete in a talent contest
19. *The Bachelor*—The American competitive reality dating game show
20. *NCIS*—The cases of the Naval Criminal Investigative Service

Box Office by Gross

1. *Real Steel*—Courage is stronger than steel.
2. *Footloose*—This is our time.
3. *The Thing*—It's not human. Yet.
4. *The Ides of March*—Ambition seduces. Power corrupts.
5. *Dolphin Tale*—Inspired by the amazing true story of Winter
6. *Moneyball*—What are you really worth?
7. *50/50*—It takes a pair to beat the odds
8. *Courageous*—Honor begins at home
9. *The Big Year*—Everyone is searching for something
10. *The Lion King*—Life's greatest adventure is finding your place in the Circle of Life

Rhetorical analyses of this media overview are somewhat troubling, concluding that the rhetoric associated with the song lyrics are void of explicit, permanent relationships. Additionally, the songs' primary foci are on "partying and hooking up." Almost nothing in these collective song lyrics refer to deeply committed and loyal relationships. Family portrayals in these selected movies are occasionally mentioned in context (e.g., courageous); however, the main themes of these movies seem to be "overcoming adversity" —be it families, baseball teams, robots, or dolphins. Not surprisingly, half of the television shows are "reality based." According to Jaffe (2005), the vast appeal to watch reality television is to experience the sense of "*schadenfreude* [a German term], which translates to the pleasure one receives at the suffering of others." For example, media consumers can delight in experiencing another's misfortune and public demise while escaping their own unremarkable lives.

This evotypical family tenet reflects media researcher Marshall McLuhan's (1994) often quoted saying that we live in a global village where "the medium is the message," only to be later argued by media researchers that both content and medium have a powerful effect on consumers. Further, Donald Ellis (1999) claims that prevalent media shapes behavior and thought. How we process and manage information and how we interact with others changes as the media in our environment changes. Sellnow (2010) reinforces this contention with her definition of mediated popular culture: "what we experience through, for example, movies, TV, songs, comic strips, and advertisements that may influence us to believe and behave in certain ways" (p. 3) and to also shape beliefs regarding how we ought *not* to behave. Today, it is daunting to consider how predominant media shape our families' behaviors and thoughts. It is even more overwhelming to speculate on the far-reaching effects that media may have on shaping and influencing the families of tomorrow.

Evotypical Family Relations Benefit from Successful Management of the Dialectical Tensions of "Fantasy Versus Reality" (Expectations)

Rapp (2008) discusses the ideology between family norms and realities. "Norms concerning families are that people should be loving and sharing within them, and that they should be protective. The reality is too often otherwise, as the recent rising consciousness of domestic violence indicates" (p. 191). Disturbing research correlates with national statistics revealing typical stresses that ordinary families endure. One study by Rubin shows that 40% of adults interviewed have at least one alcoholic parent and that 50% have been affected by parental desertion or divorce.

All of us know how harsh reality can be, individually or on families as a whole, during severe times of dysfunction or moments of minor disappointments, such as how holidays should be spent together. Sometimes, the act of fantasizing or theorizing how things *could* or *should* be different can help assuage some of the pain attached to the stark realities in family life. Braithwaite, Schrodt, and Konieg Kellas (2006) discuss the role of fantasies in conjunction with Bormann's (1985) symbolic convergence theory: "Fantasy is the creative and imaginative interpretation of events that fulfills a psychological or rhetorical need. Some fantasies include fanciful and fictitious stories of imaginary characters, yet others deal with events that that have actually happened to members of the group (or family) or that are reported in works of history, in media outlets, or in the oral history or folklore of a group" (p. 149). While these fantasies within the family are grounded in reality, they can become a helpful tool in tempering some of the disappointments and creating a more powerful vision of the future. However, fantasizing about the ideal family dynamic or situation will never bring total fulfillment, as fantasy, by the very nature of its meaning, is elusive and unattainable. Therefore, the art of "relative satisfaction" lies somewhere in between the balance of fantasy and reality.

Just as in relational dialogic theory, opposing forces exist within all relationships. Leslie Baxter's (2004) dialogical theory looks at how relationships are a place where "contradictions are managed"

stemming from opposing tensions within a system (p. 238). Because of the complexity of relationships, there can be many clusters of forces, referred to as a "knot of contradiction" (Montgomery & Baxter, 1998). Negotiating the many "knots" between fantasy and reality or hopes and disillusionment in evotypical families is challenging, yet gaining the skill of walking a razor's edge between the imaginations is a valuable skill for sustaining positive family interactions and regard.

The Charisma or Spirit Within Evotypical Families May Be Developed and Maintained by Strong Leaders, Including Hero/Heroine-Like Members Who Consistently Act Out and Narrate Their Feats to Other Family Members (Inspiration)

Heroes, or legendary family members, often serve as inspiration for evotypical families, leaving villainous behaviors to serve as examples of undesirable familial norms. Living or deceased heroic figures create a sense of belonging by moving living family members to realize similar characteristics or values within their families. Joseph Campbell (1973) writes about the path to heroism:

> A hero ventures forth from the world of common day into a region of supernatural wonder: fabulous forces are there encountered and a decisive victory won: the hero comes back from this mysterious adventure with the power to bestow boons on his fellow man. (p. 30)

As such, heroes in our families are constructed in our imaginations after they attend to difficult situations and then assist others in doing the same. The heroes of our families do not have to be flawless or possess superhuman qualities—they simply exhibit behaviors that are respectable and then have their acts followed by family members' telling and retelling stories of their various worthy feats.

Fisher (1987) discusses the power of the narrative paradigm as central to all human communication. Leoutsakas (2003) states, "Narrative reasoning is a means to . . . explain the functions of people, their societies, and institutions" (p. 59). Among those institutions is the family. Renowned family therapist Virginia Satir (1988) focuses on heroes and the roles they play in the family dynamic. Satir describes the family hero as a member of the family that holds the pride and appearance of the family in their hands and is a success that represents the entire family (Wood, 2006). These figures as sources of pride can play a forceful role in confirming the family's existence and worth while adding to a heightened sense of respect for the family system by its members. An additional benefit of familial stories is the enjoyment of their retelling and that they are often a source of entertainment at family gatherings.

The Future of the Evotypical Family Relies on Its Ability to Embrace the Paradoxical Truth That "Its Stability Is in Its Instability" (Flexibility)

An interesting paradox is created when looking at the paradigm of the evotypical family and its contradiction associated with change. The contemporary family's identity is that it is in a constant state of flux, as opposed to families throughout history that have generally experienced a considerably slower evolution. The unique aspect of present-day families are that their stability, or sense of certainty, lies within their unstable state.

We turn to researchers who have drawn on the notion of "paradox" to explain contrasts in worldviews and human behavior, especially in the fields of psychology and mental health. To quote Paul Watzlawick (1978) in his seminal work *The Language of Change*,

Chapter 2 More Than Blood: Rethinking Identities, Interactions, and the Future of Contemporary Families

> Paradox is the Achilles heel of our logical, analytical, rational world view. It is the point at which the seemingly all-embracing division of reality into pairs of opposites, especially into the Aristotelian dichotomy of true and false, breaks down and reveals itself as inadequate. (p. 99)

Furthermore, in the *American Heritage Dictionary of the English Language*, paradox is defined as "a seemingly contradictory statement that may nonetheless be true" (Pickett, 2000). "Paradox is made possible by dissociating dissociations so that the apparent and the real become so interchangeable that one cannot be discerned from the other (Foucault, 1977, p. 8). To manage a paradox, Watzlawick (1978) recommends taking a *both-and* perspective that considers both the needs and difficulties surrounding the phenomenon as well as the strengths and successes that may not, at first glance, be apparent within the phenomenon. There is something reassuring in knowing that the evotypical family system does not require survival in a fixed state—that its stability lies within its instability. With this reality, the status quo in families is always in motion and constantly challenged by critical thinkers and activists desiring change, which is viewed as a positive force.

The dichotomy in this discussion alludes to the complex patterns of evolution in families, both short and long term. Perhaps this will lead some to perceive the family system as being less stable and secure than in years past. Its structure, commitment, enactment, communication, external influences, and expectations are different, changing, and seemingly more complicated. Paradoxically, though, families always had to endure the changes and complications, such as the instability caused by the need to thrive over time. Today, however, family evolution is more rapid and adaptation more urgent. This process has become a stabilizing factor for contemporary families and attests to their resilience in the present. By reframing or altering viewpoints, once-perceived unstable family systems become more stable as changes and nuances become more typical. In families that embrace their constant instability, members appreciate the family system's ability to stay intact regardless of its invariable changes.

Evotypical Behavioral Ideas

With radical changes to the structures and interactions of families in the United States comes a necessity to reclarify family values and their accompanying behaviors. These values—some old, some new—do not ensure the continuation of evotypical families as currently constructed, but they do provide insight into what we deem "behavioral ideas" for sustaining contemporary families. In today's complex society, individual behaviors heavily influence family units, as do group interactions. While individual roles such as gender, child rearing, domestic, and so on are enacted in evotypical families, the definitional behaviors accompanying such roles are diverse and inconsistent across society. Attachments of family members, therefore, often rely on individual morality and understanding—not social acceptance. As such, behaviors like caring, sharing, supporting, and kindness remain desired within our society and specifically within the family system. Using these constructs along with the tenets of evotypical families, here are the familial behavioral requirements that we consider useful in sustaining healthy and productive families for the future:

1. Celebrate the family for what it is, not what it is not.
2. Keep the family dream alive through commitment to the family unit.

3. Recognize the family's instability and be flexible.
4. Communicate with one another utilizing various methods of sharing information (direct communication, storytelling, technology, writing, and so on).
5. Address the stress on the family that is produced by nonconformity with socially constructed standards.
6. Capitalize on family strengths and seek to change causes of weaknesses.
7. Find (create) family heroes to inspire family members.
8. Dare to take risks needed for adaption to ever-changing family dynamics (beliefs, values, attitudes, behaviors, and so on)

Each of these is discussed in the following sections.

Celebrate the Family for What It Is, Not for What It Is Not

All too often, we focus on family weaknesses and forget about the strengths of our families. We spend an inordinate amount of time trying to change family members to be or act in a manner that we think they should be or act. This often turns out to be counterproductive. All families face adversities. One strength of the family is the blending of ideas and abilities to overcome these adversities. Family members should rely on their positive instincts and beliefs that can go forward, working their ways through adversities.

Keep the Family Dream Alive Through Commitment to the Family Unit

Families often break apart when family members lose contact with each other. If family members are not committed to a family's shared dream, it is likely that they will drop out of the group physically, linguistically, or emotionally. If family members are divided over the goals and dreams of the family, the families are likely to come apart and reorganize into new familial patterns. However, if family members have shared dreams for the system to stay together, it takes dedication and a strong sense of commitment to reach those goals. It is essential for family members to be consistent with their presence and discourse with each other and share sufficient time, thoughts, emotions, and activities on a coconstructed "regular" basis.

Recognize the Family's Instability and Be Flexible

As noted, evotypical families are in a constant state of flux. This renders families unstable and family members in a continuous position of uncertainty. To cope with unexpected changes and confusion stemming from family units, family members need patience and understanding to manage the uncertainty. This takes family members with more mature, "relaxed," and "forgiving" personalities to guide family members experiencing difficulty with instability and change.

Communicate with One Another Utilizing Various Methods of Sharing Information (Direct Communication, Storytelling, Technology, Writing, and So On)

Communication is essential to all functioning groups, including families. Contemporary families, regardless of their configurations and abilities, utilize messaging to maintain their form. By using communication, from simple facial expressions to complex Internet software, family members create and maintain familial bonds. Without sharing information, family members tend to isolate, forming individual goals leading to separation from family units. When multiple members fail to communicate, there are often ruptures in those families that may or may not be repairable.

Address the Stress on the Family That Is Produced by Nonconformity with Socially Constructed Standards

In the United States, the family remains subject to regular social critique. Family analysts often provide templates for successful families. When a family unit collectively decides to disregard customary norms established by such critics, the unit is vulnerable to public scrutiny and, at times, vicious attacks. Finding ways to cope with the stress produced by these types of responses is essential for families to continue to exist. Coping may mean forming alliances with like-minded people, relocation, or relying on sympathetic extended family members.

Capitalize on Family Strengths and Seek to Change Causes of Weaknesses

Actions taken by family members reflect on family units and, as such, are perceived as positive or negative acts by other family members and immediate contacts. Actions that meet the approval of the larger groups may be considered strengths that lead to successful family bonding. Those that do not meet with approval are perceived as family weaknesses. Unfortunately, however, when the only response to behaviors is from the immediate surroundings, antisocial behaviors can develop and be treated as strengths. To capitalize on socially acceptable and legal family strengths, families must have a strong sense of right from wrong, needs from wants, and fairness from exploitation. This sense allows families to select the constructive values and behaviors needed to further their healthy existences.

Find (Create) Family Heroes to Inspire Family Members

All families need heroes. These can be members of the family (nuclear or extended) or unrelated people. Try not to select heroes based on popularity but rather choose heroes based on their values and positive actions. The acts of heroes make for great stories and can lay the groundwork for modeling members' behaviors and strengthening family bonds.

Dare to Take Risks Needed for Adaption to Ever-Changing Family Dynamics (Beliefs, Values, Attitudes, Behaviors, and So On)

As we settle into an evotypical era for families, new family dynamics often require risk taking on the members of the family. Issues such as abortion, interracial marriage, same-sex marriage, interreligious relationships, transracial adoption are not for the thin skinned—those who do not cope well with challenges to their relationships. It takes strong beliefs and perseverance to form new families and maintain them regardless of opposing outside forces. Families that withstand harassment with the aid of strong alliances often become solid and prominent community members and leaders.

Remember that stress and disappointments happen in all systems, including families. Stress can help reveal families' strengths and actually help identify what is needed to make them stronger. Often, families push through stressors without realizing the parameters, contributors, and scope of the stressors, and then they are soon repeated, creating powerfully unwanted patterns. Rather than ignoring stressors, determine the lessons you need to learn from them. In addition, pay close attention to the language of family interactions—what notions or speculations are being stated as truths. These faulty assumptions are very hard to change and can be devastating to families once things

are fixated on the most negative attributes. When the minds of members are filled with negative thoughts, negative energies result. To counteract the negativity, determine the behaviors and actions that are most important in families and voice them, making them known to others. If honesty and support are the most important to families, then be certain to practice them as individuals—in essence, model the family behaviors you wish to see in all families.

Conclusion

Today, emerging and challenging family lifestyle concerns exemplify "evotypical families," a more accurate term for conceptualizing contemporary westernized families. These include families formed, in part, through transracial adoption, same-sex parenting, anonymous or known sperm donors, third and fourth remarriages, child-free marriage, lifetime cohabitation, noncustodial mothers, singles by choice, and a host of diverging families. We contend that evotypical families are different from the earlier family units in terms of their identity, commitment, enactment, communication, external influences, expectations, inspirations, and propensity to change. Specific "behavioral requirements" for sustaining contemporary families are suggested, including family celebrations, commitment, flexibility, communication, stress management, family strength assessment, hero identification, and risk-taking behaviors.

As the views and understandings of family have changed on the U.S. landscape, so must we who study families. Research with evotypical families is now in its infancy. Certain groupings have garnered more than a fair share of attention, and there are some baseline studies reflecting common characteristics of such families. Research literature provides significant data related to gay and lesbian families, two-parent heterosexual families, adoptive families, blended families, and so on, but family communication specialists, therapists, social workers, and educators are all too often behind the learning curve surrounding family studies. Terms like "latchkey kids," "disrupted adoptions," "elder care," and "military divorce" do not represent end-stage family situations; they all represent an evolved and evolving familial state. To remain current, family researchers must remain vigilant, ever paying heed to sociocultural changes.

We must approach investigative procedures with liberal minds, closing off preconceived notions or biases regarding how families should or should not constitute their identities. When embarking on the research, it is important to consider not only which family topics or behaviors intrigue us but also how our research agendas may contribute to the existing body of family knowledge. For it is the research findings disseminated in the future and *practically applied to or in families* that will help temper the tough trials that contemporary families will undoubtedly face and will help us better appreciate continuing positive influences that families often enjoy; these are extraordinary times with exciting future prospects.

While the evotypical family is definitely in a state of flux, the intent of this chapter has been to portray its identity not as if it were in a state of decline or a major upswing but rather as an intricate network barraged with change. Whether these changes have enhanced the contemporary family's identity is worthy of reflection. One could argue that the state of the family is stronger than ever—highly resilient to its diverse problems and challenges. Or, at the other extreme, the family is fledgling and weak—on the verge of extinction. Where one's opinion lies on this continuum dictates, to a large degree, how one enacts, experiences, and values family.

Today's families are not more resilient or less resilient than families of days gone by; they are just "different" in the way their identities are created, managed, and lived. As American author and satirist James Thurber (1961) once wrote in the foreword of his book *Lanterns and Lances*, "Let us not look back in anger, nor forward in fear, but around in awareness" (p. xv); for families, the challenge will be for members to become more aware and accepting of the constant changes occurring in contemporary society; for individuals, each of us is required to take an active participatory role in doing whatever is necessary to protect and enhance this century-old institution.

Discussion Questions

1. Explain some of the ways that families have changed, both structurally and demographically, since the mid-20th century.
2. Expound on the authors' claim that "families' silence will take them out of being." Do you agree or disagree with this claim?
3. Discuss a hero/heroine or legendary member in your own family; what specific accomplishment or behavior did this member perform that provided inspiration to the family unit?
4. In your opinion, which of the eight family behavioral requirements that the authors suggest seem to be most critical to effective family interaction?
5. Do you agree with the authors' statement that "today's families are not more resilient or less resilient than families of days gone by; they are just 'different' in the way their identities are created, managed, and lived. Justify your answer.

References

Anderson, G., & Philipov, D. (2002). Life-table representations of family dynamics in Sweden, Hungary, and 14 other FFS countries. *Demographic Research, 7*(4): 67-144. doi:10.4054/DemRes.2002.7.4

Baxter, L. (2004). Relationships as dialogues. *Personal Relationships, 11*, 1-22.

Bormann, E. G. (1985, September). Symbolic convergence theory: A communication formulation. *Journal of Communication, 35*(4), 128–138.

Braithwaite, D. O., Schrodt, P., & Konieg Kellas, J. (2006). Symbolic convergence theory: Communication and symbolic convergence in families. In D. O. Braithwaite & L. A. Baxter (Eds.), *Engaging theories in communication: Multiple perspectives* (pp. 146–161). Thousand Oaks, CA: Sage.

Brown, S. K., & Bean F. D. (2005). International migration. In D.L. Poston & M. Micklin (Eds.), *Handbook of population* (pp. 347–382) New York: Kluwer Academic.

California State University, Northridge. (2012, February 15). Television statistics.'http://www.prabhupadanugas.eu/?p=26050

Campbell, J. (1973). *The hero with a thousand faces* (2nd ed.). Princeton, NJ: Princeton University Press.

Cherlin, A. J. (2010). Demographic trends in the US: A review of research in the 2000s. *Journal of Marriage and Family 72*, 403-419.

Derry, S. (1999). A fish called peer learning: Searching for common themes. In A. O'Donnell & A. King (Eds.), *Cognitive perspectives of peer learning*. Hillsdale, NJ: Lawrence Erlbaum Associates.

Ellis, D. G. (1999). *Crafting society: Ethnicity, class and communication theory*. Mahwah, NJ: Lawrence Erlbaum Associates

Endres, T. G. (2011). Notes from a lecture on family depictions in the media. In-class lecture conducted for a COMM 514, Interpersonal Communication, course at the University of Northern Colorado, Greeley, CO.

Fisher, W. R. (1987). *Human communication as narration: Toward a philosophy of reason, value, and action.* Columbia: University of South Carolina Press.

Foucault, M. (1977). *Discipline and punishment.* 1st American ed. Translated from the French by Alan Sheridan. New York: Pantheon.

Galvin, K. (2004). The family of the future: What do we face? In A. L. Vangelisti (Ed.), *Handbook of family communication* (pp. 675–690). Mahwah, NJ: Lawrence Erlbaum Associates.

Galvin, K. (2006). Diversity. In L. H. Turner & R. West (Eds.), *The family communication sourcebook* (pp. 4–9). Thousand Oaks, CA: Sage.

Gilbert, E. (2010). *Committed: A skeptic makes peace with marriage*. London: Penguin.

Heuveline, P., Timberlake, J. M., & Furstenberg, F.F., Jr. (2003). The role of cohabitation in family formation: The United States of comparative perspective. *Journal of Marriage and Family, 66*, 1214–1230.

Jaffee, E. (2005, March). Reality check. *Observer, 18*(3). http://www.psychologicalscience.org/index.php/publications/observer/2005/march-05/reality-check.html

Kukla, A. (2000). *Social constructivism and the philosophy of science*. London: Routledge.

Leoutsakas, D. (2003). *The orphan tales: Real and imagined stories of parental loss*. Unpublished doctoral dissertation, University of South Florida, Tampa.

Loving v. Virginia. (1958, 1967). U.S. Supreme Court. Appeal from the Supreme Court of Appeals of Virginia. http://caselaw.lp.findlaw.com/scripts/getcase.pl?court=US&vol=388&invol=1

Marrow, S. R. (2009, March 5). How to talk about uncertain times in your family. Interview by Amy Jacobs at WKSTT FM (recorded archives), San Luis Obispo, CA.

Martin, S. P. (2004). Women's education and family timing: Outcomes and trends associated with age at marriage and first birth. In K. M. Neckerman (Ed.), *Social inequality* (pp. 79–118). New York: Russell Sage Foundation.

Martin, S. P. (2006). Trends in marital dissolution by women's education in the United States. *Demographic Research, 15,* 537–560.

McMahon, M. (1997). *Social constructivism and the World Wide Web: A paradigm for learning,* Paper presented at the ASCILITE conference, Perth, Australia.

McLuhan, M. (1994). *Understanding media: The extensions of man* (Reprint ed.). New York: MIT Press. http://beforebefore.net/80f/s11/media/mcluhan.pdf

Montgomery, B. M., & Baxter, L. M. (1998). Dialogism and relational dialectics. In *Dialectical approaches to studying personal relationships* (pp. 155–184). Hillsdale, NJ: Lawrence Erlbaum Associates.

National Center for Health Statistics. (2009a). Births: Final data for 2006. *National Vital Statistics Reports, 57*(7). http://www.cdc.gov/nchs/data/nvsr/nvsr57/nvsr57_07.pdf

National Center for Health Statistics. (2009b). *Changing patterns of nonmarital childbearing in the United States.* Data Brief No. 18. http://www.cdc.gov/nchs/data/databriefs/db18.pdf

Pacanowsky, M. E., & O'Donnell-Trujillo, N. (1983). In S. Littlejohn & K. Foss (Eds.), *Theories of Human Communication* (pp. 314–316). Long Grove, IL: Waveland Press.

Pickett, J. P. (Exec. ed.). (2000). *American Heritage Dictionary of the English Language.* Boston: Houghton Mifflin.

Quinn, J. B. (2012). When parents move in with kids. *AARP Bulletin, 53*(7), 10.

Rideout, V. J., Foehr, U. G., & Roberts, D. (2010). *Generation m2: Media in the lives of 8- to 18-year-olds.* Retrieved from http://www.kff.org/entmedia/upload/8010.pdf

Satir, V. (1988). *The new peoplemaking.* Mountain View, CA: Science & Behavior Books.

Sellnow, D. (2010). *The rhetorical power of popular culture considering mediated texts.* Los Angeles: Sage.

Stamp, G. H. (2004). Theories of family relationships and a family relationships theoretical model. In A. Vangelisti (Ed.), *Handbook of family communication* (pp. 1–30). Mahwah, NJ: Lawrence Erlbaum Associates.

Steier, F. (1989). Toward a radical and ecological constructivist approach to family communication. *Journal of Applied Communication Research, 1,* 91–110.

Tavernise, S. (2011, May 26). Married couples are no longer a majority, census finds. *New York Times.* http://www.nytimes.com/2011/05/26/us/26marry.html

Thibaut, J. W., & Kelley, H. H. (1959). *The social psychology of groups.* New York: Wiley.

Thurber, J. (1961). *Lanterns and lances.* New York: Harper & Brothers.

U.S. Bureau of the Census. (2005). *Number, timing, and duration of marriages and divorces, 2001.* http://www.census.gov/prod/2005pubs/p70-97.pdf

U.S. Bureau of the Census. (2008). *Statistical abstract of the United States, 2008.* http://www.census.gov/compendia/statab

U.S. Bureau of the Census. (2009a). *Custodial mothers and fathers and their child support, 2007.* http://www.census.gov/prod/2009pubs/p60-237.pdf

U.S. Bureau of the Census. (2009b). Table MS-2. Estimated median age at first marriage, by sex: 1890 to the present. http://www.census.gov/population/socdemo/hh-fam/ms2.xls

Watzlawick, P. (1978). *The language of change.* New York: Basic Books.

Wood, A. (2006). *Family roles: In the addictive system.* http://therapyinphiladelphia.com/selfhelp/tips/family_roles_in_the_addictive_system.

PART 2
Communication Perspectives

Chapter 3
Family Stories: Communicative Values, Interactions, and Burdens   26
Dennis Leoutsakas, *Salisbury University*

Chapter 4
The Family that Inks Together, Links Together: Tattoos as Family Identifiers   36
Thomas G. Endres, *University of Northern Colorado*

Chapter 5
Appreciative Inquiry as a Model for Strengths-Based Decision Making in Couples and Families   49
Deborah Ballard-Reisch, *Wichita State University*

Chapter 6
Forgiveness and Reconciliation: Infidelity as a Case Study   60
Douglas Kelley, *Arizona State University*

Chapter 7
Decision Making in Dual-Career Couples: A Replication and Extension   70
Douglas C. Pennington, *Lynn Haven United Methodist Church, Panama City, Florida*
Lynne M. Webb, *University of Arkansas*

Chapter 3

Family Stories: Communicative Values, Interactions, and Burdens

Dennis Leoutsakas

My father-in-law had four brothers and one sister; all are now deceased. The six siblings from Alabama had a total of 19 children. At the rate their blood, adopted, and step-relatives are being added to the family, I've lost track of all the grandchildren and great-grandchildren. When my wife's family comes together every 2 years for their extended family reunion, I am both overwhelmed and fascinated by the event. I was orphaned at birth and have always understood family in a very different context. This is my initial reaction to her family reunions:

> Driving through the rural South, I soak in the beauty of the landscape. I think the South has gotten a "bad rap" from those living in the fast-paced northern cities. There is something calming about the peaceful nature of the terrain. Pulling into the site of the reunion, my heart begins to race. I've been with my wife for over 20 years, but I've never fully acclimated to this gathering. As soon as I stop our loaded car near the lodging, my wife pulls away the restraining seat belts, breaking free from the long drive. Immediately she starts locating the once-close but now distant, siblings, cousins, and other relatives. Story time begins. There are stories from the past, stories from the present, exciting adventure stories, and stories of pain and loss. I have been embraced by this family, so I too must share stories. It is disconcerting because I don't know how much to share. As a result, I carefully edit my stories; it's an old foster home trick—tell a story, any story, just not the whole story. After a weekend (2 full days) of sharing, we part ways. All of us, including me, look forward to meeting again in 2 more years.

As an ethnographer, oral historian, and researcher, I rely on stories to conduct my field research. I listen to individuals and family members (biological and nonbiological) discuss their past and present relationships. By using open-ended interviewing, I explore the strength of family bonds by focusing on and analyzing the stories that once-displaced children and their family members or surrogate family members tell about the childhood experiences and family-life happenings of these children when they were in foster or adoptive care.

It is clear to me that as new family configurations develop, family members rely on the most ancient of traditions—the oral tradition—to strengthen the bonds that tie families together. Lodging and clothing for protection from the elements, water and food for nourishment and growth, and contact with other living creatures throughout infancy are all basic human needs. It is through natural processes of satisfying these needs that kinship bonds develop and that communication is appreciated. For humans to get a sense of meaning in their lives, beyond the struggle for survival, they create language and story the events of their lives. Everything we know about natural and human experiences has been given to us in story fashion. Even the most sophisticated mathematical equations and inextricable religious doctrines are translated into narrative for comprehension. Stories are one of the most natural ways to express ourselves, and storytelling is a method for relating experiences and placing them into a context. Walter Fisher (1984, 1985a, 1985b, 1987, 1988, 1989) posits this as the "narrative paradigm" of human communication.

While the narrative paradigm has its detractors (Farrell, 1985; Lucaites & Condit, 1985; McGee & Nelson, 1985; Rowland, 1988, 1989; Warnick, 1987), the value of storytelling to humans is not a novel concept. From ancient cave paintings and Sumerian scripts to modern novels and broadcast news stories, humans have always sought to story their experiences. In addition, scholars throughout the ages have used the power of narrative to advance their notions (i.e., Aristotle, 1907; Barthes, 1974; Propp, 1968). Today, narrative inquiry is situated in multiple disciplines, and storytelling is utilized on all sociocultural planes. Many successful storytellers, from griots and politicians to anthropologists and ethnographers, use the work of contemporary narrative scholars to advance their craft. While the influences of narrative are not denied by today's societies, the necessity of storying for *human survival* seems to lose momentum as the species gets older and more involved with human issues on a high-tech global scale. The personal story tends to be trivialized. With this in mind, this chapter strengthens the tenet that storytelling is a necessity for kinship bonds and therefore a root communication device necessary for family, community, and global sociopolitical and ideological movements.

Family Stories: Communicative Interactions

In her edited book, *Family Communication: Theory and Research*, Lorin Badsen Arnold (2008) declares, "Without communication families wouldn't exist at all" (p. 103). She notes that communicative interactions are needed to form kinship bonds and develop rituals such as coupling, birthing, and parenting. In her writing, Arnold uses multiple works to reflect on stories as a significant communicative element within families. In the same volume, using the work of Didier Coste (1989) and W. G. Kirkwood (1992), I forward the idea that the following relationships exist between stories and family communication:

> (1) Stories help us explain what is happening in our families; (2) Stories are used by primary caretakers in families to provide examples of beliefs, values, attitudes, and behaviors; (3) As individuals, we use stories to convince other family members to recognize our points of view; and (4) Stories help us to dream, both as individual family members and as family units. (Leoutsakas, 2008, pp. 136–137)

Expanding on the notions of Coste and Kirkwood, stories are extremely important for relating and perpetuating a family history. These five interactions provide a foundation for determining the ways in which storytelling is used to develop necessary kinship bonds. The interactions can be understood as discussed in the following sections.

Stories Are Extremely Important for Relating and Perpetuating a Family History

As people seek family relationships and experiences or are birthed or placed into families, the family history is of primary importance. It helps determine the family members' identities and behaviors. Newly formed families story their experiences to form a group identity and forward their values to new family members. Established families story their experiences to justify their existence and to perpetuate values. Individuals in families, however, may have conflicting values (consider a religious figure and a criminal figure being part of the same family), but the family story remains consistent. In the minister and criminal scenario, the family story will honor one set of values and reject the other set, and the stories within the family may tell of each individual's development. The goal of the family history is to establish points around which members can psychologically and emotionally connect (or justify severing relations) with other family members. At times, the historical stories are painful, as in the case of the death of a child, and at other times, the stories are fond remembrances.

Stories Help Us Explain What Is Happening in Our Families

Many cultures, including those in the United States, have greetings that request information about family status. In English, "How are you?" or in Spanish, "Como está?" between friends often implies that a personal and family narrative is warranted. In addition, every intact family has stories about family members (the crazy aunt), the development of the family (Grandma and Grandpa's illnesses), additions to and subtractions from the family (births, adoptions, deaths, and so on), and events impacting the family (from the mundane to the tragic and/or exciting). These stories, like the families themselves, tend to evolve over time as more information becomes available. The stories are also strongly influenced by both the storyteller and the listener. The storyteller is often influenced by his or her perceived involvement in the happenings, and the story is often influenced by the depth of the connection the storyteller has with the listener (the story of little brother's first date is going to be told differently to a mentoring big brother than to his adoring but critical parents or to friends he is trying to impress). Depending on the importance of the story, it will be rendered a historical place in the family's chronicle, useful for perpetuating the family's history or used as an anecdotal story to be told on occasions such as family reunions.

Stories Are Used by Primary Caretakers in Families to Provide Examples of Beliefs, Values, Attitudes, and Behaviors

In general, all stories help forward or teach beliefs, values, attitudes, and behaviors that we hold dear. In order to preserve the family culture, some consider this the primary purpose of family stories (Jorgenson & Bochner, 2004; Stone, 1988). And while this is a primary function of family stories, some of the most canonized stories told in families of all societies are the spiritual and religious stories that have been retold for centuries. So the stories need not originate from familial experiences. Value-focused stories told within families provide a basis from which to draw positive and negative conclusions. When we read or hear stories of those in the family who do poorly because of their behaviors, the message is, "Don't act like them and you won't end up like them." When we hear or read stories about people known to the family who have excelled, the message to us is, "Be like them so we all can be proud of our family heritage." Primary caretakers use these stories as lessons, teaching through the process of sharing their beliefs, values, attitudes, and behaviors in narrative form. Naturally, some of these qualities suggested by the stories are socially acceptable and often reinforced by society (e.g., don't lie, don't steal, don't kill, and so on), but this narrative interaction can also create cultural dissonance for listeners when family values differ from social values. Children growing up in gang-style, crime-based, and institutionalized families (e.g., strict military, noncompromising police, or extremely religious families) often struggle with the paradoxes of their lives. In addition, a more subtle dissonance can be created with stories when surreptitious conflict is expressed through disparaging narrative (e.g., if your mother really loved you, she wouldn't . . . ; your stepdad doesn't care about you because if he did, he would . . .). In family relationships where blood relations do not exist, it is up to the surrogate parent figures to use stories from their own lives to create these morality narratives. Often when blood-related family members are not present, some of the anti–birth family messages are very subtle or framed as assistance, but children still get the messages. These value-laden stories, rife with negative and positive examples, assist in all stages of child development.

As Individuals, We Use Stories to Convince Other Family Members to Recognize Our Points of View

In every group, power is shared, alliances are formed, communication occurs, and negotiations take place. Families are no different than any other group. Infants and young children teach adults early on in their relationships that it is not enough for adults to be older or physically stronger to have power. All it takes is one person expressing self-will to show power fluctuations. All family members must take into account the beliefs, values, attitudes, abilities, and behaviors of the other members when expressing points of view for a family to work together well. Often individual points of view of family members are similar, thus reinforcing the bonds of the family, but there are always sticking points when family members cannot agree on a blended point of view. It is at these times that negotiation is necessary and individual family members rely on narrative persuasion to forward their points of view. Adults use such stories to get children to eat certain foods (e.g., "I used to hate fish too, then . . ."), adolescents try to convince caretakers that activities will be okay (e.g., "My friend's parents let them . . . , so I should be able to as well). This type of narrative reasoning is found throughout family constellations. At times, it is adults trying to convince children or other adults; other times, it is children trying to persuade adults or other children. While we can all come up with lighthearted persuasive stories we have witnessed, it should be remembered that many children and caregivers use stories as incendiary devices in very serious family situations or as a means to realign the family. Think how hurtful it is when adopted children say, "You're not my parents . . ." to their adopted parents. Stories related to politics, religion, personal tragedies, and traumatic histories can all be used as disengaging impeachments that sever family bonds.

Stories Help Us to Dream, Both as Individual Family Members and as Family Units

Stories from the past help families plan for the future. As family members plan for the future, they encourage hope, a basic element for human survival. If we can place an experience or several experiences into a narrative form, then we can decide what to do differently or similarly in the future. Often because of difficult childhood circumstances, adults dream of a better future for their own children and relatives. In the United States, college became highly sought after as more and more parents perceived it as a means of advancement for their children. Similarly, children will often follow the paths of adult figures in their lives who have stories they admire and want to imitate. Family dreams, however, need not be altruistic. Families positioned in war zones, ghettos, extremely high poverty areas, and other violent situations often use stories from these environments for survival. The stories are negative influencers that simply state, "Watch out for this, or the family as we know it will no longer exist." Such stories are usually followed with educational stories that show how to navigate the dangerous situations.

Family Stories: Communicative Burdens

Stories told (and often retold) within families are not without complications. Stories can be manipulated, changed over time, fabricated, and used as divisive instruments and are subject to misunderstanding or limited recall. Family stories (as with all stories) are told from a subjective point of view—the view of the teller. The stories emerge from a place in which tellers frame their stories from what they know (or think they know) based on what they remember or think they (or another person) experienced, and tellers relate the stories in such a way that they can live with the stories' outcomes and still maintain a level of credibility within the family. Fundamentally, storytellers don't want to be viewed as liars by their kinfolk unless they are telling stories for entertainment purposes. Both memory and manipulation have significant influences on our family stories. Focusing on these two burdens, it becomes obvious that family stories are crafted to meet the needs of families, and "truth" or veracity of recall often has less of an important role in family storytelling.

Memory

Many grandmothers and grandfathers, the constant brunt of forgetfulness jokes, have probably been relegated to that place in the family stories because of the biological effects of aging on memory. Memory is affected by age, but memories and the stories we tell from our memories are not exclusively affected by the aging process. Continuous research into what we remember or forget shows that our memories are affected by biology, trauma, suggestion, imagination, and sociocultural pressures (Fivush & Neisser, 1994; Loftus, 1997; Schacter, 2002; Van der Kolk & Fisler, 1995). Often, repressed memories are beneficial in coping with traumatizing events. Think of sexually abused children or returning war veterans with post traumatic stress disorder who are trying to socially adjust to their experiences. Some personalities show a high susceptibility to suggestion. There are numerous case studies exposing professionals who induced false repressed memories in patients undergoing hypnosis and police who induced false statements from witnesses through the power of suggestion.

The imaginations of children (and adults) lead storytellers to a new "truth." For example, as loved ones age or die, we often see those surrounding them begin to diminish their character defects and hold their attributes in higher esteem. In addition, remembering our own positive personal characteristics and minimizing failures is a way to reinforce the characteristics we want to develop (Carey, 2008). Finally, sociocultural pressures affect how we remember situations. Think of the 1960s—a time during which many U.S. families were divided over a broad number of issues, such as the Vietnam War and civil rights. Even with massive amounts of media footage, that era and family involvement (or noninvolvement) in the events of the era are often remembered by the actions of a few in the family, including the political leanings of the family.

Manipulation

By lying, family stories are easily altered. Whether "little white lies," lies of omission, lies arising from kindness, or totally invented narratives, lies are used to manipulate or to fabricate the family's stories. Both researchers and purveyors of popular culture agree that everyone lies (Boser, 2009; Bronson, 2008; Feldman 2009; Feldman, Forrest, & Happ, 2002; Gramzow & Willard, 2006; Kim, Kam, Sharkey, & Singelis, 2008; Kornet, 1997; Tyler & Feldman, 2005; Tyler, Feldman, & Reichert, 2006; Willard & Gramzow, 2009). Children learn to lie at early ages, and this ability is perceived as a sign of intelligence (Bronson, 2008). They often lie to avoid getting into trouble or to meet the perceived desires of adults guiding their lives. Rather than diminishing with age, lies become more complex and sophisticated with age. Think of the characteristics assigned to salespeople, lawyers, advertisers, and politicians—each spinning truths for profit. And consider how we as individuals link our self-presentations and identities to the things that we say to others and that we want to believe about ourselves. Exaggeration is not out of the question.

More collectivist cultures tend to expect members of society to lie as a sign of respect for the group culture (Kim et al., 2008). As in collectivist cultures, many of the stories told to organize, sustain, and perpetuate families contain intentionally or unintentionally manipulated elements. To protect family members from harm, we often soften our stories. Those who do not are perceived as rude, obnoxious, or brutally honest. Fabrication is often based in an effort to look good so that the storyteller is not demonized, and memory seems to reinforce the small fabrications so that they become canonized over time.

The great equalizer of false memories and manipulations of family stories is the group's memory. When stories are told in the family context, different sides of stories are exposed by individual family members. With enough witnesses to the telling and the collective memory of the story by the whole family, it is hoped that stories can remain fairly accurate (and, if not accurate, at least consistent). Still, stories told in home environments are most influenced by the designated tellers of the stories and the family members. Often the family spokesperson takes the telling position and, as such, is also placed in the role of memory keeper. Not surprisingly, most family stories can be expected to evolve over time.

I have one final comment about the storytelling process within families. Every family unit has its codes that trigger often-repeated stories. For example, when my wife is called "the matriarch of the family," it is the code for her siblings to remember that she is the firstborn—the one who is expected to remember their parents the most completely. "Matriarch" conjures up images and stories of grandparents and childhoods. These are stories of their youth, adolescence, and young adulthood—the good and the bad. Code statements are found in all families. The simple mention of an old home address can trigger the stories that surrounded that home, or a mere remark about a person causes all the old interactions with that person to resurface. Often these are enjoyable conversations because the family is looking backward in time. They do not have to cope with the stress they felt at the time of the event. Even the trauma of childhood losses can be minimized by adults when the losses are treated historically. These code words and code comments are wonderful vehicles for initiation of rich and fulfilling family conversations.

Summary

My wife's family has a strong Methodist background and thus celebrates the Christmas holidays. For many years during our early relationship, she and her siblings would gather as a family unit at their parents' home. Having grown up in foster homes and institutions, neither religion nor the religious holidays held any deep significance for me. I have few childhood memories (fond or tragic) surrounding the religious holidays of my youth. After my wife and I were together for a few years, a strange thing happened:

> Billy (named changed to protect the guilty), the youngest of my wife's four siblings, stopped by the house on Christmas Day with his family. Billy, who was married and had two young children at the time, was beginning to establish family traditions of his own. Shortly after his arrival at his parents' house, he asked if we had made "the traditional Christmas Eve chili." I, of course, had no knowledge of the traditional Christmas Eve chili, so I did not react. Strangely, however, no one else in the family seemed to know what he was talking about either, so they sat around the living room trying to help Billy sort out his memory. In the early years, they remembered the traditional home-cooked meal and leftovers. And, in the later years, they remembered the traditional Chinese dinner on that occasion, but no one knew about the traditional Christmas Eve chili. Being the youngest of his brothers and sister, the assumption was that this tradition was started after the other three siblings had left home. A check with their parents, however, produced no memory of ever having had traditional Christmas Eve chili. Yet Billy was adamant. The family was stumped. Billy finally realized he was remembering Christmas Eve dinners with his college roommate's family.

I chose this family story to close this chapter for several reasons. First, it is a wonderful example of how family stories emerge. Second, it shows the use of code words. The phrase "traditional Christmas Eve chili" is now code for the story and for anyone in the family who has a false memory. Third, it shows how family values are manifested within family stories. The story shows the importance of maintaining family traditions in my wife's family. Fourth, it shows how Billy could not convince the family of the validity of his memory because he could not furnish the other family members with enough stories about past chili-eating occasions during the holidays. Finally, and clearly, memory (with some possible manipulation) has an active role in this family story and, as such, shows how family histories get constructed from memory with the use of stories.

The traditional Christmas Eve chili story is a simple example of a set of complex processes. With today's evotypical families in the United States, family stories are far more complicated, addressing an extremely broad number of issues. Stories are constructed about family issues from past marriages to births, from divorces to addictions, from race to adoptions, and so on. Yet the oral tradition remains instrumental for making sense of familial evolution. A student presenting a poster at the Eastern Communication Association's annual conference in 2011 shows her understanding of the significance of stories when she writes,

A student presenting a poster at the Eastern Communication Association's annual conference in 2011 shows her understanding of the significance of shared stories when she notes that her family narratives contribute to her family's identity and her own self perceptions. She writes, "These processes have shaped the way we function as a group, as well as my individual sense of self. By partaking in these meaning-making processes regularly, my family is able to constantly contribute to our uniqueness as a unit and continue to uphold our identity." (Ball, 2011)

Family configurations and issues are ever expanding, and so are the stories emerging from contemporary families. In the past, I have shown how storytelling can be used to address health issues (Leoutsakas, 1996), orphaning issues (Leoutsakas, 2003, 2004), and family issues (Leoutsakas, 2008). While storytelling is an ancient tradition, it is a viable method for explaining and understanding the origins of new families, complex family issues, the development of modern families, and the activities and values of today's families.

Discussion Questions

1. What is it that makes storytelling necessary for human survival?
2. When considering the relationship between stories and family communication, why does this author believe that stories are "extremely important"?
3. Can you cite a narrative from your own family that has provided examples of beliefs or values that are endorsed by your family?
4. Explain narrative reasoning and how it may differ from individual family members.
5. How do stories help us to "dream" both as individuals and as family members? How do stories from your past help your family plan for the future?

References

Aristotle. (1907). *The poetics of Aristotle* (4th ed.). Susan H. Butcher, Trans. London: Macmillan.

Arnold, L. B. (2008). *Family communication: Theory and research*. Boston: Pearson.

Ball, H. (2011). The significance of family stories: An analysis of storytelling and other meaning making processes. Paper presented at the 102nd annual convention of the Eastern Communication Association's Undergraduate Scholar's Conference, Arlington, VA.

Barthes, R. (1974). *S/Z* (Richard Miller, Trans.). New York: Hill and Wang.

Boser, U. (2009, May 18). We're all lying liars: Why people tell lies and white lies can be ok. *US News Weekly*. http://health.usnews.com/health-news/family-health/brain-and-behavior/articles/2009/05/18/were-all-lying-liars-why-people-tell-lies-and-why-white-lies-can-be-ok

Bronson, P. (2008, February 10). Learning to lie. *New York Magazine*. http://nymag.com/news/features/43893

Carey, B. (2008, May 6). I'm not lying, I'm telling a future truth. Really. *New York Times*, D5.

Coste, D. (1989). *Narrative as communication*. Minneapolis: University of Minnesota Press.

Farrell, T. B. (1985). Narrative in natural discourse: On conversation and rhetoric. *Journal of Communication, 35,* 109-127.

Feldman, R. S. (2009). *The liar in your life: The way to truthful relationships*. New York: Twelve.

Feldman, R. S., Forrest, J. A., & Happ, B. R. (2002). Self-presentation and verbal deception: Do self-presenters lie more? *Basic and Applied Social Psychology, 24,* 163-170.

Fisher, W. R. (1984). Narration as a human communication paradigm: The case of public moral argument. *Communication Monographs, 51,* 1-22.

Fisher, W. R. (1985a). The narrative paradigm: In the beginning. *Journal of Communication, 35,* 74-89.

Fisher, W. R. (1985b). The narrative paradigm: An elaboration. *Communication Monographs, 52,* 347-367.

Fisher, W. R. (1987). *Human communication as narration: Toward a philosophy of reason, value, and action*. Columbia: University of South Carolina Press.

Fisher, W. R. (1988). The narrative paradigm and the assessment of historical texts. *Argumentation and Advocacy, 25,* 49-53.

Fisher, W. R. (1989). Clarifying the narrative paradigm. *Communication Monographs, 56,* 55-58.

Fivush, R., & Neisser, U. (Eds.). (1994). *The remembering self: Construction and accuracy in the self-narrative*. New York: Cambridge University Press.

Gramzow, R. H., & Willard, G. (2006). Exaggerating current and past performance: Motivated self-enhancement vs. reconstructive memory. *Personality and Social Psychology Bulletin, 32,* 1114-1125.

Jorgenson, J., & Bochner, A. P. (2004). Imagining family through stories and rituals. In A. L. Vangelisti (Ed.), *Handbook of family communication* (pp. 513-538). Mahwah, NJ: Lawrence Erlbaum Associates.

Kim, M., Kam, K. Y., Sharkey, W. F., & Singelis, T. M. (2008). "Deception: Moral transgression or social necessity?": Cultural relativity of deception motivation and perceptions of deceptive communication. *Journal of International and Intercultural Communication, 1*(1), 23-50.

Kirkwood, W. G. (1992). Narrative and the rhetoric of possibility. *Communication Monographs, 59,* 30-47.

Kornet, A. (1997, May/June). The truth about lying. *Psychology Today,* 52-58.

Leoutsakas, D. (1996). Assigning new meanings to traditional literature: Illustrations for HIV educators. *AIDS Education and Prevention: An Interdisciplinary Journal, 8*(4), 375-380.

Leoutsakas, D. (2003). *The orphan tales: Real and imagined stories of parental loss*. Unpublished doctoral dissertation, University of South Florida, Tampa.

Leoutsakas, D. (2004). *Contemplating fictional and nonfictional orphan stories*. Paper presented at the 29th International Board on Books for Young People (IBBY) Congress, Cape Town, South Africa, September 5-9. http://www.sacbf.org.za/congressprogramme.html

Leoutsakas, D. A. V. (2008). Storytelling as a means to communicate within the family—the orphan stories. In L. B. Arnold (Ed.), *Family communication: Theory and research* (pp. 136-142). Boston: Pearson.

Loftus, E. F. (1997, September). Creating false memories. *Scientific American, 277*(3), 70-75.

Lucaites, J. L., & Condit, C. M. (1985). Reconstructing narrative theory: A functional perspective. *Journal of Communication, 35,* 90-108.

McGee, M. C., & Nelson, J. S. (1985). Narrative reason in public argument. *Journal of Communication, 35,* 139-155.

Propp, V. (1968). *Morphology of the folktale* (2nd ed.) (Laurence Scott, Trans.). Austin: University of Texas Press.

Rowland, R. C. (1988). The value of the rational world and narrative paradigms. *Central States Speech Journal, 39,* 204-218.

Rowland, R. C. (1989). On limiting the narrative paradigm: Three case studies. *Communication Monographs, 56,* 39-54.

Schacter, D. L. (2002). *The seven sins of memory: How the mind forgets and remembers.* Boston: Houghton Mifflin.

Stone, E. (1988). *Black sheep and kissing cousins: How our family stories shape us.* New York: New York Times Books.

Tyler, J. M., & Feldman, R. S. (2005). Deflecting threat to one's image: Dissembling personal information as a self-presentation strategy. *Basic and Applied Social Psychology, 27,* 371-378.

Tyler, J. M., Feldman, R. S., & Reichert, A. (2006). The price of deceptive behavior: Disliking and lying to people who lie to us. *Journal of Experimental Social Psychology, 42,* 69-77.

Van der Kolk, B. A., & Fisler, R. (1995). Disassociation and the fragmentary nature of traumatic memories: Overview and exploratory study. *Journal of Traumatic Stress, 8*(4), 505-525.

Warnick, B. (1987). The narrative paradigm: Another story. *Quarterly Journal of Speech, 73,* 172-181.

Willard, G., & Gramzow, R. H. (2009). Beyond oversights, lies, and pies in the sky: Exaggeration as goal projection. *Personality and Social Psychology Bulletin, 35,* 477-492.

Chapter 4

The Family that Inks Together, Links Together: Tattoos as Family Identifiers

Thomas G. Endres

Eighty-year-old Phyllis Marple came from a sailing family. Her husband had been a sailor, and together they taught their children and grandchildren to sail off the coast of New England. Phyllis regularly wore a gold necklace, given to her by her husband, adorned with an anchor pendant. One day, Phyllis noticed one day that her daughter Caren had a small anchor tattooed on her foot. As the Marple grandchildren grew and began to disperse both across the United States and Europe, granddaughter Laurel wanted some way to keep connected with her family. Laurel emailed her mother and sisters Miranda and Katrina, suggesting that they each get an anchor tattoo to commemorate their shared life on the sea. The girls opted for shoulder, mid-back, or side placements, while mom located hers on her foot. When Phyllis heard this, much to the younger women's surprise, she decided that she also wanted an anchor tattoo. Caren and her girls joined Grandma at the local tattoo parlor, Inflicting Ink, as she added a third generation to the newfound family tradition. Concludes Phyllis, "When I decide something, that's it. It's done" (Marple, 2010).

Phyllis Marple's decision is not that unusual. Tattoos in general have exploded in popularity. According to Levins (1998), tattooing was the sixth fastest growing retail business in the United States during the late 1990s, and the numbers have only increased since then. Levins reported that clientele was heavily skewed toward mainstream customers, with the fastest growing demographic being middle-class suburban women. A 2003 Harris poll (Sever) found that 16% of all adults have a least one tattoo. The percentages are highest for the under-30 demographic. If you are reading this for a college course and do not have a tattoo, you are likely in the minority.

The title of this chapter offers a playful variation on the old adage, "The family that prays together, stays together." Multiple variations abound in literature and online, proposing qualities of the family that *plays* together, *camps* together, *dines* together, *bowls* together, and the like. What is proposed here is simply that the act of tattooing—getting inked—can be viewed as an activity that fosters family identification and strengthens family bonds.

DeMello (2000, pp. 161–166) lists four main reasons people report for getting tattoos: *Individualism:* to experience personal uniqueness and differentiate oneself from others; *Spirituality:* religious or not, the symbols reflect inner views of transcendence, and can be related to ceremony or ritual; *Personal growth:* symbols of self-help, empowerment, or coping with crisis; and *Sacredness of the body:* adornments and decorations, reflecting time, thought, and effort, which celebrate the human form. None of these reasons are specifically family-oriented, but neither are they family-exclusive. Family-centric tattoos can be used to express the uniqueness of one's family, its spiritual-orientation, shared philosophies toward life, or simply a mutual passion for skin art. Many tattoo aficionados believe that the body is a temple, so why not decorate it? Those aficionados have friends and families, and no doubt share their enthusiasm with them.

From a communication perspective, Modesti (2008) defines being tattooed as an act of symbolic creativity, a performance of the self and a critical tool in forming identity. She also points to cultural shifts taking place that allow tattooing to be recognized as a "meaningful and consequential presentation of the self" (2008, p. 210). Similarly, Sanders (2008) describes becoming tattooed as a "highly social act" associated with others such as family and friends (p. 41) and frequently part of a "ritual commemoration of a significant transition in the life of the recipient" (p. 43). Essentially, tattoos have lost much of the negative social stigma once associated with them, and have become for many an accepted practice for proclaiming one's identity. "When the traffic cop who stops you for speeding or the youth minister in your church sports a tattoo," quips Sanders, "the mark clearly has lost a considerable amount of stigma potential" (2008, p. x).

There are few social entities more crucial to our sense of self than our families. It is therefore not surprising that family themes and symbols crop up frequently in tattoo art. Conversely, the postmodern family is undergoing constant revision and change that for many shake the core and foundation of what it means to be a family unit. It is likewise not surprising that many turn to tattoos to create a sense of permanence and stability for their image of family.

For the sake of organization, family tattoos will be addressed under the following major headings: Family of Origin Tattoos, Family of Creation tattoos, and Family of Interaction tattoos, followed by a brief discussion of Special Cases including the dark side of family tattoos and tattoos as commemoration. These distinctions are sometimes artificial and frequently overlap depending upon what part of the family unit you are looking at. For example, one person's family of creation (e.g. father, mother, child) eventually becomes that child's family of origin, and so on. With that caveat, let's examine some of the more common forms of family tattoos.

Family of Origin Tattoos

One's family of origin is the family from which one descends. Be it one or many generations, it is a look back to and identification with one's lineage. Some cultures have developed specific tattoos to celebrate family connections. Most popularized in recent media would be the *moko* tattoos of the Maori peoples of New Zealand. Actually, the elaborate markings, often mischaracterized and wrongly appropriated by Western cultures, are not necessarily tied to bloodlines. Ellis (2008) explains that the tattoo "belongs at once to the bearer, the creator, and the people who serve as descendents from and caretakers of the patterns" (p. 194). The tattoos are as much about rank and social status as they are genealogy. Similar Pacific Islander and Polynesian cultures have adopted tattoo markings to celebrate both cultural and familial bonds. See, for example, Guy's story in Box 1.

North American culture, however, lacks such a rich symbolic tradition. Rush (2005) argues that socially sanctioned rites of passage have fallen away, so we are left to invent them on our own. Thus, tattooing becomes our form of "symbolic remembrance" (p. 59). At first glance, the most obvious symbolic representation of family would be the family's seal, or coat-of-arms. Many malls and flea markets are sure to have a vendor willing to sell you your family crest. Web sites abound purporting to investigate your lineage, and many actually allow you to purchase your surname's coat-of-arms already formatted and printable as a tattoo stencil.

> **Family of Origin Tattoos—Guys**
>
> "When they locked up our queen, that was the start of the fall of the Hawaiian people." Guy (Oahu, HI) is the son of a full-blooded Hawaiian mother and a Hawaiian-English father. He has the word "Hawaiian" tattooed on his inner arm because, as he explains, "That's my bloodline." He also has two rows of downward pointing triangles—some shaded in, some not—that descend from his left shoulder down to his wrist. He explains that traditional Hawaiian tattoos, prior to the U.S. government coup in 1893 that wrested power away from Queen Lili'uokalani, were often characterized by upward pointing triangles. The triangle shape represented both the mountains and waves of Hawaii, as well as sharp objects such as hunting knives, spears, and fish hooks. Following the coup, the triangles turned downward, "Everything went down." Some loyal Hawaiians continued to use upward pointing triangles in honor of Hawaii's original sovereignty, but Guy was told in his family to only get tattoos with triangles pointing down; "You ain't got an empire anymore, it's a state now. It's not a nation anymore." Guy's particular tattoo - the two rows of inverted triangles—is a family mark; a design created by himself and an uncle who has the same tattoo. "Somebody else," he emphasizes, "you gotta come up with another idea." The triangles alternate from light to dark, representing "heart and soul." Another unique characteristic is that a shared center line of triangles goes from top to bottom, shoulder to wrist, but the second row differs at the elbow. From shoulder to elbow, the second line is to the outside toward his back, referring to the mountains, while from the elbow to the wrist the second line is to the inside toward his abdomen, representing the ocean. "It gives me the right to say that whatever is in the oceans and on the mountain, it gives me the right to say it belongs to me—as a Hawaiian." Guy now has a son, and plans to add a row of triangles across his chest to represent his lineage "close to his heart." The design will be added down his leg as well. In fact, Guy's family tattoo will continue even beyond his death. "When I pass it's going to go on my face, and it's going to match all of this," he explains. "It's going to all be joined up together."

Dick Eastman (2001), writer for Ancestry.com, warns however that there is no such thing as a *family* coat-of-arms. He explains that a coat of arms is issued only to an individual, and not to a family. When that individual dies, their heirs may apply for the same coat of arms. Whether or not the crest is passed along is determined by an office of heralds. Arguing against coat of arms tattoos, Eastman maintains that, "At any one time, only one person may rightfully display a coat of arms." (www.ancestry.com).

The Oxford Guide to Heraldry (Woodcock & Robinson, 1988) would agree. Originally, image-laden crests were used to identify who was in a suit of armor. In Europe, though each country had various rules and degrees of complexity, a coat of arms was viewed as personal property not to be used by others. Roving minstrels, called Heralds, regulated and recorded arms. Eventually this evolved into an elaborate system of colleges and libraries. While arms generally passed down through descent of unbroken male line, the "property of particular families' arms do not belong to surnames, as is sometimes imagined" (p. 33). Thus, it is probably not advisable to purchase and permanently inscribe one's family crest simply because a vendor says it is a historically accurate representation of your family's surname. However, that should not stop anyone from using common heraldry symbols (e.g. lion, panther, griffin, fleur-de-lis, cross, dragon, eagle) in the creation of a tattoo that pays homage to one's lineage.

More recommended would be the creation of a family of origin tattoo that seeks to symbolically encode a family narrative. Bynum (1987) sets up the foundation well:

> WHEN A CHILD IS but a few hours old, it is exposed to a family tradition, not only in the customs and rituals associated with birth, but in many other forms of lore used by the

family. In the home the child first learns the lore of the greater ethnic, regional or religious group; each family also has its own lore, including tales of where the ancestors came from, stories of family misfortunes, anecdotes about interesting relatives, family expressions, jokes, recipes, names, memorabilia, gestures and even "family whistles" which are used to call the children together in a public place. This lore communicates to the child its role, the role of others in the family, the values of the family and society, and concepts or stereotypes both of its own group and of others. (p. 408)

In their study of such family lore and traditions, Arnold, Pratt, and Hicks (2004) found that positive parent-child relations are characterized by the presence of "parental voice" (e.g. value lessons, parental views) in family narratives. Children who remember the lessons and "hear" their parents' voice demonstrate greater adjustment and ability to face the challenging complexities of influences outside the family. Similarly, Fiese and Pratt (2004) argue that, "through repetitive telling there is opportunity to transform the momentary practice to a symbolic representation of family experience" (p. 410). Family of origin tattoos take the voice and the narrative and, through permanent inscription, provide an ongoing retelling of the storyline.

Consider the family who embodies the aforementioned adage about praying together and staying together. For them, the voice and narrative is one of prayer. Tattoo images such as crosses, folded hands, celestial symbols, and other forms of veneration, make real the family lore. So too the family that has a long-standing motto, many of which trace back to the age of heraldry, such as:

A good conscience is the best shield
Truth gives wings to strength
Virtue is the strongest helmet
I flourish in the rose
A tree is recognized by its fruit

In cases such as these, the actual motto could be tattooed verbatim, or a talented artist could develop a custom tattoo integrating any of the symbols—shield, wings, helmet, rose, tree—found within the wording.

Family of origin tattoos can also be more general in nature, referencing the broader cultural bloodline from which one descends. Famed tattoo artist Madame Chinchilla (1997) shares a family history example in her story of Carol, who requested a small letter "z" tattooed on her left shoulder. The tattoo is in honor of her unknown gypsy relatives who died at Auschwitz. In the concentration camps, all gypsies were tattooed with a "z" (for *zigeuner*, German for gypsy) preceding their number. As with the family crests, narratives, and mottos, this tattoo symbol was a look back to and a continuation of a family source and foundation.

Family of Creation Tattoos

Rather than looking back, some families choose themselves and the storyline they create (or procreate, with the addition of children) as the basis of their family narrative. Madame Chinchilla (1997) also shares an excellent example of a family of creation tattoo, recounting the tale of a couple who, celebrating one year of sobriety, got identical tattoos on their stomachs of torn skin with a monstrous eye peeking out. They called it "the beast within," and it served as a constant reminder of the ongoing challenge of recovery they faced in their life together.

Not constrained by mottos or symbols passed down from the previous generation, the family of creation is free to develop its own design. Some cases are quite literal, such as having family portraits inked on the body (see, for example, Angelo in Box 2). Those wishing to do portraiture are advised to seek out a competent artist; there is nothing more disappointing than having a poor rendition of a loved one permanently etched in the skin.

> **Family of Creation Tattoos—Angelo**
>
> In 1985, Angelo (Pueblo, CO) got a rose tattooed onto his left arm. Following that was a little red heart. Those original tattoos have long since been covered, and Angelo is now working on completing what's known as a French body suit, i.e. all of the torso to neck and wrists, and thighs to shorts length. That way, even though most of his body is covered, he can still cover his tattoos at work (an MA in Computer Information Systems, Angelo works as a storage engineer for Hewlett-Packard). Angelo's most significant tattoo covers his entire back. Tipping the scales near 300 pounds, it makes for an impressive canvas. The tattoo is a family portrait of his three oldest daughters - Jessica, Amanda, and Vanessa - with himself, dressed as an archangel, looking over them. Now teenagers, the tattoo shows them as young girls, all under the age of 10. "My children are my life to me," Angelo explains. "It's my representation of 'I'm their guardian.' I'll do anything to watch them." His back piece has garnered a lot of recognition and awards, even winning a national tattoo convention in 2000 in which a dozen countries participated. Angelo shares that most people are shocked when they see his back. "When they see an actual family portrait of that size, they're quite in awe." And the portrait continues to grow. He is carrying the religious symbolism to the front, depicting the battle between heaven and hell between St. Michael and the devil. One twist will be that daughter number four, Samantha, who was not around when the back portrait was done, will be portrayed as a cherub on this left upper chest. And what of these daughters? What will Angelo's reaction be if and when they decide to continue with the family of procreation tattoo tradition? "I'm not going to be a hypocrite and tell them they can't get them," he answers. "But I have asked them, when it comes time for them to get a tattoo, to get me involved so we can research it. I don't want them to be a statistic where they're older and regret it." Actually, his advice to his daughters is much the same as he would give to anyone considering getting ink; "My advice to people looking for tattoos is they've got to think of the long term." Of course, considering the size of his back piece, Angelo adds, "My theory is also 'Go Big or Go Home.'"

A safer alternative might be to create a new crest or a new family motto. This author has the Hebrew inscription אהיה אשר אהיה (roughly translated to "I will be what I will be" or "I am that I am"; what God said to Moses from the burning bush in Exodus 3:14) tattooed on his arm. Daughter Carleen has the same

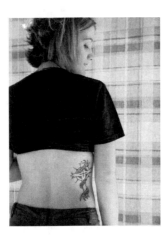

Carleen. Tattoo by Don Quintana. Photo permission by Thomas Endres.

phrase, only in Latin and conjugated in the feminine ("Sum Quae Sum") tattooed on her side. Another daughter, Kellsie, is planning her variation of the newly created family logo for her first tattoo.

When creating such a tattoo, the student of communication should pay extra care in ensuring that foreign language translations are correct, and to select visual symbols that are meaningful and appropriate to the concept being conveyed. Numerous books and websites are available regarding symbols and their interpretations. For example, the family of creation father may wish to create a tattoo design celebrating his role as a parent. Symbols for "father" include eagle, king, or sun (Biederman, 1994), or aspects of time (e.g. hourglass), or agriculture (e.g. scythe or sickle) (Cooper, 1978). Symbols for "mother" include earth, fish, grain, hen, moon, or queen (Biederman, 1994). Or, if expanded to include images of the Great Mother/Mother Goddess, "her symbols are legion" exclaims Cooper (1978, p. 109), who lists images such as: crescent moon, crown of stars, blue robe, spiral, concentric circles, water, fountains, gate, cup, basket, chalice, horn of plenty, vase, shells, pearls, dolphin, dove, swan, goose, lotus, rose, deer, and unicorn.

In designing a family of creation tattoo, many artists discourage the tattooing of names. DeMello (2000) explains that, "Names of loved ones were once a major part of a tattooist's daily bread and butter, but names are almost universally scored today by custom tattooists" (p. 92). Getting a significant other's or spouse's name tattooed is viewed as impulsive, shortsighted, and artistically unsophisticated. More important, the aforementioned Harris poll found that, while a majority of tattooed Americans have no regrets about their tattoo, of those that do, the reason most cited (16%) was due to having a tattoo of someone's name. At least a visual image, like a lion or a unicorn, can be ascribed another meaning should the named person no longer be a part of the tattooed person's life.

Family of Interaction Tattoos

The family of interaction is identified by the transactions that define them. Studied by many, Segrin and Flora (2005) summarize characteristics of this transactional family perspective: "intimacy, interdependence, commitment, feelings of family identify, emotional ties, self-defined symbols and boundaries for family membership, and an ongoing history and future" (p. 10). Such a perspective allows us to name as families groups not traditionally considered family. Families that are more than blood.

Individuals who serve together in the military. Martial artists who train in the same dojo. Actors who starred together in a movie. Popular culture is rife with such examples. Though not families in the traditional sense, these people are bound together by a common cause or activity, and choose to display that to the world through a shared inscription.

In a similar vein, some individuals get tattoos as members of a larger cultural community or family of interaction, whether or not they actually know the other members. For example, many advocates who support research on breast cancer opt for a pink ribbon tattoo. Similar marks have been found among victims of natural disasters such as floods and tornados. They are part of the larger family of survivors and their supporters who use the tattoo to encode their shared intimacy and positive affect.

Among these larger communities would be women who use tattoos as a radical form of feminist self-identification (e.g. Harlow, 2008). Tired of being objectified by their bodies, and seeking to reject the image of Playboy beauty standards, these women take ownership of their body modification, "each step rhetorically etched into the skin –to mark and break apart the passive beauty that has attempted to shroud women in silence" (194). The popular goth-inspired, indie-style burlesque group known as the *Suicide Girls* are a popular manifestation of this genre.

Perhaps the most overt manifestations of family of interaction tattoos are found in the designs of the tattoo community itself. Bonded by a mutual love and fascination for skin art, these individuals go beyond the simple one or two small and concealable tattoos found on a majority of tattooed people. Bell (1999) suggests a distinction between "*people who have tattoos*" and "*tattooed people.*" They are most readily identified by tattoos that cannot be completely covered up by clothes. Interestingly, she also suggests that, as the number of tattoos goes up, the less individual meaning ascribed to them. For heavily tattooed people, the meaning comes from the shared activity more so than the meaning of the symbols themselves. Similarly, Siorat (2005) argues that, as small tattoos become more popular, people in the body modification movement need to get bigger tattoos and body suits, as well as extensive piercings, as a way to authenticate their commitment to the act. Susan (Box 3) is a good example of the tattooed family of interaction.

Family of Interaction Tattoos—Susan

"I think if you're tattooed," says Susan, Denver, CO, "and you go to any sort of extreme, you have that common bond with somebody else who's tattooed as well." While Susan acknowledges that tattoos have become more mainstream, she still equates herself with a select community that goes beyond just getting one or two tattoos that can be easily concealed. "I guess I don't even compare myself to people that just have a little butterfly on their back." Susan's family of interaction includes those individuals who have made tattooing a lifestyle choice. The one-time professional wrestler (fans may recognize her as "Liberty" from the 1990's TV series POWW [Powerful Women of Wrestling]) is now a rock bassist—upright and electric—for various groups, and daytime traffic reporter for Clear Channel Communications. Susan's tattoos are predominantly Japanese influenced; Geishas, kanji symbols, peacocks, lions. She does have several family-specific tattoos—a portrait of her late father on her right calf and the word "Mom" on her foot (a portrait of her mother is in the works). As for family, Susan shares that, "My mom thinks my art is beautiful and that's all that matters to me." And for Susan, it *is* art. For her and members of her community, the body is a canvas. She and fellow tattooed individuals set themselves apart from others by how much time they spend in "the chair" and how much ink covers their skin. "The common denominator," she explains, "is that people want to decorate themselves into what they feel is beautiful." Susan recognizes a subculture within her community that go beyond what she is willing to do; those that tattoo their face, or who have extreme facial piercings, implants, or scarification. Barring those extremes, Susan continues to add to her canvas, most recently on her hands. She gets tattooed weekly, and concludes that "there will always be the hard core 'real' tattooed people that make it a way of life, and I consider myself one that is in it for the long haul."

The act of getting tattooed is especially noteworthy in this category. As the title of this book indicates, families are identified by more than just shared blood. Blood, however, remains a powerful and almost mystic bonding force in our understanding of familial connection. How many times have we heard or seen in movies or literature the young men or women who, in order to become "blood brothers" or "blood sisters," cut incisions into their skin and let their blood intermingle? "Blood, a symbol of life, has a magic meaning and therefore an esoteric quality," explains Grognard, adding that the purpose is to "to ensure complicity by sharing that which is most precious and vital" (1994, p. 72).

Getting tattooed can be viewed as the modern-day act of creating "blood" family. Quite simply, one bleeds as they are being tattooed. The symbolic act is accentuated by the fact that there is commitment, monetary investment, actual pain, and—literally—bloodshed. If a common bloodline did not exist prior to receiving a family of interaction tattoo, it certainly exists after.

Special Cases

Though there is overlap with the three categories above, two subcategories of family tattoos are deserving of special consideration; the dark side of family tattoos and tattoos of commemoration.

Dark Side of Family Tattoos

The examples thus far point to tattoo choices which celebrate family. But we all know that families are not always to be celebrated. Sometimes tattoos represent a breaking free from or rejection of one's family ties. Romans and colleagues (1998) reported that, among a sample of women from New Zealand, tattoos were more common in those reporting sexually abusive experiences. This is simply one example of a common phenomenon: tattoos used as a coping mechanism for re-establishing self-identity in response to traumatic family circumstances such as child abuse, infidelity, or divorce (this author has one of the latter as well).

DeMello (2000) suggests that members of the 13th Gen or Generation X get tattoos in response to family and generational stresses. She summarizes key research works and suggests the following causal factors: "disintegrated families, working mothers, failed schools, no-growth-economy, minimum wage jobs, and little-to-no chance of buying a house or achieving the level of financial security that their parents had" (p. 187). Such tattoos are the antithesis of family of origin or creation narratives. While a variant of family of interaction tattoos, it is a rebellious and anti-family variant.

A similar family of interaction variant, darker than the dojo or pink ribbon examples given earlier, would be prison and gang tattoos. Space does not permit much elaboration, as this is a book worthy topic in itself, but let's review a few examples from Valentine (2000). White supremacy gangs often have identifiable tattoos, such as the Aryan Brotherhood's shamrock with the number 666 inside. Members of the African-American gang the Vice Lords frequently get "312" tattoos, representing Chicago's area code, which is the gang's place of origin. The infamous Crips and Bloods gangs tend to have chapter specific tattoos, such as the number "83" for the Eight-Tray Gangster Crips of south central LA (p. 77). Hispanic gangs frequently display ornate tattoo designs comprised of teardrops, spiderwebs, and portraiture. But simple images also prevail, such as three dots in a pyramid shape for *mi vida loca* ("my crazy life") or happy and sad faces meaning "mess with me now, be sorry later" (p. 91). Asian gangs tend toward Eastern symbols such as tigers and dragons. Some are more specific, such as Southeast Asian gangs which have four "T" tattoos; Vietnamese for *tinh* (love), *tien* (money), *tu* (prison), and *toi* (crime) (p. 128).

Tattoos as Commemoration

Tattoos, even more so than memories, do not fade away. Rush observes, "The mind might forget an obligation but an indelible mark of that obligation . . . serves to forever *re*-mind" (2005, p. 18). Be it a family or origin, creation, or interaction narrative, the commemoration tattoo exists specifically to pay homage to a loved one. Generally, but not always, the loved one is deceased. Quite often, the tattoo takes the shape of the stickers frequently seen in the back windows of cars; the "In Memory of . . . " logos followed by a person's name and the date of their passing. This is one of the rare occasions where having someone's name tattooed is perfectly acceptable.

Sometimes, as in Viko's case (see Box 4), the act of tattooing itself is used as commemorative ritual. Most often, however, the commemoration is more iconic, with an image representing the lost loved one turned into a design. Madame Chinchilla (1997) shares the following moving story:

> One busy Saturday there was a woman who felt she had to have a tattoo. When I first saw her she was standing in the main studio with her husband holding a small Japanese box in both hands in front of her, against her belly. When I asked her if I could help her with anything, she and her husband both started to cry. I took them into my studio. Through tears and sobbing she said to me, 'I need a tattoo of a purple heart. I need it today. Please give it to me as soon as you can. Our baby died two days ago. These are her ashes. I had her by C-section. I want to be opened up and have her ashes put back inside of me, but that is unreasonable. We had to take her off life support. We held her for two hours as she died. When we were driving home I was holding the ashes on my lap, and I saw your sign with the red hearts. I knew that I need this tattoo. (p. 67)

A unique subcategory within commemoration tattoos would be tattoos designs created in memory of a truly unique member of the family, the family pet. Tovares (2010) examined how families use stories to express love for their pets. In so doing, "family members are able to create and reinforce family ties by positioning themselves as animal-lovers in opposition, although mostly playful and humorous, to those who treat animals differently" (p. 15). As we've seen, tattoos are a concrete way to make permanent a family story. While not speaking of tattoos directly, Tovares concludes

---

Tattoos of Commemoration—Viko

Viko, of San Francisco, CA, has almost 300 tattoos. His first tattoo, at age 16, was the words Punk Boy inscribed across his chest. His motivation for getting tattoos is largely in memory of his late mother. "My mom died really young," Viko explains, "She had all kinds of tattoos, and I always kind of thought she was the awesomest lady to have tattoos." He remembers watching his mother getting a tattoo of the Virgin Mary, surrounded by angels, on her back. "Just watching her get it done," he muses, "I just was so fascinated by it." Viko has six sisters that he describes as "normal" and not really into tattoos so, in honor of their mother, he decided, "I'd keep the tradition." And keep it he does. Approximately 95% of Viko's body, everything except his face, is covered with ink. Most of his tattoos are simply shapes; crosses, squares, stars, and tribal designs. Some are specific images, like clouds or flowers. Like his mother, who had tattoos of boyfriend's names, Viko also has a tattoo of a former boyfriend's name. "It was right when I turned eighteen, right when I came out, was experimenting." Years after the relationship ended, he still has the tattoo, acknowledging that it was a good experience in his life. Whether specific symbols or not, many of Viko's tattoos reflect his journey, such as his move from South Carolina to Las Vegas, and then Los Angeles, before finally settling on San Francisco. Several of his tattoos are unfinished, including one on his arm that was fully paid for, but where the artist was fired for using drugs and took off before the project was finished. Similarly, of the two sparrows on his neck, one is colored in and the other is not. He likes the fact that his tattoos, like his life, are unfinished. Viko's final tribute to his mother is in memory of his life after her passing, when he and his sisters were moved into foster care. Viko now works with foster youth. Fortunately, his work community is very accepting of his passion, so he plans to continue getting tattooed. His life, his work, and his body art are constant reflections of the lesson he learned early on from his mother, "You're free to be whoever you are."

that "All this contributes to the construction of this family's coherent collective identity that includes pets as its members" (p. 15).

Here is an example that ties it all together. Following Kate's divorce, she struggled for years to provide a good home for her two daughters as they moved from elementary school through junior high and high school. Every night, she would go for a long walk with Bailey, her yellow Labrador retriever. Years later, in a new marriage, her girls in college, and Bailey long since put to rest, Kate got a small tattoo on her foot. Three paw prints. The paws are in memory of Bailey. There are three of them to represent Kate and her two girls. The placement on her foot represents her journey, both the literal walking and figurative progression out of a bad place. One simple design signifies, commemorates, and identifies multiple family narratives.

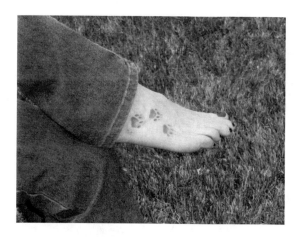

Kate. Tattoo by Don Quintana. Photo permission by Thomas Endres.

Conclusion

Tattoos are undeniably a form of communication. The tattooed body, argues Kuwahara, is socially constructed "because tattooing is a posterior inscription on the body by people's hands" (2005, p. 4). This chapter demonstrates that family, however defined, is often at the heart of that social construction. Rush (2005) takes it farther, noting that "trans-generational tattooing," such as the Marple family anchor tattoo example that started this chapter, appears "expected as a ritual in some families" (p. 60). Interestingly, in his interview with tattoo artists, mother-daughter tattoos (again, such as the Marples) were more prevalent than father-son combinations.

Such an observation is but one of many possible avenues for future research. Which family members actually get tattoos? Who initiates? What are the most common symbols? For now, the most we can do is echo Krakow's observation that, "People select tattoos that make physical—and permanent—their dreams and desires, their inner demons, their world view" (1994, p. 77). And that world view often contains family narratives. People don't always remember family stories, but tattoos provide a kind of living scrapbook. A family album engraved into the skin.

Just how commonplace family tattoos are remains up for debate. DeMello (1995) argues that both journalists and academics, by only interviewing members of the middle-class, have given the mistaken impression that the old guard of tattooed individuals (e.g. bikers, sailors, prostitutes) is gone and that tattoos now have status rather than stigma. DeMello correctly asserts that the old guard is still there. Of course, even the old guard get family tattoos. The most celebrated sailor tattoo of all time—a heart with a ribbon reading "Mom"—tops the list.

Author Photo with tattoo artist Jeanine "Lady of the Lake" Johnson.
Photo permission by Thomas Endres.

The big question, then, is where does it go from here? Perhaps the increasing popularity of tattoos in general, and family tattoos in particular, will continue on the upswing. Or, it may level out or even decrease as the years unfold. If previous generations got tattoos and a form of rebellion, but the current generation embraces the ritual, what will future generations do to make their stand? At this point in time, however, there is no end in sight. Tattoos are, and for the foreseeable future, will remain a viable communicative tool for self-identification and expression. And for those wishing to "link" to the narratives of their family of origin, their family of creation, and/or their family of interaction, the decision to "ink" remains a permanent and artistic strategy for keeping the story alive.

References

Arnold, Mary Louise, Pratt, Michael W., & Hicks, Cheryl. (2004). Adolescents' Representations of Parents' Voices in Family Stories: Value Lessons, Personal Adjustment, and Identity Development. In Michael W. Pratt & Barbara H. Fiese (Eds.), *Family Stories and the Life Course: Across Time and Generations* (pp.163-186). Mahwah, NJ: Lawrence Erlbaum Associates, Publishers.

Bell, Shannon. (1999). Tattooed: A Participant Observer's Exploration of Meaning. *Journal of American Culture*, 22(2), 53-58.

Biederman, Hans. (1994). *Dictionary of Symbolism: Cultural Icons and the Meanings Behind Them.* (James Hulbert, Trans.). New York, New York: A Meridian Book.

Bynum, Joyce. (1987, Winter). Folklore in the Family. *ETC: A Review of General Semantics*, 44(4), 408-411.

Chinchilla, Madame. (1997). *Stewed, Screwed and Tattooed*. Mendocina, California: Isadore Press.

Cooper, J.C. (1978). *An Illustrated Encyclopedia of Traditional Symbols*. London: Thames & Hudson, Ltd.

DeMello, Margo. (1995). 'Not Just for Bikers Anymore': Popular Representations of American Tattooing. *Journal of Popular Culture*, 29, 37-52.

DeMello, Margo. (2000). *Bodies of Inscription: A Cultural History of the Modern Tattoo Community*. Durham & London: Duke University Press.

Eastman, Dick. (2001, June 27). Pssst! Want to Buy Your Family Coat of Arms? *Ancestry.com*. Retrieved July19, 2011, from http://www.ancestry.com/learn/library/article.aspx?article=4133.

Ellis, Juniper. (2008). *Tattooing and the World: Pacific Designs in Print & Skin*. New York: Columbia University Press.

Fiese, Barbara H. & Pratt, Michael W. (2004). Metaphysical Meanings in Family Stories: Integrating Life Course and Systems Perspectives on Narratives. In Michael W. Pratt & Barbara H. Fiese (Eds.), *Family Stories and the Life Course: Across Time and Generations* (pp. 401-418). Mahwah, NJ: Lawrence Erlbaum Associates, Publishers.

Grognard, Catherine. (1994). *The Tattoo: Graffiti for the Soul*. Stamford, CT: Longmeadow Press.

Harlow, Megan Jean. (2008, Sept.). The Suicide Girls: Tattooing as Radical Feminist Agency. *Contemporary Argumentation & Debate*, 29, 186-196.

Harple, Miranda (2010, October) My Grandma's Tattoo: 3 Generations Discover an Indelible Family Anchor. *AARP Bulletin* (Electronic version). Retrieved July 12, 2011, from http://www.aarp.org/relationships/family/info-10-2010/grandma_gets_a_tattoo.html.

Krakow, Amy. (1994). *The Total Tattoo Book*. New York, New York: Warner Books.

Kuwahara, Makiko. (2005). *Tattoo: An Anthropology*. Oxford: Berg.

Levins, Hoag. (1998). The Changing Cultural Status of Tattoo Art: As Documented in Mainstream U.S. Reference Works, Newspapers and Magazines. TattooArtists.com. Retrieved October 3, 2005, from http://www.tattooartist.com/history.html.

Modesti, Sonja. (2008, July-September). Home Sweet Home: Tattoo Parlors as Postmodern Spaces of Agency. *Western Journal of Communication*, 72(3), 197-212.

Romans, S. E., Martin, J. L., Morris, E. M. & Harrison, K. (1998). Tattoos, childhood sexual abuse and adult psychiatric disorder in women. *Archives of Women's Mental Health*, 1, 137-141.

Rush, John A. (2005). *Spiritual Tattoo: A Cultural History of Tattooing, Piercing, Scarification, Branding, and Implants*. Berkeley, California: Frog, Ltd.

Sanders, Clinton with D. Angus Vail. (2008). *Customizing the Body: The Art and Culture of Tattooing* (Revised and Expanded Edition). Philadelphia: Temple University Press.

Segrin, Chris & Jeanne Flora. (2005). *Family Communication*. Mahwah, NJ: Lawrence Erlbaum Associates, Publishers.

Siorat, Cyril. (2005). Beyond Modern Primitivism. In Nicolas Thomas, Anna Cole and Bronwen Douglas (Eds.), *Tattoo: Bodies, Art, and Exchange in the Pacific and the West* (pp. 205-222). Durham: Duke University Press.

Tovares, Alla V. (2010). All in the family: Small stories and narrative construction of a shared family identity that includes pets. *Narrative Inquiry*, 20(1), 1–19.

Valentine, Bill. (2000). *Gangs and Their Tattoos: Identifying Gangbangers on the Street and in Prison*. Boulder, CO: Paladin Press.

Woodcock, Thomas & Robinson, John Martin. (1988). *The Oxford Guide to Heraldry*. Oxford: Oxford University Press.

Chapter 5

Appreciative Inquiry as a Model for Strengths-Based Decision Making in Couples and Families

Deborah Ballard-Reisch

Contemporary families are composed of many different vibrant shapes, colors, and forms and are no longer defined exclusively by blood or marriage ties. Models of family support and intervention, as well as the development of new interaction patterns, are necessary to reflect the values and cultures emerging within these dynamics. Appreciative Inquiry (AI) is one such model. Traditional approaches to family research and decision making often focus on solving relational problems (Fincham & Beach, 2010) or building resilience (Caughlin & Huston, 2010). AI offers a promising additional approach that emphasizes building on the strengths already existing within families (Cooperrider-Dole, Silbert, Mann, & Whitney, 2008). Based on the assumptions that every human system has something that works well (http://centerforappreciativeinquiry.net) and that people are more confident going into the future when they carry with them positive parts of the past (Hammond, 1996), AI offers families a strengths-based strategy to facilitate positive change and growth.

Expanding on the work of Mohr and Watkins (2002), the AI process described in this chapter involves five steps: (a) Choosing a positive focus of inquiry, (b) inquiring into and sharing exceptionally positive moments, (c) conceptualizing a desired future, (d) planning strategies to work toward desired outcomes, and (e) implementing and assessing strategies and progressing toward desired outcomes. The author of this chapter has found these steps useful in her work with married couples and has extrapolated their usefulness with families.

This chapter (a) provides an explication and grounding of appreciative inquiry in strengths-based approaches to change and (b) discusses a model of AI that can be used as a decision-making paradigm for families with support from examples of our work with couples.

Strengths-Based Approaches to Change

Grounded in action research (Cooperrider & Srivastva, 1987; Dick, 2011), social constructivist theory (Gergen, in Stavros & Torres, 2005, p. 7), and positive psychology (Seligman, 2002; Stratton-Berkessel, 2010), strengths-based approaches in general and AI in particular are premised on the perspective that "when people are performing in roles in which they play to their strengths, . . . performance and satisfaction increase, productivity improves, and they have [a] greater chance of achieving their full potential" (Stratton-Berkessel, 2010, p. 1). Thus, strengths-based approaches to change stand in contrast to problem-focused or deficit-focused approaches (Fincham & Beach, 2010) which, as Stratton-Berkessel (2010) advances, focus on helping people overcome weaknesses in order to be successful. From a social constructivist perspective, communicative relationships among people are viewed as the source of meaning, value and action. The constructivist principle advances that reality is socially constructed through language and in conversations; thus, critical importance is placed on relationship processes and outcomes (Gergen, in Stavros & Torres, 2005, p. 7). Focusing on a positive approach allows individuals and groups to construct more positive futures. From a positive psychology perspective, appreciative inquiry is both a way of *being* in the world and a way of *doing* in the world, a philosophy and a practice (Stratton-Berkessel, 2010, p. 2).

As noted above, a strengths-based approach is underrepresented in the scholarly research on family relationships. Fincham and Beach (2010) identify three reasons that this is the case. First, in historical context, negative events have a much stronger potential for critical impact than positive events (their example is "ignoring the grizzly bear on the path"), even life-threatening potential (p. 5). The authors argue that while generally only a comparatively small percentage of events in an individual's life are negative, managing negative issues is simply more compelling for survival than managing positive ones. They conclude that "bad is stronger than good in a disappointingly relentless pattern" (p. 6). Second, social scientists like to "help" people; "alleviating harm is inherently more ethically compelling than is promoting well-being" (p. 6), so research on how to help people has flourished. Third, the research on deficits has led to useful insights for families. Not only are social scientists motivated to help those in need, but interventions based on the negative, to solve problems or to assess the impact of negative processes, show more significant results than more positive research strategies. Based on a review of the impact of positive and negative interventions, they conclude that "it is more scientifically fruitful to study negative processes than to study positive processes" (p. 6).

Fincham and Beach (2010) not only challenge this emphasis in family research on the negative, but also call for an approach to family research that they call "relationship flourishing":

> Relationship flourishing is not merely relationship happiness, satisfaction, adjustment, or well-being. Instead, it describes a relationship that is emotionally vital; is characterized by intimacy, growth, and resilience (e.g., rising to challenges and making the most of adversities or setbacks); and allows a dynamic balance between relationship focus, focus on other family subsystems, focus on other social network involvement, and engagement in the broader community within which the relationship exists. (p. 7)

AI is one example of a strengths-based model that has the potential to support progress toward developing flourishing relationships.

Introduction to Appreciative Inquiry

Originally conceptualized to optimize communication in organizations, the key terms in AI are defined by David Cooperrider and Diane Whitney (2005) as follows:

> **Ap-pre'ci-ate**, v., 1. valuing; the act of recognizing the best in people or the world around us; affirming past and present strengths, successes, and potentials; to perceive those things that give life (health, vitality, excellence) to living systems 2. to increase in value, e.g. the economy has appreciated in value. Synonyms: VALUING, PRIZING, ESTEEMING, and HONORING.

Chapter 5 Appreciative Inquiry as a Model for Strengths-Based Decision Making in Couples and Families

> **In-quire** (kwīr), v., 1. the act of exploration and discovery. 2. To ask questions; to be open to seeing new potentials and possibilities. Synonyms: DISCOVERY, SEARCH, and SYSTEMATIC EXPLORATION, STUDY.

Cooperrider and Whitney (2005) view AI as the "search for the best in people, their organizations, and the relevant world around them" (n.p.). This and other strengths-based approaches have significant potential to assist contemporary families in negotiating transformative change.

Hammond (1996) identified seven assumptions of AI:

1. In every human situation, something works.
2. Reality is created in the moment, and there are multiple moments.
3. People have more confidence going into the future when they carry forward parts of the past.
4. Asking questions influences outcomes.
5. What people focus on becomes reality.
6. Language shapes reality.
7. Differences are important.

She and others posit that what is carried forward from the past should be positive.

In addition to the seven assumptions, Whitney and Trosten-Bloom (2003) posit eight core principles of AI reflected in Table 5.1 (derived from http://www.companyofexperts.net). Stavros and Torres (2005) add a ninth principle when emphasizing families and personal relationships.

Table 5.1 The Foundation Principles of Appreciative Inquiry

Principle	Definition
Constructionist	Reality is socially constructed through language and interaction.
Simultaneity	Asking a question initiates change.
Poetic	What we choose to study describes and creates the world we know.
Anticipatory	Images inspire actions.
Positive	Positive questions lead to positive change.
Wholeness	Bringing everyone together stimulates creativity and builds collective capacity.
Enactment	Acting as if reality is a certain way makes it so.
Free choice	Free choice stimulates excellence and promotes positive change.
Awareness	Reflexive awareness is critical.

The first five principles serve as the foundation for the AI process to be discussed below. The other four principles identify characteristics and implications of the appreciative process.

Cooperrider and Whitney (2005) summarized the foundation of AI based on these assumptions and principles. AI "is about the co-evolutionary search for the best in people.... It assumes that every living system has many untapped and rich and inspiring accounts of the positive" (p. 3). AI "involves systematic discovery of what gives "life" to a living system when it is most alive, most effective, and most constructively capable" (p. 3). For families, AI emphasizes creating positive family dynamics (Cooperrider-Dole et al., 2008) by asking an "unconditional positive question," the responses to which strengthen the family's abilities "to apprehend, anticipate, and heighten positive potential" (Cooperrider & Whitney, 2005, p. 3). Asking positive questions and visioning a desired future encourage imagination and innovation by building positive relationships among family members and accentuating past and present capabilities, potential, opportunities, and competencies. By recognizing the socially constructed nature of reality and the fundamentally important roles of language and interaction and by consciously emphasizing the positive, including identifying strengths, empowering all family members to claim a voice in the inquiry, and encouraging self-reflection in participants, AI builds on the existing strengths of families to help them strategize and move toward a desired future.

A Model of Appreciative Inquiry for Families and Couples

Based on the assumptions and principles outlined above, a five-stage cyclical, iterative, and continuing process model of AI in families, grounded in Mohr and Watkins (2002, p. 5), emerges, as shown in Figure 5.1.

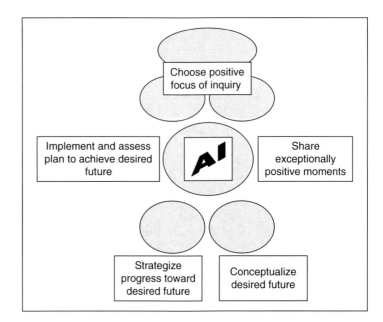

Figure 5.1: Model of AI in Families and Couples

The stages in the AI model for couples and families include the following:

1. Choosing a positive focus of inquiry
2. Inquiring into and sharing exceptionally positive moments
3. Conceptualizing a desired future

4. Planning strategies to work toward desired outcomes
5. Implementing strategies and progressing toward desired outcomes

These steps are designed to take participants from an appreciation of the strengths in what *is* to imagining *what could be*, to determining *what should be* to creating *what will be* (Cooperrider-Dole et al., 2008; Whitney & Trosten-Bloom, 2003).

Stage 1: Choosing a Positive Focus of Inquiry

Mohr and Watkins (2002) advance that the AI process begins when participants consciously choose "to focus on the positive as the basis for learning and change" (p. 5). This emphasis on the positive may be difficult for individuals, couples, or families. It is not uncommon for participants to slip easily into a deficit model, identifying concerns or problems. Distressed couples in particular have often reached the point where their relational emphasis is on *what is not working* with little attention to *what is working*. In our work, we allow some time for early venting as couples move from a deficit-based model to a strengths-based one. Overcoming any barriers to focusing on the positive is necessary for engaging the appreciative process. A useful approach is to refocus these tendencies toward what couples want more of rather than what they see as deficits or problems. If issues included an inability to release a problem orientation or anger, we have found techniques useful to helping couples get beyond those reactions.

Insights Gained: If a couple/family has difficulty letting go of the negative, the authors have found two box metaphor strategies useful in moving beyond this state:

1. *Problem orientation:* If participants have trouble moving from a problem orientation to a strengths-based orientation:
   a. Explore what strategies the partners have used in the past to manage the issue of concern
   b. Assess how effective prior strategies have been in resolving the issue
   c. Ask if they would like to try something new; introduce the theory and perspective of AI
2. *Managing anger:* Anger is not an uncommon emotion in distressed couples or families. However, anger will thwart the appreciative process. Consequently, it becomes critical to identify strategies that will assist participants in releasing their anger:
   a. Give it to God: In one of the couples with whom I worked, a participant could not get beyond the anger she felt toward her partner. She expressed her wish that God would take her anger away. The facilitator engaged that wish and asked her to close her eyes and vision putting her anger in a box and giving it to God for safekeeping, knowing that she could take it back whenever she desired to do so. The facilitator invited her to open her eyes when she had delivered the box to God. This visualization process helped this participant put aside her anger and participate in the AI process.
   b. Put it in a box: On another occasion, a nonreligious participant found that just visualizing putting his concerns and worries in a box and placing them somewhere else helped him engage in the AI process. The key was to acknowledge the issues and realize that they could be reengaged at any time but that they were not necessary to "hold" now.

The key for facilitators of AI is to meet couples where they are and assist them in shifting to or accepting an appreciative approach. Getting to the selection of a positive focus of inquiry may take one or several meetings with couples or families and may be an easy or a complex process. Once participants have agreed to try focusing on the positive, they move to the second stage.

Stage 2: Inquiring into and Sharing Exceptionally Positive Moments

The second stage in the process is grounded in self reflection (Stavros & Torres, 2005), followed by open communication with the relationship partner or other family members. Often the initial steps in this stage are done within the context of interviews. Interview templates are created for this purpose that focus on "best experiences, values, and core values" (Mohr & Watkins, 2002, p. 6). Interviews can be conducted by facilitators, by partners or family members, or by individuals themselves. They can be oral interviews, or participants can engage in journaling about the positive question that participants have agreed to focus on. In identifying exceptionally positive moments, Trosten-Bloom and Whitney (1999) encourage a focus on best experiences. Best experiences are elicited through the use of compelling questions. An example of a compelling question with subquestions for couples might be the following: "Think of a time in your relationship when you felt most supported and encouraged by your partner: What were the characteristics of that situation? How did you feel in that situation?" For families, a question might be the following: "Think about your time with your family, What are some of your best memories of times your family spent time together enjoying each other's company? Choose one and tell me/your partner/journal about it in more detail. What were you doing? How did it happen that your family enjoyed that time together? How did this impact your family relationships?" (revised from Cooperrider-Dole et al., p. 58). If partners or family members are interviewing one another, "your" can be changed to "our" in the above example. This promotes a sense of connection and common ground.

Identifying the right, positive question to move the family forward is the foundation of the AI process, as every other part of the model follows from the question. Grounded in the belief that people "move in the direction of what they study," the nature of the question is critical to launching the process in a strengths-based direction (Whitney & Trosten-Bloom, 2003, p. 134). To assist families in selecting questions, Cooperrider-Dole et al. (2008) offer guidelines and sample questions for couples and families as they approach a variety of important life events, weddings, births, and so on. In addition to being positive, Whitney and Trosten-Bloom (2003) note the critical importance of involving all concerned parties in framing the focusing question. This promotes ownership and commitment in couples and family members.

Unlike traditional problem-focused approaches that emphasize what is wrong in a relationship, this approach encourages participants to begin with a best experience, to move forward from a place of strength and positivity. As they move through the process, with an understanding of strengths as a foundation, they are able to reach greater levels of specificity and to plan precise strategies for moving forward.

The second step in this process is to ask participants to share their best experiences with one another. Those receiving the stories are asked to listen attentively but not to interrupt so that each person can feel fully heard. Receivers are then asked to affirm the participant for sharing the story. Once all partners have heard one another's stories, the emphasis shifts to identifying the strengths in each story. Addressing this question can be done either alone or in combination with a discussion of values. Questions about values might include the following: "What do you value most about yourself/your relationship/your family? What do you value most about yourself as a relationship partner/family member? What do you value most about your relationship partner/each member of your family? When you are feeling best about your relationship/your family, what is it that makes you feel that way? What is the most important thing this relationship/your family has contributed to your life?

Analyzing relationships and families in this manner allows participants to fully engage the strengths they have experienced in the relationship/family. Answers to these types of questions offer insight into what participants value about their relationship partner or family members. They might also lead to another appreciative story articulating their experiences of when all these factors came together in an empowering way. Once stories have been shared, mining them for strengths is critical so that models of capacity can be carried forward into the next stages. In our experience, it is critical to adapt this process, like the prior one, to the capacities and communication preferences of the participants. Some people respond fluidly to these types of questions. Others need time to think and reflect before they are prepared to engage. This step can be used as either a session prompt or an assignment to prepare for a next meeting. Whatever strategy is used, the first issue is to identify the characteristics in the relationship that worked well at some point in time and what made them work well. Through the sharing of positive stories about such times, couples and families also begin to embrace a collaborative, collective approach to moving toward the future.

The third step in this process is uncovering a core value or values, asking questions such as the following: "What are the core values in this relationship/family that allow you to move through difficult times? Give some examples of how you experience/live these values. If this value did not exist, how would your relationship/family be different?" As noted above, these three steps (best experiences, values, core values) can be conducted in one interview or sequentially, even across different appreciative sessions. The key is to adapt to what works for participants.

Insights Gained: A variety of timing and structural approaches may work in this stage. It is critical to adapt to the needs/perspectives of the participants:

1. Compelling questions dealing with best experiences, values, and core values might be addressed in one interview or in multiple interviews.
2. Participants might share one best experience story that encompasses elements in all three steps (best experiences, values, core values), or they may share stories about each of the steps sequentially with processing between them.
3. A variety of models for generating responses might be helpful including interviews and journaling.
4. The power in this stage is the sharing of perspectives and the collaborative identification of strengths and capacities that will move the couple/family forward in the next stages.

Once best experiences, values, and core values have been mined for strengths and capacities, the process moves to the next stage.

Stage 3: Conceptualizing a Desired Future

This stage involves visioning a desired future. It is again critical at this stage not to allow discussion to digress back into problem solving. It is not uncommon for participants to want to use their new awareness of strengths to "solve their relationship problems." It is critical that the facilitator (or the participants themselves) avoid this inclination and continue to emphasize the positive. This stage can begin with individual reflection and reporting back or with couple or family collaboration in response to probes such as the following: "What three wishes do you have for this relationship/family? What do we want to create? What would our best possible future look like?" Cooperrider-Dole et al. (2008) offer the following compelling question: "Imagine it is a year from now and you are reflecting on all the meaningful and fun-filled family times you have had together. What did you do that was new and different to ensure that each family member values the time spent together as a family? How were you able to create these special family times?" (p. 58). As with the prior stage, the critical aspect of this stage is participants collaborating to build on the positive aspects of their relationships to imagine their desired future (Stavros & Torres, 2005).

Insights Gained:

1. It is very easy in this stage for couples to digress to a problem-focused orientation. This must be avoided, as it shifts focus away from the positive.
2. While goals at this stage are general, they must also be precise so that in the next stage they can be operationalized through a precise action plan.
3. It is critical that both partners/all family members engage in visioning the future in order to sustain ownership and engagement of the process by all participants.

Once the general direction the couple/family wants to move in has been outlined, the next step involves the development of precise behavioral objectives and establishing time lines for their implementation.

Stage 4: Planning Strategies to Work Toward Desired Outcomes

Once a desired future has been envisioned, the next step in the process is action planning to move the couple/family toward that future. This stage focuses on specific steps to achieve objectives. By moving from general goals to specific objectives, participants identify behaviors they desire and are willing to undertake to move the couple/family toward their desired goal.

A couple may decide that their ultimate objective is the following: "We want to feel more connection, love, and passion in our relationship." Steps toward this objective might be incremental at first: "I will acknowledge all the little things my partner does in a day to connect with me (making the first pot of coffee in the morning, cooking dinner, or asking me to go to our favorite restaurant, enjoy a movie night, taking out the trash, and so on). Many strategies can be used to facilitate movement toward these desired outcomes. For example, one couple who wanted to appreciate one another more selected to leave "Thank You" sticky notes around the house to acknowledge what their partner did on a daily basis to contribute to their connection. A sticky note on the coffeemaker saying "Thanks! ☺" both acknowledged the act of making the coffee and created a positive connection between partners. We have also found it useful to ask couples to share with one another at the end of the day the positive contributions each made to the other's life. We typically set three as the number of positive messages to target. These affirmations create connection, acknowledge awareness of the partner's efforts, and reinforce desired positive behaviors.

Acknowledging the positive that already exists is a strong step toward building more positives in the relationship. In addition to precise actions, we have also found it helpful to identify specific time lines for movement on action items as well as specific trial periods for each item. Examples are the following:

> "Starting next week, we'll have date night on Fridays. We'll do this for the next four Fridays."

> "Starting today, we won't take any phones calls during dinner. We'll turn our phones on silent so we are not aware of missing calls and will make any follow-up calls we desire after dinner. We'll try this for a week."

"We'll all clear our schedules to go to Suzie's soccer game next Wednesday night and out for a family dinner after. We'll need to block time from 5:30 to 8:00 p.m. to meet this agreement. We'll see if this is workable and plan for following weeks."

Insights Gained: A critical step in moving toward a desired future is recognizing the elements of that future in the present. There is a great deal of power in this approach, and such acknowledgment encourages the continuance and expansion of desired behaviors:

1. Moving toward a desired future requires acknowledgment of what is working in the present.
2. Moving toward a desired future requires planning specific, incremental steps and a time line for their implementation.
3. A manageable time frame for an action allows for planned assessment, evaluation, and modification as necessary to make the steps workable.
4. Reporting back at a specified time, either to a facilitator or to one another, holds each participant accountable for her/his participation in the plan.

The final stage involves implementing, assessing, and modifying the plan to achieve the desired future.

Stage 5: Implementing and Assessing Strategies and Progressing Toward Desired Outcomes

In this and any type of relationship work, there can be a gap between intentions and behavior. Couples and families may have the best intentions, but follow-through may be a different matter. One useful strategy is to hold couples/families individually and collectively accountable for movement on planned actions designed to help them achieve their objectives. Participants may make formal agreements by writing out and signing a list of planned behaviors and time line, or they may verbally affirm their intentions. In addition, we have found progress assessments at predetermined times to be useful. Participants can check in either with the facilitator or with one another to monitor and modify agreements as necessary in order to sustain momentum. Barriers to implementation can be identified, and strategies to either meet or modify agreed-to behaviors can be developed, or, given unanticipated or nonmodifiable constraints, new agreements can be made.

Timing is critical at this stage. Short intervals between the proposed implementation and evaluation of steps taken toward the desired goal are necessary to assist participants in engaging desired behaviors, reinforcing progress, and analyzing how well desired behaviors fit into the other activities of daily living in which participants engage. Planned actions that are difficult to accomplish or that are unrealistic given other life obligations will not be sustainable and will undermine the commitment to strengths-based change. Therefore, in order to maintain forward movement toward goals and to continue, enhance, and build on strengths, participants need to engage in periodic assessments of their progress and the workability of their plans. As positive movement is made, they may also engage in further appreciative planning to identify and commit to additional behaviors that will lead toward goal achievement. This "checking in" helps participants maintain and enhance their strengths-based orientation and movement toward objectives.

For some couples, accountability through reporting back to a third party, such as a facilitator, can enhance their forward progress and the negotiation of any unanticipated issues. For others, checking in with one another is all that is needed. It is important to affirm that change is a process and that goals and progress need to be periodically assessed and, when appropriate, revised. We have found that short-term time lines assist with learning how to implement behaviors and with assessing their effectiveness. Often when couples are in the early stages of implementation, they are committed, engaged, and positive. The objective of periodic assessment at this point is to sustain this momentum. As desired behaviors become more integrated, more time can elapse between planned assessments. Later assessments can emphasize refining goals further or identifying additional objectives through engagement in additional AI.

Insights Gained:

1. To be effective, interventions must be smoothly and appropriately integrated into participants' lives.
2. Time lines for and engagement in assessment can reinforce change efforts and make them more relevant and sustainable.
3. Once appreciative skills are learned, couples can use this model to refine existing objectives or identify new ones.

Summary/Conclusion

AI is a useful model to complement problem-based and resilience-focused approaches to work with couples and families. In outlining a strengths-based model of change and decision making, AI focuses on the collaborative identification of relational strengths and utilizes them as the foundation for building a desired future. A foundation premise of AI is that people function best when they can take positive elements of the past with them into the future (Hammond, 1996). Further, as noted above, Stavros and Torres (2005) note the importance of focusing on the positive in order to move toward positive outcomes.

As outlined in this chapter, couples and families who engage in AI access a five-stage appreciative process. This process allows them to choose a positive focus of inquiry, inquire into and share exceptionally positive moments from their relationship, conceptualize a desired future, plan strategies to work toward their desired outcomes, and implement strategies and assess progress toward goals. Through the telling and hearing of each other's stories, recounting best experiences, values, and core values, participants identify what is working in their relationship. After sharing these stories, couples and family members work to collaboratively identify the existing and emergent capacities that will allow them to work toward their desired future. These strengths become the foundation for conceptualizing, strategizing, and acting to create their desired future. Combining characteristics of positive psychology, constructivism, and action planning, this collaborative process is empowering, creates ownership of the process and outcomes among all parties, and increases the likelihood that change efforts will be sustainable.

Discussion Questions

1. Stage 3 of AI requires a family to conceptualize a desired future in order to ensure positive growth. Do you believe that a family can develop if a unified idea of the future is never constructed? Why or why not?

2. In stage 1 of AI (choosing a positive focus of inquiry), the author sets forth two examples of how one may positively deal with her or his anger (i.e., give it to God and put it in a box). In what other ways can anger be positively relieved?

3. According to Fincham and Beach (2010), social scientists assert that "alleviating harm is inherently more ethically compelling than is promoting well-being." Give at least one example where society works to alleviate harm instead of promoting well-being. Do you agree with this approach?

4. In stage 2 of AI (inquiring into and sharing exceptionally positive moments), the author gives several examples of questions that reaffirm dedication to the family. Choose two of the following questions to explore your own relationships: What is the most important thing your chosen relationship or your family has contributed to your life? What do you value most about your relationship partner or each member of your family? When are you feeling best about your relationship or your family? What is it that makes you feel that way?

References

Caughlin, J. P., & Huston, T. L. (2010, March). The flourishing literature on flourishing relationships. *Journal of Family Theory and Review, 2,* 25–35.

Cooperrider, D. L., & Whitney, D. (2005). *Appreciative Inquiry: A positive revolution in change.* San Francisco: Berrett-Koehler.

Cooperrider-Dole, D., Silbert J., Mann, A., & Whitney, D. (Eds.). (2008). *Positive family dynamics: Appreciative Inquiry questions to bring out the best in families.* Chagrin Falls, OH: Taos Institute Publications.

Dick, B. (2011). Action research literature 2008–2010: Themes and trends. *Action Research, 9*(2), 122–143. http://arj.sagepub.com.proxy.wichita.edu/content/9/2/122.full.pdf+html

Fincham, F. D., & Beach, S. R. H. (2010, March). Of memes and marriage: Toward a positive relationship science. *Journal of Family Theory and Review, 2,* 4–24.

Hammond, S. A. (1996). *The thin book of Appreciative Inquiry* (2nd ed.). Bend, OR: Thin Book Publishing.

Mohr, B. J., & Watkins, J. M. (2002). *The essentials of Appreciative Inquiry: A roadmap for creating positive futures.* Waltham, MA: Pegasus Communications.

Seligman, M. E. P. (2002). *Authentic happiness: Using the new positive psychology to realize your potential for lasting fulfillment.* New York: Simon and Schuster.

Stavros, J. M., & Torres, C. B. (2005). *Dynamic relationships: Unleashing the power of Appreciative Inquiry in daily living.* Chagrin Falls, OH: Taos Institute Publications.

Stratton-Berkessel, R. (2010). *Appreciative Inquiry for collaborative solutions.* San Francisco: Wiley.

Trosten-Bloom, A., & Whitney, D. (1999). Appreciative Inquiry: The path to positive change. In M. K. Key (Ed.), *Managing change in healthcare: Innovative solutions for people-based organizations* (pp. 113–128). New York: McGraw-Hill.

Whitney, D., & Trosten-Bloom, A. (2003). *The power of Appreciative Inquiry.* San Francisco: Berrett-Koehler.

Forgiveness and Reconciliation: Infidelity as a Case Study

Douglas Kelley

Because of the threat of AIDS, he told her everything. Late one night, while on business travel, Rob had been drinking with friends. One thing led to another, and when he awoke, he realized the mistake he had made. Rob considered not telling his wife, Katie, about the one-time tryst; after all, he loved her and never planned on another breech of their relationship. However, he would have to find a way to avoid having sex with her until he could be tested for AIDS. With Katie, this would be impossible. She would immediately sense something was wrong. When he first told her, she sat stunned. Then she began to cry and told him to get out. She didn't even want to talk. And yet, after 3 months of separation and 2 years of counseling, Katie managed to forgive Rob, and together they have created a strong marriage.

Rob and Katie are working through what many psychologists believe is the most difficult issue for couples to manage: infidelity (Gordon, Baucom, & Snyder, 2005). Not all couples choose to reconcile after an extramarital affair, but those who do are confronted with the question of forgiveness. Many people struggle with forgiveness because they perceive it as "letting a wrongdoer off the hook." Yet forgiveness is a unique process that offers the potential for personal, relational, and moral restoration. As such, I begin this chapter framing forgiveness as a process of restoration. I then discuss why infidelity is particularly hurtful for most couples and offer it as a test case for understanding the potential of forgiveness as a process of reconciliation.

Forgiveness as Restoration

Forgiveness has been conceptualized as a psychological and interpersonal process (McCoullough, Pargament, & Thoresen, 2000). As a psychological process, forgiveness may be used to restore personal well-being. For example, forgiveness involves both negative and positive motivations (Fincham, Hall, & Beach, 2005); that is, forgivers experience a decrease in negative thoughts and feelings (e.g., a reduction in revenge-based thinking) and an increase in positive thoughts and feelings (e.g., feelings of empathy and compassion) toward a perceived offender. This transition from negative to positive response is also associated with positive physical and psychological health outcomes (Harris & Thoresen, 2005; Witvliet, 2005).

Vince Waldron and I (2008) make the point that individuals view their relationships as moral entities, and therefore forgiveness involves restoring the relationship's moral code. It is common for individuals to view relational behaviors as "right" or "wrong." As such, response to relational transgressions typically involves managing the moral aspect of "wrongdoing." To this end, Metts (1994) notes that romantic relationships are based on relational rules, one of which is typically monogamy. Violation of this rule, or relationship covenant (Hargrave, 1994), constitutes a moral transgression to most people. For example, extramarital affairs are not commonly viewed as inconvenient or inefficient to achieving relational goals; they are typically seen as a betrayal of the relationship agreement (Allan & Harrison, 2009) and, subsequently, a moral violation (Kelley, 2011). Therefore, Waldron and I suggest that part of the forgiveness process leading to reconciliation is renegotiation of the relationship's moral code (Kelley, 2011; Waldron & Kelley, 2008).

Viewing transgressions as interpersonal in nature raises the possibility of relationship restoration through forgiveness. Hurt is typically relational (Vangelisti, 2009). Vangelisti (1994; 2001) emphasizes the relational aspect of hurt by focusing on vulnerability and the individual's response to perceived violations of relational rules. Feeney (2009) takes an attachment theory approach to relational hurt. She proposes that in infancy, individuals form mental models of attachment that affect how they view and enact personal relationships. When these cognitive models are threatened, the reduced sense of security creates a strong emotional response and sense of personal injury. For example, an individual who perceives relationships as secure, safe places may incur significant damage to this worldview (e.g., relationship view) when experiencing a partner's infidelity. As such, significant tasks for married couples who experience an affair are reconstructing their individual relationship perspectives and deciding whether to restore the marriage relationship.

Forgiveness: Creating Conditions for Reconciliation

Forgiveness creates positive conditions for successful reconciliation but, it is important to note, *in no way demands reconciliation from relational partners*. That is, based on new information gained through the transgression period, it is possible to forgive and, yet, decide not to continue the relationship. On the other hand, it is also possible to reconcile without forgiveness. For example, after an affair, married partners may choose to stay together "for the kids" although the victim of the affair may not have forgiven the offender.

For those couples who choose to explore reconciliation after a major transgression, I examine the following definition of interpersonal forgiveness, proposed by Vince Waldron and myself (2008). My intent is to highlight and offer interpretation of key aspects that are specifically related to potential reconciliation:

> Forgiveness is a relational process whereby *harmful conduct is acknowledged* by one or both partners; the harmed partner extends *undeserved mercy* to the perceived transgressor; one or both partners experience a *transformation from negative to positive* psychological states; and the meaning of the relationship is *renegotiated*, with the possibility of reconciliation. (p. 19)

Based on this definition, four elements of interpersonal forgiveness are essential to interpersonal reconciliation: recognition of the transgression, granting undeserved mercy, transition from negative to positive response, and renegotiation of the relationship. (Waldron & Kelley, 2008).

First, for those considering reconciliation, *the transgression must be recognized and acknowledged*. Vangelisti (2009) notes that hurt is often the result of relational transgressions. As such, movement toward personal healing and possible healthy reconciliation is seldom achieved without recognition of harm done. In addition, through research interviews and conversation with individuals about forgiveness, it is clear that many who resist forgiveness do so because of a failure of forgivers to recognize "wrong" behavior. This is consistent with researcher perspectives that point out that many forgiveness-like concepts—excuse, condonation, and denial—are not forgiveness (McCullough et al., 2000). Common to these nonforgiveness concepts is lack of recognition of a perceived transgression.

The second element essential to reconciliation, *undeserved mercy*, raises the issue of relational justice. Typically, individuals view relational justice in terms of equity and fairness (Enright & Human Development Study Group, 1991). Granting undeserved mercy requires the forgiver to assess what counts as justice in the relationship and to decide whether to move beyond notions of retributive punishment. In other words, the forgiver chooses to forgive based on grace rather than merit. For deep hurts, individuals may recognize that true equity is difficult, if not impossible, to achieve (e.g., how does one "pay" for damaging another's reputation?). It is important to emphasize that forgiveness does not negate justice; rather, it exists only in conjunction with justice (Volf, 2001; Waldron & Kelley, 2008). In fact, recognition of a relational transgression is often the beginning of a renewed sense of relational justice.

Granting undeserved mercy also begins the reinstitution of conciliatory behavior in the relationship. For those relational partners interested in reconciliation, demonstration of undeserved mercy may signal the willingness of the forgiver to reengage the offending partner and renegotiate the relationship. Exline, Worthington, Hill, and McCullough (2003) suggest that forgiveness may result in future conciliatory behavior as an alternative to retribution.

A third reconciliation aspect of our forgiveness definition is the *shift from negative to positive psychological states*. Forgiveness precipitates a shift in a forgiver's response to an offender's action; that is, there is a reduction in negative response and an increase in positive response (Fincham et al., 2005; McCullough et al., 2000). Clearly, if individuals are to successfully reconcile, negative psychological and behavioral responses must diminish, and positive, conciliatory behaviors must increase. In fact, Rusbult, Hannon, Stocker, and Finkel (2005) specifically discuss sustained demonstration of prosocial responses as integral to achieving reconciliation.

Renegotiation of the relationship is the final forgiveness element that sets conditions for reconciliation. This aspect of the forgiveness process involves two essential tasks: affirmation of a desire for the relationship and establishment of transitional boundaries and renegotiation of relational rules and the relationship's moral code (e.g., "We value honesty and an exclusive sexual relationship.").

Infidelity in Marriage

Infidelity is one of the most difficult marital problems for couples to manage (Gordon, Baucom, and Snyder, 2005). Although scholars have used a variety of terms to discuss extramarital sexual activity (Allan & Harrison, 2009), I choose the term "infidelity" because of its association with the notion of betrayal.

Feelings of betrayal are a common result of infidelity. Couples often perceive infidelity as a violation of implicit or explicit expectations of exclusivity in the marriage relationship (Tafoya & Spitzberg, 2007). This violation of the relationship covenant may undermine feelings of "coupleness" or one or both partners' sense of having a unique couple identity (Allan & Harrison, 2009; Owens, 1984). Unilaterally altering the relationship may also result in the "victim" of the affair feeling cheated (Allan & Harrison, 2009); that is, without mutual consent, the nature of the relationship has been single-handedly altered.

Infidelity may also be experienced as interpersonal trauma (Gordon et al., 2005). For example, the victimized partner may experience both outwardly and inwardly directed emotion. An example of outwardly directed emotion is expression of rage toward the offending partner. Inwardly directed emotion is typically experienced as feelings of shame, depression, powerlessness, victimization, and abandonment. Loss of trust, rumination, and changes in perceptions of the offending partner may lead to an increase in communication responses (e.g., questioning and avoidance) and hypervigilance of the offending partner.

Infidelity is typically a blend of hurtful actions (Vangelisti & Gerstenberger, 2004) that break multiple relationship rules. For example, the act of infidelity may involve deception, extramarital sexual activity, and emotional closeness with a potential romantic partner other than one's spouse. These elements contribute to the perception of infidelity as betrayal. Also, because affair victims often perceive the offense as intentional (Rusbult et al., 2005), the infidelity typically elicits feelings of personal injury (Feeney, 2005, 2009). According to Feeney (2005, 2009), these feelings may result in victim distress, self-blame, and feeling unlovable. This process may trigger self-assessment and partner reassessment and orient the victim to potential relational meanings of the offending partner's behaviors. In addition, individuals who experience a partner straying from relationship guidelines may experience jealousy and damage to self-identity (Allan & Harrison, 2009). The close tie between personal identity and relationship involvement (Jamieson, 2004) inevitably leads to feelings of personal rejection. And, as one might guess, personal rejection (e.g., devaluation) is integrally tied to one's experience of relational hurt (Leary & Leder, 2009).

As alluded to previously, infidelity is not viewed solely as a violation of relational rules concerning sexual activity; it may also include implicit expectations regarding emotional involvement. It has been suggested that men are most affected by sexual involvement outside the marriage, whereas women are most affected by emotional involvement outside the marriage (Buss, Larsen, Westen, & Semmelroth, 1992; Tafoya & Spitzberg, 2007). Others propose that relational partners who see sexual and emotional involvement as highly connected are more likely to associate infidelity with betrayal (Allan & Harrison, 2009; DeSteno, Bartlett, Salovey, & Braverman, 2002; DeSteno & Salovey, 1996).

Forgiving Infidelity

Interviews conducted by Vince Waldron and myself (2008) with long-term married couples demonstrate that forgiveness is a means of reconciliation after infidelity. While couples who experience infidelity may choose not to reconcile or may find relationship and social network conditions difficult for reconciliation, our data indicate that individuals who are able to forgive may find their way to renewed relationship satisfaction and stability.

Gordon and Baucom's (1999, 2003) research (see also Gordon et al., 2005) with couples that have experienced infidelity has identified three forgiveness stages. The first stage, *impact*, includes a variety of emotional and cognitive responses. At the cognitive level, the injured party attempts to understand the transgression. Emotionally, the injured party may experience varied negative emotions, such as fear, hurt, and anger. These emotions may alternate with a sense of numbness or disbelief. The impact stage may also include behavior uncharacteristic of the victimized partner, such as punitive or vindictive responses (e.g., "I've been hurt and I want you to hurt, too.").

The second stage, *meaning*, represents the partners' attempt to make sense of what has happened and implications for the future of the relationship. At this stage, partners assess self-identity, partner identity, and the nature of the relationship within the context of new information gained through experiencing the transgression event (e.g., "You are not the person I thought you were" or "You made a mistake, but you have repented and still love me."). At this stage, partners are trying to restabilize the relationship by reducing uncertainty and restoring control (although they may not have determined the long-term nature of the relationship). As such, couple communication is characterized by questions, explanations, accounts, assurances, and promises.

The third stage, *moving on or recovery*, is characterized by deciding whether to maintain the relationship and efforts to reestablish the individual's health. This stage represents the reduction of negative emotions and "moving on" psychologically. Individuals at this stage may decide to embrace forgiveness as opposed to pursue revenge. This decision may influence the desire or willingness to reconcile the relationship. As such, partners either discuss changes if they are to continue the current relationship or decide to terminate or change the nature of the relationship (e.g., from married partners to divorced partners sharing responsibilities for joint-custody children).

Waldron and I (2008) propose seven forgiveness tasks that parallel Gordon and Baucom's three stages. I have described the overlap between the two models by using four stages and emphasizing the likely communication behaviors and restorative goals at each stage. It should be noted that each stage may occur at any part of the process and may be repeated multiple times. In addition, individuals may experience multiple stages simultaneously (e.g., *managing the impact* may take some time and involve *making sense of . . .*).

The first stage, *managing the impact*, encompasses discovery of the transgression and management of emotion. The discovery of the transgression and subsequent emotional response triggers communication oriented toward confronting the transgressor, questioning, truth-telling/confession, venting (to the offending party or a third party), and, possibly, avoidant behavior. The goal of much of the communication at this stage of the process is to restore individual well-being.

The second stage, *making sense of . . . (oneself, one's partner, the relationship)*, encompasses Gordon and Baucom's meaning stage and Waldron and Kelley's (2008) sense-making task. The predominant goal at this stage is to restore the moral order. In essence, the offended partner is trying to make sense of the partner's "wrong" or hurtful behavior, assess the role of mercy and justice, and determine future implications. Communication behaviors include discussion and explanation, questioning, listening, perspective taking, joint determination of the transgression's impact, and contextualizing the transgression in light of the relationship's past.

Third, I suggest *engaging forgiveness* as a stage that incorporates elements of Gordon and Baucom's second and third stages and Waldron and Kelley's forgiveness-seeking and forgiveness-granting tasks. From the offender's perspective, engaging forgiveness involves seeking forgiveness through apology, nonverbal sincerity (e.g., crying), restitution, or directly requesting forgiveness from the partner (Waldron & Kelley, 2005). On the other hand, the offended party may respond with empathy, listening, discussion, nonverbal displays (e.g., hugging), or directly saying, "I forgive you" (Waldron & Kelley, 2005).

Finally, *renegotiating the relationship* focuses on partner negotiation as a means of "moving on." During this time, partners explore options as to the viability of staying together. If they choose to maintain their current relationship or change the nature of the relationship, negotiation necessitates the discussion of new rules and agreeing on a moral structure that will stabilize the relationship and allow for the reestablishment of trust.

Reconciling After Infidelity

Waldron and I (2008) note that forgiveness involves relationship renegotiation "with the possibility of reconciliation" (p. 19). The distinction between forgiveness and reconciliation, held by many scholars (Kanz, 2000; Kearns & Fincham, 2004; Waldron & Kelley, 2008), is important to recognize. Many offended parties are reluctant to forgive because they believe that forgiveness requires reconciliation. They want to move past the hurt and pain of the transgression but are not ready to consider rekindling the relationship. In this light, Waldron and I (Kelley & Waldron, 2005) emphasize forgiveness as a relational repair strategy that occurs over time. Likewise, Rusbult et al. (2005) note that reconciliation is the process of enacting prosocial behaviors over an extended period of time. In essence, relational partners must realize that the relationship between forgiveness and reconciliation is often messy and deeply intertwined and occurs over a long span. In fact, our interviews with couples that successfully worked through marital infidelity revealed that forgiveness and reconciliation may take years to successfully negotiate.

Restoring the relationship is a lengthy process due, in part, to the fact that partners are confronted with two major tasks: reestablishing trust and reestablishing commitment (Rusbult et al., 2005; Worthington, 2001). Worthington and Drinkard (2000) emphasize the reestablishment of trust, through the enactment of trustworthy behavior, as central to reconciliation. They note that this does not mean the elimination of all conflict. Rather, reconciliation becomes a process of implicit and explicit negotiations that stabilize the relationship over time.

Interestingly, the process of relationship negotiation is simply an extension of normal relationship processes. I consider it useful to conceptualize all communication as a process of reconciliation (re-conciliation). Communication scholars have long recognized the constant flux of relationships as relational partners continually negotiate relational themes and dialectical tensions (Baxter, 2006; Burgoon & Hale, 1984). For example, even when partners return home from work at day's end, there is a process of reconciling, that is, reuniting and retuning the relationship. However, managing the aftermath of relational transgression may result in more explicit, direct negotiation than is typical. For example, Waldron and I (2005) discovered that severe transgressions are sometimes managed with more direct forgiveness strategies, such as conditional forgiveness (e.g., "I will forgive you if you discontinue your hurtful behavior.").

The second major task of forgiveness, reestablishing commitment, is the decision to persist in a relationship, long term, while maintaining a sense of psychological attachment (Rusbult et al., 2005). This perspective links commitment to the development of trust in the relationship. As one partner communicates and demonstrates long-term persistence and attachment, the other may become convinced of his or her willingness and ability to act benevolently in the relationship—creating a sense of trust.

The process of reconciliation has been described by Worthington and Drinkard (2000). The first of their six steps sets the conditions for reconciliation: decide to reconcile, soften toward one's partner, and forgive. The final three steps (reverse the negative cascade, deal with failures in trustworthiness, and actively build love) parallel two of the communicative forgiveness tasks that Waldron and I (2008; see also Kelley, 2011) propose: negotiate values and rules and monitor the relational transition. These tasks, which occur after a decision has been made to engage forgiveness and proceed with reconciliation, if even temporarily, focus on renegotiation of the relationship's moral structure (e.g., reestablishing trust—"We must always be honest."), relationship rules (e.g., no working late at the office with members of the opposite sex), and, possibly, long-range relationship plans (e.g., "Let's follow our dream to move to the country."). As Worthington and Drinkard (2000) note, this renegotiation process is dependent on the couple's ability to interrupt the negative communication patterns and move toward conciliatory behavior.

Our research on conditional forgiveness demonstrates additional means by which individuals try to negotiate relationships (Kelley, 1988; Waldron & Kelley, 2005). Some individuals who experience severe relationship transgressions choose to forgive by placing conditions on the forgiveness. For example, one of our respondents was asked for forgiveness by her recovering-alcoholic father. She reported, "I told him I would accept his apology, however, we both knew that there was the stipulation that he stay off the booze" (Kelley, 1998, p. 264). Often, such use of conditional forgiveness implies withdrawal from the relationship. This practice is consistent with lay definitions of forgiveness that often confuse forgiveness and reconciliation (Kearns & Fincham, 2004). Interestingly, however, recent work by Kloeber (2011) demonstrates that some individuals are able to make fine discriminations between forgiveness and reconciliation. One of Kloeber's participants, who was in a difficult situation with a drug-addicted husband, stated, "After several months of being apart I decided to start the healing process and forgive him, but end the relationship, too" (p. 60).

Waldron and I (2005) found that individuals who use conditional forgiveness often incur relationship weakening. This effect may be due to individuals in extreme situations, such as the previously described drug addiction situation, making a last-ditch effort to "save" the relationship (Waldron & Kelley, 2008), or setting appropriate and healthy boundaries. However, it may also be the case that conditional forgiveness is ineffective, at times, because it is perceived as a unilateral power move (one party sets the conditions) and signals an unwillingness to trust one's partner (Kelley, 2011).

Finally, I should note that reconciliation does not always mean a return to pretransgression status of the relationship (Rusbult et al., 2005). My research (Kelly, 1998; Kelley & Waldron, 2005) has demonstrated that reconciled relationships may be weakened or strengthened, returned to "normal," or changed in relationship type after forgiveness. In my initial forgiveness study (Kelley, 1998), the data showed that almost three-quarters of the respondents experienced some type of post-forgiveness relationship change as opposed to a return to normalcy. Some respondents even noted multiple changes such that the relationship initially went back to normal but then later deteriorated. These effects highlight the importance of conceptualizing reconciliation as a multifaceted process that occurs over time.

Final Thoughts

In a recent seminar to medical professionals, I noted that people need hope in order to survive. Forgiveness provides hope for restored individual well-being (for both the offended and the offending partner), a restored relationship, and a restored relational moral order. Many of my students who are not deeply invested in their relationships (e.g., Rusbult, Johnson, & Morrow, 1986) fail to understand why an individual would ever choose to stay in a relationship after being "betrayed" by a relational partner. Yet many individuals who have long-term, deeply invested relationships choose to try and make the relationship "work" after discovering a partner's affair. Forgiveness can be the beginning of creating a healthy space for such relationship renegotiation. The relationship challenge before us is not so much how to find the perfect partner as how to work through relationship hurt and reunite (reconcile) with relational partners who are willing to commit and create trusting relationships.

Discussion Questions

1. This chapter states that infidelity "is the most difficult issue for couples to manage." Do you agree with this statement? Why or why not? What other problems might a couple face that would jeopardize the relationship?

2. The author claims that in relationships, there can be "reconciliation without forgiveness" and gives the example of a couple staying together for the sake of their children. Do you believe that this is a healthy way to maintain a relationship? Why or why not?

3. Consider the claim, "It has been suggested that men are most affected by sexual involvement outside the marriage, whereas women are most affected by emotional involvement outside the marriage." Do you concur with this statement? Why or why not?

4. Should emotional closeness with another be construed as marital infidelity?

5. Considering Waldron and Kelley's four elements of personal reconciliation essential to interpersonal reconciliation (the transgression must be recognized and acknowledged, undeserved mercy, shift from negative to positive psychological states, and renegotiation), which one would you say is the most difficult to practice? Why? Provide an example.

References

Allan, G., & Harrison, K. (2009). Affairs and infidelity. In A. Vangelisti (Ed.), *Feeling hurt in close relationships* (pp. 191–208). New York: Cambridge University Press.

Baxter, L. A. (2006). Relational dialectics theory: Multivocal dialogues of family communication. In D. O. Braithwaite & L. A. Baxter (Eds.), *Engaging theories in family communication: Multiple perspectives* (pp. 130–145). Thousand Oaks, CA: Sage.

Burgoon, J. K., & Hale, J. L. (1984). The fundamental topoi of relational communication. *Communication Monographs, 51*(3), 193–214.

Buss, D. M., Larsen, R. J., Westen, D., & Semmelroth, J. (1992). Sex differences in jealousy: Evolution, physiology, and psychology. *Psychological Science, 3*(4), 251–255.

DeSteno, D. A., Bartlett, M. Y., Salovey, P., & Braverman, J. (2002). Sex differences in jealousy: Evolutionary mechanism or artifact of measurement? *Journal of Personality and Social Psychology, 83,* 1103-1116.

DeSteno, D. A., & Salovey, P. (1996). Evolutionary origins of sex differences in jealousy? Questioning the "fitness" of the model. *Psychological Science, 7,* 367-372.

Enright, R. D., & Human Development Study Group. (1991). The moral development of forgiveness. In W. Kurtines & J. Gewirtz (Eds.), *Handbook of moral behavior and development* (pp. 123-152). Hillsdale, NJ: Lawrence Erlbaum Associates.

Exline, J. J., Worthington, E. L., Hill, P., & McCullough, M. E. (2003). Forgiveness and justice: A research agenda for social and personality psychology. *Personality and Social Psychology Review, 7,* 337-348.

Feeney, J. A. (2005). Hurt feelings in couple relationships: Exploring the role of attachment and perceptions of personal injury. *Personal Relationships, 12*(2), 253-271.

Feeney, J. A. (2009). When love hurts: Understanding hurtful events in couple relationships. In A. Vangelisti (Ed.), *Feeling hurt in close relationships* (pp. 313-335). New York: Cambridge University Press.

Fincham, F. D., Hall, J. H., & Beach, S. R. H. (2005). "'Til lack of forgiveness doth us part: Forgiveness and marriage. In E. L. Worthington Jr. (Ed.), *Handbook of forgiveness* (pp. 207-226). New York: Routledge.

Gordon, K. C., Baucom, D. H., & Snyder, D. K. (2005). Treating couples recovering from infidelity: An integrative approach. *Journal of Clinical Psychology, 61*(11), 1393-1405.

Hargrave, T. D. (1994). Families and forgiveness: A theoretical and therapeutic framework. *The Family Journal: Counseling and Therapy for Couples and Families, 2,* 239-348.

Harris, A. H. S., & Thoresen, C. E. (2005). Forgiveness, unforgiveness, health, and disease. In E. L. Worthington Jr. (Ed.), *Handbook of forgiveness* (pp. 321-333). New York: Routledge.

Jamieson, L. (2004). Intimacy, negotiated nonmonogamy, and the limits of the couple. In J. Duncombe, K. Harrison, G. Allan, & D. Marsden (Eds.), *The state of affairs: Explorations in infidelity and commitment* (pp. 35-58). Mahwah, NJ: Lawrence Erlbaum Associates.

Kanz, J. E. (2000). How do people conceptualize and use forgiveness? The forgiveness attitudes questionnaire. *Counseling and Values, 44,* 174-188.

Kearns, J. N., & Fincham, F. D. (2004). A prototype analysis of forgiveness. *Personality and Social Psychology Bulletin, 30,* 838-855.

Kelley, D. L. (1998). The communication of forgiveness. *Communication Studies, 49*(3), 255-271.

Kelley, D. L. (2011). *Marital communication.* Cambridge: Polity Press.

Kelley, D. L., & Waldron, V. (2005). An investigation of forgiveness-seeking communication and relational outcomes. *Communication Quarterly, 53,* 339-358.

Kloeber, D. N. (2011). *Voicing conditional forgiveness.* Thesis presented in partial fulfillment of the masters in communication studies, Arizona State University.

Leary, M. R., & Leder, S. (2009). The nature of hurt feelings: Emotional experience and cognitive appraisals. In A. Vangelisti (Ed.), *Feeling hurt in close relationships* (pp. 15-33). New York: Cambridge University Press.

McCoullough, M. E., Pargament, K. I., & Thoresen, C. E. (Eds.). (2000). *Forgiveness: Theory, research, and practice.* New York: Guilford.

Metts, S. (1994). Relational transgressions. In W. R. Cupach, & B. H. Spitzberg (Eds.), *The dark side of interpersonal communication* (pp. 217-239). Hillsdale, NJ: Lawrence Erlbaum Associates.

Owens, W. F. (1984). Interpretive themes in relational communication. *Quarterly Journal of Speech, 70,* 274-287.

Rusbult, C. E., Hannon, P. A., Stocker, S. L., & Finkel, E. J. (2005). Forgiveness and relational repair. In E. L. Worthington Jr. (Ed.), *Handbook of forgiveness* (pp. 185-205). New York: Routledge.

Rusbult, C. E., Johnson, D. J., & Morrow, G. D. (1986). Predicting satisfaction and commitment in adult romantic involvements: An assessment of the generalizability of the investment model. *Social Psychology Quarterly, 49,* 81-89.

Tafoya, M. A., & Spitzberg, B. H. (2007). The dark side of infidelity: Its nature, prevalence, and communication functions. In B. H. Sptizberg & W. R. Cupach (Eds.), *The dark side of interpersonal communication* (pp. 201-242). Mahwah, NJ: Lawrence Erlbaum Associates.

Vangelisti, A. L. (1994). Messages that hurt. In W. R. Cupach & B. H. Spitzberg (Eds.), *The dark side of interpersonal communication* (pp. 53-82). Hillsdale, NJ: Lawrence Erlbaum Associates.

Vangelisti, A. L. (2001). Making sense of hurtful interactions in close relationships: When hurt feelings create distance. In V. Manusov & J. H. Harvey (Eds.), *Attribution, communication behavior, and close relationships* (pp. 38-58). New York: Cambridge University Press.

Vangelisti, A. L. (2009). Hurt feelings: Distinguishing features, functions, and overview. In A. L. Vangelisti (Ed.), *Feeling hurt in close relationships* (pp. 3-11). New York: Cambridge University Press.

Vangelisti, A. L., & Gerstenberger, M. (2004). Communication and marital infidelity. In J. Duncombe, K. Harrison, G. Allan, & D. Marsden (Eds.), *The state of affairs: Explorations in infidelity and commitment* (pp. 59-78). Mahwah, NJ: Lawrence Erlbaum Associates.

Volf, M. (2001). Forgiveness, reconciliation, and justice: A Christian contribution to a more peaceful social environment. In R. Helmick & R. L. Petersen (Eds.), *Forgiveness and reconciliation: Religion, public policy, and conflict transformation* (pp. 27-49). Philadelphia: Templeton Foundation Press.

Waldron, V. R., & Kelley, D. L. (2005). Forgiveness as a response to relational transgression. *Journal of Personality and Social Psychology, 22,* 723-742.

Waldron, V. R., & Kelley, D. L. (2008). *Communicating forgiveness.* Thousand Oaks, CA: Sage.

Witvliet, C. V. (2005). Unforgiveness, forgiveness, and justice: Scientific findings on feelings and physiology. In E. L. Worthington Jr. (Ed.), *Handbook of forgiveness* (pp. 305-320). New York: Routledge.

Worthington, E. (2001). *Five steps to forgiveness: The art and science of forgiving.* New York: Crown.

Worthington, E. L., & Drinkard, D. T. (2000). Promoting reconciliation through psychoeducational and therapeutic interventions. *Journal of Marital and Family Therapy, 26*(1), 93-101.

Decision Making in Dual-Career Couples: A Replication and Extension

Douglas C. Pennington and Lynne M. Webb

Family life in the United States has changed enormously in recent decades. Parents raising children together but outside the confines of marriage and single parenthood have increased (Mason, Fine, & Carnochan, 2004). Marriage is no longer exclusively between opposite-sex partners (Stockland, 2008). Changes in the financial stability of family life (e.g., the recent real estate crisis) means that the 1950s stereotype of families with only one adult wage earner have become far less common in lived reality (Lundberg & Pollak, 2007), leading to a dramatic increase in the number of dual-career couples (Scheider & Waite, 2005), the focus of this chapter.

The U.S. Bureau of the Census (2010) estimates that in 54.1% of U.S. married couples, both spouses were gainfully employed during 2006–2008. Indeed, Scheider and Waite (2005) note that most U.S. children under 18 are now being raised in families where both parents are employed outside the home. The growing popularity of the dual-career marriage has increased researchers' interest in the unique advantages and demands of dual-career couples, as evidenced by the number of scholarly books published on the subject in the last 10 years (e.g., Cox, 2008; Hardill, 2002; Wolf-Wendel, Twombly, & Rice, 2004).

"Dual career" refers to marriages in which both spouses are actively involved in careers and home obligations (Krueger, 1985). Sekaran (1986) described a career as an occupation demanding a high degree of individual commitment, requiring constant updating of professional knowledge, and serving as a primary source of personal fulfillment.

Social scientists have examined the attitudes and behaviors of dual-career couples, documenting the many differences between single- versus dual-career marriages (e.g., McBride & Mills, 1993) as well as the multiple advantages (e.g., added satisfaction of maintaining a home and career) and challenges (e.g., stress of balance the demands of work and family) of dual-career marriage. Much of this research examines income and spending decisions (e.g., Rubin, Riney, & Molina, 1990); another line of research examines communication in dual-career couples (e.g., Elloy, 2001). The purpose of the study described in this chapter was to unite and augment these two lines of research on dual-career couples by exploring the impact of relative income on communication during decision making within dual-career marital dyads.

Income and Spending Decisions in Dual-Career Marriages

Data from multiple U.S. national surveys indicates that spouses associate dual employment with increased equity in decision making (Amato, Johnson, Booth, & Rogers, 2003). During the first year of marriage, many spouses move from independent to collectivist monetary arrangements;

interview data indicate that the overriding factor in stability and change in marital financial arrangements is spouses' perceived ownership of income and other financial assets (Burgoyne, Reibstein, Edmunds, & Dolman, 2007). Indeed, many researchers conclude that marital bargaining power is linked to relative wage rates (e.g., Pollak, 2005) or income (e.g., Iyigun & Walsh, 2007). However, Price-Bonham (1976) reported that, in opposite-sex marriages, greater financial contributions by wives (vs. husbands) resulted in increased influence only in conventional female domains of domestic activities (e.g., home decorating and child rearing) and not in the "external domain" (e.g., selecting where the couple lives). Similarly, Krueger (1982) reported that decision-making behavior in opposite-sex, dual-career couples reflected a male-dominated orientation, even when spouses perceived themselves as adhering to the ideal of egalitarianism. More recent work reports that, in opposite-sex marriages, both men and women strain to enact appropriate gender roles in marriages where the wife earns more (Tichenor, 2005).

Decision Making in Dual-Career Couples

As early as 1974, scholars began investigating decision making between spouses (Davis & Rigaux, 1974), and their investigations remain ongoing (e.g., Durham & Braithwaite, 2009). Multiple excellent reviews of this body of research are available (e.g., Caughlin & Vangelisti, 2006). A small subsection of this body of research—the research examining decision making *in dual-career couples*—is of particular relevance to our study (e.g., Bartley, Blanton, & Gilliard, 2005). The majority of these studies employed oral or written questionnaires to collect data on spouses' perceptions. Drawing conclusions from such data can be problematic, as spouses' perceptions of their own marital communication can be inaccurate (e.g., Xu & Burlson, 2001). Almost no analyses of actual decision-making sessions between dual-career spouses have been published. Thus, very little is known about the specific communicative behavior of dual-career couples during decision-making sessions. The one notable exception to this generalization is Krueger's (1985) innovative textual analysis.

Krueger defined egalitarianism as the extent to which partners equally exhibit successful control behaviors in dyadic interaction. In five of nine couples, Krueger (1985) found less egalitarianism than the couples self-reported in questionnaires. Previous studies (Ericksen, Yancey, & Ericksen, 1979), as well as more recent research (Bartley et al., 2005), suggest that genuine egalitarianism in dual-career couples is rare.

The purpose of our study was to examine decision making in dual-career couples, with regard to patterns of control and egalitarianism. The study provides an in-depth description/analysis of the communicative process in decision making between dual-career spouses. We replicated Krueger's (1985) research and extended it in three ways. Our sample included couples with children and without children rather than focusing exclusively on childless couples, as some researchers have documented differences in marital communication behaviors based on parental status (e.g., Steil & Weltman, 1992). Additionally, we examined the relationship between spousal income and dominance in decision making, a subject of intense, recent examination (Burgoyne et al., 2007; Iyigun & Walsh, 2007; Pollak, 2005; Tichenor, 2005). Finally, we compared couples' communication behaviors when discussing marital versus child-rearing decisions, as multiple studies have documented that decision-making outcomes can vary by topic (e.g., Bartley et al., 2005). To replicate Krueger's (1985) study as well as to examine male–female differences in marital communication, we elected to sample only opposite-sex spouses. We posited four research questions (RQ):

RQ 1: Is dominance in decision making commensurate with income relative to the marital partner? Given that previous research documented associations between spousal income and influence in decision making (Burgoyne et al., 2007; Iyigun & Walsh, 2007; Pollak, 2005; Tichenor, 2005) but other research links wives earning more than husbands to decreases in wives' power within the marriage (Bittman, England, Sayer, Folbre, & Matheson, 2003; Brines, 1994; Greenstein, 2000), we queried whether partners' conversational dominance would be consistent with relative spousal income for husbands, wives, or both.

RQ 2: Are dual-career couples aware of their predominant decision-making pattern, and can they accurately identify them as either egalitarian, male dominated, or female dominated? Results of previous studies indicate that perceptions of marital equity can be influenced by and reflected in multiple factors (e.g., Bartley et al., 2005). To assess accuracy, we compared participants' self-report data to data from analyses of tape-recorded interactions.

RQ 3: Do the dual-career couples who display egalitarian decision making report higher marital satisfaction? Results of previous studies indicate that perceptions of marital quality can be influenced by multiple factors (Amato et al., 2003; Ting-Toomey, 1984). Will egalitarian decision making also influence such perceptions?

RQ 4: Do dual-career couples employ female-dominated decision making when discussing child-rearing issues? Previous studies documented male–female differences in communicative behaviors during marital conversations (e.g., Steil & Weltman, 1992) and decision making (e.g., Bartley et al., 2005). Given that wives tend to assume more responsibility than husbands for child care (Zimmerman, Haddock, Current, & Ziemba, 2003), perhaps wives dominate decision making related to child rearing.

Method

Participants

Participants were nine dual-career married couples from the southeastern United States recruited via referrals from graduate students in the communication field.[1] They self-reported as Caucasian, heterosexual, functional (not in therapy) marital dyads living together in the same abode. Length of marriage ranged from 2 to 31 years, with a mean of 16 years. This range of marital length was deemed acceptable given that a couple's methodology for handling conflict is established during the first 2 years of marriage and tends to remain constant (Galvin & Brommel, 1999; Raush, Barry, Hertel, & Swain, 1974).[2] The mean age for men was 39.8 years and for the women was 36.8 years. Each husband reported completing at least 2 years of college education. Four of the men had earned master's degrees, and one had earned a doctorate. Each wife had attended college, and six of the nine wives had earned a baccalaureate degree.

Four of the participants were ministers; four were teachers.[3] Other participants included two secretaries, two staff assistants, one registered nurse, one dentist, a self-employed businessperson, an office manager, and a county extension agent. Although Hiller and Dyehouse (1987) reported lack of agreement among research samples on a definition of the term "dual career," our sample was consistent with definitions posited by Krueger (1985), Sekaran (1986), and Goldthorpe (1987)—specifically, a marital structure in which both husband and wife are actively involved in careers and home obligations (Krueger, 1985). Six of the couples reported that the husband earned the higher salary (by $6,000 to $35,000). Three couples reported that the wife earned the higher salary (by $2,000 to $8,000). In contrast to Krueger's (1985) sample of childless couples, our sample contained only three childless couples. Thus, our sample provides a more representative view of dual-career couples.

Instruments

We employed three questionnaires. First, a demographics questionnaire assessed age, income, and family size. Second, as per Krueger's (1985) procedure, Norton's (1983) Quality Marriage Index (QMI) assessed marital satisfaction, providing evidence of reliability and external validity for the instrument. Finally, a questionnaire devised by Krueger (1985) surveyed participants' perceptions of their marital relationship and decision making.[4] Information obtained from this third questionnaire (a) provided data on couples' self-perceptions of their decision making, (b) provided a point of comparison with the coder's observation of the couples behavior during the decision-making process, and (c) complied with Norton's (1983) recommendation that evaluative, open-ended questions be included when assessing marital satisfaction via his scale.

Procedures

Given accuracy concerns about interview data from marital dyads (Beitin, 2008), we elected to collect and analyze marital dialogue as our primary data. Following Krueger's (1985) procedure, we initially telephoned each couple to ascertain willingness to participate in the study and then mailed a packet containing questionnaires, instructions, and a cassette tape. We asked participants to complete the marital satisfaction and demographic questionnaires independently. We asked the couples to select two topics for decision making, one from each of two lists. One list contained topics unrelated to children (i.e., how to spend $2,000 they won in the state lottery, how to handle a problem concerning his or her family of birth, how to celebrate an upcoming wedding anniversary, or a situation of their own creation). The other list contained topics relevant to child rearing (i.e., whether to send a child to public or private kindergarten, how to handle a problem with a child's behavior at school, whether to allow a teenage child to go with a friend's family to Europe, or a situation of their own creation involving their children). Each couple tape-recorded their two problem-solving discussions (one for each of the two chosen problems). The length of the decision-making sessions ranged from 1.6 to 20 minutes, with a mean of 6.6 minutes. The tapes were transcribed for analysis. As per Krueger's (1985) protocol, after taping their discussions, participants completed the written questionnaires described above.

Analysis

As per Krueger's (1985) protocol, one coder (a male PhD student in his late 20s) analyzed the transcripts via a language-action model (Frentz & Ferrell, 1976; Krueger, 1982). Krueger (1985) argued for the methodological validity of an interpretative approach that is more qualitative than quantitative and that employs large units of analysis in a broad context. This analysis was based on three hierarchically ordered elements: context (the interpersonal environment), episodes (topical communication sequences), and symbolic acts (speech acts). A detailed description of the analytical methodology may be found in Krueger (1982).

We analyzed the critical components of control and maintenance to identify decision-making patterns and assess the degree of egalitarianism in the couples' interaction. Krueger (1985) described control as behaviors that dominate or change the direction of conversation. We coded five behaviors as control attempts: proposing ideas or solutions, metacommunication about behavior appropriate to the task, active direction of procedural rules, disagreements, and objections.

Because of the multifunctional nature of questions, in both the Krueger (1985) study and our study, participants' questions were interpreted individually, depending on the context and observed purpose of each question. Following Krueger's procedure, we interpreted questions as control attempts if they "demanded" a response from the partner. We coded questions that requested support or permission as submissive.

Krueger (1985) operationalized maintenance as messages fostering a positive, supportive climate in the interaction. Messages of positive affect included endearment terms, back channeling, solicitousness, and support or concern for each other and his or her ideas. Negative affect, on the other hand, included such behaviors as ridicule, harsh comments, suppression of the partner, defensiveness, and oppressive behaviors. Negative affect was seen as indicative of status differentiation, and thus information on the couples' maintenance behaviors was reported to augment the information on the couples' successful control attempts.

As in Krueger's (1985) work, we created operationalizations before and occasionally during the analysis. Prior to the creation of operationalizations during the analyses, the first author consulted with Krueger via telephone. While it may appear difficult to classify dialogue using these general notions, in fact it was a simple matter to identify control and maintenance behaviors, code, and count them. We operationalized egalitarianism as the degree to which spouses exhibit an equal number of successful control attempts.

Results and Discussion

Decision-Making Behaviors Across the Sample

Preliminary analyses, employing randomization tests for two independent samples (Siegel, 1956) at $p < .05$ with power efficiency of 100%, indicated that in our sample the childless couples differed significantly from those with children in several ways. As might be expected, the couples with children were married for longer periods of time and reported higher incomes. Additionally, the childless couples had shorter conversations but provided more maintenance behaviors per minute than the couples with children. Thus, introducing couples with children into the sample may yield differing results than with a sample of childless couples.

In response to the questionnaire, all but one of the participants indicated that the topics chosen were realistic and relevant to them. When asked if the tape-recorded conversation was typical of their normal decision-making process, all participants responded affirmatively except one who suggested that being tape-recorded prompted the couple to be a little "stiff."

The couples' scores on Norton's (1983) QMI ranged from a low of 102 to a high of 136, with a mean of 119.5. Each participant indicated that he or she was "very committed" to the marriage and would "do all that I can" to make the relationship succeed. All participants predicted that their marriage will be intact "more than five years from now."

The nine couples were divided between male-dominated and egalitarian decision-making patterns. Four couples were predominantly male dominated; four couples were primarily egalitarian. One couple practiced each of the above types of decision making part of the time.

The couples varied greatly in their use of maintenance communication (support statements, agreement, back channeling, and use of endearment terms). Two couples represented the extremes: one couple displayed over five times as many maintenance behaviors per minute (5.1) and another couple less than one per minute (0.9). The mean for the participants was 2.9.

The analysis revealed less variability in the participants' use of control behaviors. The mean was 4.2 control behaviors per person per minute. At the extremes, one couple displayed 5.5 control behaviors per minute; another couple displayed the lowest number (2.6).

Decision-Making Behaviors Pertaining to the Research Questions

RQ1

Results of relevant analyses indicated that conversational dominance was not commensurate with relative income among the marital partners in this sample. Spearman's rank correlations (Siegel, 1956) were computed for spouses' relative income (ratio of husband's to wife's salary) by 12 communication variables (coder's assessment of the couple's decision-making pattern, talk time in minutes, ratio of husband's to wife's control attempts across the two conversations, ratio of husband's to wife's maintenance behaviors per minute across the two conversations, for each individual conversation, the husband's as well as the wife's control attempts per minute and maintenance behaviors per minute); all correlations were nonsignificant. Consistent with previous research (Bittman et al., 2003; Brines, 1994; Greenstein, 2000), in two of the three couples where the wife made more money than the husband, decision making was largely male dominated. The dyad who employed the most clearly male-dominated decision making among the nine couples reported that the wife earned the higher salary by the greatest margin ($8,000).

In sum, three of the wives in this study made more money than their husbands, by as much as $8,000. Only one of these three couples demonstrated egalitarianism in their decision making; the other two clearly employed male-dominated decision making. Among the six couples in which the husband earned the larger income, half practiced egalitarian decision making, including the couple in which the husband earned $35,000 more than his wife. Further, results of Spearman's rank correlations revealed no significant correlations between relative income and the communicative behaviors under study.

We offer two possible explanations for these findings. Fiscal resources other than income (e.g., greater earning potential or inherited money) may influence patterns of dominance. Alternatively, perhaps the data reflect a "reverse effect" in certain couples where compensation for unequal income is provided in decision making. The findings of this study suggest that male-dominated marital decision making is not merely a product of greater income.

RQ2

Relevant analyses indicated that most participants accurately identified their predominant decision-making pattern as either egalitarian or male dominated. The coder's analysis agreed with the participants' perceptions of their marital decision-making patterns in 78% of the cases. Both spouses in only one couple inaccurately identified their decision-making pattern. However, not all spouses shared the same vision of their decision-making processes; one-third of the couples reported differing perceptions of their decision making.

Did the couples' perceptions of their decision making match the coder's observations? Krueger (1985) found that women tended to perceive egalitarian decision making more often than either their partners or the outside observer. The conclusions of this study are different. While four of the nine wives reported egalitarianism, the coder found it evidenced in five couples. Five of the six men who reported egalitarianism demonstrated egalitarian behavior. In this study, the men and the women tended to accurately identify their dominant decision-making pattern.

The differences between Krueger's (1985) findings and our findings could result from normal variation between repeated samples of the same size. Or these findings may reflect differences in sample composition. Krueger's (1985) sample included only childless couples, in contrast to our sample, in which only one-third of the couples were childless. It may be that spouses raising children engage in more frequent joint decision making and thus develop more accurate perceptions of their actual decision-making behaviors.

RQ3

Do couples who practice egalitarian decision making report higher marital satisfaction? The mean QMI scores for egalitarian versus male-dominated couples were 124.5 and 113, respectively. However, tests to assess whether the above reported difference was statistically significant were not appropriate due to the lack of variation in the QMI scores. All couples in the sample earned QMI scores in the high range.

Krueger's (1985) reported an equivocal relationship between egalitarianism and marital satisfaction. While hypothesis-testing statistical analyses were not calculated on the data that either we or Krueger reported, the descriptive evidence (comparison of mean scores) suggests the possibility of such a relationship. Mean differences between the two groups (couples practicing egalitarian vs. male-dominated decision making) was in the predicted direction. Furthermore, the two couples with the highest score on the QMI employed clearly egalitarian decision-making patterns, while the two couples scoring the lowest in marital satisfaction employed the male-dominant pattern. More study is needed, however, before positing a correlational or causal relationship.

RQ4

Relevant analyses indicated that couples in this sample do not practice female-dominated decision making when discussing child-rearing issues. The qualitative analysis revealed that six of the nine husbands dominated the decision making on the child-rearing issues. Among the couples who generally displayed egalitarian decision making across the two conversations, three of the four demonstrated male dominance during the child-rearing decision making. However, Walsh tests with power efficiency of 87.5% to 99% (Siegel, 1956) revealed no significant differences between the husbands' and the wives' scores on control attempts per minute or maintenance behaviors per minute during discussion of the child-rearing issues. Further, Walsh tests were calculated to compare communicative behaviors in the child-rearing versus the marital discussions. The analyses revealed significant differences in length of the conversation ($p \leq .008$; M = 8.06 vs. 5.19 minutes, respectively) and husbands' control attempts per minute (5.0 vs. 4.0, respectively) but not in other communicative behaviors (husbands' maintenance per minute or wives' control attempts or maintenance behaviors per minute). Recall that the following behaviors were coded as control attempts: (a) proposing ideas or solutions, (b) metacommunicating about the task or procedural rules, and (c) stating disagreements and objectives.

Further, Spearman's rank correlations were calculated to assess the covariation among husbands' and wives' control attempts and maintenance behaviors per minute for both conversations. Results revealed only one of the possible 12 significant relationships: in the conversation on child rearing, husbands' and wives' maintenance behaviors per minute were correlated ($r_s = 0.75$, $p \leq .02$).

In sum, our study examined patterns of dominance in decision-making conversations about child-rearing issues. Although the couples in this sample spent more time discussing the child-rearing problem (vs. the other marital problem), the Walsh tests revealed no significant differences between husbands' and wives' control attempts per minute during the child-rearing discussion. Further, analyses revealed that husbands (not wives) in this sample exhibited significantly more control attempts per minute in the child-rearing discussion than the marital problem discussion. This observation suggests that, despite the conventional assignment of women to child care responsibilities (Zimmerman et al., 2003), perhaps dual-career couples tend to practice egalitarian decision making in matters related to child rearing.

Conclusions

Summary of Findings in Relation to Krueger's Results

Our study paralleled that of Krueger (1985) in focus and methodology. The results of the replication were as follows: (a) All participants in both samples stated that they would do whatever necessary to make their marriage succeed. (b) Both studies found an equivocal relationship between egalitarianism and marital satisfaction. (c) The results of the studies differed in one way: Krueger found that women were more likely than either their husbands or the coder to perceive their marital decision-making pattern as egalitarian. In contrast, in our sample, spouses of both sexes tended to identify accurately their dominant decision-making patterns. As noted earlier, this inconsistency could be due to simple variation between samples.

Our study extended Krueger's (1985) work in three ways. First, our sample included couples both with and without children rather than focusing exclusively on childless couples. Second, this study examined the relationship between spousal income and dominance in decision making. Finally, this study compared couples' communication behaviors when making marital versus child-rearing decisions. Results of the extension indicated the following: (a) Associating female dominance with child-rearing decisions may be inaccurate in dual-career couples. Husbands in our sample exhibited significantly more control attempts per minute in the child-rearing versus the marital discussions. (b) The results of Spearman's rank correlations revealed no significant correlation between relative income and communicative behavior. It is interesting to note that among the three couples in which the wives earned the higher income, only one of these couples employed egalitarianism in their decision making; the other two were clearly male dominated.

Limitations

No doubt, numerous factors influence marital decision making—too many to include in any one textual analysis. We acknowledge that many important factors that were left unexamined in our study nonetheless may have an enormous impact on spouses' behaviors in decision making. Unexamined sample variables include but are not limited to factors of region, race, ethnicity, religion, education, and culture as well as potential behavior differences between same-sex versus opposite-sex marital partners. Replication of this study with appropriately narrow samples would allow demonstration and testing of the potential influence of these factors.

Communication factors, in addition to those here examined, may influence marital decision making (e.g., argumentativeness, assertiveness, and degree of affection for the partner). As the results of this study indicate, the type of problem under discussion can affect a couple's communication behavior. While the child-rearing problems tended to provoke discussion, the marital problems, particularly the financial problems, often did not. In our study, some couples appeared to assign one spouse the primary responsibility for financial affairs. When couples employ such a division of labor, a spouse's control behaviors may reflect responsibility for a task rather than a dominant decision-making pattern in the dyad. Perhaps future studies should ask couples to discuss problems for which spouses acknowledge an equal or near-equal responsibility.

In sum, many factors that may influence marital decision making were not examined in our study. Thus, our conclusions must be interpreted with extreme caution and not generalized beyond the confines of our small, narrow sample and study. Indeed, the purpose of qualitative research is not so much to describe a population as to reveal the possibility of a range of behaviors regarding a phenomenon, in this case marital decision making. Our sample and study design do not allow us to generalize our results to how all or even most dual-career marital dyads engage in decision making all or even most of the time. The most reasonable interpretation of our findings is that they offer a description of how some dual-career marital dyads engage in decision making some of the time.

Overall Conclusions

Although the sample was small, our study's detailed analyses provided some provocative insights into decision making in dual-career couples. The results suggest the following: (a) Among dual-career couples, relative spousal income may be unrelated to dominance in decision making. (b) Dual-career couples tend to report high levels of marital satisfaction. (c) A comparison between Krueger's (1985) results and our results indicates that dual-career couples' self-reported decision-making behaviors may vary widely from small sample to small sample (nine couples). Therefore, a relatively large sample or repeated samplings of small sizes may be necessary to accurately assess this variable. (d) One sex role stereotype, associating female dominance with decisions about child rearing, may be inaccurate in dual-career couples.

Discussion Questions

1. Researchers coded five behaviors as control attempts (proposing ideas or solutions, metacommunication about behavior appropriate to the task, active direction of procedural rules, disagreements, and objections). Can you think of any additional behaviors that people may employ in efforts to control or persuade their partner(s)?

2. This study found that "in two of the three couples where the wife made more money than the husband, decision making was largely male dominated." Provide at least one reason as to why this might be the case.

3. Although child rearing is socially regarded as a female responsibility, the results of this research indicated that "husbands exhibited significantly more control attempts per minute in the child-rearing discussions versus the marital discussions." Reflect on your own family interaction growing up or on another family in your network that you observed or experienced. How do those experiences support or contradict this research finding? Explain.

4. In all of the couples, the relationship was either egalitarian or male dominated regardless of which gender obtained the higher income. In your opinion, why were there no female-dominated relationships?

Notes

Earlier versions of this chapter were presented at the annual meeting of the Southern States Communication Association, April 1990, Birmingham, Alabama, and at the annual meeting of the Speech Communication Association, November 1991, Atlanta, Georgia. The authors gratefully acknowledge the research assistance of Melissa McNab (BA, 1990, University of Florida), Julie Fenyes (BA, 1992, University of Arizona), Julie McNatt (MA, 1993, Memphis State University), Krista L. Cass (BA, 2001, University of Arkansas), and Amber M. Walker (MA, 2003, University of Arkansas).

[1]The relatively small sample size of 18 participants replicates Krueger's (1985) sample size.

[2]Obviously, couples can consciously alter their interaction patterns. For example, such a change is likely to occur with effective marital counseling. However, pending conscious change, couples may establish and maintain problem-solving patterns in their marriage.

[3]Pretests compared the ministerial couples with the nonministerial couples; a series of randomization tests for independent samples (Siegel, 1956) at $p \leq .05$ with a power efficiency of 100% revealed no significant differences in length of marriage, number of children, relative spousal income, or communicative behaviors (talk time in minutes as well as ratio [husband to wife] of the number of maintenance and number of control attempts per minute). A parallel series of tests, comparing couples in which one spouse reported being a teacher versus those couples who reported other occupations, revealed no significant differences in the

variables listed above. Thus, couples containing professions dominant in the sample failed to manifest characteristics significantly different from other couples in the sample.

[4]Open-ended questions to assess perceptions of the marital relationship included the following: How do you and your spouse usually make decisions? Who most often makes the decisions in your relationship? Was the process you went through in the taping typical of the way you usually make decisions? Did you choose a topic that was "realistic" or relevant to you and your spouse? How do you think you and your spouse compare with "traditional" male and female roles in marriage?

References

Amato, P. R., Johnson, D. R., Booth, A., & Rogers, S. J. (2003). Continuity and change in marital quality between 1980 and 2000. *Journal of Marriage and the Family, 65,* 1-21.

Bartley, S. J., Blanton, P. W., & Gilliard, J. L. (2005). Husbands and wives in dual-earner marriages: Decision-making, gender role attitudes, division of household labor, and equity. *Marriage and Family Review, 37*(4), 69-94.

Beitin, B. K. (2008). Qualitative research in marriage and family therapy: Who is in the interview? *Contemporary Family Therapy, 30,* 48-58.

Bittman, M., England, P., Sayer, L., Folbre, N., & Matheson, G. (2003). When does gender trump money? Bargaining and time in household work. *American Journal of Sociology, 109,* 186-214.

Brines, J. (1994). Economic dependency, gender, and the division of labor at home. *American Journal of Sociology, 100,* 652-688.

Burgoyne, C. B., Reibstein, J., Edmunds, A., & Dolman, V. (2007). Money management systems in early marriage: Factors influencing change and stability. *Journal of Economic Psychology, 28,* 214-228.

Caughlin, J. P., & Vangelisti, A. L. (2006). Conflict in dating and marital relationships. In J. G. Oetzel & S. Ting-Toomey (Eds.), *The Sage handbook of conflict communication: Integrating theory, research, and practice.* Thousand Oaks, CA: Sage.

Cox, F. D. (2008). *Human intimacy: Marriage, the family, and its meaning—Research update.* Boston: Wadsworth.

Davis, H. L., & Rigaux, B. P. (1974). Perception of marital roles in decision processes. *Journal of Consumer Research, 1,* 51-62.

Durham, W., & Braithwaite, D. O. (2009). Communication privacy management within the family planning trajectories of voluntarily child-free couples. *Journal of Family Communication, 9,* 43-65.

Elloy, D. F. (2001). A predictive study of stress among Australian dual-career couples. *Journal of Social Psychology, 141,* 122-124.

Ericksen, J. A., Yancey, W. L., & Ericksen, E. P. (1979). The division of family roles. *Journal of Marriage and the Family, 41,* 301-313.

Frentz, T. S., & Ferrell, T. B. (1976). Language-action: A paradigm for communication. *Quarterly Journal of Speech, 62,* 333-349.

Galvin, K. M., & Brommel, B. J. (1999). *Family communication: Cohesion and change* (2nd ed.). New York: Allyn & Bacon.

Goldthorpe, J. E. (1987). *Family life in western societies: A historical sociology of family relationships in Britain and North America*. New York: Cambridge University Press.

Greenstein, T. (2000). Economic dependence, gender, and the division of labor at home: A replication and extension. *Journal of Marriage and the Family, 62,* 322–335.

Hardill, I. (2002). *Gender, migration and the dial career household*. London: Routledge.

Hiller, D. V., & Dyehouse, J. (1987). A case for banishing "dual career marriages" from the research literature. *Journal of Marriage and the Family, 49,* 787–795.

Iyigun, M., & Walsh, R. P. (2007). Endogenous gender power, household labor supply and the demographic transition. *Journal of Development Economics, 82,* 138–155.

Krueger, D. L. (1982). Marital decision making: A language-action analysis. *Quarterly Journal of Speech, 68,* 273–287.

Krueger, D. L. (1985). Communication patterns and egalitarian decision making in dual-career couples. *Western Journal of Speech Communication, 49,* 126–145.

Lundberg, S., & Pollak, R. A. (2007). The American family and family economics. *Journal of Economic Perspectives, 21,* 3–26.

Mason, M. A., Fine, M. A., & Carnochan, S. (2004). Family law for changing families in the new millennium. In M. Coleman & L. H. Ganong (Eds.), *Handbook of contemporary families: Considering the past, contemplating the future*. Thousand Oaks, CA: Sage.

McBride, B. A., & Mills, G. (1993). A comparison of mother and father involvement with their preschool age children. *Early Childhood Research Quarterly, 8,* 457–477.

Norton, R. (1983). Measuring marital quality: A look at the dependent variable. *Journal of Marriage and the Family, 45,* 141–151.

Pollak, R. A. (2005). *Bargaining power in marriage: Earnings, wage rates and household production*. NBER Working Paper No. 11239. Cambridge, MA: National Bureau of Economic Research.

Price-Bonham, S. (1976). A comparison of weighted and unweighted decision-making scores. *Journal of Marriage and the Family, 38,* 629–640.

Raush, H. L., Barry, W. A., Hertel, R. K., & Swain, M. A. (1974). *Communication, conflict, and marriage: Explorations in the theory and study of intimate relationships*. San Francisco: Jossey-Bass.

Rubin, R. M., Riney, B. J., & Molina, D. J. (1990). Expenditure pattern differentials between one-earner and two-earner households: 1972–1973 and 1984. *Journal of Consumer Research, 17,* 43–52.

Schneider, B., & Waite, L. J. (2005). Why study working families? In B. Schneider & L. J. Waite (Eds.), *Being together, working apart: Dual-career families and the work-life balance* (pp. 3–17). New York: Cambridge University Press.

Sekaran, U. (1986). *Dual-career families*. San Francisco: Jossey-Bass.

Siegel, S. (1956). *Nonparametric statistics for the behavioral sciences*. New York: McGraw-Hill.

Steil, J. M., & Weltman, K. (1992). Influence strategies at home and at work: A study of sixty dual career couples. *Journal of Social and Personal Relationships, 9,* 65–88.

Stockland, P. M. (2008). *Same-sex marriage.* Edina, MN: ABDO Publishing.

Tichenor, V. (2005). Maintaining men's dominance: Negotiating identity and power when she earns more. *Sex Roles, 53,* 191–205.

Ting-Toomey, S. (1984). Perceived decision-making power and marital adjustment. *Communication Research Reports, 1,* 15–20.

U.S. Bureau of the Census. (2010). *Employment characteristics of families.* http://factfinder.census.gov/servlet/STTable?_bm=y&-geo_id=01000US&-qr_name=ACS_2008_3YR_G00_S2302&-ds_name=ACS_2008_3YR_G00_&-_lang=en&-redoLog=false&-CONTEXT=st

Wolf-Wendel, L., Twombly, S. B., & Rice, S. (2004). *The two-body problem: Dual-career-couple hiring practices in higher education.* Baltimore: Johns Hopkins University Press.

Xu, Y., & Burlson, B. R. (2001). Effects of sex, culture, and support type on perceptions of spousal social support: An assessment of the "support gap" hypothesis in early marriage. *Human Communication Research, 27,* 535–566.

Zimmerman, T. S., Haddock, S. A., Current, L. R., & Ziemba, S. (2003). Intimate partnership: Foundation to the successful balance of family and work. *American Journal of Family Therapy, 31,* 107–124.

PART 3
Emergence of Evotypical Families

Chapter 8
The Communicative Effort of Negotiating Unmarried Family Life: Friction and Flexibility 84
Jay Baglia, *DePaul University*
Elissa Foster, *DePaul University*

Chapter 9
Living with a Ghost: Managing Memory in Postbereaved Families 95
Christine E. Kiesinger, *George Washington University*

Chapter 10
State Disciplinary Practices and the Emergence of Coparenting Families 104
Lynn Comerford, *California State University, East Bay*

Chapter 11
Single Family: Expanding Our Understanding 114
Tiffani Baldwin, *University of Denver*

Chapter 12
Speaking About Coupleness: Relational Roles in the Conversations of Gays and Lesbians 123
Brian L. Heisterkamp, *California State University, San Bernardino*

Chapter 13
"Not 16 Anymore": Identification Challenges of Teen Parents 133
Karen E. Cirulis, *University of Nebraska at Omaha, Omaha Public Schools*

Chapter 14
Interracial and Interethnic Families 141
Francis Wardle, *Red Rocks Community College*

Chapter 15
(Not) Talking About Race and Difference in Visibly Adoptive Families 152
Sara Docan-Morgan,
University of Wisconsin–La Crosse

Chapter 8

The Communicative Effort of Negotiating Unmarried Family Life: Friction and Flexibility

Jay Baglia and Elissa Foster

Here She Comes

We had waited a long time for this child. A traumatic miscarriage (Foster, 2010) was followed by 14 months of trying to get pregnant again and then success—a pregnancy with an arduous stretch of morning sickness, a springtime of relative tranquillity (including a weeklong "babymoon" in Key West), the beginning of a hot summer, 12 hours of prelabor contractions, 30 hours of active labor, a caesarean section with its attendant drama, and, finally, our baby—"It's a girl!"—was born, on July 7, 2010, at 9:48 in the evening.

Both Elissa and baby required extra time in the hospital—Elissa in the mother/baby unit and baby about 50 yards away in the neonatal intensive care unit due to some minor difficulties. Both were destined for a 4-day stay. A July heat wave, seen if not felt through an institutional window, and a bouquet of flowers from a quick-acting relative helped set the scene for our convalescence.

As it turns out, having a baby in the United States requires piles of paperwork. We were supplied with a weighty file of forms covering everything from insurance to postnatal depression to consents for immunizations and blood work. During the morning of that first full day, we also requested from one of the nurses an Acknowledgment of Paternity (AOP) form to establish Jay as the father of our daughter.

We learned that, in our home state of Pennsylvania, when a child is born to an unmarried couple, there is no legal relationship between the father and the child. Paternity is established through the AOP form—a legal document that must be completed before the father can be listed on the child's birth certificate. The existence of the form surely confirms that institutions (in Pennsylvania at least) are prepared for variation from the marriage script; however, the online AOP form is associated with a series of links that connect users to DNA testing as well as legal services for situations in which the paternity of the child is contested. Furthermore, the form is designed to protect the baby's and mother's rights insofar as it is primarily an assurance that the father so named is legally responsible for the financial welfare of the child.

When we requested the AOP form, the nurse smiled at us indulgently. "You don't have to worry about that one," she informed us. "That's only if you aren't married."

"But we're not married," we countered.

Without judgment and without hesitation, the nurse retrieved the AOP, setting it down on a small table next to the bouquet along with the birth certificate application and other assembled literature for couples who have just welcomed their first child.

The Long View

When conceptualizing this chapter, we selected this introductory scene in order to establish the following for our readers: (a) we are not married, (b) we are often assumed to be married as a result of our demographic characteristics (white, educated, middle class, older—that is, not in our early 20s—and heterosexual), and (c) we have learned that navigating social interactions as an unmarried couple with a child entails communicative effort related to this state of being "other than expected." In the course of the chapter, we trouble the cultural habit of assuming that we and others like us (white, educated, middle class, and "older") are married, we identify the discursive violence (Foster, 2008) of demographic categories that exclude unmarried couples with or without children, and we describe some of the communicative challenges of navigating life as a family without the sanction of legal marriage. Our purpose is to share with readers what it has been like for us to discursively construct our family as unmarried partners, now parents, within the context of our local circumstances. Our attention is directed particularly to the communicative efforts we have made and the moments of interactive friction and flexibility that have characterized our social exchanges to date. By communicative effort, we mean our intentional choices of language, decisions concerning disclosure, and the expenditure of energy entailed when relating to others about our unconventional family.

In addition to the disclosure of our unmarried status, three more admissions are necessary at this juncture. First, we claim that being in a committed, heterosexual, romantic partnership in which we (a) live under the same roof and (b) parent a child but (c) are not married is an underrepresented family constellation. What has in the past been called "living together" (or, more harshly, "living in sin") and is currently referred to as cohabitation, domestic partnership, or romantic coupledom has occurred throughout history and across continents. Couples have chosen to not marry for personal, political, philosophical, and financial reasons. In some cases, marriage was not a legal option (e.g., antimiscegenation laws prevented mixed-race couples from marrying as recently as 1967 in the American South). However, the unmarried couple and, by extension, the unmarried family tend to appear in social research only in contrast to the married, such as in comparative studies of relational quality or child well-being (Coltrane & Adams, 2003; Elizabeth, 2000; Murrow & Shi, 2010). Our second admission is that we do not critique marriage; rather, our decision to remain committed yet unmarried was made for personal and political reasons that we explore throughout this chapter—reasons that we find compelling but might fall short of inspiring others to imitate. While we are part of the marriage boycott (Baard, 2003), we are distinguishing ourselves from couples described in one study as "marriage resistant" (Elizabeth, 2000). Third, we are divorced; that is, each of us was married to another person prior to our relationship. We have learned that, as a demographic category, "marital status" offers a standard menu that is not without its challenges (Foster, 2008). The choices on applications and questionnaires are almost always limited to single, married, divorced, or widowed. When called on to answer to such categories, we are forced to choose "single" or "divorced," neither of which reflects in the least our reality as a committed couple with child. Our status as an unmarried family, as shall be demonstrated in this chapter, is often relegated to an uncountable and therefore invisible category.

Through a series of personal narratives of critical incidents in our unmarried life together, we investigate what is at stake when family compositions consist of arrangements other than those recognized as state-sanctioned marriages. Using a narrative methodology that relies heavily on the assumptions of autoethnography, our cowritten stories (recalled and audio recorded by the two authors prior to writing) provide the ground for cultural analyses. Autoethnographic inquiry permits the researcher to take stories of the self as raw data that reveal cultural patterns (Chang, 2008; Ellis & Bochner, 2000; Neumann, 1996). One strength of autoethnographic research is that it makes available perceptions, emotions, and subjective sense-making processes that are not generally available through other methods of social scientific study. Often associated with narrative inquiry, autoethnography as an introspective (Ellis, 1991) method foregrounds personal experience as an avenue to meaning making with regard to larger cultural trends (Chang, 2008). Although we fall short of the evocative and literary ideals of autoethnographic storytelling (Bochner, 2000)—choosing instead to present short, descriptive examples—we share with autoethnography the intention of foregrounding the personal in order to reveal the cultural. In addition to memory, we also draw from personal documents, such as journal entries, photographs, and videotape, to reconstruct the incidents in this chapter.

The remainder of this chapter is comprised of five more critical incidents depicting examples of communicative friction and flexibility encountered in our lives as an unmarried family. We offer analyses of each narrative in succession and close with reflections on the theme of friction and flexibility along with a call for change in contemporary discursive constructions of commitment and family.

Flexibility: A Ceremony of Commitment

As a result of much discussion, we chose to mark the formal beginning of our relationship with a commitment ceremony in Elissa's native Australia in July 2003. Eighteen months earlier, Jay had proposed marriage in the presence of Elissa's family on Christmas Day. However, after considering our respective divorces and the injustice of our gay and lesbian friends being denied the privilege of marriage in most of the United States as well as in Australia, we opted to plan and participate in a commitment ceremony rather than a traditional marriage. Our ceremony took place in the Botanical Gardens in Brisbane, Queensland, and included many elements associated with weddings: rings, ceremonial dress, vows, and the attendance of our very closest family and friends. We also enjoyed what most would identify as a reception. In contrast to a wedding, our vows were offered to each other rather than being mediated by a celebrant, and there were no formal contracts with the state or any religious institution. Instead, our close friends and immediate families served as witnesses, delivering scripted lines as a formal component of the ceremony and signing a Declaration of Love document (that now hangs framed in our living room) with the following text:

> Jay Baglia and Elissa Foster have declared their love for each other and have now committed to sharing their lives together thereby creating a family. The undersigned, their friends and family pledge their support to this union, July 27, 2003.

There is nothing official about this document other than that it means a great deal to us and represents our version of a contract. By asking our friends and family to sign it in addition to attending our ceremony, we also suggest that they as the "undersigned"—by virtue of the power of a signature in our society—commit to supporting us, although there is nothing legally requiring them to do so.

Through ritualized behavior and documentation (a DVD of our ceremony created by a relative, an album of photographs, and other mementos), we hold that a social reality has been constructed. By privileging familial relationships rather than religion or the state to sanction our union as the start of a new family, we offer an alternate model. Speech act theory (Austin, 2005; Searle, 1969) identifies the "commissive" illocutionary act as having force and demonstrates how social actors employ symbolic action (including language and ritualized behaviors) to accomplish intentions. Rather than describing reality, speech acts create reality. By participating in a commitment ceremony and uttering the requisite phrases that indicate our intention to commit to each other, we are both saying something and *doing* something.

Our commitment is situated within contemporary relational discourses of marriage and family; thus, because we are unmarried to each other (Solot & Miller, 2002) in early 21st-century America, our interactions with others have the potential to expose the assumptions of these discourses. One organization—the Alternatives to Marriage Project—recognizes that couples choose not to marry for various reasons and that same-sex couples, in particular, must navigate the world as unmarried whether they like it or not. The Project also acknowledges that being an unmarried couple comes with challenges and so marshals the collective wisdom of the unmarried in order to disperse financial, legal, and social resources, including resources for the construction of a commitment ceremony. We identify our participation in a commitment ceremony as evidence of flexibility, the power of communication to open up spaces of possibility within an otherwise conservative discourse. We employed ritual in order to clarify the nature of our commitment to those closest to us; we invoke the story of our commitment ceremony to highlight our commonality with married others who have experienced a wedding, our commonality with same-sex couples who participate predominantly in commitment ceremonies or civil unions, and our difference from both types of relational experience.

Friction: The Marriage Discount

Although we are *not* married to each other, we *are* divorced. And the "divorced" dimension of our individual identities, as well as the extent to which our commitment is valued, was reaffirmed during the course of an otherwise innocent phone call to our automobile insurance agency. We guessed that having a child would lower our insurance premium—the argument being that people with children drive extra carefully. But in the months since our daughter's birth, we had not yet made the call notifying our provider of the addition to our family. So on a quiet afternoon in late April as Jay was paying bills at the dining room table, he scooped up the car insurance statement, walked into the kitchen, and dialed the 800 number of our insurance provider.

After the agent, Nathan, confirmed that the phone number Jay was dialing from coincided with the policy number provided, he asked Jay to verify some existing information about the policy—our home address, each of our birth dates and ages, and our marital status (divorced) before estimating the annual mileage for our two cars. Then Nathan asked Jay about the purpose of the call.

"I'm calling because I wanted your company to know about the birth of our child. I understand that there might be a reduction in the premium."

"Well, congratulations! Boy or girl?"

"A girl. She was born in July of last year. I'm afraid I should have called much sooner than now."

In his Texas accent, Nathan replied that he had two children himself. His were older—a boy in his late teens and a daughter in college. Jay and Nathan spoke easily with each other about how much they enjoyed fatherhood, although, clearly, the individual experiences of the two men were quite different if only by virtue of the time each had been a parent. Before long, they transitioned out of the small talk that sometimes defines good customer service, and Nathan asked, "Can I inquire why you think there is a discount for having a child?"

"Well it's just something somebody told me, or maybe I read it."

"Unfortunately we do not offer a discount for having a child," Nathan began, "although I'm sure you would like to know that there *is* a discount for being married."

"Really?" Jay replied. Then, with only a brief hesitation and anticipating a willing listener, he declared to Nathan, "I'd like you to know why Elissa and I are not married. Can I tell you?"

"Sure," Nathan responded.

"Elissa and I are not married because we want to stand in solidarity with our many gay and lesbian friends who are denied the right to marry in most of these United States. We understand that we do so at a considerable cost financially and, in some cases, socially. Nevertheless, we feel it is important to live our philosophy and our politics." (Having given this short speech many times before, Jay is quite practiced.)

Nathan was gracious in his reply, if a little tongue-tied and politically neutral. "Wow. I don't believe I've ever heard of anybody doing something like that. That's really something."

"In our way, we're actually contributing to a movement. If you have some time, you should check out a website called www.unmarried.org." Nathan thanked Jay for the information, and from a customer service perspective he (and, by implication, his corporation) had satisfied Jay's desire that they listen to his testimony, our story.

Jay had been a customer of this well-known automobile insurance company since before his divorce. When we moved in together in July 2003, following our commitment ceremony, Elissa was added to the policy. But now Nathan had more news.

"Jay, did you know that even though Elissa is on the policy, she cannot, because you two are not married, make any policy claims, nor can we discuss your policy information with her unless you've given us a power of attorney?"

"No, I didn't know that."

"I can send you the paperwork if you request it."

"Okay. I'm requesting it."

The insurance company defines each of us first and foremost by the label "divorced." For them, this is the category into which we neatly fit. It is certain that this divorce designation is a component of statistical analyses regarding, for example, driving records. This (mis)representation, then, has power beyond the fact that we pay more than we should for automobile insurance. Critical scholars have pointed out that marital status designations other than married are implicitly held as hierarchically inferior (DePaulo & Morris, 2006). Furthermore, those who populate the category of unmarried adults can be subject to interpersonal mistreatment (Byrne & Carr, 2005) or rendered invisible due to exclusionary classification systems (Foster, 2008). Made legal through a combination of licenses, contracts, and ceremonies, the modern heterosexual marriage is privileged above all other kinds of adult couplings. State-sanctioned marriages are permeated by legal and financial benefits, including tax breaks, employer benefits, insurance policy discounts, and survivor rights.

Much of the communication scholarship around divorce that employs narrative analysis is concerned with the formerly secure marital relationship in its demise (Doohan, Carrere, & Riggs, 2010; Graham 1997; Miller, 2009a, 2009b). The role of narratives in identity construction postdivorce appears in interdisciplinary journals. Hopper (1993) and Walzer and Oles (2003) consider aspects of divorce narratives in identity construction, noting that narratives facilitate the emergence of a more positive self-concept. Narrative explanations, instigated by the termination of the significant cultural institution that is marriage, allow individuals to frame their actions in ways they perceive as acceptable. Gerstel (1987) reports that the stigma attached to divorce—whether as an action pursued to end a marriage or the label of one who is divorced—has lessened considerably since the early 1970s. Nonetheless, Gerstel argues that the individual who goes through a divorce—and is, thus, a divorcee—experiences informal, relational sanctions. Citing Goffman (1963), the divorced are discounted. While not receiving a financial discount from our insurance agency, *we* are discounted—our status as "divorced" trumps our 8-year committed relationship.

Through carefully chosen openings, we attempt to perform our version of family through presentations of the kind Jay performed for the insurance agent. Mullaney (1999) notes, however, that performing identity is not exclusively the purview of the actor insofar as others make attributions that contribute to identity construction. Furthermore, individuals—and, arguably, institutions—making attributions participate in an exercise of "mental weighing" to determine which attributes count more or less. Goffman (1963) writes, "The stigmatized person learns and incorporates the standpoint of the normal, acquiring thereby the identity beliefs of the wider society and a general idea of what it would be like to possess a particular stigma" (32).

According to Goffman (1963), the natural history of a category of persons with a stigma must be clearly distinguished from the natural history of the stigma itself. A colleague of Elissa's, on learning of her divorce, declared generously, "Everyone deserves one do-over." Another noted that if Elissa and her ex had simply cohabited rather than marrying, she could simply say, "We broke up," without the accompanying sense of stigma. One could argue that the difference between the two scenarios—divorce and breaking up postcohabitation—is that the former is the end of a presumed lifelong commitment. We counter that the meaning of commitment in a marriage or an unmarried partnership cannot be assumed from the existence or lack of a signed, legal contract—neither can the meaning of the end of either type of relationship. We fully believe in the power of language and interaction to construct relationships, and we build our commitment to each other discursively every day without the benefit of the marriage banner. In this context of a strongly committed familial partnership—now extended to the love and care of a child—it is somewhat assaulting to be confronted with the social reality that our status as "divorced" outweighs our relational reality time and again.

Friction and Flexibility: Take My Partner, Please

Without exception, at the social events where we introduce each other to colleagues, relatives, and acquaintances, we use the term "partner." "This is my partner, Elissa" or "This is Jay, my partner." Most people are astute enough to know that this partnership is not a business enterprise. On the other hand, when we speak of our partners without the benefit of her or his immediate presence, more context is usually necessary to define the nature of our relationship. In either case, we acknowledge that it is not always clear to others that "partner" is not just a synonym for husband or wife. In addition, we have been surprised at how others, especially close friends and even family, often introduce one or the other of us as "Jay's wife" or "Elissa's husband." We recognize that this faux pas is not likely malicious; rather, it is merely the result of entrenched language patterns and cultural scripts. When people ask one or the other of us, "How is your wife?" or "What does your husband do?," we gauge tactically (and, it is hoped, tactfully) when to pronounce, "Actually, we aren't married," followed by our testimony of why we aren't.

In a delightful interlude during a whirlwind visit to the Southern States Communication Association Convention in Little Rock, Arkansas, Elissa encountered a new signifier to encapsulate her relationship with Jay. As she traveled alone with the baby, one of the hotel porters, Larry, had taken a special interest in ensuring a safe and easy transition into the hotel and invited her to call him for a ride back to the airport. As they made the brief journey the next day, their conversation turned to the subject of the economy and jobs—both expressing that they felt fortunate to be working. Elissa mentioned that her "partner" worked at a university in Pennsylvania that had just learned about proposed massive state cutbacks.

Larry queried, "Who is this you're talking about?"

"My partner. My daughter's father," Elissa amended, having been reminded once again how inadequate the term "partner" can be sometimes.

After a few more exchanges, Larry asked, "Is your baby's daddy worried about whether he will lose his job?"

And while the conversation continued without pause, Elissa could not help but smile inwardly and begin to reflect on what it meant to have Jay referred to as her "baby's daddy."

Considering the gentle spirit of the source and the respect with which the term was used, "baby's daddy" endowed our relationship with significance because of the existence of a child. That this significance was rendered regardless of whether we were married, cohabiting, divorced, or dating makes the term an attractive option.

Friction: "But You Can Get Married"

When our daughter was born, we had to decide about her health insurance. We decided initially to add her to both of our policies. When Jay approached his benefits office about adding our daughter, the benefits counselor asked if he wanted to add Elissa as well, presuming that our daughter's mother was also Jay's wife

"No. Elissa has her own insurance," Jay began, "and we're not married." And then, "Do you know that even though this university offers gay and lesbian employees domestic partner benefits, we do not make that same offer to heterosexual couples who aren't married? And even though I applaud this progressive thinking at my institution, I think it is unfortunate that that same benefit is not extended to heterosexual couples."

"But you can get married," the benefits counselor rationalized.

"That's true, but I'm afraid that you are missing the point," and Jay explained our position not much differently than we explain it to anybody, including our automobile insurance customer service representative, Nathan. The fact that we can get married is immaterial in light of the reasons why we are not. If we hold that participating in a cultural institution that discriminates on the basis of sexual orientation runs counter to our ethics, then we cannot get married. The extension of benefits to same-sex partners is a step in the right direction that does not go far enough. When human beings have constructed their relationships as familial and they have an abiding commitment to care for one another, then it is fitting for our institutions to support such family units however they emerge.

Flexibility: "Good Enough for Me"

About a year before our daughter was conceived, we began attending a small Lutheran church that was walking distance from our home. Although we had previously attended Unity and Universalist Unitarian churches, we were attracted by the architecture and proximity of this church. After attending several services, we found that we favored the vibe of the parishioners and the pastor's proficiency at public speaking as he delivered what we interpreted as progressive-leaning sermons. During our formal interview to join this church, we spoke candidly with the pastor about our politics concerning same-sex marriage, including our reasons for choosing not to marry. He was receptive to our views, and we became official parishioners. So when our pregnancy was obvious and the members of the congregation anticipated the arrival of the baby so positively, we knew that we would have our child baptized with this pastor as the celebrant.

Early on a weeknight in September, we welcomed our pastor into our living room to discuss the baptism. Manila folder and forms on his lap, he asked us questions, such as who the godparents would be, along with our own history of being baptized before asking a question that caught us quite off guard.

"And what is the anniversary date of your wedding?"

"Pastor, surely you remember that we are not married."

Our pastor looked momentarily confused, and we quickly reiterated the nature of our commitment and the ceremony we had undertaken 7 years prior. Jay pointed to the framed Declaration of Love over his shoulder, and Elissa retrieved our commitment ceremony photograph album. In hindsight, we are each unclear whether we referenced these artifacts as reminders or as evidence.

After expressing appreciation for the artwork rendered on the document, the pastor reminded us that during his training for the ministry, he had written a thesis on the theological basis and proposed form for a celebration of same-sex unions. He also stated that, with the addition of a single word—"lifelong"—to our declaration, we would have a document that constituted a marriage contract in the church. Despite this omission, our pastor acknowledged the sincerity of our commitment to each other and to our family and possibly asserted his own theology as much as his acceptance of us by declaring, "It's good enough for me."

We note that, as with other moments of flexibility, we perceive ambiguity and some ambivalence about the rendering of our relationship as equivalent to a "real marriage." We accept the endorsement and support that is intended by the statement, we wonder whether the same confirmation would be extended by others to same-sex couples, and we (perhaps contrarily) want to maintain the assertion that our relationship is different, if only for the sake of driving home our point that being an unmarried family comes at a price.

Conclusion: Friction and Flexibility for the Future

While by no means peripheral in American society, marriage has become less essential, especially in the regulation of property transfer, as an indication of adult identity, and as a prerequisite for child rearing (Thornton, Axinn, & Xie, 2007). The fact remains, however, that marriage is a privileged status in our society and as such is rarely addressed in public discourse. Indeed, we argue that the same progressives who recognize the privilege of whiteness (McIntosh, 1989) are far less likely to perceive their participation in the institution of marriage as a privilege. The golden age of marriage may be over (Kiernan, 2004), but for two white, educated heterosexuals to eschew marriage is to refuse a modicum of privilege.

We embrace the power of interpersonal communication to assert the existence of our family commitment outside the social framework of marriage. Because others frequently assume that we are married, considerable communicative effort is necessary as we live this "in-between" category.

We are aware that our self-presentation as a straight, white couple (along with our new addition) provokes the assumption that we are married, which we cannot always actively deny, thus affording us a significant benefit in contemporary American society that we cannot refuse.

In light of our experiences, we propose that the meaning of divorce must change along with the privileging of marriage as the pinnacle of adult commitment. Rather than a sign of a failed relationship or the failure of an individual to succeed in an institution that is itself exclusionary, divorce might be reconsidered as a necessary preface to a more successful, romantic, and familial relationship or the preface to fulfilling solitude. It is an act of discursive violence that, once married and divorced, individuals remain marked as "divorced" until remarried; there is no institutional process for expunging the label.

Language choices continue to elude us. Recently, the social networking site Facebook bridged the gap between "married to" and "in a relationship with" by including "in a domestic partnership with"; we immediately changed our virtual status to correspond to our actual one. That we share the designation of "domestic partner" with a wide range of relationship types is encouraging, and we hope that the material support of such partnerships might eventually follow the virtual. We annually celebrate the anniversary of our commitment ceremony, which is a useful example of how we might pursue more flexible discourse even if we still experience the "overwriting" of our personal meanings with dominant cultural assumptions. Specifically, couples of all kinds can celebrate "anniversaries"—and those sharing our demographic characteristics will be assumed to be married—but we might still use the ambiguity of the word to strategic advantage. Over time, perhaps the term "partner" might be used by the married and unmarried alike until there is a general acceptance that relational meaning resides with the individuals involved and society is called on merely to confirm the implied commitment.

Finally, friction and flexibility need not be thought of as existing on opposite ends of a continuum for the ways they unearth the messiness surrounding contemporary discourses of commitment. Furthermore, friction and flexibility can occur dialectically in interaction; friction can be the catalyst for conversations that open possibilities just as flexibility can sometimes mask deeply rooted assumptions that reify existing relationship hierarchies. When discussing the nature of our relationship, our communicative efforts will continue to invite others to envision a range of familial structures, including marriages, civil unions, domestic partnerships, or, perhaps, other forms of family that have yet to be named.

Discussion Questions

1. This chapter states that the "golden age of marriage may be over." What do you believe is meant by the term "golden age of marriage?" Do you agree that this "golden age" is over? Why or why not?
2. How do the authors define the term "communicative effort"?
3. According to this chapter, the stigma attached to divorce has lessened since the 1970s. What are some of the stigmas associated with divorce? Do you believe that divorce, today, is more socially accepted? Explain.
4. What are your thoughts surrounding the policy of offering gay and lesbian employees domestic partner benefits while denying benefits to heterosexual couples who choose not to marry? Is this procedure prejudicial or justified?

References

Austin, J. L. (2005). *How to do things with words* (2nd ed.). Cambridge, MA: Harvard University Press.

Baard, E. (2003, December 10). Standing on ceremony: A rites issue: Straight couples who refuse to marry because gays can't. *The Village Voice*. http://www.villagevoice.com/2003-12-09/news/standing-on-ceremony/1

Bochner, A. P. (2000). Criteria against ourselves. *Qualitative Inquiry, 6*, 266–272.

Byrne, A., & Carr, D. (2005). Caught in the cultural lag: The stigma of singlehood. *Psychological Inquiry, 16*, 84–91.

Chang, H. (2008). *Autoethnography as method.* Walnut Creek, CA: Left Coast.

Coltrane, S., & Adams, M. (2003). The social construction of the divorce "problem": Morality, child victims, and the politics of gender. *Family Relations, 52*, 363–372.

DePaulo, B., & Morris, W. (2006). The unrecognized stereotyping and discrimination against singles. *Current Directions in Psychological Science, 15*, 251–254.

Doohan, E., Carrere, S., & Riggs, M. (2010). Using relational stories to predict the trajectory toward marital dissolution. *Journal of Family Communication, 10*, 57–77.

Elizabeth, V. (2000). Cohabitation, marriage, and the unruly consequences of difference. *Gender and Society, 14*(1), 87–110.

Ellis, C. (1991). Sociological introspection and emotional experience. *Symbolic Interaction, 14*, 23–50.

Ellis, C., & Bochner, A. P. (2000). Autoethnography, personal narrative, reflexivity: Researcher as subject. In N. K. Denzin & Y. S. Lincoln (Eds.), *Handbook of qualitative inquiry* (2nd ed., pp. 733–768). Thousand Oaks, CA: Sage.

Foster, E. (2008). Communication, commitment, and contending with heteronormativity: An invitation for greater reflexivity in interpersonal research. *Southern Communication Journal, 73*, 84–101.

Foster, E. (2010). My eyes cry without me: Illusions of choice in the transition to motherhood. In S. Hayden & D. L. O'Brien Hallstein (Eds.), *Contemplating maternity in an era of choice.* Lanham, MD: Lexington Books.

Gerstel, N. (1987). Divorce and stigma. *Social Problems, 34*, 172–186.

Goffman, E. (1963). *Stigma: Notes on the management of a spoiled identity.*

Graham, E. (1997). Turning points and commitment in post-divorce relationships. *Communication Monographs, 64*, 350–368.

Hopper, J. (1993). The rhetoric of motives in divorce. *Journal of Marriage and the Family, 55*, 801–813.

Kiernan, K. (2004). Redrawing the boundaries of marriage. *Journal of Marriage and the Family, 66*, 980–987.

McIntosh, P. (1989, July/August). White privilege: Unpacking the invisible knapsack. *Peace and Freedom*, 10–12.

Miller, A. (2009a). Face concerns and facework strategies in maintaining postdivorce coparenting and dating relationships. *Southern Communication Journal, 74*, 157–173.

Miller, A. (2009b). Revealing and concealing postmarital dating information: Divorced coparents' privacy rule development and boundary coordination processes. *Journal of Family Communication, 9,* 135–149.

Mullaney, J. (1999). Making it "count": Mental weighing and identity attribution. *Symbolic Interaction, 22,* 269–283.

Murrow, C., & Shi, L. (2010). The influence of cohabitation purposes on relationship quality: An examination in dimensions. *American Journal of Family Therapy, 38,* 397–412.

Neumann, M. (1996). Collecting ourselves at the end of the century. In C. Ellis & A. Bochner (Eds.), *Composing ethnography: Alternative forms of qualitative writing* (pp. 172–198). Walnut Creek, CA: AltaMira.

Searle, J. (1969). *Speech acts.* Cambridge: Cambridge University Press.

Solot, D., & Miller, M. (2002). *Unmarried to each other: The essential guide to living together as an unmarried couple.* New York: Marlowe.

Thornton, A., Axinn, W., & Xie, Y. (2007). *Marriage and cohabitation.* Chicago: University of Chicago Press.

Walzer, S., & Oles, T. (2003). Accounting for divorce: Gender and uncoupling narratives. *Qualitative Sociology, 26,* 331–349.

Chapter 9

Living with a Ghost: Managing Memory in Postbereaved Families

Christine E. Kiesinger

I live with the ghost of my husband's dead wife.

Sometimes, this frightens me, for example, when she appears to me in a reoccurring dream. In this dream she arrives to our home demanding that I leave so that she can stay and resume her position as mother to my children and as wife to my husband. "Thanks for your help," she says coyly, while ushering me out of the house, slamming the front door behind me.

Sometimes, I actively invite her presence, and in doing so, she inspires me. Like a spirit mentor that I can connect with during quiet times, I sense that she often guides me when I am feeling lost or uncertain.

My relationship with her is fluid—always shifting and changing. At times, I feel we make a great effort to get along—that we share a sisterhood of sorts because we share the same children and husband. Other times, I experience her as an intrusion—a distraction from the work I am trying to do in helping to create a new, stable family life in her absence.

Present or absent, nothing changes the fact that I live with a ghost. Managing this fact has been complicated beyond measure.

The death of a parent in a family system with young children irrevocably shatters structures of stability and ways of being, doing, and relating within a family. In the face of the massive changes that death creates, postbereavement tasks include stabilizing the family in the absence of the deceased parent and finding new and productive ways of being a family (Baker, Sedney, & Gross, 1992). While the family works to adjust to change and build a sense of family anew, they must also find ways of communicatively negotiating the presence of the deceased parent and of honoring and remembering family life as it once was (Bryant, 2006).

In postbereaved families where the living parent marries again, a host of new, often complicated dynamics are set into motion as the family welcomes the new parent/family member into the fold. One critical and central task for the new family member, who is also the new parent, is finding productive and healing ways of managing the need to honor the memory of the deceased and the family's former ways of being a family. However, to secure his or her place in the family, the new family member must establish his or her role as the "new" parent and create a climate of appreciation and enthusiasm for the "new" life the family is creating together. Managing the tension between honoring the previous family system (which included the deceased) and negotiating a new family life is a task fraught with numerous difficulties and communicative challenges for the new family member/parent.

This chapter explores the complicated tension between the need to *remember* and the simultaneous need to *move forward* after the death of a parent. Based on my direct experience as a new spouse and parent coming into a postbereaved family system, this chapter aims to give voice to what it means not only to live with a "ghost" but also to play an active role in keeping the ghost "present" in the family system while simultaneously working hard to establish my "presence" as the new, living mother who is actively engaged in creating a new and thriving family system.

Hilary Anne Bellamy, my husband Keith's deceased wife, died abruptly in October 2002 while running the Marine Corps Marathon in Washington, D.C. Just 34 years of age, she collapsed at mile 22 of the race, the very location where my husband, Keith, was waiting with their children, Isabel, just 2 years old, and their infant son, Walker, just 9 months old. Disoriented and weak, Hilary's collapse led to a coma, and she died 2 days later of a condition called hyponatremia, otherwise known as water intoxication, or overhydration.

I met Keith 2 years later, and it was clear from the start that we would build a future together. As a professor of communication studies with expertise in the areas of interpersonal and family communication studies, I was certain that my love for this family, combined with my knowledge about family systems, parenting, and even some work I had done in the area of communicating with children about death, would ease me into a wonderful life with Keith, Isabel, and Walker.

Despite all that I knew and how deeply I loved my new husband and children, very little could have prepared me for the challenges associated with "managing" Hilary's memory and her looming presence in our lives. Nor did I realize before joining this family the role I would play in making critical decisions about how much to include and exclude her "presence" as we ventured forward together as a family.

Preserving the memory of the deceased is often best accomplished by intentionally invoking her presence through the sharing of personal stories, meaningful ritual activities, and other interactive and intrapersonal strategies (Baker et al., 1992; Braithwaite, Baxter, & Harper, 1998). However, such efforts to maintain an accessible presence of the deceased, can, indeed, thwart efforts toward creating a new, stable family life. There are times when the ghost of the deceased must be asked to depart, must be silenced, must be made "absent."

Absence

It was a Saturday evening, mid-autumn of 2007. Warm enough to keep the windows open, a soft breeze moved through our living room carrying the undeniable scent of all.

My son Walker, daughter Isabel, and my husband Keith and I were gathered together in the main living area of our home. It was an idyllic evening full of positive feelings and good cheer.

There was laughter, music, and a continuous flow of red wine for my husband and me and hot chocolate for the children.

Most vivid to me, however, is not this scene, but how I felt.

Keith and I were about to celebrate our first wedding anniversary. The children, 5 years after the unexpected and tragic death of their biological mother, Hilary, were, miraculously, thriving. My husband, utterly devastated by the death of his young wife, seemed happy and grounded in our bond.

But none of this is to say that there weren't significant challenges along the way and more challenges to come.

That evening, I looked around at the family life I was helping to create, and I felt not lost, regretful, and overwhelmed—feelings I had grown accustomed to experiencing, but instead, I felt joyous, happy, and, most of all—hopeful. I caught a glimpse of Keith as he sipped his wine and laughed, deeply, from his gut, and I thought, *"I can do this. We—are doing this."*

At one point, Isabel disappeared from the scene. I assumed she was in the bathroom, but instead she had gone to her bedroom. When she returned, she came into the kitchen. I was standing at the sink, rinsing some wine glasses. She was crying. In her hands, she held a framed photo of Hilary, her deceased mother. She handed it to me and said, *"I thought she should be down here with us."* My heart dropped. Isabel's hands were trembling as she handed the photo to me.

I stood there, paralyzed, holding the framed photo in my hands. It was one of the last photos taken of Hilary and Isabel, just 1 month prior to Hilary's death. The photo was taken during an autumn visit to Maine, and in it, Isabel and Hilary are enjoying fish at a local crab shack and sharing a bag of potato chips. This is no ordinary photo. It speaks volumes about the bond Isabel and Hilary shared. They were soul mates—truly. Their smiles matched in radiance. Isabel treasured this photo. To date, it sits prominently on her bedside table.

I stood at the sink and felt torn. Although it was just a single moment in time, this moment stands for so many similar moments when I, as "the new mom," must make important decisions about when to make Hilary a presence in our lives and when to have her remain absent.

What to do?

One possible scene plays out in my mind. I imagine the scene in this way:

I drop to my knees and wrap my arms around Isabel. I kiss her tears away. I say, "I know how much you miss your mommy . . . and I want to remind you that she is always here with us." Gently, I take Isabel by the hand and take her and the photo into the living area. I tell Keith and Walker that Isabel is feeling sad. I place the photo in a prominent area and perhaps, even light a candle close to it—further invoking Hilary's presence. The photo, the candle, and the acknowledgment of sadness grant Isabel a sense of calm.

This response feels right and noble. In it, I hear, feel, and acknowledge Isabel's sadness. With great empathy and compassion, I work to restore a sense of peace. I realize and accept that grieving the loss of a parent is an ongoing, lifelong process. I realize that we will often have to put our good times on hold—that we will likely need to pause from time to time to make space for the sadness. In this scene I imagine, I am stoic, truly grown up. I am an adult, a leader, and a supportive guide for Isabel as she navigates her way through the complicated terrain of grief.

However, something very different happened that night.

Through Isabel's sobs, I heard the sound of Keith and Walker's laughter. I thought about the heaviness of the moment—how bringing the framed photo into the main living area and sharing Isabel's sadness would ruin the lightness of the evening. I thought about how, yet again, we would enter into a scene of *memorialization*, thus destroying our *celebration* as a newly evolving family.

Although Isabel's sadness, obvious distress, and need to bring Hilary into our evening was breaking my own heart, I found myself experiencing a range of immature, selfish, yet raw and authentic feelings. First and foremost, I felt angry.

Here is a glimpse into my thoughts:

"What an intrusion! I don't want Hilary here now! This is my family now and we are making new memories! Can't you see that I am here now? Will I ever be enough?"

I found myself wanting to throw the framed photograph against the wall—to shatter future possibilities of Hilary intruding on what I very much wanted to claim as my turf, my family, and my life.

I felt threatened, as if I would never truly be a mother to these children and never truly be a wife to my husband. I felt a childish yet very real fear that I was "second" best to what would have been the "very best" had Hilary not died.

I feel the same degree of shame in writing these words now, as I did while thinking them back then.

Right or wrong, I felt these things and continue to feel this way at times. Over time, we would come to learn that Isabel's need to have Hilary present during fun, celebratory moments was less about missing Hilary and more about Isabel feeling guilty about having fun when her mother was dead—a survivor's guilt of sorts. But no matter, this scene and so many others like it illustrate the complicated position I often find myself in—a position where I, the new mom, must make decisions about how much space to make for the memory of Hilary and when to limit/constrain access to her memory for the sake of moving forward.

In the end, I rendered Hilary "absent" that night. I took the photo and placed it on a shelf, high up in the kitchen. I wrapped my arms around Isabel and told her that I was sorry that she was feeling so sad. I gently walked her back into the living area with Keith and Walker. Within a few minutes, she was smiling again, fully engaged in our family affair.

I intentionally put Hilary "away," instinctively feeling that we were doing the work of growing as a family that night. Rendering Hilary to the position of absence—even just for an evening, was what I thought best for our family. And all too often, decisions about making Hilary present or absent are made in reference to the degree to which her absence or presence assists us in growing as a family or puts us into a state of regression and/or on "pause."

In more postmodern treatments of processes of bereavement, scholars encourage a proactive "retaining" of the presence and memory of the deceased (Moos, 1995; Riches & Dawson, 1998; Silverman, Nickman, & Worden, 1992; Silverman & Silverman, 1979; Stroebe, Gergen, Gergen, & Stroebe, 1992; Walter, 1996). These models suggest that keeping the deceased alive and creating an internalized relationship with the deceased will, indeed, propel one forward and help to heal the often debilitating pain of loss. Maintaining and encouraging the presence of the "social ghost" that lives in our home is a process that has been both challenging and compelling (Gergen, 1987). However, intentionally invoking Hilary has, at times, helped me to be a better mother and has presented possibilities for resolving a range of difficult situations that would not have otherwise been available to me.

Presence

Like an angel sent down from heaven, a well-meaning neighbor warmly invites Isabel to work with her a few hours a week. Jeannie owns a modeling agency and wishes for Isabel to scan photos of prospective models into her computer. Although she knows nothing about Isabel's history, this act of reaching out to her is nothing short of a miracle. In response to the mere invitation to work, Isabel's spirits soar, and she's been granted a much-needed boost to her fragile self-esteem.

The night before she is scheduled for her first day of work, she comes to me riddled with anxiety and close to tears. "What if I can't do this?" she asks. "What if I screw up?" I recall my first babysitting job at 9 years of age—Isabel's current age—and recall having similar fears. We are all hit with some level of anxiety the night before starting a new job. I share this with her. However, I note that her fear is beyond what is expected and is potentially crippling. For Isabel, this job is about so much more than earning a few extra dollars. It is about being perceived by another as competent, valuable, good, and loved. *It is about coming to view herself as competent, wanted, good, and lovable.* Unbeknownst to our neighbor, the gesture of inviting Isabel to work is monumental, as will be the potential long-term effects should it go well.

Like Isabel, I, too, toss and turn the night before her first day on the job. Her anxiety is heartbreaking. Sleep never comes as I struggle to come up with a way to relieve her anxiety and create a space for excitement. In a half-sleep state, Hilary comes to mind.

When Hilary was 10 years old, her own mother died of a brain aneurysm. The death was devastating and life altering for all of Hilary's family but mostly for her. The only girl in a family full of boys, Hilary and her mother shared a very close bond.

Frightened by what her mother's death would come to mean for the family, the children, in response, began a small business. They created flyers offering to wash cars, mow lawns, water plants, rake leaves, babysit. An industrious spirit was born into each of them at that time—especially into Hilary, who worked hard for the rest of her life. Knowing this about Hilary, I wondered how I could convey to Isabel how similar they are. Isabel's eagerness to accept work in the face of losing playtime, extracurricular activities, matched Hilary's commitment to working hard.

The next day, I pulled a box down from a high shelf in the attic. I reached inside and into a dense pile of Hilary's jewelry. I had not visited this box in a long time. I sifted through each piece until I stumbled on what I was looking for—a collection of rings that Hilary had saved from her childhood. These were tiny pieces that would easily fit Isabel—rings that Hilary had worn when she was roughly 9 or 10 years old. The rings felt alive in my hands. Worn and somewhat tarnished, they carried the energy of Hilary's youth—her sadness, her hope, and her fierce commitment to making her life work in her mother's absence.

Before she left for work, I called Isabel into the living room. On the coffee table, I displayed five delicate rings. I explained that these belonged to Hilary and that she, like Isabel, would have eagerly accepted an opportunity to work, even at such a young age. I told her the story about Hilary going to work in the months following her mother's death and how her industrious spirit was alive and thriving until the moment of her death. I told Isabel that much like her mom, she, too, possessed this spirit. I invited her to choose a ring. I told her that when in doubt, she could look down at the ring and think about Hilary and about how she was, indeed, following in her mother's footsteps. I told her that the ring would be a reminder that Hilary would be with her as she worked.

Within moments of choosing a small gold, braided band, Isabel appeared to have grown. She stood a little taller as she walked with a new sense of confidence across the street to Jeannie's home.

I intentionally invoked Hilary's presence in this moment. Although I had similar stories to tell—stories that reflected my own industrious spirit and strong work ethic—I felt that Isabel needed something more, and this more was Hilary.

The narrative above reflects those moments when I invoke Hilary's presence, inviting aspects of her life story and experience into our daily lives. I have discovered that such invocations often help me to better "mother" my children—especially Isabel. Stories about Hilary provide important links to a part of my children's past that I did not live. Stories also offer a sense of genetic, biological, mental, and emotional "continuity" that assist my husband and me in offering our children a sense of the qualities that Hilary possessed—characteristics that they might "try on" or perhaps even "integrate" into their own identities and "visions" about the sort of people they might become. For example, as of late, Keith and I have been talking a great deal about Hilary's athletic gifts—innate physical abilities that she possessed and evolved with a lot of practice and discipline. In the telling of these stories, we see our children beginning to "test" and "try on" their own athletic personas. There has been something quite empowering for both children in holding the knowledge that perhaps, like Hilary, they possess certain innate qualities that might make them good athletes—qualities like strength, endurance, stamina, and commitment.

As I aim to illustrate in this chapter, however, a careful and continuous balance must be sought between invoking Hilary's memory and making her memory absent. We have learned that too much memorialization, too much time spent in the past, too much of her presence, both cripples and constrains the growth of our family. An overfocus on "presence" forces us "back in time" and into an orientation toward the past that is not conducive to growth. We have learned this lesson over time, particularly when faced with the very real needs of Hilary's extended family who tend to focus on Hilary and stories about her life when they spend time with our children. All too often, the children return from time with Hilary's family feeling emotionally overwhelmed and utterly exhausted. Too much memorialization forces the children into a past that they miss or struggle to remember and, thus, halts our process of moving forward together as a new family.

We render Hilary absent as we create our own family rituals and ways of being a "family." In such moments, I freely offer stories about *my* life that then become important frameworks that our children can freely access and integrate into their own life stories as they evolve as people. For example, we have talked extensively about the fact that although I did not give birth to the children, our continuous, daily interactions allow them to take in and integrate parts of who I am that then connect us in deep and enduring ways. This may explain why my daughter's voice is beginning to sound like my own or how my son's affinity for certain foods, activities, and ways of thinking about things are really rooted in time spent with my extended family. I often tell my son that although we are not blood related, he *is* a *Kiesinger* at his core.

There are rare moments, however, when Hilary and I are invited to exist comfortably together as two powerful forces in the mothering of my children. This final narrative offers a beautiful portrayal of one such moment—a moment of coexistence that is significant and one I think about often.

This narrative chronicles a final therapy session between Isabel and her therapist, Dr. Marr. In this particular session, Dr. Marr has asked Isabel, just 7 at the time, to draw a picture that tells a story of how she felt after Hilary's death. Because of its significance, this hand-drawn picture remains sealed away. It is a powerful image born out of Isabel's subconscious. The story it tells is one I treasure.

The Storm, the Sun, and the Flower: A Tale of Two Moms

In her small hand, Isabel holds a white crayon. Pressing hard, she scribbles aggressively in white across the bottom of the page. "This is snow," she tells us. Grabbing gray, she draws large, misshapen clouds across the top of the page. The scene she is creating seems stark and dire. She draws a stick figure of herself trudging through the snow. Taking a black crayon, she draws small diamond-shaped drops falling from the stick figure's eyes. This is her, crying. We continue to watch as she draws. I sit on the edge of my seat feeling anxious and wonder what the therapist is thinking. Where is she going with this?" I wonder. And then she pauses for a long time.

From the large box, she grabs a red and green crayon. She draws a small red flower with a single green leaf, pushing itself up through the snow. With confidence, she then takes a yellow crayon and draws just a hint of sunshine peeking out from under the gray mass of clouds above. "Done," she announces.

Dr. Marr is gentle with her. "Tell us about your picture, Isabel . . . what story are you telling here?" he asks.

"Well, the dark clouds and the snow is the storm that my life became when my mom died . . . it was like I was lost in the snow. I was cold and alone, and I could not find my way home."

Another part of my heart breaks as I listen to Isabel speak so eloquently and from a place of complete authenticity and truth.

"Tell us about the flower," Dr. Marr says.

"The flower is my new mom. I did not know it at the time, but she was *coming* for me, and that's her pushing up out from the ground."

Isabel continues, "The yellow is my 'old' mom, Hilary. She is like the sun, peeking out from behind a cloud, watching over me. I could not feel her at the time, but she was always there, trying to help me find my way back home."

"And look at this," Isabel says, "Just like the sun, Hilary is bringing the flower up out of the cold ground . . . she is helping my new mom grow." Isabel then announces, with a wide, toothy smile, "The End."

We all know that this is not the end. Our family continues to grapple with the fact that Hilary both lived and died.

We aim to honor Hilary's life by extracting aspects of her experience that assist our children in the launching of their own lives—a focus on narratives about her life that help to create a context from which our children can grow and realize their highest and best selves. In this way, she will always be present for us but in different ways and to different degrees. As a mother to these children, Hilary is an important resource to me in my own parenting. Although I did not know her personally, I have *come* to know her. In a proactive way, I have sought to know her as means of best integrating her into our lives in ways that don't hurt but heal and help us grow. For example, a few years ago, when Isabel was feeling guilty about the fact that she was beginning to forget her mother (she was losing memories of Hilary's voice and face), I aimed to assuage her guilt by asking Hilary's extended family and village of friends to help me to help Isabel. Together, Isabel and I composed and sent a mass e-mail that requested that family and friends send a brief story about their favorite time with Hilary and to include a photograph of Hilary and the friend/family member. Isabel set a deadline, and the entries began pouring in. Together, we constructed an album with the narratives and photos. This album is a place for Isabel to visit, whenever she chooses, and has become a powerful forum through which Isabel can both remember and come to "know" her mother in new and interesting ways. I will likely do a similar exercise with my son. Walker was just 9 months old when Hilary died. Presently, he is beginning to talk about the fact that he never really knew her. Thus, unlike Isabel, he does not struggle to remember her but rather longs to *know* her. Together we will create a project that will assist him in his own grieving process—a process not rooted in missing but rather one rooted in a desire to *know* his deceased mother.

We aim to grapple with the fact that Hilary also died, and, thus, she is absent. I arrived into the lives of these children not as a substitute for the mother she would have been but rather as a woman deeply in love with the man who would become my husband and the children who would become my own. That said, we avoid terms like "stepmother" because of the negative connotations associated with the term. We avoid terms like "old mom" and "new mom," "first mom," and "second mom." In fact, over time, the children have come to refer to Hilary as "Hilary" and call me "Mom." This was not intentional on our part but something that naturally evolved. As we go about the daily business of growing our own life together as a family, Hilary's "presence" is largely absent from the routine, mundane interactions that constitute family life. These interactions, although mundane, powerfully shape the contours and texture of family life or, even better, how it "feels" to be part of our family. To the dismay of many, we don't make visits to Hilary's grave. We do not celebrate her date of death. We address the nature of her death only when the children have questions, but we do not dwell on the various narratives about her death that are disturbing and profoundly sad. We do eat vanilla cupcakes with pink frosting each June 30, Hilary's *birth* date. We do find high places from which the children release helium balloons to heaven in hopes that she catches them and the love with which they are sent. Keith proposed to me on what would have been his 10th marital anniversary to Hilary—an engagement date chosen both to honor a past he once occupied, a past that tragically came to an end, and to embrace with enthusiasm and love a future with me. In the yard of our new home, we hope to plant a cherry tree in Hilary's honor. This tree will be a living expression of the life she led, the lives she created and ushered into this world. This will be a deeply rooted tree—one that blooms each spring—a tree symbolic of both the life we are creating together in the present and the future that will bloom and flourish before us.

In her compelling article "Mourning the Loss Builds the Bond: Primal Communication Between Foster, Adoptive, or Stepmother and Child," Barbara Waterman (2000) opens with Loewald, who writes, "Those who know ghosts tell us they long to be released from their ghost life and led to rest as ancestors. As ancestors they live forth in the present generation, while as ghosts they are compelled to haunt the present generation with their shadow life" (p. 277).

Loewald's words resonate deeply with me, as I have always felt that Hilary longs to be released from her "ghost life" and led to that peaceful place where she can exist for our children—for our family—as an *ancestor*. It is only from this place of rest that she can live on and through our lives in a productive and "present" way and not in a way that haunts, harms, or hurts. Her ancestor role, established by my husband and I, who literally "communicate" her into this role, allows Hilary to be present for us in our growth as individuals and as a family and also allows her to live forth in all that we are and shall become.

Discussion Questions

1. In this chapter, the author explores the complex dialectical tension between "absence" and "presence" as related to managing the memory of the deceased. The author's narrative suggests that creating a balance between "absence" and "presence" is central to preserving the memory of the deceased and to the process of moving forward. Can you think of other ways that the author might manage her children's need to *know* their deceased biological mother and the family's need to *move forward*?

2. How do larger, cultural, master narratives of loss, grief, and the grieving process impact the dilemma the author finds herself in whenever she feels the need to have to make decisions about making the deceased *present* or rendering her *absent*?
3. What personal experiences, understandings, and insights do you bring to your reading and interpretation of the narrative offered in this chapter?
4. What in this chapter makes you think? Feel? What sort of new understandings about loss and managing loss did this chapter grant you?
5. At the time this chapter was written, the author's children were 7 and 9 years of age. How do you think the grieving process will evolve as the children mature? The author suggests that grieving the loss of a parent is likely a lifelong process and that this process changes over time. How might the children's grieving *look* and *feel* during adolescence? Early adulthood? How might the living parents assist their children in their grieving as they move through the various developmental stages of life?

References

Baker, J. E., Sedney, M.A., & Gross, E. (1992). Psychological tasks for bereaved children. *American Journal of Orthopsychiatry, 62,* 105-116.

Braithwaite, D. O., Baxter, L. A., & Harper, A. M. (1998). The role of rituals in the management of the dialectical tension of "old" and "new" in blended families. *Communication Studies, 49,* 101-120.

Bryant, L. E. (2006). Ritual (in)activity in postbereaved stepfamilies. In L. Turner & R. West(Eds.), *The family communication sourcebook* (pp. 281-293). Thousand Oaks, CA: Sage.

Gergen, M. M. (1987, August). *Social ghosts: Opening inquiry on imaginal relationships.* Paper presented at the 95th annual convention of the American Psychological Association, New York.

Moos, N. L. (1995). An integrative model of grief. *Death Studies, 19,* 337-364.

Riches, G., & Dawson, P. (1998). Lost children, living memories: The role of photographs in processes of grief and adjustment among bereaved parents. *Death Studies, 22,* 121-140.

Silverman, P. R., Nickman, S., & Worden, J. W. (1992). Detachment revisited: The child's reconstruction of a dead parent. *American Journal of Orthopsychiatry, 62,* 494-503.

Silverman, S. M., & Silverman, P.R. (1979). Parent-child communication in widowed families. *American Journey of Psychotherapy, 33,* 428-441.

Stroebe, M., Gergen, M., Gergen K., & Stroebe, W. (1992). Broken hearts or broken bonds: Love and death in historical perspective. *American Psychologist, 47,* 1205-1212.

Walter, T. (1996). A new model of grief: Bereavement and biography. *Mortality, 1,* 7-25.

Waterman, B. (2000). Mourning the loss builds the bond: Primal communication between foster, adoptive, or stepmother and child. *Journal of Loss and Trauma, 6,* 277-300.

Chapter 10

State Disciplinary Practices and the Emergence of Coparenting Families

Lynn Comerford

Currently, around 1 million children are affected by divorce in the United States each year. In the vast majority of cases with a formal written agreement, mothers retain sole custody. However, increasingly, fathers are demanding and receiving cocustody of their children. That is, they are receiving a share of physical custody whereby they are solely responsible for their children for a certain period of time. What happens during the custody agreement process and after is an important site for researchers interested in family communication dynamics and the social forces that impact the emergence of new family forms.[1] Currently, child custody disputes form the largest percentage of domestic-relations cases and account for close to one-quarter of all legal filings, making it the largest category of court action.[2] Child custody decisions impact the majority of U.S. citizens at some point in their lives.

The ways in which child custody decisions are made is a contested site and fiercely debated. On the one hand, equal-parenting advocates argue that both split and joint physical custody better serve the best-interest standard because these custody resolutions keep fathers attached to their children and increase the frequency of child support payments. On the other hand, equity-parenting advocates (hereafter termed "maternalists") worry that a gender-neutral best-interest standard ignores the fact that women do the lion's share of child care and housework and are marginalized in market work because of it. Maternalists argue that there is little evidence that cocustody changes the behavior of fathers or that courts have the resources to turn fathers into active parents.

In this chapter, I draw from the strengths of both of these positions. I will offer another way to view the child custody decision-making process and its aftermaths by highlighting the ways in which state, as the most important communicative force in the formation of joint physical or split custodial families (hereafter called cocustodial families), benefits from this new family form. First, I will review the arguments put forth by equal-parenting advocates in custody decision making and the emergence of "gender-neutral" cocustodial families. Second, I will review the arguments put forth by maternalists (those arguing for equity in the custody decision process). Third, I will explain how both of these positions inadequately address the state's interest in controlling the day-to-day life of all family members postdivorce/separation. I will argue that the states' interest in coparenting families is best understood in term of its desire to control citizens and that this is achieved through communicative disciplinary practices, such as (a) court-imposed custody mediation, (b) family court surveillance mechanisms, and (c) the state's reconfiguration of gendered, heterosexual families. I will conclude the chapter with the observation that the debate over how to do cocustody as a day-to-day practice reflects broader concerns about social justice, marital and parenting roles, and communication.

Equality and Coparenting Families

In the United States, the parents of a child born within a marriage are joint guardians of that child, and the rights of both parents are considered equal: each parent has an equal right to the custody of the child when they separate. The U.S. Constitution allows a state to interfere with this right only to prevent harm or potential harm to the child. But joint physical and legal custody is still quite rare across the country. Those who argue in favor of an "equality" approach to the custody decision-making process desire to greatly increase the number of families in which children are jointly shared; optimistically, they would like to see the majority of families postseparation/divorce work out a 50/50 physical and legal custody agreement.

Equal-parenting advocates argue that the solution to the current gendered division of unpaid care work and paid market work is for fathers and mothers to be allocated equal joint physical custody; otherwise, the current gendered organization of domesticity will continue to be justified, sustained, and reproduced. Because market work structures encourage paternal absence in terms of actual parenting and fathers have no control over this, they should not be punished for it in a custody decision. Fathers, they argue, are necessary for children's healthy development and should have an equal right to custody regardless of their history of caretaking. Mental health professionals and custody evaluators agree and frequently favor presumptive joint custody, agreeing with recent congressional fatherhood bills that argue that "fatherlessness" is the "most consequential social problem we confront" and that no one should deny custody to fathers who want it.

Equal-parenting advocates argue that joint custody better serves the "best interest of the child" standard because it keeps fathers attached to their children and increases the frequency of child support payments. They also interpret women's desire for sole custody as contributing to a culture of gender inequality and the perpetuation of traditional gender roles. They want to subvert traditional gender roles and change social expectations and norms with respect to how children are raised. They argue that joint physical and legal custody will ignite a gender-neutral norm of parenting that involves fathers as much as mothers and that this in turn will restructure the relationship between market work and family work so that all parents can engage in both without becoming marginalized in either.

On this view, gender neutrality is necessary in child custody decision making because it is consistent with general liberal notions of equality. On a symbolic level, making equality the organizing concept underlying custody decision making ensures a more just society.

Currently, more than half of all mothers are in the workforce, new marriages break up at a rate of 50%, and nearly one-third of all births are to single women (Bumpass, 1990; U.S. Bureau of the Census, 1994). The stereotypes of the "moral" mother and the "absent" father historically have had a regulatory and normative impact on the treatment of mothers and fathers in child custody disputes (Black & Cantor, 1989; Grossberg, 1983).

Sociological and historical work on fathering makes it clear that fathering is a social construction. Each generation of fathering research appears to mold its cultural ideal of fathers according to its own time and conditions, and each deals with the gap between what LaRossa (1988) terms the "culture" of fatherhood and the "conduct" of fathers in families. Sociological and historical analyses also make it clear that fathering cannot be defined in isolation from mothering, mothers' expectations, and social expectations about child rearing in the society and that these social expectations have been fairly fluid.

As Lewis and O'Brien (1987) state, men have a less clear "job description" as fathers than women do as mothers. This suggests that father behavior is strongly influenced by the meanings and expectations of fathers themselves, as well as mothers, children, extended family, and broader cultural institutions.

Equity and Coparenting Families

Catherine MacKinnon (2006) argues that to speak of gender equality is meaningless because women live in a genders system of inequality. She explains that women are paid unequally in the workplace and allocated to disrespected work; they are targeted for rape, domestic battering, sexual abuse as children, and systematic sexual harassment and deprived of reproductive control. Women, she argues, in ways quite different from men, have a collective social history of disempowerment, exploitation, and subordination extending to the present. On this view, legally treating the sexes the same in the custody decision process, as if they were equal, disadvantages women.

Recent statistics reveal a sexual division of labor in parenting patterns,[3] and maternalists worry that a gender-neutral best-interest standard ignores this fact. Maternalists argue that there is little evidence that a joint custody standard changes the behavior of fathers or that courts have the resources to turn fathers into active parents.[4]

Carol Smart (1991) argues that the moral discourse of care is being silenced by the dominant discourse of rights and that the discourse of care is unfairly being dismissed. Maternalists see the lack of federal intervention in the family as gross neglect of women and children. They interpret the state's "hands-off" approach to "the private realm of the family" as discrimination against unpaid family work, most of which is done by women. Maternalists argue that affirmative action principles should be applied to the family context and that without a well-funded federal institutional structure of available child care and health care services, as well as adequate social and economic support systems that enable men and women to nurture and rear their children, formal equality is understood to hurt women. Because market work is stacked against mothers, calculations of child or spousal support in which courts assume that the father and mother have had equal access to the breadwinner role, on this view, are unfair. Maternalists argue that advocacy of equal treatment denies difference, requires women to adhere to masculine life patterns, and ignores evidence that equal treatment harms women.

Maternalists enter court with the belief that because children have likely received primary caregiving from their mothers whose lives are framed by powerful social forces that lead them to "choose" to become marginalized and cut off from most social roles that offer responsibility and authority, children should be "awarded" to mothers who have sacrificed economic gain to engage in care work. Maternalists believe that formal legal equality undervalues the gendered division of care work, household labor, and domestic violence and limits mothers' right to restrict contact with fathers while imposing no obligation for contact on fathers. Additionally, they point out that joint custody identifies the child's right to contact with both parents only in the postseparation family and not in the preseparation family and ignores the problems of fathers seeking revenge, retribution, and control through custody. Furthermore, maternalists find that increased paternal involvement does not automatically mean improved child outcomes or that biological fathers provide such unique nurturance that it cannot be provided by substitute caregivers. On this view, the role of custody law should recognize existing gendered inequality and move beyond the simplistic equality paradigm.

Maternalists find that granting both parents automatic joint physical custody problematic and argue that it harms the weaker party (usually mothers) (Featherstone, 1999; Fineman, 1988), is a tool of harassment by ex-partners (Chesler, 1991; Kurz, 1995), and is an excuse not to address violence against women and children (Edleson, 1999; Stark & Flitcraft, 1991). Currently, it is estimated that 2 million women in the United States are terrorized by husbands or other male partners who use violence as one way of controlling "their woman" (Johnson & Ferraro, 2005). Research indicates that children are abused in up to 70 percent of families in which violence against woman occurs (Edleson 1999; Stark & Flitcraft 1991). Women violence in domestic settings has serious negative impacts on children, including substance use, delinquent behavior, and mental health and psychiatric diagnoses, including posttraumatic stress disorder, depression, anxiety, sexual disorders, and eating disorders (Kovrola & Heger, 2003; Saunders, 2003).

Maternalists point out that fathers frequently threaten to fight for joint custody in order to gain better divorce property settlements and enforce joint physical custody in court (but not in life) in order to pay less child support. Maternalists fear that if joint custody does not enforce obligations of fathers but gives them significant rights to command how mothers do virtually all of the family work, the symbolic message is that divorced fathers are entitled to control their children without doing any of the day-to-day work of raising them. On this view, eliminating entitlements for caregivers is not a desirable feminist strategy given that there are significant power differentials between men and women. Maternalists dismiss the idea that the goal of "equality" ought to be based on accepting maleness as the norm and a denial of equality to women who are unable or unwilling to assimilate to that norm.

Child support is usually configured for 50/50 joint custody in mediation sessions. However, the high percentage of joint physical custody agreements achieved through the mediation process is not likely to be sustained because they rarely fit the behavior of families (Mason, 1999). According to Mason, very few families can maintain a 50/50 physical and legal sharing arrangement in which the child actually resides with each parent half the time because the needs and desires of parents and children often change over time. Parents move, remarry, and give in to child preferences for one parent or the other, and inevitably children drift toward a primary parent model, most often the mother. Women may find that over time a "mother drift" occurs that often mimics earlier patterns of primary child care; thus, she finds herself with de facto primary custody but de jure cocustody child support (Maccoby & Mnookin, 1992). Women and children bear the brunt of the economic fallout postrelationship; in 2000, female-headed households with children under 18 made up 52% of all poor households with children under 18 (U.S. Bureau of the Census, 2001).

The American Law Institute (ALI) is a national nonprofit group of lawyers and legal scholars who make recommendations for state legislation. For the first time, the ALI (2002) issued recommendations for states' laws on family dissolution titled "Principles of the Law of Family Dissolution: Analysis and Recommendations." They argue that the best-interest standard is met by facilitating planning and agreement, continuity of parent–child attachments, meaningful contact between children and each parent, caretaking relationships with adults who know how to care for a particular child's needs, security from conflict and violence, and expeditious and predictable legal decision making. The ALI finds that the best-interest test, as currently practiced in most jurisdictions, is not in the best interest of children if it involves a prolonged legal contest with a parade of competing psychological experts, other witnesses, and delays to custody decisions.

Fineman (1988) suggests that nonresident fathers use joint custody as a way to avoid responsibilities. For example, the economic responsibility for cocustodial parents is reduced by as much as half (California Family Code, 4330). Saving on child support may be the strongest incentive to coparent for the previously "nonprimary" parent. However, if, as Maccoby and Mnookin (1992) suggest, the postmarriage relationship between divorced parents is something that is "constructed" and not simply carried over from the marriage, there may be room for real behavior changes (in addition to financial incentives) in the coparenting family. Unfortunately, they conclude their study with the observation that "despite revolutionary changes in the law to eliminate gender stereotypes and to encourage greater gender equity, the characteristic roles of mothers and fathers remain fundamentally different" (p. 271). The differences between coparenting in law and coparenting in life are found in the day-to-day practices of the coparents themselves. Can a legal identity, in this case "cocustodial parent," change one's parenting practices significantly?

Equality or Equity: A False Dichotomy

The "equality versus equity" debate assumes a liberal conception of the state.

To argue that the state supports "equality" and/or "equity" in child custody decision making presupposes that the state acts as an impartial, neutral, objective, and legal entity. It assumes that the state has no stake other than justice and rationality. What if the state is not impartial, neutral, and objective? What if the state is an interested party that actively intervenes into the lives of citizens? What if the state institutionalizes sexism, racism, and homophobia through child custody policies? What if the state has found a way to discipline and control more of its citizens through mediation sessions and family courts?

The family, according to Foucault (1978), from the 18th century on, became an instrument of government. Foucault argues that the state was interested in finding ways to "maximizing life" and claims that this emerged from the increased ordering and disciplining of individuals in order for the bourgeoisie to maximize their class survival and continued control. The techniques the state used in the 18th century involved discourses (classifications, measurements, evaluations, controls, and so on) about objects of knowledge: the sexualization of children and female bodies, the control of procreation, and the psychiatrization of certain sexual behaviors labeled perverse. These discourses were implemented through psychiatry, medicine, law, pedagogy, economics, and demography and were supported and funded by the state and focused primarily on the family. Hence, "sex became a matter that required the social body as a whole, and virtually all of its individuals, to place themselves under surveillance" (p. 116).

Coparenting policies place all family members (fathers included) under the gaze of the state. Equal-parenting advocates and maternalists overlook the ways in which coparenting laws discipline all family members. The state places many restrictions and obligations on the behavior of both coparents and their children when heretofore "private" families become "public" and reconfigure via family court where the state sets the family schedule and monitors housing, child care, education, income distribution, and so on.

Cocustody is good for capitalism. In a capitalist system, consumption must continually expand to absorb the increased flow of goods. If there is a creation of two households, where there used to be one, consumption is increased. But consumption increases only according to income or credit. Ironically, before a divorce or breakup, there is no legal enforcement of "alimony" or "child support." Parents, free from an alimony or support order, never have to register their employment in court documents or face an automatic imposition of wage garnishment, imprisonment, suspension of professional licensing, and suspension of the license to drive for nonpayment of child support. Parents and spouses without alimony or child support orders are never harassed by private collection agencies in the collection of child support or spouse support and are not found in data-sharing computer systems that states use to track people who owe child support or alimony.

However, if alimony and child support allocations are legally enforced, it means that parents (or a parent) must earn enough income to pay them. The social construction of the parent–child relationship by the state through coparenting policies discursively reconstitutes individuals in families, family boundaries, and family economics.

Disciplining Families

Child custody mediation hearings underscore effects of self-monitoring, monitoring everyone else because they are afraid the state will intervene against their own interests. Both maternalists and equal-parenting advocates take for granted the idea that there is "the private family," a place where law does not intrude. Both maternalists and equal-parenting advocates reveal the ways in which harm is done because of law's absence in the private realm. Obscenity is protected in private, equality is not guaranteed in private, and, in private, "women who can afford abortions can get them, but those who cannot afford them get no public support, because private choices are not public responsibilities" (MacKinnon, 2006, p. 38). Both maternalists and equal-parenting advocates, for different reasons, critique family law for impoverishing women and producing and reinforcing their unequal status as a sex society-wide and for the fact that no sex equality standards have been applied to the results of divorce where women's standard of living is permitted to plummet after divorce.

The number of female-headed families in poverty increased to 3.6 million in 2002 from 3.5 million in 2001, and the poverty rate for these families was unchanged from 2001 at 26.5%. For children under age 6 living in families with a female householder and no spouse present, 48.6% were in living in poverty, five times the rate of their counterparts in married-couple families (9.7%). Custodial mothers are 44% more likely to live in poverty than custodial fathers.

Coparenting, as a technology of social control, regulates the bodies, desires, identities, and behaviors. Coparents monitor their own behavior as well as those of their coparenting partner and report legal transgressions to family court. Coparented children monitor what is going on in each home and report to their other coparent and/or a social worker or the family court judge. Other family members, friends, and community members also participate in the monitoring and disciplining of the coparenting family, prepared to speak on behalf of the family if asked. The specter of family law hovers over the coparenting family. Cocustody allows for the two new families (created from the one previously intact family) to become objects of the direct management of the state. New identities emerge as bodies are observed and managed by the sprawling apparatus of cocustody disciplinary practices.

Cocustody policies often exacerbate the feminization of poverty. Many coparenting mothers describe "coparenting in law" as quite different than "coparenting in life." The economic costs of "no-show" coparenting fathers, late child support payments, the loss of Aid to Families with Dependent Children due to losing *primary* parent status, and their having to pay for the "extra" expenses that arise when coparenting children all contribute to the feminization of poverty.

Cocustodial laws maintain the traditional heterosexual family model. As a result, single motherhood will continue to be considered deviant as cocustody seeks to replace mother-headed families. In fact, the idea of a "single mother" is defined only by her relationship (formal and legal) to the father—she is single, and no one talks about "married mother families" (Fineman, 1995, p. 148). Cocustodial families are "heterosexually repaired" by the state with cocustody policies.

Conclusion

The practices of cocustody constitute the bargaining context for men and women in good relationships as well as poor relationships because cocustody defines the possibilities of male and female behavior in a particular way within a particular structure. The fact that fathers can receive cocustody changes the bargaining position of mothers both in the life of the relationship and if the relationship ends. The impact of cocustody laws on the relative bargaining power of men and women is a function of the legal system. It is clear in the interviews that have been presented that the bargaining power of the cocustody fathers tended to be greater than the bargaining power of the cocustody mothers.

The social construction of coparenting is evolving, and contemporary mothers and fathers have a central role in this creation. The active construction of coparenting fathers and mothers themselves is not a prominent theme in the research literature, although this study suggests that it should be. More qualitative research is needed to explore the kinds of identity development and social negotiation that constitute the experience of both coparenting fathering and mothering.

Discussion Questions

1. As referenced in the chapter, how can a legal identity, in this case cocustodial parent, significantly change how one parents his or her children?
2. Explain how coparenting might act as a means of social control. How can the family's "becoming an instrument of government" potentially affect the family dynamic?

3. This author states that "the characteristic roles of mothers and fathers remain fundamentally different." In your opinion, how do these roles differ in our society?

4. The maternalist view claims that "legally treating the sexes the same in the custody decision process, as if they were equal, disadvantages women." Explain why you agree or disagree.

5. What are some of the negative impacts that children may experience when they are exposed to violence against women in a domestic setting?

References

American Law Institute. (2002). The allocation of custodial and decision making responsibility for children. In *Principles of the law of family dissolution: Analysis and recommendations* (pp. 92-408).

Black, J. C., & Cantor, D. J. (1989). *Child custody.* New York: Columbia University Press.

Bumpass, L. L. (1990). What's happening to the family? Interactions between demographic and institutional change. *Demography, 27,* 483-498.

Chesler, P. (1991). Mothers on trial: The custodial vulnerability of women. *Feminism and Psychology, 1,* 409-425.

Demo, D. (2000). Children's experience of family diversity. *National Forum, 80*(3), 16-21.

Edleson, J. L. (1999). The overlap between child maltreatment and woman battering. *Violence Against Women, 5,* 134-154.

Featherstone, B. (1999). Taking mothering seriously: The implications for child protection. *Child and Family Social Work, 4,* 43-53.

Fineman, M. (1988). Dominant discourse, professional language, and legal change in child custody decision making. *Harvard Law Review, 101*(4), 727-774.

Fineman, M. (1995). *The neutered mother and the sexual family.* New York: Routledge.

Foucault, M. (1978). *The history of sexuality: An introduction* (Vol. 1). New York: Vintage.

Grossberg, L. (1983). Who gets the child? Custody, guardianship, and the rise of a judicial patriarchy in nineteenth century America. *Feminist Studies, 9*(2), 235-260.

Johnson, M. P., & Ferraro, K. J. (2005). Research on domestic violence: Making distinctions. In *Family in transition* (pp. 506-521). Boston: Allyn and Bacon.

Kovrola, C., & Heger, A. (2003). Responding to children exposed to domestic violence. *Journal of Interpersonal Violence, 18*(4), 331-337.

Kreider, R. (2007). Living arrangements of children: 2004. In *Current population reports* (pp. 70_114). Washington, DC: U.S. Bureau of the Census.

Kurz, D. (1995). *For richer, for poorer: Mothers confront divorce.* New York:

LaRossa, R. (1988). Fatherhood and social change. *Family Relations, 36,* 451-458.

Lewis, C., & O'Brien, M. (1987). Constraints on fathers: Research, theory and clinical practice. In C. Lewis & M. O'Brien (Eds.), *Reassessing fatherhood: New observations on fathers and the modern family.* Newbury Park, CA: Sage.

Maccoby, E. E., & Mnookin, R. H. (1992). *Dividing the child: Social and legal dilemmas of custody.* Cambridge, MA: Harvard University Press.

MacKinnon, C. (2006). *Are women human? And other international dialogues.* Cambridge, MA: Harvard University Press.

Mason, M. (1999). *The custody wars.* New York: Basic Books.

Saunders, E. B. (2003). Understanding children exposed to violence: Toward an integration of overlapping fields. *Journal of Interpersonal Violence,* (4), 356–376.

Smart, C. (1991). The legal and moral ordering of child custody. *Journal of Law and Society, 18*(4), 485–500.

U.S. Bureau of the Census. (1994). *The diverse living arrangements of children.* Washington, DC: U.S. Government Printing Office.

U.S. Bureau of the Census. (2001). *People and families in poverty by selected characteristics: 1999 and 2000.* http://www.census.gov/hhes/poverty

Legal Codes Cited

California Family Code 4330

(a) In a judgment of dissolution of marriage or legal separation of the parties, the court may order a party to pay for the support of the other party an amount, for a period of time, that the court determines is just and reasonable, based on the standard of living established during the marriage, taking into consideration the circumstances as provided in Chapter 2 (commencing with Section 4320).

(b) When making an order for spousal support, whether the order is for a specific amount or simply a reservation of jurisdiction, and except in the limited number of cases where the court determines that a party is unable to make such efforts, the court shall give the parties the following admonition: "It is the goal of this state that each party shall make reasonable good faith efforts to become self-supporting as provided for in Section 4320. The failure to make reasonable good faith efforts, may be one of the factors considered by the court as a basis for modifying or terminating support."

End notes

[1] Joint legal custody means that both parents share in major decisions but individually make the day-to-day decisions when the child(ren) are with him or her. Physical custody refers to the time children actually spend with their parent(s). Cocustodial families work toward a 50/50 residential split so that the children spend equal amounts of time residing with each parent. Parents with joint physical custody have lower child support obligations in most states.

[2] Currently, nearly half of all marriages end in divorce, and each year more than 1 million children see their parents separate or divorce. The U.S. divorce rate more than doubled between 1965 and 1980, and an estimated 40% 50% of all marriages now end in separation or divorce, affecting over 1 million children annually. Although the divorce rate leveled off during the 1990s, divorce among couples with children continues to increase,

as roughly 60% of remarriages are projected to end in divorce. Today, one in three children is born to unmarried parents. Single-mother families increased from 3 million in 1970 to 10 million in 2003; the number of single-father families grew from less than half a million to 2 million. In 1960, only 9% of children under age 18 lived in single-parent homes; in 2003, this figure rose to 26%. According to the 2003 U.S. Census, there are currently 12 million one-parent families.

[3]Postrelationship parenting is gendered. Demographers project that more than half of all children born in the 1990s will spend some time in a single-parent household and that five of every six single-parent households are headed by a mother (Demo, 2000). Nonmarried women currently head over 20% of families with children (U.S. Bureau of the Census, 2001).

[4]According to Kreider (2007), between 1970 and 1990 the proportion of children living only with their mother doubled from 11% to 22%. In 1960, father-absent families numbered 10 million in the United States; today, it stands at 24 million. Ironically, this historically unprecedented shift in family composition occurred at the same time the gender-neutral best-interest standard took effect.

Chapter 11  Single Family: Expanding Our Understanding

Tiffani Baldwin

What does this title mean? What is a single family? Does the term. "single family"create an image in your mind of a single person without children? A person who lives alone but has a wide circle of friends and relatives? For many, this term may provoke thoughts of one family unit and the characteristics that define its group membership. It may bring to mind a single parent and his or her children. Perhaps it conjures up images of a home, a single-family dwelling. Most of these images likely include at least two people and possibly several more. A single person living alone is not likely to be the first image or images that spring to mind.

Always-single adults (ASAs) are those who have never been married. In 2003, almost 52 million American adults had always been single (DePaulo, 2006; DePaulo & Morris, 2005). The numbers of ASAs in our society have steadily risen over the last three decades and are expected to continue rising (DePaulo & Morris, 2005). For the purposes of defining the single individual as conceptualized in this chapter, it is important to distinguish between those people who have never been married and those who are separated, divorced, or widowed. This difference will be discussed more fully later in the chapter. Scholars agree that changing demographic trends explain this increase in ASAs, with contemporary adults marrying later if at all (Barrett, 1999; Byrne & Carr, 2005; Gordon, 2003). As a result, the single person in our society is as likely to create family as those people who are coupled.

Traditionally, family has been considered to begin with at least two people—usually two heterosexual partners who eventually procreate. Family is also typically considered to consist of those people tied by either blood or law. However, as Braithwaite et al. (2010) suggest, the family of the 21st century is substantially more diverse and varied than traditional conceptualizations permit. Recent communication research has focused on such family forms as stepfamilies (Braithwaite, Toller, Daas, Durham, & Jones, 2008), adoptive families (Galvin, 2003), and gay, lesbian, bisexual, and transgendered families (Suter & Daas, 2007), to name just a few. This chapter argues that the family created by ASAs should be included in the exciting new research directions emerging from family communication.

The relationships that ASAs engage in may serve to create unique family constellations previously unknown and certainly understudied—and have the potential to add significantly to the knowledge of scholars studying both family communication and single adults. Family scholars are calling for more research into those family relationships that are not formed through blood or law (Braithwaite et al., 2010; Galvin, 2006). At the same time, singles researchers, primarily from the discipline of psychology, are advocating for an area of research they call "singleness studies" (Byrne & Carr, 2005). Single status can significantly impact a person's life on many levels—interpersonal relationships, finances, rights and privileges, as well as overall well-being and personal and family identity formation—yet very little is known about single individuals or what it means to be single in contemporary Western society. For these reasons, DePaulo and Morris (2005) suggest that this area will be a multidisciplinary field with various perspectives playing vital roles in the field's existence.

In this chapter, I assert the importance of merging these two fields of study by examining how ASAs create family. First, I address the notion of heteronormativity as well as the dominant Western ideals of marriage and family in terms of how they pertain to singles in Western society. The stigma created by these dominant ideologies leads to a discussion of some of the prejudice facing American singles, particularly in terms of interpersonal competence and relationships. Once it is established that singles are not lacking interpersonally, I examine ways in which we might begin to conceptualize the single adult's family.

As the following discussion will demonstrate, this chapter is theoretically rooted in social constructionism. Social construction is an interpretive theory that takes as its central concern how people make sense of and create meaning in their lives for themselves and for others (Leeds-Hurwitz, 2005). In order to do this, people use significant symbols, especially language, to produce social reality. Understanding reality in this way suggests that we learn how to behave through interaction with society and society's members. As a result, dominant ideologies tend to insinuate themselves within our own values and beliefs and impact the ways in which we live our lives.

Heteronormativity, Marriage, and Family

Heteronormativity is a powerful force in defining what is valued in American society (Jackson, 1996; Turner & West, 2006; Yep, 2003). "Heteronormativity describes an ideology that assumes heterosexual experience is the normal human experience" (Suter & Daas, 2007, p. 178). In other words, the dominant institutions, values, and practices of our culture are embedded in heterosexuality and tend to extol those who adhere to heterosexual norms and punish those who deviate from them. Further, Yep (2003) suggests not only that heteronormative practices harm those who are not heterosexual but also that heteronormativity is "harmful to a range of people across the spectrum of sexualities, including those who live within its borders" (p. 48). In this way, heteronormativity is damaging to the ASA who has chosen not to engage in the heterosexual norm of marriage.

Jackson (1996) contends that the primary institution of heteronormativity is marriage. In their research on singles, DePaulo and Morris (2005) describe the ideology of marriage and family in which "marriage and family are the interpersonal versions of the American dream" (p. 77). Those who do not follow that dream are perceived to be inferior to those who do. This ideology suggests that human beings have the need for one lasting (hetero)sexual partnership. This partnership is usually idealized as marriage and considered necessary to adult interpersonal success. In fact, Erik Erikson's developmental theory suggests that an important step in the transition to adulthood involves settling into an intimate relationship and beginning one's own family (Bukatko & Daehler, 2001). This family, usually conceptualized as two people—typically a man and a woman—joining together and procreating is the idealized developmental progression in our culture. In Western ideology, the marital relationship is the one true path to interpersonal and familial happiness and success.

Byrne and Carr (2005) suggest that always-single individuals are currently caught in a "cultural lag" (p. 84). They contend that the cultural ideology of marriage has not caught up with the macrosocial changes occurring in our culture (i.e., people choosing to marry later if at all). Put another way, ideals of marriage as the gateway to adulthood and happiness are still in practice despite the changing demographic structure of our nation. This likely results in the perpetuation of stigmas surrounding ASAs and their interpersonal worth, as will be discussed below.

One of the implicit assumptions behind the dominant marriage and family ideology is that those people who choose not to follow this ideology are of less interpersonal worth (DePaulo, 2006). Society holds negative views of single adults, and many of these views involve a single person's ability to create, develop, and maintain interpersonal relationships. Common (mis)perceptions of single adults are that they lack social and interpersonal skills, in turn resulting in fewer social relationships (Barrett, 1999; DePaulo, 2006). As a result, society tends to view ASAs of the marrying age and beyond as lonely, isolated, and even deviant (DePaulo, 2006; Gordon, 2003). The assumption is that people who are not married are not married because of personal attributes. In other words, society tends to view a person who is not married as having traits that make him or her unworthy of marriage (DePaulo, 2006).

Heteronormativity and dominant ideologies dictate norms in our culture that are slow to change despite demographic trends (Byrne & Carr, 2005). Below, some of the negative effects of these dominant ideologies on ASAs will be explored.

Single Adults and Stigma

According to various scholars, the single-adult identity is impacted and stigmatized through the very definition of their status (DePaulo & Morris, 2005; Gordon, 2003). In describing always-single individuals as "unmarried" or "never married," they are defined by a relationship that they do not have. In other words, they are defined in terms of a deficit model, or as something in which they are lacking. DePaulo and Morris (2005) consider this description of singles unusual, as "it is singlehood that comes first and is then undone (if it is undone) by marriage" (p. 58). They pose a logical question: why aren't married people called "unsingle"?

In keeping with DePaulo and Morris's (2005) assertion, research demonstrates that there is a societal stigma against single people (DePaulo, 2006; Gordon, 2003). In fact, in her book *Singled Out: How Singles Are Stereotyped, Stigmatized and Ignored, and Still Live Happily Ever After*, DePaulo (2006) argues that "singlism" pervades our society. Singlism refers to the often subtle stereotyping, discrimination, and mistreatment of individuals based on their single status. Although the mistreatment of singles appears to be relatively harmless when contrasted with the psychological and physical violence that accompanies many other "-isms" in our society, it is a valuable source of study.

In past research, the term "single" often includes those individuals who have been previously married. In fact, most research on single adults is in comparison to married adults (with married adults typically being reported as healthier and happier). However, grouping ASAs with separated, divorced, and widowed adults paints an inaccurate picture of the ASA. There is often an important distinction between these different subcategories of single people, though much previous research has failed to make that distinction (DePaulo, 2006). This distinction is most easily understood in terms of the ideology of marriage and family. If a person was married in the past, they are automatically believed to have at least tried to adhere to dominant ideologies. The fact that they were once in a relationship, regardless of the reason for its current state, is enough to satisfy heteronormative ideals.

Much of the stigma surrounding singles involves their interpersonal competence and worth. For years, we have seen studies claiming the superiority of marriage over single life (DePaulo, 2006; Morris, DePaulo, Hertel, & Taylor, in press). DePaulo (2006) has systematically reviewed these studies and found that ASAs did not score significantly lower than married adults on such measures as well-being, life satisfaction, and social support. She and other scholars (DePaulo, 2006; DePaulo & Morris, 2005; Morris et al., in press) found that ASAs were often grouped with previously married individuals, bringing the overall single category score down. When taken separately, with only ASAs compared to married adults, ASAs consistently scored only slightly lower than married adults.

Scholars suggest that a possible reason always-single people score only slightly lower than married people on well-being measures is because of a strong social network that ASAs have spent most of their lives building. Research on singles suggests that a variety of relationships can provide the same benefits, maybe more, than one primary romantic relationship (Barrett, 1999; Byrne & Carr, 2005; DePaulo & Morris, 2005). These relationships include extended family, friends, coworkers, and neighbors. Clark and Graham (2005) contend that "focusing clearly on relationship issues of importance to singles lead us to new and important research. Such research ... is likely not only to advance our understanding of the lives of singles but also to be more generally informative about relationship processes" (p. 134).

Although research suggests that ASAs tend to have strong social networks that they have built throughout their adult lives, no studies were uncovered that examined how these networks may serve to help the single adult construct family. Exploring the communication factors that impact the creation and maintenance of these relationships is critical to understanding the single adult's place in family communication. But why should the single adult have a place in family communication? As this chapter purports, a person who spends their life single is just as likely to create family as those people who couple. Below, I explore conceptualizations of how nontraditional families are formed and their relevance for studying how singles create family.

Family

Floyd, Mikkelson, and Judd (2006) remind us that families provide "a host of vital roles ... in human well-being" (p. 21). How we define who our family is and how we conceptualize our family identity is important to defining who we are and how we negotiate our own personal identity. Traditional and even expanded notions of family often do not acknowledge ASAs without children. How, then, does this impact the well-being and identity of the ASA? Does the ASA not have a family? Does his or her only possibility for family come from his or her family of origin? What if that family no longer exists or is estranged for whatever reason?

Family scholars agree that defining family has become increasingly difficult (Koerner & Fitzpatrick, 2002; Turner & West, 2006). Traditionally, families have been described as potentially procreative, multigenerational, and dependent on bloodlines and genetics. In the last two decades, however, scholarship in family studies has expanded these widely held notions of family to include extended, step and blended, gay and lesbian, aging, biracial, and at-risk families (Turner & West, 2006). The discipline has traversed unexplored and often controversial terrain in these expansions and pried open the traditionally narrow definitions of family. As a result, one definition of family is hard to articulate.

Turner and West (2006) define family as "a self-defined group of intimates who create and maintain themselves through their own interactions with others; a family may include both voluntary and involuntary relationships; it creates both literal and symbolic internal and external boundaries; and it evolves through time: It has a history, a present, and a future" (p. 9). In defining intentional families, Koerner and Fitzpatrick (2002) state that a family is "a group of intimates who generate a sense of home and group identity and who experience a shared history and a shared future" (p. 71). Although these definitions are broad and appear all-encompassing, this chapter argues that they are not sufficiently expansive to allow for the family that an ASA without children might create.

The ASA may consider several different people family, but there may not be interdependence between those people. For example, Jody thinks of her two closest friends, Anne and Yvonne, as sisters. This is reciprocal in that Anne and Yvonne also consider Jody as a sister. However, though Anne and Yvonne know each other, they would not consider one another to be family. Therefore, while Anne and Yvonne help to form Jody's family identity, they do not help to form each other's. Together, the three of them do not constitute a group of interdependent intimates.

Literature on voluntary kin and discourse dependency can begin to create space for the conceptualization of family as created by the ASA. This literature extends and expands previous work on families of choice and wider families. Weston (1991) studied gay and lesbian families and suggests that families we choose are "organized through ideologies of love, choice, and creation" (p. 27). Love is suggested as both the necessary and the sufficient criterion for determining family. In addition, wider families are conceptualized as voluntary and fluid (Marciano & Sussman, 1991). Both types of family provide instrumental, emotional, and social support to their members. Although they may include kinship members, they may also exist without them (Marciano, 1991). Especially pertinent to this chapter, they allow for the creation of a family that is not dependent on primary units of two or more.

Marciano and Sussman (1991) refer to the notion that single "families are 'made' out of other affectionate and service-providing groupings" (p. 5). Weston (1991) suggests that families we choose may be centered around the individual as opposed to relying on a dyad or group as the basic primary unit. In her study, she found that families of choice were "based on ties that radiated outward from individuals like spokes on a wheel" (p. 109). As the above example about Jody illustrates, the ASA may be the only individual determining his or her family membership. In other words, family ties would extend outward from the ASA but may not be tied to other members, rendering the creation of the ASA's family a highly independent endeavor.

Taking the ideas of wider families and families of choice further, Braithwaite et al. (2010) introduce the concept of voluntary kin. They chose the term "voluntary" in order to encompass all nonblood and nonlegal kin relationships and to exemplify "the breadth of family" represented in their study (p. 4). In addition, the term "voluntary" succinctly captures the voluntary nature that may underlie many nontraditional family constellations. As a result, voluntary kin is an ideal framework from which to conceptualize the ASA's family, which likely begins with one person (the ASA) and radiates outward to members of their social network.

In order to study the relationships people describe as voluntary kin, it is important to understand the concept of discourse dependency. According to Galvin (2006), families that do not fit traditional definitions of family and kinship require much more identity work to assert and maintain individual and family identities. Such families that defy traditional definitions of family are said to be highly dependent on discourse. Certainly, all families experience and engage in some level of discursive identity construction; however, nontraditional family forms must rely heavily on discourse, or language, to create and maintain family identity boundaries. This identity boundary management is accomplished both internally (within family members) and externally (with people considered outsiders) and will be briefly explained below.

External boundary management includes labeling, explaining, legitimizing, and defending. *Labeling* refers to decisions made governing identification of family ties, titles, or positions when referring to family members to outsiders (e.g., through introductions). *Explaining* involves elaborating the labels and meanings of those labels for outsiders. In explaining, family members describe the meanings of labels and behaviors that constitute the family concept. *Legitimizing* occurs in direct response to a challenge to family identity. Family members engage in legitimizing when the genuineness of a family tie needs to be recognized by outsiders as a legitimate family link. *Defending* is a strategy taken by family members that seeks not to legitimize family bonds but rather to "shield oneself or a familial relationship from attack, justifying it, or maintaining its validity against opposition" (Galvin, 2006, p. 11).

Internal boundary management involves practices designed to maintain an internal sense of family within members. These practices include naming, discussing, narrating, and ritualizing. *Naming* describes the choices made in deciding on a name to give or to use for a family member. *Discussing* involves how family members engage in conversation about family issues pertaining to family identity. *Narrating* involves storytelling that aids in defining the family. Finally, *ritualizing* strategies involve the "doing" of family. Families use rituals to define the family through concrete behaviors. In discourse-dependent families, rituals can aid in feelings of closeness, a sense of membership, and family uniqueness.

Discourse dependency helps us understand the concept of voluntary kin in that those people who consider themselves family but are not related by blood or law must do extra linguistic work in order to create and maintain that sense of family. It is not inherent in the family form but must be talked into reality through family members. This may be especially pertinent to ASAs who may consider biological family members as family but may also include nonblood or nonlegal kin in their creation of family as well.

Braithwaite et al.'s (2010) work demonstrates a first glimpse of how voluntary kin are discursively negotiated. In their study, the researchers sought to determine how voluntary kin relationships are discursively represented given the fact that "there are no formal roles or expectations for the formation and enactment of voluntary kin relationships" (p. 6). The results show that study participants constructed their voluntary kin in four primary ways: (a) as substitute family, (b) as supplemental family,

(c) as convenience family, and (d) as extended family. These findings suggest that voluntary kin may serve as replacements to or, primarily, in addition to blood and legal kin.

Braithwaite et al.'s (2010) study underscores the importance of voluntary kin to those people engaging in voluntary kin relationships. In fact, the participants in this study "discussed voluntary kin as important sources of identity, belonging, and social support" (p. 21). As discussed previously, much of the stigma against singles includes negative perceptions of their identity and interpersonal worth. Examining the voluntary kin relationships of singles can serve to both debunk some of these myths and expand our current understanding of both family and ASAs.

Conclusion

At a time when the field of family communication is acknowledging and investigating the variety of nontraditional family forms that are becoming common in Western society, it is important to include the family of ASAs in that venture. Examining the lives and experiences of single adults from a family perspective will add a rich and unique dimension to the field. Singles scholars theorize that single adults construct their own families and, like most adults, place high value on the social relationships in their lives (Byrne & Carr, 2005; DePaulo, 2006; Fingerman & Hay, 2002). However, no research was uncovered that focuses on this particular family constellation.

The ASA population is comprised of millions of Americans who, simply by their single status, are stigmatized for not following the outdated ideologies that much of Western society still abides by. Relatively unknown is how the single adult creates family. The fact that ASAs may create a family that is centered on the individual needs to be explored further in order to paint a more complete picture of what it means to be single and part of a family in today's society. Using voluntary kin and discourse dependency as frameworks can significantly enhance this field of study and bring deeper understanding to both understudied family forms and the lives of ASAs, thus potentially enriching the lives of the millions of ASAs in Western society.

Discussion Questions

1. How do you define a family?
2. How do heteronormativity and traditional ideology regarding marriage and family impact your definition of family?
3. Do you agree or disagree that a single person without children can create a family? Have your views changed since reading this chapter? How?
4. Is it important for always-single adults to be considered as capable of creating a family form? Why or why not?
5. What are ways that single individuals in our society have been stigmatized or discriminated against?

References

Barrett, A. E. (1999). Social support and life satisfaction among the never married. *Research on Aging, 21*(1), 46.

Braithwaite, D. O., Toller, P. W., Daas, K. L., Durham, W. T., & Jones, A. C. (2008). Centered but not caught in the middle: Stepchildren's perceptions of dialectical contradictions in the communication of co-parents. *Journal of Applied Communication Research, 36,* 33-55.

Braithwaite, D. O., Wackernagel-Bach, B., Baxter, L. A., DiVerniero, R., Hammonds, J., Nunziata, A. M., Willer, E. K., & Wolf, B. M. (2010). Constructing family: A typology of voluntary kin. *Journal of Social and Personal Relationships, 27*(3),388-407.

Bukatko, D., & Daehler, M.W. (2001). *Child development: A thematic approach.* Boston: Houghton Mifflin.

Byrne, A., & Carr, D. (2005). Caught in the cultural lag: The stigma of singlehood. *Psychological Inquiry, 16*(2-3), 84-91.

Clark, M. S., & Graham, S. M. (2005). Do relationship researchers neglect singles? Can we do better? *Psychological Inquiry, 16*(2), 131-136.

DePaulo, B. M. (2006). *Singled out: How singles are stereotyped, stigmatized, and ignored, and still live happily ever after.* New York: St. Martin's Press.

DePaulo, B. M., & Morris, W. L. (2005). Singles in society and in science.*Psychological Inquiry, 16*(2-3), 57-83.

Fingerman, K. L., & Hay, E. L. (2002). Searching under the streetlight?: Age biases in the personal and family relationships literature.*Personal Relationships, 9*(4), 415-433.

Floyd, K., Mikkelson, A.C., & Judd, J. (2006). Defining the family through relationships. In L.H. Turner & R. West (Eds.), *The family communication sourcebook* (pp. 21-39). Thousand Oaks, CA: Sage.

Galvin, K. M. (2003). International and transracial adoption: A communication research agenda. *Journal of Family Communication, 3,* 237-253.

Galvin, K. M. (2006). Diversity's impact on defining the family: Discourse-dependence and identity. In L.H. Turner & R. West (Eds.), *The family communication sourcebook* (pp. 3-19). Thousand Oaks, CA: Sage.

Gordon, P. A. (2003). The decision to remain single: Implications for women across cultures. *Journal of Mental Health Counseling, 25*(1), 33.

Jackson, S. (1996). Heterosexuality as a problem for feminist theory. In L. Adkins & V. Merchant (Eds.), *Sexualizing the social: Power and the organization of sexuality* (pp. 15-34). New York: St. Martin's Press.

Koerner, A. F., & Fitzpatrick, M. A. (2002). Toward a theory of family communication.*Communication Theory, 12*(1), 70-91.

Leeds-Hurwitz, W. (2005). Social theories: Social constructionism and symbolic interactionism. In D. O. Braithwaite & L. A. Baxter (Eds.), *Engaging theories in communication: Multiple perspectives* (pp. 229-242). Thousand Oaks, CA: Sage.

Marciano, T. D. (1991). A postscript on wider families: Traditional family assumptions and cautionary notes. *Marriage and Family Review, 17*(1-2), 159-171.

Marciano, T. D., & Sussman, M. B. (1991). Wider families: An overview. *Marriage and Family Review, 17*(1-2), 1-8.

Morris, W. L., DePaulo, B. M., Hertel, J., & Taylor, L. C. (in press). Singlism—Another problem that has no name: Prejudice, stereotypes, and discrimination against singles. In T. G. Morrison & M. A. Morrison (Eds.), *The psychology of modern prejudice.* Hauppauge, NY: Nova Science Publishers.

Suter, E. A., & Daas, K. L. (2007). Negotiating heteronormativity dialectically: Lesbian couples' display of symbols in culture. *Western Journal of Communication, 71*(3), 177-195.

Turner, L. H., & West, R. (2006). *Perspectives on family communication* (3rd ed.). New York: McGraw-Hill.

Weston, K. (1991). *Families we choose: Lesbians, gays, kinship.* New York: Columbia University Press.

Yep, G. (2003). The violence of heteronormativity in communication studies: Notes on injury, healing, and queer world-making. *Journal of Homosexuality, 45*(2-4), 11-59.

Chapter 12

Speaking About Coupleness: Relational Roles in the Conversations of Gays and Lesbians

Brian L. Heisterkamp

Couples display signs indicating that they are together or are in a relationship through many forms of interaction. These displays of togetherness are often seen but unnoticed because of their routine, taken-for-granted nature. However, specific details of interaction coproduced by people indicate togetherness. Those details are the ways people "do" their relationships in public. As Fischer and Narus (1981) explain, "Relationships are interactive, interdependent and influenced by context, the situations in which they occur" (p. 452). Sexual orientation is also made available through the routine interactions that individuals produce (Land & Kitzinger, 2005). By examining interactional moments, a fuller understanding of relationships in general and same-sex relationship in particular may be specified.

Goffman's (1972) notion of "tie-signs" begins to provide an understanding of how couples produce the appearance of being a "with." Tie-signs are concerned with how people conduct themselves while together. Couples' conduct can contain evidence about their relationship. Goffman provides examples of tie-signs, such as hand holding, carrying a spouse's photograph in a wallet, or eating together in a restaurant. This explanation of tie-signs emphasizes that "withs" are achieved as interactional units rather than social-structural ones, such as "spouse" or "husband." During interaction, "two or more individuals present together have the right and duty to make some information generally available concerning their relationship" (p. 198). What interactants do that results in the perception of being a "with" or a couple becomes the question for study.

Perceptions of coupleness are often born out through the variety of roles associated with being in a romantic relationship, whether gay/lesbian or heterosexual. Roles include actions associated with decision making, family providing work, household work, and sexual interaction, to name a few (Huston, 2000). Because these roles are common to being in a relationship, they routinely appear in the conversations of couples (Goldsmith & Baxter, 1996). The mere discussion of these roles, typically associated with a close relationship, exemplifies the existence of such a relationship between the individual involved. When the couple involves individuals of the same sex, not only is a same-sex relationship displayed, but also the division of tasks within the relationship is not assumed to be based on sex. The division of activities associated with being a same-sex couple must be negotiated because few models exist (Hicks, 2008).

Lack of gender role models in gay/lesbian couples creates the possibility for less rigidity in role enactment. While this lack of gender role models may point to the less likely adoption of unconventional gender roles, studies suggest that gays and lesbians are more flexible in their behavior (Julien, Arellano, & Turgeon, 1997). Research proposes that gays and lesbians embrace flexibility in the gendered ways they describe themselves (Julien et al., 1997). For example, gay men were just as likely to describe themselves in conventionally masculine ways as they were to describe themselves as having traditionally feminine characteristics (Kurdek, 1987). Gay and lesbian couples were more likely to allocate household chores based on interest and specialization rather than on fixed roles (Kurdek, 2007). Gay and lesbian parents are also thought to engage in "degendered parenting" because personal choice and fairness rather than gender were likely to guide their division of household labor (Biblarz & Savci, 2010).

An alternative to the essentialist approach, which suggests fixed gender roles, implies "being a man or woman socially is not a natural or inevitable outgrowth of biological features, but an achievement of situated conduct" (Ferree, 1990, p. 869). This "doing" rather than "being" perspective discards the categories of masculine and feminine and rejects the expectation that gender is a stable trait in order to open broad questions for researchers in the communication discipline interested in gender (House & Dallinger, 1998). This perspective, proposed by West and Zimmerman (1987, 2009), suggests that gender is not something one is but rather something people do recurrently in interaction with others. By rebuking the notion that gender involves a set of behaviors couched into "interactional situations to produce recognizable enactments of masculinity and femininity," West and Zimmerman (1987) indicate that gender is not a regimented set of behaviors associated with one role or another but rather an emergent feature of social situations (p. 135). As suggested by Thompson and Walker (1989), this perspective enables researchers to view gender as something "evoked, created, and sustained day-by-day through interactions among family members" (p. 865).

Richer data are available for examining the interactions of intimate couples through the use of microbehavioral data rather than macrobehavioral data (Huston, 2000). This social constructionist perspective suggests that relationships are constituted in communication practices with the idea that communication constructs our social world, including our personal relationships (Baxter, 2004). Relationships and the roles we play through those relationships are constructed and can be examined by researchers through close examination of talk (Mandelbaum, 2003). As relationships are discussed, so too are matters relevant to sexual orientation and gender. Mundane discussions about roles related to work, decision making, and sexual interaction potentially convey social meanings about relationships in general and sexual orientation or gender in particular (Ferree, 1990).

Aim of This Chapter

Gays and lesbians may display gendered behavior flexibility when in the company of other gays and lesbians because such company provides a context of permissibility and social support (Fischer & Narus, 1981). When gender is not viewed from an essentialist perspective and isolated as a discrete role, researchers can explore how "gender interacts with roles such as partner, provider, homemaker, parent" (Thompson & Walker, 1989, p. 865). West and Zimmerman (1987) explain that we presume that others make their sex category available in the most decisive fashion possible so that it can be recognized, perhaps at a glance. The same can be said for relationship status (Pomerantz & Mandelbaum, 2005) and sexual orientation. Consequently, the aim of this chapter is to identify conversational activities indicative of coupleness while at the same time considering the gender and sexual orientation implications of couples' conversations.

Methodological Approach

The data examined here are from a corpus of materials involving gay and lesbian couples interacting during routine events, such as eating dinner (Table 12.1). The tapes were transcribed to first pass (words only), and then smaller sections of analytic interest were fully transcribed using conventional Jefferson notation (Hutchby & Wooffitt, 1998). The transcriptions were analyzed using discourse-analytic techniques, which treat the occurrence of ordinary activities in everyday life as problematic (Hutchby & Wooffitt, 1998; Wood & Kroger, 2000). The process involves repeated readings of the transcripts and viewings of the video recordings. Through the examination of ordinary talk details, discourse analysis seeks to uncover how conversationalists accomplish the activities of ordinary interaction. The analysis focuses on discussions involving couple role activities, including sexual interaction, decision making, household work, and so on. The extracts presented are from the larger data corpus and were selected to develop the primary analytic issue.

Table 12.1 Description of Video Recordings

Video Title	Video Length	Couples Involved
Three Gay Male Couples for Dinner	1 hour, 33 minutes	Nate and Tom Anton and Chris John and Matt
Lesbians for Dinner	15 minutes	Anton and Chris Chanda and Sarah Sandra and Lisa
Dinner with the Neighbors	1 hour, 32 minutes	Anton and Chris Mark and Dave Sandra and Lisa

Enacting Couple Roles

When couples talk about various roles in their relationships, there is often a link between that role and the couple's particular relationship category (Pomerantz & Mandelbaum, 2005). Thus, references to the roles, such as provider–providee, may be intertwined with particular relationship categories. As couples discuss roles associated with work, sexual activity, and decision making, they also make available for analysis their relationship category, sexual orientation, or gender because such discussions constitute the very categories being discussed.

Work

One topic of discussion for couples when they interact with others involves their work life, which includes work outside the home related to a career or work around the home, such as housecleaning, grocery shopping, or preparing meals. In the following extract, Lisa is responding to a question from Chris regarding the division of labor between herself and her partner Sandra.

Extract 1: "Dinner with the Neighbors"

1. Chris: =Now is that because like you're the one in schoo:l
2. °she's the one that's working °
3. Is that part of it too?↓
4. Lisa: No (.) I think the food thing is because I'm the one that cooks
5. and (.) Sandra is
6. She could (.) go without food for 16 weeks

```
 7.              [And she couldn't give a shit
 8. Mark:       [Ha ha (.) no::
 9. Sandra:     But so she knows wh- what we have [and what we need and I don't kno:w
10. Chris:                                        [what to get and that stuff
11. Lisa:       Well you could kno:w (.) [if you wanted to know
12. Anton:                               [Ha ha ha ha ha
13. Lisa:       But you choose not to know
```

In the above interaction, the couples discuss who is primarily responsible for household tasks, specifically grocery shopping. Lisa indicates responsibility for cooking because her partner Sandra could "go without food for 16 weeks." Sandra supports Lisa's statement by pointing to the fact that Lisa "knows what we have." In response, Lisa suggests that Sandra "could know" but chooses not to know. Lisa indicates that she cooks and grocery shops but also suggests that Sandra could choose to engage in those activities.

By calling attention to these activities, Lisa displays her placement in the roles of grocery shopper and cook. At the same time, she rejects her sole placement into those roles by pointing out that Sandra "could know" what is needed to grocery shop for the couple. Lisa both indicates her position in this role and rejects the idea that those duties are hers alone. Both partners could potentially share in these tasks rather than assigning them exclusively to one partner, indicating the possibility of flexibility in role enactment.

Relational phenomena, such as household division of labor, are located in this talk to the extent that Lisa and Sandra identify themselves as fulfilling certain roles. Lisa discusses her role activities and suggests that her partner could also engage in those activities. Either partner can engage in certain activities regardless of traditional notions of that role. In terms of sexual orientation or gender, the partners make their same-sex couplehood commonsensically and linguistically relevant when each refers to her cocouple member as "she" (lines 6 and 9); however, their sexual orientation and gender are not developed as interactionally relevant. For example, neither partner ties her division of household labor to either sexual orientation or gender. Rather, they account for their division of labor based on Sandra's disinterest in food.

Sexual Activity

The discussion of sexual activity between partners is one of the clearest markers of the existence of a relationship between two individuals. While a couple's sexuality is routinely a private activity, occasionally it becomes the topic of public discourse. Partners may conversationally portray their role in the couple's sexual relationship in terms of sexual appetite, initiation, and experimentation. In the following discussion of sexuality, Sandra discusses the possibility of her sexual appetite increasing in her relationship with Lisa.

Extract 2: "Dinner with the Neighbors"
```
 1. Sandra:    So like if all the sudden (.2)
 2.            I became a- the horn dog
 3.            Then she would probably =
 4. Lisa:      =be happy (.2) Oh wait
 5. Chris:     Ha ha [ha ha
 6. Lisa              [ha ha ha
 7. Sandra:    She'd probably be
 8.            You know would
```

9.   That would like [switch our roles
10. Lisa: [Like no no no no no
11. Sandra   I mean this is the theory any way

Sandra mentions that becoming a "horn dog" would be a change for her. As Sandra begins hypothesizing about Lisa's reaction to her becoming a "horn dog," Lisa completes the utterances by indicating that she would "be happy." Sandra portrays herself as the partner with a lesser need for sexual interaction, and Lisa portrays herself as potentially happy with a partner who has a higher need for sexual interaction. Lisa suggests that both partners could be "horn dogs." However, Sandra's idea of "switching" roles implies that only one partner enacts the role of having a higher sexual appetite. Here, both the idea that partners have complementary roles in terms of sexual appetite and similar roles are portrayed.

These interactions show both the fluidity of behavior in terms of sexuality and the possibility of partners sharing in the behaviors conventionally associated with a particular relational role. Neither sexual orientation nor gender is displayed to account for their different sexual appetites. Sandra and Lisa's status as a same-sex, female couple is linguistically referenced through Sandra's use of "she" (lines 3 and 7), but sexual orientation is not interactionally built to account for their sexual appetite. Indeed, the mere construction of sexual roles displays their relationship generally, but nothing specific accounts for the state of those roles.

Decision Making

Couples make a variety of decisions ranging from the serious (e.g., relocating for a partner's job) to the mundane (e.g., what to eat for dinner). By discussing their decision making, the partners show themselves as a couple. In the following extract, Matt and John converse about alcohol consumption and membership in Alcoholics Anonymous.

Extract 3: "Three Gay Male Couples for Dinner"
1. Matt: They're all in Tennessee, (1.0)
2.   but none of my °parent are in t::he program°
3. Chris: You're not are you?

4. Matt: No, I'm not (1.0) [although I don't]
5. John: He'[s under my contr]ol.
6. Anton: Hah hah hah hah
7. Matt: I don't drink because he doesn't want me to
8. °so (1.0) I haven't drink in ahh year and a half.°
9. John: There's nothing wrong with that.
10. Anton: There's no control issues going on here (.2) huh.
11. Chris: Ha ha ha ha ha

In this exchange, Matt explains that neither he nor his parents are in the "program" (i.e., Alcoholics Anonymous). As Matt begins to discuss his own alcohol consumption, his partner John explains that the reason Matt does not drink is because he is under "my control." Matt confirms this when he states that he does not drink because John does not "want" him to drink. Anton then comments that "no control issues" are going on between Matt and John, noting the apparent contradiction of the expectation that individuals make certain decisions, such as whether to drink alcohol, on their own. In associating himself with controlling his partner, John affixes the role of decision maker on himself. At the same time, Matt becomes the controlled partner in the relationship.

Both sexual orientation and gender are constructed linguistically in this interaction through the use of John's "he's" (line 5) and Matt's "he" (line 7), commonsensically indicating both are men in a same-sex relationship. While neither sexual orientation nor gender accounts for Matt's conforming to John's desire for him not to drink, their relationship provides such an accounting. As Matt begins providing an account for why he does not drink, John answers in overlap (line 5) by indicating that Matt is under his control. Several aspects point to a romantic relationship. First, the individual himself presumably makes the decision regarding whether to drink alcohol. Considering that both men are adults, John's desire for Matt not to drink is more likely one expressed in a romantic relationship, not in, for example, a friendship. In addition, the idea that one could control another is salient to a romantic relationship rather than another relationship type occurring between two adult men. While John's utterance is taken as playful by Anton (line 10) and Chris (line 11), the idea of one controlling another is still expressed. Finally, Matt provides a full explanation by commenting, "I don't drink because he doesn't want me to" (line 7). This account suggests that the relationship is the reason for Matt's decision not to drink alcohol, but beyond that, neither Matt nor John suggest why the decision was made.

Presentation of Partner

An outcome of discussing one's romantic partner is the presentation of a certain identity for him or her, either positive or negative. A concept developed by Goffman (1955) and refined by Brown and Levinson (1987), face work provides some guidance in understanding interactions when couples are actively engaged in portraying their partners. Face is the "positive social value a person effectively claims for himself [or herself] by the line others assume he [or she] has taken during a participant contact" (Goffman, 1955, p. 213). When a person's face is lost or threatened, counteractions are undertaken (Ting-Toomey & Kurogi, 1998). Face-negotiation theory suggests that people can be concerned with one's own image, another's image, or the image of both parties or a relationship (Ting-Toomey & Kurogi, 1998). Concern for a partner's face is important to different types of relationships (friendship vs. romantic relationships) and different developmental stages of a relationship (Wilson, Kunkel, Robson, Olufowote, & Soliz, 2009). The following interaction illustrates the concept of partners portraying the face of their significant other. The next extract begins with Matt responding to a question regarding his occupation.

Extract 4: "Three Gay Male Couples for Dinner"
1. Matt: I sa:y I'm a writer=
2. John: =Don't let him <f:o:o:l y:o:u>. He watches soap operas
3.   Which I got hooked into.
4. Matt: O:h (.) John you're the one who got me started on those
5.   I only wat:ched CBS

Matt responds to the question stating that he "says" he is a writer. Without any pause, John, Matt's partner, responds that Matt is fooling those present because Matt really "watches soap operas." John continues by stating that he was "hooked" into the same activity. In this interaction, Matt attempts to present himself in a relatively positive manner as a writer. His partner John, however, alters Matt's presentation, suggesting that Matt engages in a much less noteworthy activity, namely, watching soap operas.

Rather than offering a response suggesting endorsement of Matt's writing career, John relegates Matt to a soap opera–watching career. By not supporting Matt's statement that he is a writer, John also undermines Matt's endeavor to portray himself in a particular way. Additionally, John implies manipulation on Matt's part when he states that he became hooked on the same soap opera–watching activity. People hooked into doing something generally are not doing so voluntarily, suggesting some manipulation.

The following interaction, which also involves the portrayal of a speaker's significant other, includes Lisa discussing whether she would think Chris were gay when she first met him.

Extract 5: "Lesbians for Dinner"
1. Lisa: but if you said
2.   HI MY NAME IS CHRIS
3.   I would say (.2) now there's a tall straight man
4. Sandra: He he he
5. Anton: Or until he turned around and sw:ished away↑
6. All: (laughter)

In the above interaction, Lisa explains that she would believe that Chris was a "tall straight man" if he introduced himself in a loud, deep voice. After some laughter, Chris's partner Anton states that after Chris "swished away," he would be recognizable as gay. On the surface, Anton seemingly presents a negative image of his partner. Being recognized as gay would not seem to have negative consequences in an environment with all gay or lesbian individuals. Immediately prior to the above interaction, however, Lisa suggested that Anton was immediately recognizable as gay. Additionally, the ability to locate other gay/lesbian individuals in a nongay environment are common conversational topics among gay and lesbian individuals (Woolery, 2007).

Anton engages in a face-threatening act by calling into question Chris's ability to pass as nongay. These individuals construct both gender and sexual orientation as interactionally relevant. Lisa initially indicates that a man who states his name in a bold tone of voice (line 2) would be perceived as "straight." Her unstated alternative implies that gayness is marked by a softer tone of voice. Anton then provides a second characteristic of a male perceived as gay: swishing (line 5). Thus, a male with a bold tone of voice who does not "swish" is constructed as straight and able to pass. In addition, given Lisa's prior comment that Anton is easily identifiable as gay (not shown), Anton suggests competitiveness in terms of Chris's recognizability as gay surpassing his own. This interaction illustrates how the presentation of one's partner is another aspect of negotiating the actions associated with coupleness and how sexual orientation can be built more specifically than relational status as interactionally relevant.

Conclusions

This chapter presents some conversational displays of same-sex coupleness revealed through talk about various couple behaviors. From this social constructionist, discourse perspective, one can see these couples work through the creation of their relationships on a discursive, moment-by-moment basis. Primarily, what can be seen is the interactional relevance of their relationship and the linguistic construction of their gender and sexual orientation. The members of the couples present themselves in various roles involving behaviors associated with a romantic relationship, and those roles develop in conversations about the division of household labor, sexual appetite, and decision making. The interactions examined here illustrate the discussion of roles and specifically draws attention to how couples mark themselves as being in a close relationship.

Recall that these conversations took place in the private homes of gay and lesbian couples in the company of other gay and lesbian couples. This is a safe environment where one would not expect the couples to anticipate any homophobia. Additionally, because these couples know each other as couples, their explicit presentation as a couple would seemingly not be necessary. Nonetheless, the extracts examined here illustrate how individuals continue to make their identity available even to those who presumably already know that identity. By discussing aspects of their relationship, the interactants continue to build their relationship in this context.

Interpretations about the relationship that exist between these individuals emerge from the "legitimate jurisdiction" they display having over their partner (Mandelbaum, 2003). Discussing knowledge of a partner's sexual appetite and the effects that a change would have on the relationship points to a romantic relationship interpretation (extract 2). Similarly, stating an ability to control a partner's alcohol consumption suggests power over that individual. This leads to the interpretation that those interactants share a romantic relationship with one another. By discussing certain knowledge and power that they have over their partner, these interactants display a relationship easily interpreted as romantic. Overwhelmingly, these conversationalists construct their relationships, not their sexual orientation, as relevant to the interaction.

These interactions illustrate the delicacies involved in publicly crafting a relationship as couples determine what aspects will remain private versus what can be made public (Baxter, 2004). Aspects of these relationships may seem distressed. An indication that a partner's sexual appetite could be increased may indicate some conflict or dissatisfaction in the relationship (extract 2). Having one's career undermined by a partner would not seem to strengthen the relationship (extract 4). There are suggestions of either an undermining of the relationship or a problem with engaging in certain relational roles, even if they are as mundane as determining who does the grocery shopping.

Viewing relationships as being *in* communication provides an understanding that all developmental aspects of relationships occur in couples' communication. Notably, in these interactions, conflict does not ensue when comments are made regarding alternative ways in which the roles could be handled in the relationship. Rather, the couple and those present treat the interactions as play or humor, not as conflict or statements regarding dissatisfaction. By making these bold, potentially conflict invoking statements that are treated as play, the members of the couple affirm their ability to joke about the state of the roles in their relationship. By taking the risk of making light of certain aspects of their relationship, the couples affirm their togetherness and their ability to take such risks in the company of others.

Relationships-as-dialogue may also be understood in terms of the fluidity of gender roles in same-sex relationships. Others noted the benefits in terms of intimacy when both members are more androgynous than sex typed (Fischer & Narus, 1981). Rather than only indicating the presence of both masculinity and femininity, androgyny suggests behavioral flexibility and the ability to recognize the situational appropriateness of a given behavior (Fischer & Narus, 1981). Sex-typed individuals are more rigid and tend to behave primarily according to their sex role (Fischer & Narus, 1981). While not offering claims as to the self-reported sex roles of the individuals examined here, they do exhibit a similar fluidity in their couple role behaviors suggestive of the flexibility associated with androgyny. The whole complex of roles associated with a given masculine or feminine role is not given to the same person.

Discussion Questions

1. Provide several examples to illustrate the notion of "tie-signs."
2. This chapter claims that gender is something that is "evoked, created, and sustained day-by-day through interactions among family members." Do you agree with this theory? Why or why not?
3. Because gay and lesbian couples cannot allocate household chores based on gender roles, how do these couples typically negotiate the allocation of work?
4. Define "face-negotiation theory" and then give at least one example from your experience.

References

Baxter, L. (2004). Relationships as dialogues. *Personal Relationships, 11*(1), 1–22.

Biblarz, T., & Savci, E. (2010). Lesbian, gay, bisexual, and transgender families. *Journal of Marriage and Family, 72*(3), 480–497.

Brown, P., & Levinson, S. (1987). *Politeness: Some universals in language usage.* Cambridge: Cambridge University Press.

Ferree, M. M. (1990). Beyond separate spheres: Feminism and family research. *Journal of Marriage and the Family, 52,* 866–884.

Fischer, J. L., & Narus, L. R. (1981). Sex roles and intimacy in same sex and other sex relationships. *Psychology of Women Quarterly, 5*(3), 444–455.

Goffman, E. (1955). On face-work: An analysis of ritual elements in social interaction. *Psychiatry, 18,* 213–231.

Goffman, E. (1972). *Relations in public: Microstudies of the public order.* New York: Harper & Row.

Goldsmith, D. J., & Baxter, L. A. (1996). Constituting relationships in talk: A taxonomy of speech events in social and personal relationships. *Human Communication Research, 23*(1), 87-114.

Hicks, S. (2008). Gender role models ... who needs 'em?! *Qualitative Social Work, 7*(1), 43.

House, A., & Dallinger, J. M. (1998). Androgyny and rhetorical sensitivity: The connection of gender and communicator style. *Communication Reports, 11*(1), 11-21.

Huston, T. L. (2000). The social ecology of marriage and other intimate unions. *Journal of Marriage and the Family, 62*, 298-320.

Hutchby, I., & Wooffitt, R. (1998). *Conversation analysis: Principles, practices and applications*. Malden, MA: Polity Press.

Julien, D., Arellano, C., & Turgeon, L. (1997). Gender issues in heterosexual, gay and lesbian couples. In W. K. Halford & H. J. Markman (Eds.), *Clinical handbook of marriage and couples interventions*. New York: Wiley.

Kurdek, L. A. (1987). Sex role self schema and psychological adjustment in coupled homosexual and heterosexual men and women. *Sex Roles, 17*(9-10), 549-562.

Kurdek, L. A. (2007). The allocation of household labor by partners in gay and lesbian couples. *Journal of Family Issues, 28*(1), 132-148.

Land, V., & Kitzinger, C. (2005). Speaking as a lesbian: Correcting the heterosexist presumption. *Research on Language and Social Interaction, 38*(4), 371-416.

Mandelbaum, J. (2003). Interactive methods for constructing relationships. In P. Glenn, C. D. LeBaron, & J. Mandelbaum (Eds.), *Studies in language and social interaction: In honor of Rober Hopper* (pp. 207-219). Mahwah, NJ: Lawrence Erlbaum Associates.

Pomerantz, A., & Mandelbaum, J. (2005). Conversation analytic approaches to the relevance and uses of relationship categories in interaction. In K. L. Fitch & R. E. Sanders (Eds.), *Handbook of language and social interaction* (pp. 149-171). Mahwah, NJ: Lawrence Erlbaum Associates.

Thompson, L., & Walker, A. J. (1989). Gender in families: Women and men in marriage, work, and parenthood. *Journal of Marriage and the Family, 51*, 845-871.

Ting-Toomey, S., & Kurogi, A. (1998). Facework competence in intercultural conflict: An updated face-negotiation theory. *International Journal of Intercultural Relations, 22*(2), 187-225.

West, C., & Zimmerman, D. H. (1987). Doing gender. *Gender and Society, 1*(2), 125-151.

West, C., & Zimmerman, D. H. (2009). Accounting for doing gender. *Gender and Society, 23*(1), 112.

Wilson, S., Kunkel, A., Robson, S., Olufowote, J., & Soliz, J. (2009). Identity implications of relationship (re) definition goals: An analysis of face threats and facework as young adults initiate, intensify, and disengage from romantic relationships. *Journal of Language and Social Psychology, 28*(1), 32.

Wood, L. A., & Kroger, R. O. (2000). *Doing discourse analysis: Methods for studying action in talk and text*. Thousand Oaks, CA: Sage.

Woolery, L. (2007). Gaydar. *Journal of Homosexuality, 53*(3), 9-17.

"Not 16 Anymore": Identification Challenges of Teen Parents

Karen E. Cirulis

"Not 16 anymore," indeed. Wise beyond her years, "Ruby" articulates one of the simple truths of her story. Ruby is a 16-year-old high school sophomore. Cognitively, her grades and test scores indicate that she is well above average. Emotionally, she is perceptive, genuine, and courageous. Physically, she is a healthy, attractive teenager. Spiritually, she describes herself as a "believer," claiming that her "faith grounds her and gives her hope." Each of these characteristics will be crucial to Ruby's continued maturity and development, as she has recently learned that she is pregnant, and, like many other teen parents, she intuitively realizes that she is no longer an average 16-year-old—"not anymore, not like before."

Now shocked, scared, hopeful, angry, and worried, Ruby wisely realizes that her life is about to change. She will adjust to a future somewhat different than the one she and her family had envisioned. Ruby will be a teen parent; her journey will require extra focus and the love and commitment of many. No longer the center of her own universe, Ruby instead considers her responsibility to another and her recognized need for others. She will also need to rely on inner strength. The years ahead will challenge her, her family, and the new family that she will design.

Students are similar in more ways than not, yet each individual is unique in abilities, personalities, dreams, families, and so on. Life outside of school exists simultaneously along with the academic assignments in the classroom. None of us operates in a bubble, least of all teenagers. Those who become pregnant at this stage of development (cognitive, emotional, physical, and spiritual) immediately compound their developmental tasks. Focusing on the teen parent as a unique family unit is critical, as are the complexities, concerns, and challenges characterizing them.

Theoretical Consideration

The intent of this chapter is to consider the unique characteristics and challenges of becoming a teenage mother. "Family" (the family of origin, now including a teenager who becomes pregnant and decides to parent), the emerging "new family" (soon to be headed by an adolescent), and the system dynamics of those personalities, roles, developmental tasks, responsibilities, and purpose take on new dimensions and definitions.

Erik Erikson, a leading theorist in the field of life span development, defines developmental tasks common to stages throughout the human life cycle. Each age and stage of growth poses certain maturational tasks, prompting growth in identity, independence, and gradual autonomy (Santrock, 1995). Consider the cognitive, emotional, physical, and spiritual changes within an adolescent who is pregnant, *simultaneously* establishing her own "family unit" while balancing developmental tasks of adolescence and young adulthood. The teen parent thus exists in two often contradictory developmental stages. To remain physically, emotionally, academically, and socially stable while preparing for college or a career is challenging to any student. To do so while managing morning sickness, sleepless nights, sick children, financial needs, and day care can be crisis producing. The redefinition of roles in the teen's existing family can be tricky. Many innate challenges arise while accessing reputable resources or trusting community system support, such as federal and local societal agencies. These strategies are ongoing and must be managed if typical development of adolescent task completion will ensue.

A further aspect of life span theory recognizes that if a person does not fulfill the normative tasks of a particular stage, he or she eventually will return to those tasks, regardless of the timing, until mastery. Thus, the teen parent's developmental clock may become out of sync (Santrock, 1995). When a teen chooses to assume parental responsibilities while at the same time balancing the tasks of adolescent development, the importance of parents, families, schools, peers, resources, and agencies is crucial to the transition.

A pregnant or parenting teenager might automatically trigger several emotionally charged issues—premarital sex, contraception, abortion, adoption, economic stability, education, race, religion, politics, and so on. However, theory and principle pale when new reality is a loved one. Family roles change, responsibilities evolve, and developmental tasks transition in purpose and practice for the well-being of all—certainly including that of the baby.

Peer norms and societal expectations not only reflect but also dictate ultimate behaviors. The 21st-century family gives and receives messages of all kinds—especially regarding self-awareness and relationships. Adolescent girls who give up their own sense of empowerment may experience much angst, perhaps lasting far into adulthood. The power of peers, gossip, bullying, texting, and boundaryless social media can alter the very self-awareness sought.

Somehow, the adult in the teen parent emerges as he or she experiences choices, birthing experiences, parenting stories, graduations, ongoing relationships, and more. Changes are difficult for some to manage while pregnant and parenting in high school; a supportive community is crucial. Gone are the days when young pregnant women were sent out of town or forced to drop out of school. Perhaps the lives of young men as fathers-to-be have not evolved and remain double-standard strong. Opportunities for balance, growth, and mastery are most helpful at this time of a new family's life.

Mary Pipher (2001) relates how tough our society can be on adolescent girls. Pipher encourages the need to strengthen their emotional toughness and support systems. She further references a poem by Joseph Malines (1936) about a town at the top of a cliff whose townspeople kept falling off. The town magistrates debate whether to build a fence at the top of the cliff to keep people from falling off or to put an ambulance at the bottom to rescue them—the ongoing "treatment-versus-prevention" dilemma. It is critical for society to perform both, especially when dealing with adolescents. The teen parent, along with the awareness and support of others, needs stability while performing multiple roles in various life span developmental stages while, it is hoped, remaining healthy, receiving an education, and continuing to stabilize relationships with self and others.

Pipher (2001) further likens teen girls to the Shakespeare's Ophelia in *Hamlet*. Ophelia eventually dies because she could not grow—she was always the object of other peoples' lives. A teen girl moves from being a member of a peer group considering prom, clothes, and school grades to one managing pregnancy, delivering a baby, and parenthood—all within a few months. Sometimes this lack of self can be symbolized in what could be referred to as a "stuffed-animal syndrome" wherein the baby becomes an extension of the teen's self, the adolescent finding so much consolation and purpose from the baby that his or her individual development may be stifled.

Another phrase often referencing teen parents is "kids having kids." Abraham Maslow's (1943) hierarchy of human needs underlies support of adolescents. The baby is ultimately without the support of a strong parent if that parent's development flounders. Consider the analogy of the "oxygen masks on the plane." Parents are instructed to first give themselves oxygen before providing masks to children traveling in their care. These "kids having kids" need the "oxygen," or developed skills, first to save themselves as well as future generations. Learning about themselves; child development; family changes; parenting; day care selection; medical, nutritional, legal, and financial resources; child care and pediatric expertise; social service programs; and more is critical to the survival of the family unit. Focusing on the dual roles of an adolescent while also operating in an adult role can result in healthy maturation for all involved. It is not easy, but it is effective—indeed, not 16 anymore, Ruby.

Power of the Individual

To be sure, developmental challenges and emotions experienced by any teenager run the gamut; that is also true of a teen parent and his or her family systems. For the purposes of this topic, "self-centeredness" differs from "selfishness," particularly during adolescence. The reality is that adolescents must make powerful decisions—choices and consequences that will impact their lives and futures and those of their families forever. Although opinions vary relative to the entire concept of teen parenting, each entity—the pregnant girl; the baby's father; their families; schools; day care centers; charities and grant-based support systems; cultural groups; medical care; socioeconomic, legal, and religious entities; and the *baby itself*—has its own perspective.

While asking a teenager parent-to-be, "Who is your support system? Who will be there for you, no matter what?," responses (or lack of them) can be telling. The answers often reflect the development of the teen and his or her family. Honest communication with parents has always been crucial—perhaps now even more so. It is hoped that nature and nurture, along with maturation and experience (Santrock, 1995), occur together to underscore health and safety, stability, and education. An empowered individual in a supportive family is the goal.

Much like Elisabeth Kübler-Ross's (1969) well-known five stages of grief, teen pregnancy might reflect a certain grief process for all family members. A range of emotions, including shock and disbelief, bargaining, anger, depression, and acceptance, can accompany the pregnancy of anyone–consider the genuine complexity of dynamics in adolescence.

A primary developmental struggle of teens is *dependence versus independence* (Santrock, 1995), thus impacting other generations. Maturational tasks can overwhelm any adolescent and influence the family system, school, medical community, social services, and society in general. Blame is wasted. Guilt can paralyze. Anger can further displace. Indeed, the dynamics experienced by adolescent parents and their families can be many.

One cannot consider teen parenting (or much else in adolescence) without focusing on resilience. What makes a someone like Ruby resilient? Before some teens are even into abstract, logical, and formal operational thought, they are parenting. Just because there is a baby growing inside a womb does not guarantee a maturing effect, yet it often has an extraordinarily empowering effect. Linda Goldman (2006) observes that kids need encouragement, even one person who cares. It would appear that any teen parent electing to stay in school is automatically motivated to survive. Most of these individuals and families exhibit marked resilience.

Societal Consideration

The Centers for Disease Control and Prevention (2008) announced historically low numbers of infant births (367,752) recorded in 2010 to mothers between the ages of 15 and 19. However, the United States still ranks the highest in the industrialized world for teenage pregnancies. Teen pregnancy is the number one reason girls drop out of school. Since females often maintain child custody, the economic impact on their children will be multiplied (National Women's Law Center, 2007). Policymakers responded with Title IX and the Access to Education Act, wherein schools must give all students equal access to education. All states and agencies must create a plan to educate pregnant and parenting students. Statistics reveal that girls born to teen parents are nearly 33% more likely to become teen parents themselves (National Women's Law Center, 2007). Empowered schools, individuals, social groups, and families supportive of teen parent families are critical contributors.

It is fair to note an adverse opinion that adolescents who choose to parent could do better for themselves, their babies, and their extended families by focusing on one developmental stage or another—either be a teenager in high school or be a young mother, just don't try to do both. Alternative options, such as independent study programs, are available in most districts. Excellent therapies, health and pregnancy counseling, community counselors, social workers, clergy, day care centers, and school and community resources are available and can help lead one to "a new normal" (Kübler-Ross, 1969). Time, experience, and success remain as great teachers to individuals and families alike.

A corresponding topic pertinent to this chapter is that of adoption. Reputable, supportive agencies in many communities welcome the responsibility and trust involved in that decision. An evident concern is the apparent misunderstanding of many students regarding adoption versus foster care. Adoption and foster care are not the same. Healthy options for all must be made.

"Mary" is another outstanding young woman committed to education. A daughter of immigrant parents, Mary wanted a high school diploma "more than anything!" Her dream was to eventually become a physician. However, she had recently become pregnant and was told by her parents that she would now be on her own with her new husband. The family's practiced religion required that they be married; besides, two more mouths to feed was "impossible" for her parents to manage. Again, the family, in its presence or absence, is critical to all. Mary's family of origin soon moved to another city to find work, and Mary and her new husband stayed. She was one motivated freshman; school attendance was no problem. Her husband was employed, and they did the best they could. But he had a temper; his poor anger management skills sometimes threatened Mary's safety and stability. Often, she would appear at school with a bruise or in tears. Abuse reports were filed with legal authorities by the school counselor and administration, though in those years a formal complaint of domestic violence needed to be submitted by the victim herself regardless of age or marital status—not likely in this case, especially as a young teen who was completely dependent on her husband and the father of her child. Today, law enforcement would respond differently; charges would be filed automatically.

Mary had personal fortitude, even stubbornness, and an unbelievable resilience; she was amazing (even puzzling) to many. Mary did not quit; she chose self-advocacy, education, and family. At graduation 4 years later, she posed for photos alongside her husband and their three children. Mary beamed tearfully as she proudly donned cap and gown, diploma in hand.

Power of the Group

Besides Ruby and Mary, there are many others. While education is a primary focus, considering the whole student in this process is essential. Some are children with adult lives, others seemingly just the opposite. Keeping the eyes on the prize of a diploma, via resilience, safety, and success, is the work of many. Many learning environments offer pertinent teen parenting curricular classes for credit. Through small-group intentional guidance, student assistant team meetings, and so on, students and families can effectively communicate and experience support. School counselors practice confidentiality through the concepts of (a) in loco parentis, (b) substantial interest and need to know, and (c) qualified privilege. As with all students, there is a special duty to exercise care in protecting a student's right to privacy; health and pregnancy and choices certainly require professionalism and judicious communication ("Ins and Outs of Ethics and Law," 2012).

Consider the following anonymous comments taken from a teen parenting in-class assignment:

> "The most important person in the world is my mother."
> "If only I could drive my car or get a good night's sleep."
> "I don't like vomiting every morning."
> "This year I hope to graduate with honors, and I will!"
> "I like teachers who don't put me down because I'm pregnant."
> "When I'm alone, I like to watch Disney movies."
> "I wish I could disappear."
> "My mom says my baby is a mistake."
> "I take pride in my son, and I know I'm a great mom."
> "It makes me angry when I think of my baby's dad."
> "I feel nervous when I hear people whisper."
> "I do care, but some days I'd rather hit everybody."
> "I wish I could go back in time before I got pregnant."
> "My baby is the best thing that ever happened to me, but this is hard."

Some of these comments are poignant, others playful. Clearly, the need exists for a strong developmental focus in supporting individuality and group concerns among teen parents, their families of origin, and their new families. The roller-coaster changes involved in many teen parents are stressful by nature, especially as experienced among other peer groups. Likewise, the tales of students helping each other cannot go unnoticed. Once a new student showed up in school and privately shared with a peer in her teen parenting class that she and her two children were out of food. That evening, another young woman in the class showed up at her door bearing infant formula. "Family" takes on a new definition, and "more than blood" means something else entirely.

The teen parent and family (including the existing family unit prior to the adolescent's pregnancy as well as the new subsystem soon to become parented by the adolescent) represent "more than blood" in its very existence. Individuals and families vary. Many factors impact interpersonal family communication platforms. How many multigenerational families in our society live together, easily communicate, and are mutually supportive? Although this may have been more common in previous generations, the encouragement to move out and be independent is a Western concept intended to assist in the maturation and socialization of the young adult. Supportive familial components within and around an extended multigenerational family can be very meaningful and powerful for all involved.

Family roles are flexible according to purpose and necessity. On occasion, teenagers' parents have punished, ceased responsibility, stopped the relationship, and severed ties in the event of a pregnancy. Some angry and disappointed parents in shock have told their daughters to leave home, move into the boy's house, and so on, but eventually emotions *usually* cool and families unite. In such fragile cases, social reporting systems have thus responded in kind, and minor students are then cared for by legal, social, and extended families. It is sometimes true that the physical presence of baby encourages feelings of acceptance and "family" communication reopens. Regardless, generations may continue to be affected in a variety of ways when a teen pregnancy occurs.

Meet "Cindy," a bright, distractible "will-o'-the-wisp" whose mother had died prior to Cindy's freshman year. As the firstborn daughter of her family, she exhibited resilience in a rather confrontational manner, accompanying it with humor, sarcasm, and even a certain charm. Perhaps there exists a correlation of a student in early to mid-adolescence who experiences the death of a close family member and being potentially vulnerable to the possibility of a later unplanned pregnancy. Literature dealing with grief references loss during adolescence as a fragile time to reaffirm life and its purpose, sometimes influencing its accompanying risks. Suffice it to say that Cindy was affected by "life's unfairness." Cindy recognized the importance of building the kind of life that she and her mom had dreamed for her, "without babies until the time was right." However, she and her boyfriend chose to parent their much-loved son. She chose to become a good mother in the absence of having her own mother in her life. Yet struggles and joys of all kinds ensued. To cope with the challenges, Cindy wrote tender poetry as an emotional release in times of her loneliness. Her poetry was as genuine as she was. Cindy was able to graduate from high school and later college despite the difficult circumstances of her adolescence.

Along with all parental relationships, the role of significant adult women in the lives of teen parents is noteworthy. It may be confirmed that a female teen parent can most assuredly benefit from supportive, trustworthy, and respected female role models. Likewise, a male teen parent can benefit from the positive mentoring and modeling of a respectful, committed, mature male role. Family roles and individual personalities impact each and every family dynamic, and the ensuing stories eventually play out. As stated in Robert Frost's (1915) poem *The Death of the Hired Man*, "one can always go home to *family*—it's where they have to take you in." Crises tend to ultimately bring the best and the worst out of all. Unfortunately, teen pregnancy might also be blamed as the "straw that finally broke this family's back," and fragmentation or divorce may occur.

Final Considerations

Each of us has some form of "family" that contributes or indeed impacts our lives. Families, too, not only reflect the society in which they exist but also project behaviors, beliefs, and values back into that culture. Genetic DNA is surely contributive to a family, but it can also be anything *but* a "family maker," and the term "parenting" indicates so much more than just what follows pregnancy and birthing. Very often, in any society and with all ages concerned, it is the "more-than-blood" components that powerfully contribute to "family making." Neighborhoods, charities, churches, foundations, day care centers, medical teams, community agencies, social services, and school systems might ultimately perform as *perfect* extensions (not substitutes for) of "family members." In the lives of teen parents, the importance of blood and more-than-blood support systems, "family" support, cannot be overstated. No two teen parents' stories are the same; no two families are the same. The power of *one* reigns supreme, but the power of *a few* in support of each other and of the children can be crucial to this population in particular. Making a positive difference in the life of a teen parent can impact generations.

Adolescence is a time of change and challenge, a favorite of many (this author included) though not an easy stage of development. Therefore, does the teen parent represent a "family at risk," a "family to be at risk," or both? Inviting and involving the support of all extended family members is critical to the success and health of all involved. Ruby, Mary, and Cindy all shared similar stories with emphases in resilience. Yet each young woman was unique. Investments of time and attention can accrue to the benefit of *all* family members.

For the purposes of this chapter, "more than blood suggests all family systems that surround pregnant or parenting teens. These unique families can be powerful when comprised of focused, resilient others. Loving, capable, and promising teen parents are capable of surviving and thriving; they have done so throughout the ages. Defining future generations based on choices made by its members, at any age, can be daunting. If challenges are honestly acknowledged and encouragement exists, all families can benefit. Societal tensions need not overpower the reality of a developing family, including multiple generations of "children." They merit society's wisdom and energy. The positive impact of his or her support systems, immediate and extended family, school personnel, medical care, and child care options may be crucial.

This author, acknowledging her perspective as an advocate (a counseling educator), has been privileged to be a member of an educational system striving to empower adolescents as they transition and establish the next generations of family. Regardless of the perspective or focus of the reader, the concept of a "teen parent family" merits specialized study. What better gift to a child of any age than stable, loving, healthy, educated parents who are likewise members of a cohesive family—of "blood" and "more than blood"—willing and able to care for self, baby, and others? Society most assuredly stands to benefit from individual or corporate support in making such a difference. It was the intention of this chapter to enlighten and encourage the characteristics unique to the teen parent family. "Blood" is only a single characteristic of that family. Commitment, courage, and community are integral to teen parent families and all who respectfully learn from them.

Discussion Questions

1. What new awareness does Ruby experience when she uttered, "I'm not 16 anymore"?
2. Discuss some of the pros and cons of adolescents remaining in high school as they parent.
3. Name three critical referrals in a community that are often supportive of teen parents and children.
4. Discuss the similarities and differences among the three teen moms (Ruby, Mary, and Cindy) highlighted in this chapter.
5. If you were a teen parent, what support would you appreciate as an adolescent? As an adult?
6. What can parents do to teach younger adolescents to avoid pregnancy, sexually transmitted diseases, and so on?

References

Frost, R. (1915). *The death of the hired man.* http://www.poetryfoundation.org/poem/173525

Goldman, L. (2006). *Raising our children to be resilient.* New York: Routledge.

"Ins and Outs of Ethics and Law." (2012). *ASCA School Counselor, 49*(5).

Kübler-Ross, E. (1969). *On death and dying.* New York: Macmillan.

Malines, J. (1936). "The fence or the ambulance." In H. Felleman (Comp.), *Best loved poems of the American people.* New York: Knopf Doubleday Publishing Group.

Maslow, A. (1943). A theory of human motivation. *Psychological Review, 50,* 370–396.

National Women's Law Center. (2007). *When girls don't graduate we all fail.* http://www.nwlc.org/sites/default/files/pdfs/when_girls_dont_graduate.pdf

Pipher, M. (2001). *Reviving Ophelia, saving the selves of adolescent girls.* New York: Ballantine.

Santrock, J. W. (1995). *Life-span development* (5th ed.). Madison, WI: Brown and Benchmark.

U.S. Centers for Disease Control and Prevention. (2008). "Education update." In *Million dollar babies.* Washington, DC: Author.

Chapter 14

Interracial and Interethnic Families

Francis Wardle

Over the years, the definition of family has expanded greatly (Berger, 2009). We now have a variety of structures that are recognized by most people as a family, from gay and lesbian couples, teen families, extended families, and grandparents raising children (Brooks, 2011). While Western society has become far more accepting of a range of definitions of family, in many ways some of the oldest taboos still linger. These taboos are not about structure—two men, two women, grandparents, teens, extended families, single parents, foster and adoptive families, and so forth; they are about people from different racial and ethnic backgrounds creating families (Gallup Poll, 1991).

Taboos Against Interracial and Interethnic Marriage

Historically in Europe and North America, taboos against certain combinations in marriage have been deep seated and powerful. These include income discrepancy, social class differences, and people with different religious backgrounds, diverse educational backgrounds, and interracial and interethnic relationships. In other societies and cultures, taboos also included people from different geographic areas, tribal differences, and breaking prearranged marriages by parents or tribal leaders. Many of these taboos still exist, to a greater or lesser degree, in today's global societies (Crohn, 1995). Some societies still practice prearranged marriages; certain religious groups, both in this country and worldwide, have strict taboos against marrying outside their religion; and almost all societies have taboos against interracial and interethnic marriage—depending, of course, on each society's social construction of race and ethnicity. For example, I have a good friend from Sierra Leone who recounts that, in her country, there is a taboo against people from the upper class (blacks descended from African Americans) marrying lower-class Native Africans (M. Dufor, personal communication).

In the United States, there continues to be strong opposition to interracial and interethnic marriage and families (Gallup Poll, 1991; Root, 1996; Spickard, 1989). By interracial and interethnic, I mean parents who come from different U.S. racial and ethnic backgrounds, as defined by the U.S. census (i.e., white African American, Asian white, Native American/African American, and so forth) (U.S. Bureau of the Census, 2000). It should be noted that an interracial or interethnic marriage in the United States might not be considered one, in say, Brazil and vice versa. These taboos exist across all possible family structures, however radical or alternative they otherwise appear.

Interracial/Interethnic Families: From Dysfunctional to (More) Common

According to Spickard (1989), free blacks married whites during the colonial period of this country. As different minority groups either voluntarily came, were forced to come to this country (black slaves, Japanese, Filipino and Chinese workers, Portuguese fishermen, and so on) or already lived here—Native Americans and Mexicans—a dynamic tension developed between whites and people of color. Part of this friction was fueled by sexual relationships and marriage, both legal and illegal (Spickard, 1989). Certain legal realities exasperated this dilemma. Two of the more obvious ones were that only Japanese men were allowed to immigrate to this country, thus almost forcing interracial unions, and, since most blacks were slaves, they were not free to marry nonslaves (Spickard, 1989). An additional element was the commonly held belief of the intellectual and moral superiority of people of northern European descent compared to people of color (Grant, 1916).

Added to these tensions were the more benign relationships (formal and informal) between people from various minority groups. The most obvious of these was Native American and Mexicans in the Southwest; however, the number of contemporary African Americans with Native American ancestry belies this phenomenon between African American and Native Americans (Wardle & Cruz-Janzen, 2004).

The Civil War

While the Civil War was a landmark event in the liberation of black slaves, the creation and support of the Jim Crow laws guaranteed that blacks and other racial minorities would remain second-class citizens in this country (Wardle & Cruz-Janzen, 2004). Further, the activities of the Ku Klux Klan—ostensibly to enforce the laws and rules of Jim Crow—lead to the lynching of many black men, supposedly because of their immoral desires for white women. However, while these laws and behaviors kept black and white Americans apart, Japanese in the West were marrying whites and producing an entire population of productive Asian American citizens (Spickard, 1989).

Other historical events that impacted this issue were the Mexican-American War, the subsequent creation of American territories and states in the Southwest, and the forced resettlement of Native Americans onto reservations. The Dawes list and other legislation were used to define membership in various Indian tribes (Wilson, 1992).

Loving v. Virginia

The 1965 civil rights legislation put an official end to the Jim Crow laws and legal discrimination against blacks and other racial and ethnic minorities in this country. However, it was not until the 1967 Supreme Court decision of *Loving v. Virginia* that state laws against interracial marriages were deemed unconditional. As a result of this decision and considerable interaction between whites and African Americans and other minorities, particularly in colleges and universities, interracial marriage increased dramatically. Many viewed interracial marriage as a symbol of post–civil rights America (Ness, 2001; Root, 1996).

One of the results of this increase was the creation of the multiracial movement (Brown & Douglass, 2003; Wardle, 2005). At its height in the 1980s and early 1990s, there were 80 interracial support groups scattered throughout America and Canada. These groups "provided a safe place to talk, dispelled stereotypes regarding interracial marriage, allowed multiracial children to claim their full identity, and provided a forum for multiracial adults to share their life experiences with each other and new interracial couples with children" (Brown & Douglass, 2003, p. 111).

This movement also inspired a range of national publications, including *Interrace, Interracial Voice, Biracial Children*, and *New People*, along with the official publications of many of the support groups. A variety of books dedicated to the topic were also produced, including the seminal books by Maria Root (*Racially Mixed People in America* [1992] and *The Multiracial Experience: Racial Borders as the New Frontier* [1996]).

The election of Barack Obama, the product of an interracial family, as president of the United States has also given some credibility and profile to interracial families. However, it would not be accurate to suggest that interracial families and relationships are considered typical or common, especially from the perspective of academic scholarship.

Academic Resistance to Interracial and Interethnic Marriage

The catalog for the conference of the American Association of Marriage and Family Therapists (AAMFT) in Atlanta, Georgia, on September 23–26, 2010, is titled "Marriage: Relational and Societal Perspectives." I conducted an informal count of the conference seminars, poster sessions, and plenary sessions. This count, from highest to lowest, of sessions related to families is LGBT (lesbian couples, gay families, and bisexual and transgender members of a family) (15), violence (12), military families (11), divorce (8), Latino (7), African American (5), Native American (3), adoptive (3), and Asian (2). If a session covered more than one area, I counted them in both categories. Not a single session was devoted to families (of any kind) with parents from different racial or ethnic backgrounds. The closest was one session on transracially adoptive families.

The sixth edition of the *Publication Manual of the American Psychological Association* (American Psychological Association, 2010) contains within it six pages under the heading "Reducing Bias in Language," which includes, gender, sexual originations, racial and ethnic identity, disabilities and age (pp. 71–77). While the section under race and ethnicity provides detailed explanations about various words used to describe blacks, Hispanics, or Latinos and alternative ways to discuss Native Americans, there is absolutely no discussion of the appropriate label for individuals or couples from more than one of these single-race/ethnicity groups. This is absolutely amazing given (a) the variety and misunderstanding of labels for this group (i.e., biracial, bicultural, mixed race, mixed heritage, multiracial, multiethnic, interracial, and interethnic) and (b) the fact that some authors still use the totally unacceptable term "mulatto" (Spencer, 2010).

I published a study examining 12 child development textbooks with a copyright date of 2005 or later (Wardle, 2007). Since the 2000 U.S. Census allowed people for the first time to "check more than one race" and the Genome Project has shown that race is not a biological construct, I hypothesized that these books would include in them material on the rapidly increasing group of mixed-race children in this country (Wallace, 2004). While all of the books I studied included discussions of children from all the American single-race groups, only two discussed mixed-race children to any degree (Wallace, 2005).

The second edition of the *Handbook of Research on Multicultural Education* (Banks & Banks, 2003) has 49 chapters included in it. One of these 49 chapters is on mixed-race students and the other 48 on single-race/ethnicity students, and these chapters often reinforce the hierarchical and "hypodescent" approach to categorizing and describing the American population.

The book *The Process of Parenting* (Brooks, 2011) includes a chapter titled "Parenting in Complex Family Structures" (p. 441). This chapter includes gay and lesbian families, adoptive and foster families, but no interracial families. The book also indexes African Americans, Native Americans, Latinos, Asian Americans, Middle Eastern Americans, European Americans, and Puerto Rican families, but there is nothing under mixed race, multiracial, interracial, or biracial. For a 2011 edition of an American book on parenting, this is unbelievable.

The Taboo of Crossing the Color Line

Interracial and interethnic relationships are increasing in this country and have been since the civil rights movement and the *Loving v. Virginia* Supreme Court decision. More and more people are crossing the color line to marry and have children (Ness, 2001; Root, 1996; Wallace, 2004).

However, while we seem to be pushing the definition of the various acceptable structures of marriage and families in many directions—the AAMFT (2010) catalog even lists a session titled "Single African American Mothers with Multiple Fathers" (of their children) (p. 27)—we are still very resistant to challenging the deep-seated taboo against people from different racial and ethnic backgrounds marrying and raising a family. And it seems that the academic community—particularly the disciplines of sociology and education—while embracing all these new family constellations, have systematically ignored families that have challenged the racial and ethnic taboo of crossing the color line (Wallace, 2004). Wallace believes that this is due to (a) their relatively small numbers, (b) the essentialist definition of race and the view that racial groups are somehow discrete and exclusionary, and (c) the one-drop rule (p. x). The academic literature has virtually no discussion of this topic other than the literature describing the many pitfalls of these constellations (Gibbs, 1987) and current literature that affirms group belonging and racial loyalty (Tatum, 1999).

Not Politically Correct

One of the central hallmarks of studies in diversity, social justice, and critical theory is a focus on power, power relationships, and power hierarchies (Derman-Sparks & Edwards, 2010; Nieto, 2004; Tatum, 1999; Wallace, 2004). In this view, heterosexual white men are at the top of the power structure and privilege and women of color at the bottom. Those at the top have power; those at the bottom are oppressed. Race, gender, sexual orientation, disability, and non-Christian religious affiliation are placed along this neat hierarchy, as determined by their distance from mainstream, white society (Gupta & Ferguson, 1997). Institutions, educational programs, policies, and initiatives are then interpreted from the point of view of the group within this list (Pai & Adler, 1997).

However, this neat system cannot handle a family comprised of two people from opposing positions in the hierarchy as well as children who are products of these relationships (Pittinsky & Montoya, 2009). What do you do with an interracial family like mine—a white, higher-educated, heterosexual male and a black/Chickasaw women? There is no way to discuss this except to say that, by definition, it is an unequal and therefore unhealthy relationship. Because racial groups are placed on this hierarchy—white at the top and black at the bottom (Daniel, 1996)—any interracial family totally disrupts this neat view of society (Pittinsky & Montoya, 2009).

Racial and Cultural Loyalty

The National Association of Black Social Workers (NABSW, 2003) has historically opposed transracial adoption because they believe that placing black children in white homes destroys African American culture and places these children at risk of racial identity confusion and white harassment. James and Cherry Banks (2004) discuss a concept that comes from Erik Erikson known as "in-group" and "out-group" membership. This is a process and pattern of behaviors designed to develop and maintain group loyalty and belonging. William Cross (1987) calls this "reference-group orientation." There is considerable literature on the topic of minority race group loyalty. The arguments for creating and maintaining group loyalty in minority groups are (a) that the only way minorities can withstand the oppressive, white majority is through group power and solidarity and (b) that individual minorities develop their own racial identity and strength through a positive and active relationship with their reference group (Cross, 1987; Tatum, 1999).

Not So Inclusive

It is no accident that the 2010 catalog of the AAMFT conference on marriage has no sessions addressing issues unique to interracial families. The 2010 edition of the *Publication Manual of the American Psychological Association* does not discuss terms for multiracial individuals and families, and *The Process of Parenting* (Brooks, 2011) totally ignores interracial families. When it comes to exploring and rejecting racial and ethnic taboos, academics are not only conservative and traditional but also prime supporters of these traditional views of marriage and family. Ironically, it is the public that is leading the change of domestic relations. As Maria Root (1996) so accurately states, racial borders are the new frontier.

Challenging Societal Norms

Because of the racist history of the United States and Europe—along with all of the Americas—interracial and interethnic families challenge many societal norms. However, because race and ethnicity are political and social constructs and differ from country to country, my discussion of this topic will focus on the United States. These relationships—and the children they produce—challenge many societal rules, deep-seated values, and social constructs. Interracial families challenge the following:

- The view that interracial marriage is somehow biologically and socially unnatural (Olumide, 2002; Sickels, 1972) and the idea that multiracial children are dysfunctional and academically unsuccessful (Poussaint, 1984).
- The view that interracial marriages are less successful than single-race marriages.
- The view that mixed-race people are what Stonequist (1937) calls "a marginal man" and that they exhibit hybrid degeneracy.
- The rule of "hypodescent" (the one-drop rule) (Daniel, 1996).

- The very concept of race and racial borders (Root, 1996). The Genome Project has shown that race is not biological; research suggests that no one is of only a single race (Alves-Silva et al., 2000) and that we subscribe to outdated and incorrect views of DNA and genetics (Daniel, 1996).
- Essentialist views of race and racial identity (Fish, 2002) and the validity of the U.S. Census Bureau's racial categories.
- The single-race approach to multicultural educational and diversity training (Banks & Banks, 2004).
- The view that it is only whites who are racists and prejudiced and the myth that interracial families experience racism and disaffection from only the white side of their family (Wardle, 1999).
- Those who are opposed to interracial relationships because of past injustices (i.e., the rape of black slaves by white slave masters).
- The view by many sociologists and educators that race and ethnicity are the same as culture (Derman-Sparks & Edwards, 2010; York, 2003).
- The belief that children of color cannot succeed in our "racist" schools.
- The idea, deeply held by many scholars, that individual identity is solely the product of "reference-group orientation" and that individuals who do not subscribe to "racial group belonging" are lost and dysfunctional and lack a healthy racial identity (NABSW, 2003; Tatum, 1999).
- The view that racial difference in the United States are too deeply ingrained to be overcome, at least on an individual level (NABSW, 2003).
- The view that only black families can teach children of color to withstand the hostility of mainstream, white America (NABSW, 2003).
- The belief that racial differences are more difficult to overcome than other differences, including language, religion, nationality, income, and so forth.
- The view that white men engage in relationships with women of color only for sexual gratification and will not develop permanent social relationships.

The Reality of Interracial and Interethnic Families in America

Maybe more than any other societal norm, racism continues to raise its ugly head in America (Nieto, 2004). As I have already suggested, the expansion of different constellations of the family and the radical shift to a more inclusive definition of family have not substantially challenged these racial borders. Multiracial families experience racism and harassment from all directions (Wallace, 2004). Harassment begins when individuals decide to date across racial borders, and this behavior continues when they become grandparents; even strangers assume that these grown individuals are maids caring for their own grandchildren.

Remember, however, that these borders are not just black and white—they include Asian/Hispanic, Native American/black, Korean/Native American, and so forth. It could also be argued that these relationships include intertribal (Dine and Tohono O'odham) and international (Chinese/Korean) relationships. These relationships must also overcome deep historical, social, and political antagonism and distrust (Root, 1996).

Dating

When teens and young people date across racial and ethnic boundaries, the amount of resistance they face depends on the social group to which they belong. Certain high school and college groups are very integrated, and people are almost expected to date across racial borders. Other groups, such as religious and some work-related groups, are extremely segregated, and crossing over causes a great deal of friction and harassment from peers of single-race groups. Added pressure often comes from the families of both participants (Wardle & Cruz-Janzen, 2004).

Becoming a Family

There is a great deal of change between dating and becoming a family (whether through formal marriage, living together, or creating a formal partnership). The commitment tends to ratchet up the harassment from friends and especially relatives. Again, however, it is not just white relatives who object (if the family includes a white person). There is considerable literature that describes the opposition of black women to black men–white women relationships (Root, 1996; Winters & DeBose, 2003).

Raising Children

Raising multiracial and multiethnic children adds a whole new dimension to the reality of multiracial families in America. Some of these new realities include the following:

- Resolving different cultural practices used in raising children (Wardle, 1999).
- Addressing the deeply held belief that only the parent of color knows how to raise the children because a central task is teaching the child how to withstand white racism (NABSW, 2003).
- The need to teach mixed-race children about their multiracial identity, which must include the minority side of the family. This is particularly difficult for single, white mothers of mixed-race children.
- The question of identity in a race-fixated society. Parents take three positions: black or the identity of the parent of color if not Black, no race (human), and multiracial. This issue can become quite contentious, especially if relatives become part of the debate. Often the minority parent (and relatives) advocate the first position for historical, loyalty-to-group, and "society-sees-them-as black" arguments. The white partner will often accept this view. However, a growing number of psychologists support the belief that mixed-race children should be raised with their full racial and cultural heritage (Bowles, 1993; Brandell, 1988).
- Educating teachers and other professionals who work with children about the unique needs of mixed-race children (Wallace, 2004; Wardle, 1996).
- Finding a variety of ways to help their children integrate diverse heritages into a positive, healthy, secure identity. Limited research suggests that mixed-race children are at risk of school failure, drugs, and mental illness due to harassment from single-race peers and adults (Udry, Li, & Hendrickson-Smith, 2003).

Healthy Families

Along with all the other skills and values that single-race parents must use, both in their relationships with each other and with their children, interracial and interethnic partners must continually resist racism from within and from without. Some of the approaches that healthy families use include the following:

- Avoiding using race and racism in discussions and conflicts. It is very easy to resort to racial argument when in the heat of a discussion, but this is not helpful.
- Being assertive with friends and relatives. Not only do interracial partners have to withstand society, but they also have to protect their relationship from the harassment of friends and extended family. These conflicts are not just with the white side of the family. They learn to choose friends who are tolerant.
- Being proactive with schools. Many schools—and the professionals who work for them—lack understanding of the unique characteristics and needs of interracial families. They are often highly insensitive to a parent who objects to the single-race school forms and the focus on single-race holidays and curriculum content (Cortes, 1999). Many interracial parents actively engage their children's schools by providing training and advocacy and initiating new policies and curriculum activities.
- Making efforts to expose their children to both sides of the family. Because the children must integrate two or more cultures, heritages, and backgrounds, interracial parents provide opportunities for exposure to all sides of their family. They do not prefer one side to the other. In families where only one side of the child's background is represented (e.g., single, white mothers of biracial children), the parent finds a way to expose the child to his or her minority background: clubs, schools, neighborhood organizations, friends, and so forth.

Conclusion

Over the last several years, our definition of marriage and family has expanded. In fact, as Berger (2009) suggests, it is more helpful to look at the function of marriage (what it provides to children, adults, and society) than to focus on its various structures. However, disapproval of interracial and interethnic marriage and families has not radically improved with this change. Surprisingly, a resistance to this increasingly popular family choice in America is led by academia. Because diversity and equity issues focus on social justice, critical pedagogy, and overall power relationships, academics tend to be confused by these interracial relationships. Further, these relationships—and the children they produce—challenge deep-seated societal and academic constructs, from racial categories and the "one-drop rule" to group loyalty and single-group racial politics.

Within this context, multiracial families are not only increasing in number but also asserting their healthy relationships and their right to raise children as they choose with the combined biological and cultural identity of both sides of the family. Further, these families are educating the rest of society, including schools and psychologists, about the unique needs and characteristics of their family unit.

Discussion Questions

1. The author provides numerous examples of "taboo combinations" in marriage. In your opinion, which three do you perceive as the most socially opposed?
2. The National Association of Black Social Workers opposes transracial adoption on the grounds that it will cause identity confusion and allow for white harassment. Do you agree with this "rationale"? Why or why not?
3. This chapter criticizes the lack of an appropriate label for individuals or couples from mixed- or multiple-race/ethnicity groups. What term do you feel is the most commonly used today? What term would you propose using?
4. Do you believe that maintaining group loyalty within minority groups is a positive way to foster individual identity, or does it reinforce racial lines? Explain.

References

Alves-Silva, J., Santos, M. S., Gulmaraes, P. E., Ferreira, A.C., Bandrlt, H. J., Pena, S. D., & Prado, V. F. (2000). The ancestry of Brazilian mtDNA Lineages. *American Journal of Human Genetics, 67,* 444–461.

American Association of Marriage and Family Therapists. (2010). *Marriage: Relational and societal perspectives.* Alexandra, VA: Author.

American Psychological Association. (2010). *Publication manual of the American Psychological Association.* Washington, DC: Author.

Banks, J. A., & Banks, C. A. M. (Eds.). (2003). *Handbook of research on multicultural education* (2nd ed.). Hoboken, NJ: Jossey-Bass.

Banks, J. A., & Banks, C. A. M. (Eds.). (2004). *Multicultural education: Issues and perspectives* (5th ed.). Hoboken, NJ: Wiley.

Berger, K. (2009). *The developing person: Through the lifespan.* New York: Worth.

Bowles, D. D. (1993). Biracial identity: Children born to African American and white couples. *Clinical Social Work Journal, 21*(4), 417–428.

Brandell, J. R. (1988, October). Treatment of the biracial child: Theoretical and clinical issues. *Journal of Multicultural Counseling and Development,* 176–186.

Brooks, J. (2011). *The process of parenting* (8th ed.). New York: McGraw-Hill.

Brown, N. G., & Douglass, R. E. (2003). Evolution of multiracial organizations: Where we have been and where we are going. In L. I. Winters & H. L. DeBose (Eds.), *New faces in a changing America. Multiracial identity in the 21st century* (pp. 111–124). Thousand Oaks, CA: Sage.

Cortes, C. (1999). Mixed-race children: Building bridges to new identities. *Reaching Today's Youth, 3*(2), 28–31.

Crohn, J. (1995). *Mixed matches: How to create successful interracial, interethnic and interfaith relationships.* New York: Fawcett Columbine.

Cross, W. (1987). A two-factor theory of black identity development in minority children. In J. S. Phinney & M. J. Rotheram (Eds.), *Children's ethnic socialization* (pp. 117-134). Newbury Park, CA: Sage.

Daniel, G. R. (1996). Black and white identity in the new millennium: Unsevering the ties that bind. In M. P. P. Root (Ed.), *The multiracial experience: Racial borders as the new frontier* (pp. 121-139). Newbury Park, CA: Sage.

Derman-Sparks, L., & Edwards, J. O. (2010). *Anti-bias education for young children and ourselves.* Washington, DC: National Association for the Education of Young Children.

Fish, J. M. (Ed.). (2002) *Race and intelligence: Separating science from myth.* Mahwah, NJ: Lawrence Erlbaum Associates.

Gallup Poll. (1991, August). For the first time, more Americans approve of interracial marriage than disapprove. *Gallup Poll Monthly, 311,* 60-64.

Gibbs, J. T. (1987). Identity and marginality: Issues in the treatment of biracial adolescents. *American Journal of Orthopsychiatry, 57*(2), 265-276.

Grant, M. (1916). *The passing of the great race: The racial basis of European History.* New York: Charles Scribner & Sons.

Gupta, A., & Ferguson, J. (1997). *Culture, power, place: Explorations in critical anthropology.* Durham, NC: Duke University Press.

National Association of Black Social Workers. (2003). *Preserving families of African ancestry.* http://www.nabsw.org/mserver/Preserving Families.aspx.

Ness, C. (2001, March). Multiracial pride shows up in new census: Mixed-heritage now recognized. *San Francisco Chronicle,* pp. A1, A17.

Nieto, S. (2004*). Affirming diversity: The sociopolitical context of multicultural education* (4th ed.). Boston: Allyn & Bacon.

Olumide, J. (2002). Raiding the gene pool. In *The social construction of mixed-race.* Sterling, VA: Pluto Press.

Pai Y., & Adler, S. A. (1997). *Cultural foundations of education* (2nd ed.). Upper Saddle River, NJ: Merrill.

Pittinsky, T. L., & Montoya, R. M. (2009). Is valuing equality enough? Equality values, allophilia, and social policy support for multiracial individuals. *Journal of Social Issues, 65*(1), 151-163.

Poussaint, A. P. (1984). Study of interracial children presents positive picture. *Interracial Books for Children Bulletin, 15*(6), 9-10.

Root, M. P. P. (Ed.). (1992). *Racially mixed people in American.* Newbury Park, CA: Sage.

Root, M. P. P. (Ed.). (1996). *The multiracial experience: Racial borders as the new frontier.* Thousand Oaks, CA: Sage.

Sickels, R. J. (1972). *Race, marriage, and the law.* Albuquerque: University of New Mexico Press.

Spencer, R. (2010). Militant multiraciality: Rejecting race and rejecting the convenience of complicity. In J. O. Adekunle & H. V. Williams (Eds.), *Color struck: Essays on race and ethnicity in global perspective* (pp. 155-172). New York: University Press of America.

Spickard, P. (1989). *Mixed blood: Intermarriage and ethnic identity in twentieth century America.* Madison: University of Wisconsin Press.

Stonequist, E. V. (1937). *The marginal man: A study in personality and culture conflict.* New York: Russell and Russell.

Tatum, B. D. (1999). *Why are all the black kids sitting together in the cafeteria?* New York: Basic Books.

Udry, J. R., Li, R. M., & Hendrickson-Smith, J. (2003). Health and behavior risks of adolescents with mixed-race heritage. *American Journal of Public Health, 93*(11), 1–6.

U.S. Bureau of the Census. (2000). *U.S. Census 2000.* Washington, DC: Author.

Wallace, K. R. (Ed.). (2004). *Working with multiracial students: Critical perspectives on research and practice.* Greenwich, CT: Information Age Publishing.

Wardle, F. (1996). Multicultural education. In M. P. P. Roots (Ed.), *The multiracial experience: Racial borders as the new frontier* (pp. 380–391). Thousand Oaks, CA: Sage.

Wardle, F. (1999). *Tomorrow's children: Meeting the needs of multiracial and multiethnic children at home, in early childhood programs, and at school.* Denver: Center for the Study of Biracial Children.

Wardle, F. (2005). History of contemporary multiracial movement, part 1. *Interracial Voice.* http://www.webcom.com/~intvoice/wardle6.html

Wardle, F. (2007). Multiracial children in child development textbooks. *Early Childhood Education Journal, 35*(3), 253–259.

Wardle, F., & Cruz-Janzen, M. I. (2004). *Meeting the needs of multiethnic and multiracial children in schools.* Boston: Allyn & Bacon.

Wilson, T. P. (1992). Blood quantum: Native American mixed bloods. In M. P. P. Root (Ed.), *Racially mixed people in America* (pp. 108–125). Newbury Park, CA: Sage.

Winters, L. I., & DeBose, H. L. (Eds.). (2003). *New faces in a changing America. Multiracial identity in the 21st century.* Thousand Oaks, CA: Sage.

York, S. (2003). *Roots and wings: Affirming culture in early childhood programs* (Rev. ed.). St. Paul, MN: Redleaf Press.

Chapter 15

(Not) Talking About Race and Difference in Visibly Adoptive Families

Sara Docan-Morgan

This chapter focuses on communication in families formed through international, transracial adoption. These families, formed through what Galvin (2006) calls "visible adoption," are distinct from the traditional model of family in two main ways. First, rather than being of the same race or a combination of the parents' race, visibly adopted children's race differs from that of their parents. Second, instead of being born and bonded through birth, adopted children come to their adoptive families through legal transactions, paperwork, and fees. Yet despite these differences from the traditional family, the bond rendered by adoption is assumed to be permanent and familial. These characteristics result in interactions that show the power of language to create or diminish a sense of family identity.

An understanding of communication in visibly adoptive families would be incomplete without basic knowledge of how these families came to occupy their current place in society. The history of transracial adoption in the United States is complicated, political, and controversial, and it is not possible to examine it in full here. However, a brief background will demonstrate how adoption, like the institution of family itself, undergoes continual change and how visibly adoptive families came to be culturally situated as common yet not fully "normal."

Although adoption may seem like a recently popular practice in the United States, families have been formed through legal adoption since the Massachusetts Adoption of Children Act was passed in 1851 (Adoption History Project, 2007). Racial "matching" and secrecy characterized the majority of adoptions for the next 100 years as parents sought to adopt children who looked like them and kept their children's adoptions secret. Then, in the mid-1950s, Harry and Bertha Holt adopted eight children from South Korea and subsequently founded Holt International adoption agency, the country's largest international adoption agency (Holt International, 2011). In addition, Operation Babylift in 1975, which brought nearly 3,000 children to the United States from Vietnam, also increased the number of international adoptees in the United States (Precious Cargo, n.d.). Stories—some of which were fabricated (Sachs, 2010)—of Korean and Vietnamese "orphans" compelled American families to adopt children of another race. At the same time, white families were further persuaded to adopt internationally given the legalization of abortion and society's increasing acceptance of single motherhood, both of which made it challenging to find healthy, white, adoptable infants.

Today's adoptive families are often characterized by racial difference given that adoptive parents tend to be white, and adoptable babies tend to be racial minorities, whether they are domestically or internationally adopted. Not surprisingly, this racial difference, along with the lack of biological ties to one another, impacts communication both within the family and with those outside the family. In previous research, I have examined adoptees' experiences with two types of interactions resulting from these deviations from the traditional family form: racial derogation (Docan-Morgan, 2010a) and intrusive interactions (Docan-Morgan, 2010b).

Before examining these interactions, it is important to note that the significant presence of visibly adoptive families in American society suggests that the practice of transracial, international adoption has gained increased acceptance over the past decades. Yet research by Suter (2008), Suter and Ballard (2009), and Docan-Morgan (2010a) suggests that adoptive parents and adoptees face interactions with strangers and family members that highlight the widespread assumption that ideal nuclear families are comprised of members who are biologically related and racially homogeneous. Examining the research on adoptive families' experiences with racial derogation and intrusive interactions will illuminate a striking paradox: that although visibly adoptive families may have become more common, they remain outside of many people's vision of the "normal" family. As a result, these families may need to use communication to create and sustain a sense of family identity more than single-race families who have children solely through birth.

Racial Derogation

Background

The purpose of this investigation (Docan-Morgan, 2010b) was to explore adult Korean adoptees' experiences with racial derogation, the extent to which they avoided disclosing these experiences to their white parents, and the reasons, if any, for this avoidance. Racial derogation was defined as "instances where the adoptee is the victim of malevolent and/or essentializing comments or questions related to his/her race" (Docan-Morgan, 2010b, p. 4). Using transcribed in-depth interviews and qualitative, online survey responses, this study examined how adoptees' self-disclosures about experiences with racial derogation were impacted by the fact that their parents were white.

Previous studies had not systematically examined adoptees' experiences with racial derogation or racially charged comments despite the fact that adoptive parents and adoptees reported the occurrence of racially derogatory comments consistently (e.g., Bartholet, 1992; Fujimoto, 2002; Suter, 2008; Tessler, Gamache, & Liu, 1999). In addition, Galvin (2003) placed the study of adoptees' experiences with racial derogation as one of the key elements of her communication research agenda for international and transracial adoption.

Theoretical Foundation

Experiences with racial derogation are not unique to transracial adoptees; however, the composition of transracially adoptive families—in contrast to single-race families—may create a situation wherein racial derogation elicits in adoptees a sense of isolation and difference from one's family. Communication privacy management (CPM) theory (Petronio, 2002; Petronio & Caughlin, 2006) states that communicators own their private information and experiences and that they learn and develop rules about what to disclose, to whom, and when.

Related to the development of privacy rules, research on topic avoidance suggests that communicators may avoid talking about conversational topics in order to preserve intimate relationships (Caughlin & Afifi, 2004; Guerrero & Afifi, 1995a). With regard to families, Guerrero and Afifi (1995b) outlined four general reasons why parents and children tend to avoid discussing certain topics with one another: (a) *self-protection* (i.e., wanting to avoid judgment, criticism, embarrassment, and vulnerability), (b) *relationship protection* (i.e., the desire to avoid conflict, eliciting anger, or deescalating the relationship), (c) *social inappropriateness* (i.e., the tendency to avoid topics that one perceives as socially inappropriate for discussion), and (d) *parent unresponsiveness* (i.e., avoiding a topic because of the perception that one's parent will be unresponsive or think that the issue is trivial or lacks relevant knowledge necessary for handling the problem).

Overall, CPM and topic avoidance provided useful lenses for examining the development of privacy rules surrounding adoptees' experiences with racial derogation. This study aimed to explore whether adoptees' development of privacy rules was impacted by their parents' race and whether their parents' past communication set a precedent for future disclosure.

Results

All participants recalled experiencing racial derogation at one time or another, most commonly during their primary and/or secondary school years. Participants reported three main types of racial derogation: *appearance attacks*, *perceived ethnicity attacks*, and *physical attacks*. Appearance attacks targeted adoptees' racialized (or presumably racialized) features. For example, participants reported having children pull their eyes back in a horizontal fashion to mock the shape of Asian eyes. They also recalled being called names such as "flat nose" or "slant eyes" and having their black hair mocked. In perceived ethnicity attacks, the aggressor referenced essentializing cultural beliefs or stereotypes about Asians. Such attacks included racial epithets, such as "chink," "Chinese," "Jap," and/or "nigger," as well as having children mock karate moves in their presence. In addition, many participants recalled having children recite a singsong chant: "Chi-*nese*, Japan-*ese*, dirty knees, look at these." Finally, physical attacks involved acts such as the throwing of rocks, tripping the adoptee, and/or fighting.

Overall, the adoptees in the current study reported that they developed privacy rules that kept them from telling their parents, who were white, about their experiences with racial derogation. They offered several reasons for the development of this privacy rule.

First, many participants avoided the topic of racial derogation due to what Guerrero and Afifi (1995b) label *parent unresponsiveness*. Adoptees expressed a belief that their parents would not be able to respond in a way that they, the adoptees, found to be comforting or helpful. Whereas some participants reported past negative experiences disclosing to their parents, others *perceived* that because their parents were white, they would inherently not be able to understand adoptees' racialized experiences.

Some participants had not had negative past experiences sharing with their parents; they simply *perceived* that their parents' responses would not be helpful and thus chose to avoid the topic of racial derogation. For example, one participant reported, "I have encountered many acts of discrimination or racism throughout my life. I never let my parents know about any of them … I don't think my parents could contribute much of any advice to any of my past experiences because they don't know what it's like to be in my shoes." These participants perceived their parents to lack knowledge of how to respond to racial derogation given that they, as white people, had not experienced it.

Other participants recalled disclosing a racially based experience or feeling with their parent(s), who responded in a way that the adoptee did not find to be helpful. These participants subsequently decided to avoid disclosing experiences with racial derogation to their parents. One female participant shared similar experiences, writing of her experiences as a preteen, "I usually cried in reaction [to racial derogation] and would run away. I usually didn't tell my parents after they happened because they never said anything that helped." Another participant reported being told by her parents to have "thick skin" and to not "get her shorts in a bunch" when she was called racial names. As a result, she avoided disclosing her experiences with racial derogation, even when it escalated to four months of daily appearance, ethnicity, and physical attacks.

These examples of past parent unresponsiveness confirm CPM's premise that individuals learn privacy rules through interaction (Petronio, 2002). As Petronio and Caughlin (2006) write, "The decisions to reveal or conceal are predicated on rules that stem from many different spheres of influence" (p. 38). Indeed, one "sphere" that appears particularly influential is past experiences of self-disclosing to one's parents. One participant stated his rule explicitly, reporting, "The issue of race was not allowed to be discussed at home. We weren't allowed to talk about our differences."

Other participants chose to not tell their parents about experiences with racial derogation because they desired to "fit in" or "blend in" with the white family and community surrounding them and experiences with racial derogation made them stand out. One female respondent wrote, "I didn't want to people to notice that I wasn't white." Such a response underscores the strong desire many Korean adoptees felt to assimilate and blend in. The result was topic avoidance about race.

Importantly, although participants chose to avoid discussions of race with their parents, they wanted to be able to talk with their parents about these topics. They appeared to feel the dialectic expressed by Petronio and Caughlin (2006): They wanted to avoid the topic of racial derogation because it highlighted their difference, yet they wanted to be able to disclose their experiences and receive support. Indeed, adoptees who reported that they felt the need to avoid the topic of race or racial derogation with their parents often expressed feelings of loneliness, isolation, and/or anger.

Some participants, however, reported that they felt open in talking with their parents about experiences with racial derogation. For example, one participant characterized herself as always feeling "very comfortable" talking with her parents about issues related to adoption, race, and racial derogation. She recalled her father's response when she and her sister, who was also a Korean adoptee, were teased about their "Chinese" eyes on the bus:

> And I remember coming home . . . and telling our parents and we'd be crying, you know, "Why did they tease us, why did they do that?" and again them being just amazingly really cool. And I also remember my dad . . . said, "Let's come up with something that you can, you know, how you can respond." . . . I just thought this was so cool. [laughs]

Adoptees who said that they had positive past experiences disclosing feelings about or interactions involving race were less likely to avoid these topics in conversations with their parents than did those who did not report such experiences. If they encountered racial derogation or had questions about their adoption, they reported talking with their parents about these topics and receiving what they perceived as helpful, empathic responses. This finding is important in that it suggests a meaningful connection between one's family communication orientation (e.g., levels of openness and emotional expressiveness) (Matsunaga, 2008) and the tendency for children to engage in topic avoidance.

Participants who reported disclosing regarding racial derogation based their decision on past, positive experiences of self-disclosure with their parents. In contrast to participants who reported topic avoidance, these participants developed the privacy rule that disclosing these experiences to one's parents is beneficial.

Intrusive Interactions

Background

Privacy rules and topic avoidance regarding racial derogation suggest communication challenges *within* visibly adoptive families. Yet visible racial differences may also present communicative challenges with people *outside* the family. Both adoptees (e.g., Trenka, 2003) and researchers (e.g., Suter, 2008) have documented interactions wherein people outside the adoptive family question or comment on adoptive family members' relationships with one another.

Consequently, Docan-Morgan (2010a) examined intrusive interactions, which can be defined as "interpersonal encounters wherein people outside the immediate family question or comment on the adoptee and/or the adoptive members' relationships with one another" (p. 139). During intrusive interactions, families are asked by those outside the family (e.g., strangers and school officials) to speak to their family's composition (Galvin, 2003). Questions such as "Is she your real daughter?" or "How much did she cost?" may become unsurprising for visibly adoptive families. Past literature, including research and adoptee accounts, suggested that adoptive parents and adoptees find these interactions disconcerting and invasive at times (Fujimoto, 2002; Register, 1991; Suter & Ballard, 2009; Trenka, 2003). Using the same method as Docan-Morgan (2010b), this study explored Korean adult adoptees' reported experiences with intrusive interactions while growing up and how their adoptive parents responded to outsiders' questions or comments.

Theoretical Foundation

This study aimed to extend Galvin's (2006) concept of discourse dependency, which emphasizes the importance of language in constituting and reaffirming family ties. According to Galvin (2006), families are *discourse dependent* to the extent that they use interaction and language to constitute and reconstitute themselves as a family. Transracially adoptive families may be thought to be *highly* discourse dependent because of their visible racial differences and lack of biological ties to one another (Galvin, 2006).

Discourse dependency in families is comprised of two processes: *internal* and *external boundary management practices* (Galvin, 2006). Whereas internal boundary management refers to the communicative processes *within* the family that serve to constitute family identity, external boundary management practices refer to the discourse used to explain the family to persons *outside* of it. These processes allow family members to create a sense of family identity or cohesion among themselves as well as to legitimize their relationships to outsiders.

Intrusive interactions require discursive responses from adoptive family members that both acknowledge the person who made the comment and reaffirm familial ties. These responses can be seen as examples of external boundary management strategies. Previous research (Suter, 2008) examined parents' perceptions of intrusive interactions and their external boundary management strategies, yet prior to Docan-Morgan (2010a), none had explored adoptees' perceptions of intrusive interactions and of their parents' responses.

Parents' external boundary management appears to be important to some adoptees, who expect their parents to respond in some way, perhaps by setting up discursive boundaries against outsiders' queries. For example, an 18-year-old Korean adoptee interviewed by Fujimoto (2002) expressed anger when a sales clerk asked her father, "Where did you get a pretty young thing like that?" (p. 271), and her father did not reply. Her anger resulted primarily from her father's choice to ignore the question. Indeed, parental responses can be extremely important to many adoptees, whose way of seeing themselves and their adoptive families may be impacted by how their parents respond to issues of race and racial difference (Evan B. Donaldson Adoption Institute, 2000; Fujimoto, 2002).

Results

Participants reported several types of intrusive interactions, including *relational comments/questions, compliments, stares, mistaken identities/relationships,* and *adoptee-only interactions*. In relational comments/questions, adoptees reported receiving questions or comments from strangers that inquired into and/or expressed judgments about the relationships among their adoptive family members. Consistent with Galvin's (2006) claim that outsiders challenge the "relatedness" of nontraditionally formed families, adoptees reported facing questions and comments that discursively challenged or questioned the genuineness of the adoptive family identity. Participants reported being in places such as the grocery store and having strangers ask their parents questions such as "Is that your daughter?," "Where did you get him/her?," or "Where are they from?" Those who had one or more siblings also adopted from Korea reported often being asked whether their siblings were their "real" sister or "real" brother. Although such questions could be viewed as innocently curious, the adoptees in this study viewed them as confusing and frustrating because they challenged the legitimacy of their family. Like the adoptive parents in Suter's (2008) study, participants found that these interactions questioned their beliefs that their families were real and legitimate. These interactions also highlighted that adoptive family identity is highly discourse dependent and perceived as more fragile than family bonds formed through blood relations.

Participants also reported that their families received compliments about the adoptees' or the family's appearance. For example, one participant reported that in grocery stores, strangers "would ask, they would say like, 'Oh, she's so cute! Asian babies are so cute!' Like one time I guess this lady told my mom like, 'I should get one!'" Notably, both adoptees report these interactions secondhand, which suggests that these intrusive interactions were viewed as significant enough to have become narratives within the family.

Both relational comments/questions and compliments were reported to elicit a variety of responses from adoptees. Particularly when these interactions were directed at the *parents* rather than the adoptees, they left some participants feeling somewhat objectified and essentialized.

In U.S. culture, where Asian Americans continue to be regularly represented through racial stereotypes, the importance of such feelings should not be minimized, as they exist within a historical, cultural context of racialization (Lowe, 1996).

In addition to interactions where the adoptee and his or her family were approached by strangers, participants also reported perceiving that others outside the family were staring at them. One interviewee stated, "Um, I just remember waiting in line for maybe like a ride or a movie, and we would get some stares from other people as they were passing by. They'd just like shoot us a quick glance like, like maybe for two seconds longer than they should." These stares were reported to elicit anger and discomfort, as they highlighted the difference between transracially adoptive families and single-race, nonadoptive families.

Instances when adoptees were mistaken for nonmembers of the family or instances when family memberships were misinterpreted also arose as a theme in participants' reports. These interactions are included as results because they require family members to engage in external boundary management by labeling the adoptee as a member of the family and/or providing an explanation. With regard to mistaken identities, participants reported being mistaken for foreign exchange students, refugees, newly arrived Korean immigrants, and housecleaners. In other instances, rather than mistaking the *identity* of an adoptee, outsiders misconstrued the adoptee's *relationship* with members of the family. Some female participants reported being mistaken for their brother's girlfriend or their father's wife, and one male participant reported that he was often mistaken for the boyfriend of his sisters. Not surprisingly, participants reported that these encounters made them uncomfortable. Whereas mistaken identities called into question the adoptees' identities as Americans or citizens of their countries, mistaken relationships called into question their relationships with their family members. These two identities—ethnic and familial—are central to one's self-perception, and it is therefore unsurprising that this type of intrusive interaction was particularly challenging for participants.

Participants also reported intrusive interactions in their families' absence. These encounters tended to occur with peers who knew who the adoptees' parents were, but some of these interactions involved teachers. Primarily, adoptees reported receiving questions from peers about their adoption, such as "Do you know your Korean parents?" and "How did you parents find and get you?" Other participants reported that school projects, such as creating "family trees," were uncomfortable because they required adoptees to talk explicitly about their families.

Some adoptees, however, were not particularly bothered by questions about their adoption and did not find them to be particularly intrusive. One participant recalled, "I remember swinging on the swings on the playground and telling someone that I was born in Seoul and my Korean name and when I was adopted. In many ways, it was not a big deal." Thus, the meaning of relational comments or questions is subjective and dependent on factors including the adoptees' personality and the person asking the question. Similarly, the adoptive parents in Suter and Ballard's (2009) study reported that they consider factors such as who is asking the question and what the question is when deciding whether to respond to intrusive interactions.

Adoptees reported that their parents used several types of external responses when faced with intrusive interactions. In general, these external boundary management strategies were reported to reaffirm adoptive family identity and included *labeling and explaining, defending, and joking.*

Labeling and explaining, both strategies identified by Galvin (2006), were reported as the most common responses to relational questions. In these encounters, adoptees reported that their parents labeled them as their child (e.g., "This is my daughter, ———.") and explained that the child was adopted from Korea. Parents were often reported to have responded with a great deal of pride in their children. One participant recalled the following:

They would always reply, "[Our son] is from Korea," then they would take a look at me proudly and continue on how handsome and intelligent I was. My parents always were willing to talk to people about me. In all the conversations they had about me, I could always tell my parents were proud of me because it is written all over them and I still see that today, so I feel very fortunate.

Participants reported that they were satisfied with their parents' and siblings' external boundary management strategies. They felt their families handled these interactions well, were pleased with the way their parents labeled and explained their relationships, and saw these responses as indicators that their family members were proud of them.

Joking surfaced as another external boundary management strategy. Because joking involved humorous but evasive responses to intrusive interactions, it may be viewed as an additional external boundary management strategy, one not identified by Galvin (2006). One participant recalled that her mother often used joking in addition to labeling and explaining when faced with intrusive questions, saying,

[My mom] would just be like "Yeah, we adopted them and they're our family and that's my daughter," and she would just make funny jokes like "Why can't you tell it's my daughter? We have the same nose," or she would just say funny things like that. She would always try to lighten the mood so we'd never really focus on it too much, I guess.

Importantly, this participant positions her mother's response as being directed *both* at the person asking the question and at her and her siblings. Her mother's jokes responded to the asker, but they also were intended to keep her and her siblings from focusing on the outsider's comments or question; in other words, these jokes served as both internal and external boundary management strategies.

Discussion

In reviewing research on visibly adoptive families' experiences with racial derogation and intrusive interactions, this chapter aims to shed light on some of the communicative challenges that these families may face because of their racial differences and lack of biological ties to one another. These challenges may arise because of outsiders' challenging comments or questions, adoptees' understandable desires to "blend in," or real or perceived shortcomings in family members' communication with one another. Regardless, it is apparent that although visibly adoptive families have become more common, they are often compared to antiquated visions of "normal" families"—those with two parents of the same race who have children through birth.

The reality of the American demographic has challenged the nuclear, single-race model of family and brought to light different family compositions, many of which can be viewed as "normal" to the people whose lives they reflect. Results from Docan-Morgan (2010b) suggest that although some adoptees had negative experiences talking (or trying to talk) about race with their adoptive parents, others reported that their parents offered helpful responses. This latter result suggests that racial difference does not need to prohibit open, supportive communication about race in visibly adoptive families. Even as these families become more common, it remains critically important for white adoptive parents to not minimize issues of race and difference but instead to make intentional efforts to convey openness about race and to attempt to empathize with their children's experiences as racial minorities.

In addition, results from Docan-Morgan (2010a) supported Suter's (2008) findings, suggesting that members of adoptive families experience intrusive interactions and may perceive them to be challenging to their sense of family identity. Thus, although definitions of family are changing and evolving, visibly adoptive families remain subject to outsiders' comments and queries. As time passes, it is hoped that tomorrow's vision of family will expand even further, allowing more visibly adoptive families to communicate openly about difference with one another yet remain free from unwanted scrutiny, questions, and comments.

Discussion Questions

1. When faced with such identity threats as external intrusive interactions, what three external boundary management strategies may help reaffirm the family identity?
2. Recall various reasons why adoptees experiencing racial abuse would avoid telling their parents about it and thus create "privacy rules?"
3. This chapter states that transracial families are "highly" discourse dependent because of their visible adoption. In what areas might the discourse of a transracial adoption family prove more crucial to forming and protecting the family identity than in families with the same racial background?
4. Families with visible adoption are frequently obligated to answer questions about their relational ties or other questions surrounding the adoption(s). Do you believe that these questions hinder or help preserve the family's unity? Explain.

References

Adoption History Project. (2007). *Adoption history in brief.* http://pages.uoregon.edu/adoption/topics/adoptionhistbrief.htm

Bartholet, E. (1994). *Family bonds: Adoption and the practice of parenting.* New York: Houghton Mifflin.

Caughlin, J. P., & Afifi, T. D. (2004). When is topic avoidance unsatisfying? Examining moderators of the association between avoidance and dissatisfaction. *Human Communication Research, 30,* 479-513.

Docan-Morgan, S. (2010a). Korean adoptees' retrospective reports of intrusive interactions: Exploring boundary management in adoptive families. *Journal of Family Communication, 10,* 137-157.

Docan-Morgan, S. (2010b). "They don't know what it's like to be in my shoes": Topic avoidance about race in transracially adoptive families. *Journal of Social and Personal Relationships, 27,* 1-20.

Evan B. Donaldson Adoption Institute. (2000). *The gathering of the first generation of Adult Korean adoptees: Adoptees' perceptions of international adoption.* http://www.adoptioninstitute.org/proed/korfindings.html# summary

Fujimoto, E. (2002). South Korean adoptees growing up in white America: Negotiating race and culture. In J. N. Martin, T. K. Nakayama, & L. A. Flores (Eds.), *Readings in intercultural communication: Experiences and contexts* (2nd ed.). Boston: McGraw-Hill.

Galvin, K. M. (2003). International and transracial adoption: A communication research agenda. *Journal of Family Communication, 3,* 237-353.

Galvin, K. M. (2006). Diversity's impact on defining the family: Discourse-dependence and identity. In L. H. Turner & R. West (Eds.), *The family communication sourcebook* (pp. 3–19). Thousand Oaks, CA: Sage.

Guerrero, L. K., & Afifi, W. A. (1995a). Some things are better left unsaid: Topic avoidance in family relationships. *Communication Quarterly, 43,* 276–296.

Guerrero, L. K., & Afifi, W. A. (1995b). What parents don't know: Taboo topics and topic avoidance in parent-child relationships. In T. J. Socha & G. Stamp (Eds.), *Parents, children, and communication: Frontiers of theory and research* (pp. 219–245). Hillsdale, NJ: Lawrence Erlbaum Associates.

Holt International. (2011). *Holt has always been about the children: A historical perspective.* http://www.holtinternational.org/about/historical.shtml

Lowe, L. (1996). *Immigrant acts: On Asian American cultural politics.* Durham, NC: Duke University Press.

Matsunaga, M. (2008). Parents don't (always) know their children have been bullied: Child-parent discrepancy on bulling and family-level profile of communication standards. *Human Communication Research, 35,* 221–247.

Petronio, S. (2002). *Boundaries of privacy: Dialectics of disclosure.* Albany: State University of New York Press.

Petronio, S., & Caughlin, J. P. (2006). Communication privacy management theory: Understanding families. In D. O. Braithwaite & L. A. Baxter (Eds.), *Engaging theories in family communication: Multiple perspectives* (pp. 35–49). Thousand Oaks, CA: Sage.

Precious Cargo. (n.d.) *Operation Babylift.* http://www.pbs.org/itvs/preciouscargo/babylift.html

Register, C. (1991). *Are those kids yours? American families with children adopted from other countries.* New York: Free Press.

Sachs, D. (2010). *The life we were given: Operation Babylift, international adoption, and the children of war in Vietnam.* Boston: Beacon Press.

Suter, E. A. (2008). Discursive negotiation of family identity: A study of U.S. families with adopted children from China. *Journal of Family Communication, 8,* 126–147.

Suter, E., & Ballard, R. (2009). "How much did you pay for her?": Decision-making criteria underlying adoptive parents' responses to inappropriate remarks. *Journal of Family Communication, 9,* 107–125.

Tessler, R., Gamache, G., & Liu, L. (1999). *West meets East: Americans adopt Chinese children.* Westport, CT: Bergin & Garvey.

Trenka, J. J. (2003). *The language of blood: A memoir.* St. Paul, MN: Graywolf Press.

Endnotes

This chapter was adapted with author permission from Docan-Morgan, S. (2010). "They don't know what it's like to be in my shoes": Topic avoidance about race in transracially adoptive families. *Journal of Social and Personal Relationships, 27,* 1–20, and Docan-Morgan, S. (2010). Korean adoptees' retrospective reports of intrusive interactions: Exploring boundary management in adoptive families. *Journal of Family Communication, 10,* 137–157.

PART 4
Family Experiences from a Distance

Chapter 16
On the Evolution of Togetherness and Living with Two Hearts   164
Vinita Agarwal, *Salisbury University*
Suchitra Shenoy, *De Paul University*

Chapter 17
Family Relationships as More Than Blood: Military Families as Dialectics and Discourses   174
Erin Sahlstein, *University of Nevada–Las Vegas*
Katheryn C. Maguire, *Wayne State University*

Chapter 18
Ex-Prisoners Are Coming Home: A Reentry Court's Family Focus   183
Jeralyn Faris, *Purdue University*

Chapter 19
Family as an Academic Motivator for African American and Ghanaian Students' University Attendance   192
Eletra S. Gilchrist, *University of Alabama*

Chapter 16

On the Evolution of Togetherness and Living with Two Hearts

Vinita Agarwal and Suchitra Shenoy

Physical copresence has emerged as an important lens to conceptualize geographical distances in relationships. Often classified as long-distance relationships, the notion of copresence allows us to reimagine distances through a discursive lens (Merolla, 2010; Werner & Baxter, 1994). Our chapter takes two related but conceptually distinct narratives of examining copresence in relationships. In the first section, "Three Phases of Evolution of Togetherness," the first author integrates advancing communication technologies, the sense-making processes of distance-as-discourse, and negotiation of copresence to propose the three phases of evolution of togetherness challenging commonly held beliefs about copresence, communication, and technology in relationships. In the section "Living with Two Hearts," the second author focuses on examining her family through relationships, drawing on the appeal "to consider the importance of multiple influences on communicative behavior when studying human relationships" (Floyd, Mikkelson, & Judd, 2006, p. 37) and adopting a relational dialectical approach to the negotiation of family relationships (Baxter, 2004).

In our chapter, we draw on our individual experiences to examine copresence in relationships. In the sections below, we present each narrative in turn. In conclusion, we tie in our parallel yet distinct discourses into a cohesive whole that illuminates the unique challenges and common grounds shared by long-distance relationships.

Three Phases of Evolution of Togetherness

In the narratives in this section, I talk about the process of nurturing my relationships at home in the United States and my family in India. My narrative interrogates how our criteria for defining and maintaining relationships at a distance challenge prevalent assumptions of family, such as the following: face-to-face interactions are the normative mode in intimate relationships (O'Sullivan, 2000), communication should be frequent and in depth for close relationships to thrive (Parks, 1995), or even that small talk/casual talk on a daily basis is a presumed relational necessity (Duck & Pittman, 1994). My narrative examines these through the emerging frame of distance-as-discourse to highlight the unique, emergent nature of presence/copresence and distances in relationships. The narrative contributes to the paucity of research on adult children, specifically distance communication with the larger family (grandparents, nieces/nephews, and parents).

As I come from a military family (my father was a fighter pilot in the Indian air force), geographically separated relationships due to dual career couples, telework (Leonardi, Treem, & Jackson, 2010), school, or military appointments defining the familial landscape of American life in the 21st century (Sahlstein, 2010) ring intimately familiar to me. In family communication scholarship, growing numbers of long-distance family relationships have signaled an emerging interest in examining the experiences of geographically separated relationships, or relationships characterized with physical copresence. Along with problematizing the notion of "distance" and "long-distance relationships" or "geographically close" relationships (Merolla, 2010, p. 37), recent scholarship has called for a multiperspectival, nuanced examination of distance-as-discourse.

Through the lens of the distance-as-discourse approach, distance communication in recent scholarship has been conceptualized as "communication that constructs meanings of distance, [looking] for when distance is referenced and constituted in talk, [such that] the context in which the communication takes place does not need to be at a distance" (Sahlstein, 2010, p. 112). Copresence experiences in relationships are based on the five linear and cyclical temporal concepts of amplitude, scale, pace, sequence, and rhythm categorize differences according to duration, frequency, emotional intensity, and routineness of separations (Merolla, 2010). Unlike a decade ago, advances in communication technologies and the processing power of mobile devices have had a deep influence on negotiation of communication in relationships at a distance, challenging us to (re)examine temporal modes of conceptualizing distance. The narratives here reveal how the possibility of constant contact offered by richer media with greater social presence (e.g., video chat via mobile devices) along with evolving meanings of distance play into blurring traditional dichotomies of presence/copresence.

Narratives of Three Phases of Evolution of Togetherness

Distance is a contested concept in relationships today, and part of the tension stems from grappling with discursive notions of presence and separation, geographical or physical. These tensions are compounded when we bring in cultural norms. Traditional families in India have privileged the notion of family as those bound by ties of blood, living under one roof until the daughter was married and left for her (often husband's) house or the son married and either moved to set up another home or continued as part of one large family unit with the parents. The notion of the contemporary Indian family includes retired older parents living without their children, children setting up their own homes, and single-parent family structures. My story most closely resembles the second case. Through the initial years of getting acculturated to life in the United States, first in my role as a homemaker, then as an international graduate student, and finally professionally in the academia as a professor, my narrative ties together the contexts of balancing my family with my husband's long-distance work commutes and our relationships in India.

In this context, the criteria of duration, frequency, routineness, and emotional intensity allow me a tangible framework by which to grasp at the notion of separation and copresence. It was with our move to the United States that transnational distances with my family in India sharply broke the routineness of copresence, such as of being able to casually drop by my mother's house. Hitherto, in India, being their only daughter, my parents had showered all the care and undivided attention on me. I had been the center of their universe, and my family was deeply protective of me in a way that would suggest I never grew up. Given that I had no immediate family in the United States, it took my family in India a long time to get used to my decision to leave for that country, in their eyes so far away from all that had been familiar to me.

On reflection, it may be the geographical distances that most tangibly conceptualized copresence and relational separation for me. The conversations at weekly intervals with my family in India during my initial years in the United States slowly brought in a sense of individual identity and a form of relational distinctness that I had been unable to meaningfully achieve while in India. Traditional theoretical perspectives such as the social presence theory (Short, Williams, & Christie, 1976) or the cues filtered out perspectives (Culnan & Markus, 1987) suggest lack of nonverbal cues and interactivity limits the nature of personal information shared, yet online emancipatory spaces allow us to enact empowerment through disrupting familiar enactments of roles and social practices (Agarwal & Buzzanell, 2008). If I was able to reconfigure the norms of traditional role practices, it was because of negotiating the twin tensions of separations and distances with my family in India and my husband's commute in the United States. Balancing presence/copresence in family relationships made me aware of both my strengths in a way I had not been before and the poignancy of family bonds that I never had an occasion to miss while in India. In my graduate student years, my telephone conversations with family in India and with my husband during his travels for work made up for in duration and frequency what they could not through a compression of spatial distances.

When I started audiovisual media chats over Skype with family in India, it felt like an ideal mediated environment because of the richness of their affordances (Burgoon et al., 2002), their only real marker being carrying the laptop screen across the room. At times, if our underlying conversational goal was to talk, share, and connect, our video Skype conversations were humdrum and meandering. I would study, prepare lectures, grade, do household chores, play with the dog, and so on, while in India my mother might have her breakfast, interact with the neighbors, or play with my niece. At such moments, given the seamless audiovisual nature of the medium, the experience of being together was heightened by our virtual copresence. Through these chats, I felt complete, feeling eventually that I was able to be copresent in my family happenings and gatherings in India.

Similarly, frequency was based on the need to get together as opposed to a cost-based decision. On occasion, we would connect several times a week; other times, with semester deadlines, several weeks would pass by without anyone noticing that we had not talked. A consistency of routine was reassuring on occasion; on others, just the ability to be in touch as often as needed was enough. For my relationships, establishing the audiovisual dimension of the video chat has been instrumental in transforming my sense of togetherness. In the end, what my family in India and I came to miss most about our parallel yet cocreated transnational family worlds was the baseline level of togetherness that lent our lives the rich texture and nuance that came from distances-as-context and distances-as-construct merged together—when I could drop by her home without a moment's thought.

As my husband and I sought to manage physical colocation within the same roof even as we balanced our family and two fledgling career paths in the United States, we found ourselves saying good night many weeknights over the phone. Definitions of long-distance student relationships examine criteria ranging from physical parameters such as mileage (Carpenter & Knox, 1986) to nights spent in separate residences (Gerstel & Gross, 1984) to individual perceptions of distance (Dellman-Jenkins, Bernard-Paolucci, & Rushing, 1994). As an international student, the meaning of physical distance changed with time for me. The initial period, which I would like to call *the naming of distances* phase, was when I felt the separation most acutely in its physical, geographical embodiment. Distances felt tangible, laden with a very real weight of copresence and separation that almost felt like a physical pain. Slowly, though, with the busyness of graduate education and family, the routineness of spending a few weeks and, at times, a few months apart changed the nature of distance to a perception of copresence. This phase symbolized the *creation of togetherness* phase in my life.

In the *creation of togetherness* phase, our relationship embraced the spatiality of distance such that we constructed a dimension of copresence, a hyperpersonal relational sphere of togetherness, regardless of duration, frequency, or routineness of our interactions. Building on a foundation of copresence/noncopresence, we gradually made a meaningful whole of their opposites, *a creation of togetherness* that was more than just geographical colocation. While a line of research has argued that relationships drawing on computer-mediated communication are not rich enough to convey the complex information (Daft & Lengel, 1984) characterized by interpersonal or face-to-face communication, Walther (1996) has proposed that "combinations of media attributes, social phenomena, and social-psychological processes [l]ead CMC [computer-mediated communication] to become 'hyperpersonal'" (p. 5). It is this dimension of togetherness we still draw on when my husband commutes. Today I manage my academic career and my family, we have a home in a small town, and my husband is able to maintain a biweekly (or more) commute home. Given this stable rhythm, it is impossible to delineate where physical copresence ends and virtual copresence begins. Our lives weave into and apart through the virtual/geographical, much as if we were in the same geographical space.

Distances in relationships, I have come to learn, are a coconstructed phenomena, an artifact of the blending of two minds, given form by the actual, more elusive sense of togetherness in the relationship. Technology—rich, hyperpersonal, or not—is ultimately quite tangential to personal, intimate relationships. Perhaps this phase is best described as the *coconstructed spatiality of intimacy*. Our time as a family spent watching a Sunday show on television is as routine as an evening spent saying good night via Skype or to the telephone or a spontaneous instant-messaging chat while at office. Technological affordances do not imbue our relationship with additional form or meaning. Perhaps relational intimacy (as opposed to task-related communication) is characterized less by notions of media richness or copresence and more by the *coconstructed spatiality of intimacy* where perpetual and ongoing meaning construction, sustained in a spatiality of nuance and the mundane, defines the relational form.

Three Phases of Evolution of Togetherness: Concluding Thoughts

Distance communication is a nascent, fledgling field of inquiry. In my narrative here, distances are conceptualized as a discursive, coconstructive continuum of meaning. On the one end, in the phase of *the naming of distances*, all distances are meaningful, spatial, geographical, and temporal, yet, as we continue to meditate on their location in our lives, on the other end, they offer a space for *cocreating a spatiality of intimacy* all its own. Examining the concept of distances as a noun and of distance a form of discourse, my meditations on distance have challenged me to question our deepest assumptions of relationships, family, cultures, and norms. Even as there is no one semantic anchor to norms in relationships, the process of negotiating distances in family relationships on the one hand embodied a potential for empowerment and identity that eluded me in India; on the other hand, they imbued my life with a *coconstructed spatiality of intimacy* in my home in the United States.

My relationship with my family in India, however, continues to fluctuate between the *naming of distances* phase, the *creation of togetherness* phase, and the *coconstructed spatiality of intimacy* phase. While normative theories of social presence, media richness, or those of noncopresence and relationship cycles suggest the many lenses through which we can conceptualize distances in family relationships, my narrative suggests that the meaning of the three phases can be cocreated only within the body of each relationship, uniquely negotiated by the participants, through a continuous process of constructing intimacy.

Living with Two Hearts

The theory of relational dialectics aims to make sense out of competing discourses in everyday communication across contexts. According to this viewpoint, as we communicate, we create multiple meaning systems that often lead to contradictory messages. Individuals encounter discursive struggles as they sort through the "simultaneous fusion, and differentiation of different systems of meaning, or discourse" (Baxter & Braithwaite, 2008, p. 351). Drawing on Russian sociologist Bakhtin's theory of dialogism, Baxter (2004) developed and applied the relational dialectics theory to family communication. This theory views communicative life as being inherently embedded within contradictory forces. Families engage in an interplay of multiple opposing perspectives where some voices dominate and others get marginalized (Baxter, 2006). Positioning relational dialectics as a theory of discursive flux, Baxter (2004) explains that the theory takes a constitutive approach to communication—an approach that asks "how communication defines, or constructs the social world, including our notions of 'self' and 'family'" (Baxter, 2006, p. 138). In other words, family communication, when viewed dialectically, is a careful enactment of change, contradiction, and connection and the opposing forces that get embedded within.

Narratives of Living with Two Hearts

Scholars of family communication have acknowledged the challenges and instability in defining "family" (see Floyd et al., 2006; Galvin, 2006). Personally, I face no such anguish. I accept Floyd et al.'s (2006) concept of viewing the family from a role lens based on "emotional attachment and patterns of interaction" (p. 26), a psychosocial definition that argues "that people who perform instrumental tasks, such as providing nurturance, care giving, and support, are family" (p. 27). The use of this inclusive definition, for me, allows the recruitment of my beloved uncles and grandmothers into the "family" fold. However, for the purpose of this chapter, I will use the term "family" to pertain to my parents and sisters.

Growing up as the second of three daughters, the quintessential middle child, my search for significance within my family, especially in my formative years, was a constant struggle. Even as I quarreled with my sisters over shoes and clothes and argued with my parents over retrospectively irrelevant issues, I was always conscious of the strength of our bonds, the warmth of our love for each other, and the unmistaken concern in every reprimand or punishment. At age 16, after winning multiple leadership awards at a Rotary Club–sponsored event, when the president of that club proposed the idea of my applying to their international youth exchange program, my parents gave permission in a heartbeat, a decision that surprised my relatives given that that would mean my living in a foreign country (I chose Japan) for an entire year. To my sisters and me, it merely reaffirmed our parents' unwavering faith and confidence in us.

The bonds with my sisters only grew stronger with age. I felt close to my older sister, with whom I had a reciprocal secrets-sharing relationship. I could be the immature, crazy, younger sister if I wanted to, and I could also morph into my mature, empathic listener and adviser self when the situation presented itself. With my little sister, the performative aspects of my roles switched. I was her older sister first and felt extremely protective of her. I would advise her, scold her, praise her, and awaken her to harsh realities while still breaking into random dance sessions in our living room to loud music, a craziness that continues to this day. From someone who constantly struggled to accept her birth order as the middle child, extremely sensitive to unfairness, real or imagined, I have now come to appreciate that psychological position's unique vantage point. I believe that journey could not have been traversed had it not been for my parents and sisters allowing for me to quietly tread my developmental stages, through interactions and experiences (Sabourin, 2006), making mistakes and learning many lessons along the way.

In 2001, "I" decided to come to the United States to pursue my master's degree. I place the "I" in quotes because even though I was the executor of that decision, the master puppeteers of that action were all my family members, collectively. The year I returned from Japan, my older sister left for the United States to pursue her master's. I knew then that I would join her abroad just as I had followed her footsteps through school plays, debate competitions, other extracurricular activities, and academic achievements. My parents and little sister enabled that decision by providing financial and emotional support. I still remember my father standing outside the U.S. consulate in the rain, holding an umbrella but refusing to move from his position lest I missed his coming out of the building. When I did emerge, getting his confirmation, my father's first call was to my mother to tell her that I had indeed gotten my visa. My mother's excitement at the other end of the line, at the prospect of my future in the United States, did not betray her inner concerns about my going so far away from our home and her heart.

As any international student will attest, getting a visa to study abroad long term is not even half the battle for those in close-knit families. It is the going away, the bidding farewell, the tug at your heart, that reminds you of the countless birthdays and anniversaries you will miss going forth, that feeling in the pit of your stomach when you hear about your parents' ill health over the phone and numerous other moments like these that are the bigger emotional tensions and contradictions of a long-distance relational life. Today, 10 years later, having spent all of my 20s in the United States, I literally grew up, living a schizophrenic life, rooted in the dilemma of a heart torn between my native land (India) and my adopted one (the United States), straddling dual spaces often strife with ambiguities, discontinuities, irrationalities, and self-imposed logics.

Words like "culture shock" and "homesick" were never a part of my vocabulary until 1997, when I first left home to go live in Japan for a year. That year was when I had my first real tryst with long-distance relationships. Living in the United States, thanks to having experienced and successfully navigated homesickness in Japan, I was better prepared to take on this second international adventure. Falicov (2005) eloquently wonders, "If home is where the heart is, and one's heart is with one's family, language, and country, what happens when your family, language, and culture occupy two different worlds?" (p. 399). She further explains that although the realities of a transnational life are often challenging when it comes to maintaining familial relationships, technology has enabled immigrants to continue to remain connected to their homelands and relatives. In fact, she poignantly states, "Because lives and relations are linked across borders, transnationalism offers an attractive, and at times deceiving, imagined possibility of living with two hearts rather than with one divided heart." Therein lays my answer (and the title of my essay). I do not have to choose. I could continue living with two hearts just as I have been for several years now. This dually appropriated hybrid identity has served me well. Elsewhere (Shenoy, 2011), I have discussed the convoluted enactment of my multiple selves as a transnational nomad. For now, however, I take consolation in the ready availability (speaking from the location of someone who is highly cognizant of her privileged life) of new technologies that help maintain long-distance connections and enable me to recharge my emotional batteries, a process essential to the successful maintaining of a transnational lifestyle (Falicov, 2007).

I consistently use telephone calls and e-mails to communicate with my family. Handwritten letters that I exchanged with my family when I lived in Japan, however, are some of my most prized possessions even today. I believe that instant technologies, such as e-mail, can never replace or replicate the sentiments felt when holding a physical letter addressed to you (perhaps an experience that a younger generation will never understand), but I made my peace with this arrangement a long time ago in order to maintain connections with my Indian heart.

My long-distance technology-enabled conversations with my family have often been a struggle between wanting to assert my newfound independence and accepting the absolute reality that familial bonds may loosen but will never break and that, interestingly, that third, in-between space is a home I will inhabit with little complaint. Even as I call my mother to ask about recipes or homemade cures for the common cold, as a rule, I do not let any sad emotions show. In moments of loneliness or when I have had unfavorable news, I experience a strong urge, simultaneously wanting to stay connected while having to force a neutral, almost emotionless state of calm to protect my family from worrying. This dialectic of connection–disconnection is something I continually navigate to this day. In a related context, Sabourin (2006) refers to the need to connect as the centripetal force and the need to separate as the centrifugal force and explains that "both these needs occur simultaneously, meaning that families are not *either* close *or* distant but rather *both* close *and* distant (p. 54, emphasis in the original).

In all the discontinuities of relational maintenance that I have encountered, from Japan until now, despite the overlapping and multilayered themes of changes, contradictions, and connection-related ambiguities, we have always remained a close-knit family looking out for one another and often switching roles as the situation demanded. From a traditional parent–child relationship, my parents and my sisters and I continually blur the adviser–advisee roles. I first witnessed my own significance in the family structure rise after my older sister left for the United States. My parents, who hitherto consulted my sister on major decisions, now sought out my opinions. Likewise, once I left for the United States, my little sister rose to that position. With all the years elapsed between us, we now engage in a multidirectional, cross-generational advice–support–encouragement give-and-take. Falicov (2005) claims that "the extent to which transnational relationships provide instrumental and affective support becomes limited to extraordinary or occasional circumstances, as opposed to daily interactions" (p. 401), but that reasoning has not diluted our relational bonding, and we take solace in the firm belief that we are all doing the best we can to nurture those bonds because we want to, because we care, and because we love each other.

In conclusion, Prasad (2006) opines that with regard to our family life, it is "but natural to give credence to theories and anecdotal accounts that validate the choices we have made" (p. 8) as adults. I see my narrative as firmly embedded within the dialectical perspective of family communication. Turner (2003) rightly observes that a dialectical perspective "maintains that what characterizes relational life is ongoing tension between contradictory desires" (p. 29). My familial reality, through all the emotional distances covered, is that relational dynamics get (re)negotiated over time. This dynamism, I believe, is what makes the improvisational nature of these situations (Sabourin, 2006) that much more appealing to me. That we give each other the space we need and want to carve a calm between the demands of autonomy and connection and of stability and change is a significant marker of a family life that is confident and secure in the maturity of its relationships and collective identity.

Living with Two Hearts: Concluding Thoughts

In this narrative, physical and emotional distances created due to transnationalism enabled cross-generational and multidirectional communication between the parents and daughters, showing how relationships are not linear. Ambiguities, building connections, contradictions, and change in general are what make up relational lives. These observations are in concert with Turner's (2003) four basic assumptions of dialectical family lives, which state that "a) relationships are not linear; (b) relational life is characterized by change, (c) contradiction is a fundamental fact of relational life, and (d) communication is central to negotiating relational contradictions" (p. 29).

Distances and Relationships

That relationships are complex is unquestionable. In fact, those of us who traverse long distances in pursuit of myriad objectives implicitly accept the nuances that accompany transnational relational maintenance. As international students who came to the United States for higher education and work and progressively made our lives and homes in this country, we continually navigate the multitude of interactions that are fluid as much as they are dynamic. While the first author's narrative suggests that implied within spatiality are the meandering tensions of continually negotiating identity, temporality, and presence, the second author examines distances through the dialectically cocreated processes of change and contradictions. In the end, both narratives suggest that, despite being temporally and spatially separated from our families in India, it is in the ongoing negotiation of distance-as-discourse and in the dialectically cocreated processes of change and contradictions that we experience connections, intimacy, and togetherness.

Discussion Questions

1. How do the three phases in the "Three Phases of Evolution of Togetherness" illustrate the coevolving nature of distances in relationships? Do you agree that technology is ultimately tangential to negotiating distances and copresence in relationships? How? How not? Do you think that newer, emerging forms of mobile communication technologies hold the potential to redefine copresence in relationships?

2. In "Three Phases of Evolution of Togetherness," what characteristics of technology heighten or limit the experience of virtual relational copresence for the author in each of the phases? In what way does the hyperpersonal characteristic of computer-mediated communication define distances and relationships for the author in the *creation of togetherness* phase?

3. How does the author's narrative in "Living with Two Hearts" reflect on and represent the connections, contradictions, and changes inherent in her familial relational interactions?

4. In "Living with Two Hearts," what does the author mean when she says she "grew up living a schizophrenic life, rooted in the dilemma of a heart torn between my native land (India) and my adopted one (the United States)"? What is she alluding to in that statement? How does she eventually negotiate the challenges of such a life?

5. In what way are the central ideas surrounding copresence in the narratives of "Three Phases of Evolution of Togetherness" and "Living with Two Hearts" related? In what way are they distinct?

References

Agarwal, V., & Buzzanell, P. M. (2008). Spatial narratives of the local: Bringing the *basti* center-stage. In R. Gajjala & V. Gajjala (Eds.), *South Asian technospaces* (pp. 123–134). New York: Peter Lang.

Baxter, L. A. (2004). A tale of two voices: Relational dialectics theory. *Journal of Family Communication, 4,* 181-192.

Baxter, L. A. (2006). Relational dialectics theory: Multivocal dialogues of family communication. In D. O. Braithwaite & L. A. Baxter (Eds.), *Engaging theories in family communication: Multiple perspectives* (pp. 130-145). Thousand Oaks, CA: Sage.

Baxter, L. A., & Braithwaite, D. O. (2008). Relational dialectics theory: Crafting meaning from competing discourses. In D. O. Braithwaite & L. A. Baxter (Eds.), *Engaging theories in family communication: Multiple perspectives* (pp. 349-361). Thousand Oaks, CA: Sage.

Burgoon, J. K., Bonito, J. A., Ramirez, A., Jr., Dunbar, N. E., Kam, K., & Fischer, J. (2002). Testing the interactivity principle: Effects of mediation, propinquity, and verbal and nonverbal modalities in interpersonal interaction. *Journal of Communication, 52,* 657-677.

Carpenter, D., & Knox, D. (1986). Relationship maintenance of college students separated during courtship. *College Student Journal, 20,* 86-88.

Culnan, M. J., & Markus, M. L. (1987). Information technologies. In F. M. Jablin, L. L. Putnam, K. H. Roberts, & L. W. Porter (Eds.), *Handbook of organizational communication: An interdisciplinary perspective* (pp. 420-443). Newbury Park, CA: Sage.

Daft, R. L., & Lengel, R. H. (1984). Information richness: A new approach to managerial behavior and organizational design. In L. L. Cummings & B. M. Staw (Eds.), *Research in organizational behavior* (Vol. 6, pp. 191-233). Homewood, IL: JAI Press.

Dellmann-Jenkins, M., Bernard-Paolucci, T. S., & Rushing, B. (1994). Does distance make the heart grow fonder? A comparison of college students in long distance and geographically close dating relationships. *College Student Journal, 28,* 212-219.

Duck, S. W., & Pittman, G. (1994). Social and personal relationships. In M. L. Knapp & G. R. Miller (Eds.), *Handbook of interpersonal communication* (pp. 676-695). Thousand Oaks, CA: Sage.

Falicov, C. J. (2005). Emotional transnationalism and family identities. *Family Processes, 44*(4), 399-406.

Falicov, C. J. (2007). Working with transnational immigrants: Expanding meanings of family, community, and culture. *Family Processes, 46,* 157-171.

Floyd, K., Mikkelson, A. C., & Judd, J. (2006). Defining the family through relationships. In L. H. Turner & R. L. West (Eds.), *The family communication sourcebook* (pp. 21-39). Thousand Oaks, CA: Sage.

Galvin, K. M. (2006). Joined by hearts and words: Adoptive family relationships. In K. Floyd & M. T. Morman (Eds.), *Widening the family circle: New research on family relationships* (pp. 137-152). Thousand Oaks, CA: Sage.

Gerstel, N., & Gross, H. (1984). *Commuter marriage: A study of work and family*. New York: Guilford Press.

Leonardi, P. M., Treem, J. W., & Jackson, M. H. (2010). The connectivity paradox: Using technology to both increase and decrease perceptions of distance in distributed work arrangements. *Journal of Applied Communication Research, 38,* 85-105.

Merolla, A. J. (2010). Relational maintenance during military deployment: Perspectives of wives of deployed U.S. soldiers. *Journal of Applied Communication Research, 38,* 4-26.

O'Sullivan, P. B. (2000). What you don't know won't hurt ME: Impression management functions of communication channels in relationships. *Human Communication Research, 26,* 403–431.

Parks, M. R. (1995). Webs of influence in interpersonal relationships. In C. R. Berger & M. E. Burgoon (Eds.), *Communication and social influence processes* (pp. 155–178). East Lansing: Michigan State University Press.

Prasad, G. (2006). *The great Indian family: New roles, old responsibilities.* New Delhi: Penguin.

Sabourin, T. C. (2006). Theories and metatheories to explain family communication. In L. H. Turner & R. L. West (Eds.), *The family communication sourcebook* (pp. 43–60). Thousand Oaks, CA: Sage.

Sahlstein, E. (2010). Communication and distance: The present and future interpreted through the past. *Journal of Applied Communication Research, 38,* 106–114.

Shenoy, S. (2011). Navigating the third space with double consciousness: South Asian Indian women in the American workplace. In A. Gonzalez, M. Houston, & V. Chen (Eds.), *Our voices* (5th ed., pp. 71–76). London: Oxford University Press.

Short, J. A., Williams, E., & Christie, B. (1976). *The social psychology of telecommunications.* New York: Wiley.

Turner, L. H. (2003). Theories of relational communication. In K. M. Galvin & P. J. Cooper (Eds.), *Making connections: Readings in relational communication* (pp. 20–31). Los Angeles: Roxbury.

Walther, J. B. (1996). Computer-mediated communication: Impersonal, interpersonal, and hyperpersonal interaction. *Communication Research, 23,* 3–43.

Werner, C. M., & Baxter, L. A. (1994). Temporal qualities of relationships: Organismic, transactional, and dialectical views. In M. L. Knapp & G. R. Miller (Eds.), *Handbook of interpersonal communication* (2nd ed., pp. 323–379). Newbury Park, CA: Sage.

Chapter 17

Family Relationships as More Than Blood: Military Families as Dialectics and Discourses

Erin Sahlstein and Katheryn C. Maguire

With the 10-year anniversary of 9/11 and the daily information circulated in the public sphere about casualties, deployment cycles, and family reunions, the prominence of the American military family in the 21st century is evident. Deployments have increased in "optempo," or frequency (Keller et al., 2005), with U.S. military families experiencing several wartime deployments and other military-related separations (e.g., trainings) (Tanielian & Jaycox, 2008). The research in this area spans several disciplines and decades (for excellent reviews of the research, see the edited collections of Castro, Adler, & Britt, 2006; MacDermid-Wadsworth & Riggs, 2011), and communication researchers recently started focusing on this very important family type with Operation Iraqi Freedom and Operation Enduring Freedom (e.g., Frisby, Byrnes, Mansson, Booth-Butterfield, & Birmingham, 2011; Joseph & Afifi, 2010; Merolla, 2010; Sahlstein, Maguire, & Timmerman, 2009; Wilson et al., 2011). The majority of military family research focuses on traditionally defined families (military spouses [e.g., Merolla, 2010] or military parents and their biological children [e.g., Lincoln, Swift, & Shorteno-Fraser, 2008]). In this chapter, we present alternative perspectives for viewing military families—ones that consider family as something more than blood or legal relations between family members.

Across the research on military families and family research in general, scholars use some typical definitions for what is a family. A common definition of family includes blood, or genetic, ties (Floyd, Mikkelson, & Judd, 2006), but, as the title of this book reflects, families might also be considered as more than individuals bound by blood. In this chapter, we argue that families should be thought of in terms of the communication that (re)constructs these relationships both at the level of interpersonal communication within families and at the level of discourses about families. Guided by relational dialectics theory (RDT) (Baxter, 2011; Baxter & Montgomery, 1996), we offer two alternatives to typical familial definitions—family as contradiction and family as discourse.

Using the military family as our case and starting point, we exemplify these new definitions, or lenses, for thinking about families. Throughout this chapter, we will use examples from our research on military family communication, specifically military wives' experiences, as the particular case to exemplify dialectical concepts. Our explication incorporates relevant data from interviews we conducted with 50 military wives whose husbands had recently deployed to Iraq or Afghanistan. We conclude the chapter by suggesting lines of inquiry for family communication scholars interested in military family research.

Families as More Than Blood Ties

Families are typically defined, both in scholarly research (Segrin & Flora, 2005) and in lay terms (Baxter et al., 2009), using at least one of three categories: biogenetic, sociolegal, and role (Floyd et al., 2006). A commonly identified definition of family is one of blood ties—those who are related by genetics or reproductive capacity. Floyd et al. (2006) outline two criteria for deciding family boundaries based on biogenetics: (a) whether partners share genetic material (e.g., parents and their children or siblings) and (b) the extent to which two individuals in a relationship are reproductively capable. The former is relatively clear, but the latter needs elaboration. In order to be considered family, according to the second criterion, partners must at least have the potential to produce children as well as provide for them until their adulthood; therefore, marriages are considered families given their real or potential production of offspring. The biogenetic definition of family, while common and relatively objective, is not the only definition of family that individuals use in their everyday lives.

Another definition is a given society's legal definition, or what Floyd et al. (2006) term the sociolegal definition. Families, in this case, are those that "carry legal recognition . . . in either common, statutory law, or both" (Floyd et al., p. 29). While some family relationships have "no civil or criminally enforceable obligations or privileges" (e.g., siblings) (p. 29), they are considered family when compared to other legally sanctioned relationships (e.g., partners in a corporation) (p. 29). Opposite-sex marriages and parent–child relationships clearly fall into this category, as do adoptive relationships, domestic partnerships, civil unions, and common-law and same-sex marriages in states where they are legal. While biogenetic ties are often the basis for sociolegal definitions, certainly recognition of nontraditional relational forms that are based in the third conceptual lens for defining family is coming about with more frequency (e.g., same-sex marriage; Baxter et al., 2009).

Family membership may also be determined through the roles individuals play in their relationships (Floyd et al., 2006). Individuals might say, for example, that their friends are "like family" to them, and their claims are based in the emotional connections they hold with these people as well as the types of interactions they have with them (e.g., friends giving each other the same kind of support given to siblings) (Floyd et al., 2006). The role definition is akin to social constructionist, or constitutive, approaches to family; how people feel and behave is what defines the relationship and not only genetics connections, reproductive potential, or the law. According to the role definition, family is what individuals feel and see as family.

In the military family research, scholars operationally define family based on the sociolegal and biogenetic definitions (i.e., legally married couples and their biological children), rarely stretching them beyond their limits (e.g., extended family such as grandparents or siblings) or taking into consideration other family forms (e.g., cohabitating partners or same-sex couples). The role perspective is scarcely reflected in military family research but does come into play when scholars look at communicative processes such as social support, coping, and relationship maintenance and include military family members' experiences with individuals who are not legal or biological family (Maguire & Sahlstein, 2012). Researchers have also focused on support groups, such as in the U.S. Army's Family Readiness Groups (FRGs), where military spouses help one another cope with the challenges of deployment (Di Nola, 2008; Orthner & Rose, 2003, 2007; Sahlstein & Maguire, 2011).

While all three definitions are and have been useful for family communication scholars and laypeople alike, we present two additional approaches to family that come from an RDT perspective

(Baxter & Montgomery, 1996). First, we will discuss families in terms of their contradictions using the first iteration of RDT (RDT 1.0; Baxter & Montgomery, 1996), and then we present the family as discourse approach using the second iteration of RDT (RDT 2.0; Baxter, 2011).

Families as Dialectics

In addition to treating family as the lived experiences of individuals who are connected through blood, by society, and/or because of their roles, we might consider families as patterns of dialectics, or contradictions, that individuals experience with specific others using RDT 1.0. Contradictions are opposing yet unified forces within a relationship that are shaped in but that also shape the communication between relational partners, such as the dialectic between autonomy and connection (Baxter & Montgomery, 1996). While this concept might appear to be included within the role definition presented above, as contradictions are patterns of interaction that certainly bring with them affective responses to others, there are a few key distinctions in the assumptions that go along with each. First, Floyd et al.'s (2006) examples of interaction patterns that reflect a role definition privilege "good" interaction types and do not necessarily connote all interaction patterns. They cite two examples used in the literature: Fitzpatrick and Caughlin's (2002) psychosocial task definition where "people who perform instrumental tasks, such as providing nurturance, care giving, and support ... [who are] characterized by strong ties of interdependence and commitment," are family, and Wamboldt and Reiss's (1989) definition that families are groups of people who have "strong ties of loyalty and emotion" (p. 27). Both of these definitions cited by Floyd et al. (2006) emphasize actions or emotions that value bonding and connection with the implied devaluing of difference or separateness, or what relational dialectics scholars term monologic, or one-sided, views of relating (Baxter & Montgomery, 1996). These ideas for what constitutes family reflect idealized or privileged notions of how families should act and not necessarily how they typically occur. They also do not recognize how communicative patterns typically deemed as distancing or counterproductive (e.g., topic avoidance) may also promote bonding and connection. RDT 1.0 offers an approach that reflects complexities of family life by including less ideal forms of communication. RDT 1.0 scholars seek to identify and understand dynamics relational partners struggle with in their everyday lives, such as how to stay connected as a family while maintaining autonomy as individual members of society, and they would not include in their analyses only those interaction patterns that favor connection or reflect loyalty (e.g., offering social support).

RDT 1.0 is founded in four key concepts (i.e., contradiction, praxis, totality, and change), but for the purposes of this chapter, the most important of these is the contradictions relational partners experience as a result of trying to negotiate two opposing yet unified forces, needs, or desires (Baxter & Montgomery, 1996). Contradictions, or dialectics, manifest in theoretically an infinite number of ways; however, researchers often report that families deal with a similar set of dialectics: certainty–uncertainty, autonomy–connection, and openness–closedness (Baxter, 2006).

We published a study that used RDT 1.0 to understand military wives' experience across predeployment, deployment, and postdeployment stages (Sahlstein et al., 2009). We reported that within each deployment phase, one contradiction seemed to dominate. In predeployment (i.e., the period beginning with official orders and ending when the soldier departed for duty), wives' reports overwhelmingly reflected contradictions of uncertainty–certainty. These wives dealt with, for example, the need for predictability in a period when certainty was questioned with changing deployment dates and fears about their future marital stability. Wives spoke of "pushing away" their husbands in order to gain some certainty, while others struggled to communicate their uncertainties to their husbands. During deployment, they dealt with the contradiction of autonomy–connection. Wives with children, for example, had to face life without their partner and co-parent, and they shared stories of how they developed new patterns that adjusted to life without their husbands. In some cases, wives privileged their independence by creating lives of their own. Other wives maintained a balance between their connection to their husbands and their autonomous lives back home. Finally, openness–closedness defined the postdeployment period. Other communication research on military families, albeit not using RDT 1.0, reports difficulties with expression and concealment (Frisby et al., 2011; Joseph & Afifi, 2010). The wives in our study reported dealing with a range of communication struggles after their husbands returned. Some wives had no problems with their communication, while others conflicted with their husbands in terms of what could be talked about, with whom, and when.

While an RDT 1.0 approach to studying family communication is quite useful for understanding the complexities of familial dynamics, scholars who use this approach focus on the patterns *within* the family. RDT 1.0 research has examined families in a variety of forms (e.g., stepfamilies, lesbian families, and fictive kin), but using the context as the basis for inquiry about other variables, while common across family communication research, is not without its critics. Because of its treatment of the relationship as the context where communication takes place, scholars have referred to this type of research as taking a container approach to studying personal relationships (Baxter, 2004; Baxter & Braithwaite, 2008). The military-as-context approach is dominant in military family research as well as other relationship types that experience periods of separation (e.g., commuter marriages) or that exist in states of physical distance (e.g., online relationships) (Sahlstein, 2010). Military family researchers look for how the communicative patterns or other variables are unique within this context and seek to improve military family functioning, which ultimately benefits military objectives (e.g., service members are focused during their missions when their personal lives are stable). Critics of the container approach advocate shifting the research gaze from how family members talk to each other to how families are talked about. We revisit the initial three definitions of family presented by Floyd et al. (2006) to introduce a fifth approach—family as discourse.

Families as Discourse

Floyd et al. (2006) discuss how the three definitions (i.e., biogenetic, sociolegal, and role) might come into "pronounced tensions during extraordinary circumstances" (p. 27) when one definition might trump another. For example, many state's sociolegal definitions of marriage do not allow public recognition of a relationship between two women who feel and act like they are married to one another (role definition). Another example is when one sibling might say to another, "You don't act like my brother. My best friend is more like a brother to me than you!" In this example, the role definition dominates the biogenetic. A far more common conflict of definitions is when the biogenetic definition silences constructions of families as defined by actions, not their blood. For example, a stepdaughter might lash out at her stepmother who is trying to punish her by saying, "You're not my real mom. I don't need to answer to you." These examples show how the definitions, or discourses, of family might compete in everyday life. Instead of using the definitions to create contexts in which to study communication patterns, their use in talk becomes the focus, in particular when certain discourses can be identified as dominant.

Baxter (2011) updated RDT by giving "a central place to discourse, or the systems of meanings by which social realities are shaped" (p. 39), displacing somewhat the conceptualization of dialectic, or contradiction, emphasized in RDT 1.0. While a complete description of RDT 2.0 is beyond the scope of this chapter, we guide our discussion with the main focus of this approach, which is to identify competing discourses in talk (e.g., what is a family and what is not a family). For the purposes of this chapter, we took an ad hoc discursive approach to our data and asked, "What discourses appear to dominate wives' talk about military family life?" We immediately noted two discourses in their talk about deployment experiences: (a) what it means to be a "good wife" or "good military wife," which is close to if not interanimated with (b) what it means to have "good" marital or familial communication throughout deployment.

Those who have had an association with the military during their lives will attest to the fact that the military culture is unique (Britt, Adler, & Castro, 2006; Ender, 2006). Like other organizations, each military branch provides information and other resources, formally and informally, to new members for learning about the culture. For example, one of our sisters, who is a U.S. Air Force wife, was provided a "complete social guide" for what it means to be a wife on her husband's entry into the branch (Crossley & Keller, 2009). Military branches also provide special training sessions for spouses about to go through a deployment, including guidelines for how spouses can support their husbands or wives across these difficult periods. Thus, what it means to be a good military wife is communicated in numerous ways within these communities. A primary way in which our interviewees articulated what this means was through "being supportive" of their husbands and the military. Several women described how good wives become an extension of their husband (i.e., they wear their husband's rank) and/or form a unit or team with their husband where he has his duties and she has hers.

We also noted for many of the women we interviewed that being a good military wife included helping other military wives and families, which typically translated into participating in the unit's FRG. Most of the wives we interviewed lived thousands of miles away from their blood relatives and personal friends, so the FRG was a place where these women could serve as "fictive kin" (i.e., individuals who feel and act like family but who are not biologically or legally related to them) for one another. They could also help support other soldiers: "We got some stuff for [them] cuz [single soldiers] not coming home to anything and some of the wives didn't make it in and that kinda thing so I thought, well you know what, I'll go greet them" (13E, lines 2503–2505). Helping others was consistently constructed as good-wife behavior. Also, participating in the FRG was a way to cope with their own stress during the deployment without necessarily involving their husbands, which was another sign of being a good wife—not bothering one's husband with stressors from home. "[It helped me cope with my stress by] just the [helping] spouses and doing things with the FRG to help soldiers out and get ready for it" (1K, line 437). Research also supports our interviewees' notion that good military wives participate in FRGs: "The FRG is indeed a potential force multiplier for spouses, especially in terms of helping spouses adjust to the demands of Army life and potentially contribute to spouse support for the readiness and retention of the Soldier" (Orthner & Rose, 2007, p. 11).

We found that wives reinforced the construction that to be a good wife, women should participate in the FRGs through their talk that showed disdain for wives who did not become actively involved in their FRGs. Some wives, typically officers' wives and others with significant roles in the FRGs, talked about other wives deciding not to participate. One wife said, "No, [wives not participating] doesn't stress me out because people that want to be involved are involved, and the people that don't want to be involved that's fine" (2E, lines 399–402). This woman's comments seem to indicate that good wives "make time" for the FRG and that, for those who do not, "that's their decision." Wives who stayed put perceived wives who went home during deployment (i.e., they moved close to or in with their families, such as parents, siblings, or in-laws) as weaker than wives who stayed in proximity of their husbands' bases.

On the other side of this issue, wives who did not participate in the FRGs constructed the more "gung ho" wives as too dependent on the military because they made "the FRG . . . their whole life" (18E, line 397) and tried to wear their husbands' rank when around other wives (9e). These women were, however, in the minority of our data set. Overall, a good military wife, at least in part, meant working with their husbands and the military to help promote strength and resiliency.

A second and closely related discourse to the first was what constitutes good or appropriate military wife communication. This often meant that wives communicated support for their husbands' goals and excitement over deploying, even if that meant silencing their fears and uncertainty. Wives also spoke of good spousal communication during deployment as supportive and non–stress inducing for their husbands, even when in some cases the wives would have benefited from talking to their husbands about problems occurring stateside. Wives and other family members are told that they should avoid bringing up conflicts or anything negative when communicating with the deployed service member. Erika shared how she did not follow these rules, making her, what she called, the "anti-Christ" wife:

> I was not being pleasant on the phone, and I wasn't trying to help him in any way. I was just only looking for help. I wasn't trying to give him any help. I was like the anti-Christ wife, like in terms of what they tell you to do as wife of deployed soldier. I wasn't doing anything [that you're supposed to do]. (17A, lines 839–844)

Good military wife communication during deployment also meant for many of our interviewees that they acted as the stateside "eyes and ears" for their husbands, subsequently telling their husbands what went on while they were gone. Participation in the unit FRG was an important site for gaining information that could then be shared with the husbands. Julia, an FRG leader and career army wife, in some cases advised her husband in his decisions to take men out of combat:

> We would talk about the best way to execute things and the best way to handle different situations and um maybe a suggestion on for instance I knew of a situation that was going on here with a spouse and it was serious incident and I wanted to let him know so he could tell one of his pilots they need to take the guy out of the cockpit. Don't let the guy fly. Because of the family's issues, he's a safety hazard. So we've always worked like that together to avoid a bad situation by listening to how people are doing. (2E, lines 411–432)

During postdeployment, many wives constructed good communication as that which is "on the same page" as their husbands. These women reported having open lines of communication with their husbands throughout the deployment process and felt that their marriages were "back to normal" since they were reunited. Here, good communication meant agreement or being free of conflicts, which is somewhat troubling given that the reintegration phase likely brings up changes in the marriage or household that need to be addressed. Wives who reported disjointed or conflictual communication during postdeployment seemed to feel that this was abnormal or problematic, thus reiterating the notion of good communication as smooth talk where partners are similar in their interaction patterns.

While revisiting our interviews with a discursive approach in mind was interesting and productive, it was not what we set out to accomplish when we gathered the data. In the final section, we outline some directions for future research using the approaches of families as dialectics and families as discourses as our guides.

Future Research

Previous research has opened the door for future studies of military family dialectics and discourses. In our case, while we planned to identify contradictions of deployment, we did not interview military wives with the intention of identifying the dialectics of being a military family or the dominant, marginal, and competing discourses in their reports. Therefore, we suggest that researchers interested in taking dialectical or discursive approaches to family, military or otherwise, consider the following lines of inquiry. First, researchers should collect and analyze transcripts of families talking about what it means to be a family. Shifting from studying the communication within families to closely examining how people talk about families is necessary when taking an RDT 2.0 approach (Baxter, 2011). With respect to military culture, researchers could look at how family goes beyond the biological and/or sociolegal definitions of family within particular contexts. Service members might be asked to talk about the family-type relationships they have with other service members and their families. We strongly encourage family researchers to ask participants to discuss the complexities of family life to identify dominant discourses. Within the military, this would involve looking into what it means to be the active duty member versus the spouse or child. It could also mean asking what the differences are between officers and enlisted members or living on base versus off base. Another line of inquiry could be to look closely at how dominant discourses inform relationships with civilians. Similar to Bergen's (2010) work concerning how the master narratives, or discourses, of marriage affect commuter wives' interactions with people who question their relationship status, military family researchers could investigate how spouses and even military children are called on to defend their family situation given that military families, with their frequent moves and separations, depart from what are considered "normal" families. Finally, we suggest studying the media coverage concerning military families as another site for identifying dominant discourses with respect to this important family type. We hope that future research continues to identify functional communication within military families dealing with deployment, but we strongly encourage researchers to consider new ways of studying families and communication, most notably using RDT 2.0 to identify discourses about families.

Discussion Questions

1. Which four key concepts constitute the relational dialectics theory?
2. According to this article, what are some characteristics that denote a "good military wife"?
3. There is a strong code of conduct among military wives that encourages a unique culture for the wives of the deployed. Can you think of any other profession that fosters a distinctive culture among the families of those involved in the profession? Explain.

References

Baxter, L. A. (2004). A tale of two voices: Relational dialectics theory. *Journal of Family Communication, 4,* 181-192.

Baxter, L. A. (2006). Relational dialectics theory: Multivocal dialogues of family communication. In D. O. Braithwaite & L. A. Baxter (Eds.), *Engaging theories in family communication: Multiple perspectives* (pp. 130-145). Thousand Oaks, Sage.

Baxter, L. A. (2011). *Voicing relationships.* Thousand Oaks, CA: Sage.

Baxter, L. A., & Braithwaite, D. O. (2008). Relational dialectics theory: Crafting meaning from competing discourses. In L. A. Baxter & D. O. Braithwaite (Eds.), *Engaging theories in interpersonal communication: Multiple perspectives* (pp. 349-361). Thousand Oaks, CA: Sage.

Baxter, L. A., Henauw, C., Huisman, D., Livesay, C. B., Norwood, K., Su, H., et al. (2009). Lay conceptions of "family": A replication and extension. *Journal of Family Communication, 9,* 170-189.

Baxter, L. A., & Montgomery, B. M. (1996). *Relating: Dialogues and dialectics.* New York: Guilford.

Bergen, K. M. (2010). Accounting for difference: Commuter wives and the master narrative of marriage. *Journal of Applied Communication Research, 38,* 47-64.

Britt, T. W., Adler, A. B., & Castro, C. A. (2006). Military culture: Common themes and future directions. In T. W. Britt, A. B. Adler, & C. A. Castro (Eds.), *Military life: The psychology of serving in peace and combat (Volume 4: Military culture)* (pp. 231-234). Westport, CT: Praeger Security International.

Castro, C. A., Adler, A. B., & Britt, T. W. (Eds.) (2006). *Military life: The psychology of serving in peace and combat (Volume 3: the military family).* Westport, CT: Praeger Security International.

Crossley, A., & Keller, C. A. (2009). *The Air Force wife handbook: A complete social guide.* Marietta, GA: ABI Press.

Di Nola, G. M. (2008). Factors afflicting families during military deployment. *Military Medicine, 172,* v-vii.

Ender, M. G. (2006). Voices from the backseat: Demands of growing up in military families. In C. A. Castro, A. B. Adler, & T. W. Britt (Eds.), *Military life: The psychology of serving in peace and combat (Volume 3: The military family)* (pp. 138-166). Westport, CT: Praeger Security International.

Fitzpatrick, M. A., & Caughlin, J. P. (2002). Interpersonal communication in family relationships. In M. L. Knapp & J. A. Daly (Eds.), *Handbook of family relationships* (2nd edition) (pp. 726-778). Thousand Oaks, CA: Sage.

Floyd, K., Mikkelson, A. C., & Judd, J. (2006). Defining the family through relationships. In L. H. Turner & R. West (Eds.), *The family communication sourcebook* (pp. 21-39). Thousand Oaks, CA: Sage.

Frisby, B. N., Byrnes, K., Mansson, D. H., Booth-Butterfield, M., & Birmingham, M. K. (2011). Topic avoidance, everyday talk, and stress in romantic military and non-military couples. *Communication Studies, 62,* 241-257.

Joseph, A. L., & Afifi, T. D. (2010). Military wives' stressful disclosures to their deployed husbands: The role of protective buffering. *Journal of Applied Communication Research, 38,* 412-434.

Keller, R. T., Greenberg, N., Bobo, W. V., Roberts, P., Jones, N. & Orman, D. T. (2005). Solider peer mentoring care and support: Bringing psychological awareness to the front. *Military Medicine, 170,* 355–361.

Lincoln, A., Swift, E., & Shorteno-Fraser, M. (2008). Psychological adjustment and treatment of children and families with parents deployed in military combat. *Journal of Clinical Psychology, 64,* 984–992.

MacDermid-Wadsworth, S., & Riggs, D. (Eds.) (2011). *Risk and resilience in U.S. military families.* New York: Springer.

Maguire, K., & Sahlstein, E. (2012). In the line of fire: Family management of acute stress during wartime deployment. In F. C. Dickson & L. Webb (Eds.), *Communication for families in crisis: Theories, methods, strategies* (pp. 103–127). New York: Peter Lang.

Merolla, A. J. (2010). Relational maintenance during military deployment: Perspectives of wives of deployed U.S. soldiers. *Journal of Applied Communication Research, 38,* 4–26.

Orthner, D. K., & Rose, R. (2003). Dealing with the effects of absence: Deployment and adjustment to separation among military families. *Journal of Family and Consumer Science, 95,* 33–37.

Orthner, D. K., & Rose, R. (2007). *Family readiness group involvement and adjustment among Army civilian spouses.* Washington, DC: Army Research Institute for the Behavioral and Social Sciences.

Sahlstein, E. (2010). Communication and distance: The present and future interpreted through the past. *Journal of Applied Communication Research, 38,* 106–114.

Sahlstein, E., & Maguire, K. C. (2011, February). *Comfort, cliques, and clashes: Dilemmas Army wives face when interacting within a family readiness group during wartime.* Paper presented at the annual meeting of the Western States Communication Association, Monterrey, CA.

Sahlstein, E., Maguire, K. C., & Timmerman, L. (2009). Contradictions and praxis contextualized by wartime deployment: Wives' perspectives revealed through relational dialectics. *Communication Monographs, 76,* 421–442.

Segrin, C., & Flora, J. (2005). *Family communication.* Mahwah, NJ: Lawrence Erlbaum Associates.

Tanielian, T., & Jaycox, L. (Eds.). (2008). *Invisible wounds of war: Psychological and cognitive injuries, their consequences, and services to assist recovery.* Santa Monica, CA: Rand Corporation.

Wamboldt, F., & Reiss, D. (1989). Defining a family heritage and a new relationship identity: Two central tasks in the making of a marriage. *Family Process, 2,* 317–335.

Wilson, S. R., Wilkum, K., Chernichky, S. M., MacDermid, Wadsworth, S. M., & Broniarczyk, K. M. (2011). Passport toward success: Description and evaluation of a program designed to help children and families reconnect after a military deployment. *Journal of Applied Communication Research, 39,* 223–249.

Chapter 18

Ex-Prisoners Are Coming Home: A Reentry Court's Family Focus

Jeralyn Faris

As a recent Reentry court graduate, a woman named Teanna explains in court how the program, coupled with her strong determination to put her life back together, has earned her the right to be a part of society again. She tells the court that she has met, and in some cases exceeded, the requirements of the Reentry program in an effort to resume her roles as a mother, employee, and citizen. The program showed her that the life she was living as an alcoholic and addict was no longer what she wanted for herself. Teanna now wants to show others that living a life of crime and addiction does not have to be the end for them; that if she can overcome addiction, they can too. She says that completing the Reentry program has been a blessing and she feels confident that she now knows how to live without drugs.

Teanna is one of approximately 730,000 individuals who are released annually from U.S. federal and state prisons (West, Sabol, & Greenman, 2010). She has returned to her home community and reunited with her family while voluntarily participating in a reentry problem-solving court (PSC). Many incarcerated mothers report plans to become the primary caregivers of their children on their release (Arditti & Few, 2006; Mumola, 2000), and most inmates who are fathers plan to have an active role in their children's lives (Edin, Nelson, & Paranal, 2004; Shannon & Abrams, 2007). However, these expectations are often unmet (Hairston, 2007), as many ex-prisoners find the reuniting process discouraging and the reentry process more difficult than anticipated and often find themselves among the number of over 67% of ex-prisoners who are in legal trouble within 3 years of their release (U.S. Department of Justice, 2009).

The high rate of recidivism has prompted the formation of reentry PSCs, a strategy implemented to reform the reentry process for ex-prisoners as they return to their communities (Berman & Feinblatt, 2005; Clark & Neuhard, 2005; Miller & Johnson, 2009; Travis, 2005). A critical aspect of a reentry PSC is enabling ex-prisoners to reunite with children and families, a strong motivation that can increase the likelihood of ex-prisoners becoming law-abiding citizens in their communities. This chapter begins with a brief overview of the research related to incarceration and families. Second, a description of a local reentry PSC (based on a 3-year qualitative study) provides background. Finally, an ethnographic study of a reentry PSC public courtroom session with accompanying analysis demonstrates the saliency of family reunification in terms of blood relationships and also how court participants often develop family-type relationships with their cohorts.

Incarceration and Families

The explosive growth of persons incarcerated in the United States in the past 30 years has had a dramatic impact on children and families. More than 1.7 million children had one or both parents in federal or state prison in 2007 (Glaze & Maruschak, 2008). Wildeman (2009) asserts that "parental imprisonment has emerged as a novel—and distinctively American—form of childhood disadvantage" (p. 276). Research has shown that the children of criminal offenders are more likely to experience poor academic performance, exposure to domestic violence, extreme poverty, delinquency, drug use, and psychopathology (Comfort, 2008; Foster & Hagan, 2007; Krisberg & Temin, 2007; Murray & Farrington, 2008; Phillips & Dettlaff, 2009; Trice & Brewster, 2004). However, ill effects are often felt by all members of the family—children, parents, spouses and partners, and caregivers of children.

Whole communities suffer the "collateral consequences" of a resident's incarceration (e.g., economic hardship, loss of social capital, depression, posttraumatic stress syndrome, and so on), and the impact of incarceration has fallen disproportionately on families of color (Glaze & Maruschak, 2008). African American children are nine times more likely and Latino children three times more likely to have a parent incarcerated than is a white child (Krisberg & Temin, 2007). Braman (2004), Comfort (2007, 2008), and Wildeman (2009) provide extensive and insightful reviews on the wide range of the unintended punitive effects of prisoners' incarcerations on their families. Further reading of these sources can provide understanding of what Krisberg and Temin (2007) refer to as a "growing social time bomb" that requires "enlightened social policies" (p. 189). Reentry PSC programs are a strategy of social policy reform that deserves closer examination. Furthermore, observing how ex-prisoners interact with, support, and challenge one another in the course of their program yields insights into ways in which visions of "family" often extend to other-than-blood relationships in which others are seen as playing the roles of "parent" or "child," "brother" or "sister."

Description of a Local Reentry PSC

In 2005, a circuit court judge in a Midwest county decided to initiate plans for a reentry PSC. From his bench, he was well positioned to see who came into court over and over again over a period of years and who was caught in the revolving door of the criminal justice system. A sociology professor helped design the program, and the structure, procedures, and policies were delineated. At the time of this writing, this reentry PSC has been in existence for nearly 5 years. During that time, there have been a total of 80 participants with 40 having graduated, 21 expelled, and 19 current participants, and only 5% of the graduates have been rearrested (compared to over 67% nationwide; U.S. Department of Justice, 2009).

The process begins while an inmate is in state prison. Persons who are interested in voluntary participation in the reentry PSC can petition for a sentence modification. Most participants have been incarcerated for at least 2 years and have 2 or more years left to serve of their original sentence at the time of the application. The county prosecutor reviews the application and has the discretionary power to reject the modification request, prevent an inmate from an early release from prison, and thus exercise his or her role as a protector of public safety. The prosecutor voices his or her approval or rejection of an inmate's request for modification at the weekly reentry team meeting. The team convenes and meets with the presiding judge for a staff meeting on Mondays at 8:00 a.m.

Team members include the reentry court case manager, representatives from police agencies, probation, representatives of the prosecutor and public defense offices, mental and physical health treatment providers, education and housing personnel, service agency volunteers, and a university researcher/volunteer.

When participants are accepted into the reentry PSC program, they sign a participation agreement and are placed in the work-release facility, a place where they are housed and remain under strict surveillance while they are in the process of reentering the community. The first week after their release from prison is referred to as "Community Transition Week," and participants face many requirements: obtaining an identification card and a library card, initiating participation in required treatment programs, registering to vote, and applying for entitlement programs such as food stamps and Medicaid. Empirical studies show that a person's participation in a community (e.g., voting and using library services) while receiving support services increases his or her social capital and thus provides stake in society (Manza & Uggen, 2006; Wolff & Draine, 2004). Therefore, the program is designed to include aspects of community involvement at the very beginning of a participant's reentry. The most important determinant of a person's readiness to leave the work-release facility is acquiring a job and maintaining employment for a minimum of 30 days.

The ex-prisoners engage in a cluster of programs—cognitive-behavioral therapy, substance abuse treatment, education and employment assistance, and housing services. A participant's progress is monitored weekly by a case manager who is responsible only for reentry participants, and each individual in the program is initially required to check in daily with the case manager or a representative in the community corrections office. The case manager schedules drug and alcohol tests and reports each participant's progress or setbacks to the reentry team in the form of a written report each week. The team discusses each participant's reports and advises the judge as to responses they feel are appropriate (e.g., specific rewards and sanctions to be delivered to specific participants).

When the team meeting concludes, the judge enters a public courtroom where the current participants are waiting for a session that lasts 90 minutes. These sessions are where the "front-stage performances" of the court take place (Faris, Miller, & Johnson, 2009). Individual participants are called to a podium with a microphone in front of the judge's bench, and each man and woman engages in dialogue with the judge. During these public conversations, the judge queries participants about jobs and family relationships and listens to the reading of essays prepared by participants as requested. The judge also issues sanctions to those who have violated regulations during the previous week, sometimes announcing, for example, that the person must complete 4 hours of work crew before the next court session or write a one-page essay on an assigned topic. These sanctions are usually in response to a participant's failure to check in with the case manager, tardiness at work, or absence at a required meeting. If a person's offense is more serious (e.g., drug abuse relapse or getting fired from a job for good reason), he or she may be cuffed by the bailiff in the courtroom and taken to the county jail. All participants witness these court interactions, and the court session is open to the public. In fact, supporters of the participants (usually family members) are encouraged to come and are often present along with members of the team who sometimes choose to extend their service to be present for the courtroom sessions. The following ethnographic description (using pseudonyms) and accompanying analysis is based on a typical day in reentry court that serves to demonstrate the salient role of family and surrogate family relationships in the reentry PSC program.

Importance of Family: An Ethnography of a Reentry Public Courtroom Session

It is a hot, humid summer day in 2010, and the reentry court session is held on the third floor of a stately, century-old courthouse with tall ceilings and beautiful oak woodwork. Eighteen ex-prisoners are seated in the jury box and the front row of the gallery. Their case manager sits at the defense table, and other members of the reentry team sit in the gallery and at the prosecutor's table, while several family members sit in the back rows of the gallery. The judge enters the courtroom at 9:00 a.m., having just completed his meeting with the reentry team. He walks to the front of the courtroom and activates the computer program that records the morning's proceedings and then takes his seat behind his bench. He is not dressed in judicial robes, indicative of his desire to support, not merely pass judgment on, the individuals he addresses in the courtroom.

Everyone present is familiar with the procedures that will unfold during the next 90 minutes. As the judge calls out each of the reentry participants' names, they make their way to the podium at the center of the courtroom and enter into dialogue with the judge. The ex-prisoners are men and women who served time in the state prisons with time served ranging from 2 to 20 years. All of the participants are nonviolent offenders but are at high risk of reoffending because of addictions to alcohol and drugs, low job skills and education levels, and few resources. Some of them are nearing completion of the 18-month reentry court program and looking forward to "graduation," while others have only recently been released from prison and are only beginning the process of reentry to the community.

The judge begins the session by announcing that no sanctions will be issued this day, and he congratulates them on a good week. He then calls Dan (5 months in the program) to the front and asks, "What's new?" Dan's description of his trip to an amusement park with his 6-year-old daughter draws laughter from others in the courtroom. The judge notes, "It's clear how much she means to you. When you talk about her, you smile. You clearly have a commitment to restoring the relationship." Dan's follow-up comment illustrates the motivation that he receives from the relationship: "When I put her first, everything else is like a walk in the park!" The judge then explains to everyone that he and the reentry team monitor progress not only by observing how the participants live and work but also by whether they are learning to put others first and meet their needs. He commends Dan for his progress and his decision to give more time to his daughter and concludes his conversation with the statement that such behavior can help "reduce the risk of returning to a criminal lifestyle." The judge is aware of the literature on the importance of family as a motivating factor in reducing recidivism (Edin et al., 2004; Nurse, 2002) and uses his discourse to bring the point home to the participants.

Matthew (2 months in the program) is the next man called to the microphone, and the judge asks what he learned from his sanction that had been meted out for Matt's hour-late tardiness for a check-in. This ex-prisoner served 8 hours cleaning a 7-mile stretch of highway on a hot day and remarks that he will not be late for check-in again. The judge then inquires about his 8-year-old daughter, and Matt describes the joy of having her over to swim and watch a movie the day before. Referencing Dan as an example, the judge encourages Matt to recognize that he has the opportunity to exhibit the same "commitment to renewing the relationship" with his daughter. In one sense, the ex-prisoners become a sort of "family" to one another as they model good behavioral changes, encourage, challenge, and hold each other accountable. In this dialogue, the judge is taking advantage of the influence of Matt's peers in the reentry court program.

When the judge calls Katy (5 weeks in the program) to the front, they first discuss how her job at a fast-food restaurant is going, and she exclaims, "I love my job!" He reminds her of his ABC job program: "A" refers to "any" job, "B" refers to a "better" job, and "C" refers to a "career" job. The judge then asks Katy what she expects to do in the next 6 months, and she assures him that she hopes to have a better job. Her second goal is to talk with her 13-year-old daughter every night in efforts to rebuild trust. She then explains that her daughter "is waiting for Mom, missing that figure in her life." The judge counsels her, "No one needs that more than a 13-year-old, but be careful to be a mother, not a pal," and he elaborates on his meaning. In this conversation, we observe that the judge offers realistic words of warning and wisdom. Penal paternalism (see McCorkel, 2004) is one way some researchers describe a judge's effort to play a father role to some offenders, and, at times, a paternalistic approach is evident and valuable to the participants in the reentry PSC.

Joe, a young man who has been in the program for 10 months and has been sanctioned much more frequently than most participants, is the next participant to stand in front of the judge. Joe's offenses on the program range from being fired from jobs for laziness to being late to a number of meetings. Although he has a mother who resides locally, she tends to enable Joe in his misbehaviors. At this court session, Joe has completed 16 hours of work crew (a sanction given 2 weeks ago), volunteered on two community projects, been commended by those who supervised him, and is working long hours at his new job. Based on these reports, the judge announces that Joe is released from the work-release facility to return to his apartment. The other participants break out in applause, laughter, and shouts of encouragement. The judge then asks Joe, "Why are all these people smiling?" Joe describes his experience in the mental health group therapy session with his peers the week before: "I was on the hot seat. They all told me things I needed to hear." One of the other male ex-prisoners seated in the jury box adds, "We were brutally honest." And Joe quickly agrees with a firm "Yes!" As laughter in the courtroom dies down, the judge remarks, "When someone slacks, it drags everyone down. I'm with them [pointing to the other participants]." Everyone, including Joe, laughs again. His cohorts laugh with him in the sort of way a family finds relief and joy in seeing someone progress out of difficulty as he or she receives edification, encouragement, and loving support. The judge concludes the conversation by asking Joe if he is "on track now" and adds his parting edification to Joe not to consider himself "on a plateau but to keep climbing." Joe can do that with the help of his reentry "family."

Luis is nearing completion of the reentry court program but has recently had surgery for a chronic health problem. As he steps to the front, he greets the judge, who immediately inquires about his health and his new job. Luis has just landed a career job and reports that fellow employees are making sure he does not lift. He then volunteers that he has lots of good news: his family has moved in with him, and he proudly declares, "I'm seeing my children everyday, I've been clean three years tomorrow, and I have a good job with a retirement package and benefits. It doesn't get any better than that!" Everyone applauds and rejoices with Luis. The judge then states, "I am concerned for your health. You're the best judge of your own body. Be careful and pay attention to what it is telling you." Luis reports that his mother says the same thing, and the judge quips, "Well! I know I'm right if I'm saying what your mother says!" Again, we see how much family means to Luis in his efforts to become a contributing member of the community, and we observe the judge's paternalism.

Jerry (in the program 5 months) comes to the podium and reads aloud his essay, assigned by the judge: "The Nugget I got from Living in Balance [the mental health group therapy class]." Much of what he reads focuses on family:

> The therapy has really helped me to concentrate on the bigger goals in life. It helps to talk to my daughters on the phone when I'm upset with life on life's terms. I would love to see my daughters again! I know if I don't live a balanced life for myself, I can't be there for my kids as a father. . . . Today I have goals and plans for my life. I want to get my GED, go to college, and be a dad to my children.

As is the usual pattern, everyone in the courtroom applauds when Jerry finishes reading his essay, but, as is often the case, the judge tells him this was a good first try. Next time, he is to come with an essay that details a specific incident that illustrates Jerry's application of what he read today. In the next essay, we will most likely hear more about his daughters or steps he is taking to achieve "a balanced life" so that he can be there for them.

The judge calls Adam (5 months in the program) to the front. This middle-aged man has spent the most time in prison—20 years—of any of the participants in the history of this reentry PSC. His first time in court, he did not recognize his sisters, who had come to offer support. While in prison, he chose to remain as isolated as possible. Adam needs a lot of support, but it has become clear in the first months of his participation that he relies too heavily on one of his sisters. Today's dialogue with the judge demonstrates the situation clearly. The judge asks him if he called the police when his moped was stolen a few days ago, and Adam reports that he had his sister call. The judge uses it as a teaching moment about "acquiring living skills":

> You don't want to call the police, Adam, but every member of a community needs to be able to call the police. This is not your sister's responsibility. Part of the challenge is when you see something wrong, you call the police. One concern the team has is that your sister is too involved, and you are dumping responsibility on her. You need to acquire living skills. The police station is only six blocks away from where it was stolen, but you didn't report it immediately. Make an appointment with Captain Baker. Take your manual and registration information as quickly as possible today and report the crime yourself.

In this discourse, we see how family can unwittingly present a barrier to Adam's progress. The balance between support and assisting someone like Adam in gaining autonomy is an important goal (Faris et al., 2009). Self-agency must be learned by Adam, and his sister will also be learning how to assist in ways that can strengthen his ability to acquire necessary living skills (Travis, 2005; Wolff & Draine, 2004).

In the remainder of the court session, several other participants have their time with the judge, and short references are made to family, but most of the focus is on job situations. When George (only 2 months in the program) is called to the podium, the judge asks him about his work and is told that he is enjoying his new job pouring concrete. He has worked 111 hours in the past 2 weeks and is pleased that he is getting caught up in child support payments. The judge asks about his children and whether he is spending time with them. George states that he is not yet able to see his children, ages 8 and 10. The judge then reiterates what has been a theme for the court session today: "We've heard how important it is to reestablish relationships with your children. Do you want to be a part of their lives?" George answers with a strong voice, "Most definitely." The judge then encourages him by affirming the steps George is taking: "You have a financial responsibility. That is the first step. You are making progress. How do you feel about paying child support?" George explains how it gives him a sense of pride because he is providing for his children in a way that he could not when he was in prison. As George proceeds to contribute to his family's needs, he will earn the right to spend time with them and continue to experience an increase in his own sense of self-worth (Edin et al., 2004; Murray & Farrington, 2008; Phillips & Dettlaff, 2009).

One participant was not present in court. Fred has been in the program for over a year, has never been sanctioned, and is soon to graduate. Today, he is in the hospital with a blood clot and pneumonia, and the case manager announces that Fred would like to have visitors. After the judge dismisses the court, many of the participants gather to make plans for who will visit Fred and at what time. The reentry court "family" works to encourage and provide support to one of their own who is suffering.

Conclusion

The discourses that occur in one session of a reentry PSC public courtroom session illustrate the reality of the conclusions made by many criminal justice researchers and practitioners: family relationships are an important factor in an ex-prisoner's success or failure in becoming a law-abiding, contributing citizen as he or she reenters his or her community. This ethnographic study demonstrates that parents are often highly motivated to reunite with their children. The reentry PSC program assists them in a gradual process of building trust and reuniting in realistic ways, holding them accountable, and enabling them to gain the tools needed to assume the responsibilities of parenting.

The court session ethnography also illustrates that "family" is not defined only by blood. For the ex-prisoners in this program, family includes each other as they assist and support one another, speak truth in ways that urge one of their own to develop better work habits and responsibility, and offer cheers and applause to deserving cohorts. In speaking with graduates of the program, I know that these relationships continue after they are released from the program.

Communities across the United States need to consider how to best assist men and women who have served time in our prisons. Reentry PSCs offer a type of reform that is greatly needed in our criminal justice system. The reality of the numbers of incarcerated parents ought to motivate implementation of more reentry PSCs in more jurisdictions. After all, men and women like Teanna *are* coming home.

Discussion Questions

1. Review the problem-solving court's strategy for reintegrating prisoners into society. Briefly outline each step mentioned. For example, how does a prisoner enter the program? What are requirements for graduation and so on?
2. This chapter notes that incarceration has profound "collateral consequences" on the community and family. What might be some of these "consequences" regarding the community and the family of the incarcerated individual?
3. Studies have shown that voting, using library services, and receiving Medicaid greatly improve the rate of successful reintegration for prisoners. Provide several reasons why these factors may assist reintegration.
4. What offenses can lead to reprimand, and what are some examples of punishment? What offenses can lead to expulsion from the program?
5. This chapter references the term "growing social time bomb." What do you believe is meant by this term?

References

Arditti, J. A., & Few, A. L. (2006). Mothers' reentry into family life following incarceration. *Criminal Justice Policy Review, 17*, 103–123.

Berman, G., & Feinblatt, J. (2005). *Good courts: The case for problem-solving justice.* New York: New Press.

Braman, D. (2004). *Doing time on the outside: Incarceration and family life in urban America.* Ann Arbor: University of Michigan Press.

Clark, C., & Neuhard, J. (2005). Therapeutic jurisprudence and problem solving practices positively impact clients, the justice systems and communities they serve. *St. Thomas Law Review, 17*, 781–810.

Comfort, M. (2007). *Doing time together: Love and family in the shadow of the prison.* Chicago: University of Chicago Press

Comfort, M. L. (2008). Punishment beyond the legal offender. *Annual Review of Law and Social Science, 3*, 271–296.

Edin, K., Nelson, T. J., & Paranal, R. (2004). Fatherhood and incarceration as potential turning points in the criminal careers of unskilled men. In M. Patillo, D. F. Weiman, & B. Western (Eds.), *Imprisoning America: The social effects of mass incarceration* (pp. 46–75). New York: Sage.

Foster, H., & Hagan, J. (2007). Incarceration and intergenerational social exclusion. *Social Problems, 54*, 399–433.

Glaze, L. E., & Maruschak, (2008). *Parents in prison and their children.* Bureau of Justice Statistics Special Report. http://www.ojp.usdoj.gov/bjs/pub/pdf/pptmc.pdf

Hairston, C. F. (2007). *Focus on children of incarcerated parents: An overview of the research literature.* Baltimore: Annie E. Casey Foundation. http://www.aecf.org/KnowledgeCenter/Publications.aspx?pubguid={F48C4DF8-BBD9-4915-85D7-53EAFC941189}

Krisberg, B., & Temin, C. E. (2007). The plight of children whose parents are in prison. In B. Krisberg, S. Marchionna, & C. Baird (Eds.), *Continuing the struggle for justice: 100 years of the National Council on Crime and Delinquency* (pp. 185–190). Los Angeles: Sage.

Manza, J., & Uggen, C. (2006). *Locked out: Felon disenfranchisement and American democracy.* New York: Oxford University Press.

McCorkel, J. (2004). Criminally dependent? Gender, punishment, and the rhetoric of welfare reform. *Social Politics, 11,* 386–410.

Miller, J., & Johnson, D. C. (2009). *Problem solving courts: New approaches to criminal justice in the United States.* New York: Rowman & Littlefield.

Mumola, C. J. (2000). *Incarcerated parents and their children.* Washington, DC: Bureau of Justice Statistics. http://www.ojp.usdoj.gov/bjs/pub/pdf/iptc.pdf

Murray, J., & Farrington, D. P. (2008). Effects of parental imprisonment on children. *Crime and Justice: A Review of Research, 37,* 133–206.

Nurse, A. M. (2002). *Fatherhood arrested: Parenting from within the juvenile justice system.* Nashville: Vanderbilt University Press.

Phillips, S. D., & Dettlaff, A. J. (2009). More than parents in prison: The broader overlap between the criminal justice and child welfare systems. *Journal of Public Child Welfare, 3,* 3–22.

Shannon, S. K. S., & Abrams, L. S. (2007). Juvenile offenders as fathers: perceptions of fatherhood, crime, and becoming an adult. *Families in Society: The Journal of Contemporary Social Service, 88,* 183–191.

Travis, J. (2005). *They all come home: Facing the challenges of prisoner reentry.* Washington, DC: Urban Institute Press.

Trice, A. D., & Brewster, J. (2004). The effects of maternal incarceration on adolescent children. *Journal of Police and Criminal Psychology, 19,* 27–35.

U.S. Department of Justice, Office of Justice Programs. (2009). *Reentry.* http://www.reentry.gov

Wildeman, C. (2009). Parental imprisonment, the prison boom, and the concentration of childhood disadvantage. *Demography, 46,* 265–280.

Wolff, N., & Draine, J. (2004). Dynamics of social capital of prisoners and community reentry: Ties that bind? *Journal of Correctional Health Care, 10,* 457–490.

Chapter 19  Family as an Academic Motivator for African American and Ghanaian Students' University Attendance

Eletra S. Gilchrist

For many children, family members are the first major influence on how children see themselves in the present and what they aspire to be in the future. Children's behaviors are often influenced by the communication they hear from their parents and other family members. For example, immediate families often guide children's understandings of the importance of education by instructing the offspring on the likely benefits linked to obtaining an education and the potential challenges associated with not receiving an education (Watkins, 2006). In addition to influencing children's behaviors, family members also offer direct definitions that impact children's racial, cultural, and ethnic identities. This is especially true in the African American family, where many parents and grandparents teach their African American children to take pride in the strength and struggle that has defined their collective history in America (Mosley-Howard & Evans, 1997). Many African American families also feel that it is their duty to teach children that racism still exists in the United States, and one way to help counter a tainted history of racism and oppression is through education (Mosley-Howard & Evans, 1997).

The benefits of knowledge have long been recognized. During the time of slavery, most slave states in the American South enacted laws that made it a crime for enslaved black people to learn literacy skills for fear that slaves would spread abolitionist materials, forge passes, and initiate revolts (Williams, 2005). By keeping the slaves uneducated, the slave owners could theoretically maintain control. In more modern times, anthems and slogans expressing "knowledge is power" radiate throughout black communities in the United States. In an effort to garner support for historically black colleges and universities, the United Negro College Fund adopted the campaign slogan "A Mind Is a Terrible Thing to Waste" in 1972, and since its inception, not only has this slogan become part of the American vernacular, but African American families all across the country have stressed it to the younger generations (Ad Council, n.d.). It is important to note, however, that the importance of education among blacks is not limited to blacks living in the United States but instead can be traced to the motherland of Africa, where black families are on an urgent mission to encourage their offspring to seek higher education in the hope of establishing a brighter future for themselves and their family (Liddell, Barrett, & Henzi, 2003). The black family serves as a source of great knowledge for black children and can impact the children's decisions on a number of issues, including the choices they make regarding education (Liddell et al., 2003). Because family is perceived to be a powerful, enduring, and persuasive force in the lives of black children living in both the United States and Africa (Clark, 1983; Liddell et al., 2003), this chapter explores how family serves as an academic motivator for African and African American university students to pursue a college education. The relevant literature initially addresses structures of the African and African American families, followed by an overview of academic motivation.

African and African American Families

For as long as scholars have documented African family practices, researchers have noted that African families practice communal child care. In other words, African families believe that it truly takes a village to raise children, and nurturing and caring for children are collective responsibilities shared among family members. Collins (2000) calls this practice of communal parenting "othermothering" (p. 178), which involves networks that operate on an informal basis in a variety of contexts, including churches, social clubs, and the workplace. African families pride themselves in having intimate networks comprised of relatives and friends (though primarily female) who provide parenting and child care assistance and, consequently, facilitate extended family structures (Collins, 2000). Because of othermothering and other acts of extended family care, "family is the domain of both primary attachment and primary fear" in many African societies (van Dijk, 2002, p. 180).

Researchers have historically perceived a connection between African Americans and their ancestral past in many areas, including family practices. Sudarkasa (1998), for example, posited that extended family values and practices of African Americans are kinship categories derived from and "juxtaposed to the heritage of Africa" (p. 91). African Americans inherited a history of strong kinship ties from their African ancestors, and presently one of the most significant features of African American families is the extended family structure and salient family values (Billingsley, 1993; Hill, 1997). Similar to African families, African American families often relationally define the family to include non-blood-related individuals forged by economic necessity as well as racial, historical, political, and social factors (Angel & Tienda, 1982; Mutran, 1985). Thus, fictive kin are just as important as blood relatives in African American families as they are in African families. Although the similarities between African American families and their African ancestors are duly noted, recent research has unveiled many differences between the two groups' family structures (Gilchrist & Camara, 2012; McDonald, 2010).

There are some features of African American families that are rarely characteristic of African families, including female-headed households and unwed mothers. According to Benokraitis (2007), the percentage of single-parent African American households has doubled in the last three decades. In contrast, female-headed households and unwed mothers are not characteristic of traditional African family structures (Gutman, 1976). The value placed on family members is another major difference between Africans and African Americans. For example, in Africa, motherhood is viewed as the "pinnacle of womanhood" and a "site of power for Black women" (O'Reilly, 2004, p. 10). In contrast, African American women have been saturated with powerfully negative images, spanning the strong *Matriarch*, hypersexualized *Jezebel*, overly assertive *Sapphire*, and subservient *Mammy* (Collins, 1999; Gilchrist & Camara, 2012), which have degraded their position in the family.

Notable differences are also seen in the roles that African and African American families play in their children pursing higher education. Equitable access to education for all African children represents a constant challenge, as females, people with disabilities, those living in poorer and more remote communities, and individuals restricted by certain family customs have traditionally encountered educational barriers (Teferra & Altbach, 2004). In spite of these barriers, African parents are generally highly invested in their children's schooling (Liddell et al., 2003). African parents encourage their children to pursue education in the hope that they will receive employment and improve their living conditions and, consequently, help support their families (Amuah, personal communication, May 21, 2012). About 45% of African children who find work remain in their communities and use their immediate social and labor capital to enhance their homes and families; when the children do leave their communities and families for work, about two-thirds of them send regular remittances home (Liddell et al., 2003). Hence, in spite of issues with access and the financial challenges associated with obtaining an education, African families greatly encourage their children to seek education in order to obtain jobs and support the family. In response to their parents' encouragement, many African children follow their parents' guidance and attend school because cultural norms dictate that offspring should be loyal to external influences, especially members of one's family, tribe, or group. As stated by Riccio (2008), extended families in Africa "represent the most important source of never-ending special obligations" (p. 221).

While many children in Africa often face challenges receiving equitable access to education, African Americans who were once barred from learning to read and write during the antebellum slave days now earn academic degrees from the most prestigious colleges and universities. African Americans currently make up a little more than 12% of the U.S. population, yet data from the U.S. Department of Education, National Center for Education Statistics (2009), report that African American students made up more than 13% of the total enrollment in degree-granting U.S. institutions in 2007, and the percentage continues to rise. Like African parents, many African American parents encourage their children to pursue an education but for different reasons—topping the list is an almost guaranteed higher earning potential. Data compiled by the U.S. Department of Education, National Center for Education Statistics (2008), report that median earnings for full-time employed young adults in the United States, ages 25 to 34, rose as education level increased between 1995 and 2006. Specifically, young adults with at least a bachelor's degree in the United States consistently had median earnings higher than those with less education, and this pattern held true regardless of race or gender. Hence, many African American families view "schooling and education as a means of empowerment and upward social mobility," and the families often verbally and nonverbally convey these thoughts to their children (Watkins, 2006, para. 47). Barnett (2004) interviewed a sample of African American students enrolled at an Ivy League university and found that 98% of the respondents reported that their parents were the main motivating forces in their decision to attend college, and for 96% of the students, the decision to attend college was made well in advance of high school. Research has further found that African American families instill in their children the belief that there is a relationship between schooling and future success and prosperity (Sanders, 1998; Watkins, 2006). Thus, African American children are encouraged by their families to pursue education in order to fulfill their individual goals and to become leaders, independent, and prepared for the future (Barnett, 2004). As one parent put it who was interviewed by Watkins (2006), "Your job [as an African American student] is to make those grades and the world is yours" (para. 55).

In sum, the relevant research on African and African American families suggests that though there are similarities between the two groups' family structures, there are also many noticeable differences, especially when it comes to the motivations that families have for encouraging offspring to seek education. Some scholars argue that differences in family practices and ideologies between Africans and African Americans are due to time and distance in that there has been more than 400 years of space between Africans, African Americans, and colonial rule. There appears to be many facets of African culture, traditions, and family practices that did not survive transitions to the New World. Although African Americans have a historical connection to Africa, previous research has determined a rift in the family lessons and practices shared between people in the African homeland and the Diaspora in America (Billingsley, 1993; Gilchrist & Camara, 2012; McDonald, 2010; Uzoigwe, 2008). This potential disconnection and findings from the previous literature on African and African American families give probable cause to theorize discrepancies in the extrinsic and intrinsic motivators that inspire students' university attendance. Hence, an exploration of the literature on academic motivation is warranted.

Academic Motivation

Academic motivation explores the reasons that inspire students to seek education. Previous research infers that academic motivation is a key determinant of academic performance and achievement (Green, Nelson, Martin, & Marsh, 2006; Linnenbrink & Pintrich, 2002). The principal theory supporting academic motivation is Deci and Ryan's (1985) self-determination theory of motivation (SDT), which posits that humans have an innate desire for stimulation and learning from birth that is either supported or discouraged within their environment. According to this theory, motivation is not a unidimensional construct but rather a multidimensional perspective comprised of three degrees of self-determined behavior: intrinsic, extrinsic, and amotivation (Deci & Ryan, 2000).

Intrinsic Motivation

Intrinsic motivation refers to the drive to pursue a goal based on the pleasure or satisfaction derived from it. Intrinsically motivated individuals voluntarily participate in an activity without experiencing external pressure to do so and without expecting rewards (Deci & Ryan, 1985; Vallerand et al., 1992). Intrinsic motivation is perceived as a global construct that can be differentiated into three specific motives: (a) *to know*, (b) *to accomplish*, and (c) *to experience stimulation*.

Intrinsic motivation to know (IMTK) refers to engagement in an activity "for the pleasure and satisfaction that one experiences while learning, exploring, or trying to understand something new" (Vallerand et al., 1992, p. 1005). IMTK is related to constructs of curiosity, exploration, and the epistemic need to know and understand. Second, *intrinsic motivation toward accomplishment* (IMTA) is viewed as engagement in an activity for the pleasure and satisfaction derived when trying to excel, to reach a new standard, or to create something new. According to Barkoukis, Tsorbatzoudis, Grouios, and Sideridis (2008), individuals predisposed to this type of motivation focus on the *process* instead of the *outcome* of an activity and seek to feel competent and creative. Finally, *intrinsic motivation to experience stimulation* (IMES) includes involvement in an activity because it is fun and exciting and yields positive sensations (Vallerand et al., 1992).

Extrinsic Motivation

Extrinsic motivation refers to pursuing a goal out of a sense of obligation or to obtain rewards. Extrinsically motivated individuals often participate in activities because of external pressures. Here, people engage in a behavior because it is considered a means to an end (Deci & Ryan, 1985; Vallerand et al., 1992). Similar to intrinsic motivation, extrinsic motivation is a multidimensional construct consisting of three components: (a) *external regulation*, (b) *introjection*, and (c) *identification*.

External regulation (EMER) refers to behavior that is controlled by specific external contingencies. In other words, people are motivated to participate in an activity to gain rewards or to avoid punishment (Deci & Ryan, 2000). *Introjection* (EMIN) is another form of extrinsic motivation that involves more internalized involvement with an activity. "At this stage, behaviour is not yet self-determined, but the individual is beginning to internalise the reasons for his/her actions" (Barkoukis et al., 2008, p. 40). Thus, EMIN represents a partial internalization in which regulations are internal, but they have not really become assimilated to the self. According to Deci and Ryan (2000), introjected regulations are "within the person, but still relatively external to the self" (p. 236). Because these regulations are partially internalized, the behaviors are likely to persist over time. With EMER, the behavior is motivated by contingent consequences that are administered by others, but with EMIN, the contingent consequences are administered by the individuals themselves (Deci & Ryan, 2000). As such, individuals motivated by EMIN participate in certain activities because their involvement evokes certain self-inflected emotions, such as feelings of self-worth, shame, or pride (Deci & Ryan, 2000). *Identification* (EMID), the third type of extrinsic motivation, refers to involvement in an activity because people recognize and accept the underlying value of the behavior. In other words, with EMID, the behavior is valued and considered important to individuals because it is a part of their identity or value system (Deci & Ryan, 2000).

Amotivation

Amotivation (AMOT) involves the absence of motivation or drive to pursue a goal due to individuals' failures to establish contingencies between their behavior and the activity. These individuals participate in activities, yet they lack specific goals and purposes (Barkoukis et al., 2008). In other words, amotivated individuals' involvement in an activity is not the result of their will (Deci & Ryan, 1985). Amotivation stands in contrast to both intrinsic and extrinsic motivation because it represents the lack of both types of motivation and, thus, a lack of self-determination with respect to the target behavior (Deci & Ryan, 2000).

The literature on academic motivation implies that the intrinsic, extrinsic, and even amotivation reasons for pursuing higher education is not a monolithic experience for all students, especially African American and African students, who represent two different cultures. According to Trenholm and Jensen (2008), members from different cultures often have varied answers to the following questions: "To whom should I be loyal? To myself or to others? Do I owe allegiance to my family, clan, or company, or should my first allegiance be to myself?" (p. 376). Answers to these questions can aid in understanding how African American and African families function as academic motivators in the pursuit of higher learning. However, it is impossible to study people from every country within the continent of Africa. West Africa is a location in which extended kinship continues to e.ween blacks in Africa and in the United States (MacLean, 2002; Oyewumi, 2003). Therefore, Ghana is the geographic region chosen to study family as an academic motivator because Ghana was the center of British slave trade and approximately 2 million Africans were transported from Ghana to the New World (Thomas, 1997). Toward that end, the following research questions are asked:

RQ 1: Will African American or Ghanaian families of origin prompt students to report more intrinsic motivations for seeking a college education?

RQ 2: Will African American or Ghanaian families of origin prompt students to report more extrinsic motivations for seeking a college education?

RQ 3: What primary motivations will African Americans students report for pursuing higher education?

RQ 4: What primary motivations will Ghanaian students report for pursuing higher education?

Method

Participants

A purposive sample of 206 university students from the United States and Ghana participated in this study. The sum participants included 103 African American undergraduate students from a midsize southern university in the United States who self-reported being from an African American family of origin. The African American sample was comprised of 63 males and 40 females who had a mean age of 21. The African American students also included 21 freshmen, 23 sophomores, 33 juniors, 18 seniors, and 8 students who classified their education level as *other*. The sum participants also included 103 Ghanaian undergraduate students from a large university in Ghana who self-reported having a Ghanaian family of origin. There were 69 male and 34 female Ghanaian participants, including 10 freshmen, 5 sophomores, 26 juniors, 55 seniors, and 7 participants who labeled their year in school as *other*. The Ghanaian students' mean age was 24.

Procedure and Instrumentation

To recruit the purposive sample of U.S. students from African American families of origin, the principal investigator corresponded with student organizations comprised of a predominant African American membership, such as the Black Student Association and the National Pan-Hellenic Council, which is a coordinating body for the historical African American fraternities and sororities. After contacting the organizations' advisers and student leaders, the principal investigator was granted permission to administer the survey. The principal investigator also asked the members to refer additional students; thus, some (i.e., ~20%) African American survey respondents were obtained through snowball procedures.

The purposive sample of students from Ghanaian families of origin was obtained when the principal investigator participated in a study abroad program in Ghana. A team of researchers, professors, and students was granted permission by officials at the University of Ghana to collect data during the program. To recruit students, the principal investigator and student assistants canvassed the campus and solicited students to participate in the study. The Ghanaian students were recruited from various classrooms, the library, bookstore, and informal settings on campus.

Once the participants were recruited, they first completed a consent form, followed by a demographic sheet that asked for the participants' family of origin, sex, race, age, and year in school. Each student then completed the Academic Motivation Scale (AMS),[1] which took about 10 minutes to complete. The AMS was developed by Vallerand et al. (1992) and consists of 28 items that probe students to respond to the following question: "Why are you going to college?" Each item on the AMS is rated on a scale ranging from 1 (does not correspond at all) to 7 (corresponds exactly). Based on self-determination theory, the AMS consists of seven subscales, reflecting one subscale of amotivation, three ordered subscales of extrinsic motivation (external regulation, introjected, and identified), and three unordered subscales of intrinsic motivation (to know, toward accomplishment, and to experience stimulation).

An example of an AMOT item is "I once had good reasons for going to college; however, now I wonder whether I should." A sample EMER item is "because with only a high-school degree I would not find a high paying job later on." A sample EMIN item is "to prove to myself that I am capable of completing my college degree." An example of an EMID item is "because this will help me make a better choice regarding my career orientation." A sample IMTK item is "because I experience pleasure and satisfaction while learning new things." A sample IMES item is "for the 'high' feeling that I experience while reading about various interesting subjects." An example of an IMTA item is "for the pleasure that I experience while surpassing myself in my studies."

After students completed the AMS, they were instructed to write out and explain their main motivation for seeking higher education. This question was asked in order to complement the survey responses and arrive at a more complete understanding of students' overall academic motivation.

Data Analysis

AMS: Vallerand et al.'s (1992) research identified the AMS as a multidimensional scale comprised of a seven-factor subscale structure: (a) AMOT, (b) EMER, (c) EMIN, (d) EMID, (e) IMTK, (f) IMES, and (g) IMTA. Factor analyses performed by this study also found seven factors, with each loading at .60 or higher. Initial research by Vallerand et al. also indicated that the AMS generally had good internal consistency with Cronbach's alpha ranging from .83 to .86 of the subscales, with the exception of the extrinsic motivation identified subscale, which had an internal consistency of .62. Test–retest reliability measures over a 1-month period ranged from .71 to .83 (Vallerand et al., 1992). Subsequent to Vallerand et al., other researchers have found the AMS to also have good internal consistency with Cronbach's alpha ranging from .70 to .86 (Cokley, Bernard, Cunningham, & Motoike, 2001), .86 to .88 (Sobral, 2004), and .77 to .90 (Fairchild, Horst, Finney, & Barron, 2005). This study followed suit and had good internal consistency with Cronbach's alpha for the subscales ranging from .74 to .83 when the AMS was given to the African American students and .78 to .85 when the survey was administered to the Ghanaian students. Table 19.1 presents the descriptive statistics of the AMS for the African American and Ghanaian students.

Content Analysis: In order to complement the survey data, an open-ended question probed participants to explain their main motivation for seeking higher education. From the written responses, the goal was to categorize occurrences of extrinsic and intrinsic motivators. Thus, quantitative content analysis was the appropriate data analysis procedure. According to Neuendorf (2002), *content analysis* is a "summarizing, quantitative analysis of messages that relies on the scientific method (including attention to objectivity-intersubjectivity, a priori design, reliability, validity, generalizability, replicability, and hypothesis testing) and is not limited as to the types of variables that may be measured or the context in which the messages are created or presented" (p. 10). In other words, content analysis is a prime method for quantitatively summarizing message content.

Frey, Botan, and Kreps (2000) recommend using two coders to enhance a study's validity when performing content analysis. Thus, two trained research assistants performed the content analysis by following a coding process suggested by Frey et al. (2000). Initially, the coders unitized the students' statements into *syntactical distinctions*; this form of unitizing involves coding textual data based on discrete units of language, such as particular words, phrases, or sentences (Neuendorf, 2002). Specifically, the data were coded into the seven categories outlined in the AMS by Vallerand et al. (1992). Thus, as described earlier, the seven content categories included (a) AMOT, (b) EMER, (c) EMIN, (d) EMID, (e) IMTK, (f) IMES, and (g) IMTA. Because the categories of EMER, EMIN, and EMID

Table 19.1 Descriptive Statistics for the Seven AMS Subscales for African American ($N = 103$) and Ghanaian Students ($N = 103$)

Subscale	α	M	SD	Min	Max
African American Students					
EMER	.74	6.08	1.01	2.00	7.00
EMIN	.83	4.88	1.63	1.00	7.00
EMID	.79	5.67	1.36	3.00	7.00
IMTK	.83	5.47	1.14	1.50	7.00
IMES	.82	4.93	1.09	1.00	7.00
IMTA	.78	5.21	1.15	1.75	7.00
AMOT	.74	1.77	1.18	1.00	5.50
Ghanaian Students					
EMER	.83	5.74	1.33	1.25	7.00
EMIN	.81	5.37	1.19	1.00	7.00
EMID	.85	6.27	0.72	1.00	7.00
IMTK	.79	5.38	1.24	2.00	7.00
IMES	.79	4.49	1.35	1.25	7.00
IMTA	.79	4.83	1.40	1.00	7.00
AMOT	.78	1.69	1.10	1.00	6.00

collectively refer to extrinsic motivations and the categories of IMTK, IMES, and IMTA holistically relate to intrinsic motivations, two additional content categories were added to account for intrinsic or self-serving motivating factors (INTR) and extrinsic or other-oriented (EXTR) motivating factors, yielding a total of nine content categories. For the second step in the content analysis process, the coders individually read the students' responses and looked for key words, phrases, or sentences reflective of the nine categories. Because individual words, phrases, and sentences were observed in each student's written responses, it was possible for one student to indicate multiple motivating factors behind his or her university attendance. After analyzing the written statements, each syntactical distinction was then coded into one of the nine content categories that best reflected its content. There was high intercoder reliability with data from the African American students (Cohen's kappa = .80) and the Ghanaian students (Cohen's kappa = .86). In the third step, the coders negotiated discrepant codings until consensus was reached. Analyzing the data comprised the fourth and final stage of the content analysis. Here, coders counted the number of syntactical codings in each of the nine categories for both the African American and Ghanaian students to obtain a quantitative typology of the students' motivational factors for attending college. Table 19.2 lists the number of syntactical codings for both groups resulting from the content analysis.

Table 19.2 Number of Syntactical Codings for African American and Ghanaian Students

Type of Motivation	African American Students[a]	Ghanaian Students[b]
EMER	56 (24.3%)	73 (27.1%)
EMIN	7 (3.0%)	11 (4.1%)
EMID	16 (7.0%)	27 (10.0%)
IMTK	20 (8.7%)	49 (18.2%)
IMES	7 (3.0%)	3 (1.1%)
IMTA	16 (7.0%)	13 (4.8%)
AMOT	6 (2.6%)	5 (1.9%)
INTR	77 (33.5%)	19 (7.1%)
EXTR	25 (10.9%)	69 (25.7%)
Total	230 (100%)	269 (100%)

Note: Percentage of the total number of syntactical codes is in parentheses.
[a] $N = 103$.
[b] $N = 103$.

Results

The first research question queried whether African American or Ghanaian families of origin would prompt students to report more intrinsic motivations for seeking a college education. According to the AMS, intrinsic motivation is measured based on three constructs: IMTK, IMES, and IMTA. With IMTK, the means were slightly higher for the African American students ($M = 5.47$, $SD = 1.14$) than the Ghanaian students ($M = 5.38$, $SD = 1.24$). However, results from an independent-samples t-test yielded no significant findings, $t(204) = .57$, $p = .57$, suggesting that African American and Ghanaian families of origin do not differ as motivators for students to attend college in order learn or acquire knowledge. Based on IMES, African American students had a higher mean ($M = 4.93$, $SD = 1.09$) than Ghanaian students ($M = 4.49$, $SD = 1.35$), and an independent-samples t-test supported this statistically significant difference, $t(204) = 2.57$, $p < .01$. This implies that compared to students from a Ghanaian family, students from an African American family are more motivated to attend college for fun and excitement. According to IMTA, the last intrinsic construct, African American students had a higher score ($M = 5.21$, $SD = 1.15$) than the Ghanaian students ($M = 4.83$, $SD = 1.40$), $t(204) = 2.12$, $p < .05$. These figures indicate that in comparison to students from a Ghanaian family, students from an African American family are more motivated to attend college because they desire to excel, reach a new standard, or create something new from their college experience. The three intrinsic constructs combine to give the students from an African American family of origin an average score of 5.20 ($SD = 0.96$) and students from a Ghanaian family of origin a mean score of 4.89 ($SD = 1.21$). These findings suggest that African American families of origin intrinsically motivate students to attend college more than Ghanaian families of origin, and this assertion is supported by a statistically significant independent-samples t-test, $t(204) = 2.00$, $p < .05$.

The second research question asked whether African American or Ghanaian families of origin will lead students to report more extrinsic motivations for seeking a college education. The three constructs of EMER, EMIN, and EMID make up extrinsic motivation, according to the AMS. The African American students scored higher on EMER ($M = 6.09$, $SD = 1.01$) than the Ghanaian students ($M = 5.74$, $SD = 1.01$), and this was supported by an independent-samples t-test, $t(204) = 2.14$, $p < .05$, which suggests that students from African American families of origin are more motivated by external pressures to attend college in order to gain rewards or avoid punishments compared to students from Ghanaian families of origin. Based on EMIN, another extrinsic construct, Ghanaian students had a higher score ($M = 5.37$, $SD = 1.19$) than African American students ($M = 4.88$, $SD = 1.63$), $t(204) = -2.48$, $p < .01$, implying that students from Ghanaian families are more motivated than students from African American families to attend college because of the self-inflicted positive or negative feelings that accompany their college attendance and performance. According to the EMID construct, Ghanaian students had a higher motivation ($M = 6.27$, $SD = 0.72$) than African American students ($M = 5.67$, $SD = 1.36$), $t(204) = -3.95$, p .01, indicating that compared to students from African American families, students from Ghanaian families are encouraged to attend college so that they can acquire important skills and behaviors necessary to their career and competence as a worker. The three extrinsic constructs combine to give Ghanaian students a mean score of 5.79 ($SD = 0.86$) and African American students an average of 5.55 ($SD = 0.94$). This finding is supported by a statistically significant independent-samples t-test, $t(204) = -1.97$, $p < .05$. The results suggest that, overall, students from a Ghanaian family of origin are more extrinsically motivated to attend college than students from an African American family of origin.

To complement the findings from the AMS and further explore how African American and Ghanaian families influence students' academic motivation, an open-ended question probed participants to explain their main motivation for pursuing higher learning. Quantitative content analysis was used to code the responses from both the African American and the Ghanaian students into the following nine content categories, as suggested by the AMS: (a) AMOT, (b) EMER, (c) EMIN, (d) EMID, (e) IMTK, (f) IMES, (g) IMTA, (h) INTR, and (i) EXTR.

Academic Motivation of Students from African American Families per the Content Analysis

The content analysis resulted in 230 syntactical distinctions for the students of African American families of origin that were each coded into one of the nine motivational content groups. From greatest to least motivation, the following sections describe each of the content categories and offer examples of written responses from the African American students.

INTR: Of the 230 syntactical codes, African American students reported being motivated to attend college most for intrinsic or self-serving reasons ($n = 77$; 33.5%). Comments that stressed independence from one's family, self-sufficiency, and providing for oneself were coded into the INTR category. Example comments were "I want to be able to take care of myself," "I want to stand on my own two feet one day without help from anyone else," and "My main motivation to stay in college is so I can support myself when I graduate and not have to rely on help from my family."

EMER: The second-highest motivator for students from African American families of origin who are attending college was external regulation, which involves extrinsic motivating factors ($n = 56$; 24.3%). This category reflects external pressures that motivate the students to attend college in order to gain a reward or avoid a certain punishment. Statements categorized into this content category included "Without a college degree, many people don't qualify for jobs and if they do then they aren't high paying jobs," "I know that a college degree will make me more marketable when searching for a job," and "I want to make millions! and I can't do it without an education. I'm tired of being broke." One student adequately summed up the essence of EMER by stating, "My motivation for attending college is that I know the rewards that come in the end."

EXTR: Per the African American students' statements, extrinsic or other-oriented reasons were the third-highest motivator prompting their college attendance ($n = 25$; 10.9%). Statements that suggested supporting one's family, being a good servant to the community, and taking care of others' needs were coded in the EXTR category. Representative statements included "My mom is my main motivation. I want to make her proud and take care of her," "So I can help student athletes get into school on a scholarship, unlike myself," "My motivation is my family and my goal is to make them happy," and "I come from a household in which my mom doesn't have a high school education and my dad has an addiction and I know a college education will keep me from bringing my family up in a struggling household."

IMTK: Ranking in the middle, students from African American families reported intrinsic motivation to know as another motivating factor behind their college attendance ($n = 20$; 8.7%). This content category comprised statements about the satisfaction and pleasure derived from learning or expanding one's knowledge level. Specific statements included "I love the experience one can gain from college through learning," "I love learning and gaining more wisdom," and "I feel that knowledge is power and a mind is a terrible thing to waste."

IMTA: Accomplishment, an intrinsic motivating factor, also moderately motivated the African American students to attend college ($n = 16$; 7.0%). Statements that stressed that the students were trying to excel, reach a new standard, or create something new were coded in this category because the statements reflected that the students were motivated more by the process of attending college than by the actual outcome of obtaining an education. The following statements made up this category: "I am bettering myself as a person," "I love finding out I can do stuff that I didn't think I could," "To make myself a more marketable and polished individual that can excel in any environment," and "For personal satisfaction."

EMID: EMID tied with accomplishment as a moderate motivator for American American students' college attendance ($n = 16$; 7.0%). This content category included behaviors that were valued and considered important to the students, especially concerning their career choice and their competence as a worker. Some African American students who were motivated by EMID said, "Education is the passport to the future, for tomorrow belongs to the people who prepare for it today," "My main motivation for being in college is to study computers and future technology to further me in the business world," and "To receive a higher level of education that will be needed in corporate America."

IMES: To experience stimulation, an intrinsic motivation, was among the least reported factors that motivated students from African American families to attend college ($n = 7$; 3.0%). Here, students said they found the college experience to be fun and exciting. One student said, "The experience of college life is one of no other." Another student said, "My main motivation for attending college is to play sports." One other student added, "I love hanging out with my fraternity brothers. Being with them makes my college experience fun and fulfilled."

EMIN: EMIN tied IMES as one of the least reported reasons why African American students are motivated to attend college ($n = 7$; 3.0%). The extrinsically motivated introjected category included statements reflecting contingent consequences imposed by the students on themselves that led the students to feel either negatively or positively about themselves based on their college attendance and performance. According to the students, many of them wanted to prove to their family members that they could excel at higher learning: "To prove to my mother, brothers, and everybody else that said I couldn't do it [that I could do it]," "To prove to others that I can succeed in life and be a better person than them," "I want to be proud of myself," and "To finish what I started."

AMOT: Per the African American students' written comments, amotivation occurred the least ($n = 6$; 2.6%). Statements making up this category suggested that students did not know why they were attending college. One student said, "When I graduated from high school I never thought I would attend college." Another student said, "It used to be to graduate. Now, I don't know." Other comments included "I'm here because it's close to home" and "I hate school; don't know why I put myself through this torture."

In sum, the third research question inquired the primary motivation that African Americans students have for attending college. Per the content analysis, more than one-third of African American students' encouragement for pursing higher education is based on intrinsic or self-serving reasons that will make them independent from the care of their families.

Academic Motivation of Students from Ghanaian Families per the Content Analysis

There were 269 syntactical distinctions for the students from Ghanaian families resulting from the content analysis. Each of the syntactical distinctions was coded into one of the nine motivational content groups. Ranging from greatest to least motivation, the following sections present examples of the Ghanaian students' written responses.

EMER: Of the 269 syntactical codes, students from Ghanaian families reported being motivated to attend college most for external regulation, an extrinsic motivation ($n = 73$; 27.1%). The Ghanaian students listed several reasons why they were motivated to attend college to either acquire some reward or prevent some form of punishment. Specific statements were "My college degree will enable me to get a good job. This will also enable me to have a good income in the nearest future," "I simply want to be a medical doctor and earn a lot of money," "My motivation for attending college is that those who attend colleges/universities normally get a responsible job compared to a high school dropout," "It is not easy to survive in life without any meaningful education," and "I believe that in whatever you do, education makes it better."

EXTR: The Ghanaian students listed extrinsic or other-oriented reasons that stressed family, society, and the community as the second-highest motivator encouraging their college attendance ($n = 69$; 25.7%). Specific statements included "To be a responsible person in my neighborhood . . . and to cater for [*sic*] my wife and kids and my parents," "My motivation for attending college is to pursue the course of humanity especially the oppressed in the economy and societal perspectives," "To achieve the highest academic standard needed to help in the development of an agenda for my nation, continent, and the world as a whole. I want to bring about quality standards of living to mankind," "To challenge the status quo regarding the philosophy and general psychology of Ghanaians. And to prove that Blacks can lead the rest of the world," and "To help build a better Ghana later in the future."

IMTK: In third place, Ghanaian students listed intrinsic motivation to know as one of their top motivations for attending college ($n = 49$; 18.2%). Statements that suggested the students derived pleasure and satisfaction from learning included "My motivation is to read and study more books and documents about scholars in order to acquire more knowledge to broaden my horizon," "To be exposed to a wide spectrum of knowledge and [I] hope to learn more," and "My motivation to go to college has nothing to do with money with regards to salary at work. [I want to] achieve that personal satisfaction that comes with being the best and having a knowledgeable view of aspects of society and certain fields of study."

EMID: As a moderate motivating factor for college attendance, the extrinsic motivation of identification ranked fourth with the Ghanaian students ($n = 27$; 10.0%). Sample statements reflecting behaviors that are valuable to the students and potentially important to their career and overall future included "I can stand out [*sic*] and say that the courses that I am reading at college are actually motivating me. Courses like economics broaden my horizon and scope of thinking about economics and social problems," "I am exploring my personal potential and preparing myself for future endeavors," "To train myself and be able to make better decisions about my life choices," and "I am becoming a critical thinker that can make strategic decisions in my businesses after school."

INTR: Reflecting another moderate motivator, the Ghanaian students reported that intrinsic or self-serving reasons are also driving forces in their college attendance ($n = 19$; 7.1%). According to one student, "What motivates me to be in school is to be able to achieve my dreams and make a better life for myself." Another student said he was attending college to "achieve the status I want to." One other student stated, "My main motivation for attending college is the fact that a high prestige is attached to a person who attends college in our part of the world."

IMTA: Intrinsic motivation to accomplish rounded out the middle by ranking sixth per the Ghanaian students' reported motivations for college attendance ($n = 13$; 4.8%). To review, this category comprised statements that the students were trying to excel, reach a new standard, and create something new and were motivated more by the process of attending college than by the actual outcome of obtaining an education. Example comments consisted of the following: "I am able to really think, understand, and analyze my present situation," "I feel happy when I understand new concepts and also when I discover new ideas," "I am adding value to myself," and "I go to college to discover new things that were unknown and to improve my value."

EMIN: Introjection, an extrinsic motivation, ranked among the Ghanaian students' least reported reasons for attending college ($n = 11$; 4.1%). Statements reflecting contingent consequences imposed by the Ghanaian students on themselves that led them to feel either negatively or positively about themselves based on their college attendance and performance included "Education is civilization and I feel proud to be on course [sic] of civilization," "Attending college will enable me to accomplish what I desire to accomplish in life, feel respected, [and] boost my self confidence and self-esteem," and "To prove to myself and my family that I can make it." One female Ghanaian student said, "I want to empower myself as a woman."

AMOT: Ranking next to last was amotivation ($n = 5$; 1.9%). Five of the 269 syntactical codes suggested that the Ghanaian students did not know why they were attending college. Sample statements included "I don't know," "It is a waste of time. I want to go to the military. I do not need to be here. The school does nothing to motivate the students. There is no internet, the school lacks its ability to inspire students," and "Well in Ghana because almost everybody does it, but for me if I had been brought up elsewhere maybe on another continent I would have cared not so much for education."

IMES: To experience stimulation, an intrinsic motivation, persuaded the Ghanaian students to attend college the least ($n = 3$; 1.1%). The only three reported statements that suggested that learning was exciting and stimulating were "For the opportunity to interact with people," "To associate with people who have similar interests," and "Learning is fun!"

The fourth research question queried the main motivation prompting Ghanaian students to attend college. According to their written comments, students from a Ghanaian family of origin are encouraged to attend college primarily because of extrinsic or other-oriented motivations, as reflected in EMER and EXTR each accounting for approximately one-fourth of the impetus behind Ghanaian students' college attendance. In particular, Ghanaian students are prompted to pursue higher learning in order to help their families and promote their country.

Discussion

The primary goal of this investigation was to explore how family serves as an academic motivator for African American and Ghanaian university students in pursuing a college education. Initially, as probed by the first research question, African American families of origin motivate their offspring to pursue higher education primarily for intrinsic reasons. This result is logical for a couple of reasons. First, the United States is a rather autonomous nation that stresses independence, self-sufficiency, and obtaining individual goals (Trenholm & Jensen, 2008; Triandis, 1995). Hence, it is not surprising that African American students are internally motivated to attend college because intrinsically motivated individuals voluntarily participate in an activity (such as pursuing higher education) for self-serving reasons (Deci & Ryan, 1985; Vallerand et al., 1992). This finding also concurs with previous research on the African American family that asserts that many African American families perceive education as a means of empowerment and upward social mobility (Sanders, 1998; Watkins, 2006). Hence, these families encourage their children to seek education in order to become independent and reach their individual goals (Watkins, 2006).

In response to the second research question, the data suggest that Ghanaian families of origin motivate their children to pursue higher education primarily for extrinsic reasons. This finding aligns with previous research on extrinsic motivations that posits that individuals participate in an activity (such as attending universities) because of external pressures or a sense of obligation or to obtain rewards (Deci & Ryan, 1985; Vallerand et al., 1992). Also, as mentioned in the literature on African families, cultural norms dictate that Ghanaians should be loyal to their family, tribe, or group, and they should be subordinate to external influences. As stated by Riccio (2008), the extended family and household in Ghana "represent the most important source of never-ending special obligations" (p. 221). In light of previous literature on extrinsic motivation and Ghanaian family and cultural values, the finding that Ghanaian families encourage their children to attend college for external reasons is plausible.

The third research question pondered the main motivation that African American students have for attending college. More than one-third of the students' written content was comprised of intrinsic or self-serving motives. The students stressed via their narrative accounts that they were attending college to take care of themselves, be independent, and not have to rely on anyone else for financial support—all motives reflective of the autonomous, individualistic, and independent cultural values found in the United States (Triandis, 1995). This finding is also not surprising given that median earnings for full-time employed young adults in the United States tends to rise as education level increases (U.S. Department of Education, National Center for Education Statistics, 2008), substantiating the link between education and financial freedom. Furthermore, this finding aligns with previous research that has asserted that families are the main encouragements that guide African American students in the direction of college by stressing to the children early on a connection between education and leadership, independence, and preparedness for the future (Barnett, 2004).

The fourth research question explored the key motivation driving Ghanaian students to pursue higher education. Data embedded in the students' written statements suggest that Ghanaian students are swayed by extrinsic or other-oriented motives. In particular, Ghanaian students are persuaded by family loyalty and obligations to educate themselves. Their narrative statements were laced with references to taking care of their family; representing their country, tribe, or clan; and making their families proud—all motives consistent with Ghanaian cultural values that reflect communal and family living (Riccio, 2008). As articulated by van Dijk (2002), primary attachment for Ghanaians lies with the family. Hence, it is plausible that Ghanaians desire to educate themselves in order to provide for their families of origin, which nearly 70% of African offspring accomplish by using their education and employment gains to support their families and enhance their communities (Liddell et al., 2003). Unfortunately, the returns to Ghanaian parents who invest in their children's education are not always guaranteed. According to Amuah (personal communication, May 21, 2010), University of Cape Coast professor, "The employment situation in Ghana is dire. People have graduated to get better jobs, but 10 years later they do not have better jobs. But they come to the university with the *hope* that a better future will come." In spite of the dire and unpredictable employment prospects, Ghanaian families still invest in their children's future and advise them to pursue higher education in the hope that they will be able to give back to their families and communities one day. Liddell et al. (2003) refer to the investment strategy that these families contribute toward their offspring's education as "bet-hedging" in that the families aim to educate all offspring to a level where employment opportunities are enhanced (p. 62), subsequently increasing the likelihood of the family's financial survival.

Limitations and Recommendations

While this study provides a more in-depth understanding of how family serves as an academic motivator for African American and Ghanaian university students to seek higher learning, it is not without limitations, and one limitation is of a methodological nature. To enhance the study's validity, the survey responses were complemented with an open-ended question that probed students to explain their main motivation for attending college. The students' narrative statements derived from this method augmented the survey data and, consequently, enhanced our understanding of how lessons learned from families can motivate students to pursue a college education. While the students' written comments were invaluable to the research objectives, it is advisable to triangulate the data with qualitative assessments. Perhaps interviews or focus groups can be conducted with the two groups under study following their completion of the survey. In sum, triangulating the survey findings with some form of qualitative analysis would facilitate a deeper understanding of how the students' families have really impacted their decisions to seek higher learning.

Universities and classrooms are becoming increasingly diverse and interdependent. According to Marklein (2008), the number of American students studying abroad is up nearly 150% compared to just a decade ago. Likewise, the number of international students enrolled in American colleges and universities in 2008–2009 increased by 8% from previous years, marking an all-time high (Rajka, 2010). Because students are venturing out and seeking diverse educational opportunities, it could also be telling if future researchers interviewed Ghanaian students who are studying in the United States and African American students studying in Ghana or other parts of Africa to explore whether their families impacted the motives behind their pursuing higher learning in different countries. Also, most of the students in this study were in the same age category and were classified as traditional students. Future research could gain a better understanding of the roles families play in motivating traditional and nontraditional students to pursue higher learning by comparing and contrasting data obtained from students representing different age-groups.

Conclusion and Implications of Research Findings on African American and Ghanaian Families

The study explored how the family serves as an academic motivator for African American and Ghanaian university students to pursue a college education. Findings suggest that students from African American families of origin are prompted to attend college mainly for intrinsic or self-serving reasons, which will position them to become independent of their family's care and financial support. In contrast, students from Ghanaian families of origin generally are motivated to seek a college education for extrinsic or other-oriented motives, which will increase the likelihood of their being able to provide for their families, tribe, or community. Data from this study suggest that families of origin do indeed impact why black students seek higher learning, lending support to previous research that has argued that the black family educates and impacts many of the decisions that children make (Mosley-Howard & Evans, 1997). Findings from this study, however, suggest that African American and Ghanaian families are encouraging their youth to pursue education for two different reasons related to the family. For African American families, the goal is for the children to obtain a higher education in order to become independent from the family's financial support, whereas for Ghanaian families, the objective is for the offspring to obtain an advanced degree so that they can become competitive in the job market and, subsequently, provide the family with financial support.

These research findings are meaningful in that they document clear differences in how African American and Ghanaian families communicate the roles and expectations of family in the educational process. As such, the data from this study contradict researchers, such as Sudarkasa (1998), who has advocated a historical connection between African Americans and their African heritage regarding family values and practices. In contrast, findings from this investigation lend support to more current research that has noted many observable differences in the family structures and practices of African Americans and their African ancestors (Gilchrist & Camara, 2012; McDonald, 2010; Uzoigwe, 2008).

In the past, describing the family structures of African Americans and Africans as dissimilar may have been perceived as illogical because African Americans have a historical connection to Africa. However, findings from this study suggest that what was once considered illogical and atypical regarding assumptions of discontinuity in African and African American family practices has become common.

This study has added to the growing body of knowledge that asserts that a rift now exists in the familial similarities of people in the African homeland and the Diaspora in America. As such, findings from this study allege that the contemporary African American family is slowly becoming disconnected from its African ancestors, and this perceived disconnect has grave ramifications concerning family cohesion. Researchers have long referred to the modern-day African American family as a cohesive unit that serves as a powerfully persuasive force in the lives of its members (Clark, 1983; Liddell et al., 2003). However, findings from this study imply that members of the once highly cohesive African American family are perhaps becoming more independent and self-centered. Unlike many African families that are motivated to pursue academics in order to support the collective family unit, it appears that members of the contemporary African American family view education as a springboard to severing ties, especially financial ties, with the family. Only time will reveal the true impact that seeking higher learning for independent and self-serving motives has on the contemporary African American family's cohesiveness. In the meantime, one thing is clear: "Power and justice . . . are linked to educational excellence and equity for disenfranchised groups," such as Africans and African Americans (Watkins, 2006, para. 3). Hence, the intrinsic and extrinsic benefits associated with higher learning are likely to inspire the continual pursuit of higher learning within black families.

Discussion Questions

1. What similarities exist between the overall African and African American family structures and practices?
2. What is the main motivation that African American families have for encouraging their offspring to pursue higher education?
3. What is the main motivation that Ghanaian families have for encouraging their offspring to pursue higher education?
4. Why does the author argue that a rift now exists in the familial similarities of people in the African homeland and the Diaspora in America?
5. What does the author identify as a potential consequence of the contemporary African American family's becoming disconnected from its African ancestors?

References

Ad Council. (n.d.). *United Negro College Fund (1972–present).* http://www.adcouncil.org/default.aspx?id=134

Barkoukis, V., Tsorbatzoudis, H., Grouios, G., & Sideridis, G. (2008). The assessment of intrinsic and extrinsic motivation and amotivation: A validity and reliability of the Greek version of the academic motivation scale. *Assessment in Education: Principles, Policy and Practice, 15,* 39–55.

Barnett, M. (2004). A qualitative analysis of family support and interaction among black college students at an Ivy League university. *Journal of Negro Education, 73*(1), 53-68.

Benokraitis, N. (2007). *Marriages and families* (6th ed.). Upper Saddle River, NJ: Prentice Hall.

Billingsley, A. (1993). *Climbing Jacob's ladder: The enduring legacy of African American families.* New York: Simon and Schuster.

Clark, R. (1983). *Family life and school achievement: Why poor black children succeed or fail.* Chicago: University of Chicago Press.

Cokley, K., Bernard, N., Cunningham, D., & Motoike, J. (2001). A psychometric investigation of the academic motivation scale using a United States sample. *Measurement and Evaluation in Counseling and Development, 34*(2), 109-119.

Collins, P. H. (1999). Mammies, matriarchs, and other controlling images. In J. Kournay, J. Sterba, & R. Tong (Eds.), *Feminist philosophies* (2nd ed., pp. 142-152). Upper Saddle River, NJ: Prentice Hall.

Collins, P. H. (2000). *Black feminist thought: Knowledge, consciousness, and the politics of empowerment.* (2nd ed.). New York: Routledge.

Deci, E. L., & Ryan, R. M. (1985). *Intrinsic motivation and self-determination in human behavior.* New York: Plenum.

Deci, E. L., & Ryan, R. M. (2000). The "what" and "why" of goal pursuit: Human needs and the self-determination of behavior. *Psychological Inquiry, 11,* 227-268.

Fairchild, A., Horst, S., Finney, S., & Barron, K. (2005). Evaluating existing and new validity evidence for the academic motivation scale. *Contemporary Educational Psychology, 30*(3), 331-358. doi:10.1016/j.cedpsych.2004.11.001

Frey, L., Botan, C., & Kreps, G. (2000). *Investigating communication: An introduction to research methods* (2nd ed.). Boston: Allyn & Bacon.

Gilchrist, E. S., & Camara, S. (2012). Cultural *dis*/continuity in African-American and Ghanaian mothers' voices and identities. *Journal of Intercultural Communication Research.*

Green, J., Nelson, G., Martin, A. J., & Marsh, H. (2006). The causal ordering of self-concept and academic motivation and its effect on academic achievement. *International Education Journal, 7,* 534-546.

Gutman, H. (1976). *The black family in slavery and freedom, 1750–1925.* New York: Pantheon Books.

Hill, R. (1997). *The strengths of African American families: Twenty-five years later.* Washington, DC: R & B Publishers.

Liddell, C., Barrett, L., & Henzi, P. (2003). Parental investment in schooling: Evidence from a subsistence farming community in South Africa. *International Journal of Psychology, 38*(1), 54-63.

Linnenbrink, E. A., & Pintrich, P. R. (2002). Motivation as an enabler for academic success. *School Psychology Review, 31,* 313-327.

MacLean, L. M. (2002). Constructing a social safety net in Africa: An institutionalist analysis of colonial rule and state social policies in Ghana and Côte d'Ivoire. *Studies in Comparative International Development, 37*(3), 64-90.

Marklein, M. B. (2008, November 17). Record number of U.S. students study abroad, in diverse locations. *USA Today.* https://www.usatoday.com

McDonald, P. B. (2010). The differences that bind us: An informal diasporan conversation. In D. A. Brunson, L. Lampl, & F. Jordan-Jackson (Eds.), *Interracial communication: Contexts, communities, and choices* (pp. 19-32). Dubuque, IA: Kendall/Hunt.

Mosley-Howard, S., & Evans, C. (1997). *Relationships in the African American family.* Paper presented at the Conference of the International Network on Personal Relationships, Oxford, OH.

Neuendorf, K. A. (2002). *The content analysis guidebook.* Thousand Oaks, CA: Sage.

O'Reilly, A. (2004). *Toni Morrison and motherhood: A politics of the heart.* New York: State University of New York Press.

Oyewumi, O. (2003). *African women and feminism: Reflecting on the politics of sisterhood.* Trenton, NJ: Africa World Press.

Rajka, B. (2010). *Open doors 2009: Report on international educational exchange.* New York: Institute of International Education.

Riccio, B. (2008). West African transnationalisms compared: Ghanaians and Senegalese in Italy. *Journal of Ethnic and Migration Studies, 34*(2), 217-234. doi:10.1080/13691830701823913

Sanders, M. (1998). The effects of school, family, and community support on the academic achievement of African American adolescents. *Urban Education, 33*(3), 385-409.

Sobral, D. (2004). What kind of motivation drives medical students' learning quests? *Medical Education, 38*(9), 950-957. doi:10.1111/j.1365-2929.2004.01913.x

Sudarkasa, N. (1998). Interpreting the African heritage in Afro-American family organization. In K. V. Hansen & A. Garey (Eds.), *Family in the US: Kinship and domestic politics* (pp. 91-104). Philadelphia: Temple University Press.

Teferra, D., & Altbach, P. G. (2004). African higher education: Challenges for the 21st century. *Higher Education, 47,* 21-50.

Thomas, H. (1997). *The slave trade. The story of the Atlantic slave trade: 1440–1870.* New York: Simon & Schuster Paperbacks.

Trenholm, S., & Jensen, A. (2008). *Interpersonal communication* (6th ed.). New York: Oxford.

Triandis, H. C. (1995). *Individualism and collectivism.* San Francisco: Westview Press.

U.S. Department of Education, National Center for Education Statistics. (2008). *The condition of education 2008* (NCES 2008-031), Indicator, 20. http://nces.ed.gov/fastfacts/display.asp?id=77

U.S. Department of Education, National Center for Education Statistics. (2009). *Digest of Education Statistics, 2008* (NCES 2009-020), table 226. http://nces.ed.gov/fastfacts/display.asp?id=98

Uzoigwe, G. (2008). A matter of identity: Africa and its Diaspora in America since 1900, continuity and change. *African and Asian Studies, 7*(2-3), 259-288. doi:10.1163/156921008X318718.

Vallerand, R. J., Pelletier, L. G., Blais, M. R, Brière, N. M., Senécal, C., & Vallières, E. F. (1992). The academic motivation scale: A measure of intrinsic, extrinsic, and amotivation in education. *Educational and Psychological Measurement, 52,* 1003-1017.

van Dijk, J. (2002). Religion, reciprocity and restructuring family responsibility in the Ghanaian Pentecostal Diaspora. In D. Bryceson & U. Vuorela (Eds.), *The transnational family: New European frontiers and global networks* (pp. 173-193). Oxford: Berg.

Watkins, A. P. (2006). The pedagogy of African American parents: Learning from educational excellence in the African American community. *Current Issues in Education* 9(7). http://cie.ed.asu.edu/volume9/number7

Williams, H. A. (2005). *Self-taught: African American education in slavery and freedom.* Chapel Hill: University of North Carolina Press.

Endnote

[1] The survey was completed in English for both the African American and Ghanaian students, as English is the official language in both Ghana and the United States.

PART 5
Families in Grief and Loss

Chapter 20
The Boundary Management and Family Identity Issues in Postbereavement Remarried Families 214
Carrie L. West, *University of Denver*

Chapter 21
The Life of a "Twinkie": Performing Race as a Korean Adoptee 224
Gina Bacon, *University of Utah*

Chapter 22
Obstacle or Opportunity? Reflections on Rhetorical Resilience Following Family Crises 234
Sherilyn Marrow, *University of Northern Colorado*
Nancy J. Karlin, *University of Northern Colorado*
Betty Burdorff Brown, *University of Northern Colorado*

Chapter 20

The Boundary Management and Family Identity Issues in Postbereavement Remarried Families

Carrie L. West

Just before midnight, on the day before my 29th birthday, I was shocked when I answered the doorbell to find our county coroner. He had come to notify me of my husband's death in a car accident caused by icy roads a few hours earlier. In a matter of seconds, my life changed forever. I went from being a wife and mother to being a widow and an only parent to two boys. From that moment, I have been reconstructing my view of family. I had unwillingly joined a group that no one wants to be a part of and a group that was much larger than I was aware. In the United States, approximately 4.5% of the population is widowed (U.S. Bureau of the Census, 2003). Also, in 2000, 4% of single parents had been widowed, and of those households, about 14% included children under the age of 12 (U.S. Bureau of the Census, 2003).

The death of a spouse is one of the most stressful life events (Holmes & Rahe, 1967; Norris & Murrell, 1990). Yet as I worked through the daunting task of adjusting to my new life, I realized how little support there was for bereaved families. For example, I attended a support group for newly single people, but I was the only widow in a group of recently divorced individuals. Also, I attended a bereavement program run by Hospice. Although they offered some helpful advice for dealing with loss, the Hospice organization focused primarily on families affected by long-term illness and focused on the grieving process for only the first year after death (interview with Dr. J. William Worden [L. M. Veglahn, Interviewer], Hospice Foundation of America, March 12, 2008).

Contact with friends and family was frequent in the first few months following my husband's death. Some brought food, some called or dropped by, and others offered to take the kids for a few hours. After a few months, although relationships with my family and my spouse's family remained constant, many friends returned to their normal lives, and I felt as though I was expected to do the same. Gradually, I adapted to my new life and was ready to think about moving forward and possibly remarrying. Eventually, I began dating and discovered that I was confronted with situations for which there were no support groups. I needed answers to some very basic and practical issues about dating, being an only parent, and, later, remarriage and incorporating my former family with my new family. Most support available to myself and to bereaved spouses is designed to help with the grieving process. However, these groups and programs do not address questions about how to move forward beyond the initial year or so of grieving. One difficulty I found was that I did not know how my new family was supposed to look. I did not know anyone else in my situation. The only widowed people I knew were elderly, and the only single parents I knew were divorced. In fact, some therapists have suggested that bereaved families refer to fictionalized accounts of families formed after the death of a spouse and parent because there is a lack of good models for these family types (Bryant, 2003). The lack of good support and role models highlights the need for investigation into the processes and challenges that bereaved spouses and families encounter when developing new relationships and new families.

It is not uncommon for widows and widowers with school-age children to date and remarry after the death of a spouse. Bishop and Cain (2003) reported that 2 years after the death of a spouse, 17% of surviving parents with school-age children were either engaged, living with someone, or remarried and that, within 5 years, almost half (47.5%) were remarried or cohabitating. The construction and blending of a new family can be one of the most challenging tasks faced by a bereaved spouse, especially those with children. Surviving spouses make choices about how to define their family and extended family and how to include their deceased spouse's family. These families rely on discourse to communicate family identity both within the family and to outsiders.

Now, 12 years later, I am part of the growing number of families whose membership goes beyond the connections of blood and law and who make daily choices about how to define my family and extended family. I am a remarried widow with school-age children, and I am acutely aware of the lack of research on this unique family form. As a widow, only parent, and wife, I have firsthand perspective of the challenges I have encountered while blending my old and my new families. As a scholar, I wanted to learn from the experience of others with similar life circumstances.

After obtaining the necessary institutional approval, I conducted in-depth, semistructured interviews with two individuals, a widow and a widower, whose children were very young when they experienced the unexpected death of their spouse. The female participant, Tara, lost her 31-year-old husband 7 years ago to an illness that appeared and killed her husband over the course of only a few days. Tara had two daughters at the time of her husband's death. One daughter was almost 2 years old, and the other was only 5 weeks old. The male participant, Jeff, lost his 23-year-old wife when he was 26 and 6 years prior to the interview. Jeff's wife was killed in a car accident when his two boys were 4 years old and 6 months old. Each interview lasted between 2 and 3 hours, and interview questions were directed at discovering the most difficult issues each participant faced and the strategies they have devised to deal with those issues. The main questions and follow-up discussion during the interviews were informed by my own experience.

After the interviews were transcribed, I made notes and diagrams to distill the most salient issues mentioned, noting both the frequency and the emphasis and emotion attached to each issue. While there are far too many ideas to fully address in this chapter, I have chosen two lenses through which to describe some of the most prominent parts of the discussion. First, I found several practices mentioned repeatedly in both interviews that align with those identified by Kathleen Galvin (2006) as used by discourse-dependent families to construct and maintain family identity. Second, in some cases, within the process of constructing family identity, privacy management theory (Petronio, 2002) can add to our understanding of these families' struggle to balance the sharing and protecting of private information when interacting with outsiders as well as family members.

The contemporary family is a complex and dynamic relational structure in which connections are made based on more than simply blood, or biological, relationships. Families additionally determine membership based on a combination of laws, roles, and choices. As the everyday practices and definition of families change, our understanding of more complex families must also evolve. As Galvin (2006) explains, "A growing number of U.S. families are formed through differences, visible or invisible, rendering their ties more ambiguous to outsiders as well as to themselves" (p. 3). When family ties are unclear, it is necessary for family members to communicate and explain connections to outsiders and to affirm those connections within the family. In Galvin's discussion of complex families, she explains, "as families become increasingly diverse, *their definitional processes expand exponentially, rendering their identity highly discourse dependent*"(p. 3, emphasis in the original). The discursive processes defining family connections occur through communication with outsiders as well as within the family (Galvin, 2006). Stepfamilies of all kinds rely heavily on discourse to negotiate, build, and maintain their family identity as they blend multiple families into a new family unit.

Of primary concern to the identity of blended families is boundary negotiation, in other words, who belongs in the family and what role each member plays. Galvin (2006) identified stepfamilies as a discourse-dependent family type and thus more likely to rely on discourse to construct their family identity than families fully defined biogenetically. Galvin examined discursive practices that family members use to construct their family identity internally as well as externally and identified four strategies for each. Even though these strategies are used by all types of stepfamilies and, to a lesser extent, by all families, there are unique or nuanced ways in which different types of stepfamilies may employ these practices. As discourse-dependent families are replacing other family types as the norm, communication scholars are delving into blended families and, often, into the communicative processes in stepfamilies.

Stepfamilies

Census data show that in 2000, there were more than 4 million stepchildren under the age of 18 living in the United States, while another 2 million were identified adopted (U.S. Bureau of the Census, 2003). The increased prevalence of alternative family forms has led family communication researchers to investigate blended and stepfamilies. Research has focused primarily on how divorce and remarriage affects family members because divorce rather than death is the most common circumstance prior to remarriage (Cherlin, 1992). Even so, approximately 1.2% of all children in the United States less than 18 years of age were living with a widowed parent in 2000 (U.S. Bureau of the Census, 2003).

Up to this point, family communication scholars have investigated primarily communication processes and issues as members adjust to a stepfamily after divorce (Braithwaite, Toller, Daas, Durham, & Jones, 2008; Coleman, Ganong, & Fine, 2000; Galvin 2006; Kellas, LeClair-Underberg & Normand, 2008). Members in stepfamilies must find ways to deal with additional stresses and risks associated with changing roles, relationships, and circumstances (Hetherington & Stanley-Hagen, 2000). Additionally, members of stepfamilies must manage uncertainty and complexity of their family relationships, particularly in the early stages after divorce and remarriage (Hetherington & Stanley-Hagen, 2000). When stepfamilies are considered as a homogeneous group, however, we lack information that leads to understanding some key differences between divorced remarried and bereaved remarried families.

The experience of children in stepfamilies formed after the death of a parent is similar to those in other stepfamilies, but their unique family history may change the way they approach a new family. In fact, in some ways, the transition to a stepfamily may be easier. For example, they can more easily move forward as they accept their loss as final rather than hoping for a parental reunion, have less anger toward the parent who left, can grieve more openly, experience fewer feelings of abandonment (Worden, 1996), and avoid feeling like they have torn loyalties between parents (Portrie & Hill, 2005). These differences necessitate a more nuanced understanding of these particular types of stepfamilies.

One approach to understanding stepfamilies has been put forth by Galvin (2006). She suggested that discourse-dependent families use eight types of strategies to negotiate their family identity and boundaries. These strategies are divided into external and internal boundary management. External strategies consist of *labeling*, *explaining*, *legitimizing*, and *defending*, and the internal strategies are *naming*, *discussing*, *narrating*, and *ritualizing*. This chapter will address only the boundary management strategies used for managing family identity with outsiders. Labeling, the first strategy identified by Galvin, represents one of the most useful and most difficult practices for stepfamilies formed after the death of a parent and spouse.

External Boundary Management

Labeling

A label "becomes a way to organize our experiences, to understand ourselves and others in relation to us" (Cait, 2006, p. 88). Galvin (2006) defines labeling as "the identification of the title or the position one uses when talking about or introducing a family member" (p. 10). Tracy (2002) considers labeling to be "the forms people select to address others and refer to self, they present their view of the existing relational identities..." (p. 51). More than simply differentiating one individual from another, terms of address reveal meaning about relationships, including levels of intimacy, legitimacy, and identity (Bergen, Suter, & Daas, 2006; Emihovich, 1981; Kellas et al., 2008).

Labels, names, and terms of address serve a very meaningful role in family relationships and can be used as both internal and external strategies for managing family identity. Choosing a form of address for one's family members helps establish the relational expectations the individual has of that family member, and identity is constructed and reinforced through the selection of terms of address (Bergen et al., 2006; Kellas et al., 2008; Tracy, 2002).

The selection of who is included in the category of *family* and the selection of terms of address for family members serves to "channel thinking in certain directions, to make actions seem sensible or potentially problematic" (Tracy, 2002, p. 58). The choice of a term of address is particularly important since it can impact feelings about a relationship. For example, terms of address can manage tensions and accomplish face work (Goffman, 1967), show solidarity (Kellas et al., 2008), and help outsiders make sense of the relational ties (Galvin, 2006). In addition, terms of address are sometimes chosen to relieve tension or make others happy, even though they do not accurately represent how a family member feels about the relationship (Kellas et al., 2008). Labeling clearly communicates crucial information about relationships, but appropriate labels do not exist for all stepfamily relationships (Ganong & Coleman, 2004).

One particularly difficult task in remarried bereaved families is the choosing of a last name for family members. In families, the choice of last names is a rhetorical one that can legitimize a relationship to others. "The choice of a last name upon marriage communicates affiliation and bonding or being a part of a group" (Carbaugh, 1996). This presents a problem, however, in bereaved remarried stepfamilies. In bereaved remarriages, the ex-spouse is no longer present to maintain connection to their family members. It is left to the surviving spouse to maintain the link with the deceased's family because the person who ties the spouse and in-law family together is absent.

When marrying, the choice to change one's last name is usually a symbolic act to show family union (Boxer & Gritsenko, 2005). On remarrying, the bereaved spouse is presented with a new set of challenges. Retaining the deceased's last name can signify solidarity with the children or a connection to the deceased spouse and their family, but this fails to show solidarity with the new spouse. If a widow(er) chooses to change his or her children's last name to a family last name, he or she risks hurting the deceased's family. If he or she changes his or her own last name to signify the union between himself or herself and his or her spouse, this may make the children feel as if they are not part of the family because their last names are different and may confuse teachers and others when the question of children's last names is addressed (Tracy, 2002). Beyond the choice of last names for family members, families also make meaningful choices about the labels used when talking to outsiders.

A recent study of stepfamilies and terms of address by Kellas et al. (2008) found that even the participants, who at first claimed that familial terms of address did not matter to them, acknowledged during the interview that at some point in their life the terms of address were very important. Usually, instances cited were when they were communicating relationship ties.

In many stepfamilies, choosing terms of address for members and extended family can be complex and tricky when speaking to outsiders. This is partially because there are no definitive labels, and choices are influenced by context, relationships, and the consideration of the feelings of others. The participants whom I interviewed identified the question of names and labels as one that they find particularly challenging and were interested to know the "right" answer to the question about what to call their deceased spouse and his or her family members.

An example of this is differentiating between the spouse one is married to and the deceased spouse. Participants explain that in the absence of a better option, they sometimes use words like "current" or "new" hesitantly because these labels give the impression that the spouse is filling a space that was vacated by the deceased spouse and lacks permanence.

A further illustration of this can be seen in bereaved remarried stepfamilies. The familial terms once used to refer to the in-laws may become awkward. Legally, the surviving spouse is tied to someone else. However, when introducing a former father-in-law, for example, Jeff said, "I usually just say, hey, this is my father-in-law." But occasionally his current father-in-law and his former father-in-law are in the same place, such as for a holiday celebration. Then it is difficult to differentiate between the two without offering an explanation that involves private information he does not want to share with just anyone. This situation becomes particularly problematic when family relationships are labeled in public ways, such as the Family Link application on Facebook. When Jeff's former father-in-law tagged him as his son-in-law, Jeff was concerned about how his current father-in-law would feel about the designation since they both have access to his profile.

Tara shared a story that illustrates this point as well. She was introduced at a family wedding, by her late-husband's brother, as his sister-in-law. Subsequently, she introduced her husband. This led to confusion and questions about the relationships, made her feel uncomfortable, and led to awkward explanations. She was confronted with the choice of whether to take the time to clearly explain her family's history to a casual acquaintance. This example also demonstrates how labeling often occurs simultaneously with decisions about how much and what to explain to outsiders.

Explaining

According to Galvin (2006), explaining "involves making a labeled family relationship understandable, giving reasons for it, or elaborating on how it works" (p. 10). An explanation is usually given in response to a nonhostile questioning of a family relationship. Instances of this often occur when the children are starting classes with a new teacher or in casual conversation when, as Jeff said, "You see that look on their face, and they're noticing that things don't quite add up." Then family members must choose if and how much private information to disclose about family relationships. When representing the family to outsiders, members presume ownership of their private information (Petronio, 2002) and can use explaining strategies to balance the personal and private while claiming their family identity.

One example addressed by privacy management theory (Petronio, 2002) is when parents of bereaved children feel that it is important for their child's teacher to know their situation. Both participants explained that they often choose to share this information when they anticipate that it will help explain unexpected or emotional behaviors by the child or when they anticipate that the child may share and it may be confusing or uncomfortable for a teacher or a friend's parent.

Another example mentioned by Tara and Jeff is when casual acquaintances notice that the parents have not been married as long as the children are old or that the last names of the children and one parent are different from those of the other parent. Often, the outsider will say something alluding to divorce, such as "How often do the kids see their dad?" At this point, the family member being questioned has to decide if he or she should explain the misconception, share private information, or just let it go.

A problem Jeff encountered when disclosing that his child's parent is deceased is that people then often become curious and feel like it is okay to ask extremely personal questions about the death of the parent and the situation with other family members. An often unintended yet particularly harsh result of this is that the bereaved spouse is now open to judgment about his or her handling of the situation, such as remarriage. This response seems different than in the case of a divorce, where it seems that people would more or less feel like they know what happened or do not want to pry.

Finally, the participants explained that they sometimes chose to disclose their personal situation when it might help to connect with another individual struggling with the death of a loved one. For example, Jeff works with youth and adolescents and, on more than one occasion, has been able to connect with a grieving child because of his willingness to disclose his personal situation as a means of connecting. When sharing and explaining aspects of a bereaved family relationship, family members often make attempts to legitimize the relationship as well.

Legitimizing

Legitimizing is when families use recognized laws or customs to prove the genuineness of relationships (Galvin, 2006). Legitimizing is the strategy that came up least frequently in these interviews, perhaps because the participants are remarried and thus are legal kin. This is also simplified because the children's biological deceased parent is absent from all interactions, so there is no competition for the place of "real" mom or dad. Both Jeff and Tara mentioned that they expected to deal with statements like "You're not my *real* mom/dad" from their children as they get older. Currently, the question of legitimacy takes a slightly different form.

For instance, Tara's first-grade daughter was tasked with filling out her family tree for a school assignment. She was struggling with the project and asked Tara, "Whose names do I write on Daddy's side of the paper?" In this case, Tara gave her the option of choosing one of her fathers (her biological father, whom she barely remembered, or her stepfather). She chose to divide the boxes in two and record both of their family trees. As a final statement on her project, Tara's daughter also hyphenated her own name on the paper to claim ties to both her biological father and her stepfather. While explaining and legitimizing are often used in response to nonhostile questions, Galvin (2006) suggests that there are other strategies utilized in response to more challenging remarks.

Defending

One such strategy is defending, which is used in multiple forms as stepfamilies defend their family identity. The challenge that was described as most meaningful to these participants is the challenge that comes, not to the new family but rather to genuineness of the old one. For example, it is common for outsiders to express their disapproval about the surviving spouse's moving on to a new relationship "so quickly" or even at all. To the others and myself, there seemed to be an expectation of a long mourning period. Regardless of how long participants waited before remarrying (1 to 4 years), both experienced negative judgment about how quickly they had remarried. These judgments implied that the new marriage was a negative reflection on their quality of their relationship with their deceased spouse. As Tara explained, "For some reason, because my spouse is dead, and we're not divorced, people feel like they have the right to judge . . . you should have been by yourself for 5 years and really struggled. . . . It might seem quick to outsiders but from the inside, on your own, friends have all left, you're doing everything by yourself . . . 7 years feels like 20 years."

Frequently, members of a bereaved family feel as if they have to defend their relationships with their new family. One such example often occurs in conservative or religious environments where there is a negative stigma around divorce. Participants expressed tension around choosing whether to disclose their family relationships to clarify a misconception that they are divorced. As Jeff explained, "When you are divorced, people assume you were at least part of the problem; when your spouse dies, they want to help you." In response to particularly offensive remarks, the disclosure could even be used as a weapon to shame others for their insensitive remarks by "dropping the bomb."

Feelings of defensiveness increase significantly when privacy boundaries around a spouse's death are crossed without permission. As Jeff explained, at the time of his wife's death, her accident was fairly public and covered in the newspapers. Because the details of her death were very public and there were many people involved in memorials, the matter did not feel as private. However, as time has passed (and it has now been 6 years since her death), he considers and wants her death to be more private. Now he does not want to discuss and, consequently, relive her death with outsiders.

Unfortunately, once access has been granted to private information and outsiders have been allowed into the most personal details of a widow's or widower's life, it can be particularly difficult to rescind access and reestablish privacy boundaries.

Discussion

Bereaved and remarried families face unique relational challenges when compared to other stepfamilies in the ways that they incorporate their old and new families. Because they are not as common as other types of stepfamilies, these differences have gone largely unnoticed and unstudied, particularly in the communication field. These families draw on multiple communicative strategies to continuously manage their identity with outsiders, such as labeling, explaining, defending, legitimizing. This process is complicated by their own needs for privacy and concern for others' feelings.

One of the limitations of this study is the small sample size. However, results highlight difficult situations not found in other stepfamilies, and these participants desire guidance and coping strategies for dealing with their unique communication issues.

Since many scholars agree that the death of a spouse is one of the most difficult and stressful life experiences an individual will encounter, research into how bereaved spouses and families adapt to their loss is clearly important. However, the next phase of a bereaved spouse's life, one that is equally important yet often overlooked, is that of dating and remarriage. Often surviving spouses date and remarry within 2 years of the death of a spouse (Schneider, Sledge, Schucter, & Zisook, 1996), but remarriage may be especially complicated for these individuals because many of the negative effects for children who have lost a parent do not surface until a year or more after their parent's death (interview with Dr. J. William Worden [L. M. Veglahn, Interviewer], Hospice Foundation of America, March 12, 2008). Therefore, stepfamily adjustment occurs during a turbulent and crucial time for family and individual identity of all family members. One way bereaved remarried stepfamilies meet these challenges of family identity is through discourse, particularly by labeling, explaining, defending, and legitimizing their family connections. Family communication scholars can assist these families by extending the investigation of stepfamilies to bereaved remarried stepfamilies and to the processes and coping strategies used in family development.

Discussion Questions

1. In what ways, other than those mentioned in the chapter, might stepfamilies that are formed after divorce differ from those that are formed after the death of a spouse and parent?

2. Other than strategies for managing family identity, what are some issues or questions that communication researchers should investigate related to bereaved remarried families?

3. How would you advise bereaved remarried parents to solve the question of last names for family members?

4. How might the age of the children at the time of their parent's death influence the decisions about sharing the family's history and relational connections?

References

Bergen, K. M., Suter, E. A., & Daas, K. L. (2006). "About as solid as a fish net": Symbolic construction of a legitimate parental identity for nonbiological lesbian mothers. *Journal of Family Communication, 6,* 210-221.

Bishop, S., & Cain, A. (2003). Widowed young parents: Changing perspectives on remarriage and cohabitation rates and their determinants. *Omega: Journal of Death and Dying, 47,* 299-312. doi:10.2190/N50W-AGNC-OMXA-EP9B

Boxer, D., & Gritsenko, E. (2005). Women and surnames across cultures: Reconstituting identity in marriage. *Women and Language, 28,* 1-11.

Braithwaite, D., Toller, P., Daas, K., Durham, W., & Jones, A. (2008). Centered but not caught in the middle: Stepchildren's perceptions of dialectical contradictions in the communication of co-parents. *Journal of Applied Communication Research, 36,* 33-55. doi:10.1080/00909880701799337

Bryant, L. E. (2003). *Stepchildren's perceptions of the contradictions in communication with stepfamilies formed post bereavement.* PhD dissertation, University of Nebraska-Lincoln.

Cait, C. A. (2006). Identity development and grieving: The evolving processes for parentally bereaved women. *British Journal of Social Work, 38,* 322-339.

Carbaugh, D. (1996). *Situating selves: The communication of social identities in American scenes.* New York: State University of New York Press.

Cherlin, A. J. (1992). *Marriage, divorce, remarriage: Social trends in the United States.* Cambridge, MA: Harvard University Press.

Coleman, M., Ganong, L., & Fine, M. (2000). Reinvestigating remarriage: Another decade of progress. *Journal of Marriage and Family, 62,* 1288-1307.

Emihovich, C. A. (1981). The intimacy of address: Friendship markers in children's social play. *Language and Society, 10,* 189-199.

Galvin, K. M. (2006). Diversity's impact on defining the family: Discourse dependence and identity. In L. H. Turner & R. West (Eds.), *The family communication sourcebook* (pp. 3-19). London: Sage.

Ganong, L. H., & Coleman, M. (2004). *Stepfamily relationships: Development, dynamics, and interventions.* New York: Kluwer Academic/Plenum.

Goffman, E. (1959). *The presentation of self in everyday life.* New York: Doubleday.

Hetherington, E. M., & Stanley-Hagen, M. (2000) Diversity among stepfamilies. In D. Demo, K. Allen, & M. Fine (Eds.), *Handbook of family diversity* (pp. 173-196). New York: Oxford University Press.

Holmes, T., & Rahe, R. (1967). The Social Readjustment Scale. *Journal of Psychosomatic Research, 11,* 213-218. doi:10.1016/0022-3999(67)90010-4

Kellas, J. K., LeClair-Underberg, C., & Normand, E. L. (2008). Stepfamily address terms: "Sometimes they mean something and sometimes they don't." *Journal of Family Communication, 8,* 238-263.

Norris, F. H., & Murrell, S. A. (1990). Social support, life events, and stress as modifiers of adjustment to bereavement by older adults. *Psychology and Aging, 5,* 429-436. http://www.apa.org/pubs/journals/pag/index.aspx

Petronio, S. (2002). *Boundaries of privacy: Dialectics of disclosure*. New York: State University of New York. Press.

Portrie, T., & Hill, N. R. (2005). Blended families: A critical review of the current research. *Family Journal, 13,* 445–451. doi:10.1177/1066480705279014

Schneider, S. S., Sledge, P. A., Schucter, S. R., & Zisook, S. (1996). Dating and remarriage over the first two years of widowhood. *Annals of Clinical Psychiatry, 8,* 51–57.

Tracy, K. (2002). *Everyday talk: Building and reflecting identities.* New York: Guilford Press.

U.S. Bureau of the Census. (2003, October). *Adopted children and stepchildren: 2000.* Washington, DC: Author.

Worden, J. (1996). *Children and grief: When a parent dies*. New York: Guilford Press.

Chapter 21

The Life of a "Twinkie": Performing Race as a Korean Adoptee

Gina Bacon

Twinkie: A golden coloured small sponge cake with a [white] creamy filling.
(Word Web Online)

I am what some may call a twinkie: yellow on the outside, white on the inside. Generally meant as a derogatory racial term, I decode it as an accurate description. I am just under 5 feet tall and have brown skin, black hair, and dark-brown eyes. I look about as Asian as one can get. I would say that my height (or lack of height) came from my dad and my thick black hair from my mom, but my dad is 6 feet tall, and my mom has fine, medium-brown hair. They are both (Cauc)asian. I am not the only twinkie or (Cauc)Asian in the world. Asian adoption has become fairly common, especially in the United States. However, I can speak only to my experience, so this chapter serves as the voice of one twinkie: Gina Bacon.

My parents' race differs from my own. My exterior is like a small yellow sponge cake, soaking up the American culture that surrounds me. My interior is white, like the cream that makes a twinkie distinct and full of flavor but is never actually seen from the outside. Both parts never mix and block each other from being one solid color. In other words, my "yellow" body gets in the way of my "white" experience. At the same time, my "white" inside does not allow me to be fully "yellow." Words like "minority," "oppression," and "marginalization" are used to describe my Asian body. "Privilege," "patriarchy," and "dominance" describe my white inside.

Most people, especially in academia, recognize that race is not biological but rather a social construct. Yet, as hard as people may try to decrease the impact that skin color has on individuals, we cannot deny that race plays a significant part of our self-concept because we live in a "race-conscious society" (Fogg-Davis, 2002). After all, almost every survey has a little race box to check. It is almost metaphorical. By checking the box, you are being put into a box. You are marking who you are, where you come from, and where you stand in society (Table 21.1).

Table 21.1 Stereotypical Associations with Racial Categories

> **Select One:**
> ☐ Caucasian (privileged, ideal)
> ☐ Black American (criminal, ghetto)
> ☐ American Indian (alcoholic, spiritual)
> ☐ Asian American (martial arts master, studious)
> ☐ Hispanic American (lazy, illegal)
> ☐ Other/Unknown (unrecognized, unimportant)

Note. Each assigned stereotype list is not comprehensive. The author listed them from general knowledge and is using the stereotypes to demonstrate how arbitrary meanings can be constructed when forced to choose a specific racial category.

Based on my skin color, I check "Asian American." However, my cultural background does not come from South Korea. My parents' ancestors came from Germany, England, Switzerland, and Scotland. I do not share my family's bloodline because I am not racially mixed with one parent white, the other Korean. So what is my racial identity? When society tells me that I am supposed to speak Korean and know about the culture, how do I explain that my parents are white without feeling shame or guilt? I am writing about my story as a Korean adoptee because I check the Asian American box but fit better in the Caucasian box, yet I cannot check that box because I am Korean. So I should really check the "Other/Unknown" box because I do not fit into any other racial category. Through writing this chapter, I will attempt to place my identity in this multicultural yet heavily racialized society.

I am not the first Korean adoptee to attempt such a task. Some Korean adoptees have written books about their experiences being adopted. Trenka (n.d., para. 7) identified seven to be exact. Only seven adoptees have shared their story in 50 years of adoption. While more adoptees are telling their stories, there is still a small percentage being disseminated. By writing this autoethnographical chapter through performative writing, I hope to add more to the limited conversation that international adoptees have started. Korean adoptees share unique experiences that most do not and cannot understand. I write to raise awareness, identify with other adoptees, and explore the connotations of "race," "identity," "stereotype," and "family." Each adoptee has a different story, but our silenced and/or misunderstood voices have a place in dominant family discourse.

International adoption challenges the concept of the "all-American family."

Heterosexual, monoracial norms are changing as gay marriage, single parenting, divorce, in vitro fertilization, and adoption increase. The "family" is not breaking down; it is in a state of transition. I write from the position that my (Cauc)asian family is no different from any other monoracial family. Although racial difference cannot be denied or silenced, family is not solely dependent on biology. Race is, after all, a social construction arbitrarily based on skin pigmentation. Nixon (2009, para. 12) states that South Korean adoptees constitute the largest group of transracial adoptees. Around 160,000 children were adopted from 1953 to 2007, mostly into the United States. Transracial adoption (especially from South Korea) is no longer a family anomaly; it is common. Yet stories of South Korean adoptees are not widely disseminated. This chapter aims to bring one Korean adoptee's voice into a canon of family stories.

I use an autoethnographic approach because I live the experience of a Korean adoptee every day. Autoethnography "positions personal narrative and lived experience as the text, or data, for a particular study" (Meyer, 2007 p. 19). By recalling memories of my life, my body is the text in which I will analyze, criticize, and explore the significance of racial identity, stereotypes, and performativity from an international adoptee's standpoint. Undoubtedly, I write about my family because they shaped and continue to shape who I am. While challenging the significance of racial identity, I also challenge the insignificance of race when it comes to love and connection to my family.

Definitions of performance have expanded from the arts to a more inclusive position of performativity. Performance ethnographers assume that humans are essentially performing, which examines how people "constitute and sustain their identities and collectively enact their worlds through roles and rituals" (Conquergood, 1992, p. 27). Studying members of society in terms of performance positions researchers in a unique position of seeing how individuals change behavior according to their social, cultural, and political context.

The field of performance studies talks about performance with the interest of "uncovering truths about the cultural environments of the performers and performance being discussed—truths[,] anthropological, ethnographic, sociological, economic, political" (Bacon, 1996, p. 358). By studying how people perform in different contexts of our hegemonic society, a richer understanding of privilege, behaviors, and attitudes can be produced. Performance ethnography is used to "see how meaning, identity, and culture are made—how self and other are constituted in everyday life" (Warren, 2001, p. 200). My goal is to use my body as a text in which to study how I perform race in a society that assumes that race signifies culture and how people react to and/or reject my performances. Fox (2007) asserts that performative writing is "one way that marginalized academians may demonstrate creative control of their subjectivities" (p. 6). By narrating my life experiences, I can solidify my standpoint in a cultural and academic context while adding another voice to the small chorus of international adoptees living in a white-dominated world.

"Noh" More Korea: How I Became "Twinkified"

Noh Eun Joo was born in Seoul, South Korea. She was the oldest among one boy and one girl. Composed and of medium build, Eun Joo had a round face and was thin and cute. At 18 years old, she attended high school as a third grader, similar to being a senior in the United States. On May 5, 1986, Eun Joo's life changed forever. She gave birth to a healthy baby girl. However, she felt that she could not raise her baby normally as a young and unmarried student. She thought her baby "had better be adopted to a good family for the sake of her baby's future." So, on May 8, 1986, Eun Joo never saw her baby girl again.

I am the baby girl that Eun Joo gave up for adoption. The above paragraph contains all that I know about the brave woman who gave me life. After just 3 days of having a daughter, she placed me in the Angel Baby Home. About 4 weeks later, I was put under the care of foster parents for 3 months. Then, on September 9, 1986, I grew wings and flew to Seattle, Washington, and was united with Theresa and Richard Bacon, otherwise known as Mom and Dad. I went from a daughter to orphan to foster child and back to a daughter once more.

My parents, two older brothers, and extended family waited for me at the airport. According to my parents, I was the only baby not crying when the plane of Korean adoptees arrived. Pictures reveal that I was wide eyed with curiosity and surprisingly peaceful and calm. Being surrounded by white faces did not alarm my baby self. They were my family from the moment I was carried off the airplane and placed into my mother's arms; they were my "real" family, not my "adopted" family. As a 4-month-old baby, I did not seem to notice or care that my family was white, a color so different from the brown I had been surrounded with. Yet growing up and seeing other families made me realize that my family was quite unique.

Most people can literally see themselves in their parents. They might have their mother's nose or father's eyes and can attribute most of their physical persona to a specific family member. Even personality traits are linked to genetics. Seeing these similarities are, in my opinion, highly taken for granted. Why? Because I cannot. The only information I have about my birth mother and father is what is written in my adoption papers. My birth mother was 18 years old when she gave birth to me. At the time, she was "composed and of medium build. She [was] thin and cute. She [had] a round face." There is no information about my birth father. I assume he had a pointier chin since my face is more oval. Yet I will never know about the physical characteristics passed on to me beyond the undetailed description of my birth mom. Although her genetic attributes are unknown, she did give me a name.

Contrary to the majority of sons and daughters, I was born with a name that does not identify who I am in this world. McKerrow (1989, p. 455) writes that naming is a rhetorical act that gives meaning to the abstract. Therefore, the emergence of names is not based on truth but rather contingently, or incidental. Although names are merely symbolic, they carry significant meaning for people's identity. In theater, actors play many different identities. I began acting at the age of 13 and found that it is rare to play a character who shares your legal name. In every production or scene, I am no longer "Gina," I am ———. My body stays the same, but one simple word changes my entire being. I perform differently onstage than I do in the real world. I am a separate identity, another person.

Similar to my various personalities onstage, I perform a different person as Gina Renae Bacon than the name given to me at birth—Noh Hyeong Kyeong (last name Noh). It means "wise and shining." Noh Hyeong Kyeong is neither who I am nor who I perform. Noh Hyeong Kyeong lives in South Korea, understands the language, and was raised by her Korean family. She knows about the Korean culture. She is Asian. Gina Renae Bacon lives in the United States of America. She speaks English, was raised by her Caucasian family, and knows about her Western culture. She is (Cauc) Asian. Noh Hyeong Kyeong is me, so I try to embody my Asian heritage. Gina Renae Bacon is also me, so I act and perform what I know—white. The disconnect between my Asian and white selves creates my "twinkie" status.

When did I become a "twinkie"? On the day my family brought home their little girl from Korea. Since arriving in the United States, my Korean name and American name have struggled to identify who I am. People assume that I am Hyeong Kyeong, so I try to embody her for them. Then I say my name, "I'm Gina, nice to meet you," and reveal that I do not speak Korean, and my Asian performance is rejected. "Performing race is ultimately performing self in the face of history and in the company of others—and negotiating the problems and pitfalls of claiming and maintaining membership" (Alexander, 2004, p. 25). Since neither of my names represents who I am, what racial membership am I trying to claim? Who do I perform, Noh Hyeong Kyeong or Gina Renae Bacon? And, perhaps more important, what performance is the most accepted?

Twinkie in the Making: Discovering Race

As a young child, I did not see myself as Asian. I did not know what Asian was. But I do remember certain memories that made me realize that I was different and that separated me from the white population. Willink (2007, p. 22) writes that remembering as performance brings bodies into the present and offers possibilities for transformation. It "mobilizes new possibilities into bodies, current life, and future conversation" (p. 23). Remembering my childhood informs how I performed race (or was forced to perform) before even knowing what race was. By telling memories, my remembered body can act as a means for understanding and transforming my present self, thereby adding insight to the concept of race in our multicultural society.

Before kindergarten, I attended a day care where my mom worked. I have only one distinct memory of being there. A woman brought out large sheets of white paper for the girls to make dresses. We were going to perform Cinderella that day. One of us got to be Cinderella, while the others had to play the evil stepsisters. I *really* wanted to be Cinderella but almost instinctively knew that I would not be picked because I did not look like her. Unsurprisingly, a cute blonde girl got the part, and I was stuck as an ugly stepsister. A racial consciousness or identity begins to internalize at about 4 years old (Simon & Alstein, 1992, p. 133). I was probably around that age when this happened. Although I did not identify myself as Asian back then, my racial identity began to form through comparing and being compared by the white others that surrounded me.

Interestingly enough, I have never *felt* different from my family and friends. I have only looked different. My physical appearance leaves me unable to be Caucasian but only because our racialized society cannot accept the (Asian) part of my identity. The Evan B. Donaldson Adoption Institute conducted a study of first-generation Korean adoptees and found that 78% of the participants saw themselves as Caucasian or wanting to be Caucasian as children (Nixon, 2009, para. 6). In another study, 11% of Korean adoptee adults identified themselves as Caucasian over Korean or Korean American (Freundlich & Lieberthal, 2000, para. 10). Similar to these adoptees, I *would* consider myself Caucasian. Yet people around me cannot accept that identity because Asian American connotes someone from Asia living in America, whereas Caucasian simply connotes American. So why can't I just be American? Consider the simple question, "Where are you from?" Here might be a typical conversation between two white acquaintances:

White 1: "Where are you from?"
White 2: "Vancouver, Washington."
White 1: "Oh, great. That's a nice city."

This is a typical conversation between a white acquaintance and me:

White 1: "Where are you from?"
Me: "Vancouver, Washington."
White 1: "Oh. But I mean, where are you *really* from?"
Me: "South Korea."
White 1: "Wow. So, you speak Korean."
Me: "No."
White 1: ". . ." (silent and confused)
Me: "Well, I'm adopted . . ."

For me, a simple "where are you from?" actually implies "tell me about your exotic culture." Why can't I be considered American? My physical body does not let me. I imagine my experiences growing up have been fairly similar to my white peers. Yet my yellow outside created a barrier that separated me even more from the many issues that face young people. Fogg-Davis (2002) writes that "race, as indicated by skin color, facial features, and hair texture, is therefore an extremely poor predictor of human compatibility in friendship, romance or adoption" (p. 20). In my case, "race, as indicated by skin color, facial features, and hair texture," is an extremely good predictor of jealousy and comparison between me and my white peers.

Yellow Sponge Cake in a White Creamy World: (Un)able to Perform White

There will always be one clear memory I have from kindergarten. While walking under the covered area during recess, four or five boys approached me. Not knowing how I moved, my body was suddenly pinned against the brick wall, unable to push past the boys that put me there. They started yelling things at me. Scared and with tears streaming down my face, I caught the eye of one of my classmates, Casey, between the boy's bodies. I desperately pleaded for help with my eyes but watched him continue to walk by while watching me. After the boys let me go, my friend Kaylyn suggested telling the recess aid what happened, but I did not follow her advice. Instead, I told my family what those boys did and said to me. Much to my surprise, they did not seem upset. I even remember them laughing. I shared my hurt, and my family did not share my pain. I will never forget that day.

I will never forget that the boys pinned me to a wall but have no recollection of what they actually said to me. As an adult, my mom later told me what happened and explained that I was upset not by their physical actions but rather their words. Apparently, the boys said, "You have a round face" over and over. They read my text (my body) and vocalized what they found. My family did not have a big reaction because the statements that hurt me so much were true. They reminded me that I do have a round face. My parents did not want me to feel ashamed of that. Their casual reaction was to help me realize that the boy's "insults" were not insults at all. I remember being confused because I expected them to feel sorry for me. Now I am grateful for their calm reaction and understand why they did not validate my hurt feelings. I did have a round face. There is nothing hurtful about that. Yet, if the boys just vocalized a true statement about my physical body, why did their particular reading create tears?

Being trapped by boys was frightening, but I was hurt by what they said to me. They pointed out my physical difference like I was a freak, ugly and unnatural. I would never look like them or be the "pretty" girl in class. These thoughts did not formulate in kindergarten, but I recognize the same feelings of pain and disappointment about my physical body now. I will never be the blonde, oval-faced, blue-eyed girl that society deems beautiful. Granted, most girls cannot reach the tall, skinny ideal of beauty that the media force on us. Yet my short, yellow body removes me farther from the white ideal my friends and family possess.

I do not feel different from my peers until I cannot perform like my peers. My yellow exterior does not hinder my ability to run a mile, act onstage, or swim laps at a pool. It does not hinder my ability to connect and identify with my white friends. I do not feel like an outsider or outcast because I am Korean. I feel like them; I feel white. My inability to perform white happens when looking at myself in a photograph or gazing into a mirror. It happens when I go shopping with my friends and find one shirt that fits while they find six. My Asian body puts me in the kids' section at the shoe store, keeps my feet from touching the ground on city buses, and forces me to realize that I am not like my friends.

My friends are tall, have eyelids, can wear bright yellow and orange, can buy age-appropriate clothing, and do not have to stand on a chair to reach the high cupboards. When the media tell me that beautiful is tall and white and everyone around me fits that description, my body serves as a reminder that I will never be close to the ideal of beauty. Participants of Freundlich and Lieberthal's (2000) study made comments like "I felt that I wasn't pretty because I didn't meet the Western ideal of beauty" and "I did not consider myself attractive because I was not Caucasian." To find beauty in my short brown body, small brown eyes, and plain black hair while being surrounded by beautiful white women is a difficult task. Supposedly, Asian women are exotic to members of Western culture. Exotic and submissive are two common stereotypes linked to Asian women. Yet I cannot even be those because I grew up in Washington State in a culture that aims for equality and individualism.

White Cream Flavors the Yellow Sponge Cake: (Un)able to Perform Asian

I watched a show called *The Naked Truth* at my school. The show aimed to break down several stereotypes through various monologues. Two monologues really affected me. I watched an Asian woman break down the stereotype of being a quiet, smart, Asian girl who slips silently through the crowd. Another monologue showed the difficulty of having an Asian accent because people assume that you are unintelligent or incapable of correctly performing tasks. These two monologues got me thinking: my parents never pressured me to do well in school, and I cannot even fake a good Asian accent. Watching these performances made me realize how (un)Asian I really am. People read my body and assume that I have Asian parents and can speak a different language. When meeting people who expect me to be yellow on the inside *and* out, I feel shame for not embodying a typical Asian woman. I cannot blame or be offended by their readings of my physical body. Multiracial families are uncommon, and it might be strange to assume that every person of color is adopted. However, my inability to perform Korean should not be cause for guilt or shame.

Warren (2001, p. 186) (re)constitutes whiteness by examining an incident that occurred in one of his classrooms. He writes that race is not located in the body but rather is a discourse that produces whiteness through social interaction. Warren then narrates a situation when his student, Karen, reveals her whiteness by using a racial term. She told the class that someone in a "rice burner" (Asian car) started a horrible accident on the road. The class, which did not have a single Asian student, became very uncomfortable and offended. The term "rice burner" perpetuates Asian stereotypes. Yet if I was in that classroom, I would not be offended. Is that because I do not identify as a *real* Asian person or because I *am* Asian and am allowed to think that it is funny? Everyone assumes the latter, but my inside screams the former.

People read my body and expect me to be Asian, but, according to our multicultural and racialized society, I do not live up to that expectation. I met a Korean woman who, on hearing that I did not speak Korean, said, "Shame on you!" An older gentleman at my parent's church saw me and said, "Ni hau." Interactions like these occur monthly. I simply cannot perform Asian. My knowledge of Korean culture comes from school projects. I cannot pronounce my own Korean name and am not familiar with Korean cuisine. I cannot speak a convincing Korean accent. I am looked down on. I am "whitewashed." I am a twinkie that cannot be fully Asian, whatever being Asian means. But I still try to embrace my yellow exterior. I still try to make my performance believable.

Yellow Sponge Cake Hides White Cream: Embodying Stereotypes

People assume that my name should be Noh Hyeong Kyeong rather than Gina Renae Bacon. So, many times I attempt to embody her for them to make *myself* feel more Asian. There is a stereotype that Asian people are intelligent and studious. I do not believe that there is an "A student" gene. Perhaps there is, but my limited knowledge about genetics cannot make any conclusions. People tell me that I get good grades because I am Asian. It is the equivalent of my saying, "You can play the flute because you're white." Being white has nothing to do with a person's musical talent, and being Asian has nothing to do with getting a good test grade, though even I find myself agreeing with those who say, "It's because you're Asian." While these comments are mainly in jest, there is some truth to the statement—not in the sense that all Asians have a "do well in school" gene but that some people perceive Asians as intelligent simply because of their exterior appearance. Even though stereotypes negatively generalize individuals of a specific group, I feel more like a legitimate Asian person because of my grades. I embrace stereotypes because they make me feel like I belong. I find myself trying to perform yellow while simultaneously attempting to hide my white inside.

As previously mentioned, Warren (2001) wrote about a student who called someone's car a "rice burner." If any car embodies that racial description, it is my middle brother's sleek, dark green Tiburon. Red dragons tattoo the sides of his car, while red flame decals burst from the hood. Green lights illuminate the tires, while blue and black lights fill the interior. It looks like a car used in *Fast and the Furious*. My white brother, however, does not necessarily look like the type to drive such an "Asian"-looking vehicle. I, on the other hand, do. When my brother lets me drive his car, I feel more Asian. For some reason, putting my physical body in the driver's seat of his car makes me feel like I can belong. Having "yellow" skin does not make me feel Korean, but driving a "yellow"-associated car with my "yellow" skin does. Physical accessories like cars and hairstyles influence readings of my body, which in turn influences my own perception about my racial identity. My efforts at being yellow on the outside *and* inside generally fail. Because I cannot rid my white inside, I perform what it is like to be Korean. My Asian performances may seem believable, but when it comes down to the truth, they are just performances.

Ingredients—Yellow Cake *and* White Cream: Performing and Embracing "Twinkie"

I perform white and Asian, but both are not accepted. I look too Asian to be white but do not act "yellow" enough to be Asian. My inability to be one or the other only solidifies my position as both. I was born in South Korea and am proud of my heritage. I live in the United States and am proud of my white family. "A narrative of personal experience is not a clear route into 'the truth' . . . such stories are intensely personal, they are thoroughly shaped by cultural conventions" (Atkinson & Delamont, 2006, p. 166). Writing about my racial experiences does not end in a distinct conclusion about society, racism, stereotypes, or identity. But the journey of this chapter raises awareness about the disconnect between skin color and culture. Members of society assume that I am Asian, which is a stereotype of its own. Just because I look Korean does not mean that I know about the culture. Nor does it mean that I *should* know about the culture.

Children's House International (n.d.), a Ferndale, Washington, adoption agency, emphasizes the need for parents to educate adopted children about their original culture. I agree that children should know where they were born and learn about where they would have been raised. Adopted children of color are different because they come from a separate country and were conceived from different parents. At the same time, they are no different from biological children in the parent's eyes. At least I am no different from my brothers in my parent's eyes. My mom tried talking to me about South Korea and my adoption, but I lived here, so my knowledge about the country seemed irrelevant. My family was and is my family. My home is my home. My life was not meant to be in South Korea. My birth mother hoped that I would have a good life in the United States, and that is just what I got. Whether I am yellow, white, purple, or green, my family and I are no different from one another. I am their daughter, not their *adopted* daughter.

Lev (2004) writes that "loving and well intentioned white parents are failing their children of color" (p. 100). She believes that children feel separate from others who look like them and do not look like them. As an adopted child of color, I *am* separate from Asian Americans and white Americans. Separate does *not* mean less or worse. Our racialized society tries placing people into boxes, but adoptees cannot fit. I perform two different races in an attempt to "fit in" when I should not have to fit in at all. My white upbringing and Asian exterior make me unique. My (Cauc)asian family is my *real* family. They do not see my Asian body; they see Gina. I am a twinkie and do not want to be anything else. Society has a difficult time accepting my "yellow" outside and "white" inside as a package, but through giving my "twinkified" body a voice, individuals may rethink the way we label people of color.

Discussion Questions

1. Has someone ever incorrectly assumed characteristics about you based on skin tone, race, or other physical attributes? Have you made incorrect assumptions about someone else? How were you or others affected by these experiences?
2. What are positives and negatives of self-identifying with a racial, gendered, or other identity labels?
3. What effects (if any) does the reappropriation of derogatory labels have on self-identity, perceptions of others, and societal understanding of constructed groups of people?
4. International adoption is prevalent in the media due to public figures like Angelina Jolie and Madonna. How, if at all, does the media portrayal of international adoption affect public views of transracial adoptee families?
5. Have you ever embraced or tried to escape a stereotype associated with your physical body? Why or why not?

References

Alexander, B. K. (2004). Racializing identity: Performance, pedagogy, and regret. *Cultural Studies: Critical Methodologies, 4*(1), 12-27.

Atkinson, P., & Delamont, S. (2006) Rescuing narrative from qualitative research. *Narrative Inquiry, 16*(1), 164-172.

Bacon, W. A. (1996). The dangerous shores—One last time. *Text and Performance Quarterly, 16*, 355-358.

Children's House International. (n.d.). http://www.childrenshouseinternational.com

Conquergood, D. (1992). Review essay: Ethnography, rhetoric, and performance. *Quarterly Journal of Speech, 78*(1), 80-97.

Fogg-Davis, H. (2002). *The ethics of transracial adoption.* New York: Cornell University Press.

Fox, R. (2007). Skinny bones: Thin gay bodies signifying a modern plague. *Text and Performance Quarterly, 27*(1), 3-19.

Freundlich, M., & Lieberthal, J. K. (2000). The gathering of the first generation of adult Korean adoptees: Adoptees' perceptions of international adoption. http://www.adoptioninstitute.org/proed/korfindings.html#detail

Lev, A. I. (2004). Parenting in the gray area. *In the Family, 10*, 100.

McKerrow, R. E. (1989). Critical rhetoric: Theory and praxis. *Communications Monographs, 56*, 91-111.

Meyer, M. (2007). On remembering the queer self: The impact of memory, trauma and sexuality on interpersonal relationships. *Sex Cult, 11*, 18-30.

Nixon, R. (2009, November 8). *New York Times.* http://www.nytimes.com/2009/11/09/us/09adopt.html

Simon, R. J., & Alstein, H. (1992). *Adoption, race, and identity: From infancy through adolescence.* New York: Greenwood.

Trenka, J. (n.d.). *Why write?* http://www.languageofblood.com/whywrite.html

Warren, J. T. (2001). The social drama of a "rice burner": A (re)constitution of whiteness. *Western Journal of Communication, 65*(2), 184-205.

Willink, K. (2007). Domesticating difference: Performing memories of school desegregation. *Text and Performance Quarterly, 27*(1), 20-40.

Chapter 22

Obstacle or Opportunity? Reflections on Rhetorical Resilience Following Family Crises

Sherilyn Marrow, Nancy J. Karlin, and Betty Burdorff Brown

> A man to be greatly good, must imagine intensely and comprehensively; he must put himself in the place of another and of many others; the pains and pleasures of his species must become his own. (Shelley, 1874)

As the revered poet Shelley penned nearly two centuries ago, when we "put ourselves in the place of another and of many others" and empathize accordingly, the worst and best of human emotions may be known. As we strive for the "greatly good," we vicariously experience our species' contrasting states of "pains and pleasures"; and, as investigators of human communication, we remain curious about our species' affiliating rhetoric that distinguishes the two states.

And so it is with the challenge of studying human "resilience"—a complex descriptor that requires individuals affected by adversity to "imagine intensely and comprehensively" their futures, along with acting on and communicating on their thoughts. It is certain that we, as human beings, are likely to experience crises or troubled times throughout life—events that are irreversible and experiences that, for better or worse, alter our personal paradigms. But why is it that some individuals or families are able to recover from crises more effectively than others? What communication practices are used that propel families to move forward with their lives following crises instead of succumbing to the adversity? What factors preclude the survivors' perceptions of the crisis as either an obstacle or an opportunity?

To gain better insight into the topic of communication and resilience, it is necessary to probe further with a formal research plan. To that end, this study investigates the following: (a) assumptions of family, resilience, and communication; (b) two original research reports on individuals surviving crises of Hurricane Katrina (Gulf Coast, 2005) and individuals surviving three earthquakes in Vina Vieja, Peru (2007); and (c) the development of a typology of "resilience rhetoric"—the associating expressed communication that individuals and families may practice during and following crises that empower them to "bounce back" and move forward with their lives (Marrow, 2010).

Assumptions of Family, Resilience, and Communication

Family Defined

This chapter will look at the concept of family resilience and its accompanying rhetoric, but clarification of the term "family" is needed first. According to Patterson (2002), "a family system is two or more individuals (family structure) and the patterns of relationship between them (family functioning). Within the United States, there is considerable variability in family structure, reflecting diverse family forms (e.g., couples who are heterosexual, homosexual, married, remarried, cohabiting, with or without children; separated, divorced, or always single adults with children" (p. 234).

Jorgenson (1989) defined "family" in terms of an experiential quality. She states, "My own research experience suggests that 'family,' in its 'potent' sense, refers, typically, to a quality of experience realized in interpersonal relationships which may, in turn, be grounded in any of several criteria. Some respondents cited *emotional solidarity* as the key consideration; for others, *patterns of routine contact* was the important criterion; occasionally, respondents made reference to *mutual expectations of reciprocity and exchange*" (p. 33):

> A family is a self-defined group of intimates who create and maintain themselves through their own interactions and their interactions with others; a family may include both voluntary and involuntary relationships; it creates both literal and symbolic internal and external boundaries, and it evolves through time: It has a history, a present, and a future . . . families can be biologically, legally, or socially derived, although these categories overlap. (Turner & West, 2002, p. 8)

> A family is a social group of two or more persons, characterized by ongoing interdependence with long-term commitments that stem from blood, law, or affection.(Baxter & Braithwaite, 2006, p. 3)

An additional consideration of the term "family" has been defined by Marrow as "a network of linked individuals, genetic or loyal, with a memory and outlook that willingly share cognition, communication, and emotion unique to their cultural norms." Using this definition, the notion of family members includes its biological members as well as those influencers who are "more than blood" and may be deemed familial from "loyal" or emotional connections, such as partners, mentors, significant others, companions, good friends, and so on. Members are unified or "linked" by their "cultural norms" of shared "cognition, communication, and emotion"—practices of thoughts and feelings that may help them thrive during routine or adverse times; family members call on their "memory" or recollection of their perceived experiences, whether joyous, painful, or somewhere in between, to help fuel active expressions that will, ideally, secure the family's "outlook" or positive future. Because of the likelihood that crises or at least discomfort will be experienced by all families at one time or another, it is critical to recognize and honor the past and present strengths of the individual families that will help them weather the difficult times and thus maintain their existences.

Resilience Defined

In order to properly discuss resilience, we need to understand the basic meaning of the term and then consider its application to the family structure. There are many different definitions of the term "resilience," stemming from psychology studies in the 1940s and recently applied to the study of disasters. To begin, the ability to "bounce back" following a challenge or loss is one suggested definition of "resilience" (Werner & Smith, 1992); positive adjustment outcomes is another (Luthar, Cicchetti, & Becker, 2003). Klein, Nicholls, and Thomalla (2006) regard "resilience" as a term "derived from the Latin word *resilio*, meaning 'to jump back'" (p. 35).

Manyena's (2006) discusses the evolvement of disaster resilience as a "gradual refinement" from more outcome oriented to more process oriented. He writes, "Undoubtedly, earlier authors were thinking of resilience as a process to reach an outcome. However, use of the upcoming terms 'cope,' 'bounce back,' 'withstand' or 'absorb negative impacts' to return to 'normal' within the shortest possible time, tend to emphasize a reactive stance" (pp. 437–438).

More recent definitions validate the notion of process when discussing resilience: "Resilience is the capacity of a system to continually change and adapt yet remain within critical thresholds" (Stockholm Resilience Center, 2007), and "Resilient people do not let adversity define them. They find resilience by moving towards a goal beyond themselves, transcending pain and grief by perceiving bad times as a temporary state of affairs" (Marano, 2003).

Resilience After Natural Disaster or Traumatic Event

Resiliency study is a growing body of research suggesting that individuals are typically resilient after traumatic events (Almedom, 2005; Bonanno, Galea, Bucciarelli, & Vlahov, 2007). Unfortunately, the factors that promote resilience are limited (Bonanno et al., 2007). Although socioeconomic status (SES) is often cited as a barrier to resilience following a natural disaster, SES may not be the most important factor in long-term psychosocial recovery. For example, Ticehurst, Webster, Carr, and Lewin (1996) reported that lower SES was not related to greater psychosocial distress among older adults after an earthquake. Additionally, personal and social relationship characteristics might have more influence on resilience than age. For one group of centenarians, underlying factors of psychological resilience, such as self-efficacy and optimism, suggested that resilience might last into very old age (Jopp & Rott, 2006).

Mancini and Bonanno (2006) noted that "although people may possess characteristics that are globally associated with resilience, whether people actually exhibit resilience in the face of potential trauma can only be defined in terms of their actual outcome after a potentially traumatic event" (p. 972). They discuss the heterogeneity of resilience after the attacks on September 11, 2001, in New York City. They state the following:

> Resilience was most prevalent among married as opposed to unmarried, divorced, or separated individuals. Resilience was also more common among younger people and males rather than females. Some surprising findings also emerged in these data. For example, although whites showed relatively high levels of resilience, the highest proportions were among Asian Americans. Additionally, although years of education showed a direct relationship to resilience and more education was associated with more resilience, personal income showed a more complex association with resilience. People at low income levels tended to have less resilience and people at higher levels more. However, resilience was less common among people who had moderately high income. (p. 976)

Mancini and Bonanno (2006) also discuss posttraumatic stress disorder (PTSD) and the relationship of this disorder to resilience. Based on their study done following the September 11 attacks, they note that "the majority of persons exposed to violent or life threatening events do *not* go on to develop PTSD, and a surprising proportion demonstrate resilience to such experiences" (p. 975).

Norris, Friedman, Watson, Byrne, et al. (2002) showed that "undoubtedly, the condition most often assessed and observed in these samples was PTSD (109 samples, 68%)" (p. 211).They later state that "the effects of disasters are diverse and require responses that address a myriad of outcomes, including psychiatric disorders, generalized distress, physical illness, and various interpersonal problems" (Norris, Friedman, & Watson, 2002, p. 248).

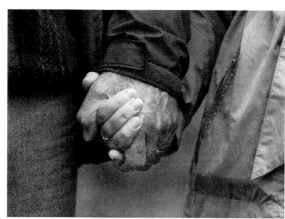

Resilience in the Context of Family

Moving from a more organizational perspective on resilience to that of a family perspective, the American Psychological Association (2012) regards resilience as the process of adapting well in the face of adversity, trauma, tragedy, threats, or even significant sources of stress—such as family and relationship problems, serious health problems, or workplace and financial stressors. Walsh (1996) looks at resilience in the context of families as "the ability to withstand and rebound from crisis and adversity" (p. 261). Black and Lobo (2008) contend that family resilience occurs due to the "successful coping of family members under adversity that enables them to flourish with warmth, support, and cohesion" (p. 33).

In a quantitative study done by Lietz (2006), Walsh's perspective on resilience is referenced: "the term resilience is described as the capacity to rebound from adversity strengthened and more resourceful" (p. 4). [BRO1]This definition suggests that resilience involves two phenomena: first, that a system is experiencing adversity, which is also referred to in this study as high risk, and, second, that the system is able to avoid negative consequences typically associated with that risk in a way that promotes growth" [BRO2](p. 576).

In a second study done by Lietz (2007), the process of resilience for families is examined using a qualitative analysis. The authors identify the stages in the resilience process as (a) survival, (b) adaptation, (c) acceptance, (d) growing stronger, and (e) helping others. While communication skills are assumed for all of the stages, discourse between family members is mentioned only during the survival stage. The communication in this stage is described as "expressing thoughts and feelings about difficulties through verbal and nonverbal forms of communication" (p. 149).

The majority of studies on family resilience reveal that one of the factors in resilience is communication. "There is no universal list of key effective, protective, and recovery factors, but a review of recent research and literature recognizes recurrent and prominent attributes among resilient, healthy families. These factors include: a positive outlook, spirituality, family member accord, flexibility, communication, financial management, time together, mutual recreational interests, routines and rituals, and social support" (Black & Lobo 2008, p. 37).

Silberberg (2001) contends that, in difficult times, "strong families are able to adapt to changing circumstances and have a positive attitude towards the challenges of family life. They deal with these challenges by means of communication—talking things through with each other; supporting each other in times of need and/or seeking outside support when it is beyond the family's capability to deal with the situation; and togetherness—pulling together to form a united front and to find solutions" (p. 55). Cardona (2004) noted that the lack of communication is a factor for risk in disaster resilience. Manyena (2006) expounds on this claim by writing that "deficient information, communications and knowledge among social actors, the lack of institutional and community organization, weaknesses in emergency preparedness, political instability and the absence of economic health in a geographic area, are all factors in generating greater risk" (pp. 435–436).

Walsh (2003) states, "Communication processes foster resilience by bringing clarity to crisis situations, encouraging open emotional expression, and fostering collaborative problem-solving. It must be kept in mind that cultural norms vary considerably in the sharing of sensitive information and expression of feelings" (pp. 11–12). What is appropriate and normative in one culture may not be acceptable or welcomed in another.

Marrow (2010) regards family resilience as more than brick-and-mortar repairs and returns to the routine; it also includes a collection of behaviors and rhetoric, displayed and expressed within the family, that positively reframes the event(s) and allows foregrounding of the family's present strengths and accomplishments.

Continuing along this line, Finkenauer, Engels, Branje, and Meeus (2004) examined relational satisfaction in families and discovered the importance of communication to the family unit. One of their findings revealed that "families who disclosed more had more satisfactory relationships" (p. 207). But even in families where disclosure is high, the question(s) remain: What role does a family's communication behavior play in the way a natural disaster or traumatic family event affects them? What types of communication during or after the event move a family toward resilience and recovery? What types of disclosure or rhetoric are more helpful than others?

In view of the many definitions and orientations of resilience, there are multiple approaches for assessing resilience within the family. Identifying the objective of the measurement and its relationship to the many variables that constitute or contribute to resilience may be challenging. According to Ganong and Coleman (2002), "More research is needed that helps build models of family resilience or that compares competing views empirically" (p. 348). To specifically address the research question of the role that communication plays in natural disaster resilience, we have called on our original research from two natural disasters areas: the Gulf Coast after Hurricane Katrina and Vina Vieja, Peru, after three earthquakes.

Research Study 1: Hurricane Katrina

In an effort to better understand how families react to a natural disaster and its impact on family relations, a study was conducted consisting of survey research and extensive qualitative interviews that addressed the rhetoric and narratives voiced by the Hurricane Katrina survivors. One year following the 2005 disaster, participatory research was conducted in Metairie, Louisiana, a community just north of New Orleans, with a volunteer, convenience sample ($N = 38$) of older adults affected by the hurricane; semistructured interviews and structured surveys were the instruments used. Questionnaires assessed the impact of social support, self-efficacy, locus of control, and mood. Open-ended questions were used to assess measures of personal loss and experiences before, during, and after Hurricane Katrina.

Participants for the study included 18 males (47.4%) and 20 females (52.6%) with a mean age of 71.3 ($SD = 6.25$ years, range = 59–85). The majority of participants were married ($N = 28$, 75.7%), three were divorced/separated (8.1%), six were currently widowed (16.2%), and one did not report. The length of time for current marital status had a mean of 39.3 years ($SD = 16.6$, range = 1.5–58 years). Widows had reported being widowed from 1.5 to 20 years ($M = 11.1$ years). The two individuals who had reported being divorced had been so for between 28 and 30 years ($M = 29$ years). Five of the participants had served in the military (16.1%). No significant change took place in the number of individuals living in each household as a result of Hurricane Katrina ($M = 1.94$, $SD = .612$ before; $M = 2.0$, $SD = .771$ after). The overall length of time living in the New Orleans region ranged from 3 to 80 years ($M = 62.3$ years, $SD = 16.2$). The majority of participants were Caucasian ($N = 35$, 92.1%), two indicated Native American (5.3%), and one indicated Hispanic (2.6%). Distribution of income ranged from $10,000 to over $70,000 per year. The most frequently reported income level was $30,000 to $40,000. All but one respondent reported they were Catholic ($N = 36$, 97.3%) with one additional individual indicating Jewish background.

Survey data obtained from the elders having experienced Hurricane Katrina suggests a relationship between resiliency after a natural disaster and overall positive mood states. Additionally, the more years of education, the lower reported mood states of tension, depression, anxiety, frustration, and total mood disturbance scores. Participants also indicated high levels of self-efficacy for belief in their ability to perform the tasks necessary to cope, a strong belief that their behavior would lead to desired outcomes, and a belief that performing these tasks was an important part of coping. Participants also reported a fairly strong belief in their ability to influence events encountered. Additionally, the social support reported by participants centered on assistance that was interpersonal, encouraging, and non–problem focused rather than on instrumental and practical help given during the year after the hurricane. This suggests that the resiliency to cope with disaster may, in part, reside with the perception that one is cared about and socially supported by others, even though the actual care may not be directly related to the disaster itself (Marrow, Karlin, Collins, Bentz, & Goldschmidt, 2008).

Questions for the qualitative portion of the study were developed as a result of a pilot discussion with three women (ages 60, 65, and 71) who had experienced Hurricane Katrina and had since relocated to Colorado. Information from the discussion/field notes was translated into formal interview questions. The interview questions were shown to the three pilot group women for feedback, and on revision a 29-question interview was created. Sample questions included the following: Describe your "darkest hour" or worst time that was (or is) affiliated with this event. Were there any words of support or inspiration that you heard or read that have helped you cope with this event? Describe how you have tried to relieve your stress. Overall, how has Hurricane Katrina impacted you, now one year later? Can you recall a story or an incident that best describes how you are experiencing or "getting through" the aftermath of Hurricane Katrina? A primary finding of this study was that many survivors of Hurricane Katrina were able to positively reframe the event and regarded the disaster as "an opportunity" to demonstrate individual and family strengths after the crisis (Marrow, Goldschmidt, Green, & Donnelly, 2007).

Eight themes emerged from the qualitative interviews, five of which were conceptually linked to the quantitative measures of self-efficacy, emotional support, and physical stamina. The specific emergent themes demonstrating strengths included the following:

1. Emotional support
2. Task management
3. Heroic displays
4. Physical stamina

5. Communication commitment
6. High concern for others
7. Strategies for the future
8. Opportunistic reframes of the event

The first theme or strength referred to the emotional support that family members gave to other affected family members. One very telling research question asked of the participants was, "What was their greatest source of support, during and after the hurricane?" Participants who were married identified their spouses as their greatest source of emotional support:

"Both my wife and the man upstairs."
"My husband."
"And my husband gave me support."
"I couldn't have gotten through this without my wife."

All of the research participants had grown children, many of whom lived within driving distance of New Orleans but far enough away from the hurricane's path that they were safe. With the exception of one of the participants, all of them evacuated ahead of the hurricane. Many of them stayed with their children in cities away from the storm:

"We evacuated with my son and daughter-in-law and their three children."
"We went to a friend of my daughter-in-law. They welcomed us, the whole family, with open arms."
"We stayed at our son's house. I mean, we had three families there, and everybody was compatible. You know we had absolutely no problems at all."

In fact, many were forced to stay for several weeks and even months before returning to the New Orleans area. Having the emotional support of their children also helped them deal with the disturbing effects of the damage their homes endured. Without exception, the participants were thankful that their families did not suffer any injuries or deaths and that there was only property damage, which, as almost all participants said, "can be replaced."

The second family strength identified was the task management of those participants who had children who "came to the rescue" of their parents. The participants, who had children who responded to their aid, were clearly the ones who had been able to rebuild their physical structures the quickest. The research team heard stories of family members who responded from different states and did demolition work, carpentry work, interior design work, and so on. Some of the responding family members brought supplies for the jobs, as the supply of lumber, sheetrock, and roofing materials was in high demand in the damaged area and difficult to obtain:

"As soon as we could get back to our house, our daughter and her friend drove a van from Texas loaded with sheetrock. Without her and her friend's help, we never could have started rebuilding so soon."

It was clear that without the task management support from family members, the recovery of these affected families would have been stalled. As an example, during interviews, several of the participants pointed out specific families who had been able to perform repairs quickly after the storm, even after suffering severe damage. They explained that without their children coming to help, they would still have repairs to do and would still be living in trailers, like many others were still doing. Essentially, the participants who received the aid of their children were able to showcase their family's talents in the area of construction and repair.

The third overall theme relating to family strengths was that of heroic displays. Responding to the damage caused by Hurricane Katrina enabled the participants' children to rise to new heights of heroism from their parents' perspectives—essentially passing the torch from one generation to the next. One woman consistently referred to her son as a "pillar of strength," her "Rock of Gibraltar." Many stories were told by the participants of how their sons or daughters "just took over" the rebuilding effort and "unselfishly helped them" get through their "trying ordeal."

The fourth family strength theme that emerged was physical stamina. The destruction caused by Hurricane Katrina provided participants an opportunity to display their own physical stamina and fitness to their family members. The senior citizens who were in good enough physical condition to assist with the reconstruction of their homes were deservedly proud of that accomplishment, thus enabling them to demonstrate their fitness and health. This was an additional factor identified by the participants who assisted in the swift completion of repairs. The participants who had children respond to the area to assist with construction performed their repairs quickly. The participants who were still in good enough physical condition to do their own repairs were still ahead of those in the study who had been tasked with hiring out all the repair work:

"I put in my own patio; I didn't want to wait for a construction crew. The concrete squares were heavy, but I was able to do it. I stay in real good shape; I lift weights every day. . . see these muscles?"

A fifth family strength theme was communication commitment. Review of the data indicated that the communication strengths among the research participants and their families allowed them to manage the stress created by the storm. All of the participants were required to negotiate with representatives of the government or insurance companies. The successful negotiators received what they perceived as fair settlements for their losses. Additionally, the affected family members assisted in crisis support for their families. Several participants supported the notion that returning to family rituals with their children was important for them to return to a normal life. Even if their homes were not livable, they learned that maintaining their family traditions made it possible for them to maintain a sense of togetherness, in turn reminding them that the important possessions in life are family, not the replaceable or repairable possessions damaged and destroyed in the hurricane:

"We tried to be as normal as possible. And we also made an effort to not let the aftermath get us down. If one of us would get down, the other one would call us on our negative attitude and help us get back up."

"To give you an idea, on Tuesdays we always have a family night. I'm fortunate that everybody in my family lives here, and on Tuesdays we get from 20 to 27 people over at the house."

"We call each other at least once a week, if not more. We use our cell phones more now than ever and just talk so we can hear each other's voices . . . just to hear their voice helps."

"We all talk a lot to each other because we want to know how everybody's doing."

The sixth family strength theme revealed by the data is a high concern for others. Several participants remarked about how the storm contributed to caring for one another:

"My worst fear while we were away was, when I couldn't get in touch with half my family. I've got five children and six little grandchildren, and I couldn't get in touch with all of them. Cell phones weren't working, and my son, I didn't know where he was."

"It was that part that was stressful for me. Not so much the damage to my house as to where were my children."

"As long as my family was safe, the house could blow away, you know you could get over it."

Another female participant described how well she and her spouse were being treated by strangers throughout the ordeal:

"We were going to sleep on the road when a lady told us about this shelter. They were really good to us. We would go to dinner at a church, and they would give the kids free toys. You wouldn't think that people are like that, but they are."

It appeared that the ordeal of Hurricane Katrina allowed or triggered many others to extend themselves and show their generosity and concern. Those outreach efforts and simple kindnesses were greatly appreciated by the study participants.

A seventh theme that emerged concerned strategies for future crisis. Few of the participants had an evacuation plan in place prior to Hurricane Katrina. They had all experienced many hurricanes but had never experienced anything close to what this storm brought them. In fact, many of them waited until the last minute to leave. Unfortunately, this was what most of the residents in the New Orleans area also did. Consequently, as several participants said, "What should have taken two hours to drive, took us over 12. Everyone was trying to get out at the same time." Because of the traffic jams encountered and caused by last-minute evacuees, many feared that they would be stranded on a highway when Hurricane Katrina hit shore:

"The worst part of the whole thing, besides what Katrina did, was getting out of town."

"It was terrible. It was a nightmare. Sitting in that car for that long. But we have a plan now. My kids made us come up with one should we get hit again. But I don't think we will get hit again."

As a result of the difficulties encountered due to poor or insufficient planning, many of the research participants formed strategies to evacuate earlier in case of future need and knew where they would be going ahead of time rather than making last-minute plans. Many of these plans included going to their children's homes earlier or, at the very minimum, notifying their family members of their whereabouts. While some participants gave general indications that they would not leave—"I'll stay for another one; I won't leave"—other participants voiced specific plans for action in a hurricane:

"We will go to Texas to his sisters and leave early like we've always done."

"We have a Hurricane procedure, and we have a routine. You board up your windows, you close up your house, you shut off your electricity, you bat down the hatches, pick everything up. That is what you do for a hurricane."

"It would have to be another category 5 to move me."

The majority of the participants stated they would leave earlier next time and had a definite plan. This prevailing sentiment—having a plan of action for future disasters—seemed to have a calming effect on most participants on articulation. Vocalization of these plans was made with a strong sense of conviction and certainty. While there were no severe self-denigrations for not having executed carefully calculated plans before Katrina, many responded with certainty of their future plans should another hurricane occur.

The eighth family strength theme that emerged from the study was opportunistic reframes of the event. This theme reflects the unique capabilities of the human mind to foreground the positive aspects of a situation and background its negative aspects—to regard a crisis as a learning opportunity in which to grow. The following participants' remarks attest to the paradigm shift or altering of the lens when discussing the aftermath of Hurricane Katrina:

"Well I found out how little I really need and how unimportant some physical things are. We don't need three closets of clothes, which is what I had. [chuckle] You could get by with a lot less. What's important, is needs of today... not material things."

"You see all these other people and can see how much worse off they are than you."

The realization that one could be around family members in times of crisis was very comforting and reassuring to the participants, as voiced by these participants:

"A pleasant surprise of this is that we were able to live with our daughter and son-in-law. That was very accommodating. Very open to us staying there and not feeling like we were putting them out."

When another participant was asked about what was different in her life post-Katrina, she responded,

"Oh, I think my attitude is a lot better... because I found out that, uh, you can't dwell on things that you can't do anything about, you know. Live for today."

When discussing surprises that had resulted from their lives since Katrina, responses were varied:

"Well, I like my new living residence. I'm living in an apartment which I never had before. It's in a very convenient area that's close to a lot of things that I can walk to. That's very pleasant. I can go sit by the river, watch the boats and drink coffee or a glass of wine."

One participant discussed the adverse relationship he had had with his kids and mentioned how the hurricane brought them together:

"It gave us the ability of our family to... help them [their children], where before our children wouldn't even have considered taking help from us."

One participant reflected on how the event changed his overall perception of his family membership:

"Quite frankly during things like that [Hurricane Katrina], you do find out who you are you know, who's a member of your family and who's not. And we found out who's not. See... ' cause we are family people you know... families."

Another response referenced how the hurricane gave this male participant the "opportunity" to appreciate his family's togetherness:

"The best thing about the hurricane, is the family working together. We got each other through it... whether in silence, in anger, in dismay, we did it together. Even though my son wasn't with us, we kept in contact, we knew where he was... ..we just stayed together."

Research Study 2—Vina Vieja

The second study of resilience continues the investigation on specific psychological, rhetorical, and behavioral strengths patterned by successful global families following times of crises, specifically in Peru. During June 2010, quantitative and qualitative data were gathered in Vina Vieja from those who experienced a devastating earthquake on August 15, 2007, and two subsequent earthquakes in January 2010. These earthquakes ranged from 5.7 to 7.9 on the Richter scale, creating psychological and physical unrest throughout the population of Peru. Similar to the Katrina research methodology, semistructured interviews and structured surveys were the instruments used. Questionnaires assessed the impact of social support, self-efficacy, locus of control, and mood. Open-ended questions were used to assess measures of personal loss and experiences before, during, and after the earthquakes. Participants for the Peruvian study included 13 males (54.3%) and 19 females (37.1%), with three not reporting gender (8.6%). A mean age for those who participated was 43.0 years ($SD = 20.98$, range = 18–85). Just over half of the survey participants were married ($N = 19$, 54.3%), one was divorced/separated (2.9%), one was widowed (2.9%), two were separated (5.7%), 11 never married (31.5%), and one did not report. The length of time for current marital status had a mean of 23.0 years ($SD = 13.8$, range = 2.5–53 years). The overall length of time living in Vina Vieja ranged from one month to 80 years ($M = 62.3$ years, $SD = 16.2$). All village inhabitants were Peruvian (total population estimated at 186). Income ranged from 10 to 6,000 Sols per year for participants. At the time of data collection, the exchange rate was 1.00 Sols = 0.36 U.S. dollars. The most frequently reported yearly income level was 1,000 Sols. The mean number of years of education reported was 8.2 years ($SD = 4.0$, range = 0–16 years). Fourteen participants reported being a practicing Catholic (40%) (Karlin, Marrow, Weil, Baum, & Spencer, 2012).

The findings from the Peruvian study are similar to the themes that emerged from the Katrina study, as previously named. The following themes were derived primarily from the qualitative interview transcripts, direct field observation notes, and partial findings from the quantitative analysis of the study:

1. External locus of control
2. Minimal presence of heroism
3. Lack of initial social support
4. Physical stamina
5. Minimal communication commitment
6. Concern for others
7. Acknowledgment of plans for the future
8. Opportunistic reframes of the event

The first overall theme from Vina Vieja relates to external locus of control. Differing from Katrina research, this study revealed the villagers' emphasis on external locus of control; few believed that their fate was in their own hands. The participants reflected a deterministic screen that embraced learned helplessness and the belief that "God's will had been done." Many of the participants felt they were being punished for by God for "something they did":

"Earthquake took hope away . . . cold, afraid."

When asked, "What would you do differently from the first time if there was another earthquake? one female responded,

"Oh, well, what we will do, it will be what God wants. May He decide, see. . . .the only way is what He wants. Here it is only what the Lord wants. If He crushes us, well, what will we do?"

One male participant who had lived in Vina Vieja his entire life stated,

"To live, to continue on. If there is an opportunity to rise up and fix what is broke. We would do that if possible, but we don't have a way to do it. It's sad, that this has happened to us and there is nothing we can do to recuperate."

Another male participant stated,

"Earthquake was like a nightmare, a punishment."

The second theme was the minimal presence of heroism around the times of natural disaster. The Vina Vieja participants spoke of few glorifications of heroes within their community during the earthquakes; there were clearly no external accolades of any one figure *during* the earthquake that stood out. The interviewees expressed resounding sentiments of resentment and neglect by their governmental officials, often with no reference to heroic ways:

"No one came to my house, my place in Peru, they give no importance to the small towns."
"Help delayed—they did not know about us."

However, two to three years after the earthquake, a presence of heroism evolved with those providing assistance and working in the area, interviewees becoming "heroes" in the minds of the Peruvians after the earthquake:

"Now we are more united, much good happened, that is,, community center, kitchen, and dining room built by Iliana [Diaz] and Partners of America."

A third theme of lack of initial social support was found. In opposition to emotional support findings from Katrina, the Peruvian focus was primarily on and with family members; there was no consensus on how soon the villagers received help from their employer and/or their government. Recollection of help and gratitude was inconsistent among the recounts of the study participants:

"We are so hidden back here . . . help received was little . . . nothing we can do to recuperate."
"Help after a week, so little help . . . three weeks without anything."
"State had not been helping."
"Mayor of Chincha did not want to help; not many people came to help."
"Help from Bamar [their employer] for 15 days, with food and clothing."

Physical stamina in the face of disaster was noted as a fourth theme. Interviewees discussed great physical demands on them following the earthquake. Most had headaches and exhaustion but went back to work anyway, as it seemed expected of them; all were used to long hours and hard work:

"So tired. . . . We're going to work to repair what was lost."

In comparison, Katrina survivors rose up to the level of physical demand to their own astonishments; a new behavior of strength was exhibited and therefore contributed to their high levels of self-efficacy and self-empowerment.

A minimal communication commitment was seen as a fifth theme. For the most part, this formal interview process was the first time the Peruvian study participants talked about the event from its onset three years ago:

"This is the first time I was asked to talk."
"There was 15 days of silence, without any communication . . . everything gone silent."

Only a few of the participants ($N = 4$) stated that they had talked with their family about the earthquakes:

"We talked about everything in our family and still do."
"We need to share to keep the family together."

One participant mentioned talking to a professional psychologist about it, but that was not the norm. All but one Peruvian participant in the sample wanted to express their thoughts and feelings to the interviews. Both verbal and nonverbal behaviors were present in the interview.

Concern for others was seen as the sixth theme. The Peruvian villagers were moving toward unity. They were mostly still focusing on family (not friends) and community. "We helped each other . . . we became more of a community" were statements cited often during the interviews. "There was good and bad; we were together like a community."

Acknowledgment of plans for the future was the seventh theme. There was much rhetoric around forward thinking and survival modes; that is, there was considerable hope for the next generation and the importance of getting their children educated:

"With a little help, the children are growing up, we can continue on."
"Community continues to be prepared, help each other."
"We will improve this community and move forward."
"I will fix up this house and educate my children."

The middle generation and the senior generation had little mention of hope for their futures; however, there seemed to be a polite surrender or resignation by them to accept the status quo and hope for the best for their children. One female remarked,

"We are almost bad receivers of help, do not value it . . . but thank you [to the researchers] for coming."

Another male spoke:

"No future plans; will stay in region of Vina Vieja."

The final theme included opportunistic reframes of the event. A major contrast occurred in this category, comparing the data for Katrina and Peru. There was little mention of this by the Peruvians, as the villagers' perceptual concept of opportunity and resilience was limited; however, one notable quote from a participant was the following:

"My advice for those going through this kind of problem: is to have optimism; to have faith in God. Always think about the future—we have our paradise here and while we have life, we have to move forward; in this way, we are going to accomplish what we want."

Another participant, Rosa, who often traveled outside the community, responded differently:

"The people who have lived through this type of disaster need to think positively. Life does not end when disaster occurs. Those of us with health. . . life, have to continue to fight because the end of the world has not come. The end of the world is when our life ends."

These qualitative themes reflect on where the villagers saw and how they heard themselves in terms of recovery. Collectively, their sentiments feature contradictions between obstacle and opportunity. These contradictions confront their desires for independence and their realizations that they need help; they note their challenges of determining obstacle versus opportunity and hopes of how they could move forward with their lives amidst the slow signs of progress. This thematic perspective of obstacle/opportunity is unique to this Peruvian culture and not to that of the Hurricane Katrina study; being in a poor, rural environment such as Vina Vieja, the villagers, with their fewer freedoms, must undoubtedly question their possibilities, privileges, and rights associated with the estranged concepts of resilience and recovery. Because of differences that exist between the participants of Hurricane Katrina and Vina Vieja, any comparisons are an attempt to begin to identify patterns of similarity and difference to assist in the creation of a rhetorical model of resilience.

Resilience Rhetoric Model

It is necessary to address how these two research investigations might help us move toward a model or typology of rhetoric, known as "resilience rhetoric," specifically in families following disaster. In other words, what does a resilient population's talk, or rhetoric, sound like? Is it different than someone who is not progressing toward recovery or someone experiencing difficulty in overcoming the challenges affiliated with resilience?

In building a model for resilience rhetoric, several components will be addressed: (a) resilience intrinsic questions, (b) resilience extrinsic responses, (c) oral interview guide, (d) typology of resilience rhetoric, and (e) value of resilience rhetoric typology.

In the first component of the model, resilience intrinsic questions, the communication is examined from the perspective of the "lived self" or the subject who has experienced the event. How would he or she approach the opportunities for resilience building? In other words, what questions may this "lived self" ask, intrinsically, when facing the aftermath of a disaster? These questions may or may not be externalized when approached with offers of help. Might he or she reject or embrace support from others? The questions that the "lived self" may internalize, along with the presumed core sentiments affiliated with the questions, are listed below. (These questions are not necessarily sequential in the person's thought process or delivery.)

Resilience Intrinsic Questions
1. Why must you bother me?
• This refers to the person, or the "lived self," who is adamant against receiving any one else's help, refuses external assistance, and wants to move toward resilience in a very private, individual way, if at all. (sentiment of disdain)
2. What do you have for me that I need or want?
• This reflects a more selfish approach in its directness and clarity that the "lived self" is now a taker, or a user of the system; a sort of entitlement approach toward resilience. (sentiment of disdain)
3. What do I have to do to get something in return?
• This is likened to a "vending machine approach" (Payne, 2005) where the dominant voice of the "lived self" considers what must be put into the system to get something out of it—the cost and reward to attain this state of resilience. The individuals are at least interested in their role evoking some kind of positive change. (sentiment of hope)

4. How can I help myself and/or others?
• This constitutes a true spirit of cooperation, a willingness to unite, a coming together to help one and all. This encompasses the barn-raiser approach (Payne, 2005) toward resilience as "an additive mold—better to be a barn-raiser where communities have shared understanding and common vocabulary to be willing and motivated to make changes" (p. 182) (sentiment of hope)
5. How can this experience enhance my life?
• This question addresses the opportunity for the "lived self" to capitalize on this event or to reframe the event in positive ways; this stance moves toward self-actualization or the ability to maximize misfortune into a favorable reflection. (sentiment of hope)

The individual's answers to these questions reflect, in part, the degree of willingness toward resilience, or notion of moving forward; in other words, the answers show the individual's stance on the crisis and the degree in which he or she perceives the event as more of an obstacle or as an opportunity.

Resilience Extrinsic Responses

The second component for discussion is the resilience extrinsic responses of the sender or "lived self." The rhetoric spoken by the "lived self" reflects the degree of resilience orientation of obstacle or opportunity.

Resilience Extrinsic Responses
Lived Self-Rhetoric
• Orientation toward resiliency • Proclivity toward change and progress • Personal expectation for quality of life • Level of life satisfaction • Vision for the future • Enactment of value system • Level of regard for self and others

Analyses of these intrinsic questions/answers and extrinsic referents are then subsumed into the larger category of the resilience rhetoric framework and are taken into consideration for the overall assessment of resilience achieved.

Oral Interview Guide

The third component of the model is the oral interview guide. The initial tool used to elicit answers from the participants in these research studies was an interview guide consisting of several questions. Now in its third version (following conflation of interview guides used in studies 1 and 2), the guide consists of generalized questions to be asked of affected individuals following adverse situations.

Chapter 22 Obstacle or Opportunity? Reflections on Rhetorical Resilience Following Family Crises

Oral Interview Guide

Audiotape #: _____

1) Identify the members of your immediate household who shared your experience of the event.
2) Describe how you were involved in the event.
3) Describe your physical reaction to the event.
4) Describe how you perceived your safety risks during this event.
5) What did you/your family do to become physically safe before, during, and after?
6) Describe your emotional reactions to the event(s) before, during, and after.
7) Explain how you and others in your family or household talked about the event before, during, and after, if applicable.
8) Explain how you and others in your family or household experienced silence before, during, and after the event, if at all.
9) Explain how you and others in your family or household acted or behaved following the event.
10) What particular words or phrases, if any, do you remember saying before, during, and following the event?
11) What particular words or phrases, if any, do you remember others saying when the event happened, during, or following, if applicable?
12) Following the event, has time ever been set aside for communication between you and others in your household (i.e., family meetings, scheduled phone calls, and so on)? If so, please describe.
13) Describe your "darkest hour" or worst time that was (or is) affiliated with this event.
14) What did you do to get through the darkest hour of this event?
    a. How did you talk to yourself through this?
    b. What was said to others in your household or family?
    c. What did you *do* during this time?
15) Were there any words of support or inspiration that you heard or read that have helped you cope with this event? Please describe.
16) How were you able to pull yourself together through this event?
17) What has worked, and what hasn't worked?
18) Describe how you and your family talked with each other during this event.
    a. What worked? What didn't?
19) How did you find the emotional strength to get through this event?
20) How did you find the physical strength to get through this event?
21) Who would you say is your greatest source of support to you at this time? Family, friends, other?
22) What words or talk were shared with you that helped you (if applicable)? By whom?
23) On a scale of 1 to 10 (10 = most togetherness), how would you rate your family or household's sense of togetherness? Before this event? after this event? How did that change in number "happen"? Please elaborate.
24) What has changed in your life following the event?
25) How would you describe the role that communication or talk has played in your coping or getting through the event?
26) Describe how you have tried to relieve your stress.
27) How much of your normal activity or routine has come back following the event? Please describe.
28) Please share any changes that have occurred in your life as a result of this event (i.e., sleeping patterns, finances, employment, friends, relatives, moods, attitudes, temperament, and so on).
29) Have you developed a plan should another crisis occur? If so, describe the plan.
30) On a scale of 1 to 10 (10 = high), how would you rate your ability to recover or "bounce back" from the event? Please elaborate.
31) Please describe any pleasant surprises that have resulted in your life following the event? Unpleasant surprises or disappointments?
32) Overall, how has the event impacted you?
33) What concerns, if any, do you still have that are related to the event?
34) Can you recall a story or an incident that best describes how you are experiencing or "getting through" the aftermath of the event?

Typology of Resilience Rhetoric

The fourth component of the resilience rhetoric model is the resilience rhetoric typology, developed from the thematic analyses from research studies 1 and 2. As previously stated, eight overall themes related to resilience were found. Questions to determine the degree/level of resilience have been created in accordance with each theme. These questions are considered for use by a consultant or volunteer supporting a trauma-stricken community or individual and are aimed to determine the interviewee's orientation to resilience, a readiness to accept change in connection to life satisfaction. The themes and target questions (in the present tense) fall under a categorical framework called the "typology of resilience rhetoric."

Typology of Resilience Rhetoric	
Themes	**Target Questions**
1. Locus of control	• Do people feel that they are in control of their own destiny? • Are people owning their power and ability to move forward? • Are people able to make decisions or plan what they needed to do? • What examples of healthy self-esteem are shown versus helpless victimization? How are these expressed? • Are people able to voice progress from one to another after the first shock of the event or crisis passed? Or do they remain in the same deterministic screen?
2. Heroism	• Is anyone serving as a hero or dominant person toward progress and change? If so, how is he or she described? • What does he or she do? • Does the hero act alone to motivate, involve, or persuade others?
3. Social support	• Does anyone provide assistance or help? If so, who? What kind of assistance or help is being given? • To what degree is the support from others appreciated or valued? • Does the support encourage independent recovery? Dependence?
4. Physical stamina	• See item 1, locus of control: How is this seen related to physical strength and endurance? • Is there a physical ability to rise to the demands of the situation? • Are physical strengths and stamina owned? Helplessness?
5. Communication commitment	• How is a commitment to communication shown? • How does the overall communication affect the sender? The receiver? • Are certain terms repeated in conversation and interviews? • Is there a reluctance to talk? • Is there a willingness or eagerness to tell personal stories? • Are those interviewed seeking consolation or sympathy?
6. Concern for others	• Is concern for others shown? If so, how? • Is this expressed in physical assistance or service? • Is this expressed by sharing of goods and services? • Are individuals seen (or described) offering comforting words? • Emotional support? Speaking words of comfort?

7. Acknowledgment of future plans	• How do survivors address hope for their lives? • Are disappointments and complaints being expressed? • Are concrete needs being revealed? • Is there a focus on the disaster without an ability to look beyond? • How do survivors express plans for their tomorrows?
8. Opportunistic reframes of event	• How is the situation or event being described? • How are words/terms used to express either opportunities or obstacles? • How is hope being described? Hopelessness? • How is opportunity or hopefulness surrounding event manifested into positive talk?

As a result of our investigations, we claim these questions real and recognize how the power of language can move victims of trauma to recovery, sway motivation, and influence positive choice. This typology is to be used as a guideline when assessing the overall level of resilience displayed individually or collectively by community members.

The fifth and final component of this model is the value of resilience rhetoric typology. These questions promote value in our quest for developing this integrated system, examining the self-talk and interpersonal talk that is related to measurable recovery.

Value of Resilience Rhetoric Typology
Value Qualities
• Examine the concept of resilience that transcends culture interpretation • Assess the activity without indictment of the individual or culture • Speak to the collective voice; rather than just the individual • Sanction multiple methods of investigation for the study of resilience • Synthesize otherwise fragmented findings into a more comprehensive and applied rhetorical model that helps promote resilience

Discussion

Together, these two research studies have practical implications for substantiating a model of resilience rhetoric—the system of parts framed above. First, all of the resounding themes were communication based and were derived from the participants' spoken language. In Hurricane Katrina, participants believed strongly in "their way, or style" of recovering from the event and voiced their successes with much conviction and pride. Regarding the Vina Vieja survivors, all of the participants appeared honored to be included in the study and were highly eager to communicate their stories in the hope that they would help others in crises. Second, our findings provide a framework for what resilience actually sounds like, *communicatively*, from two selected populations that had varying levels of resilience. The participants' words, sentiments, explanations, interpretations, and revelations that yielded the recurring eight themes provide a beginning typology of a family resilience rhetorical model. Additionally, it is important to include the participants' actions *along with the supporting language*, which contributed to those actions. The questions in the typology model incorporate both the actions and the supporting language. For example, our findings suggest that much self-motivation was required by the participants in the initial aftermath to clean, repair, relocate, recover, and so on. Perhaps examining the intrapersonal communication that initially drove these participants' actions and behaviors remains an integral piece of the model.

While the results of these two research studies are limited in scope and population, they offer valuable insights into the complexities of resilience. Collectively, this grand study reinforces the importance of natural disaster survivors reaching out to and communicating their needs with others. Moreover, the present qualitative and quantitative research fills a conceptual gap pertaining to understanding factors that influence resilience, as is critically seen in the cases of Hurricane Katrina and Vina Vieja earthquake survivors, and moves us closer toward justifying use of this overall resilience rhetoric model. This research supplements practical implications for programs that assist young and old alike after crisis situations and stresses the importance of the individual culture while noting some important constructs of resilience across cultures.

In conclusion, we believe that a resilience rhetoric model can be useful to better assess the level of progress toward an individual or family resilience. Use of this integrated rhetorical model could accelerate the healing process and, ideally, help the participants and their families to experience support from themselves and others, triumph over despair, and, ultimately, move forward, positively, with a renewed spirit and vigor.

Discussion Questions

1. Discuss the many diverse definitions of "resilience" as presented in this chapter. Compare and contrast your own definition of "resilience" with those of the authors.
2. Recall an experience in your life when you were faced with adversity. What factors made you view your situation as either an obstacle or an opportunity?
3. In your opinion, how does the communication within the family unit impact resilience and recovery following a traumatic event?
4. Discuss the qualitative themes of resilience discovered in the Hurricane Katrina and Vina Vieja findings. In your experience, which of these themes seemed most significant? Why?

References

Almedom, A. M. (2005). Resilience, hardiness, sense of coherence, and posttraumatic growth: All paths leading to "light at the end of the tunnel"? *Journal of Loss and Trauma, 10,* 253–265.

American Psychological Association. (2012). *The road to resilience: What is resilience?* http://www.apa.org/helpcenter/road-resilience.aspx

Black, K., & Lobo, M. (2008). A conceptual review of family resilience factors. *Journal of Family Nursing, 14*(1), 33–55.

Bonanno, G. A., Galea, S., Bucciarelli, A., & Vlahov, D. (2007). What predicts psychological resilience after disaster? The role of demographics, resources, and life stress. *Journal of Consulting and Clinical Psychology, 75*(5), 671–682.

Cardona, O. D. (2004). *Disasters, risk and sustainability.* Unpublished manuscript.

Finkenauer, C., Engels, R., Branje, S., & Meeus, W. (2004). Disclosure and relationship satisfaction in families. *Journal of Marriage and Family, 66*(1), 195-209.

Ganong, L., & Coleman, M. (2002). Family resilience in multiple contexts. *Journal of Marriage and Family, 64*(2), 346-348.

Jorgenson, J. (1989). Where is the "family" in family communication? Exploring families' self-definitions. *Journal of Applied Communication Research, 17*(1-2), 27.

Karlin, N., Marrow, S., Weil, J., Baum, S., & Spencer, T. (2012). Social support, mood, and resiliency following a Peruvian natural disaster. *Journal of Loss and Trauma: International Perspectives on Stress, Coping, 17*(5), 470-488.

Klein, R. J. T., Nicholls, R. J., & Thomalla, F. (2003). Resilience to natural hazards: How useful is this concept? *Environmental Hazards, 5,* 35-45.

Lietz, C. (2006). Uncovering stories of family resilience: A mixed methods study of resilient families, part 1. *Families in Society, 87*(4), 470.

Lietz, C. (2007). Uncovering stories of family resilience: A mixed methods study of resilient families, part 2. *Families in Society, 88*(1), 147-155.

Luthar, S. S., Cicchetti, D., & Becker, B. (2003). Research on resilience: Response to commentaries. *Child Development, 71*(3), 573-575.

Mancini, A., & Bonanno, G. (2006). Resilience in the face of potential trauma: Clinical practices and illustrations. *Journal of Clinical Psychology, 62*(8), 971-985.

Manyena, S. B. (2006). The concept of resilience revisited. *Disasters, 30*(4), 433-450. http://www.ncbi.nlm.nih.gov/pubmed/17100752

Marano, H. (2003, May 01). The art of resilience. *Psychology Today.* Retrieved from http://www.psychologytoday.com/articles/200305/the-art-resilience

Marrow, S. (2010). *Communication resilience and the family: The known and unknown.* Research colloquium, School of Communication, University of Northern Colorado.

Marrow, S., Goldschmidt, B., Green, C., Donley, M. (2007) "Psychosocial Factors and Rhetoric of Resilience in Hurricane Katrina Survivors." Paper presented at the Western Communication Association Conference, Seattle, WA.

Marrow, S., Karlin, N., Collins, S., Bentz, A., Goldschmidt, B. (2008). Reframing resilience: Rhetoric of social heroism as voiced by elderly Hurricane Katrina survivors. In *Social Sciences Interdisciplinary Society Conference Proceedings* pp. 253-256.

Norris, F., Friedman, M., & Watson, P. (2002). 60,000 disaster victims speak: Part II. Summary and implications of the disaster mental health research. *Psychiatry: Interpersonal and Biological Processes, 65*(3), 240.

Norris, F., Friedman, M., Watson, P., Byrne, C., Diaz, E., & Kaniasty, K. (2002). 60,000 disaster victims speak: Part I. An empirical review of the empirical literature, 1981-2001. *Psychiatry: Interpersonal and Biological Processes, 65*(3), 207.

Patterson, J. (2002). Integrating family resilience and family stress theory. *Journal of Marriage and Family, 64*(2), 349-360.

Patterson, J. (2002). Understanding family resilience. *Journal of Clinical Psychology, 58*(3), 233-246.

Payne, R. (2005). *A framework for understanding poverty*. Highlands, TX: Aha! Press.

Shelley, P. B. (1874). *The poetical works of Percy Bysshe Shelley*. London: Edward Moxon, Son & Co.

Silberberg, S. (2001). Searching for family resilience. *Family Matters, 58,* 52.

Simon, J., Murphy, J., & Smith, S. (2005). Understanding and fostering family resilience. *Family Journal, 13*(4), 427–436.

Stockholm Resilience Centre. (2007). What is resilience. http://www.stockholmresilience.org/research/whatisresilience.4.aeea46911a3127427980004249.html

Turner, L., & West, R. (2002). *Perspectives on family communication* (2nd ed.). Boston: McGraw-Hill.

Walsh, F. (1996). *Strengthening family resilience* (2nd ed.). New York: Guilford Press.

Walsh, F. (2002). A family resilience framework: Innovative practice applications. *Family Relations, 51*(2), 130–137.

Walsh, F. (2003). Family resilience: A framework for clinical practice. *Family Process, 42*(1), 1.

Walsh, F. (2007). Traumatic loss and major disasters: Strengthening family and community resilience. *Family Process, 46*(2), 207–227.

Werner, E. E., & Smith, R. S. (1992). *Overcoming the odds: High-risk children from birth to adulthood*. Ithaca: New York University Press.

PART 6
Physical and Mental Health Considerations in the Family

Chapter 23
Reframing Addiction 256
Nicholas Fittante, *A.C.T. Family Counseling, Ontario, California*
Dennis Leoutsakas, *Salisbury University*

Chapter 24
When Family Blood Kills: Reflections on the Criminal Dangers of Confused Family Allegiances 264
Brad Goldschmidt, *University of Northern Colorado/Greeley, Colorado, Police Department*

Chapter 25
Intimacy and Connection: Parents Being Challenged from a Child's Disability 271
Stacy L. Carter, *Texas Tech University*
Narissra Maria Punyanunt-Carter, *Texas Tech University*

Chapter 26
A "Sounding Board and a Safety Net": Privacy Boundary Management between Adolescents with Insulin-Dependent Diabetes and Their Parents 278
Jeanette Valenti, *University of Denver*

Chapter 27
Defining Caregiving Relationships: Using Intergenerational Ambivalence Theory to Explore Burden Among Racial and Ethnic Groups 289
Angela C. Henderson, *University of Northern Colorado*

Chapter 28
Implications of Family Communication on Nutritional Health and Obesity of Children 304
Wanda Koszewski, *University of North Dakota*

Chapter 23

Reframing Addiction

Nicholas Fittante and
Dennis Leoutsakas

Just as family dynamics continue to evolve, so too do our methods for treating addicts within families. It is our opinion that psychologists and clinical therapists trained in the tradition of the medical model of addiction treatment may find themselves troubled at some of the contemporary rejections of traditional theoretical foundations. This paradigm shift growing out of postmodern thought represents a truly admirable and welcome change from a problem-focused model to a strengths-based model that can be embraced by all who work in the mental health fields. In our work with addiction and substance abuse, it is often the continued negative frames of reference that keep the addictive process ongoing.

The devastation that occurs to the individual and his or her family makes up the references that keep the individual believing that recovery is a hopeless cause. Recovery from addiction is tied to the restructuring of meaning in the addict's life. The success of the addict is reliant on support she or he receives (and accepts), often from family members, during that restructuring process.

One of the most important and, at times, more difficult tasks in treating clients with substance abuse is reframing how they look at the world. We have established that how we view the world and ourselves affects our behavior. If we honestly think that we are failures, it will be harder to stay clean or sober. If we think the world is a tough place and we have to battle hard each and every day, it will be so much easier to justify a drink or two so that we can unwind after a "hard" day.

Patterns of thinking are just that—patterns. They have been learned and reinforced over time. Like many people, addicts often have histories of negative experiences that keep them anchored to those past negative experiences and are often convinced that they are incapable of changing. These changes, however, are not impossible to accomplish, just difficult.

Recovery from addiction may be understood in terms of a total redefinition of the meaning of the addict's life. Just as their entry into the addictive process redefined who and what they were, so too their emergence from that world of addictive definitions and meanings is an important part of the process of recovery. We might say that the addict's life was reframed—redefined—by the experience of addiction. The task of recovery itself is redefining the lives of substance abusers so that, reframed, their lives and family related experiences can proceed without destructive and addictive substances.

In the present-day discussions about "addictions" in the world and the tendency to seek more and more pharmaceutical or medically based answers to controlling moods and behavior, we are still not succeeding to curb alcoholism or addiction. And whether we argue that we have diminished some use in some ways for some people, we are, as a society, finding new ways to amuse ourselves (e.g., gambling, Internet porn, and so on). We are not suggesting that these activities are good, bad, right, or wrong, just that they have always occurred, are occurring, and will continue to occur.

To us, it is more about "what results are we getting?" Are the results we get from these activities the results we want individually or as a society, or not? Do we even know what else to do if not what we are already doing? Yet, experts keep adding more pills and methodologies to "cure" addictions in a world that believes that there are entirely too many unreliable methods already. What are we not paying attention to? There must be something just beyond our line of sight that we are not able to see because of our focused attention on the things we are trained or conditioned to see.

We have known many of our colleagues in the world of addictions who question the systems, methods, policies, and so on. Most of us have been frustrated at one time or another. Maybe that is because we care. We know we care. We care about the results we get. We care about the happiness, sadness, and lives of the people we encounter. We care that people hurt so badly that they hurt others in the process of their addictions and their struggle to survive by whatever means. We care because we have been there.

There is no reason for us to think that anyone doing recovery work cares any more or any less than we do, and that is why we keep looking for the next best or better thing, is it not? We also believe that as long as we focus on sets of behaviors and strategies, maybe we are limiting the possibilities of seeing our way beyond the present-day thinking. Our addictions however, may simply be addressed within the complexity of early (or lack thereof) family experiences. It is generally agreed upon that addictions are most probably rooted in our beliefs, values, and attitudes about who we are as individuals, as people, and quite possibly, even about who we are as a species.

To repeat the quote attributed to Albert Einstein, "We cannot resolve the problems of today at the same level of thinking that created them." If we are to solve social and environmental dilemmas, we must behave differently. If we are to solve behavioral dilemmas, we must step outside the behaviors to develop strategies. If we are to resolve capability or strategic dilemmas, and desire lasting change, we must reconsider the beliefs, values, and attitudes that are driving them. Too often, using the modern medical model of addiction treatment, we seek a pill to cure our addictions and this method seems relatively ineffective.

We question the effectiveness of present-day addiction treatments and their ability in moving humans along the path to wellness and really living. The statistics and trends are not glowing. Much of the therapy is geared for simple survival in a socially palatable manner, accepting the lowest common denominator for being alive—an existence based in mediocrity and, in many ways, stuck in the repetition of past stories. Is it possible that our models in the world of rehabilitation and who we are in this world are not wrong, but insufficient in guiding us to our greatest potential? Similar to our young, the addicted and their families must be retrained to consider and believe in the vast scope of possibility. We know that for ourselves, in our addictions, we failed to see that there were other kinds of conversations possible. It is only in the present, long removed from our addictions, that we are able to consider possibilities as we continue to learn and, at times suffer, from our periods of past addictions.

This chapter draws on selected literature from the fields of family therapy, child and adolescent therapy, developmental psychopathology, theories of addiction and recovery, neurolinguistic programming, and general psychiatry. It is a synthesis of the authors' perspectives and experiences as child, adolescent, adult and family therapists/educators who began their careers more than 35 years ago. We too have both struggled with addictions, and we were introduced to a therapeutic community model of treatment in the 1970s. At that time, this was a grassroots experience in recovery, founded on the Synanon model and the "Synanon Game" which was heavily based on confrontation and accountability (Yablonsky, 1965). At times, very harsh treatment for those who opposed the house rules was the norm. In fact, we were so much a part of the concept back then that Nick became a staff member and eventually directed one of the residential facilities in Parksville, New York, for a dozen years. Dennis, who was a resident while Nicholas was the community's director, graduated from the program and went on to work at, and eventually direct, a therapeutic community in another state.

Now, as opposed to then, the program appears to have a more constructive approach: the therapeutic community is a style of treatment that engages the whole person in the recovery process for a long period of time and challenges the individual to have a full, positive life with healthy supportive relationships and satisfying responsibilities. We both want to believe that we had something to do with shifts in the treatment mentality and therapeutic approaches of the times—albeit not very well received in the moment.

One of Nicholas' most important realizations is that, as long as he continued to focus on addictions as the "thing" that it was made out to be, or as a set of behaviors and characteristics that certain people exhibit (including himself), he continued to be frustrated in his efforts at making a real difference in clients' lives as well as in his own. One of Dennis' most important realizations is that he is so much more than an addict. These realizations have linked us together for life. Even when we believed strongly in programs, structures, educational training in clinical treatment, and best practices that supported our efforts, we still kept falling short of making the difference that we held as possible.

So we kept looking for more, for a better or best method, generally acknowledging that we felt alright about the quality of people we were becoming and the skills we possessed. Yet we continued to search because we could not help feeling like most people coming through "the system" were leaving it prematurely. They were not ready, or were being set up for the big one—"failure" or "relapse" which for almost certain would destroy their families (and in some cases be a matter of life and death). In time, we have learned that it has never been about good or bad counselors, centers, systems, or methods, but that with all recovery processes, there is a whole other conversation that continues in the addict's head. It is one that modern therapists seldom have with their clients because it goes beyond all addictions, attitudes and behaviors; it is a conversation about significant past experiences, values, and beliefs.

We believe that knowing who we truly are cannot be comprehended by narratives at an environmental or behavioral level. Only when we allow ourselves to have conversations at the deeper levels of past experiences/values/beliefs can we start to have some clue about our attitudes, how we present ourselves, and why we perceive the world as we do. We are left wondering how long and how difficult it will be, if not impossible, to address addictions at environmental and behavioral levels with therapeutically designed statements like, "Just say no!" or "keep coming to meetings." For us, expectations of change cannot be forthcoming without first facing and managing deeply situated and long-held experience, beliefs, and values that we all carry within ourselves, as people, as a society, and as a species.

As we continue to consider what is best for us, in living a life that supports the essence of the beings that we are, and we continue to unmask our own truths about ourselves, we are reminded and in awe of the possibilities that lie ahead of us. We are amazed by the number of choices we have from moment to moment to moment. As with all things in life, up to and until we are courageous enough and willing to have a different kind of honest conversation about what we feel, what we experience, what we see, what we hear, and what we think with or without our addictions, we will continue to create repetitious results—or die trying. In the remainder of this chapter we will candidly discuss some current recovery models and our perceptions of how they can have meanings for the future of families. It is not a typical research endeavor; it is our thoughts based on experiential work from a combined 70 plus years in the field of addictions recovery. Whole families, regardless of their configurations are affected by addicted family members and our goal with the following discussion is to help improve the future of family life.

Understanding Recovery

Defining Addiction

In trying to define addictive dependence, health professionals tend to use psychiatric understandings that rely on a psychological sense of need for a substance or behavior (American Psychiatric Association, 1994; Bolstad and Hamblett, 2010). Although there are questions about addiction being hereditary, most addiction specialists seem to agree that recovery is possible and addicts are not doomed to a lifetime immersed in their addictions. Addictions come in all forms and most people are addicted to something. We all know people who can't stop shopping, eating candy, whitening their teeth, collecting books, and so forth. There are fine lines between consistency, habits, and addictions. While consistency and habits tend to be less harmful, addictions tend to be more destructive to familial relationships. This is because constant behaviors and ongoing habits are considered choices and manageable; addiction is viewed as a psychological need that is out of control.

The majority of addicts struggle with their addictions because they are caught in a tension that tears them apart like an aging rag. There is a part of them that does not want to use or inflict hurt on loved ones, but there is another part of their inner selves that is driven to continue feeding the addicted self, experiencing some measure of gratification from their addictions. If addicts do not exhibit this tension then their psychological problems are greater than their addictions. In terms of substance abuse alone, one study notes that at any given time, 6–7% of all Americans, qualify for a diagnosis of dependency (O'Brian and McKay, 1998). This study includes only substances often abused on the street, such as alcohol, cocaine, cannabis, and opiates, but did not measure prescribed pharmaceuticals, nicotine, caffeine, food, or behavioral dependencies. Once all addictions are grouped together, one can only imagine the impact on our families and communities. As is well known, many families around the world suffer in silence from the ongoing repercussions of multiple addictions.

The Disease Model & Addiction

Believing addiction to be a disease tends to reinforce the impossibility of recovery. If addictions are a disease, then they are genetically implanted, organically driven, and like cancers or AIDS, behaviorally unmanageable. Yet, it is possible to present case study after case study that proves otherwise. The authors refer readers to the opening paragraphs of this chapter and we too believe that recovery is possible. Through belief and value restructurings, behavioral modifications associated with addictions are made possible.

Medications & Addiction

In highly technocratic medical and pharmaceutically driven societies there is an unwritten law: If given an option between a machine, a pill, or a behavior change, choose the pill or the machine first; they are far easier than behavioral change. Probably there is no greater example of this for addictions than smoking cessations. We have gum, patches, mechanical cigarettes, and all other sorts of devices to assist with nicotine addiction and yet people continue to smoke. While the United States has made outstanding strides in reducing cigarette consumption, the world has yet to catch up and every generation produces a new crop of smokers.

Medications have not worked well in curbing alcohol or drug addictions, and this includes antabuse (Disulfiram), which makes consumers violently ill when they come in to contact or consume alcohol. The best documented results of such a dramatic treatment are shown in a 7 year study completed in Europe where antabuse is more commonly used. The drug was shown to be successful for approximately 50% of the recipients (Krampe, et al, 2006). The reason for this level of success is attributed to changes in habits and support for the alcoholics during the time they were using the drug. Once again the authors draw the readers' attention to the opening paragraphs of this chapter when their recovery processes originated in a ". . . program [that now] appears to have a more constructive approach: the therapeutic community is a style of treatment that engages the whole person in the recovery process for a long period of time and challenges the individual to have a full, positive life with healthy supportive relationships and satisfying responsibilities." Instead of using antabuse or any other medication or technologies as deterrents, the authors both began their journeys of recovery by reframing their own experiences, values, and beliefs.

Ending Addiction

Prison guards and jailers have a well-know axiom, that the best prisoner is an old prisoner. In the same manner, time is the best cure for addiction to substances; one either changes or dies. Studies continue to show that while treatment methods can be helpful, most people recover from their dependencies on their own (Peele, 1989; Prochaska, et al, 1994; Ragge, 1998; Schachter, 1982; Trimpey, 1996). This expectation seems to hold true for most addictions, but the majority of families sheltering addicts cannot afford to wait for a recovery process to unfold; the expenses, the hurts, and the possible losses of loved ones are too great. As such, treatment and recovery programs continue to flourish.

Addiction & Recovery

By now it should be understood that we are not "hucksters" for any particular brands of treatment for addictions. Let us be clear, we are well aware that over 80% entrants do not complete their treatment programs (Trimpey, 1996). And even the most promising recovery program will fail if the addict is not prepared to let go of experiences, values, and beliefs leading to their addictions. Regardless of the type of programs that addicts encounter, there are possibilities for successes and failures. Since we both believe that internal changes are at the core of recovery, we want readers to consider what it will take to construct an environment of recovery. Prochaska, et al, (1994), forward the idea that there are six stages for successful change. Alcoholics Anonymous and Narcotics Anonymous along with all the other 12-step programs suggest there are 12 stages for successful change. Brief motivational counseling suggests four sessions are enough to initiate change (Finney and Moos, 1998), while at the other end of the spectrum, therapeutic communities rely on years of treatment and aftercare. In the 1970s, one therapeutic community was so cult-like that some its members came to believe they could never leave because they were incapable of surviving in a world full of addictions and dishonesty (Morgan, 1999). We are more practical.

As we have noted several times in the course of this chapter, recovery is made possible by reframing addicts' experiences, values, and beliefs. Many therapists and programs do this utilizing a variety of methods. Most therapists use ongoing counseling to help addicts explore their inner selves. As they uncover experiences, values, and beliefs related to addictions they suggest changes and contracts within families. This form of treatment is reliant on perceptive analysts and habit forming experiential alternatives to disenchant addictive values. Counselor driven treatment also depends on a single point of view so supplemental group work and family counseling can be beneficial.

Common 12-step programs rely on the 4th and 8th steps to achieve this task: *Step 4 - Made a searching and fearless moral inventory of ourselves*; and *Step 8 - Made a list of all persons we had harmed, and became willing to make amends to them all* (AA World Service, Inc., 2002). With these two activities, all addictive beliefs and values can be exposed and hopefully healthy recovery can begin. Unfortunately, the reframing process is surrounded by a stream of self-negating dialogue. Words like "powerless" and a need for a directive "sponsor" tend to disable recovering addicts by placing them in positions of perceived helplessness. Supportive "home groups" and family attendance in like-minded environments such as Alanon and Narcanon, seem to be beneficial. With 12-step programs it is important for addicts to see past, "the foot of the sick bed." For recovery to be possible, they must be able to imagine themselves as healthy, recovering, and successful individuals.

Other programs such as neurolinguistic programming (NLP) and brief motivational interviewing (BMI) rely on two major elements for addiction recovery: *Contemplation* and *Commitment* (Bolstad and Hamblett, 2010). Contemplation is getting addicts to a state of readiness and commitment is when addicts make the initial efforts to be different from their addicted selves. From these positions, counselors, whether inpatient or outpatient, can hopefully identify the experiences, beliefs, and values that led to the addictive attitudes and behaviors and provide desirable alternatives to them. Time and environmental considerations are the greatest threats to these types of programs. They are often insurance or cash based, so brief in their implementation. Addicts have little time to habitualize their recoveries.

Finally, therapeutic treatment communities have phenomenal recovery outcomes for those who complete their programs. Not surprisingly, however, less than 10% of entrants successfully complete the program. The time needed to habitualize new beliefs, values and experiences is a major cause for disillusionment among treatment seekers. Homesickness, and limited opportunities are also discouraging factors. For the most part, residential expenses for such communities are sustained by public funding or extremely high admission fees. There is often minimal family interfacing, so the recovered addicts often exhibit new values and beliefs to their families. This can be extremely disconcerting to family members who can no longer read the intentions of their loved ones. For the communities to have continued success, greater integration of the family into the treatment process is warranted.

Conclusion

Research shows that successful assistance for family members struggling to end an addiction is very different from the nonproductive, psycho-babbling, negative labeling, superficial approaches of the recovery industry. Families and their addictive relatives need to be perceived as meaning makers. As we continue to apply new meanings to our lives, our existence remains in a constant state of flux. Addictions therefore are also subject to redefinition. The reframing of the experiences, beliefs, and values that lead to addiction is the most crucial task in guiding individuals through recovery. Through the use of personal flexibility and imagination, addicts, family members, and substance abuse treatment professionals can reframe the meaning of events and perceptions in such a way as to enhance the process of recovery.

One of the more difficult tasks in drug rehabilitation and drug and alcohol treatment is training addicts to adapt to new perceptions of themselves. In addition, their footing in the world is often unstable. How they view their positions in their environments will affect their beliefs and ultimately their behaviors. If they honestly think that the individual, family and or world is funnier or cooler when they use drugs and alcohol, it will be harder for them to stay sober. As stated earlier, "Patterns of thinking are just that—patterns." They have been learned and reinforced over time and many of the addicts' patterns originated in earlier familial life. They are not impossible to change, just difficult. Just like the magnetic feelings associated with sex or eating a meal when hungry, so too are the feelings associated with drugs or alcohol, making the patterns of addicts seem stronger and more difficult to change. The most decisive element of recovery from addiction, however, is the restructuring of meaning in the addicts' lives—including the addicts' family lives. Indeed, the entire rehabilitation venture is founded on developing a series of personal narratives, internally retold, that are designed to make fruitful recoveries believable.

Discussion Questions

1. Many "evotypical" families have members addicted to drugs and/or alcohol. What does the author suggest be done to assist the addicted family members?
2. Addiction is not exclusive to drugs or alcohol. What treatment methods suggested by the author can be applied to other addictions (e.g. gambling, overeating, sexuality, etc.)?
3. Many 12-Step programs are common in Western culture. What are some of the benefits and problems faced by those participating in 12-step programs?
4. List the surprising facts presented in this chapter?
5. What is the most central (and probably the most difficult) issue leading to addiction recovery?

References

AA World Service, Inc. (2002). "The twelve steps of Alcoholics Anonymous." Service material from the *General Service Office*. Retrieved from www.aa.org/en_pdfs/smf-121_en.pdf

American Psychiatric Association (1994). *Diagnostic Criteria From DSM-IV™*. Washington, DC: American Psychiatric Association.

Bolstad, R. & Hamblett, M. (2010). "Transforming Recovery." International Society of Neuro-Semantics. Retrieved from http://www.neurosemantics.com/meta-states/transforming-recovery-nlp-and-addiction

Finney, J. W. and Moos, R. H. (1998). "Psychosocial Treatments for Alcohol Use Disorders." In Nathan, P. E. and Gorman, J.M. *A Guide To Treatments That Work*, 156–166. New York: Oxford University Press.

Krampe, Henning; Stawicki, Sabina; Wagner, Thilo; Bartels, Claudia; Aust, Carlotta; Ruther, Eckart; Poser, Wolfgang; Ehrenreich, Hannelore (2006). "Follow-up of 180 Alcoholic Patients for up to 7 Years After Outpatient Treatment: Impact of Alcohol Deterrents on Outcome". *Alcoholism: Clinical and Experimental Research* 30 (1): 86–95.

Morgan F. (March 29, 1999). "One big dysfunctional family." *Salon Magazine*. Retrieved from http://www.rickross.com/reference/synanon/synanon2.html

O'Brien, C. P. and McKay, J. (1998). "Psychopharmacological Treatments of Substance Use Disorders." *In* Nathan, P. E. and Gorman, J. M. *A Guide To Treatments That Work*, 127–155. New York: Oxford University Press.

Peele, S. (1989). *Diseasing of America*. Boston: Houghton Mifflin.

Prochaska, J. O., Norcross, J. C. and Diclememnte, C. C. (1994). *Changing For Good*. New York: William Morrow & Co.

Ragge, K. (1988). *The Real AA: Behind the Myth of 12 Step Recovery*. Tucson: See Sharp Press.

Schachter, S. (1982). "Recidivism and self-cure of smoking and obesity." *American Psychologist*, (37), 436–444.

Trimpey, J. (1996). *Rational Recovery*. New York: Simon & Schuster.

Yablonsky, L. (1965). Synanon: *The Tunnel Back*. Baltimore: Penguin Books.

Chapter 24

When Family Blood Kills: Reflections on the Criminal Dangers of Confused Family Allegiances

Brad Goldschmidt

I am Lieutenant Brad Goldschmidt. I have worked for the City of Greeley, Colorado, Police Department for almost 30 years, having spent the majority of my career working in the Detective Bureau, first as a detective, then as a sergeant, and, finally, as a lieutenant. The city of Greeley has a population of approximately 90,000. The police department has 146 sworn officers. My time in the detective's area has been working or supervising the Crimes Against Person's Unit. During my tenure at the Greeley Police Department, I have been the lead detective or supervised the investigation of more than 50 homicides. In many of these homicide investigations, I have observed and become aware of deceptive communication patterns within families, specifically how often family members engage in lies to protect another family member, even when the guilt of that family member was not in question.

We must ask ourselves this: As a society based on laws, where does our responsibility rest when a family member has broken the law? Are we devoted and responsible to the family member at all costs, even if it means intentionally deceiving to cover up the most horrendous of antisocial laws, that of murder?

Family members lying to police or encouraging family members who are suspected of crimes to lie to police occurs from time to time—perhaps more than we, as citizens of a law-abiding society, would like to think. I have seen many examples of this family boundary violation in my career. For example, during a murder that I was investigating, a juvenile suspect was being interviewed by police, and his mother was with him in the interview room. When the detective stepped out of the interview room, the suspect's mother instructed her son to make up a story and lie to the police to account for the injuries to the victim and in no way admit to causing the injuries that killed the victim. The victim in this case? She was only 2 years old.

Communication privacy management theory (Petronio, 1991) suggests that people characterize private information as "theirs," something they own. When this private information is shared, those with whom it is shared become shareholders of the information. We expect to have complete control over our private information. Research has shown that family members control a boundary regulating private information that is shared with those outside the family (Morr, 2002; Petronio, 2002). Everyone knows that once information is shared with others, they lose control over it, particularly if the information is shared with the police. The Fifth Amendment to the U.S. Constitution grants every individual the right to not incriminate him- or herself; however, the Constitution does not grant us the right to lie.

Conversation orientation (Koerner & Cvancara, 2002) is defined by the degree to which families create a climate where all family members are encouraged to participate in unrestrained interaction about a wide assortment of topics. Families that have high conversation orientation spend a lot of time interacting with each other and share with each other their individual thoughts and ideas. Conversely, families at the low end of the conversation orientation dimension interact less with each other, and there are only a few topics discussed within the family. Associated with high orientation is the belief that open and frequent communication is essential within the family. Families holding this view value the exchange of ideas, and parents will have frequent conversations with their children as the main means to educate and socialize them. On the other hand, families with low conversation orientation do not believe or engage in sharing ideas; activities and values are not necessary for the functions of the family or for the education and socialization of the children (Koerner & Cvancara, 2002).

I have seen evidence of these orientations in adult gang members teaching their children to always lie to the police when being questioned about their involvement in criminal activity. This pattern of lying is very difficult to overcome when questioning one of these individuals who is suspected of committing a crime or who may be a witness to a crime. It is assumed that they have been taught from early childhood to never cooperate and to always lie to the police when being questioned, regardless of their involvement.

These evil perceptions of law enforcement, once instilled in young children, are difficult if not improbable to positively reframe. This is due, in part, to the power of social group membership and the psychological barriers that may result. According to Dombeck (2012), psychological barriers are comprised of our own perceptions, ideas, and beliefs that enable us to define our social group membership as well as our own self concepts and identities. We are all part of a social group that contains subgroups. Each layer of those groups and subgroups maintains a particular level of hierarchy. Parents function as a powerful level within the subgroup of a family, particularly over their children.

One case in particular stands out to me as an example of family members lying to protect their own. Similar to the example of the mother instructing her juvenile child to deceive the police, the mother in this next subgroup participated in deception as well as encouraging it from her son. This is a case that took 14 years to solve, primarily because the body of the victim was never found. It was a case where family allegiances were markedly misplaced, where more than one family member lied to protect the guilty. One lie occurred the day of the crime; more lies occurred to create a fictitious alibi. The following is a detailed account of the investigation and trial.

Sandoval Case: 1995–2011

At approximately 9:00 p.m. on Thursday, October 19, 1995, Mary Ellen Tournai, the mother of 23-year-old Kristina Sandoval, arrived at the Greeley Police Department to report her daughter missing. Mary Ellen reported that Kristina had met with her estranged husband, John Sandoval, earlier that morning. She also reported that Kristina and John were in the process of a divorce and lived in separate homes and that Kristina had just begun a new career as a registered nurse at the local hospital and worked the late shift. She went to meet John after her shift ended. Kristina had arranged to call her sister, Susan, after she met with John to let her know that she was alright. She feared meeting with John, as he was very possessive and at times violent and did not want the divorce. Kristina never called her sister, and nobody ever heard from or saw Kristina again.

Detectives from the Greeley Police Department were familiar with John Sandoval and knew of his previous law enforcement contacts regarding criminal offenses. On hearing that Kristina was reported missing and was last seen with John Sandoval, detectives Keith Olson, Clay Buckingham, and myself immediately began to investigate.

Detectives met with Mary Ellen and learned that she had been to John's house looking for Kristina. While there, she talked with John's Aunt Gabby, who also lived at John's house. She said that John was not at home and that she had not seen him since early morning when she left for work. Gabby told Mary Ellen that she had not seen Kristina, but before she left for work, John told her that Kristina was coming over that day. Mary Ellen saw a jacket draped over a chair in the kitchen. She recognized this jacket as Kristina's, as she had just purchased it for her. Mary Ellen knew that Kristina would not have voluntarily left the house without her jacket on a late November day. Mary Ellen took the jacket from John's house and brought it to the police department.

There were three primary detectives who began this investigation: Keith Olson, Clay Buckingham, and myself. We contacted neighbors of John Sandoval and learned that one of the neighbors reported hearing what was believed to be a gunshot earlier in the day. At about 1:00 a.m., we knocked on John Sandoval's door. Gabby answered and said that John was not home and that she had not seen him all day. She would not allow us into the house to search for evidence of what may have happened to Kristina. I requested officers be assigned to conduct surveillance on the house.

At about 5:45 a.m., while still dark and very cold, the surveillance officer radioed and informed us that a vehicle had stopped in front of John's house and that one person was seen exiting the car and entering the house. Detectives Buckingham and I immediately responded to that location, arriving in 4 minutes. I went to the door while Detective Buckingham went to look in the car. I knocked on the door, which was again answered by Gabby. I told her that I needed to talk to John. She told me that John was in the shower and that she would tell him I was there when he was out.

I felt strongly that foul play had occurred, that something bad could have happened to Kristina, and that John was a potential suspect. I also knew that if he had done something to injure or kill her, showering would quickly remove any trace evidence that may have existed. While I did not want to allow him to shower, I did not feel that there were currently exigent circumstances for me to enter someone's home without a warrant. That quickly changed.

Detective Buckingham called me over to the car and told me to look in through the windows. The car was a hatchback, and as I shined my flashlight into the car, I saw a white 5-gallon bucket with a white plastic bag inside of it, and next to the bag was a shovel, a spade-type shovel used for digging. The most alarming thing about the shovel was that it was wet, as if it had recently been washed or used to dig in a wet area. There was also a small amount of mud on the shovel.

I went back to the door and loudly knocked again. Gabby again returned to the door, and I told her I needed to speak with John immediately. She turned and walked through the kitchen and stood in a hallway. From where I was standing, I saw that a door was opened near where she stood, and I saw a person (or the shadow of a person) move past where Gabby was standing. Gabby returned to me and told me that she must have been mistaken; John was not home after all. (This was a lie to protect her nephew.)

Based on the information I had at this point, I immediately entered the home to locate John. Detective Buckingham entered behind me. Knowing John's past and also knowing that John had previously possessed guns, I loudly announced our presence as police officers and told John to step out and talk to us. I also called for additional officers to cover the outside of the residence. Within a minute of entering the home, I heard some banging coming from a room in the hallway. We opened the door and saw that John was in the process of jumping headfirst through the bedroom window. We ran out the front door to find that John had been stopped by one of the officers outside the house. I saw that John was wearing only a pair of blue jeans and a white T-shirt. He had on no jacket, nor was he wearing any socks or shoes. The temperature was well below freezing. He was taken into custody and immediately requested to speak with his attorney.

John was taken to the police department and placed in an interview room. While there, I observed numerous fresh fingernail scratches on his neck and chest. He would not make any statements as to what he had done with Kristina.

Massive and frequent searches immediately commenced attempting to locate Kristina. These searchers were comprised of personnel from local police, sheriff's, and federal agencies as well as family members and volunteers, many of whom had never even met Kristina. The searches continued frantically at first in hopes of finding Kristina alive. But as days passed, so did our hope that she was alive. The search to rescue a person passed to searching for the recovery of Kristina's body. We searched frequently for several months, but as winter took hold, hope of finding her faded, and searches diminished. While we never gave up hope of finding her remains, the places to search lessened, although searches continued for several years after that night.

John had been arrested the night of Kristina's disappearance on a different offense that he pled guilty to and was sentenced to prison. In this other case, he had illegally entered the homes of three young women, one of whom found him in her bedroom when she returned home. He served about 6 years in prison for that offense. When he was released, he moved to Las Vegas, Nevada.

The district attorney at the time of this offense believed that a conviction for murder was unlikely without Kristina's body; consequently, John was not charged with Kristina's death. Fourteen years after Kristina's disappearance, the detectives who had originally been involved in this investigation went to the then current district attorney and asked him to review the case. This was done, and the district attorney felt that after 14 years of absolutely no contact involving Kristina, his office could prove her death and that John had indeed killed Kristina.

An arrest warrant for the arrest of John Sandoval was completed. On June 18, 2009, Keith Olson and I went to Las Vegas to arrest John for the murder of Kristina. John was taken into custody by Las Vegas police officers. He was handcuffed and standing on the street as I made my way toward him. As he noticed me walking toward him, he looked at me, turned away, and did a double take. I immediately knew he recognized me and knew why I was there. I told him he was under arrest for the first-degree murder of Kristina. His reply: "Get me my attorney."

John was extradited back to Colorado to face the charge of murdering his estranged wife, Kristina. He arrived in Colorado on August 7, 2009. As part of the investigation, a detective, Mike Prill, was assigned to this case, and one of his duties included listening to recorded jail phone calls and visitor contacts John had while in jail. During these phone calls and visits, Detective Prill heard and documented many instances of John and his mother, Mary, talking in code and discussing possible lies to be told on his behalf to create his alibi for use in the upcoming trial.

Listed below are a few of the verbatim conversations that John had with his mother. These conversations occurred over the course of a year while John was in jail awaiting trial. Keep in mind that John and everyone he met with at the jail or talked to on the phone knew that their conversations were being recorded. Detective Prill interpreted these conversations as very guarded, and often they reminded the other that they were being recorded:

> John asked if Mary remembered a person, Ray's friend, [Mary did not], John said, "Ask Roy if he can get a hold of her, you know when you were saying about having witnesses that, you know, can say where I was, well, there's a possibility. You know what I'm saying?" Mary said yes.
> Mary said to John she knows, "You've forgotten, but there's some critical alibis" that she is aware of. Mary said she is in contact with the provider of that alibi.
> Mary told Sandoval, "It's been 15 years and you know you've forgotten a lot of that day, who you were with all that day, in the morning and in the afternoon, and Rico and, ya know? It's like, well every time he came up here he always came over and spent a couple hours over here [she spoke in Spanish at this point]." During all of this Sandoval is repeating, "Yeah, yeah, yeah." Sandoval told Mary to tell all of this to his attorney and they both mumbled in unison, indicating they knew the call would be listened to.
> Mary discusses a change of venue for his hearing, John asks a completely off topic question, asking, "the sewer pipe in your backyard that I was working on, did the city tell you to change that, or did we just . . . well I broke it cause we were doing the backyard." Mary said no, the city didn't order it and she confirms it was a sewage line that broke, creating mud everywhere.
> John said his attorneys have asked him, "How good is that going to be?" John said, "It doesn't matter how good it's gonna be, she knows that I was there from a certain amount of time to that morning, because I was there that night working on the damn thing."
> John says, "As to who I was with that night, from when I left my house and I went to point a, to point b, to point c, and then I came to your house and was there from that time at night to that time in the morning when I went back to my house."

The detectives on this case spent several days investigating when and if this sewer issue occurred. They did find that there had been a sewer line break near the time Kristina was killed. However, when Mary testified during her son's trial that John was at her house the night Kristina disappeared digging up the sewer line, this fictitious alibi fell through after the detectives proved that it did not occur near the time of the murder. This lie was unsuccessful in an attempt to convince the jury that her son did not kill Kristina.

Chapter 24 When Family Blood Kills: Reflections on the Criminal Dangers of Confused Family Allegiances

There are several occasions during these conversations that Mary begins babbling incoherently, as if using some type of code. We were never were able to determine the reason for this. Here is one example:

> Mary says they should subpoena Dave [a retired police officer], "To show the fact that, you know, that was in there, you know. Why did you dada, dada, dada, dada, dada, dah? And why did you dada, dada, dada, dah, because dada, dada, dada, dada, dada, da!" [I have included this verbatim to demonstrate how Mary speaks so often in these calls and visits, never articulating a point presented as relevant.]

After a monthlong trial, on August 6, 2010, 15 years after Kristina's disappearance and death, John Sandoval was convicted of the first-degree murder of his estranged wife. The jury took only 7 hours of deliberation to reach the verdict.

Not everyone who, we (the police) encounter lies to us, and as a society based on laws and the importance of truth, I came into this career believing that most people are honest. I still believe that; however, I have come to narrow that belief that most law-abiding people are truthful. The power of the family dynamic, especially in these confused systems, is strong and distorted; when the truth is abandoned for the "sake of the family," criminal dangers, even tragedies, can occur. Acting out on confused family allegiances can be disastrous; its practice can kill. That is not to say that most family members of suspects who are arrested for serious crimes encourage them to tell the truth of their involvement. Many encourage their family members to invoke their right against self-incrimination, which is a fundamental right granted by the U.S. Constitution and is completely different from lying.

The questions for us all to ask are these: What makes family members tell lies for those that commit the most horrendous of crimes? How do these confused allegiances ultimately sabotage the family? Why are these allegiances so integral to the family structure that they would condone and encourage telling lies for one another, even when one family whose daughter, sister, aunt, and friend was killed and her remains never found? Even then, knowing what Kristina's family was going through, the lies continued.

The murder of Kristina cannot be changed. The conviction of John was a just verdict, even with the lies that were told in an attempt to thwart justice. However, I often ask myself, If just one person from that family had encouraged the truth—if John's mother had not confused family allegiance with her duty to live within society's rules—what could have been different about this case? Would Kristina's family, at the very least, been given the opportunity to fully grieve their loss and provide a proper burial for their loved one? In this case, when "family blood killed" and confused family allegiances were created, justice for a murder victim was delayed. But, in spite of this, after many years of agony and grief for the victim's family, justice prevailed.

Discussion Questions

1. What characteristics would be present in a family that maintains a high level of conformity orientation?
2. Families with low conversation orientation do not believe that sharing ideas and values is necessary for the education and socialization of children. In what other ways might these children become educated and socialized?

3. In your family, what is the dialogue surrounding the police and cooperation with law enforcement?
4. This chapter poses the question, "Are we devoted and responsible to the family member at all costs, even if it means intentionally deceiving to cover up the most horrendous of antisocial laws?" Explain your thoughts and your possible actions if one of your family members allegedly broke the law. What situational factors might change your willingness to cooperate with police?

References

Dombeck, M. (2012). *Boundaries and dysfunctional family systems*.

Koerner, A. F., & Cvancara, K. E. (2002). The influence of conformity orientation on communication patterns in family conversations. *Journal of Family Communication, 2*(3).

Chapter 25

Intimacy and Connection: Parents Being Challenged from a Child's Disability

Stacy L. Carter and Narissra Maria Punyanunt-Carter

Editor's note: The following chapter is an example of a research proposal designated to investigate specific challenges presented to parents' relationships within families of disabled children, rather than a completed study; note its integral parts that will assist in the successful outcomes once the proposed research is conducted.

Introduction/Problem Statement

Communication patterns and intimacy between couples are greatly challenged once the couple welcomes their first child. There are time restraints, work schedules, household chores, and romantic relationships that are tested to their breaking point. These difficulties are increased 10-fold with couples having children born with specific learning and developmental disabilities, mostly depending on the severity of the disability. Within these families, not only must the child be supervised and monitored at all times, but the situation persists over long periods of time, and the child has difficulty growing into an individual independent of parental supervision. This creates strain on all relationships within the family, specifically the relationship between the parenting couple:

> The diagnosis of a chronic illness or disability in a child represents a major stressful life event for all family members, yet the diagnosis is but one point in the family's ongoing experience with the ill child. (Canam, 1993, p. 46)

Research Question

What are the specific challenges presented to parents' relationships within families of disabled children?

Through an evaluation and examination of this research question, an effective communication resolution can be created in order to facilitate successful communication techniques within these romantic relationships, alleviating much frustration and communication apprehension within the affected families. Successful communication in these circumstances can also be used in future communication training and evaluation in an attempt to help families in the future. The purpose of this project is to identify the specific communication frustrations and limitations of these families so that examination can be done to find specific techniques and training practices that can improve these situations.

Definition of Keywords

Disability—A medical condition diagnosed as a result of the inability to perform common, everyday routines adequately. Condition can range from severe, such as cerebral palsy, to mild, such as attention deficit disorder. The disability in this study serves as the independent variable; the initial cause of the communication frustration within the specific romantic relationships.

Routine—The everyday events and actions that are necessary to human function, such as showering, preparing dinner, or getting dressed.

Romance—Feeling of intense love or desire, often resulting in affection and sexual activities. The romance in this study refers to the parents' closeness with one another during alone time, away from outside distractions. Romance is evaluated in terms of length, satisfaction, and frequency.

Parent–child communication—Interaction techniques between a mother or father and their child. Communication occurs on a daily basis, ranging from assignment of duty, chores, casual conversation, guidance, and social support.

Parent communication—Communication between the parents of the child, often between a mother and father, occurring on a daily basis. Communication often results in feelings of contentment.

Strain—Frustration or pressures from a specific force within the family. In this instance, the communication difficulties result from the independent variable of the child's disability. The family members often feel guilty or frustrated because of the circumstance.

This research study is designed to solve a practical problem that has been scarcely examined in the past: to identify specific communication limitations within parents' relationships of children with disabilities in the hope of finding communication alternatives and practices that can settle many of these frustrations. Limitations to this study can be the identification of respondents and the reliability of the research findings. With such a sensitive subject matter being researched, it is to be expected that many respondents may choose to not participate fully or honestly. In order to be sure that the participants are fully aware that their personal information will not be disclosed, interviewees will be personally assured that confidentiality will be maintained. No names or identities will be asked during the interview process, and respondents will be given the option to participate or not. Consent forms will be provided, describing the purpose, design, and goals of the research project, and handed out in a lengthy amount of time before the interviews are conducted in an attempt to prepare the respondents for their interview. The preparation time will also allow the respondents time to think about their communication techniques and routines with their partners, hopefully making them aware of techniques that they, subconsciously, may be doing.

Literature Review

The basis of this research proposal is founded on the idea that the relationship between the mother and father of a disabled child forms an important foundation in the child's development and growth over the life span. Communication between both parenting partners is crucial to the development of their entire family, and both parents should maintain constant contact with one another, keeping each other abreast of problems or issues within the home:

> Partners' communication with one another will have a positive effect on their overall view of their marriage, and directly result their views of marital satisfaction. (Knapp & Daly, 2002, p. 643)

Thus, "Marital satisfaction seems to be a strong predictor of positive family coping with stressors associated with family care of a disabled child" (Friedrich, 1979).

While there is little research into the specific relationships of parents of disabled children, there is an abundance of previous work that evaluates the specific families' adaptations and beliefs regarding such instances.

Trute (1990) concluded, after an exhaustive, cross-sectional sample of 88 families containing young, disabled children, that these families struggle with the same challenges and discourse as those of any other family with developmentally healthy children. Many of the results of stress and frustration within these families were similar to that in other families. Time restraints and communication difficulties are frequent due to the addition of children to the family, not the disability alone.

Trute (1990) also concluded that parents' relationships with one another can have a strong effect on the coping success throughout the entire family:

> Marital satisfaction seems to be a strong predictor of positive family coping with stressors associated with family care of a disabled child. . . . The significant role of the parental subsystem as the executive center or pivotal hub of the family seems particularly evident in families containing disabled children. (p. 292)

Mothers and fathers of disabled children are more likely to suffer from challenges and adversities than families with healthy children. Mild to moderate levels of stress and anxiety, coupled with lower incomes, are more frequent in families with children having disabilities (Sloper, 2001). Sloper (2001) concluded that parents of these children are also more likely to suffer from many different emotional difficulties, such as self-blame and guilt, indicating that these parents are knowledgeable and aware of support services provided to their child and to themselves but are reluctant to take advantage because of feelings of inadequacy and the need for self-punishment. Research also shows that many parents are reluctant to use services for themselves: They will go to great lengths to obtain appropriate help for their children but may view support for themselves as an admission of failure as a parent (Sloper, 2001).

Service support is an area of great frustration to many parents. There are many different services available to families with disabled children; however, there are inadequate resources pertaining to these services, and service confusion and frustration can sometimes make the chore of choosing a service more difficult than easy:

> Areas where over one third of parents report unmet needs include: information and advice about services, the child's condition and how to help the child; financial and material support with housing and transport; and practical help with breaks from care. (Sloper, 2001, p. 90)

Time restraints have also been mentioned as a key factor in the stress and strain on the parents' relationship. Most of the day is spent caring for the child since the child, depending on age and severity of disability, is very dependent on the parent interaction for daily activity. However, in addition to the time restraints during the day, frequent sleep problems occur with children having disabilities, taking more time away from the parents' romantic relationship and alone time. Sloper (2001) evaluated this frequency in the United Kingdom in 2001 and found that there are many different training activities in that country that can educate parents and prepare them for this problem.

Previous research has analyzed the importance of the parents' attitudes in regard to their children's disabilities. This attitude is very important to the child's improvement and development:

> The child's sense of self is inextricably tied to the accomplishment of the psychosocial developmental tasks and if parents focus on the illness or disability to the exclusion of the child's developmental needs, the child's development is likely to be thwarted. (Canam, 1993, p. 48)

Another researched topic has examined the effects of home schooling on children with disabilities. Many children with learning disabilities are forced to be home schooled because they are unable to take courses in public schools, whether they be too fast paced and, in some cases, unavailable entirely. Home schooling may place more strain on the caregiver in the home. This is another factor contributing to stress and lack of time for other activities. Home schooling requires hours of work and dedication on the part of the student and teacher. Harniss, Epstein, Bursuck, Nelson, and Jayanthi (2001) evaluated the success of this type of schooling on the student, learner, and families. They concluded that for the home-schooling process to work, the parents must be the most active team member in the process, resulting in many hours of work and effort in order to ensure the student's success in the program.

Finally, Hammer, Tomblin, Zhang, and Weiss (2001) examined the specific instances with specific language impairment (SLI) in children. SLI is a developmental disability, impairing the child's ability to speak and use effective language, becoming evident primarily in the second year of life. Their study examined the importance of parent–child communication in these homes, closely evaluating the relationships within the home. The study concluded that parents who engaged frequently with their children, treating the child as if he or she had no disability, typically formed the same bonds and connections with their children as in the households with no SLI case. This study provides overwhelming evidence that the parent–child communication is a necessary component in the child's development and progression throughout the life course. Thus, the parents' communication with one another takes a backseat to the parent–child relationship. In order for the child to experience the rewards from an effective relationship with their parents, both parenting partners must communicate openly, keeping each other aware and involved in the child's activities. This study will evaluate this much more closely, documenting the importance of the parent–child relationship and the strain created as a result.

Methods

The research design in this study will be based on a qualitative interview analysis based on the personal experiences from each participant. The interview/survey type analysis will allow for personal recollection and thought, and since every participant has this or her own experience and ideas, the interview session will allow for open-ended responses, giving the researcher a more personal, in-depth look into the lives of those being studied. Since this is a personal subject, the interviewer will present clear, unbiased questions that are to make the participants comfortable. At any time, the participant will be free to leave and discontinue the survey should he or she feel threatened or uncomfortable in any way.

Data obtained for this research study will be obtained by contacting potential interview respondents through the local school districts. There are many special education programs in the Lubbock Independent School District as well as other school districts in the area. Permission must be obtained prior to the study by the superintendent of the Lubbock district and by the specific teachers within the special education program. If necessary, letters can be mailed out notifying parents of the study through their children during school time, then an initial meeting should be conducted with all of the parents together in order to answer any questions or concerns that they might have. Since there is the possibility of low participant turnout, several attempts to contact parents should be made, notifying them of the meeting time and place. It will be at this meeting that the consent forms will be handed out. After consent is gained from all participants, interview times can be set up. A meeting room or area should be reserved ahead of time for the interview session to take place, and there should be plenty of room with little distractions to keep participants focused.

Interview participants should include both active parents of the disabled child, likely the mother and father. It will be necessary for both parents to be in attendance so that an adequate amount of information is provided into each specific relationship and so that communication techniques can be evaluated based on both perspectives. The sample size should be as large as possible. Five research assistants should be available to administer the interviews, more or less to fit the sample size. They should be trained in confidentiality, and each should be aware of the participants' rights and wishes to remain entirely anonymous. With participation limitations, 50 to 100 participants will constitute an adequate amount of information for this study. Each participant should have a child who suffers from a developmental learning disability—one that creates a unique situation within the home.

Interview questions will be designed to document as much insight into the personal, romantic relationships beyond the initial disability affecting the participating families. Both partners should be allowed to answer the same questions separately so that they are not intimidated and more likely to answer the questions honestly without reprimand. Participants will be read the following instructions before the interview is conducted:

> Thank you so much for taking the time to participate in this research study. Your participation will help us develop insight into the personal relationships of parents with children having learning disabilities. Through the completion of this study, new training opportunities can be created to improve romantic relationship communication to help parents in the future. Please answer the questions to the best of your ability, as openly and as honestly as possible. If, at any time, you wish to forgo the interview, you may leave, and your interview answers will be disregarded. Your complete anonymity will be maintained, and you will not be obligated to anything in the future.

The questions are to be open ended, allowing plenty of time for participants to think, in depth, about the sample questions.

Interview Questions

Are you satisfied in your romantic relationship?

Are you frequently frustrated by a lack of alone time?

How often do you disagree on parenting styles or issues within the home?

Are you satisfied with the amount of romance in your relationship?

Do you disagree often?

Do you feel like you take a backseat to parenting issues within the home? Are you in control of them?

Do you feel like your relationship is strained due to your child's disability?

Do you feel guilty for circumstances within the home?

Are you satisfied with your relationship's intimacy?

Overall, are you satisfied with your relationship?

Is there anything that you would change?

Based on the information obtained, the independent variable is the child's disability, and the dependent variable is marital satisfaction, guilt, romance, intimacy, and lack of alone time in a romantic relationship.

In order to ensure reliability and validity, a second interview can be conducted if participants are willing to continue with this process. The test–retest approach will check for consistency with interview answers, helping to ensure that all answers are reliable. Unfortunately, with so many participants and the needed face-to-face interaction, it will be difficult to have each participant return for a second interview.

Data will be analyzed by examining the interview responses, documenting the similarities and differences within them. Any unusual responses should be given special attention, and there should be plenty of time allowed for careful review of each relationship's characteristics. The more instances of communication frustration and disagreement should signal to the researchers that a correlation with the child's disability could possibly exist. It should also be taken into account that many of the relationship frustrations are similar to the parents of healthy children as well. This lays the foundation for future research into the similarities and differences into the different family types.

Conclusion

Because of the intense stress and emotional strain created in families due to a child's disability, it is our hypothesis that communication and/or relationship tension is likely to occur within parents' romantic relationships. This study is designed to examine specific families and their raw, honest feelings about the subject. It should give researchers insight into these specific cases, allowing us room to create future research studies that can make training and support systems possible in the future. This study should take place over the course of one year, and it is hoped that by then we can gain useful information that can help families in the future.

Discussion Questions

1. How does this chapter define "disability"?
2. What are some of the challenges that parents of disabled children might face?
3. Why are parents of disabled parents often reluctant to take advantage of parental support services but are willing to engage services for their children?

4. Recall several of the negative and positive aspects of home schooling disabled children.

5. What communication behaviors should parents utilize in order to strengthen their relationship?

References

Canam, C. (1993). Common adaptive tasks facing parents of children with chronic conditions. *Journal of Advanced Nursing, 18,* 46-53.

Friedrich, W. N. (1979). Predictors of the coping behavior of mothers of handicapped children. *Journal of Consulting and Clinical Psychology, 47,* 1140-1141.

Hammer, C. S., Tomblin, J. B, Zhang, X., & Weiss, A. L. (2001). Relationship between parenting behaviours and specific language impairment in children. *International Journal of Language and Communication Disorders, 36*(2), 185-205.

Harniss, M. K., Epstein, M. H, Bursuck, W. D, Nelson, J., & Jayanthi, M. (2001). Resolving homework-related communication problems: Recommendations of parents of children with and without disabilities. *Reading and Writing Quarterly, 17,* 205-225.

Knapp, M. L., & Daly, J. A. (Eds.). (2002). *Handbook of interpersonal communication* (3rd ed.). Thousand Oaks, CA: Sage.

Sloper, P. (2001). Models of service support for parents of disabled children. What do we know? What do we need to know? *Child: Care, Health and Development, 25*(2), 85-99.

Trute, B. (1990). Child and parent predictors of family adjustment in households containing young developmentally disabled children. *Family Relations 39*(3), 292-297.

Chapter 26

A "Sounding Board and a Safety Net:" Privacy Boundary Management Between Adolescents with Insulin-Dependent Diabetes and Their Parents

Jeanette Valenti

July 31, 1993, was a memorably awful day for my family. My brother had a collision with a car that totaled his bike (luckily he was unharmed), my sister found her treasured opal necklace crushed in the garage, and I was diagnosed with type 1 diabetes. That day was an obvious turning point in my life. My brother and sister were able to procure a new bike and necklace, but we had no luck in finding a new pancreas for me. Having diabetes requires rigorous planning and treatment, and sometimes I have to remind myself that it is not just *my* disease but also a condition that affects the important people in my life. Chronic illness of any kind affects not only the patient, but their interpersonal partners as well.

One of the areas of relational difficulty surrounding chronic illness is that of privacy. Especially in families, which are typically highly interdependent, there are concerns about what the person with the disease should disclose and what he or she can keep private. Looking back on my teenage years with diabetes, I was satisfied with the amount of privacy I enjoyed. As I have had conversations with my mother about that time period, however, I was surprised to learn that although I was usually perfectly fine with the flow of information between us about diabetes issues, she was not. She trusted me, but since she did not want to "nag" about my diabetes treatment or blood glucose levels and I did not volunteer a great deal of information, she was left feeling concerned about my health on a regular basis. This type of privacy dilemma is common in families where chronic illness is present, particularly during adolescence.

Insulin-Dependent Diabetes Mellitus

Insulin-dependent diabetes mellitus is a well-known chronic illness and familiar to most people. It is also known as "childhood diabetes" or "juvenile diabetes" because it is typically diagnosed during childhood or adolescence. It is is an autoimmune disease, which means that it is the result of the body's destruction of pancreatic cells that produce insulin, leaving the body without insulin (Hanna & Guthrie, 2001).

Type 1 diabetes is fatal without artificial insulin administration. Multiple daily insulin injections or inhaled insulin are a few methods of receiving the required doses, although insulin pumps are increasing in popularity as the new preferred system of administering insulin. In addition to insulin, insulin-dependent diabetes mellitus must be treated or "controlled" through a routine of blood glucose monitoring, dietary calculations, and regular exercise (Cerreto & Travis, 1984; Schilling, Grey, & Knafl, 2002; Wennick & Hallstrom, 2006).

When diabetes is not controlled, the complications are alarming and intense (Schilling et al., 2002; Wennick & Hallstrom, 2006). When the body experiences a lack of insulin, glucose is unable to enter the cells of the body and remains in the bloodstream, thus causing glycosuria (highly elevated blood glucose levels). Frequent glycosuria can lead to early development of vascular complications, retinopathy, neuropathy, cardiac arrest, blindness, diabetes-related hospitalizations (including emergency room visits), and death (Cerreto & Travis, 1984; Wennick & Hallstrom, 2006).

Teenagers with Diabetes and Their Parents

Adolescence is often a time for negotiation between parent and teen about what is or is not disclosed, a process of change within the communication between parent and child. Teenagers with diabetes and their parents face an interesting challenge in the process of navigating adolescence. Parents and teenagers must balance commonly occurring adolescent issues (e.g., changing emotions, behaviors, and desires) *and* focus on transitioning diabetes control from the parent to the adolescent. Transitioning control involves the teen's taking increased responsibility for his or her diabetes treatment regimen and experiencing more independence from the parent in performing his or her diabetes management (Hanna & Guthrie, 2001).

Unfortunately, many teenagers and parents struggle with establishing what is acceptable and unacceptable in the discussion of diabetes care and treatment (Hanna & Guthrie, 2000a, 2000b). Commonly, there are difficulties in negotiating what areas about diabetes the teen can keep private and what the teen needs to tell the parent. For example, a parent may ask the teenager what his or her blood glucose levels were that day in an effort to ensure good metabolic control. The adolescent, however, may resent the questions and perceive them as an intrusion of privacy, lack of trust, and a threat to independence (Hanberger, Ludvigsson, & Nordfelt, 2006) and therefore avoid diabetes conversations.

Too much privacy may lead to inadequate care for the adolescent because the parent may not be aware that he or she needs medical help. Not enough supervision (e.g., too much privacy) may also result in a teenager's lax adherence to his or her treatment program as he or she learns to take control of the disease without adequate parental guidance (Hanna & Guthrie, 2000a, 2000b; Hutchinson & Stafford, 2005).

Communication Privacy Management Theory

Communication privacy management (CPM) is a theory that addresses the complex question of disclosure in relationships, "to tell or not to tell" (Petronio, 2002, p. 1). Divulging private or personal information is rarely a simple choice; rather, it is a series of maneuvers requiring the weighing of situational demands and the needs of ourselves and others. CPM posits that private disclosures are dialectical and provides a framework to understand how people manage the tension between revealing and concealing.

One of the basic suppositions of CPM involves the definition of private information. CPM maintains that private information is the *content* of what is revealed through disclosure. Through the process of sharing private information, people may achieve social control, express themselves, foster intimacy, or relieve a burden (Petronio, 2002).

A second theoretical supposition discusses the use of the boundary metaphor to describe privacy (Petronio, 2002). A boundary is used to differentiate between what is public and private. Within CPM theory, privacy is defined as "the feeling that one has the right to own private information, either personally or collectively" (Petronio, 2002, p. 6). Boundaries may be altered over time according to life span changes (such as the open boundaries a child has vs. the closed boundaries an adult may have) or relational needs (such as enlarging a family or getting to know a new relational partner) (Morr-Serewicz, Dickson, Morrison, & Poole, 2007).

Research Questions and Methodology

Research Questions

Although research has been done in the area of families with a teenager who has diabetes, little to no empirical research has been conducted that examines privacy as a construct in the transition of care from parent to child. It is important to investigate how privacy boundaries are established and negotiated in order to determine what practices of privacy management foster independence for the adolescent while still maintaining adequate metabolic care.

Research in the area of diabetes control clearly positions the role of parental support as an important factor in the transition of diabetes care. It is especially important to study parent–adolescent relationships because they combine the expectation of disclosure and the mutual dependency that occurs within families, especially within the parent–adolescent dynamic.

Research questions for this study were developed based on existing literature about parent–adolescent relationships, diabetes research, and data from a pilot study conducted prior to this research study (Valenti, 2007). Questions focused on the preferences for open and closed privacy boundaries between parents and adolescents with insulin-dependent diabetes, the most frequent areas of boundary turbulence, and issues of boundary negotiation that affected the transition of diabetes control from parent to child.

Methods and Procedures

Twelve families took part in this study, for a total of 24 participants (12 parents and 12 adolescents). Participants for this study were parents and their teenage children who had insulin-dependent diabetes (ages 13 to 17 years). Data were collected from semi-structured individual telephone interviews. Interview protocol developed from issues and themes previously derived from a pilot study (Valenti, 2007) and research literature from the areas of privacy, chronic illness, family communication, parent–child relationships, and adolescent development. Interview data were analyzed using a thematic analysis technique developed by Owen (1984).

Results and Discussion

Two major overarching themes emerged in this study. The first major theme that came out was the idea that parents wanted reassurance that their children's metabolic health was acceptable. For example, parents would allow their children more privacy if diabetes was in control. If parents perceived that their children's diabetes was not in control, they would engage in information-seeking behavior to try to help their children.

The second major theme that appeared was the viewpoint of disclosure from adolescents. Teenagers wanted to be in control of their diabetes information and be the initiators of diabetes-related conversations and disclosure with their parents. For example, teenagers mentioned that diabetes was their own personal disease, so they should be the ones to have control over diabetes-related discussions. Both themes were present in all the parents' and adolescents' discussion of experiences, and both themes were supported by the less dominant themes that surfaced.

Preference for Open and Closed

In CPM, privacy rules are developed based on individuals' needs and desires about private disclosure (Petronio, 2002). For example, would it be more beneficial for a communicator to reveal a piece of information or conceal it? Knowing the preferences for open or closed boundaries lends understanding to how and *why* privacy rules are developed to protect the degree of boundary permeability.

The two major themes in this study suggest that parents typically prefer open boundaries (to ensure that their children are healthy), while teenagers prefer closed boundaries (to maintain control over their information). Both parents and teenagers, however, expressed that their preferences for open or closed boundaries varied. Desires and needs surrounding disclosure situations related to the amount of risk associated with sharing or hiding diabetes information.

Risk–benefit ratios are one factor in how privacy rules are developed. People attach risk amounts (high, medium, or low) to private information. High-risk information, for example, would involve drastic consequences (e.g., shame or punishment) if the information were revealed (Petronio, 2002). If information is considered by the individual to be high risk, thick and closed privacy boundaries will be constructed around that information. Low-risk information would typically have more permeable boundaries because the consequences of disclosing would not be severe.

There are several types of risk associated with disclosure, such as stigma risks, security risks, face risks, and relational risks (Petronio, 2002). In this study, forming rules for open and closed boundaries centered primarily on security risks. Security risks involve the formation of privacy boundaries around information that might cause perceived harm to self or others (Petronio, 2002). Parents in this study viewed too much privacy about diabetes information as a security risk because their children's metabolic control might suffer (which supports the first major theme in this study). Teenagers viewed disclosure in the light of a security risk because they might be punished or lose privileges if some diabetes information was revealed (thus supporting the second major theme in this study).

Closed Boundaries The primary reason that adolescents did not share diabetes information was because parents often had a negative response to the teenager's disclosure; many teenagers felt like their parents did not trust them when they shared negative diabetes information. Marie (17 years old) spoke of the fear of blame or punishment she had telling her mother about problematic blood glucose levels:

> Usually if I go over 400, I know she's going to know so I just tell her right out. But if I have a series of 200, 300 over a series of days, maybe a week or something like that, I think what am I doing wrong? *It's my fault.* She's going to be *mad* at me! (Marie, p. 7, lines 2-5)

Katie (17 years old) also mentioned that her parents would sometimes get upset when they found out she had made a mistake and would prefer to keep her mistakes to herself. She related that sometimes her parents got distressed when she forgot to test her blood or her levels were not in range:

> When I have really high blood sugars and I'm sick they like lecture me about it. I would rather just deal with it myself. (Katie, p. 2, lines 18–23)

Teenagers talked about that, although it was obvious that parents would know some diabetes information based on behavior and symptoms (such as an extremely high blood glucose level), teens did not want to share all of the problematic diabetes information. When a teenager can control whether he or she shares problematic glucose information with parents, the teenager has the control over whether he or she will be punished.

Another aspect of security risks perceived by teenagers in this study is the notion of doubt or disappointment from their parents as a result of their diabetes disclosures. Many teenagers felt like their parents did not trust them when they shared diabetes information. None of the parents in this study had diabetes, and sometimes adolescents were reluctant to share diabetes information because they felt as though parents did not understand. With this perceived lack of understanding from parents came an expressed lack of confidence in the teenager's ability to care for him- or herself. Marie (17 years old) says, that her mother sometimes lapses into the "I know best" mode in reference to Marie's diabetes. In response to this behavior, Marie related:

> "And I tend to get really mad and want to say, "No you don't! You have not been there!" And then, like I don't want to say anything to her about my diabetes because she acts like she knows more than I do. (Marie, p. 10, lines 3–6)

Jeanne (15 years old) also expressed that her mother would sometimes express a lack of confidence in Jeanne's ability to control her diabetes, which prompted her to prefer closed boundaries. For example, she often had a snack when she felt her blood glucose level dropping, but her mother told her that, according to her current glucose level, Jeanne shouldn't have any food. Jeanne shared her frustration:"

> Sometimes I wish she could just know what it feels like and know that I am going to get low and I know I'm gonna. She just doesn't know that I actually know I guess, so I wish she would just leave me alone" (Jeanne, p. 3, lines 7–18)

This supporting theme of disappointment as a result of disclosure correlates to both the first theme (parents want reassurance of their children's health) and the second theme (teens want control of their health information) of this study. When parents see that their children's health is suffering, they feel the need to intervene in order to help their children. If adolescents can decide what to tell and not tell, teenagers can experience more independence about treating their diabetes.

Parents, although wanting enough information to ensure their children's health, also had preferences for developing privacy rules for closed boundaries about diabetes information. They recognized the value of having their children take responsibility for their own diabetes, which included not disclosing *all* diabetes information. Cindy discussed that she simply needed to know that her child's blood glucose levels were acceptable: "We came to the part where okay, I'm not going to monitor you [daughter], but *you have to be able to tell me* 'I'm low' or 'I'm high.' That was one thing we did come to an agreement with" (Cindy, p. 5, lines 5–8).

Part of parents' wanting their children to have increased responsibility and closed privacy boundaries was their desire to better prepare their children to leave home. For example, Mary said,

"She's doing it all on her own. You know? So I'm glad she's doing that, because I know that here in a year and a half she's going to be all on her own" (Mary, p. 4, lines 1–5). Another parent, Andrea, also discussed the role of privacy in preparing her children to leave home. Her first son, who also had diabetes, was unprepared to monitor himself, and Andrea felt the need to constantly call him. The arrangement did not work for mother or son, so Andrea developed a new plan:

> "So now with the second one [child with diabetes], I am making sure he is okay but I am really making the effort to *have him come to me* about diabetes stuff. So hopefully he will be more prepared when he leaves for college and so will I. (Andrea, p. 6, lines 15–21)

Open Boundaries Although it may be surprising after hearing about teenagers' desire to maintain privacy and independence, most teenagers in this study also reported a strong desire to maintain some open boundaries with their parents about diabetes information. Adolescents preferred to keep open privacy boundaries with their parents in order to handle life circumstances. Life circumstances are situations that require adaptations to a new set of events (Petronio, 2002). These adaptations usually encompass changes in privacy boundaries. In this study, teenagers adapted their privacy boundaries to match *diabetes* circumstances, such as when their blood glucose levels were high or low and they needed extra help and support.

Katie (17 years old) discloses information and relies on her parents to jump in and help if there is a problem. If she was having difficulties with high blood glucose patterns she would confide in her parents and ask for help and her parents would intervene.

Rachel (17 years old) also remarked that her mother was able to help her when things were not ideal. "If I had a high or low and then I'll tell her, and she'll try to figure out everything that went on that week to help" (Rachel, p. 4, lines 13–17). Parents can play a positive role in helping with their children's diabetes care when their teenagers share information.

Teenagers also discussed their preference for sharing information with their parents, or keeping open boundaries about certain diabetes information, in order to have their parents empathize or share in exciting events. In CPM theory, expressive needs involve the role of disclosure in filling an individual's need to express feelings and thoughts (Petronio, 2002). Sharing thoughts and feelings or disclosing certain information helped teenagers fill their expressive needs. Brandon (17 years old) said,

> "My A1C was 6.7, and they [parents] were pretty excited. Super excited. They were all "Good job." We went out for ice cream and it was just nice to have the pressure off and tell them since they knew how much hard work it took to get it [A1C] there. (Brandon, p. 6, lines 14–17)

Brandon was able to share his great news with his parents and express his thoughts and feelings, which earned their congratulations and support. Jeanne (15 years old) also mentioned expressing her feelings to her mother and receiving support from her mother as a confidant. For example, on days where her blood glucose levels were staying too low, she would call her mother and burst into tears. Telling her mother about the issue, however, was due to Jeanne wanting support and not about having her mother need to know. As she called to simply tell her mother she was low, she was also filling her need to express and disclose her feelings. It is clear that adolescents appreciated the support of their parents when they decided to disclose diabetes information. Since teenagers in these circumstances were the ones making the decision to share diabetes information with their parents, the second overarching theme of this study was supported.

Parents agreed that as long as their children had good metabolic control, it was acceptable for them to have increased responsibility, independence, and privacy. If, however, parents recognized (through observing their children's symptoms and behavior) that their children's metabolic control was unacceptable, more supervision was warranted. This supporting theme about privacy rule development with open boundaries coincides with the first major theme in this study.

One parent, Chelsea, illustrated the idea that she could not allow her child to have open boundaries with diabetes information because he was not taking adequate care of himself. Her son told her he needed to have privacy and freedom. Her response:

> But I . . . I told him I couldn't give that to him at that point. He has to take responsibility. He has to show me that he can take care of his diabetes. *And right now he isn't.* (Chelsea, p. 3, lines 12–18)

In Chelsea's case, open boundaries were required so that her son could maintain adequate health. Even though her son wanted closed boundaries, Chelsea could not agree since his health was at risk. In situations such as this, when parents and children disagree about privacy boundaries, boundary turbulence takes place.

Boundary Turbulence

Another research question inquired about the most frequent areas of boundary turbulence between parents and adolescents with insulin-dependent diabetes. Although there was some agreement between parents and teenagers about when boundaries changed and how negotiations took place, boundary turbulence still occurred. Turbulence occurs when boundary coordination is unsuccessful and illustrates the idea that boundary coordination is a difficult process.

The most common area of boundary turbulence was the everyday conversations about diabetes. Children reported that their parents asked too many questions, while parents mentioned that children were too protective about their diabetes privacy. Both parents and teenagers frequently used terms such as nagging, badgering, and bugging to describe their everyday conversations about diabetes.

The majority of parents mentioned that their child would rarely initiate conversations about diabetes care and that they would consistently be the one seeking information. Parents discussed being puzzled about why their child did not initiate diabetes conversations or disclose more about their diabetes. Kathryn said about her daughter with diabetes:

> She is always so stubborn and stuck on being independent and private, and all I want to do is to help her. She just wants to do everything herself and not tell me anything about it. I don't see the crime in letting me know that she is okay. (Kathryn, p. 5, lines 11–17)

Although parents acknowledged that they knew that their children resented their questions, they still engaged in diabetes conversations (supporting the first theme in the study). Kris mentioned, "He'd [son] probably call it nagging, but as his parent I *have* to ask what his results [blood glucose] were and if he remembered to bolus." (Kris, p. 2, lines 23–25) Another parent, Andrea, also described her child's reactions to her questions about diabetes care as a lot of eye rolling.

Adolescents in the study described at length their irritation at their parent's questioning. Dawn (14 years old) discussed the conversation that she and her mother had consistently repeated about her diabetes. "She was driving me nuts. So I just told her to leave me alone." (Dawn, p. 2, lines 17–21) Kelley related that she felt as though her parents were nagging her constantly.

Although most adolescent participants mentioned feeling annoyed at the initiation of diabetes conversation from their parents, a few teenagers mentioned deeper concerns in reference to boundary turbulence. Kelley (16 years old) said,

> I'm going to be leaving the house in like a year. I need them to kind of like, wean me off gradually and they're not really. I think if they're reminding me every day I'm not going to remember for myself. (Kelley, p. 8, lines 4–5)

Kelley expressed her concern that the boundary turbulence with her parents might interfere with her abilities to take care of herself.

The consequences of boundary turbulence within the parent–adolescent relationship can extend beyond irritating interactions and interfere with the teenager's preparation for self-care after leaving home. If privacy is not successfully managed and independence is not positively established, drastic health results may be the consequence.

Transitioning Control

The relationship between parent and child is important in maintaining the adolescent's metabolic control and in helping the teenager positively and correctly take over diabetes care. Participants discussed success stories as situations where the metabolic health of the teenager was adequate and the relationship between parent and child was not damaged as a result of diabetes boundary turbulence. "Failures," or unsuccessful transition processes, were considered to be occasions where boundary turbulence affected the health of the teenager and/or put a strain on the relationship between parent and teenager.

Success Stories

In success stories, it is clear that privacy management practices and boundary turbulence were effectively handled. If there was disagreement about diabetes conversations and disclosure of information, parents and their children tried to solve the problem rather than engage in a demand/withdraw pattern (Milnitsky-Sapiro, 2006). One of the most successful communicative tactics for managing privacy and transitioning control involved striking a communicative compromise. For example, Brandon (17 years old) said that he set up an agreement with his mom that involved her backing away as long as his glucose levels were acceptable. Claire (16 years old) talked about the journey she undertook with her mother about transitioning control. For 7 years her mother had been consistently asking Claire if she was checking her blood sugar and giving her insulin, even getting up in the middle of the night to check Claire's glucose level. Finally Claire asked her mother to be less integrated in her care, and her mother agreed to let Claire try it for a week. Claire was surprised at how easy the transition was, considering how involved her mother had been for so long:

> So she checked it and made sure I was doing everything okay and that was the end of it. It wasn't this whole huge blow out or discussion or anything. (Claire, p. 6, lines 1–4)

Both Brandon and Claire mentioned that they were experiencing boundary turbulence, or disagreements, with their parents about diabetes information. They handled that disturbance by communicating with their parents about their privacy needs. Brandon's and Claire's parents (respectively) responded with a solution that would also meet their needs to be reassured that Brandon and Claire were taking care of themselves.

Parents and children agreed that setting up a situation so that children could prove they had the capability to take care of themselves was key in being able to allow more privacy. This problem-solving technique is especially effective because, as per the two guiding themes of this study, parents have reassurance that their children can take care of diabetes more independently (through the children proving they were taking care of themselves), while children were the ones exercising control over their diabetes information and treatment.

Another important aspect of transitioning care, however, was continued parental involvement even after the child had demonstrated that he or she could take care of him- or herself. Involvement from parents was a key issue because, first, parents needed to know that their children were healthy and, second, children did need occasional guidance from their parents to remain healthy. A parent, Rich, said that although his child was independent, his role as a parent still required supervision of his child because sometimes his daughter would get complacent about her daily glucose levels:

> She'll get into a track where 200 is okay, 250 is not bad, so you know we'll just have to knock it back down. She'll get comfortable with some higher levels of blood sugar readings and that is why we just keep talking to her about 'em. (Rich, p. 8, lines 3–7)

Boundary permeability needs to be such that parents have adequate information to help their child stay healthy, such as Rich's experience monitoring his daughter's blood glucose levels. Boundaries also need to be impermeable enough, however, so that teenagers feel independent, like Brandon and Claire. As all participants mentioned, it was important to communicate their *expectations* of boundary permeability and disclosure. For example, Brandon and Claire (supporting the second overarching theme) spoke with their parents about establishing more privacy and independence with diabetes information. In turn, their parents discussed (supporting the first theme) that more privacy and independence was acceptable as long as the teenagers were showing responsibility and good metabolic control.

One of the most indicative statements of success came from Beth, who described her worry and relief as a parent to watch her daughter take control of her own diabetes but also expressed that she was available for disclosure in case her daughter needed help:

> I think I'm just a . . . I'm a sounding board and a safety net still. . .she is taking care of herself along with talking to me about it, so I'm the safety net if anything happens. She knows she can come to me. (Beth, p. 8, lines 9–14)

Although Beth's daughter did have privacy, it is clear that the rules for boundaries around diabetes information were still permeable, so Beth was comfortable with the amount of information she received as a parent. Since she knew her daughter had good metabolic control, Beth allowed her to take control over sharing her diabetes information. This example demonstrates both major themes in this study.

Failures

Not all parents and teenagers reported a smooth or successful diabetes care transition process during adolescence. The supporting theme that was present in the failure stories was the idea that one or both of the overarching themes of this study was not present in the relationship. For example, either teenagers felt as though they did not have control over their diabetes information or parents felt as though their teenagers did not have good diabetes control. Boundary turbulence was the result of parents and teenagers not meeting their needs for privacy.

A "failure" is an instance when boundary turbulence leads to a damaged relationship between parent and child and/or the child's health is at risk. Several parents described situations in which their relationships with their children suffered and their children's metabolic control was compromised. The primary theme in their stories of difficult transitions is a lack of communication about privacy expectations and boundary turbulence. In unsuccessful situations, parents and children also reacted negatively to one another rather than finding a solution to the turbulence. One parent, Chelsea, described the negative reactions and exchanges with her son as always a fight. One day she gave up and told her son he was on his own, just as he had wanted. As a result, her son went into his room, took off his insulin pump, and said that since his mother didn't care, he didn't care. Chelsea then described her son's self destructive behavior of eating without giving insulin and not testing his blood. She was understandably distraught as she related:

> He's *killing* himself. And he *is*. (Chelsea, p. 3, lines 5–19)

The major themes are present in this situation; Chelsea did not feel as though her son was healthy, so she intervened and reduced his amount of privacy in attempts to help control his health. Her son, wanting freedom and privacy, resented the intrusions and rebelled against her. It is important to note, however, that the role of a parent was still crucial in the transition of diabetes care. Chelsea's son mentioned that he did not care about his disease because his mother did not care.

Chelsea's statement that her son was "killing himself" was not overly dramatic. Even if a child experiences poor metabolic control for a few months, complications from that failure can last a lifetime. As a result of consistently high blood glucose levels, vascular complications, retinopathy, neuropathy, blindness, and kidney damage can occur (Cerreto & Travis, 1984; Gage et al., 2004; Wennick & Hallstrom, 2006). For the health of the teenager, both during adolescence and throughout life, boundary turbulence and diabetes disclosures between parents and children need to be addressed as part of the diabetes treatment process.

Conclusion

This study provides an important step in learning more about the role that privacy plays in the transition of diabetes care from parent to child. The overarching themes of this study illustrate that parents still need to know diabetes information, while adolescents still need to feel ownership and responsibility for their own diabetes information. Both parents and teenagers seemed to agree that diabetes disclosures between parents and children were important in maintaining good metabolic control for the teenager and comfort for the parent. Disclosure situations were the most effective when the adolescent had control over how and when diabetes information was discussed. In this way, the privacy needs of both teenagers and their parents are met.

This study focused on the relationship between teenagers with diabetes and their parents, but it can be useful when examining other teenager–parent relationships. Although diabetes is not a privacy issue in most families, there are other issues that are problematic in reference to disclosure. Parents and teenagers might have difficulty negotiating what the teen needs to tell the parent and areas in which the teen can maintain privacy. The overarching themes of this study could be applied with other topics where parents and teenagers negotiate about what information is required for comfort for the parents but also allows the teenager privacy.

Discussion Questions

1. Adolescence is typically a time when parents and children clash about issues of privacy and independence. Reflecting on your own experiences, what areas or topics typically cause the most boundary turbulence? How was that turbulence handled or resolved?
2. What (and how) might other chronic illnesses, disabilities, handicaps, or physical limitations impact the privacy and independence between parents and their adolescent children?
3. After reading this chapter, what advice would you give to a parent and his or her teenager who are struggling with privacy issues? Be creative with your ideas and suggestions.

4. In addition to diabetes or another chronic illness, what factors might affect the satisfaction a parent and child experience about privacy and independence during adolescence?
5. At what other times of life might an individual struggle with issues of privacy with families or relational partners?

References

Cerreto, M. C., & Travis, L. B. (1984). Implications of psychological and family factors in the treatment of diabetes. *Pediatric Clinics of North America, 31,* 689–709.

Gage, H., Hampson, S., Skinner, T., Hart, J., Storey, L., Foxcroft, D., et al. (2004). Educational and psychosocial programmes for adolescents with diabetes: Approaches, outcomes, and cost-effectiveness. *Patient Education and Counseling, 53,* 333–346.

Hanberger, L., Ludvigsson, J., & Nordfelt, S. (2006). Quality of care from the patient's perspective in pediatric diabetes care. *Diabetes Research and Clinical Practice, 72,* 197–205.

Hanna, K., & Guthrie, D. (2001). Parents' and adolescents' perceptions of helpful and nonhelpful support for adolescents' assumption of diabetes management responsibility.*Issues in Comprehensive Pediatric Nursing, 24,* 209–223.

Hanna, K., & Guthrie, D. (2000a). Adolescents' perceived benefits and barriers related to diabetes self-management, part 1. *Issues in Comprehensive Pediatric Nursing, 23,* 165–174.

Hanna, K., & Guthrie, D. (2000b). Parents' perceived benefits and barriers related of adolescents' diabetes self-management, part 2. *Issues in Comprehensive Pediatric Nursing, 23,* 193–202.

Hutchinson, J. W., & Stafford, E. M. (2005). Changing parental opinions about teen privacy through education. *Pediatrics, 116*(4), 966–971. http://www.ncbi.nlm.nih.gov/pubmed/16199709

Milnitsky-Sapiro, C. (2006). Brazilian adolescents/conceptions of autonomy and parental authority. *Cognitive Development, 21,* 317–331.

Morr-Serewicz, M. C., Dickson, F., Morrison, J., & Poole, L. (2007). Family privacy orientation relational maintenance, and family satisfaction in young adults' family relationships. *Journal of Family Communication, 7,* 1–20.

Owen, W. (1984). Interpretive themes in relational communication. *Quarterly Journal of Speech, 70,* 274–287.

Petronio, S. (2002). *Boundary of privacy: Dialectics of disclosure.* New York: State University of New York Press.

Schilling, L., Grey, M., & Knafl, K. (2002). The concept of self-management of type 1 diabetes in children and adolescents: An evolutionary concept analysis. *Journal of Advanced Nursing, 37,* 87–99.

Valenti, J. (2007) *Transitioning control: Privacy boundary management between adolescents with diabetes and their parents.* Unpublished manuscript.

Wennick, A., & Hallstrom, I. (2006). Swedish families' lived experiences when a child is first diagnosed as having insulin-dependent diabetes mellitus: An ongoing learning process. *Journal of Family Nursing, 12,* 368–389.

Chapter 27

Defining Caregiving Relationships: Using Intergenerational Ambivalence Theory to Explore Burden Among Racial and Ethnic Groups

Angela C. Henderson

Specific Aims and Purpose

The National Alliance for Caregiving (2009) estimates that currently there are at least 43.5 million adult caregivers, equivalent to 19% of all adults, who provide unpaid care to an older adult family member or friend. In addition, during the last few decades, several social and demographic trends have redefined the caregiving roles of middle-aged adults. The rising costs of health care, the increased longevity of the elderly and subsequent growth of the elderly population, changes in the levels and timing of fertility, and the increase in women's labor force participation have created unprecedented demands on the caregiving population (Cherlin, 2010). These trends will require caregivers to occupy multiple roles at the same time, such as being a multigenerational caregiver (caring for both children *and* older adults), holding a career, and maintaining a healthy marriage. While past research has examined the effects of multiple roles on caregivers' well-being (Dautzenberg et al., 2000; Dunham & Dietz, 2003; Edwards et al., 2001; Rozario, Hinterlong, & Morrow-Howell, 2004; Voydanoff & Donnelly, 1999), results are somewhat conflicting as to whether these additional responsibilities harm or enhance caregivers' lives. This project attempts to dissect the conflicting results about burden and caregiving using the framework of intergenerational ambivalence theory (IGA) (Luescher & Pillemer, 1998). This framework is useful because it takes into account the context of the relationship, the conflicting feelings toward the care receiver, and the racial, ethnic, and cultural constraints surrounding the caregiving relationship. Indeed, most research in this area has reported that patterns of perceived burden are highly dependent on the racial and cultural background of the family and the relationship of the caregiver to the care receiver. Thus, it is imperative to explore how burden varies across these structural and contextual characteristics. The purpose of this research is to examine definitions of caregiving relationships based on race and ethnicity, gender, and culture.

Theoretical Framework

The main premise of this research depends on the racial and ethnic cultural backgrounds of caregivers, giving weight to how individual caregivers define burden, whether they perceive burden, and why or why not. Because of the complexities associated with caregiving for a loved one, it is important to take into account the unique perspective of the caregiver as well as provide a theoretical model for understanding how and why they became the caregiver and their feelings toward that relationship. IGA (Luescher & Pillemer, 1998) stresses the different experiences of each respondent and how his or her perceptions and viewpoints are colored by culture, expectations, and personal experience. This will allow the project to take into account specific cultural propositions about caregiving that may depend on race and ethnicity.

Luescher and Pillemer (1998) introduced IGA theory into gerontological study by suggesting that family members can feel hate and love for a family member at the same time, especially in a caregiving relationship. Thus, concomitant feelings of duty, love, and obligation toward caring for older adults can exist in caregiving relationships. This theory considers both individual- and the structural-level feelings of ambivalence, suggesting that family members experience contradictions in relationships that cannot be reconciled. This may include personal feelings of love and concern that occur on the individual level and the obligations of a career and other nuclear family duties that occur on a social-structural level. Ambivalence theorists maintain that the theoretical concepts derive out of a weakened set of social norms for how to deal with intergenerational conflicts such as caregiving needs. This leaves family members feeling a sense of fragmentation and uncertainty regarding how social relations should be conducted.

This model is very appropriate for studying caregiving relationships because it requires using in-depth interviewing and other qualitative techniques in order to capture the existence of a conflictual ambivalent feeling. While scholars in this area maintain that ambivalence can be measured on both quantitative and qualitative levels, quantitative research is challenging because the researcher must be able to identify ambivalent feelings—even if respondents are not consciously aware of them. Therefore, this theoretical model is very appropriate for qualitative work because it allows for in-depth discussion and requires the researcher to identify ambivalent feelings when respondents cannot. Consequently, the possibility of ambivalent feelings surfacing hinges on three factors: (a) the discussion of the caregiving dyad (interview), (b) the researcher's perception and analysis of the relationship (interview/transcriptions), and (c) the cultural norms of the racial and ethnic group being studied. It is well known that perceptions of familial obligation vary significantly by race and ethnicity—one group may or may not readily admit negative feelings towards their family members. Each participant will bring different cultural norms, background, and expectations to the interview. As a result, this theory is highly appropriate for this research because it will allow us to tap into those unique perceptions and feelings.

Depending on these distinctive experiences, perceptions and responsibilities of adult children may reveal the pressures of having to raise their own children at older ages, help out with their own aging parents, and maintain a successful career in order to support family needs. This taps into the other aim of this research—identifying disadvantage among those who do not have equal access to resources. We already know that the majority of caregivers are women (Call, Finch, Huck, & Kane, 1999), but we also must take into account the socioeconomic and racial/ethnic differences that may be influencing these caregiving relationships as well. Aside from race and ethnicity, this research will also examine gender differences in caregiving relationships. Taken together, IGA theory provides a very useful framework within which we can examine the issues that this research hinges on. Those issues include but are not limited to the fact that (a) women leave the workforce more often than men to take on caregiving responsibilities (in addition to child care responsibilities), (b) women are "expected" to be the carers in the family, (c) women are disproportionately represented in low-wage jobs, and (d) racial and ethnic minority groups are socioeconomically disadvantaged to whites *and* are much more likely to have nontraditional, extended kin family networks. Each of these reasons lends itself to an in-depth examination of which caregivers are experiencing burden (male or female, black/white/Hispanic) and how that definition is related to socioeconomic status, cultural background, and social inequalities. Indeed, a qualitative approach is necessary to examine these patterns in order to understand whether it is even necessary to study "burden" among caregivers.

Literature Review

Much of the literature on caregiving suggests that burden is a preexisting condition that all caregivers experience and examines differences in burden among racial and ethnic groups (Cox, 1999; Dilworth-Andersen, Williams, & Cooper, 1999; Farran, Miller, Kaufman, & Davis, 1997; Fredman, Daly, & Lazur, 1995; Hennessy & John, 1996; Wood & Parham, 1990; Young & Kahana, 1995). In addition, research has been restricted to single-generation caregivers or white-only or elite samples, such as those on Medicare (Avioli, 1989; Call et al., 1999; Walker, Pratt, Shinn, & Jones, 1990).

Because few studies have systematically examined multigenerational caregivers, much less racial differences within this group, we know relatively little about how burden is perceived or experienced in this population. The American Association of Retired Persons (AARP, 2001) estimates that one-fifth (22%) of adults in this age-group are "caught in the middle" of caring for both their own children as well as elder relatives. Studies have also shown that the makeup of multigenerational caregivers is strikingly segregated: only 19% of whites are multigenerational caregivers, compared to 28% of African Americans, 34% of Hispanics, and 42% of Asian Americans (AARP, 2001). In addition, the vast majority (77%) of caregivers are female (Call et al., 1999). Sociological research has revealed that the socialization of women to be more expressive and to feel obligated to give care to older parents or spouses has contributed to the higher number of women in the caregiving role (Walker, 1992). Structurally, paid women are able to leave the labor force to care for family members at a lower cost to their families, thus making them more "available" to do caregiving when needed (Connidis 2001; Walker, 1992). Demographically, age stratification also plays a role in the number of female caregivers—women have lower mortality rates, marry men who are older than they are, and, because health problems increase with age, are much more likely to be caring for their older spouse (Walker, 1992). Thus, women's experiences are very central to the study of multigenerational caregiving.

While these demographics suggest that caregiving is primarily "women's work," this population is very diverse and experiences burden, family-related stress, and caregiving responsibilities very differently. For instance, caring for one's parents or in-laws is a cultural norm for Asian Americans (AARP, 2001), which helps explain the high incidence of multigenerational caregivers. This group is also more likely to have the smallest social support system yet reports the lowest burden when it comes to caring for older adults. Thus, a unique relationship between cultural expectations, social support, and low levels of burden exists among Asian Americans. Multigenerational African American caregivers, on the other hand, are the most likely to have extended social support systems, yet they also report being overwhelmed by a sense of family responsibility. Examining racial and ethnic differences is crucial in understanding multigenerational caregiving.

Caregiving and Burden—Racial Differences?

Few studies have systematically examined race and caregiving. This is critical because, traditionally, kinship ties among African Americans—indicated by joint residency, visiting, and the exchange of mutual aid among kin—are much stronger than they are for whites (Hays & Mindel, 1973; Ladner, 1998). African Americans of all ages are more likely than whites to live in an extended family household (Hofferth, 1984) and also demonstrate a greater reliance on family than on formal care, as shown by lower formal service utilization (Mindel & Wright, 1982) and greater social support networks than whites (Haley et al., 1995). In addition, Asian, Hispanic, and African Americans are traditionally more likely than whites to feel that children should help their older parents, and reciprocal obligations of help from kin are more salient among these racial and ethnic groups (AARP, 2001; Mutran, 1985).

In addition to these culturally embedded tendencies to have closer kinship relationships than whites, racial and ethnic minority groups have also been shown to experience different gender norms than whites. What has been defined as an "early" transition for female adolescents into parenthood is considered to be on-time behavior for some cultures (Hamburg, 1986). Burton (1996) examined African American families' transition into parenthood and found that this group experiences much earlier entry into parenthood than whites. This research also suggests that multigenerational caregiving is not only more common among African American families but also on the verge of becoming an *expected* behavior for girls in late adolescence. Burton (1996) also found that middle-aged African American mothers are caring not only for their own parents and children but for their grandchildren as well.

This brings our attention to another dimension of multigenerational caregiving. In another study of caregiver effort and satisfaction, Lawton, Rajagopal, Brody, and Kleban (1992) report that African American caregivers expressed greater caregiving satisfaction and less burden, depression, and perceived intrusion than whites. Greater caregiver effort among African Americans was associated with more satisfaction, which confirmed the researchers' hypothesis of a "parallel channel" relationship: Positive affect was differentially affected by satisfactions.

Other research examining both African American and white caregivers of family elders has revealed a few differences in their reported stress outcomes. Morycz, Malloy, Bozich, and Martz (1987) found that although both groups of caregivers reported similar stress levels, predictors of strain differed. For African American caregiving women, strain was related to economic stability, and for white caregiving women, strain was related to additional responsibility. This makes sense because we know that African Americans as well as Hispanic Americans are socioeconomically disadvantaged in comparison to whites (Lima & Allen, 2001). Thus, if they are more likely to be members of multigenerational households and disadvantaged economically, the logical conclusion might be that they experience more burden than white caregivers.

However, while a few studies report that African Americans perceive economic strain as their main source of "stress" in caregiving for two generations, this conclusion is not upheld in the literature (AARP, 2001). Most minority groups perceive caregiving as a natural part of life, while white caregivers are more likely to report that they feel burdened because of the caregiving tasks (Haley et al., 1995). These differences are vital when examining multigenerational caregivers, who tend to have lower levels of education and income than their single-generation caregiving counterparts (AARP, 2001). Research also suggests that socioeconomic and racial/ethnic minority status may contribute to role overload and affect social relationships in many ways, and cultural norms and values can either complicate or mitigate this strain (Burnette, 1999).

This generates several research questions: (a) Who is more likely to be a multigenerational carer—white, Hispanic, or African Americans? (b) Do racial and ethnic minority groups define their caregiving relationships as burdensome (i.e., do they use the term "burden")? (c) How do racial and ethnic minority groups *define* disadvantage (i.e., are there socioeconomic difficulties or other barriers to using formal caregiving services)? (d) Does gender play a role in how burden is defined by caregivers?

The present research will address these issues, identifying how and why caregivers report feeling "burdened" by the caregiving relationship, including differences between men and women as well as between Hispanic, white, and African Americans.

Research Design and Sample

This project utilized in-depth interviews with six caregivers in West Texas and eastern New Mexico cities. Caregivers were included in the sample if they were caring or had cared for a family member either inside the home or if they spent a considerable amount of time caring for and visiting the family member in a formal setting. This study was not limited to multigenerational caregivers but instead recruited all caregivers and then explored differences between those who were multigenerational carers and those who were not.

Respondents were recruited in a variety of ways. Some were found through contacts with adult college students in sociology classes at a local university, through personal contacts in the community with the principal investigator, and through snowballing techniques. In order to fairly compare the three groups, an even number of caregivers from each racial and ethnic group was recruited, yet due to an illness, only one Hispanic caregiver was interviewed, along with two African American and three white caregivers. Each respondent was contacted over the telephone and asked for an interview.

The total sample consisted of four female caregivers and one male caregiver. The mean caregiver age was 51. The caregivers had a variety of occupations, including a substitute teacher, school secretary, two office managers, and one retired caregiver. Respondents were interviewed at a variety of stages in their caregiving careers. At the time of the interview, two of the care recipients were receiving care informally in the caregivers' homes, one was in a nursing home, and two were deceased. Three of the respondents were married, one was widowed, and one was single. Four of the five caregivers were providing multigenerational care during their time as a caregiver. The caregivers were providing care to a wide range of family members; two of the caregivers were providing care for their mothers, one for her grandmother, one for her father, and one for her mother-in-law. The health problems of the care receivers also varied significantly, including dementia, prostate cancer, lung disease, diabetes and heart failure, and a brain aneurysm.

The primary investigator conducted semistructured interviews, usually in a restaurant or coffee shop suggested by the caregiver. Interviews were audio recorded and usually lasted about 1 hour. Open-ended questions were asked about the entire caregiving career on a variety of topics, including how the caregiver defined the relationship; how they saw their role as a caregiver; the ways in which they contributed to the care receiver's well-being emotionally, psychologically, and financially; feelings of reciprocity; and decisions about formal care. Each of the interviews was transcribed for analysis, which involved identifying how each caregiver told his or her individual story, with specific attention paid to emerging patterns associated with IGA theory (i.e., how caregiving relationships are defined, how definitions of caregiving duties compare between racial/ethnic groups in relation to reported "burden," and so on). The three racial groups were also compared to one another.

Results

Two-thirds of the caregivers interviewed were providing multigenerational care, three of them white women and one a Hispanic American woman. However, the multigenerational caregivers discussed the extra responsibilities differently—two of the caregivers reported having "extra help" because of the children in the household, and one reported the additional responsibilities as burdensome. However, the caregiver who did report extra burden appeared to be involved in especially taxing caregiving situations, whereas the others reported a more positive relationship with the care receiver overall. One multigenerational caregiver, a white woman caring for her father, repeatedly used the pronoun "we" instead of "I" to describe the caregiving tasks:

> We were caregivers for about a year, but for the most part, that only involved doctor appointments, and . . . we would all just help out with household chores . . . we made sure he had transportation whenever he needed it . . . there were also times when we would bring him home and have him stay for a few days if he was really having bad days and nights . . . then we would take him back to his apartment and . . . stay there with him . . . Edward [caregiver's husband] always stopped by his apartment on his way home from work and he would have a cocktail with him and watch the news . . . Robert [care receiver] used to love that . . . they both did.

This caregiver went on to describe how her husband and children would take turns spending time with him during the day and how she would split the nights with her husband. She describes how they were a "tremendous support during his last days, both to him and me."

Another multigenerational caregiver, a Hispanic woman, reported similar feelings about her husband's emotional support as well as their help visiting the care receiver, her mother, in the nursing home:

> My husband has been amazing, he's always asking "how's your mom?" and if I'm going to be home late, he calls me and asks me if he wants to leave some dinner for me, and he makes dinner if I won't be there, and he's just been so supportive . . .

This caregiver also commented on how her teenage daughter was helpful in providing emotional support to the care receiver as well:

> she's real close to her grandma . . . she was volunteering at the church the other day and she bought some stuff, . . . from the little church store, and she said 'you're going to have to take this to grandma, take this to her because I'm not going to be able to go.

This caregiver and the one above attributed their positive situations to additional social support, which was not available to the other multigenerational caregiver. The final multigenerational caregiver, a white woman caring for her mother-in-law, described the situation very differently; she laments job opportunities that she could have taken had she not become a caregiver; the difficulties of juggling a teenage son; her husband, who traveled often with his job; and her own health issues:

> I never actually quit work to take care of David's mother. . . . I was working the two positions at the office, having a teenager at home, dealing with my mother's two hip replacements and heart conditions . . . dealing with my own health issues that included not being able to have children, a hysterectomy, and related chemical imbalances and depression.

In addition, this caregiver described a time when she had her own mother on one floor in the hospital, and her husband's mother on a different floor. She explained how difficult this was, given that her husband traveled three out of four weeks every month.

This contributed to the very taxing day-to-day strains of providing for her family and the adjustments she had to make just to survive:

> And at one point I put her on Meals on Wheels because . . . I just . . . I just . . . I was barely cooking for us, much less anybody else.

Thus, "burden" is very relevant for multigenerational caregivers who lack additional social support.

Themes

Several other themes emerged from these data that supported IGA theory. The four most common themes that were revealed in these data were the presence of (a) a love/hate relationship; (b) role conflict from other obligations, such as children, marriage, or career; (c) difficulty making decisions about the care receiver's care; and (d) the closer the relationship between the caregiver and care receiver, the easier it was to sacrifice time and effort to provide the care. Each of these themes is described below.

Love/Hate relationship: All but one caregiver described the relationship with the care receiver as complex, mainly because the caregiver cared deeply for the care receiver and it was a struggle to watch their health decline. In addition, each mentioned that the effort to provide care became overwhelming at times; one of them stated that being a caregiver requires compassion and patience. The caregivers hated having to watch their loved ones decline but were also glad to be able to do it. One caregiver talked about the difficulty of leaving the role of "daughter" to become the role of "nurse":

> At that point, it was easier for me to see him more as a patient and not as my father. I had to detach my emotional feelings as a daughter and become more of a nurse in order to be able to fully care for him. . . . He even started calling me "Nurse Ann" . . . [laughs]

This caregiver goes on to say that playing the role of nurse actually helped her detach herself from the situation, but she still struggled with the guilt associated with doing so:

> I was . . . more able to deal with my dad's situation if I detached myself emotionally. . . . There still are times that I wonder if I did the right thing. . . we still hugged and kissed him and told him we loved him, but . . . I don't know . . . I may have let him down by not being more of his daughter at that time.

Three of the other caregivers described similar situations wherein her relationship with the care receiver suddenly changed when they became the primary caregiver. The white caregiver who provided care for her mother-in-law recalls how close they both were until she became the primary caregiver and her mother was hospitalized:

> I ended up having to clean her after she would have an accident in bed, . . ., and after that . . . and I think I kind of resented it, and it wasn't even her fault. But when the tables turned and I became a true . . . caretaker . . . she became dependent on me . . . our relationship kinda changed.

Another caregiver, an African American woman, talked about how her relationship with her grandmother (the care receiver) changed because her grandmother still saw her as a child. This woman described herself as being a "difficult" child, and her grandmother often brought up things that she used to do as a teenager that made her feel guilty. She says,

> To her, I'm still more or less a teenager, so . . . it's like . . . a lot of the things I had to deal with my own self because the memories would sometimes come back to her, and . . . to hear her just sitting alone and talking about things . . . about me, that I have chose to forget . . .

This caregiver described how she would be brought back to the times she was a teenager, which was difficult for her. She described going to her room to pray, thinking, "she can't help herself, she can't help herself," and I think that's the key to really being a caretaker . . . is understanding whatever is going on, the person can't help themselves."

One caregiver in this study, an African American male caring for his mother, did not describe his relationship with his mother in a negative way. He did have significantly more social support than other caregivers in the sample, utilizing help from his sister, his 24-year-old nephew who spent 6 to 7 hours a day with the care receiver, and other family members. When asked whether he could be a caregiver without all that extra help, he admits that the role might become a burden if he were ever to have to care for her by himself:

> It would be a lot harder [if my sister and nephew weren't around to help]. Yeah, a lot harder. I mean . . . I've often thought about what would I do if, you know, because you know, there are no guarantees.

He continues on to say that he would give it his "all" if he had to take full responsibility for his mother, but clearly felt torn:

> How am I going to handle this, if I'm left with the burden . . . left with the . . . responsibility, rather than a burden, of caring for my mother?

It is telling that this caregiver used the term "burden" but corrected himself because he did not want to portray the situation as burdensome. However, even he admits that social support is pertinent in maintaining a positive outlook on the caregiving bond.

Role conflict: Two of the caregivers also discussed how the caregiving role affected other areas of their lives—particularly career and child rearing. Not surprisingly, the caregivers who brought up role conflict were those multigenerational between caring for older adults as well as children. The multigenerational Hispanic caregiver talks about how her job has been very flexible to allow her to spend time during the day with her mother. She admits that juggling children, a full-time job, and her marriage is hard, and she has days where she does not want to go see her mother in the nursing home.

The white multigenerational woman caring for her mother-in-law talks about managing the conflicting roles of mother, wife, and caregiver while holding a career and maintaining her own health. On top of managing these roles, this caregiver experienced discrimination as a female caregiver. When she tried to recruit her husband to go along with her to doctor's appointments and visit his mother in the nursing home, the care receiver got upset:

> I would just make him [go], and she didn't like that at all . . . because he was missing his work time, and she would just throw a fit when I would have him come and help me . . . she didn't want him to have to miss work . . . and her doctor's appointments, we always had to sit there for 2 to 3 hours.

Difficulty making decisions: Another aspect of IGA theory, difficulty making decisions, surfaced in all the caregiving relationships. The African American male caregiver stressed how difficult it was taking the doctor's advice to put his mother in a nursing home. He described the year while he and his family were visiting her daily as very difficult not only on himself but also on his sister because she and their mother "were like sisters." Thus, the decision to pull their mother out of the nursing home was difficult because of what they were seeing their mother go through in the nursing home. They wanted to be able to offer her the care she needed at home, but they also needed to make major renovations to the house where she would be living:

> the first thing . . . I will never forget . . . the first thing I bought for that room . . . was a piece of linoleum because we agreed that linoleum would be the thing to put on the floor . . . rather than re-carpet it b/c she urinates a lot.

In addition, this caregiver described that after he got his first check from social security, he bought her a television and a stereo system because he knew his mother enjoyed those things. His sister and her husband paid to have the living room finished, and so, together, they did what they could to get her house ready for her to come home. The way in which he described these efforts was full of care and concern for doing the best thing for his mother:

> I can't even begin to tell you . . . that was just our way to show her gratitude . . . it wasn't . . . it wasn't . . . a whole lot, but it was things I thought were necessary to get things off the ground.

While it was financially taxing for the family to get preparations made to bring their mother home, they also knew that she belonged at home:

> She was just not getting the one-on-one [in the nursing home], and I know the nursing home is not designed to give every person out there the one-on-one . . . and I just feel so much at ease. . . I just found myself just crying . . . and . . . [gets distant] . . . for the year that she was gone.

Another caregiver doing multigenerational work, a white female, talked about how she wondered if she was "doing right" by her father by not putting him in a nursing home, which was what he had wanted. He had not wanted to "burden" his family, but his daughter talked about how she loved him too much to put him in a home. She said,

> I wonder now, if I may have given my dad the opportunity to just give up at that point. . . . When the doctor told him that he wasn't going to admit him to a home, my dad's shoulders

> just drooped and he looked as if he was gonna cry . . . after that, my dad's personality
> changed and he went downhill fast.

She lamented about whether or not she "did things correctly", and hoped that by *not* putting him in a nursing home, she encouraged him to give up, because she felt that deep down, he didn't want to burden her:

> My only concern is that my dad may have given up too early. . . . I guess in that sense, I
> was thinking as a daughter who loved her father and didn't want anyone else to take care of
> him but us, his family. But in his heart, he didn't want us to see him go through the changes
> that he knew he would be going through.

The other white caregiver was more certain of the decision she made to stop providing primary care because it was too hard on her. She describes the process that she went through after being told by the physician that if she admitted her mother-in-law to a nursing home, "it'll kill her":

> [near the end] I finally told the family that I could not do any more . . . and [my husband]
> had told me several years before . . . I had wanted to put her in a nursing home, because I
> was running out of gas, and he said "It'll kill her" and I believed him . . .

After years of caregiving for her mother-in-law, the home health care nurse finally suggested that the caregiver admit the care receiver to the nursing home because she was getting even too difficult for the nurse to manage.

For the African American caregiver with her children grown, she says the burden of caring for her grandmother "fell on" her, and she wonders about her life before she had to move in with her grandmother and care for her:

> I have to admit,. . . I go through, and think . . . I gave up my job, everything, . . . to come
> here. And sometimes I think she thinks that she's doing me a favor by letting me live with
> her, and I have to accept that.

This caregiver went on to say she felt like she was on a mission, completing a "task" she had been assigned, and she wanted to do the best job she was able to:

> I try to do it well, and to the best of my ability, and like I said, I do have to deal with my
> own feelings and emotions and things like that. I can't fault her for it.

The other caregiver, a Hispanic woman, also discussed difficulty making decisions about her mother's care, but because of the seriousness of her mother's condition (a brain aneurysm), she felt she had little choice in admitting her to a nursing home, where she "would receive the proper care."

Closeness of relationship: Several caregivers discussed the closeness of the relationship as a major part of the caregiving relationship with the exception of the caregiver who took care of her mother-in-law. One caregiver in particular, the multigenerational Hispanic woman, discussed how she loves her caregiving duties and has always felt very close to her mother yet is not sure if she could provide care for her in-laws if she were asked to:

> I don't know that I would do for my mother-in-law what I do for my mother . . . it scares
> me . . . my mother's so . . . they're like night and day, and I don't know that I could take
> care of my mother-in-law . . . she's so cranky!

Similarly, the white multigenerational caregiver who provided care for her mother-in-law often has had to provide informal care for her mother, which she reported having enjoyed very much because she describes the relationship as much closer and more pleasant than with her mother-in-law.

The African American male caregiver described similar feelings for his mother, saying that his day "wouldn't feel complete" without seeing his mother every single day:

> There's not a morning that God doesn't wake me up and I don't go over there, I'm headed that way, to my mother's house . . . because uh, it's just that it's become a ritual, or a habit. That I just . . . I just . . . I don't feel like my day is full unless I go over there and see her.

Discussion and Conclusions

The purpose of this research was to examine whether racial, ethnic, or gender differences existed among caregivers who experience intergenerational ambivalence—having conflicting feelings about the responsibility of caring for an aging loved one. This research also highlighted differences experienced by multigenerational caregivers or those with multigenerational caregiving duties.

First, while no racial differences emerged in terms of reported burden, results indicate that racial differences do exist among caregivers yet operate along different pathways. For the caregivers in this study, religion and spirituality were discussed only by African American caregivers in light of their caregiving duties as well as with their coping strategies. Both African American caregivers openly stated the belief that they were providing care for their relatives because God had called them to do so. In addition, the female African American caregiver cited her spirituality and prayer time as a time of coping and healing for her when the caregiving responsibilities were too overwhelming. Neither the Hispanic nor the white caregivers mentioned spirituality when discussing their caregiving duties.

However, this does not mean that spirituality and religion served as a "buffer" for the African American caregivers' tendency to report burden; it may be that the African American caregivers tend to access religion more than the other racial and ethnic groups as a way to cope with the situation. The female African American caregiver was quick to state that her caregiving relationship was very difficult at times, yet she turned to her spirituality in order to cope with the additional strain. Thus, African Americans are not necessarily *less* likely to report burden in caregiving situations; simply stated, they may be more likely to use religion as a way to deal with the situation.

The other caregivers reported using other coping strategies to deal with the caregiving situation, most of which revolved around being able to take a break from the duties once in a while. Indeed, the presence of a support system is imperative to providing caregivers with resources to cope with the relationship on a day-to-day basis. If a caregiver had extra help, he or she was less likely to report feeling overwhelmed by the caregiving duties. Only the caregivers without support reported burden repeatedly in their interviews, which was not tied to race or ethnicity in this study. The absence of an extended social support system seemed to be a recurrent theme for those who tended to report feeling burdened by the caregiving situation.

The four propositions of IGA theory were highly supported by these data. The most notable theme that emerged from these data revolves around the closeness of the relationship. For those caregivers who reported having a close relationship with the care receiver, the relationship was less likely to be perceived as a burden. On the other hand, for those who reported having a strained or somewhat distant relationship with the care receiver, burden was much more likely to surface in the conversation about the relationship. Thus, while no racial differences emerged in this study, it is clear that the social support system and closeness of the relationship serve as very powerful mechanisms that can buffer the "burden" associated with caring for an older family member.

In conclusion, the relationships between race and ethnicity, gender, and definitions of the caregiving bond are very complex. The results support the idea that social support functions for different caregivers in different situations. While the idea that race and ethnicity affect perceived burden is not directly supported, this research revealed different pathways that operate for different racial and ethnic groups, such as the use of religion or spirituality to manage the "burden" of caregiving. In addition, while only a few of the caregivers used the verbatim concept of "burden" in the discussion of caregiving, many of the caregivers still discussed coping mechanisms—such as God, prayer, or social support—to deal with their added responsibilities.

In addition, no gender differences were revealed outright, with the exception that the male caregiver hesitated in using the word "burden" to describe his relationship with his mother. Yet, as mentioned above, he did discuss ways in which he deals with his mother's condition—by using prayer, his faith in God, and his social support system.

Limitations

Because of time constraints, this study is limited in its scope. Only five caregivers were interviewed, and the study area is limited to West Texas. In addition, it is important to note that some of the caregivers may have found it hard to confide about their caregiving "burden" to a young white researcher. In a discussion of qualitative research, DeVault (1999) points out that "outsiders" to research areas and locations may find it hard to "know the nuances" of the target population simply because the researcher is not a part of the everyday activities of that group. Being without the tools to fully understand one's culture may sacrifice the researcher's interpretation as well as the participant's willingness to share.

Again, no striking racial differences were found in this study, which may be due to the small sample size or limited region. In addition, due to an illness during the interview time frame, the second Hispanic caregiver was unable to complete the interview, so there is not an even number of each racial and ethnic group included in the study.

Another limitation of this research is that it is limited to caregivers as opposed to those who chose formal versus informal care for their loved ones. Future research might also address the concerns and viewpoints of those who made the decision to *not* provide informal care at home and compare those decisions to caregivers who are doing work at home. The gender/race/ethnicity interaction may be more robust in such a comparison study.

Future Directions

Overall, this project generates several new research ideas that should be tested. First, how does religion function for African American caregivers? Is it a coping mechanism, or do religious African Americans self-select into caregiving duties? Second, more male caregivers should be interviewed to further test whether gender differences exist in perceived (and willingness to report) burden. Third, how does burden manifest in caregiver's lives? Does role conflict or strain increase or decrease among (a) caregivers with more social support, (b) caregivers who report being religious or spiritual, (c) caregivers with more income, or (d) caregivers with children in the home? Finally, given the frequency that caregivers reported ambivalent feelings toward the caregiving relationship, the concept of ambivalence in intergenerational relations should be studied in more depth. For instance, are the four components of IGA theory causally prior to one another? Is closeness of the relationship tempered by the difficulty making decisions, which results in a love/hate relationship developing? Each of these questions opens new and interesting questions for future research.

Discussion Questions

1. In the last few decades, what social and demographic trends have changed the caregiving roles of middle-aged adults?
2. What four themes were present in all of the caregiving relationships in this study?
3. Name some of the reasons why 77% of caregivers today are female?
4. All the African American and white caregivers reported increased "strain"; however, this extra stress was due to different factors. What was the difference between the causes of the "strain"?
5. Under what conditions were caregivers more likely to describe their caregiving as a "burden"?

References

American Association of Retired Persons. (2001). *In the middle: A report on multicultural boomers coping with family and aging issues*. Washington, DC: Belden Russonello and Stewart.

Avioli, P. S. (1989). The social support functions of siblings in later life. *American Behavioral Scientist, 33*, 45-57.

Burnette, Denise. 1999. Social Relationships of Latino Grandparent Caregivers: A Role Theory Perspective. *The Gerontologist*, 39(1): 49-59.

Burton, L. M. (1996). Age norms, the timing of family role transitions, and intergenerational caregiving among aging African American women. *The Gerontologist, 36,* 199-208.

Call, K. T., Finch, M. A., Huck, S. M., & Kane, R. A. (1999). Caregiver burden from a social exchange perspective: Caring for older people after hospital discharge. *Journal of Marriage and the Family, 61,* 688-699.

Cherlin, A. (2010). Demographic trends in the United States: A review of research in the 2000s. *Journal of Marriage and the Family, 72,* 403-419.

Connidis, I. A. (2001). *Family ties and aging.* Thousand Oaks, CA: Sage.

Cox, C. (1999). Race and caregiving: Patterns of service use by African American and white caregivers of persons with Alzheimer's disease. *Journal of Gerontological Social Work, 32*(2), 241-255.

Dautzenberg, Maaike G. H., Diederiks, Jos P. M., Philipsen, Hans, Stevens, Fred C. J., Tan, Frans, E. S., Vernooij-Dassen, Myrra J. F. J. 2000. The Competing Demands of Paid Work and Parent Care: Middle-Aged Daughters Providing Assistance to Elderly Parents. *Research on Aging,* 22(2): 165-187.

DeVault, M. L. (1999). *Liberating method: Feminism and social research.* Philadelphia: Temple University Press.

Dilworth-Andersen, P., Williams, S., & Cooper, T. (1999). The contexts of experiencing emotional distress among family caregivers to elderly African Americans. *Family Relations, 48,* 391-397.

Dunham, Charlotte Chorn and Bernadette E. Dietz. 2003. ""If I'm Not Allowed to Put My Family First": Challenges Experienced by Women who are Caregiving for Family Members with Dementia." *Journal of Women and Aging,* vol.15, #1.

Edwards, A. B., Zarit, S. H., Stephens, M. A. P. & Towensen, A. (2002). Employed family caregivers of cognitively impaired elderly: An examination of role strain and depressive symptoms. *Aging & Mental Health*, 6(1), 55-61.

Farran, C. J., Miller, B. H., Kaufman, J. E., & Davis, L. (1997). Race, finding meaning, and caregiver distress. *Journal of Aging and Health, 9,* 316-333.

Fredman, L., Daly, M. P., & Lazur, A. M. (1995). Burden among white and black caregivers to elderly adults. *Journal of Gerontology: Social Sciences, 50B,* S110-S118.

Haley, W. E., West, C. A. C., Wadley, V. G., Ford, G. R., White, F. A., Barrett, J. J., et al. (1995). Psychological, social, and health impact of caregiving: A comparison of black and white family dementia family caregivers and noncaregivers. *Psychology and Aging, 10,* 540-552.

Hamburg, B. A. (1986). Subsets of adolescent mothers: Developmental, biomedical, and psychosocial issues. In J. Lancaster & B. Hamburg (Eds.), *School-age pregnancy and parenthood* (pp. 115-145). New York: Aldine de Gruyter.

Hays, W. C., & Mindel, C. H. (1973). Extended kinship relations in black and white families. *Journal of Marriage and the Family, 35,* 51-57.

Hennessy, C. H., & John, R. (1996). American Indian family caregivers' perceptions of burden and needed support services. *Journal of Applied Gerontology, 15,* 275-293.

Hofferth, S. L. (1984). Kin networks, race, and family structure. *Journal of Marriage and the Family, 46,* 791-806.

Ladner, J. A. (1998). *The ties that bind: Timeless values for African American families.* New York: Wiley.

Lawton, M. P., Rajagopal, D., Brody, E., & Kleban, M. H. (1992). The dynamics of caregiving for a demented elder among black and white families. *Journal of Gerontology, 47,* S156-S164.

Lima, J. C., & Allen, S. M. (2001). targeting risk for unmet need: Not enough help versus no help at all. *Journal of Gerontology, 56B*(5), S302-S310.

Luescher, K., & Pillemer, K. (1998). Intergenerational ambivalence: A new approach to the study of parent-child relations in later life. *Journal of Marriage and the Family, 60,* 413-425.

Mindel, C. H., & Wright, R., Jr. (1982). The use of social services by black and white elderly: The role of social support systems. *Journal of Gerontological Social Work, 4*(3-4), 107-125.

Morycz, R. K., Malloy, J., Bozich, M., & Martz, P. (1987). Racial differences in family burden: Clinical implications for social work. *Journal of Gerontological Social Work, 10,* 133-154.

Mutran, E. (1985). Intergenerational family support among African Americans and whites: Response to culture or socioeconomic differences. *Journal of Gerontology, 40,* 382-389.

National Alliance for Caregiving. (2009). Caregiving in the U.S.: A focused look at those caring for someone age 50 or older. http://assets.aarp.org/rgcenter/il/caregiving_09_es50.pdf

Rozario, Philip A., Nancy Morrow-Howell, & James E. Hinterlong (2004). Role Enhancement or Role Strain: Examining the Impact of Multiple Roles on Family Caregivers. *Research On Aging, 26* (4), 413-428.

Voydanoff, P., & Donnelly, B. W. (1999). Multiple roles and psychological distress: The intersection of the paid worker, spouse, and parent roles with the role of the adult child. *Journal of Marriage and the Family, 61,* 725-738.

Walker, A. (1992). Conceptual perspectives on gender and family caregiving. In J. Dwyer & R. T. Coward (Eds.), *Gender, families, and elder care* (pp. 34-46). Newbury Park, CA: Sage.

Walker, A. J., Pratt, C. C., Shinn, H., & Jones, L. L. (1990). Motives for parental caregiving and relationship quality. *Family Relations, 39,* 51-56.

Wood, J. B., & Parham, I. A. (1990). Coping with perceived burden: Ethnic and cultural issues in Alzheimer's family caregiving. *Journal of Applied Gerontology, 9,* 325-339.

Young, R. F., & Kahana, E. (1995). The context of caregiving and well-being outcomes among African American and Caucasian Americans. *The Gerontologist, 35,* 225-232.

Implications of Family Communication on Nutritional Health and Obesity of Children

Wanda Koszewski

There was a saying that families who eat together stay together. There is some truth to that saying, at least when it comes to nutrition. Research has shown that families who eat together do have a higher nutritional quality of a diet than do families who do not. Hammons and Fiese (2011) found that sharing more than three family mealtimes per week was beneficial. The benefits they reported included a reduction in overweight, eating unhealthy foods, disordered eating, and an increase in eating healthy foods. What is the family meal? According to Corbin (2008), the family meal is "a place for shared social interaction, a chance to learn and teach, a time to explore food, and a place to build family unity" (p. 1).

Prior to the 1960s, the typical evening included time set aside for a family meal. This daily ritual, then considered essential time for the family to meet together consistently each evening to share a home-cooked meal, unfortunately succumbed to the busy and hectic lifestyle of modern America (Cinotto, 2006). Now there are basketball practices, dance lessons, extensive hours at the office trying to meet deadlines, increasing numbers of single-parent families, and more women working outside the home all acting as deterrents to families sitting down together to share a meal on a daily basis (Cinotto, 2006; Patrick & Nicklas, 2005; Story, Neumark-Sztainer, & French, 2002). There is reason to encourage families to sit down together for meals. Studies have shown the value of family meals in a wide variety of different aspects of health. It has been found that family meal frequency is inversely related to many different high-risk behaviors, such as substance abuse, sexual activity, depression or suicide, antisocial behaviors, violence, school problems, eating disorders, and the initiation of alcohol consumption at a young age (Eisenberg, Neumark-Sztainer, Fulkerson, & Story, 2008; Neumark-Sztainer, Eisenberg, Fulkerson, Story, & Larson, 2008; Fisher, Miles, Austin, Camargo, & Colditz, 2007; Fulkerson et al., 2006). Increased frequency of family dinner corresponds to higher grade-point averages, commitment to learning, positive values, social competencies, and positive identity (Eisenberg, Olson, Neumark-Sztainer, Story, & Bearinger, 2004; Fulkerson et al., 2006).

Studies have shown that family mealtimes do in fact impact the nutritional intake of the children in the family. Children whose families eat meals together in the home more frequently consume more grain, fruit, vegetables, fiber, and several beneficial vitamins and minerals, including calcium, folate, iron, and vitamins A, C, E, B_6, and B_{12}. They were found to consume less saturated fat, trans fat, soda, and fried foods. The foods that they ate also had a lower glycemic load, which measures food's tendency to raise blood sugar (Gillman et al., 2000). Not only is this true for children living in the home, but these healthy dietary habits learned during family mealtimes carry on even after children have grown and are living on their own. A study performed by Larson, Neumark-Sztainer, Hannan, and

Story (2007) collected data from high school students in 1998–1999. More data were then collected in 2003–2004 from the same sample group. The data looked at several factors, including frequency of family meals and diet quality. Results from the study showed that those who consumed family meals together more frequently during their adolescent years had a higher intake of fruit and vegetables, including dark-green and orange vegetables. In addition, frequency of family mealtime in female subjects during time 1 was correlated with an increase in consumption of calcium, magnesium, potassium, vitamin B_6, and fiber during time 2. In males, there was a correlation between frequency of family mealtimes at time 1 and consumption of calcium, magnesium, potassium, and fiber during time 2. It was also found that a high frequency of family mealtimes during time 1 was negatively associated with soft-drink consumptions in both males and females during time 2 (Larson et al., 2007). These studies show not only the immediate impact of family mealtime on the nutritional intake of the children in the home but also how the behaviors learned during the family mealtimes persist, even into the adult years. This implies that there is a positive impact that family mealtime has on behavioral factors impacting the food choices that children and adolescents are making.

Several other behaviors besides food choices can impact how children and adolescents eat. Other studies have shown not only that food choices are better for those who consume meals with their families regularly but also that they eat at a slower pace and are able to better learn how to follow internal satiety cues (Gillman et al., 2000). By learning to follow the hunger and satiety cues of the body, this could potentially prevent the consumption of excess calories and therefore reduce the risk of overweight or obesity later on in life.

Family mealtimes play a significant role in environmental factors that shape the eating habits of children in the home. It has been found that although individuals are born with an innate preference for sweet and salty foods, the strongest influence of food preferences that eventually shape the eating habits of children is the family, especially the parent who is preparing the meals (Skinner, Carruth, Bounds, & Ziegler, 2002). Even at a young age, children are willing to try a new or unfamiliar food more readily when an adult is present and eating that same food as well (Harper & Sanders, 1975). It has also been shown that when someone is presented with a new food, social facilitation, such as family meals, leads to faster acceptance of a food (Visalberghi & Fragaszy, 2001). This shows the impact that interaction during family mealtimes has on the acceptance of new and potentially more nutritious foods. Boutelle, Birnbaum, Lytle, Murray, and Story (2003) performed a study that showed that the family meal environment led to the development of eating patterns, even into the adult years. These findings provide strong implications of the effectiveness in family mealtime environment and interaction during meals in developing healthier eating habits, even as the children in the family age and become adults themselves.

Obesity Problem

Good nutrition is essential to healthy growth and development among youth (Lytle & Hearst, 2009). However, evidence suggests that current dietary behaviors and practices in children and adolescents have detrimental consequences on their health (Flynn et al., 2006). Without proper nutrition and physical activity, people increase their risk of weight gain with the odds of becoming overweight or obese escalating as long as poor diet and sedentary behaviors continue (Flynn et al., 2006). Obesity is strongly associated with recent changes in lifestyle and dietary habits, such as the low cost of and easy access to foods containing high amounts of fat and sugar (Benzeval, Taylor, & Judge, 2000). Obesity most commonly begins in childhood between the ages of 5 and 6 and increases during adolescence. Studies show that children who are obese between the ages of 10 and 13 have an 80% chance of becoming an obese adult (American Academy of Child and Adolescent Psychiatry, 2011). According to the Centers for Disease Control and Prevention, among children 6 to 11 years of age, the prevalence of obesity has more than doubled over the past 20 years, increasing from 6.5% to 17.0% (U.S. Department of Health and Human Services [USHHS], 2012a).

Obese youth are prone to risk factors for cardiovascular diseases, such as high blood pressure or high low-density lipoprotein cholesterol (USHHS, 2012b). They are also at a greater risk for sleep apnea, bone and joint problems, social and psychological problems, and developing associated adult health problems, including type 2 diabetes, heart disease, stroke, cancer, and osteoarthritis (USHHS, 2012b). In addition, data suggest that rates of obesity differ depending on a child's race and ethnicity. For example, obesity rates are higher among Mexican American boys, non-Hispanic black girls, and American Indian youth (USHHS, 2012a). Furthermore, physical inactivity is associated with an increase in obesity and chronic diseases (USHHS, 2012a). Research shows that older children engage in less physical activity than younger children overall, with less than one-third meeting recommended physical activity guidelines by the time they are 15 years old (Nader, Bradley, Houts, McRitchie, & O'Brien, 2008).

Healthy lifestyle habits, including healthy eating and being physically active, have been shown to lower the risk of becoming obese (USHHS, 2012b). Teaching children the benefits of eating healthy foods encourages them to develop and maintain healthy eating habits. Likewise, teaching children the benefits of physical activity and health self-image can help them develop lifelong health-protective habits. In addition, however, in order to teach adolescents how to eat healthy, messages must be communicated in a relevant manner.

Obstacles to Healthy Eating

Obstacles to healthy eating are multifaceted. Data suggest that many people cannot measure the nutritional quality of a meal—a problem compounded in our society by increased dining out and consumption of fast foods and prepackaged meals. Data also suggest that while we may be aware of the nutrient content of a particular food, we lose track of that nutrient content when foods and ingredients are combined in unknown portions. Consumers, who often have no concept of appropriate portion size, typically eat three large meals a day, drink sugar-sweetened beverages, and snack between meals (Kennedy, Blaylock, & Kuhn, 1999). Moreover, while caregivers generally want to provide healthful food for their families, most have never learned to cook and fail to provide meals that meet daily dietary recommendations (Kennedy et al., 1999). In addition, recent studies have reported that adolescents have poor eating habits that do not meet current dietary recommendations (Story et al., 2002).

In obese children, family structure and family eating behaviors have an important role with respect to the onset and maintenance of the family children being overweight and obese. Children learn by observing and imitating their parents. Parents serve as role model for their children and therefore have great influences over their child's eating behaviors. Parents influence their child's eating style and behavior (Puder & Munsch, 2010). Williams (2011) noted that parents influence their children's healthy behaviors in five areas: (a) availability and accessibility of healthy foods, (b) meal structure, (c) adult food modeling, (d) food socialization practices, and (e) food-related parenting style.

Family Mealtime, Weight Status, and Obesity

With these studies showing the impact that family mealtime has on the nutritional intake of the children in the family, it is not surprising that several other studies have found that frequency of family mealtimes has an impact on their weight status as well. Taveras et al. (2012) performed a study that looked at associations between frequency of family meals and overweight status. The results from their study showed that at baseline, those who ate family dinner most days or every day had a decreased prevalence of being overweight when compared to those who reported eating dinner with their family never or some days. Gillman et al. (2000) looked at measures of diet quality in comparison to frequency of family mealtime as well as the weight status of those children surveyed. The results from their study showed that those who consumed family dinner never or some days had an average body mass index (BMI) of 19.5. Those who reported eating family dinner most days had a BMI of 19.2, and those who reported eating family dinner together every day had an average BMI of 19.0. Although these data did not demonstrate whether the findings with regard to BMI and frequency of family dinner were significant, there was a trend that showed a decreased BMI with increased frequency of family dinner. A study done by Sen (2006) found that those youth who reported never eating dinner as a family had the highest mean BMI and percent overweight when compared to those who reported consuming dinner with their family.

With all of these studies showing the correlation between frequency of family meals and improved diet quality and decreased risk of being overweight in children and adolescents, there is compelling evidence to show the benefits of eating meals as a family on a regular basis. With the implications for the impact of family meals, it might be worth encouraging more frequent family meals as a way to improve the nutritional intake and perhaps even help prevent further increases in the prevalence of obesity and overweight in children and adolescents. Considering the health complications that can be brought on by obesity, perhaps family mealtimes could prove to be a beneficial tool in improving not only the weight status and nutrition of children and adolescents but also their overall health and prevention of various obesity-related diseases. Also, since family meals impact children and adolescents up into their adult years, the effects of an increase in family mealtimes could prove to have long-lasting benefits on the health of not only the younger but also the adult population.

Over the past 30 years, there has been an alarming increase in the prevalence of obesity in children and adolescents (Cinotto, 2006). Between the years 1980 and 2002, the number of

overweight individuals in this population has tripled (Eisenberg et al., 2008; Patrick & Nicklas, 2005; Story et al., 2002). One factor that impacts this pattern is poor diet quality (Fulkerson et al., 2006; Neumark-Sztainer et al., 2008). Only 2% of school-aged children are meeting their dietary recommendations for their food groups, and the quality of their diet tends to decrease as they move into adolescence (Fisher et al., 2008). A corresponding trend with adolescent overweight and poor diet quality is a decline in the frequency of meals eaten as a family (American Dietetic Association, 1995; Eisenberg et al., 2004). As a result, many studies have been performed to assess the impact of frequency of family meals on either weight status or quality of diet of adolescents (American Dietetic Association, 1995; Burgess-Champoux, Larson, Neumark-Sztainer, Hannan, & Story, 2009; Flegal, Carroll, Ogden, & Johnson, 2002; Ogden, Flegal, Carroll & Johnson, 2002; USHHS, 2012b). The results of these studies have been promising, showing that an increase in the frequency of family meals corresponds with lower BMI, increased intake of several beneficial nutrients, and a reduced consumption of several less beneficial foods (American Dietetic Association, 1995; Burgess-Champoux et al., 2009; USHHS, 2012b).

The most important goal for managing obesity in children and young people is that of weight maintenance—a short-term issue but a lifelong process. A holistic approach needs to be taken to intervention, as simplistic interventions that target one form of sedentary behavior have not been shown to be effective. It is preferable to provide appealing opportunities to be physically active and to eat more healthily and thereby encourage intrinsic motivation to make lifestyle changes, as there is greater likelihood of these behaviors being maintained.

Care needs to be taken so that an unhealthy preoccupation with weight is not encouraged and so that the possibility of stigmatization is not increased. Firm rules and occasional treats are the ideal diet strategy, along with an unwavering emphasis on the positive rather than any form of criticism or communication of failure. In relation to this, psychologically based interventions should fully utilize positive behavioral approaches. Interventions should aim to create long-term behavioral change and the promotion of children's positive self-esteem and increased confidence. They should also offer support to address possible bullying, to improve family communication, and to provide parental support and empowerment (Cullen, 2011).

One study found that those adolescents who reported eating family dinner most days or every day had a decreased prevalence of overweight when compared to those who reported eating dinner with their family never or some days (Burgess-Champoux et al., 2009). Gillman et al. (2000) found that frequency of family meals corresponded with an increased consumption of grain, fruit, vegetables, fiber, and several beneficial vitamins and minerals, including calcium, folate, iron, and vitamins A, C, E, B_6, and B_{12}. Frequency of family meals was also found to be inversely related to consumption of saturated fat, trans fat, soda, and fried foods. Even those families who watched television but still consumed regular meals as a family showed nutritional benefits over those who did nit consume dinner together regularly as a family (Gillman et al., 2000). Another promising study showed that those adolescents who consumed regular meals with their families had higher intakes of fruits and vegetables, even in their adult years when they were living away from home (Burgess-Champoux et al., 2009). Hammons and Fiese (2011), based on a meta-analysis, found that the frequency of shared family meals was significantly related to the nutritional health of children, youth, and adolescents. They reported that sharing a family meal at least three times or more per week resulted in children and adolescents more likely to be of normal weight and to have healthier dietary patterns than those who did not. The other benefit they reported in this study was that the engagement of disordered eating behaviors was reduced by 35% in families who ate more than three meals per week together. This has several implications for improving the weight status and nutritional intake of children and even helping them as they grow up and live on their own. Families who had a child of healthy weight spent more time engaged with each other during the meal, expressed more positive communication, and considered mealtimes more important and meaningful than families who had a child who was overweight or obese (Fiese, Hammons, & Grigsby-Toussaint, 2012).

Tips for Make Meals and Family Time

Over 40% of the typical American food budget is spent on eating out, with family meals often being relegated to holidays and special occasions. Aside from costly effect on the family budget, eating out has been shown to be generally associated with poor food choices with the consumption of high-fat, high-calorie, low-nutrient-dense foods. Growing scientific evidence indicates that fewer family meals may translate to increased obesity risk and poor nutritional status, especially among children. But getting this message out to busy parents in a way that will convince them to spend more time at the dining room table with their children is problematic at best. Cason (2006) noted that family mealtimes are associated with more positive dietary intake and healthful behaviors among adolescents. Family meals can facilitate family interaction, communication, and a sense of unity. Because of the multiple benefits of eating meals together as a family, professionals working with youth and families should emphasize the importance of family meals. Promoting the family meal can improve dietary quality, reduce overweight, and improve educational and social outcomes.

When the U.S. Department of Agriculture (2011) developed the MyPlate nutritional program, emphasis was placed on family mealtime and encouraging parents to be role models to their children. They recognized that it takes time and effort to bring families together for mealtimes but in the long run is well worth it with regard to the nutritional health and well-being of the family members. Three main tips in making mealtime a family time are as follows:

- Start eating meals together as a family when your children are young. This way it becomes a habit.
- Plan when you will eat together as a family. Write it on the family calendar.
- You may not be able to eat together every day. Try to have family meals most days of the week.

Corbin (2008) suggested that family mealtimes need to be made a priority, show flexibility, involve everyone, be planned ahead, and be positive. She suggested that family mealtimes are a time

Photo courtesy of Sherilyn Marrow

to connect—to talk, listen, and laugh as a family. Research has shown that families have better communication and a stronger bond when they eat together (Eisenberg et al., 2008; Fisher et al., 2008; Fulkerson et al., 2006; Neumark-Sztainer et al., 2008). Make sure to turn off the television and work with families on tuning into each other and not electronics.

Families receive multiple, sometimes competing messages regarding nutrition and dietary habits. Many factors influence parental perceptions of child feeding practices. It is important that parents and their children talk about what they think about the information they learn in school, on the Internet, and other sources since there is so much nutrition misinformation today. Parents play an essential role in guiding the eating habits, weight status, activity levels, and body image of their children (Rhee, 2008). Because parents provide the most important psychosocial influences in the lives of their children, working with parents to increase their essential nutrition and physical activity knowledge and skills should strengthen their positive influences, ultimately leading their children to healthier lifestyles, lower obesity risk, and long-term health benefits. Obesity prevention efforts may want to consider targeting family functioning, such as communicating, problem solving, closeness, and behavioral control, as a way to improve their children's health and weight outcomes. Obesity interventions may want to include education for families about the importance of family communication, structure/roles, problem solving, and closeness/warmth.

Discussion Questions

1. Research has suggested that families who eat at least five meals per week together have better diets, improved diet quality, and indirectly a lower body mass index. How do you go about helping families eat at least five meals per week together?
2. Positive family functioning can improve dietary practices and weight in families. What techniques or suggestions might be developed to help families improve their family functioning and family communication patterns?
3. How do families develop safe environments so that they can discuss positive and negative food, nutrition, and health information often coming from unreliable sources?
4. How can positive family communication help reduce the obesity epidemic? If you were to develop an obesity prevention program, what would you include with regard to family communication?

References

American Academy of Child and Adolescent Psychiatry. (2011). *Facts for family: Obesity in children and teens. No. 79.* http://www.aacap.org/galleries/FactsForFamilies/79_obesity_in_children_and_teens.pdf

American Dietetic Association. (1995). *Food, physical activity, and fun: What kids think.* Chicago: Author.

Benzeval, M., Taylor, J., & Judge, K. (2000). Evidence on the relationship between low income and poor health: Is the government doing enough? *Fiscal Studies, 21*(3), 375–399.

Boutelle, K. N., Birnbaum, A. S., Lytle, L. A., Murray, D. M., & Story, M. (2003). Associations between perceived family meal environment and parent intake of fruit, vegetables, and fat. *Journal of Nutrition Education and Behavior, 35*(1), 24–29.

Burgess-Champoux, T. L., Larson, N., Neumark-Sztainer, D., Hannan, P. J., & Story, M. (2009). Are family meal patterns associated with overall diet quality during the transition from early to middle adolescence? *Journal of Nutrition Education and Behavior, 41*(2), 79.

Cason, K. L. (2006). Family mealtimes: More than just eating together. *Journal of the American Dietetic Association, 106,* 532–533.

Cinotto, S. (2006). "Everyone would be around the table": American family mealtimes in historical perspective, 1850–1960. *New Directions for Child and Adolescent Development, 2006*(111), 17–33.

Corbin, A. (2008). *Make mealtime family time.* Purdue Extension Nutrition Fact Sheet, CFS-748-4-W, 1–2. http://www.extension.purdue.edu/extmedia/CFS/CFS-748-4-W.pdf

Cullen, K. (2011). A review of some of the existing literature on obesity in children and young people and a commentary on the psychological issues identified. *Obesity in the UK: A Psychological Perspective, 56.*

Eisenberg, M. E., Olson, R. E., Neumark-Sztainer, D., Story, M., & Bearinger, L. H. (2004). Correlations between family meals and psychosocial well-being among adolescents. *Archives of Pediatrics and Adolescent Medicine, 158*(8), 792.

Eisenberg, M. E., Neumark-Sztainer, D., Fulkerson, J. A., & Story, M. (2008). Family meals and substance use: Is there a long-term protective association? *Journal of Adolescent Health, 43*(2), 151–156.

Fiese, B. H., Hammons, A., & Grigsby-Toussaint, D. (2012). Family mealtimes: A contextual approach to understanding childhood obesity. *Economics and Human Biology.*

Fisher, L. B., Miles, I. W., Austin, S. B., Camargo, C. A., Jr., & Colditz, G. A. (2007). Predictors of initiation of alcohol use among US adolescents: Findings from a prospective cohort study. *Archives of Pediatrics and Adolescent Medicine, 161*(10), 959.

Flegal, K. M., Carroll, M. D., Ogden, C. L., & Johnson, C. L. (2002). Prevalence and trends in obesity among US adults, 1999–2000. *Journal of the American Medical Association, 288*(14), 1723–1727.

Flynn, M. A. T., McNeil, D. A., Maloff, B., Mutasingwa, D., Wu, M., Ford, C., et al. (2006). Reducing obesity and related chronic disease risk in children and youth: A synthesis of evidence with "best practice" recommendations. *Obesity Reviews, 7*(Suppl. 1), 7–66.

Fulkerson, J. A., Story, M., Mellin, A., Leffert, N., Neumark-Sztainer, D., & French, S. A. (2006). Family dinner meal frequency and adolescent development: Relationships with developmental assets and high-risk behaviors. *Journal of Adolescent Health, 39*(3), 337–345.

Gillman, M. W., Rifas-Shiman, S. L., Frazier, A. L., Rockett, H. R., Camargo, C. A., Jr., Field, A. E., et al. (2000). Family dinner and diet quality among older children and adolescents. *Archives of Family Medicine, 9*(3), 235.

Hammons, A. J., & Fiese, B. H. (2011). Is frequency of shared family meals related to the nutritional health of children and adolescents? *Pediatrics, 127*(6), e1565–e1574.

Harper, L. V., & Sanders, K. M. (1975). The effect of adults' eating on young children's acceptance of unfamiliar foods. *Journal of Experimental Child Psychology, 20*(2), 206–214.

Kennedy, E., Blaylock, J., & Kuhn, B. (1999). *On the road to better nutrition: America's eating habits: Changes and consequences.* Washington, DC: U.S. Department of Agriculture, Economic Research Service, Food and Rural Economic Division.

Larson, N. I., Neumark-Sztainer, D., Hannan, P. J., & Story, M. (2007). Family meals during adolescence are associated with higher diet quality and healthful meal patterns during young adulthood. *Journal of the American Dietetic Association, 107*(9), 1502.

Lytle, L. A., & Hearst, M. O. (2009). Examining the state of the science of prevention of childhood obesity. *Current Nutrition and Food Science, 5*(2), 134-148.

Nader, P. R., Bradley, R. H., Houts, R. M., McRitchie, S. L., & O'Brien, M. (2008). Moderate-to-vigorous physical activity from ages 9 to 15 years. *Journal of the American Medical Association, 300*(3), 295-305.

Neumark-Sztainer, D., Eisenberg, M. E., Fulkerson, J. A., Story, M., & Larson, N. I. (2008). Family meals and disordered eating in adolescents: Longitudinal findings from project EAT. *Archives of Pediatrics and Adolescent Medicine, 162*(1), 17.

Ogden, C. L., Flegal, K. M., Carroll, M. D., & Johnson, C. L. (2002). Prevalence and trends in overweight among US children and adolescents, 1999-2000. *Journal of the American Medical Association, 288*(14), 1728-1732.

Patrick, H., & Nicklas, T. A. (2005). A review of family and social determinants of children's eating patterns and diet quality. *Journal of the American College of Nutrition, 24*(2), 83-92.

Puder, J. J., & Munsch, S. (2010). Psychological correlates of childhood obesity. *International Journal of Obesity, 34*, S37-S43.

Rhee, K. (2008). Childhood overweight and the relationship between parent behaviors, parenting style, and family functioning. *Annals of the American Academy of Political and Social Science, 615*(1), 11-37.

Sen, B. (2006). Frequency of family dinner and adolescent body weight status: Evidence from the National Longitudinal Survey of Youth, 1997. *Obesity, 14*, 2266-2276. doi: 10.1038/oby.2006.266

Skinner, J. D., Carruth, B. R., Bounds, W., & Ziegler, P. J. (2002). Children's food preferences: A longitudinal analysis. *Journal of the American Dietetic Association, 102*(11), 1638-1647.

Story, M., Neumark-Sztainer, D., & French S. (2002) Individual and environmental influences on adolescent eating behaviors. *Journal of the American Dietetic Association, 102*(Suppl. 3), S40-S50.

Taveras, E. M., Rifas-Shiman, S. L., Berkey, C. S., Rockett, H. R., Field, A. E., Frazier, A. L., et al. (2012). Family dinner and adolescent overweight. *Obesity Research, 13*(5), 900-906.

U.S. Department of Agriculture, Center for Nutrition and Public Policy. (2011). *Developing healthy eating habits: Making mealtime family time.* http://www.choosemyplate.gov/preschoolers/healthy-habits/making-mealtime-family-time.html

U.S. Department of Health and Human Services, Centers for Disease Control and Prevention, National Center for Health Statistics (2012a). *Child obesity facts.* http://www.cdc.gov/healthyyouth/obesity/facts.htm

U.S. Department of Health and Human Services, Centers for Disease Control and Prevention, National Center for Health Statistics (2012b). *The growing problem.* http://www.cdc.gov/obesity/childhood/problem.html

Visalberghi, E., & Fragaszy D. (2001). Do monkeys ape? Ten years after. In K. Dautenhahn & C. Nehaniv (Eds.), *Imitation in animals and artifacts* (pp. 471-499). Boston: MIT Press.

Williams, J. E. (2011). Child obesity in context: Ecology of family and community. *International Journal of Exercise Science, 4*(2), 1.

PART 7
Family Ties and Influences

Chapter 29
The Impact of Communication Technology on the Family   314
Cheryl Pawlowski, *University of Northern Colorado*

Chapter 30
The "Plugged-In" Family: The Dialectics of Digital Technology in the Everyday Life of Families   322
Charles Soukup, *University of Northern Colorado*

Chapter 31
Pathways to Marital Satisfaction in Interfaith and Interracial Marriages   332
Patrick C. Hughes, *Texas Tech University*
John R. Baldwin, *Illinois State University*
Bolanle Olaniran, *Texas Tech University*

Chapter 32
Mother and Daughter-in-Law Relationships: For Better or for Worse?   341
Paul Yelsma, *Western Michigan University*

Chapter 33
"I Want to Be a Marcks": Generativity in Relationships between Uncles and Nephews   353
David E. Weber, *University of North Carolina–Wilmington*

Chapter 34
Navigating a Mother–Daughter Relationship   366
K. T. Aldridge, *University of Northern Colorado*

Chapter 35
Media Depictions of Adoption Narratives   372
Beth M. Waggenspack, *Virginia Tech University*

Chapter 36
From Isolation to Connection: Former Sex Workers Conceptualize Family and Familial Interactions   386
Jennifer Mayer, *University of North Texas*
Brian K. Richardson, *University of North Texas*

Chapter 37
Mothering at the Boundaries: When Relative Being is More Important Than Being a Relative   398
Deborah Eicher-Catt,
Pennsylvania State University–York

Chapter 29  The Impact of Communication Technology on the Family

Cheryl Pawlowski

Mention the family in conjunction with the 1950s, and many people conjure images of Mom, Dad, and children gathered around the dinner table sharing a meal and lively conversation. This idealized concept of the family was popularized by the mass media and still produces a longing by many for perceived "simpler times."

By contrast, today's family may appear stressed, fragmented, and even on the verge of becoming obsolete. Meals are often eaten alone in front of the television or computer. What little "family time" left is frequently interrupted by cell phone calls and text messages.

Beyond the evolution of gender roles and other family dynamics, one of the biggest impacts on family interaction has been the advent of a variety of new technologies. For better or worse, computers, cell phones, television, and other devices have changed how parents and children spend their time. Further, although technology has often held the potential to increase leisure time—and, presumably, time spent with loved ones—research indicates that modern technologies have frequently gobbled up any gains they provide in disposable time. When we do have free time, we are increasingly likely to spend it alone—using technology.

"The convenience and accessibility of modern technology contributes greatly to the 'privatizing' of leisure," says Tom Sanders, a researcher on *Bowling Alone*, by Harvard professor Robert Putnam (Gandossy, 2007). "Technology makes it easier to get what we want, when we want it, while remaining entirely alone."

Equally important, communication technologies have significantly changed the roles of family members. In past generations, adults were the primary keepers of both social and informational knowledge. As a result of this role, maturity and experience naturally resulted in a higher status within the social order. In other words, "elders" were respected and admired for their wisdom and knowledge; youths were adults in training.

These roles have essentially been turned on their head. The human brain is no longer required to be the primary repository for knowledge. Facts are now more easily (and some would say more accurately) stored within various forms of communication technology, such as the Internet. Given this change, those who are better at computing and navigating communication technologies are likely to experience increased status and power. Children and adolescents, for example, are typically quicker to understand and adopt new technologies. Modern youths may therefore view parents and grandparents as less relevant than in earlier times. Some would argue, however, that while young people have better access to data, modern communication technologies do not bestow the emotional maturity required to fully process and apply such knowledge.

Communication Technology: A Historical Perspective

The history of communication technology is nearly as old as humankind itself. From cave paintings and the advent of the written word to cell phones and the Internet, humans have continually striven to improve and expand the ways in which they communicate.

Generally, the development of communication technologies following the advent of the spoken word can be divided into three major epochs. The first era was marked by the development of the written word by the Greeks between 800 BC and 500 BC. Writing was a major technological advancement, allowing communication over long distances and the recording of information with more precision than oral histories. While the written word had little direct impact on most families, it allowed societies to standardize general rules of morality and gender roles. It also redefined the family as a copartner with spiritual leaders and the community for the socialization of children through the development of religious texts and other documents (Aries, 1962; Eisenstein, 1979).

The invention of the printing press by Johannes Gutenberg in the 15th century signaled a new era in communication technology. Previously, the written word was the exclusive domain of religious and some political leaders. The printing press provided the masses direct access to information. It also served to isolate the family unit. Educated parents became the family's primary moral agent, no longer having to rely solely on the interpretations of religious leaders.

Although today we think of electronic media as cell phones, computers, televisions, and radios, the first true electronic communication technology is significantly older. Introduced in 1843, the telegraph whet consumers' appetites for immediate access to information and heralded a new age in communication technology. It also changed the family in fundamental ways, allowing a more dispersed society and prompting individuals and families to view themselves as part of a broader, even national or global, community.

The first true "mass communication" electronic technologies emerged during the first half of the 20th century. They allowed information to be disseminated beyond in the confines of local communities with lightening-fast speed. Further, the aural and visual aspects of these technologies tended to lend authority, credence, and immediacy to the information they provided. These technologies have had profound impacts on the family, conveying what has become known as "popular culture" to both children and adults with little or no filtering. Further, both technologies are primarily one-way communication devices, controlled almost exclusively by the marketplace. Many experts see this as changing the role of the family from a primary socialization unit to a product consumer group.

The fact that computers, the Internet, and related technologies allow two-way communication might, on the surface, suggest they are more likely to empower families to influence their members. This, however, has not yet been the case. In fact, computers and related technologies have established a dichotomy that many scholars see as further eroding the power of the family. The physically solitary nature of computer use has increased privacy within the context of the family, yet the Internet and social media have reduced the privacy of the individual on a macrolevel. In other words, parents, spouses, and siblings may know relatively little about other family members' virtual lives, while relative strangers—from social network "friends" to online retailers—are privy to vast amounts of knowledge about the individual.

Technology and the Family

The impact of broadcast and communication technologies—now collectively called information and communication technologies (ICTs)—within the family unit is rapidly expanding. Throughout the history of human civilization, the family unit has played a variety of vital roles to support and socialize members. The family has traditionally been involved with the management of members' time and resources; its members have communicated, interpreted, and filtered society's cultural narrative; it has helped define and indoctrinate members into specific gender roles; it has advised and guided family members regarding sexual matters; and its members have often served supportive roles similar to friendships (Pawlowski, 2000).

During the second half of the 20th century, many of these roles were usurped by mass media technologies, such as television, which still remains a major factor in the family. Consumers spent about half their leisure time, or about 11% of their lives, in front of the television, according to the U.S. government's American Time Use Survey (Johnson, 2005). The amount of time taken from other activities and this level of exposure to a technology designed to market products by establishing them as popular culture requirements are bound to change individual and family dynamics. The growth of cable programming and the shear number of program options—including adult-oriented offerings—means that television will continue to be a powerful force within the family for the foreseeable future.

When it comes to assuming traditional family responsibilities, however, television now has a host of relatively new competitors. Family roles have evolved over millions of years as tools to support and socialize family members. Yet many researchers contend that computers, cell phones, and related media are rapidly undermining the family's influence.

The speed at which these technologies are encroaching on traditional family responsibilities is truly amazing, frequently leaving scholarly research in the dust. Changes from Internet use for professional purposes in the late 1980s and early 1990s to casual Web surfing, e-mail, social media, cell phones, texting, and Twitter have happened so quickly that there is relatively little empirical knowledge about how these developments affect individuals and families. Many researchers are now attempting to tackle this new frontier even as new technologies make "older" ones—those two or three years old—obsolete. Other family scholars are attempting to extrapolate from research on earlier technologies, such as radio, television, and early computing, to predict the impact of these changes.

Mobile Communication Devices

In little more than two decades, ICTs have inserted themselves into nearly every facet of family life. Take the cell phone, for example. Mobile or cellular phones were a luxury for a select few until the mid-1990s. Over the past decade, however, they have become almost a necessity. A survey by CTIA, an international wireless communication association, found that 90% of wireless device users report having the technology with them almost constantly (Lanigan, 2009).

In 2011, 83% of American adults had cell phones, and 35% had smart phones that allowed mobile Internet access (Smith, 2011). About 60% of adolescents ages 13 to 17 now have cell phones (Johnson, 2006), and a Pew study revealed that 27% of youths ages 13 to 17 have mobile devices that allow them to go online (Lenhart, 2011). Most young mobile phone users get their first cell phone around age 12 or 13.

Parents typically cite safety as the top reason to buy youths cell phones. "Parents love kids to have mobile phones," said Glen LeBlanc, research director for wireless services at NPD Group. "It's an electronic leash." Geser (2006) notes that many cell phone users willingly sacrifice privacy for the perceived safety that cell phones provide by allowing instant access to others. In fact, nearly half of all parents of young cell phone users have used the devices to monitor their child's location (Lenhart, 2011).

The sense of security that cell phones provide comes with some significant trade-offs. About 20% of teenagers, for example, use cell phones and online technology to send sexually explicit pictures of themselves to others. John Grohol, an expert in online psychology issues, attributes this trend to the "online disinhibition effect." People say and do things in cyberspace they would not do in the real world. Grohol also notes that nearly a quarter of teens report that technology makes them more forward and aggressive. Other research suggests that adolescents often use their cell phones to increase their privacy and exclude parents from their social interactions and culture (Lanigan, 2009).

Half of adolescent cell phone users keep their phones on during school hours, and nearly a third admit to sending and receiving texts in class (Lenhart, 2011). Texting by youths has other implications. The Nielsen Company reports that American teenagers send and receive nearly 3,276 text messages per month, or about 110 texts per day. This habitual use of text features is rapidly becoming a 24-hour phenomenon. A Pew Research Center study found that 80% of teens typically sleep with their cell phones on or near their beds. Other research by the John F. Kennedy Medical Center sleep laboratory found that teens sent an average of 33.5 e-mails and texts overnight, significantly affecting their sleep (Teitell, 2011). This trend of being "on call" 24/7 is leading to anxiety, distraction in school, falling grades, repetitive stress injury, and sleep deprivation, say physicians and psychologists (Parker-Pope, 2009).

Protecting children from the downsides of cell phone technologies is a challenge for many parents. Two-thirds of parents say they have looked at their child's cell phone content. Yet only 26% of parents of young cell phone users limit the number of texts their child send and receive (Lenhart, 2011). It is interesting to note that one study found that 61% of parents claim they impose limitations on ICTs but that only 38% of children said these rules are regularly enforced (Lanigan, 2009).

The social impact of cell phone technologies on the family unit and on individuals is far more difficult to pin down. While some research suggests that, overall, cell phones have been detrimental to the family unit, other experts claim they offer significant benefits.

Geser (2006) identifies the cell phone as an "antievolutionary device," promoting "premodern patterns of social life" by allowing people to shut out their surroundings and interaction with strangers to concentrate on individual, one-to-one relationships. In addition, he asserts that cell phones help users reestablish the casual, informal communication patterns of communal life. Geser notes that other researchers have described the cell phone as an "umbilical cord" between parents and children that spans physical distances. Therefore, parents can still carry out their roles as "caregivers" even while they are at work or engaging in other activities apart from their children. The constant ability to communicate via cell technology also releases users from more rigid, formal time constraints. Geser argues that the resulting attitude spills over to other areas, such as schools and workplaces, with less emphasis on punctuality.

Geser and others are not totally complimentary toward mobile technologies. Geser (2006) suggests that the cell phone is changing social norms and rules with mixed results. Users, for example, now expect instant responses and more frequent contact since time and distance are becoming less relevant. "One higher order consequence of wireless communication is that it makes us more responsible, for both our own actions and those of people for whom we have assumed responsibility," says author James Katz. "In effect, we become more subject to social control" (Geser, 2006).

Geser goes on to note that cell phones may isolate users from wider social contacts and may decrease their overall independence. "Anywhere and any time, we can evade unfamiliar contacts in public places, bridge time gaps of loneliness and avoid reliance on our own judgment by contacting our loved ones at home" (Geser, 2006).

Other research appears to support these assertions. According to the Pew Research Center's Internet and American Life Project, 42% of cell phone owners used their phones for entertainment when they were bored (Smith, 2011). In addition, 13% of cell owners pretended to use their phones to avoid interacting with the people around them.

Computers and the Internet

The various permutations of computer use have received equally conflicting reviews. An estimated 61.8% of U.S. households own computers, and 86.7% of those households access the Internet (National Telecommunications and Information Administration, 2004). Users spend an average of 15.3 hours online each week, typically communicating with others via e-mail and other applications, and gathering information such as news and product details. More than half of users report the Internet as their most important source of information (Lanigan, 2009).

When it comes to computer use, families often experience significant conflicts. These disagreements typically focus on adolescents' time spent using computer technologies, the potential negative effects of computer use, and conflicting perceptions of expertise between parents and youths (Blinn-Pike, 2009).

Just behind e-mail, the most ubiquitous use of computers is to utilize social media websites such as Facebook, MySpace, and LinkedIn. In fact, 65% of adults who use the Internet also use social networking sites, and more than 60% of young adults—those age 30 and under—use such sites on a daily basis. Nearly a third of baby boomers ages 50 to 64 are daily social network users (Madden & Zickuhr, 2011). "Social networking sites continue to cement their place as a significant part of mainstream online life," says Zickuhr, a Pew research specialist and coauthor of the report.

Despite some sites' age restrictions, preteens are also logging on to social media sites at a significant rate, providing personal information and interacting with other users who may be much older. For example, more than 7.5 million youths under 13 are Facebook users, and about 5 million are 10 or younger (Dixon, 2011).

These sites are especially popular among girls and young women. While 56% of girls in one large-scale survey said that social networking makes them feel closer to their friends, 68% of girls said that they had also had negative experiences associated with social networking (Salmond & Percell, 2011). This may help account for a decline in use by some youths. The percentage of young social media users who send or post messages on these sites actually dropped by more than 10% between 2006 and 2009 (Lenhart, 2011).

Although a variety of kinds of businesses have proliferated on the Internet, as an industry pornography is one of the most wildly successful online endeavors. Two-thirds of men ages 18 to 34 visit Internet pornography sites at least once per month, and each second more than 28,000 Internet users are viewing pornography online (Eberstadt & Layden, 2010).

Pornography is hardly a new phenomenon. In fact, it dates back to the time of cave painting. Yet many experts set Internet pornography apart from previous forms of sexually explicit materials. Eberstadt and Layden (2010), for example, note that Internet pornography is far easier to obtain than printed materials, and an online volume of pornography far exceeds any previous media. This volume has also created competition among providers, resulting in ever more explicit depictions of sexual acts.

In testimony before the U.S. Senate's Subcommittee on the Constitution, Civil Rights, and Property Rights Committee on Judiciary, Jill C. Manning, MS, noted that Internet pornography can have a profound impact on families (Manning, 2005). Among the deleterious effects Manning cites are decreased parental time and attention due to the time spent using pornography, increased risk of children encountering pornographic material, increased risk of parental separation and divorce, and increased risk of parental job loss and financial strain. Further, Manning (2005) notes that Internet pornography decreases marital intimacy and sexual satisfaction, increases the likelihood of infidelity, and can result in a devaluation of monogamy, marriage, and child rearing.

Conclusion

The lack of research and resulting data on the social implications of ICTs makes it difficult to develop any solid predictions about their long-term effects on the family. That said, there are clearly some early trends in usage that may offer some broad insights.

On the positive side, mass communication technologies, mobile communication devices, and computers offer the potential to increase family interaction by keeping members connected. They can also allow members to access a vast treasure trove of knowledge that can enhance family life. In addition, they can facilitate spontaneous interactions by allowing families to coordinate plans and identify activities and events that they can participate in together.

Well over half of ICT users say, however, that communication technologies have reduced time spent with family members. One reason for this may be that these technologies and the expectation placed on users of constant availability blur the boundaries between families and the outside world (Lanigan, 2009). This is especially true in terms of work–family boundaries. They also often allow relatively unfettered access to family members—including children—by the outside world. Research suggests that many parents are more reluctant to impose and protect family boundaries related to ICTs. This task is frequently complicated by the fact that children often know more about such technologies than their parents.

ICTs have also become a new source of conflict in many families; however, some research suggests that ICTs may often simply express preexisting family dysfunction (Lanigan, 2009). For example, pornography and social media may be used to meet sexual and emotional needs that a well-functioning family typically provides.

While these trends may be perceived as ominous signs of the family's demise as a primary social unit, such predictions have been made about nearly all previous communication technologies, including the written word, the printing press, and the telegraph. Early indications suggest that ICTs may continue to significantly change family life, but it may also be that we are currently in a period of transition and adjustment. The family, as in the past, may simply adapt to these new technologies and eventually integrate them successfully into its role of socialization and support of its members.

Discussion Questions

1. What are the three main eras of communication technology development following the advent of the spoken word?
2. What is the main reason cited by parents for purchasing mobile communication technologies for their children?
3. Name three potentially positive effects of mobile technology on the family.
4. Identify two potentially negative impacts of computer technologies on the family.
5. What are the three most popular uses of the Internet?
6. On balance, do you think information and communication technologies benefit or hurt families? How so?

References

Aries, P. (1962). *Centuries of childhood: A social history of family life.* New York: Vintage Books.

Blinn-Pike, L. (2009). Technology and the family: An overview from the 1980s to the present. *Marriage and Family Review, 45*(6-8), 567–575.

Dixon, S. (2011). Editor. *Journal of Developmental and Behavioral Pediatrics, 32*(7), 520.

Eberstadt, M., & Layden, M. A. (2010). *The social costs of pornography.* Princeton, NJ: Witherspoon Institute.

Eisenstein, E. L. (1979). *The printing press as an agent of change.* New York: Cambridge University Press.

Gandossy, T. (2007). Technology transforming the leisure world. In *Current sociology.* Thousand Oaks, CA: Sage.

Geser, H. (2006). Is the cell phone undermining the social order? Understanding mobile technology from a sociological perspective. *Technology and Policy, 19,* 8–18.

Johnson, B. (2005, May 2). How U.S. consumers spend their time: A U.S. government study of a day in the life of America. *American Demographics*.

Johnson, B. (2006, March 20). Understanding the "generation wireless" demographic. *American Demographics*.

Lanigan, J. D. (2009). A sociotechnological model for family research and intervention. *Marriage and Family Review, 45*(6-8), 587-609.

Lenhart, A. (2011). *"How do they even do that?" Myths and facts about the impact of technology on the lives of American teens*. http://www.pewinternet.org/Presentations/2011/Apr/From-Texting-to-Twitter.aspx

Madden, M., & Zickuhr, K. (2011). *65% of online adults use social networking sites*. http://www.pewinternet.org/Reports/2011/Social-Networking-Sites/Report/Part-1.aspx

Manning, J. C. (2005). *Senate testimony*. http://judiciary.senate.gov/hearings/testimony.cfm?id=e655f9e2809e5476862f735da10c87dc&wit_id=e655f9e2809e5476862f735da10c87dc-1-3

National Telecommunications and Information Administration. (2004). *A nation online: Entering the broadband age*. http://www.ntia.doc.gov/reports/anol/NationOnlineBroadband04.htm#_Toc78020930

Pawlowski, C. (2000). *Glued to the tube: The threat of television addiction to today's family*. Naperville, IL: Sourcebooks.

Salmond, K., & Percell, K. (2011). *Trends in teen communication and social media use: What's really going on here?* http://www.pewinternet.org/~/media//Files/Presentations/2011/Feb/Pew%20Internet_Girl%20Scout%20Webinar%20PDF.pdf

Smith, A. (2011). *Americans and their cell phones*. http://www.pewinternet.org/Reports/2011/Cell-Phones.aspx

Teitell, B. (2011, March 27.). Connected, exhausted: Texting teenagers who stay "on call" all night pay the price in lost sleep. *Boston Globe*.

Chapter 30

The "Plugged-In" Family: The Dialectics of Digital Technology in the Everyday Life of Families

Charles Soukup

In an episode of the popular television program *Modern Family* titled "Unplugged," on seeing a breakfast table filled with cell phones, laptop computers, and portable video game players, the family's matriarch demands that the family discontinue their use of new technologies for 1 week (by setting up a friendly wager) (Levitan, 2010). She is concerned that the family no longer engages in pleasant family conversation, as each member is isolated within his or her digital technology. Predictably, situation comedy high jinks ensue with family members sneaking around the house with their various digital devices. After this brief rupture in their domestic routines (the wager is resolved with the father "relapsing" with his laptop), by the end of the episode the family returns to the familiar habits of their various communication technologies.

Today, parents use technology for family communication throughout their children's lives: the digital video of a fetus via ultrasound (now in high definition), the baby monitor in the first days after birth, the cell phone surveilling the teen out on Friday nights, the Skype videoconferences with the child away at college, and the Facebook photo updates of their grandchildren. To put it simply, for many Americans, family life is increasingly dominated by digital technology. The "plugged-in" family faces a number of dialectic tensions that help explain why families lament dissatisfaction with the use of technology in their everyday lives yet, despite this apparent dissatisfaction, adopt digital technologies at an increasing rate. Via a representative case study concerning the family dinner, I hope to reveal the emergent dialectical tensions of digital media devices in contemporary family life.

Over the past several years, book chapters in anthologies such as *The Handbook of Family Communication* and *The Family Communication Sourcebook* have lamented the scarcity of research concerning the dynamic communication processes associated with new media in the family (Bryant & Bryant, 2006; Jennings & Wartela, 2004). In fact, reviewing literature between 2000 and 2011, there is a consistent call for more research in this "understudied" area (see Hughes & Hans, 2001; Mesch, 2006). I share these lamentations, as only a handful of studies have emerged since these anthologies and articles were published. As the research concerning family communicative applications of digital technology is in its infancy, this chapter intends to chart the terrain of families and digital technology as a means of fostering new areas of research and new lines of thought. Digital technology, once a relatively small part of family life, is now a routine and consistent facet of many families' daily lives. In this respect, the plugged-in family represents a kind of evotypical family.

A Few Initial Points of Clarification

I deliberately use the term "digital technology" rather than more limiting terms such as "information technology" or "mobile devices" because of the obvious media convergences of recent years. Interoperability is the norm with content and applications moving between smart phones, tablet computers, notebook computers, desktop computers, video game consoles, and high-definition televisions rather seamlessly. In 2011, it seems a bit peculiar to make harsh distinctions between various machines that increasingly perform the same functions such as accessing social networking, watching television programs and movies, listening to music, videoconferencing, and so on. Interoperability is dependent on digitization (Evens, 2003). In simplest terms, the "digital" refers to numerical representation via binary code (Manovich, 2001). For the purposes of this chapter emphasizing everyday communication practices, the technical details of digitization are not relevant. More practically for everyday communication practices, due to the tremendous interoperability/convergences offered by digital technology, various digital devices should be viewed as a whole rather than distinct machines with distinct qualities, applications, or implications. Of course, extensive research has explored the role of more traditional (analogue) broadcast media, particularly television (this literature is examined in chapter 29 in this volume).

In addition, this chapter warrants an initial caveat. The technologies highlighted in this chapter are often relatively "cutting-edge" devices associated with so-called early adopters. In complex postindustrial Western societies with vast chasms between rich and poor as well as considerable cultural/sociological differences, not all families are represented by the bourgeois upper-middle-class experiences (so vividly portrayed by *Modern Family*) of early technological adoption. Nonetheless, recent evidence suggests that the so-called digital divide is shrinking across various groups within Western societies with Internet access and mobile devices now in the hands of people from remarkably diverse geographic, economic, and ethnic backgrounds (Castells, Fernandez-Ardevol, Qiu, & Sey, 2007). For instance, while people from different age-groups may emphasize different activities via digital media (e.g., social networking, e-mail, research, or shopping), today just about everyone is using digital technology (Jones & Fox, 2009). Further, evidence indicates that African Americans and Hispanics are now relatively early adopters of smart phone technology (Castells et al., 2007). In fact, rather than an exceptional segment of society, Western cultures are now *filled* with early adopters of technology.

Finally, at the outset, I caution readers against neo-Luddite, dystopian views of technology suggesting that digital media are *inherently* contrary to happy, satisfying family life. In fact, research indicates that the assumption that "media cause children to become antisocial, violent, unproductive" is pervasive among parents (even media- and technologically savvy parents) (Horst, 2010, p. 150). Certainly, technology can be a source of dissatisfaction and alienation in families. Nonetheless, technology can also be a source of renewal, a means to sustain ties at a distance, offering unique opportunities for creative and satisfying family interaction. Most important, digital technology, for better or worse, is now the *reality* for families. Attempting to stop the flow of technology and/or completely disconnecting from our machines not only is unrealistic but would mean disconnecting from our careers and social lives—basically, disconnecting from the society at large. While we may long for Thoreau's Walden (I certainly have occasionally fantasized about such a utopian pastoral life), for most of us a remote cabin in the woods is not a realistic domestic life in the 21st century.

Digital Technology in the Family Home

Since the turn of the 21st century, American families live in increasingly media-saturated homes (Jennings & Wartella, 2006). As Horst (2010) observed, "In effect, a large share of young people's engagement with new media—using social network sites, instant messaging services, and gaming—occurs in the context of home and family life" (p. 150). Initially, I simply want to sketch the major technological processes at play (and at work) in the everyday life experiences within the domestic home.

Families' integration of technology into everyday life echoes larger trends concerning the proliferation of digital media across American culture. A group of researchers from Ball State University's Center for Media Design estimated that "adults are exposed to screens—TVs, cellphones, even G.P.S. devices—for about 8.5 hours on any given day" (Stelter, 2009). Mobile phones saturate American culture, as "85% of Americans now own a cell phone. Cell phone ownership rates among young adults illustrate the extent to which mobile phones have become a necessity of modern communications: fully 96% of 18–29 year olds own a cell phone of some kind" (Smith, 2010). Further, 76% of Americans own a computer, with the greatest statistical increases in laptop ownership (Smith, 2010). With the emergence of inexpensive flat-screen high-definition televisions, American homes are filled with television screens (often connected to video game consoles, DVD players, and so on). Today, the average American home has more televisions than people (Bauder, 2006) and there are now more televisions in the United States than there are people (Starr, 2009).

Certainly, media technologies have been significant in the family home since (at least) the 1950s. Further, research in the early 1990s by Lindlof (1992) suggested that personal computers produced complex meanings within families. Digital screens in the contemporary plugged-in family differ from previous media forms because, today, every family member has his or her own personalized television, mp3 player, computer, and smart phone "fostering privatization and individualization of media use" (Jennings & Wartella, 2006). Rather than sharing a *family* television, telephone, or computer, family members now stare at their own personalized digital screens.

Most significant, complex meanings are associated with the technologies that fill the contemporary family home. Based on the initial research into technology and the family, these meanings cluster around a few key themes. First, the boundaries and rules associated with technology in the home are consistent sources of conflict among parents and children. Caron and Caronia (2007) concluded that, "once they are integrated into family routine, NICTs [new information and communication technologies] lead parents and children to constantly redefine boundaries for the family institution" (p. 201). The second, closely related theme is a complicated ambivalence concerning technologies in the home. Schiffrin, Edelman, Falkenstern, and Stewart (2010) called this a "a new Internet paradox" in which "individuals report less fulfilling communication online but continue to increase the amount of time they communicate with others online" (p. 305). Finally, technological objects are associated with routine and habitual daily practices. As Stern and Messer (2009) concluded, "What we found in this study is that people use the technologies available to them to fill the niches in which they believe they are most useful" (p. 671).

The general idea that can be gleaned from the themes of these various interdisciplinary studies into technology in the family is that technologies are closely integrated into the everyday lives of family members. Therefore, in this chapter, I am interested in the unique communicative dynamics *between* family members with digital technologies in their everyday lives. By "everyday life," I simply mean the routine temporal and spatial relationships in the family—mundane practices within the time and space of daily life (e.g., "everyday" family rules, rituals, patterns of talk, and so on). Of course, with myriad technologies and countless everyday practices, the topic of technology in the everyday lives of families can seem overwhelming in scope. For the sake of clarity and focus, I will emphasize examples from a daily practice associated (in some form) with all families—the family dinner.

Case Study: The Dialectics of Family Dinner

For Americans, the family dinner has come to represent the possibilities of both the tight-knit cohesiveness and the unraveling disintegration of the family unit. The family dinner offers a compelling representative anecdote to focus attention on the unique dynamics of digital technology in families. In Burke's (1969) conceptualization, a representative anecdote is a "summation" or "prototype" (pp. 60–61) of a complex phenomenon or process—in this case, the role of digital technology in everyday family life.

With their flair for the obvious and uncontroversial, pop culture and self-help literature consistently point to the family dinner as a kind of panacea for what ails families. The family dinner represents at least two important signifiers for Americans: the nightly routine of coming together and sharing food over a discussion of the day's events and the major holiday celebration (Thanksgiving, Christmas, Easter, Independence Day, and so on) when extended family gather together for a large meal. Pervasive iconography dominates our understanding of the family dinner with nostalgic images in Norman Rockwell paintings and classic television programs such as *Happy Days* and *The Andy Griffith Show* (both of which continue to run daily on cable television) featuring friendly banter around family dinners. The argument is both simple and clear: Happy families eat dinner together without technology/media, while unhappy families eat dinner as individuals while plugged into technology (Gibbs, 2006). As self-help gurus and bloggers almost uniformly argue, technology is a major reason that families fail to have meaningful conversations around the dinner table (or anywhere else for that matter).

Having nightly dinner together as a family is in that rare class of practices such as sending your grandmother a birthday card or flossing your teeth daily that no reasonable person could disagree with. Interestingly, despite its obvious benefits, the family dinner continues to be a source of conflict for families—conflict increasingly revolving around technology (Caron & Caronia, 2007; Edley & Houston, 2011). The family dinner actually involves a wide range of important issues facing individuals within Western cultures: obesity and high-sugar, high-fat diets; the stresses of increasingly demanding postindustrial work; the "McDonaldization" and standardization of consumer products by multinational franchises; and so on. Of course, technology is related to all of these issues, but my focus here is more interpersonal than macrocultural—I am interested in how family members relate to one another in everyday life.

Dialectical vacillation appears to be essential to the experiences swirling about digital technology and family life. For real people facing the unique challenges of the 21st-century technological family, the fluid dialectical ebb and flow of balancing many demands vividly represents their experiences (Golden, 2009; Ling & Donner, 2009). While I certainly do not have the space to inventory the remarkably generative set of ideas and research conclusions that have emerged from dialectic theory, I will highlight a few key theoretical threads that have unique salience to digital technology in families. First, dialectics emphasize the perpetual and ongoing process of change. Baxter (2004b) argued, "Instead, relational dialectics, like dialogism more generally, displaces the notion of a center with a focus on ongoing centripetal–centrifugal flux. There is no center, only flux" (p. 186). Perhaps no material objects in everyday life represent *change* better than new technologies, which, of course, evolve at a dizzying pace. The tremendous flux of technology lends itself to dialectic theory. In addition, dialectics highlight the processual and social constructivist nature of relationships. As Baxter (2004b) explains, "Relationships are close not because preformed selves are revealed but because the parties' selves are given shape through relating" (p. 187). In very similar ways, we give shape to the meaning and function of technologies by interacting with and through these technologies in our everyday lives. Facebook or text messaging have meaning and value only when people integrate these technologies into their daily practices. In addition, technology, like dialectics, is also about the unexpected, sometimes moving in unpredictable directions as new cultural formations emerge often via convergences (e.g., the rapid proliferation of Facebook or Twitter in families). Baxter (2004a) likens dialogic dialectical processes to jazz as "the interplay of utterances takes the interactants to places unforeseeable at the beginning of the conversation and in unscripted ways" (p. 11). In line with dialectical theory, interaction with technology is also highly ritualistic, evoking complex contradictions. As Baxter (2004a) defines, "A ritual, then, is a joint performance in which competing, contradictory voices in everyday social life are brought together simultaneously" (p. 13). Ritualized contradictions seem ever present in the integration of technology in everyday life—as represented in the following dialectical tensions associated with technology in the family.

Autonomy–Control

The dialectical struggles of adolescents over autonomy are a common rite of passage within Western societies. As Horst (2010) observed, "The anxiety surrounding the integration of new media into the home also reflects concerns about independence, separation, and autonomy that, at least in the context of Western societies, occur during the teenage years" (p. 152). While parents lament the unknown qualities of their children's technological world (e.g., what are they doing in a video game community, who are they talking to on Facebook, and so on), children lament the constant surveillance of their parents over their technology use (Caron & Caronia, 2007). Technology is a consistent source of battles over control in families. Based on interviews with families about mobile technology, Caron and Caronia (2007) described "a complex dialectic between the parental duty to exercise control and children's rights to independence and freedom" (p. 208). Researchers have consistently observed the struggles over establishing rules and boundaries for access to a wide range of technologies (television, video games, telephone, and so on) in the home (Jennings & Wartella, 2006). More specifically, Mesch (2006) found that "our most salient finding was that adolescent–parent conflict over Internet use was widespread" (p. 489). A dynamic negotiation process concerning the child's freedom to choose when and where to use media devices and parent's control over this media use has been unfolding in families for quite some time. Horst's (2010) research echoes the stories of my students who describe a constant threat of parental surveillance of their social networking and text messaging. Like Foucault's often-cited panopticon, the parent does not actually have to watch every move the child makes with their media devices—children are disciplined simply by the *possibility* of surveillance.

Somewhat ironically, parental surveillance of social networking and mobile devices can actually offer children greater freedom by allowing the child more time spent away from home and the physical presence of their parents (Caron & Caronia, 2007). In fact, empirical observations (Horst, 2010) indicate that the rules associated with new media are based on a number of specific, situational factors, such as (a) the unique needs of family members (single parents providing latchkey kids cell phones), (b) changes in a family's monthly budget due to professional changes (the number of minutes allocated for texting or mobile phone use), (c) parents growing familiarity with new media devices, or (d) the evolving responsibility/irresponsibility demonstrated by children with social networking or text messaging. As both technologies and children continue to develop, parents have found it necessary to maintain fluidity with boundaries and rules based on the emergent dynamics in the home and family.

Family meals clearly represent the dialectical vacillation associated with autonomy and control. While few parents consciously create family norms that involve everyone sitting at the breakfast table staring at individualized digital screens, due to dynamic dialectical processes, they wake up one day and see their family tethered to smart phones, laptops, and video games while eating their Cheerios. Many parents try to establish firm rules about mealtime, such as no television or no computers at the dining room table, but, due to life's demands and the pressures of children, parents often bend these rules (Golden, 2009). As technology allows children more time away from home, presumably children (especially teens and even "tweens") are eating more meals away from home with greater decision-making power over their food choices. Simultaneously, technologies, functioning as an electronic leash or collar, allow parents to surveil their children's eating practices away from the home.

As an unpredictable dialectical process, more people feel "controlled" by their technology. The increasingly popular practice of families "unplugging" from technology for a weekend indicates a desire to regain a sense of control over technology (Rubin, 2010). In addition, an almost endless variety of "life management" apps (offering an "illusion of control") are available for smart phones and tablet computers (see the iTunes or Android app stores), suggesting that people are feeling the dialectical vacillations associated with control/powerlessness over technology in the everyday lives of families (Edley & Houston, 2011). These issues of autonomy–control also blend into the blurring boundaries associated with technology in families.

Family–Nonfamily Boundaries

Communication research has effectively documented the ways that digital technologies blur the private and public domains (Caron & Caronia, 2007). For instance, telework is increasingly common in Western societies with professionals bringing their work into the home (Edley & Houston, 2011). This blurring, like most implications of new technology, can facilitate both productive/healthy communication practices in families as well as destructive/unhealthy practices in families. Cell phones can create "spillover" between work and family that some people perceive as negative (Chesley, 2005). Further indicating an ambivalent dialectical vacillation, based on survey data, more than half of respondents believe that a mobile phone used for both work and social interaction "helps them to balance their family and working lives" (Wajcman, Bittman, & Brown, 2008, p. 642). Multitasking is another form of blurring boundaries: "with the blackberry, users tried to do more than one thing at once," leading to "work-family interference" or "overlap" (Middleton, 2008, pp. 36–37). While technology keeps us in "perpetual contact" (Katz & Aakhus, 2002) with work, it *also* keeps us in perpetual contact with family.

Meals become an interesting ritual performance of the blurring between work and family life. Telework creates dialectical dynamics for family meals. Indicating a conflicting state of attention or multitasking between family and work, research indicates that only a small portion of people turn off their mobile phones during mealtimes (Wajcman et al., 2008). The employee might feel an inclination to have his or her smart phone at the dinner table to address any urgent work issues. On the other hand, diners once stuck at the office or in traffic are now in the home with the family. Further, the "private" lives of families are now increasingly public via digital media, as "what used to be 'family' business is now available to a multitude of Facebook friends" (Edley & Houston, 2011, p. 209). In terms of family dinner, it is not uncommon to find the menu and even recipes of family dinners on Facebook. For instance, some of my Facebook friends, often vegetarians or vegans, will proudly post weekly meal plans on their Facebook page, sometimes with photographs of their meals. These examples suggest a greater permeability of family boundaries with a constant dialectical overlapping and interweaving of various public/private domains of everyday life.

Connection–Disconnection

Despite conventional wisdom concerning the inherent impersonalness of new technology, it appears that technology can be a mechanism for building intimacy/closeness as well as creating feelings of separation and detachment (Bryant & Bryant, 2006). In this regard, the movement between connection and disconnection via technology in families has been described as dialectical in nature. As Christensen (2009) observed, "This tension between ICT 'bringing together the family' versus 'distributing family members' was expressed by the participants' ambivalent attitude towards children's use of media technologies" (p. 449). Research indicates that cell phone use, while encouraging greater mobility and movement outside the home, can also increase connectedness between family members via mobile expressions of affection (Wei & Lo, 2006). Text messaging between family members at different locations can sustain a sense of intimacy despite physical distance (Wajcman et al., 2008). The practice of frequent texts, mobile phone calls, e-mails, and so on throughout the day has become normative in many families (Christenson, 2009). When engaging in a discussion about texting with my students, many admitted that they send romantic partners and close friends many short messages (e.g., "this class is soooo boring" or "I hate rainy days") throughout their school day or workday. In our discussion, we realized that the content of these messages is actually quite irrelevant because the relational message is always the same: "I'm thinking about you." Similarly, digital devices have an important role for nonresidential parents to maintain daily contact with their children (Edley & Houston, 2011). Mobile phones are also often used for microcoordination in families by efficiently managing scheduling on the move (Castells, et al., 2007; Katz & Akhaus, 2002). While families may foster cohesiveness with digital technology, families also often experience a state of "absent presence" when "one is physically present but is absorbed by a technologically mediated world of elsewhere" (Gergen, 2002, p. 227). Technologies allow people physically near one another to be mentally miles and miles away.

The family dinner vividly represents these tensions. For instance, a text message during dinner could bring an embodied family member into a state of absent presence while sitting at the dinner table. On the other hand, receiving a text message while sitting alone among the neutral white walls of a company's generic conference room eating lunch can actually create a sense of connectedness while physically apart. Mobile devices can also serve an important role in microcoordinating schedules to enable family members to find an hour in their busy schedules to meet face-to-face for a family dinner (Chistensen, 2009). The mobility, absent presence, and perpetual contact associated with digital media encourage tremendous dialectical fluidity concerning connectedness and disconnectedness in families.

Conclusion

Due to the rapid evolution of digital media, observations and conclusions about technology in the family must be made with a fair amount of contingency and tentativeness. A few things seem relatively clear. Families will continue to integrate digital technology into their everyday lives in meaningful ways. In addition, the communicative applications of these technologies will be filled with contradictions, ambivalences, and complexities. In this respect, the phrase "plugged in" (as referenced in the title of this chapter) has two important meanings. The popular meaning of "plugged in," of course, references being connected to technology. A second meaning, as highlighted by Merriam-Webster.com, is "to remedy (a deficiency) as if by inserting a plug <trying to *plug* the gaps in their understanding>." My hope is that the families already plugged into technology also become plugged into understanding the implications of technologies in their everyday lives.

Discussion Questions

1. What other dialectical tensions are associated with families and technology? (e.g., singular focus-multitasking, embodied-virtual, and so on)?
2. How do families make decisions when adopting new technologies?
3. How do families manage their technology use?
4. How do the dialectical vacillations associated with new technology in families impact family members' overall satisfaction?

References

Bauder, D. (2006, September 21). Average home has more TVs than people. *Washington Post.* http://www.washingtonpost.com/wp-dyn/content/article/2006/09/21/AR2006092101007.html

Baxter, L. (2004a). Relationships as dialogues. *Personal Relationships, 11,* 1–22.

Baxter, L. (2004b). A tale of two voices: Relational dialectics theory. *Journal of Family Communication, 4,* 181–192.

Bryant, J. A., & Bryant, J. (2006). Implications of living in a wired family: New directions in family and media research. In L. Turner & R. West (Eds.), *The family communication sourcebook.* Thousand Oaks, CA: Sage.

Burke, K. (1969). *A grammar of motives.* Berkeley: University of California Press.

Caron, A., & Caronia, L. (2007). *Moving cultures: Mobile communication in everyday life.* Montreal: McGill-Queen's University Press.

Castells, M., Fernandez-Ardevol, M., Qiu, J., & Sey, A. (2007). *Mobile communication and society: A global perspective.* Cambridge, MA: MIT Press.

Chesley, N. (2005). Blurring boundaries? Linking technology use, spillover, individual distress, and family satisfaction. *Journal of Marriage and Family, 67,* 1237–1248

Christensen, T. (2009). Connected presence in distributed family life. *New Media and Society, 11,* 433–451.

Edley, P., & Houston R. (2011). The more things change, the more they stay the same: The role of ICTs in work and family connections. In K. Wright & L. Webb (Eds.), *Computer-mediated communication in personal relationships* (pp. 194–221). New York: Peter Lang.

Evens, A. (2003). Concerning the digital. *Differences: A Journal of Feminist Cultural Studies, 14,* 49–77.

Gergen, K. (2002). The challenge of absent presence. In J. Katz & M. Aakhus (Eds.), *Perpetual contact: Mobile communication, private talk, public performance* (pp. 227–241). Cambridge: Cambridge University Press.

Gibbs, N. (2006, June 4). The magic of the family meal. *Time.* http://www.time.com/time/magazine/article/0,9171,1200760,00.html

Golden, A. (2009). A technologically gendered paradox of efficiency: Caring more about work while working in more care. In S. Kleinman (Ed.), *The culture of efficiency* (pp. 339–354). New York: Peter Lang.

Horst, H. (2010). Families. In M. Ito (Ed.), *Hanging out, messing around, and geeking out* (pp. 149–194). Cambridge, MA: MIT Press.

Hughes, R., & Hans, J. (2001). Computers, the Internet, and families: A review of the role new technology plays in family life. *Journal of Family Issues, 22,* 776–790.

Jennings, N., & Wartella, E. (2004). Technology and the family. In A. Vangelisti (Ed.), *Handbook of family communication* (pp. 593–609). Mahwah, NJ: Lawrence Erlbaum Associates.

Jennings, N. A., & Wartella, E. A. (2006). Advertising and consumer development. In N. Pecora, J. P. Murray, & E. Wartella (Eds.), *Children and television: 50 years of research.* Mahwah, NJ: Lawrence Erlbaum Associates.

Jones, S., & Fox, S. (2009, January 28). *Pew Internet and American Life Project.* http://www.pewinternet.org/Reports/2009/Generations-Online-in-2009.aspx

Katz, J., & Aakhus, M. (2002). Conclusion: Making meaning of mobiles—A theory of Apparatgeist. In J. Katz & M. Aakhus (Eds.), *Perpetual contact: Mobile communication, private talk, public performance* (pp. 301–318). Cambridge: Cambridge University Press.

Levitan, S. (Executive Producer). (2010). Unplugged. *Modern Family.* Los Angeles: ABC Television

Lindlof, T. (1992) Computing tales: Parents' discourse about technology and family. *Social Science Computer Review, 10,* 291–309.

Ling, R., & Donner, J. (2009). *Mobile communication.* Cambridge, MA: Polity Press.

Manovich, L. (2001). *The language of new media.* Cambridge, MA: The MIT Press.

Mesch, G. (2006). Family characteristics and intergenerational conflicts over the internet. *Information, Communication and Society, 9,* 473–495.

Middleton, C. (2008). Illusions of balance and control in the always on environment: A case study of blackberry users. In G. Goggin (Ed.), *Mobile phone cultures* (pp. 28–41). London: Routledge.

Rubin, G. (2010). Find a way to unplug from technology, or, how to escape the cubicle in your pocket. *Psychology Today.* http://www.psychologytoday.com/blog/the-happiness-project/201003/find-way-unplug-technology-or-how-escape-the-cubicle-in-your-pocke

Schiffrin, H., Edelman, A., Falkenstern, M., & Stewart, C. (2010). The associations among computer-mediated communication, relationships, and well-being. *Cyberpsychology, Behavior, and Social Networking, 13,* 299–306.

Smith, A. (2010, October 14). *Americans and their gadgets.* http://www.pewinternet.org/Reports/2010/Gadgets.aspx

Starr, M. (2009, July 22). More TVs than humans. *New York Post.*http://www.nypost.com/p/entertainment/tv/item_3UM2vSI2DGw2q7XiJ1PdwK;jsessionid=762EB4CD645C5CA7A14CF1BEA877D33F

Stelter, B. (2009, March 26). 8 hours a day spent on screens, study finds. *New York Times.* http://www.nytimes.com/2009/03/27/business/media/27adco.html

Stern, M., & Messer, C. (2009). How family members stay in touch: A quantitative investigation of core family networks. *Marriage and Family Review, 45,* 654–676.

Wajcman, W., Bittman, M., & Brown, J. (2008). Divisions families without borders: Mobile phones, connectedness and work-home.*Sociology, 42,* 635–652.

Wei, J., & Lo, V. (2006). Staying connected while on the move: Cell phone use and socialconnectedness. *New Media Society, 8,* 53–72.

Chapter 31

Pathways to Marital Satisfaction in Interfaith and Interracial Marriages

Patrick C. Hughes, John R. Baldwin, and Bolanle Olaniran

Religious and racial intermarriage is increasingly common in the United States, and racial and religious homogeneity appear to be less important in the selection of a romantic relationship partner than decades ago. Whitehead and Popenoe (2001) forecast this "marrying out" pattern to continue to increase at the turn of the century, and recent data have validated this trend (Sahl & Bateson, 2011; Taylor et al., 2010). In most cases, the literature brackets intermarriage according to race, culture, ethnicity, or religion. However, in many instances of intermarriage, partners differ in both race and religious backgrounds, yet few have considered the relationship processes among partners who are both religiously and racially different. It may be that overlapping identity differences may compound the issues faced by intermarriage as well as the relationship dynamics of these interracial and interfaith families (Haji, Lalonde, Durbin, & Vaveh-Benjamine, 2011; Hecht & Baldwin, 1998).

Marriages that are interracial, interfaith, or both may be less stable than homogamous marriages (Bystydzienski, 2011; Knobloch & Carpenter-Thune, 2004). Some evidence suggest that "racial and religious heterogamy detract from marital stability, but the effects are nearly twice as large for religion" (Heaton, 2002, p. 79). Some have stated that intermarried individuals are more prone to divorce (Leslie & Letiecq, 2004; Yoshida & Busby, 2011). It is possible that, in addition to causing conflict, differences in race or religion in a marriage may also influence couples' communication, such as during conflict negotiation. Therefore, we take a conceptual or "pathways" perspective in describing some of the relational dynamics of this emerging family type by discussing, theoretically, the underlying cultural and religious dimensions to these relationships. Additionally, we provide results from a small study examining the impact of perceived and real cultural and religious differences between the partners' on their relationship processes in interracial and interfaith marriages and families. These pathways invite you to integrate your conceptualizations of interfaith and interracial marriages as both religious and culturally unique relationships.

Intercultural, Intergroup, "Third-Culture," and Religious Characteristics of Interfaith and Interracial Marriages

The *intercultural* aspect of the relationship refers to real differences between groups of people based on culture, such as in ways of thinking, communicating, or behaving (Hecht, Jackson, & Ribeau, 2003). Partners often deny the existence of such differences in their relationships (Bustamente, Nelson, Henricksen, & Monakes, 2011; Karis, 2003). Many sources on intervention and remediation for intermarried couples advocate an awareness of cultural differences, for example, in terms of perceptions of hierarchy, communication differences, role division, family boundaries, and so on (Sandage, 2011). Scholars often attribute lack of marital stability or satisfaction to racial and religious differences between partners (Heaton, 2002; Poulson, 2003). Partners may differ in terms of value orientations (Crohn, 1998), the meaning and importance of marriage (Dainton, 1999), or the level of connection to families of origin (Timmer, Veroff, & Hatchett, 1996).

The *intergroup* aspect pertains to perceptions of differences simply because one perceives the other to be a member of another group. This relates to intergroup perception, stereotypes, and group-based prejudice. These three issues should be present whether the marriage is interfaith or interracial. Research suggests that the greatest difficulty for interracial marriages within the United States will be the reaction of family and community members to the relationship rather than real cultural differences. Several researchers have determined that intermarried couples may feel stigma or a sense of loss resulting from racism (Chan & Wethington, 1988; Lewandowski & Jackson, 2001; Rosenblatt & Tubbs, 1998; Tubbs & Rosenblatt, 2003). Despite a fair level of overall support for interracial relationships in particular found in some studies (e.g., Killian, 2003; Zebroski, 1999), one study found a sense of social isolation in leisure activities, perceived largely in terms of racism (Hibbler & Shinew, 2002). The same patterns seem to hold for interfaith couples (Greenstein, Carlson, & Howell, 1993). Some suggest that partners themselves may hold prejudicial attitudes toward the partner's group (Allport, 1954; Falicov, 1995). In times of stress, racial identities rather than real cultural differences might become salient (Killian, 2002), influencing marital stability or satisfaction (Chan & Wethington, 1998).

Families and couples create their own cultures (Dodd & Baldwin, 2002), interpreting, filtering, and importing aspects of their respective cultures and the dominant culture (Gushue & Sciarra, 1995). Some have called this a "third" culture or a "relational" culture. Partners may either already see themselves similar in group and cultural terms prior to interfaith or interethnic dating or marriage or converge toward one another during the relationship. Thus, interfaith partners may become more secularized (Voas, 2003), shift to a more moderate denomination of the religion of origin (Lazerwitz, 1995), or alter their level of commitment (Sherkat, 2004). Still, some researchers have found the importance of maintaining one's identity of origin for the increased satisfaction of the relationship (Bell, Bouie, & Baldwin, 1990; Leslie & Letiecq, 2004).

Religion involves more than worship style; it also includes different lifestyles, values, and cultures (Chinitz & Brown, 2001) that may be sources of conflict. Interfaith marriages are found to be less stable and more likely to end in divorce than same-faith marriages (Lehrer & Chiswick, 1993). Interfaith partners also claim to experience greater social difficulty and stress in the religious upbringing of their children (Chinitz & Brown, 2001; Williams & Lawler, 2000). For instance, differences between Judaism and Christian denominations are more pronounced than those between various Christian denominations. Religious heterogeneity is positively correlated with conflict and hence lower marital satisfaction (Chinitz & Brown, 2001).

Level of religious involvement may also be important to a marriage relationship. Beyond the phenomenon of religious shift prior to marriage or during marriage (Sander, 1993; Sherkat, 2004; Voas, 2003), in Williams and Lawler's (2003) study of 1,512 interviews, religious differences proved to be the greatest predictor of marital satisfaction. Shehan, Bock, and Lee (1990) found that Catholics who were in same-faith marriages were more likely to attend mass, and Williams and Lawler (2001) found partners in interreligious marriages to report lower religiosity and emphasis in religion in child raising. Such differences may impact a relationship if the partners feel themselves going in different spiritual directions.

As indicated above, interfaith marriages sometimes transcend differences in faith. This may be because partners do not hold their religious identities with high salience (Hecht et al., 2003), or it may be that partners in such relationships have "internalized" their religion. Allport (1966) suggests that an individual's religious orientation might be intrinsic or extrinsic. Religiously intrinsic people are said to be more spiritual and thus more flexible and open or tolerant of different viewpoints than religiously extrinsic people who are less spiritual, flexible, and tolerant of others. The religiously extrinsic orientation argument is consistent with the findings that highly religious individuals rated the "self" to be better on nonreligious attributes than did less religious individuals (Rowatt, Ottenbreit, Nesselroade, & Cunningham, 2002). Also, a study of intermarried Catholics led to the conclusion that, while being in an interfaith marriage by itself "did not significantly affect Catholics' marital happiness," an interaction effect demonstrated that those Catholics who reported more frequent mass attendance reported a lower marital satisfaction (Shehan et al., 1990, p. 77). A difference in religious orientation (rather than a difference in faith or denomination) may have greater consequences on interpersonal interaction, especially where religion is a salient feature of the interpersonal relationship (Allport, 1966; Hughes, 2004; Hughes & Dickson, 2005, 2006).

Intermarried couples face cultural and religious difficulties that are both similar and unique to other types of relationships (Root, 2001). The fourfold approach we introduce suggests that conflict in intermarriage—or any relationship—will be based on individual factors, on cultural expression (i.e., real cultural differences), or on intergroup factors (i.e., the perceptions of group identity by the partners and surrounding family or community) as well as the religious orientations of the partners. The next section of this chapter, first, describes results from a small-scale empirical case study in which we examine these influences on intermarried partners' reports of marital satisfaction and, second, applies our theoretical approach to the findings.

The Effects of Cultural and Religious Dynamics on Reports of Marital Satisfaction in Interfaith and Interracial Marriages

We conducted a small study intended to demonstrate the impact of the cultural and religious factors described here on the quality of interfaith and interracial marriages (contact the first author for a complete copy of this unpublished research report). To this end, we surveyed 334 people who were in an interfaith/interracial marriage. We surveyed both European American and African American males ($N = 186$) and females ($N = 148$) from both Christian and Jewish religious denominations: Christian (50.0%), Jewish (41.9%), and not reported (8.1%). We asked the participants to report on their communication conflict preferences, strength of religious commitment, preference for practicing their faiths, and marital satisfaction.

The results of this study suggest that interfaith and interracial married partners' relational dynamics may be influenced in part by the four factors described in the first section of this chapter. For instance, Jewish participants reported significantly more demand–withdraw communication (one partner pursues a resolution over a conflict, while the other partner avoids addressing the matter) ($M = 25.67$, $SD = 9.0$) than non-Jewish (Christian) participants ($M = 21.22$, $SD = 9.0$) ($t = -4.11$, $df = 305$, $p = .001$). African Americans reported significantly more demand–withdraw communication ($M = 23.24$, $SD = 9.87$) than European American participants ($M = 19.9$, $SD = 8.9$) ($t = -2.32$, $df = 332$, $p = .02$) and less marital satisfaction ($M = 103.36$, $SD = 22.78$) than

European Americans in this study ($M = 117.47$, $SD = 14.9$) ($t = 4.47$, $df = 332$, $p = .0001$) (for an introduction to demand–withdraw communication, see Christensen, 1988).

Overall, participants reported that their extrinsic religious orientation was indirectly related to their reports of marital satisfaction ($r = -162$, $p = .003$). That is, the more partners reported the need to practice their faiths in an interpersonal context with others, the less happy they were in their interfaith marriage (Spanier, 1976). Conversely, participants' reports of intrinsically practicing their faiths were directly related to reports of marital satisfaction ($r = .316$, $p = .0001$) (Allport, 1966). In other words, participants who internalized their religious identity were happier in their interfaith and interracial marriages. Finally, African American partners in interfaith/interracial marriages reported higher strength-of-faith scores ($M = 35.24$, $SD = 5.37$) than European American participants ($M = 31.88$, $SD = 6.96$) ($t = 3.84$, $df = 332$, $p = .0001$) (Plante & Boccaccini, 1997).

Conclusion

The results from this exploratory study on the impacts of the cultural and religious factors described in the first section of this chapter on relational dynamics and overall quality of interfaith/interracial marriages suggests that participants may interpret conflict through a cultural lens—in which conflict might be either experienced and perceived as more direct, include more withdrawal, or both. Such differences might become relevant not only in Jewish–Christian marriages but also in African American–European American relationships.

The present findings extend this notion to suggest that African Americans and members of some groups that may be defined both religious and ethnically (i.e., Jewish) may bring communication patterns from their home cultures into the relationship. This conclusion is theoretically interesting for a couple of reasons. First, writers have already noted that much of African American communication style is related to African histories and cultures (Hecht et al., 2003), such as the focus on the power of the word (*Nommo*; Weber, 1994). Perhaps a directness of speech in Jewish culture, in a parallel sense, is related to the *dugri* speech common in Israel (Katriel, 1986). The difficulty with this interpretation is that Jewish identity might relate either to ethnic identity or to a religious orientation and, if the latter, might refer to a belief in a set of doctrines or to a sense of belonging to a religious heritage.

A second reason the findings are interesting is that, regardless of the origin of cultural conversational norms at least in terms of conflict communication, the possibility that marital partners may avow more similar cultural elements, and the wide differences within cultural groups, a large number of Jewish and African American partners may still take cultural values into the relationship with them. These cultural values include both preferred conflict strategies (for both groups) and strength/importance of religion (for African Americans). The findings, for example, suggest that the importance of either church or spirituality fundamental to African American culture (Hecht et al., 2003) extends to those who are intermarried. Indeed, it may be that, if romantic partners validate each other's identities (Collier & Thomas, 1988), even those who feel and express their cocultural identity strongly may still engage in intergroup romance. That is, someone can perceive him- or herself strongly to be "African American" but also intermarry.

At the same time, African American intermarried partners reported a lower marital satisfaction than European Americans. To borrow from the cocultural theory of Orbe (1998a, 1998b), African

Americans who hold and express their identity more strongly, such as through extrinsic religion, may feel more of a tension in an interracial relationship, feeling a dual loyalty (to spouse and ethnic group) that can be fully understood only from the standpoint of someone in the relationship. Because many whites in society may suspect the motives of African Americans involved in intermarriage, African Americans in such marriages may face the emotional burden of dealing with stereotypes and negative attributions (despite the fact that research suggests that the main reason for interethnic dating is attraction for the other person) (Lampe, 1982). At the same time, the results echo a trend found in homogamous marriages (Acitelli, Douvan, & Veroff, 1997; Adelman, Chadwick, & Baerger, 1996), where African Americans in same-race marriages also report lower marital satisfaction than European Americans. Thus, the finding may relate to African American and European American perceptions of the marriage—an expression of cultural beliefs.

Furthermore, the findings highlight the different content that partners can hold toward their religious identities and the relationships that content has with other aspects of the intermarriage. Specifically, two partners holding the same religious identity (e.g., Christian) might hold it differently, one focusing on external form (extrinsic) and the other on spirituality (intrinsic). For some who are intermarried religiously, religious identity may be more of a symbol of identification—they are "born, married, and buried" in a church. They can "pass" for a member of another religion or keep their identity hidden, similar to Gans's (1979) notion of *symbolic ethnicity*. For these people, religious identity has low intensity and low salience and will not be an issue of consideration for their marital satisfaction. In the present study, partners who avow their identity (at the "individual," or psychological, level) (Hecht, 1993) extrinsically were less likely to be satisfied in intermarriage, perhaps because the salience of their religious identity was stronger in relation to the salience of their relational identity. Those who avowed their religious identity intrinsically were more satisfied, perhaps because their conceptualization of the content of their religious identity allowed for the inclusion of their interfaith partner within that identity.

Partners who are dating interreligiously or interethnically have many things to talk about including values, child-rearing practices, and financial obligations to family, but the present study again highlights the deep nature of culture, with implications for talk: An "iceberg" model of culture would also allow partners to discuss notions of what constitutes good logic in an argument, what is the value and meaning of conflict (Collier, 1991), and, from the present study, what are culturally or individually preferred styles of conflict. Partners can discuss how they sense their identities (at different times and in different contexts), how those identities relate to their relationship together, and how they relate to economic, cultural, and social power relationships between cultural groups. Finally, partners can discuss the topic of religion but not just in terms of doctrinal differences. Partners should have a concept of what religion means to the other person, whether their respective faiths are intrinsic or extrinsically held, and the strength of their partner's faith. In the end, either "culturally" or "religiously," partners need to know that they are going down the path in the same direction—or that, if they are keeping their paths separate but united, they are both comfortable with and respect the path of the other.

Discussion Questions

1. How do the authors conceptualize interfaith and interracial marriages?
2. In what ways are real and perceived cultural differences contrasted, and how might each differently impact marital satisfaction?
3. The results show that cultural and religious identities may affect perceptions of conflict in interfaith and interracial marriages. What are some other relational communication processes (i.e., social support and self-disclosure) that may be similarly affected by these identities?
4. What are some practical questions that intermarried partners may ask each other to better understand their partner's cultural identity, preferences for religious practice, and strength of religious commitment?
5. What are some other "paths" that intermarried couples may take to better understand the religious and cultural aspects of their marriages?

References

Acitelli, L. K., Douvan, E., & Veroff, J. (1997). The changing influence of interpersonal perceptions on marital well-being among African American and white couples. *Journal of Social and Personal Relationships, 14,* 291–304.

Adelman, P. K., Chadwick, K., & Baerger, D. R. (1996). Marital quality of African American and white adults over the life course. *Journal of Social and Personal Relationships, 13,* 361–384.

Allport, G. W. (1954). *The nature of prejudice.* Reading, MA: Addison-Wesley.

Allport, G. W. (1966). The religious context of prejudice. *Journal for the Scientific Study of Religion, 5,* 447–457.

Bell, Y. R., Bouie, C. L., & Baldwin, J. A. (1990). Afrocentric cultural consciousness and African-American male-female relationships. *Journal of Black Studies, 21,* 162–189.

Bustamente, R. M., Nelson, J. A., Henricksen, R. C., & Monakes, S. (2011). Intercultural couples: Coping with culture-related stressors. *The Family Journal, 19,* 154–164.

Bystydzienski, J. (2011). *Intercultural couples: Crossing boundaries, negotiating difference.* New York: New York University Press.

Chan, A. Y., & Wethington, E. (1998). Factors promoting marital resilience among interracial couples. In H. I. McCubbin, E. A. Thompson, & J. E. Fromer (Eds.), *Resiliency in Native American and immigrant families* (pp. 71-87). Thousand Oaks, CA: Sage.

Chinitz, J. G., & Brown, R. A. (2001). Religious homogamy, marital conflict, and stability in same-faith and interfaith Jewish marriages. *Journal for the Scientific Study of Religion, 40,* 723-733.

Christensen, A. (1988). Dysfunctional interaction patterns in couples. In P. Noller & M.A. Fitzpatrick (Eds.), *Perspectives on marital interaction* (pp. 31-52). Clevedon: Multilingual Matters.

Collier, M. J. (1991). Conflict competence within African, Mexican, and Anglo American friendships. In S. Ting-Toomey & F. Korzenny (Eds.), *Cross-cultural interpersonal communication* (pp. 132-154). Newbury Park, CA: Sage.

Collier, M. J., & Thomas, M. (1988). Cultural identity: An interpretive perspective. In Y. Y. Kim & W. B. Gudykunst (Eds.), *Theories in intercultural communication* (pp. 99-120). Newbury Park, CA: Sage.

Crohn, J. (1998). Intercultural couples. In M. McGoldrick (Ed.), *Re-visioning family therapy: Race, culture, and gender in clinical practice†*(pp. 295-308). New York: Guilford Press.

Dainton, M. (1999). African-American, European-American, and biracial couples' meanings for and experiences in marriage. In T. Socha & R. C. Diggs (Eds.), *Communication, race, and family: Exploring communication in black, white, and biracial families* (pp. 147-165). Mahwah, NJ: Lawrence Erlbaum Associates.

Dodd, C. H., & Baldwin, J. R. (2002). Family culture and relationship differences as a source of intercultural communication. In J. Martin, T. Nakayama, & L. Flores (Eds.), *Readings in cultural contexts* (2nd ed., pp. 279-288). New York: McGraw-Hill.

Falicov, C. J. (1995). Cross-cultural marriages. In N. Jacobson & A. S. Gurman (Eds.), *Clinical handbook of couple therapy* (pp. 231-246). New York: Guilford Press.

Gans, H. (1979). Symbolic ethnicity: The future of ethnic groups and cultures in America. *Ethnic and Racial Studies, 2,* 1-20.

Gushue, G. V., & Sciarra, D. T. (1995). Culture and families: A multidimensional approach. In J. G. Ponterotto, J. M. Casas, L. A. Suzuki, & C. M. Alexander (Eds.), *Handbook of multicultural counseling* (pp. 586-606). Thousand Oaks, CA: Sage.

Haji, R., Lalonde, R. N., Durbin, A., & Vaveh-Benjamine, L. (2011). A multidimensional approach to identity: Religious and cultural identity in young Jewish Canadians. *Group Processes and Intergroup Relations, 14,* 3-18.

Heaton, T. (2002). Factors contributing to increasing marital stability in the US. *Journal of Family Issues, 23,* 392-409.

Hecht, M. L. (1993). 2002: A research odyssey toward the development of a communication theory of identity. *Communication Monographs, 60,* 76-82.

Hecht, M. L., & Baldwin, J. R. (1998). Layers and holograms: A new look at prejudice. In M. L. Hecht (Ed.), *Communication of prejudice* (pp. 57-84). Thousand Oaks, CA: Sage.

Hecht, M. L., Jackson, R. L., III, & Ribeau, S. (2003). *African American communication: Exploring identity and culture* (2nd ed.). Mahwah, NJ: Lawrence Erlbaum Associates.

Hibbler, D. K., & Shinew, K. J. (2002). Interracial couples' experience of leisure: A social network approach. *Journal of Leisure Research, 34,* 135-156.

Hughes, P. C. (2004). The influence of religious orientation on conflict tactics in interfaith marriage. *Journal of Communication and Religion, 27,* 245-267.

Hughes, P. C., & Dickson, F. C. (2005). Communication, marital satisfaction, and religious orientation in interfaith marriages. *Journal of Family Communication, 5,* 25-41.

Hughes, P. C., & Dickson, F. C. (2006). The relational dynamics of interfaith marriages. In L. Turner & R. West (Eds.), *Family communication: A reference of theory and research* (pp. 373-388). Thousand Oaks, CA: Sage.

Karis, T. A. (2003). How race matters and does not matter for white women in relationships with black men. In V. Thomas, T. A. Karis, & J. L. Wetchler (Eds.), *Clinical issues with interracial couples: Theories and research* (pp. 23-40). New York: Haworth Press.

Katriel, T. (1986). *Talking straight: Dugri speech in Israeli Sabra culture.* Cambridge: Cambridge University Press.

Killian, K. D. (2002). Dominant and marginalized discourses in interracial couples' narratives: Implications for family therapists. *Family Process, 41,* 603-618.

Lampe, P. E. (1982). Interethnic dating: Reasons for and against. *International Journal of Intercultural Relations, 6,* 115-126.

Lazerwitz, B. (1995). Denominational retention and switching among American Jews. *Journal for the Scientific Study of Religion, 34,* 499-506.

Lehrer, E. L., & Chiswick, C. U. (1993). Religion as a determinant of marital stability. *Demography, 30,* 385-341.

Leslie, L. A., & Letiecq, B. L. (2004). Marital quality of African American and white partners in interracial couples.*11,* 559-574.

Lewandowski, D. A., & Jackson, L. A. (2001). Perceptions of interracial couples: Prejudice at the dyadic level. *Journal of Black Psychology, 27,* 288-303.

Orbe, M. (1998a). *Constructing co-cultural theory: An explication of culture, power, and communication.* Thousand Oaks, CA: Sage.

Orbe, M. (1998b). From the standpoint(s) of traditionally muted groups: Explicating a co-cultural communication theoretical model. *Communication Theory, 8,* 1-26.

Plante, T. G., & Boccaccini, M. T. (1997). The Santa Clara strength of religious faith questionnaire. *Pastoral Psychology, 45,* 375-387.

Poulson, S. S. (2003). Therapists' perspectives on working with interracial couples. In V. Thomas, T. A. Karis, & J. L. Wetchler (Eds.), *Clinical issues with interracial couples: Theories and research* (pp. 163-177). New York: Haworth Press.

Root, M. P. (2001). *Love's revolution: Interracial marriage.* Philadelphia: Temple University Press.

Rosenblatt, P. C., & Tubbs, C. Y. (1998). Loss in the experience of multiracial couples. In J. H. Harvey (Ed.), *Perspectives on loss: A sourcebook* (pp. 125-135). Philadelphia: Brunner/Mazel.

Rowatt, W. C., Ottenbreit, A., Nesselroade, K., Jr., & Cunningham, P. A. (2002). On being-holier-than-thou or humbler-than-thee: A social psychological perspective on Religiousness and humility. *Journal for the Scientific Study of Religion, 41,* 227–237.

Sandage, S. J. (2011). Relational spirituality, differentiation of self, and virtue as predictors of intercultural development. *Mental Health, Religion, and Culture, 34,* 21–39.

Sahl, A. H., & Bateson, C. D. (2011). Race and religion in the Bible Belt: Parental attitudes toward interfaith relationships. *Sociological Spectrum, 31,* 444–465.

Sander, W. (1993). Catholicism and intermarriage in the United States. *Journal of Marriage and the Family, 55,* 1037–1041.

Shehan, C. L., Bock, E. W., & Lee, G. R. (1990). Religious heterogamy, religiosity, and marital happiness: The case of Catholics. *Journal of Marriage and the Family, 52,* 73–79.

Sherkat, D. E. (2004). Religious intermarriage in the United States: Trends, patterns, and predictors. *Social Science Research, 33,* 606–625.

Spanier, G. B. (1976). Measuring dyadic adjustment: New scales for assessing the quality of marriage and similar dyads. *Journal of Marriage and the Family, 38,* 15–28.

Timmer, S. G., Veroff, J., & Hatchett, S. (1996). Family ties and marital happiness: The different marital experiences of black and white newlywed couples. *Journal of Social and Personal Relationships, 13,* 335–359.

Tubbs, C. Y., & Rosenblatt, P. C. (2003). Assessment and intervention with black-white multiracial couples. In V. Thomas, T. A. Karis, & J. L. Wetchler (Eds.), *Clinical issues with interracial couples: Theories and research* (pp. 115–129). New York: Haworth Press.

Weber, S. N. (1994). The need to be: Socio-cultural significance of African American language. In L. A. Samovar & R. E. Porter (Eds.), *Intercultural communication: A reader* (6th ed., pp. 337–347). Belmont, CA: Wadsworth.

Whitehead, B. D., & Popenoe, D. (2001). *The state of our unions: The social health of marriage in America.* Piscataway, NJ: Rutgers University and National Marriage Project.

Williams, L. M., & Lawler, M. G. (2000). The challenges and rewards of interchurch marriages. *Journal of Psychology and Christianity, 19,* 205–218.

Williams, L. M., & Lawler, M. G. (2001). Religious heterogamy and religiosity: A comparison of interchurch and same-church individuals. *Journal for the Scientific Study of Religion, 40,* 465–478.

Williams, L. M., & Lawler, M. G. (2003). Marital satisfaction and religious heterogamy: A comparison of interchurch and same-church individuals. *Journal of Family Issues, 24,* 1070–1092.

Yoshida, K., & Busby, D. M. (2011). Intergenerational transmission effects on relationship satisfaction: A cross-cultural study. *Journal of Family Issues,* 1–21.

Zebroski, S. A. (1999). African American-white intermarriages: The racial and gender dynamics of support and opposition. *Journal of African American Studies, 30,* 52–61.

Chapter 32

Mother and Daughter-in-Law Relationships: For Better or for Worse?

Paul Yelsma

Marriage ceremonies provide a host of opportunities for "more-than-blood" relationships to develop between newlyweds and their in-laws. For decades, many jokes have abounded about the difficulties associated with getting along with mothers-in-law. According to Duvall's (1954) on-the-air radio listener survey, the mother-in-law relationship appears to be the most difficult to achieve. Unfortunately, Duval provides almost no scientific information pertaining to the difficulties that family members may experience with daughters-in-law. Other scholars (Komarovsky, 1964; Landis & Landis, 1963; Wallin, 1954). also report that many disharmonies appear to exist between mothers-in-law and daughters-in-law. Both groups of women almost always have strong emotional bonds with the same man, and they are usually expected to develop satisfying relationships with each other in ways that, it is hoped, maintain their affectionate bonds with their son or husband.

The formation of a mother-in-law/daughter-in-law relationship provides many opportunities for each person to contribute to either an open atmosphere of expression or a closed atmosphere of repression. Galvin (2004) described the rapidly changing culture of the extended American family as being similar to "permanent white water," with few guidelines or rules existing to facilitate effective communication patterns between mothers-in-law and daughters-in-law. Although these adult women are "joined together" as if they were related by law or blood (Whitaker, 1976), they often begin their relationship journey with relatively ambiguous communication guidelines or rules, yet they are expected to develop satisfying relationships with each other. For example, most newly married couples (men and women) lack experience or knowledge in determining the most appropriate names or labels for addressing or referring to their mother-in-law (or father-in-law). The daughters-in-law often experiment with various names or labels, such as Mrs. Smith, Jane, Mom, Eric's mother, or Grandma, or they simply avoid using labels altogether in an attempt to gain joint agreement on an appropriate and meaningful appellation (Jorgenson, 1994). Even knowing how to talk to each other on the phone appears to result in positive mother-in-law/daughter-in-law relationships (Jackson & Berg-Cross, 1988). Most women would benefit from understanding more about the communication behaviors that contribute to the harmony or disharmony that emerges between mothers-in-law and daughters-in-law.

Within most family systems, many of the in-laws will inevitably experience varying degrees of tension, stress, conflict, or dissatisfaction (Canary, Cupach, & Messman, 1995; Linn & Breslerman, 1996). Conflicts between adult women, at least between mothers-in-law and daughters-in-law, appear to be greatest during the "getting-acquainted period," when younger women are attempting to develop and enhance their own personal identities and autonomies (Baruch & Barnett, 1983). The older women appear to maintain relatively stable or established patterns of interacting with others.

Daughters, as well as daughters-in-law, are thought to experience difficulties establishing their own personal identities with their mothers or mothers-in-law (Adelson, 1998). The relationships appear to stabilize as the younger women learn to contextualize themselves by constructing relatively unique, personal relational experiences with the older women.

At least traditionally, the responsibility for establishing, maintaining, and repairing personal relationships with extended family members has been relegated to the family "kin keepers," who are frequently the mothers-in-law and daughters-in-law. Despite the pressures placed on them, very little is known about the ways in which these adult women create an effective expressive atmosphere (expression of emotion) or develop communication satisfaction that is rewarding to them. Rarely do other family members help mothers-in-law and daughters-in-law establish good relationships when tensions arise. Tensions are likely to take place for several reasons: (a) The coconstruction of two adult women's personal relationships with each other occurs almost involuntarily as they commence an ongoing relationship with each other as "strangers" (Galvin & Cooper, 1990); (b) because the women may have high levels of emotional involvement and commitment with their children and grandchildren, probabilities exist for their having an involved long-term relationship with each other that sometimes lasts longer than does the marriage that created the relationship (Vangelisti, 1993); (c) mothers-in-law and daughters-in-law usually have strong emotional attachments with the same man (son/husband) but may not share the same cultural or social values or belief systems with each other on other important matters (i.e., financial decisions, religious practices, health care practices, or discipline of children). These discrepancies may have notable consequences on establishing, maintaining, and repairing functional interpersonal relationships with the son/husband and with each other; and (d) even though most women are predominately nurture oriented, there is often a degree of contention between adult women who want to obtain and maintain a relatively finite amount of interaction time, personal affection, or unmediated attention from sons/husbands (Linn & Breslerman, 1996).

Duvall's (1954) study of radio respondents reported the following relationship characteristics associated with mother-in-law influences within families: being (a) meddlesome and interfering; (b) possessive and demanding; (c) nagging, criticizing, and complaining; (d) indifferent and uninterested; (e) immature, childish, and dependent; (f) uncongenial and disagreeable about traditions; (g) thoughtless and inconsiderate; (h) pampering, taking sides, and spoiling; (i) intrusive and abusive of hospitality; (j) self-righteous and superior; and (k) overtalkative and gushing. More recently, Horsley (1997) provided further insight into problematic concerns within in-law relationships, such as (a) lack of approval, even though family members initially appeared to like the fiancé; (b) blaming the daughter-in-law (or son-in-law) for controlling their "child"; (c) loyalty issues when one member of the couple does not give equal visitation time to his/her spouse's family; (d) undefined roles that may cause stress while evolving from a parent–child relationship into an adult–adult relationship; and (e) "holidays from hell," where any of the first four problems may be exacerbated by the heightened emotional expectations and arousal associated with spending holidays with the in-laws.

Conventional wisdom tells us that the relationship that mothers-in-law and daughters-in-law develop will ultimately influence their satisfaction with each other as well as with other long-term family members, such as the son/husband and child(ren) or grandchild(ren). Yet the patterns of communication that enhance building and maintaining satisfactory personal relationships between mothers-in-law and daughters-in-law are noticeably understudied. Attempts to address the scarcity of research on these patterns in mother-in-law and daughter-in-law relationships have just begun.

Fingerman (1998) suggests that mothers and adult daughters can build effective relationships with each other through "finding constructive means of dealing with problems in their relationships" (p. 133). For example, making joint decisions about how to share information and emotions with each other and other family members may be one way of enhancing their relationship. One of the overarching issues pertaining to the regulation of affective expressions many adult women have with each other is their "desire to shape the relationship context in which emotions are experienced . . . and [develop an] acceptance of the need to regulate [their] own emotions as well" (Fingerman, 1998, p. 135). Nastasee-Carder's (2003) research regarding mother and daughter-in-law pairs and their needs to regulate emotional expression suggests that mother-in-law influence on occurrence of conflicts between newlyweds is minimal; respect for each other's privacy contributes to positive in-law relationships; and moodiness and demanding, interfering behaviors foster negative feelings toward the other in-law. Kivett's (1989) findings on solidarity of mothers-in-law and daughters-in-law bolster the more recent findings. She suggests that, in general, the contemporary results "do not support the usual negative generalizations regarding the mother-daughter-in-law relationships, especially as they relate to expression of affection" (p. 26). Daughters-in-law who have the most contact with mothers-in-law report strong feelings of closeness and agreement (Jackson & Berg-Cross, 1988; Kivett, 1989).

Compelling challenges of communicating effectively with in-laws involve learning communication behaviors that facilitate receptive listening and recalibrating or reframing one's own thoughts and emotions when interacting with others who may have different cultural patterns of expressing their emotions (Galvin & Brommel, 2000). According to Meyerstein (1996), expressive and respectful communication within the newly formed family system often include (a) inviting and accepting a stranger or newcomer into one's family, (b) managing the dialectical tension of family of origin loyalty and including the nonblood partner into the family, (c) allowing the newcomer to maintain his or her own values, (d) allowing the newcomer to have his or her own lifestyle without imposing the host family's expectations on the newcomer, (e) dealing with the dialectical tensions of autonomy and connectedness between the generations within the family, (f) renegotiating the "child"–parent relationship so that it can develop into an adult child–parent relationship, (g) understanding the difference between love for one's partner and love for one's in-laws, (h) and learning to adjust from having familiar young adults leave home to having unfamiliar young adults join the family. We add another perspective suggesting that host family members and new arrivals develop communication carriers (common themes or interests) that do not rely entirely on the events, activities, or interests of children or grandchildren as primary carriers of interaction.

Another compelling challenge in effectively communicating with in-laws involves knowing ways to develop communication satisfaction and maintain a positive affective expressive atmosphere. At least for women, the creation of an affective expressive atmosphere most likely will foster opportunities to successfully share one's own thoughts and emotions and provide opportunities to be a receptive listener to the thoughts and emotions of others. The sharing of information and emotions that enhances one's own growth as an individual and promotes either the growth or the inclusion of another within the kinship network seems to be a fundamental necessity for the effective functioning of complex family systems. The underlying premise of this present research is based on the perspective that the ability to establish a positive, emotionally expressive atmosphere with an adult female family member will most likely contribute to one's communication satisfaction with that person.

Past research between mothers-in-law and daughters-in-law, as noted above, has focused mainly on problems or difficulties associated with in-law relationships (Duvall, 1954; Silverstein, 1992), conflicts within the family relationships (Horsley, 1997; Meyerstein, 1996), and difficulties that daughters-in-law and sons-in-law have in knowing effective ways to address their mothers-in-law and fathers-in-law (Jorgenson, 1994). Focusing on communication characteristics that contribute to positive mother-in-law and daughter-in-law relationships is essential in understanding the diverse cultures within the continually changing American family.

The Present Study

Communication satisfaction is essentially the subjective feelings one achieves from interpersonal encounters with others, or the outcomes within relationships that promote positive feeling between people (Onyekwere, Rubin, & Infante, 1991). In addition, there appears to be an association between communication satisfaction and communication competence (Canary & Cupach, 1988; Onyekwere et al., 1991; Spitzberg & Hecht, 1984). Thus, each person's perception of the attractiveness of the relationship, as well as their own communication behaviors, influences the degree of communication satisfaction that they may derive from the relationship. Considering the body of research described above, our study focuses on the mother-in-law and daughter-in-law perceptions of positive, emotionally expressive atmospheres and the communication satisfaction they have developed. The second aim is to identify the specific communication behaviors that are predictive of communication satisfaction and expressive atmosphere in these relationships.

Rationale and Hypotheses Driving the Present Study

Interdependence theory (Kelly et al. (1983) contends that the thoughts, feelings, and behaviors shared within relationships influence the degree of connectedness between the participants. Mothers-in-law and daughters-in-law are expected to develop an effective relationship with each other, as if they were virtually in a "bloodline" relationship, as well as with other family members, and to function as the predominant kin keepers in the family. The interdependence or connectedness that is often presumed to arise from a mother-in-law and daughter-in-law relationship emerges from the communication behaviors that contribute to the expressive atmosphere and communication satisfaction they experience with each other.

A basic premise of reciprocity theory holds that communication behaviors from one person promote similar types of communication behavior from the person with whom he or she interacts (Gouldner, 1960; McCroskey & Richmond, 2000). When one person initiates expressive communication in a mutually interdependent relationship, the other person will most likely reciprocate similar behaviors. The reciprocity of emotionally expressive behaviors is critical in shaping the course of personal relationships (McCroskey & Richmond, 2000). Given the likelihood that a relatively high degree of interdependence will prevail between mothers-in-law and daughters-in-law and that they will engage in reciprocal emotionally expressive behaviors with each other, the following hypotheses are presented in this research:

H1: Mother-in-law perceptions and daughter-in-law perceptions of the communication satisfaction with each other will be significantly similar.

H2: Mother-in-law perceptions and daughter-in-law perceptions of the affective expressiveness atmosphere with each other will be significantly similar.

A discussion of these interrelationship experiences necessitates addressing the impact that specific communication behaviors have on two major outcomes: the communication satisfaction derived from the relationship and the affective expressive atmosphere created within it.

Research Methods

Data Collection

Initially, mothers-in-law and daughters-in law were recruited from different geographical regions of southwestern Michigan. After being assured that their identities and the information that they provided would be confidential, those consenting to participate answered questionnaires and agreed to provide locating information for their corresponding in-law (dyadic partner). Nearly two-thirds of the participants were contacted through face-to-face interactions, while the remainder were contacted by telephone or through the mail because they lived in different regions of the United States. If the partner was receptive to providing responses to the questionnaire, she did so and returned the materials.

These partners were matched by code numbers on their questionnaires, resulting in 66 mother-in-law and daughter-in-law pairs in which each woman embraced a personal relationship with the same man (son/husband).

Analyses of Data

As expected, the ethnic identities of the mothers-in-law and daughters-in-law were very similar. A series of between-groups analyses of variance were computed in an attempt to determine whether any of four biographical variables (education, yearly income, faith- community activity, and marital status) had any bearing on either mothers-in-law or daughters-in-law mean scores on communication satisfaction or affective expressive atmosphere. No significant differences were found between mother-in-law or daughter-in-law levels of educational achievement and their communication satisfaction or affective expressive atmosphere, although, as expected, in most categories the daughter-in-law had attained higher levels of education than the mother-in-law. Data pertaining to the yearly financial income of the two groups of women revealed no significant association with either groups' communication satisfaction scores or their affective expressive atmosphere scores. Daughters-in-law, however, did report having slightly higher yearly incomes than their mother-in-law. There were no significant differences in communication satisfaction or affective expressive atmosphere between either mothers-in-law or daughters-in-law based on their levels of participation in faith-community activities, although older women did report having significantly more participation than the younger women.

No evidence was found that indicated the various levels of marital status data of the two groups of women were significantly associated with their communication satisfaction or their affective expressive atmosphere. Length of time daughters-in-law had been married was not significantly correlated either with their own communication satisfaction or with that of their mother-in-law, nor was it significantly correlated with the affective expressive atmosphere of either group. Scatter plots for daughter-in-law level of communication satisfaction and affective expressive atmosphere largely revealed that high levels occurred near the beginning of the mother-in-law association and continued through the course of the relationship. Again, barring a few outlying scores, scatter plots for mothers-in-law reveal that high levels began to build slightly later, peaking several years into the mother-in-law association and continuing throughout the relationship. The longevity of the daughters-in-law association with mothers-in-law is not significantly associated with either group of women's communication satisfaction or affective expressiveness.

Results

Hypotheses Analyses

Two independent paired t-tests were conducted to determine the extent of similarities that existed between each of the variables (communication satisfaction and affective expressiveness atmosphere) for mothers-in-law and daughters-in-law. Hypothesis 1 conjectured that the communication satisfaction achieved by mothers-in-law and daughters-in-law during their interactions with each other would be significantly similar. Hypothesis 1 was supported. Hypothesis 2 conjectured that the mother-in-law and daughter-in-law affective expressiveness atmosphere achieved in their relationship would be significantly similar. Results from a paired t-test indicated that mothers-in-law did report perceiving significantly higher levels of affective expressive atmosphere within the relationships than did the daughters-in-law; thus, hypothesis 2 was not supported.

A correlational analysis of each group's perception of their own communication satisfaction and expressive atmosphere reveals that these two constructs are highly correlated: in each group, communication satisfaction was significantly correlated with expressive atmosphere. These results indicate that a high level of statistical association exists between one's own communication satisfaction and one's expressive atmosphere. Continuing results from the research questions may shed light on the influence that specific in-law communicative behaviors have on the communication satisfaction and expressive atmosphere of the other in-law.

Post Hoc Analyses

By assessing only paired mothers-in-law and daughters-in-law, it is possible that either a positive or a negative response bias was not being addressed. Presumably, unpaired persons (those who did not return usable materials, while their associated in-law did) could have had either considerably higher or lower levels of perceived communication satisfaction or expressive atmosphere than their in-law. Thus, post hoc t-tests were computed between the mother-in-law and daughter-in-law pairs, who both returned usable materials, and the unpaired mothers-in-law and daughters-in-law. No significant differences were found between mean scores of communication satisfaction or expressive atmosphere for either the mother-in-law or the daughter-in-law group, therefore offering no suggestion of response bias.

Discussion

Although past research associated with mother-in-law relationships has focused primarily on problems and difficulties with mother-in-law relationships, more recent attempts to understand mother-in-law and daughter-in-law relationships have begun to examine the importance of forming positive first impressions and learning effective ways that in-laws can address each other. By identifying communication patterns that promote an affective expressive atmosphere within this context, the family sciences may provide useful insights toward developing effective and satisfying in-law relationships. This study attempted to determine whether mothers-in-law and daughters-in-law shared similar perceptions of the communication satisfaction and affective expressive atmosphere that they developed with each other. It also attempted to examine the influence that their self-reported communicative behaviors had on the communication satisfaction and expressive atmosphere of their in-law. Identifying the specific communication behaviors that are associated with communication satisfaction and affective expressive atmosphere between mothers-in-law and daughters-in-law is essential in understanding and improving continually changing American family cultures.

All but two of the biographical characteristics between the two groups of in-laws were similar. Only two intuitive, expected differences emerged: Mothers-in-law were significantly older, and daughters-in-law had received more formal education. Biographical characteristics appear to have little influence on the development of effective relationships.

Results from the present study confirm Nastasee-Carder's (2003) findings that most mothers-in-law and daughters-in-law apparently do not change their overall first impressions of each other. The length of time the daughters-in-law had been married was not significantly associated with perceived communication satisfaction or affective expressive atmosphere of either mother-in-law or daughter-in-law, suggesting that the first impressions that adult female in-laws form of each other have a lasting impact on the status of their relationships.

Although both groups of women had similar levels of communication satisfaction with each other, mothers-in-law reported experiencing significantly higher levels of expressive atmosphere than did the daughters-in-law. No causality can be inferred regarding whether mother-in-law perceptions of the expressive atmosphere were high *because* the daughter-in-law interactive behaviors led to a more positive expressive atmosphere than did those of the mothers-in-law. In a like manner, no causality can be determined regarding whether the mothers-in-law perceived their expressive atmosphere of their relationship with their daughters-in-law to be more positive *regardless* of daughter-in-law interactive behaviors. Fischer (1983) observed that mothers-in-law were less likely than daughters-in-law to recognize conflicts within their relationships. Having once been a daughter-in-law, perhaps, they are more forgiving of differences that may occur between themselves and members of the next generation.

Although communication satisfaction for these in-law associates appears to be similar, the daughters-in-law reported experiencing a significantly lower level of generalized communicative atmosphere within the relationship than did the mothers-in-law. An examination of specific communication behaviors sheds light on this influential relationship. As reported above, nine mother-in-law communication behaviors significantly influenced daughter-in-law communication satisfaction. Several reasonable conclusions may be drawn from these results. A mother-in-law could enhance communication satisfaction of her daughter-in-law by monitoring the following communicative behaviors: reducing nervous mannerisms in her speech, curtailing her argumentative style, avoiding being very encouraging to other people and slighting the daughter-in-law, and being mindful that when she is easily communicating with strangers, she may be slighting attention that could be given to her daughter-in-law. Apparently, when mothers-in-law report being able to encourage other people and communicate easily with strangers, daughters-in-law find these behaviors vying with quality time and attention that could be directed toward them and perhaps even underlining the shortcomings of the in-law communication relationship.

Mothers-in-law may also enhance the communication satisfaction of their daughters-in-law by consciously practicing the following five communicative behaviors: being friendly by verbally acknowledging the contributions of the daughters-in-law, revealing personal things about themselves, laughing easily, reacting in ways that let the daughter-in-law know she is listening, and gesturing when she is communicating. Furthermore, mothers-in-law could enhance the expressive atmosphere with their daughters-in-law by monitoring the following communicative behaviors: reducing nervous mannerisms in her speech and minimizing those behaviors that leave a definite (strong) impression on people.

In a similar manner, daughters-in-law could enhance communication satisfaction with their mothers-in-law by curtailing their own argumentative style. Additionally, daughters-in-law could enhance the expressive atmosphere with their mothers-in-law by readily expressing admiration toward the mother-in-law. These results bolster Nastasee-Carder's (2003) contention that sincerity, kindness, respect, and maturity are important characteristics in facilitating positive mother-in-law and daughter-in-law relationships. She also reported characteristics that contribute to challenges within these in-law relationships, including moodiness and demanding and interfering behaviors.

The results from this study do not support many of the findings from previous research reports (Duvall, 1954; Horsley, 1997; Meyerstein, 1996) that suggest that communication satisfaction might be lower for daughters-in-law. However, daughters-in-law perceived lower levels of affective expressive atmosphere within their relationships than did mothers-in-law. Fischer (1983) has suggested that mothers-in-law who are older may be more dependent on social support from younger persons and less likely than daughters-in-law to acknowledge stresses or differences within their relationships.

This desire for social support may occur as mothers-in-law consider the pragmatic needs of establishing support or an expressive atmosphere with their daughters-in-law that will ultimately influence their sons as well as their grandchildren.

Study Limitations

The study of perceptions on affective expressiveness in human relationships is inherently entangled with the challenge of teasing out the individuals' actual affective expressive behaviors versus their perception of their behaviors. Self-reported assessments of affective expression are confounded by the concern that, regardless of the "bona fide" communication processes that transpire between people, how each person interprets and feels about the interactions within the relationship may be as meaningful to her or him as any objective measure of the communication partner's perceptions of the interaction.

The perceived impact of emotional expressions has far-reaching consequences beyond the actual verbal or nonverbal behavior. At a time of stress or conflict, one's perceptions of a few harsh or inappropriate behaviors could easily alter myriad very pleasant previously shared expressions. Intuitively, any close relationship can be quickly changed with a few single bursts of speech on a sensitive subject area. Clearly, this study did not focus explicitly on "objective" affective expressions that take place between mothers-in-law and daughters-in-law in an attempt to identify the ratio of positive affective expressions that it takes to alter a few negative affective expressions. Thus, the use of self-reported perceptions provides only one perspective on the actual impact of communication within the in-law relationship, which often involves many interactions that may take place over long periods of time. The self-assessment of ongoing, complex, changing relationships continually poses challenges for relationship researchers.

Another limitation involves utilization of volunteer subjects who may be more receptive to report on the "successes" of the in-law relationship than those who are reluctant to report on their unsuccessful relationships. This study provides very little information about those in-law relationships that have degenerated in both communication satisfaction and affective expressive atmosphere. Nonetheless, comparisons between the mean scores for women whose partners did not return usable questionnaires and the means scores for pairs who did return usable data revealed no significant differences in either expressive atmosphere or communication satisfaction.

Future research should consider examining the impact that specific communication behaviors with others, such as fathers-in-law and sons-in-law, have on communication satisfaction and expressive atmosphere. Studies designed to assess the impact of affective expression between husbands' communication satisfaction with mothers-in-law may reveal insights concerning how husband and wife communication satisfaction may be enhanced by developing insights into the affective expressive atmosphere they have with their parents. In addition, examination of communication behaviors and their effects on families attempting to incorporate a mix of cultures and languages and those facing changes resulting from the death or disability of a family member may be fruitful and beneficial.

Conclusion

Even though early folk wisdom has suggested over the years that one of the most difficult in-law relationships within the family involves those interactions with mothers-in-law (Duvall, 1954), this notion was not supported. The communication satisfaction of mothers-in-law and daughters-in-law was essentially the same: If either woman reported being satisfied with the female relationship, so did the other.

The levels of affective expressiveness, however, were significantly different. The reasons mothers-in-law perceived higher levels of expressive atmosphere with their daughters-in-law are not entirely clear. The perceptions a mother-in-law possesses about her own contributions to the expressive atmosphere with a daughter-in-law appear to be as influential to her own communication satisfaction as are the daughter-in-law's communication behaviors.

Clearly, the most challenging opportunities facing a young married couple are in learning how to achieve and maintain a satisfactory marriage. Approximately half of all the divorces occur in the first 7 years of marriage (Cherlin, 1981). Despite Meyerstein's (1996) conjecture that some of these marriages may dissolve because of in-law problems, the results from this study show no indication that daughters-in-law involved with divorce and second marriages have any more difficulties with their mothers-in-law than those in first marriages. The findings from this study suggest that if mothers-in-law and daughters-in-law effectively express their emotions with each other, they will most likely experience both high communication satisfaction and affective expressive atmosphere in the relationship.

Perhaps another challenge facing newlyweds is in learning how to develop affective expressive atmospheres with both mothers-in-law and fathers-in-law that will facilitate the young couple's own marital satisfaction. Future research is needed to examine the impact that daughter-in-law and mother-in-law communication satisfaction may have on the marital behavior of husbands/sons.

More evidence is being amassed (for example, see Gottman & Levenson, 2000) suggesting that learning new means of effectively expressing positive emotion is important within family relationships. In those family ties that are characterized as positively emotionally expressive, one's ability to generate an affective expressive atmosphere with another seems to prepare the stage for what ultimately transpires within the relationship.

Findings from the present study identify several enhancing communication behaviors and a few debilitating behaviors associated with mother-in-law and daughter-in-law communication satisfaction and affective expressive atmosphere. The ability of mothers-in-law and daughters-in-law to create a *positive-feeling tone of acceptance* that reveals an understanding of the other person's emotional state seems to be an underlying orientation influencing their communication satisfaction with each other. Studies that further our understanding and development of a positive feeling tone of acceptance with in-laws are critical to helping family members function effectively within our continually changing society.

Discussion Questions

1. According to this chapter, the mother-in-law/daughter-in-law relationship is one of the "most difficult to achieve." What reasons did the author give that might explain this occurrence?

2. In Duvall's radio survey, what negative characteristics did respondents report mother-in-laws displaying with regard to family influence?

3. Results from this study suggest that both mother-in-law and daughter-in-law have similar levels of communication satisfaction; however, mother-in-laws reported experiencing higher levels of "expressive atmosphere." Why do you believe this might be the case?

4. In what ways could a mother-in-law enhance the communication satisfaction of her daughter-in-law?

References

Adelson, M. J. (1998). Mothers and daughters: Secrets and lies. *Journal of Clinical Psychology, 7,* 389–399

Baruch, G., & Barnett, R. C. (1983). Adult daughters' relationships with their mothers. *Journal of Marriage and Family, 45,* 601–606.

Canary, D. J., & Cupach, W. R. (1988). Relational and episodic characteristics associated with conflict tactics. *Journal of Social and Personal Relationships, 5,* 305–325.

Canary, D. J., Cupach, W. R., & Messman, S. J. (1995). *Relationship conflict: Conflict in parent-child friendship and romantic relationships.* Thousand Oaks, CA: Sage.

Cherlin, A. J. (1981). *Marriage, divorce and remarriage.* Cambridge, MA: Harvard University Press.

Duvall, E. M. (1954). *In-laws, pro and con: An original study of interpersonal relations.* New York: Association Press.

Fingerman, K. L. (1998). Tight lips? Aging mothers' and adult daughters' responses to interpersonal tension in their relationships. *Personal Relationship, 5,* 121–138.

Fischer, L. R. (1983). Mothers and mothers-in-law. *Journal of Marriage and Family, 45,* 187–192.

Galvin, K. (2004). The family of the future: What do we face? In A. L. Vangelisti (Ed.), *Handbook of family communication* (pp. 647–672). Mahwah, NJ: Lawrence Erlbaum Associates.

Galvin, K. M., & Brommel, B. J. (2000). *Family communication: Cohesion and change.* New York: Addison-Wesley Longman.

Galvin, K. M., & Cooper, P. J. (1990). *Development of involuntary relationships: The stepparent-stepchild relationship.* Paper presented at the annual meeting on the International Communication Association, Dublin, Ireland.

Gottman, J. M., & Levenson, R. M. (2000). The timing of divorce: Predicting when a couple will divorce over a 14-year period. *Journal of Marriage and Family, 62,* 737–745.

Gouldner, A. W. (1960). A norm of reciprocity: A preliminary statement. *American Sociological Review, 26,* 151–178.

Grant, J. A., King, P. E., & Behnke, R. R. (1994). Compliance-gaining strategies, communication satisfaction and willingness to comply. *Communication Reports, 7,* 99–108.

Hecht, M. L. (1978). The construction and measurement of interpersonal communication satisfaction. *Human Communication Research, 4,* 253–264.

Horsley, G. C. (1997). In-laws: Extended family therapy. *American Journal of Family Therapy, 25,* 18–27.

Jackson, J., & Berg-Cross, L. (1988). Helping the extended family: Mother-in-law and daughter-in-law relationships among black women. *Family Relations, 37*(3), 293–297.

Jorgenson, J. (1994). Situated address and the social construction of "in-law" relationships. *Southern Communication Journal, 59,* 196–204.

Kelley, H. H., Berscheid, E., Christensen, A., Harvey, J. H., Huston, T. L., Levinger, G., et al. (1983). *Close relationships.* New York: W. H. Freeman.

Kivett, V. R. (1989). Mother-in-law and daughter-in-law relations. In: J. A. Mancini (Ed), *Aging Parents and Adult Children.* (pp. 17-32). Lexington, MA, Lexington Books.

Komarovsky, M. (1964). *Blue-collar marriage.* New York: Random House.

Landis, J. T., & Landis, M. G. (1963). *Building a successful marriage* (5th ed.). Englewood Cliffs, NJ: Prentice Hall.

Linn, R., & Breslerman, S. (1996). Women in conflict: On the moral knowledge of daughters-in-law and mothers-in-law. *The Norham Foundation,* pp. 291-217.

McCroskey, J. C., & Richmond, V. P. (2000). Applying reciprocity and accommodation theories to supervisor/subordinate communication. *Journal of Applied Communication Research, 28,* 278-289.

Meyerstein, I. (1996). A systemic approach to in-law dilemmas. *Journal of Marital and Family Therapy, 22,* 469-480.

Nastasee-Carder, A. (2003, November). *Between image and reality: An analysis of the mother-in-law and daughter-in-law relationship.* Paper presented at the annual meeting of the National Communication Association, Miami Beach, FL.

Norton, R. W. (1983). *Communicator style: Theory, application, measures.* Beverly Hills, CA: Sage.

Onyekwere, E. O., Rubin, R. B., & Infante, D. A. (1991). Interpersonal perception and communication satisfaction as a function of argumentative and ego-involvement. *Communication Quarterly, 39,* 35-47.

Silverstein, J. L. (1992). The problem with in-laws. *Journal of Family Therapy, 14,* 399-412.

Spitzberg, B. H., & Hecht, M. L. (1984). A component model of relationship competence. *Human Communication Research, 10,* 575-599.

Vangelisti, A. L. (1993). Communication in the family: The influence of time, relational prototypes and irrationality. *Communication Monographs, 60,* 42-54.

Vangelisti, A. L. (2004). *Handbook of family communication.* Mahwah, NJ: Lawrence Erlbaum Associates.

Wallin, R. (1954). Sex differences in attitudes to "in-laws": A test of a theory. *American Journal of Sociology 59,* 466-469.

Whitaker, C. (1976). A family is a four-dimensional relationship. In P. J. Guerin Jr. (Ed.), *Family therapy: Theory and practice* (pp. 182-192). New York: Gardner.

Chapter 33

"I Want to Be a Marcks": Generativity in Relationships between Uncles and Nephews

David E. Weber

A thought experiment for you: Reflect on what you learned as a member of your family—frame the scope, history, or size of the term "family" however you care to. Start making a list of the lessons—consequential or minor, grand or trivial. For me, one trivial lesson is this: Don't place your kitchen trash can under the kitchen sink. In the house where I grew up, that is not where you would have found it. To this day, my trash can rests in a corner of my kitchen—precisely as it did in the house I lived in as a youngster. In contrast, a lesson far grander in scope is my recognition of the tension that I enduringly negotiate and renegotiate between my father's insistence that one must always tell the truth, period, and my mother's addendum, "but sometimes it doesn't hurt to have a little bit of larceny in your heart."

Now, on the list (probably quite a long one), isolate those lessons taught to you by members of your family who are senior to you (in contrast to those taught by family members in your age range or younger). Those lessons are enactments of *generativity*—in a family, "adults' concern for and commitment to the next generation" (de St. Aubin, McAdams, & Kim, 2004, p. 4). Generativity most markedly results from the intentional ministrations, instructions, guidance, and interventions of a parent as well as social learning that you accomplished by observing actions taken and communication choices made by a parent. Milardo (2005) proposes, though, that generativity can also occur in the context of relationships that parents' offspring construct with parents' siblings—that is, the relationships involving nieces or nephews and uncles or aunts—and as an example adapts the concept of generational buffer (Kotre, 2004) to delineate several roles uncles may play in the lives of siblings' offspring:

> *Mentors* are practical guides, individuals who model action, teach skills, [and] provide guidance or support. . . . The *keeper of meaning* refers to individuals concerned with preserving a family's traditions. *Intergenerational buffers* can be viewed as family members who have firsthand knowledge of parents and their children and who can intercede on behalf of a parent with a child, or vice versa. (p. 1227)

After the birth of her fourth child, Lillian Marcks, my maternal grandmother, began telling her daughter (Beverly, my mother, born in 1917) and three sons (Jerry, born in 1918, Keith in 1923, and Dane in 1926) to always stay together and take care of one another. Lillian, who died in 1980 at the age of 86, repeated this admonition to her offspring even near the end of her life. Beverly, Jerry, Keith, and Dane complied with Lillian's request: Surely, few sibling quartets remain as close

353

as my mother and her three brothers always were. One by one, during and after World War II, they migrated from Buffalo, New York, to California. Throughout their lives in California, mostly in Los Angeles (my hometown) and adjacent cities, they spent a great deal of time together and seemed to derive joy from doing so.

What follows is a recounting of key events that, across the nearly six decades my life has spanned, constitute my experience of being nephew to my mother's three brothers—my uncles Jerry, Keith, and Dane. By exploring these events, I propose to examine generativity in such relationships.

I Knew That Keith Flew Airplanes

By the time I was 5 years old, I could not remember having met Keith, although our lives surely would have already intersected—at a family party, say, when he would have first seen his sister's son. What I did know was that Keith flew airplanes. I loved the idea of airplanes and flying. Whenever an aircraft would drone overhead, Mom or Dad would point to the sky, saying, "Look, David, an airplane." One day, watching a plane cruise under the clouds, I asked my father, "Is that Uncle Keith's airplane?" "No," Dad replied, "Uncle Keith lives up north, and that's where he flies his airplanes." (At the time, Keith was an airline pilot.)

At about 3:00 one afternoon, Dad awoke me from a nap. "Come on, let's meet Uncle Keith," Dad said. Slightly groggy, I walked from my bedroom into the living room holding Dad's hand. We stopped in front of a tall man—slender, dark hair, big smile—who extended his hand warmly toward me. "This is your Uncle Keith," Dad announced, adding, "the flyer." Keith said hello with a slightly nasal, smiling, midrange voice. My father encouraged me to shake his hand. Affection, awe, and desire to please filled me in that moment when I, at age 4, first met the mysterious and charismatic Uncle Keith. Keith stayed at our house overnight—years later, I presumed he was passing through Los Angeles on business.

The next morning I woke up 6.00 or so, as I normally did, and began playing with toy soldiers—again, an early morning routine. I heard a soft scratch at my door—and in walked Keith, beaming. He had seen the light coming from my doorway. He sat right down on the floor across the battlefield from me and played with my soldiers, instructing me about how to best deploy the troops (Keith was a military veteran), their vehicles, and heavy weapons. I was enchanted by Keith's good nature and his ability to take my playing as seriously as I did. Never had an adult, specifically my parents, done this (that I could recall).

Woolen Overshirt, Tartan Design

The earliest memory I have of Jerry occurred another afternoon not too much later. Jerry hunted, fished, built homes throughout Los Angeles County, and drove an immaculate forest-green pickup truck with his surname, Marcks, and a phone number stenciled onto the side. Hearing conversation in the den a few yards from my bedroom, I wandered toward the chatter. I saw a tall, well-built man with a crew cut. His clothes smelled of cigarette smoke. He wore thick, metal-rimmed glasses. His suntanned skin showed off white teeth when he smiled. Sitting next to him, his wife (named Paula) wore identical clothing—blue jeans, sturdy shoes, and a heavy woolen overshirt with a red tartan design. They had just come back to Los Angeles from a camping trip and wanted to give my mother some fresh trout they had caught just that morning. As I walked into the den, the three of them—Jerry, Paula, and my mother—began laughing, scaring me because I had no sense of what made them laugh. Jerry greeted me with a handshake, his hand consuming mine, his voice a fond growl. I felt somewhat intimidated.

One Saturday morning when I was 13, Jerry showed up at our house. "I want to teach David to shoot," he declared to my mother, and despite my mother's distaste for firearms, Jerry drove me to a firing range. We stood in a shooting lane, Jerry holding a revolver as if it were a sacred object. He explained, "This is a tool and you treat it with respect," and showed me how to check whether a revolver was loaded—"Never hand a gun to anyone unless you are willing to put that gun to your own head and pull the trigger."

Almost an Older Brother

For the first half dozen or so years of my life, Uncle Dane lived with his parents—Loretta and my grandfather—about half an hour from my house. A little more than 30 years old in the late 1950s, Dane often picked me up at nursery school and, later, kindergarten as a favor to my mother. I thought of him as almost an older brother.

Dane addressed me as "buddy," which I liked. "Hey, buddy," he would say, as I climbed into his car on a day he would collect me, "let's take a drive. Your mom gave me a couple of errands to do on my lunch break." (For a few years after his discharge, he worked in retail clothing and entered the banking business, where he hit his stride professionally.)

During those early years of my life, Dane wore a heavy ID bracelet with an elaborate closure. Like his brother Jerry, Dane smoked. In one high-spirited sweep, he would flick open his stainless-steel lighter, flame a cigarette tip, inhale and exhale, and snap the lighter shut as he spoke and laughed. After work, Dane typically removed his tie and dress shirt and wore just his T-shirt atop dress trousers, a keychain draped elegantly alongside the pleats. One late afternoon, Dane poked his head through the doorway to my bedroom, grinning as I lay under the covers. From his T-shirt and neatly slicked-back dark hair emanated the smell of tobacco smoke and his aftershave lotion, an inexpensive brand called Pinaud. "So, buddy, your mom says you're not feeling well," he intoned in mock sympathy. "Did you cut yourself shaving?"

One early afternoon, in Dane's passenger seat as we wound along Olympic Boulevard, he casually announced, "Your Uncle Dane's getting married, buddy! But don't tell anyone." I solemnly promised, "I won't."

A week or two later, my mother reported at dinner that Dane and Marlene, whom he had been dating for several years, had returned that day to Los Angeles after having eloped. True to my vow of silence, I did not mention that I knew this was due to happen.

Conflicted Departures and Rocky Transitions

For my father, the fragrance of night-blooming jasmine settling around you after dark always represented southern California. An attorney reared in Brooklyn, uprooted by conscription and three years of service in the U.S. Army, Dad earned an honorable discharge as a second lieutenant and moved to "the Coast," where he first smelled the bewitching jasmine. He had not really minded leaving New York. Not long after settling in Los Angeles, he began falling out of touch with virtually everyone (other than pro forma contact with his seven siblings) he had known "back East" before the war.

In contrast, my mother and uncles had conflicted departures and rocky transitions in their moves from New York to California. Throughout the years, each of them—especially Dane and my mother—visited Buffalo a few times every few years. Their ties to kin in Greater Buffalo and to their closest friendships constructed antebellum remained strong long after my father ceased to consider himself a transplant and thought of himself as a Californian.

A few months after Pearl Harbor, Jerry left Buffalo with his young wife, Paula. A fundamentally physical man (Jerry normally worked bare chested at his construction sites, could drive a nail full in with only two or three blows of a hammer, and astound onlookers at Lions Club banquets with his sinuous grace on a dance floor) Jerry had poor eyesight. It kept him out of military service—a shameful situation according to U.S. sociocultural mores holding mainstream sway during World War II. To escape the scorn he felt that some Buffalo folk aimed at him, he sought work in the opportunity-filled defense industries of Greater Los Angeles. Jerry and Paula drove westward in their 1937 Buick. The travails of that journey west—encounters with bad roads, gas rationing, and awful food and lodging en route—blended with the anxiety and exuberance characteristic of youth in transition during wartime. They made it to California, Jerry found a good job at McDonnell-Douglas Aircraft as a draftsman, and their adventure on the road became part of family lore. In 1960, Jerry proposed to Paula that they and their 12-year-old daughter drive across the United States—a rite of passage for young families for a few decades after the war. Paula's first reaction was an astonished, "Again?"

Beverly, my mother, came west next. To end a brief, imprudent marriage, Beverly had divorced in the late 1930s. In that era, divorcées often met with social disapproval in conservative Buffalo. In 1943, wanting a fresh start, she boarded a train in Buffalo and headed for Los Angeles. Traveling by train across the continent was a long, exasperating journey, with passenger trains routinely sidetracked to give right of way to troop trains pelting eastward or westward to ports of embarkation to war zones. She soon settled in an apartment near downtown Los Angeles, rooming with a girlfriend from Buffalo who preceded her west.

During the last year or so of the war, while serving in the U.S. Navy as a fighter pilot, Keith enjoyed a carnal wartime romance with a beautiful young elementary school teacher named Eleanor. She lived in San Diego (roughly 120 miles south of Los Angeles) near Keith's air base. In late 1944, Keith received orders to catch up with an aircraft already in combat in Philippine waters. By the early summer of 1945, he had returned to the U.S. mainland. He reignited his casual relationship with Eleanor, formally ending it when he received his honorable discharge from the navy and returned to New York to resume undergraduate studies at the University of Buffalo that the war had interrupted. He planned to earn a law degree.

In the fall, however, Keith received a phone call from Eleanor's angry, protective father that Eleanor was pregnant. A day or so later, on a crisp morning and afternoon, Keith and his dad walked around campus, discussing various options—which in 1945 numbered two: either leave New York and marry Eleanor in California or bring Eleanor east from San Diego to get married and live in New York. Without exploring Eleanor's preferences, Keith and his dad agreed that she should come east, where Wynn was born in 1946. Keith withdrew from school to begin life as a husband and father. But still restless, he decided that his young family would thrive in California. They lived in southern California briefly while Keith finished up his bachelor's degree at a small private college there, then moved to northern California.

New Wings, Irresistible Bonhomie, and *The Racing Form*

All his life, few have been able to resist Keith's glibness. Not long after settling in northern California, he talked his way into a job with Trans World Airways as a flight engineer and, eventually, a pilot. In those days, airlines and air cargo companies had mountains of applications from discharged military pilots with several years of experience flying big bombers or cargo aircraft for hours and hours, week after week, from land bases in Europe and Asia. Keith, in contrast, knew only nimble, single-engine, single-seat carrier-based fighter aircraft. But his irresistible bonhomie got Keith in with one of the best airlines in the United States and assignments with crews flying out of San Francisco.

Indeed, Keith's glib charm kept Dane out of harm's way during the war—or so Dane always claimed. Dane was drafted and sworn into the U.S. Army soon after receiving his high school diploma in 1944. He expected he would become an army infantry replacement destined for the European Theater of Operations, its massive casualty rates promising a negligible life expectancy. At Buffalo Central Station, a gloomy Dane sat on his suitcase one afternoon, surrounded by a couple of hundred other army recruits, all of them having waited for hours already for transport to a training camp.

Dane suddenly heard Keith's signature greeting, "Hey, brother, what's buzzin'?" Arriving by surprise in Buffalo earlier that day and sent to the station by my grandmother, who envisioned a quick brotherly reunion, Keith loomed over Dane on the station platform, grinning. Keith had come to Buffalo on furlough, his flight training just completed, new golden metal aviator wings gleaming over the left breast pocket of his crisp naval officer's uniform.

Keith declared that being in the army was no way to fight a war, especially in the European Theater. "Who's your boss?" Keith asked his kid brother, and Dane pointed to a heavy-set, 50-ish army noncommissioned officer, a master sergeant, whom Keith then approached.

"Sergeant," intoned Keith, "my brother and I come from a long line of navy men. My father served aboard a destroyer in the last war." Not true: My grandfather was exempted from military service in World War I. "His father served in the navy for almost 30 years and was with Dewey in Manila." Also untrue: My maternal great-grandfather operated a struggling fishing camp in the Adirondacks his entire working life. "I am on flight status awaiting orders to join the fleet. You understand we just can't break this family tradition. There must be some way to get my brother out of your branch of service and into my family's."

The master sergeant gazed at Keith, whose gold collar bars, glowing bright and untarnished in the low-angled sunlight, indicated he was an ensign—the navy's lowest officer rank. Old noncommissioned officers disdain untried boy officers despite being outranked by them. But Keith's earnest argument worked. Yes, agreed the master sergeant, family tradition means something. He began stamping and signing a sheaf of papers, thereby releasing Dane from the army and directing him to navy offices in downtown Buffalo for further orders.

Ultimately, then, Dane served 2 years not as an army infantry replacement in the winter fight at the Battle of the Bulge but as a navy seaman assigned as a driver for an admiral in a New Orleans shore billet. The admiral dispatched Dane each morning to fetch aspirin, hot coffee, and *The Racing Form* and taught Dane how to handicap the ponies.

In the Viewing Room Until Dawn

My Uncle Dane moved back into his childhood home after the navy discharged him. He caught up with old friends, themselves back from the service, and worked contentedly in retail. Also contentedly, my grandfather had gradually migrated from working outdoors as a master carpenter and venerated contractor to a secure and successful indoor job at a bank, assessing the value of commercial and residential properties. Lillian, though, missed having all of her children close at hand. She insisted the three of them move to California. Grandpa begged Grandma to agree to postpone relocation just another couple of years so that his pension from the bank would start up. But my grandmother had grown up in an orphanage in Buffalo, New York. She believed that no one may hold family at arm's length for mercenary reasons. So my grandparents and Dane packed up their lives and followed the trail westward. Dane did most of the driving. My grandparents never again had financial security.

Jerry and my mother helped them settle in Los Angeles. These were boom years for construction in southern California. Jerry's small, growing construction business acquired a succession of contracts, and Jerry took Grandpa into the business as a partner. Jerry revered his father. Growing up, Jerry would watch silently from a corner of the kitchen when his father's workmen assembled there to receive the wages that Grandpa scrupulously counted out for them. Any bills and coins left over, my grandfather kept. If no money remained, the family would eat macaroni and cheese or grilled cheese sandwiches for dinner the next several nights. On family road trips, Beverly, Dane, and Keith would argue about who sat where but not Jerry: Everyone understood his seat was directly behind my grandfather, the driver.

Because no one knew the construction business better than my grandfather did, Jerry did not mind that after having worked for almost a decade indoors, Grandpa had lost stamina, physical strength, and speed or that he had no contacts in Los Angeles from which to generate business. Paula minded, however. She kept the books and watched revenue go into my grandfather's pocket, with little measurable benefit to the business. In 1958, after hearing Paula insist once again that his father was hurting business, Jerry fired his dad. Eighteen months later, my grandfather suffered the first of several strokes, from which, in 1966, he died. When my grandfather passed, Jerry was quietly inconsolable. Paula had to physically force him away from the casket during official viewing hours at the funeral home, and even so, Jerry returned that night and persuaded the funeral home caretaker to let him sit in the viewing room until dawn.

In a crisp, rough, honest voice, Jerry told me these tales for the first time as we drove along a curvy mountain road in the southern California high desert in the mid-1990s. For Jerry, the meaning of actions and the contours of memories were set once they became the past and were not up for negotiation or revision, and regret endures.

"I Want to Be the First Guy They Come to for a Loan"

One Christmas, Dane proposed that he and I go to lunch before school reconvened in January. I was 13 years old. My mother dropped me off at the bank where Dane worked, a manager (soon to be vice-president) in the loan department. "Hey, buddy," he smiled as I walked to his desk, "I want to introduce you to some people." I pretended to be an adult as I shook hands with administrative staff, managers, tellers—all of whom seemed unduly delighted to meet Dane's nephew. Several of them knew my mother, and told me how much they liked her.

This was my first exposure to the business world. Over the years, I had visited my dad's law office but almost always on weekends, when he would catch up on work and I would amuse myself with the office machines. A weekday in my dad's office consisted of hushed utterances filtering into corridors, a random bell softly summoning an administrative assistant, an occasional chuckle from a man's chest during a telephone conversation, and the smell of leather, tobacco smoke, and furniture polish. At Dane's bank, however, commerce unfolded in a lively manner. I watched Dane talk with secretaries as well as with businessmen discussing loans. It seemed to me that "work" consisted of laughing, making jokes, engaging in chatter, and occasionally issuing a brief instruction in an arch or amused tone.

That first lunch with Dane, as well as during the many thereafter (even while in college, I had lunch with Dane twice a year, at Christmas and during the summer), Dane greeted one passerby after the other by name as we walked to the restaurant. Men would hail Dane from the opposite side of the street, and Dane would shout back a greeting or wisecrack. At the dining establishment, the maître d' and waiters knew Dane well and hovered near him; businessmen on their way in or out stopped by our table to exchange pleasantries with Dane—some of them earnest and others arch.

During one of our first lunches, I exclaimed, "You know everyone, and they all like you!"

"Well, buddy, I try to stay on the good side of everyone," Dane replied. "If any of these fellas start thinking about a loan, I want to be the first guy they come to."

Family Holiday Rounds

From the late 1950s and into the early 1970s, in southern California, the family holiday rounds began with Thanksgiving. My mother first hosted the feast in about 1957, taking over for my grandmother. My mother assigned each of my uncles the same duty year after year at our feasts.

Jerry carved the turkey. He treated his carving tools, meticulously cleaned and sharpened, as respectfully as he did his firearms. He would let me watch him but only if I stood safely several feet away. Jerry would narrate his actions, explaining to me how to angle the blade to ensure that well-sized, steaming slices of turkey might drop neatly onto the carving board.

Dane mashed the potatoes. He swirled the blades of a handheld electronic beater through potatoes laced with warm milk, melting butter, and seasoning. When the adults had taken seats at the large dining room table, my cousins and I would group ourselves around it while Keith rose, held a glass of wine high, and offered a toast to us all. Then my dad would offer a blessing, and after that, we cousins would retire to our own table.

Christmas Eve unfolded at Dane's home. He chatted with each family member briefly, laughing and encouraging each of us to have seconds before he moved on to the next person. Jerry wore a bowtie that Paula had made by hand, the wings shaped like holly leaves with red plastic berries wrapped around the middle. When he arrived wearing his tie, everyone laughed as if we had never seen the goofy accessory before. After dinner, Dane displayed for us the gifts his bank customers had given him: cordovan attaché cases, bottles of excellent whiskey, electronic devices (shavers, tape recorders, and portable radios), and fountain pens. As Dane displayed that Christmas's haul, Jerry would pretend to steal one of the gifts—usually a bottle of especially good scotch. He and Dane would conduct a mock tug-of-war, Dane feigning possessive indignation.

The Perfect Male Takes Me Under His Wing

I often ate dinner at Keith's in the mid-1970s. I was out of college and, for a time, at loose ends. Keith took me under his wing. He almost always cooked pot roast. He taught me to roast a tomato over the gas flame on the range and then cut it up into the salad. "The skin comes right off, it's easier to eat, and gals like it that way," he explained. Keith had moved from near San Jose to Los Angeles in 1970. Eleanor and Keith divorced that year after a quarter-century of restive marriage—serial philandering on both their parts—and he relocated to Los Angeles as a real estate agent and developer. Following his divorce, Keith had nothing but opportunity to indulge his apparent natural inclination to seduce, delight, and cater to women and ultimately madden them with anger, jealousy, indignation, and grief. Almost everything he did seemed to be in service to his quest for what he always referred to as "gals." He would go out with one woman—"She's a super gal!"—and not long after be with another despite having seemed so happy with the previous woman.

At the time, I considered Keith the perfect male. He was always busy, always making new friends, all of them as confident and cheerful as Keith. No one ever said no to Keith, it seemed. His will would always prevail. He traveled, avidly played tennis and skied, and went out with several different women each week in addition to the "super gal" he was dating at the time. During these years, my father made a toast to Keith at a family party very close to Keith's birthday. "Keith," he said, after raising his glass to his brother-in-law and shaking his head, "I don't know what you do for blood."

One weeknight, Keith arranged a blind date for me with a young woman named Katherine, about 2 years my senior. She and I met at Keith's apartment, from where we three plus one of Keith's male friends drove to a charity event in the friend's car. Katherine stepped into the backseat—followed by Keith. I sat in the front with my uncle's friend. I could hear Keith cooing to Katherine, "Do you mind if I hold your hand? Oh, your hand is so warm." It sounded as though Keith were seducing the "gal" he had wanted to set me up with. At the event, I did have the opportunity to get acquainted with Katherine, and I thought I detected some interest on her part. We four later returned to Keith's apartment for a nightcap. Then Keith's friend left. I stayed, waiting for a moment when I could privately say good night to Katherine and request her phone number. At about 11:30, though, Keith said, "Dave, I think you'd better get on your way, I know you're up early tomorrow for work." (At the time, I was a teacher in the Los Angeles Public Schools.) He stood up, guided me to the door—with Katherine smiling behind his shoulder. Within moments, I was alone on the porch.

The next evening, I called Keith. "I thought you were fixing me up with Katherine," I complained.

"Well, that was the plan," Keith replied, "but when she showed up at my place, I realized what a super gal she was, and—well, at any rate, she was a couple of years older than you, you don't want that!" Keith and Katherine ended up dating briefly.

I noticed that I began to get an upset stomach after dining at Keith's. I thought it was the way he cooked meat—too much fat, perhaps, left in the juice. Then I realized it was tension: I could not relax because I could never be like Keith, and in my 20s, I so wanted to be the charming, confident, athletic combat veteran who had seen and done it all that Keith was.

Cutty Sark, Handguns and Penmanship

The best days with my uncles were when the four of us built a mountain cabin in the Angeles National Forest. The three brothers always agreed that those years in the forest formed them into a trio more tightly knit than they had been since childhood. My grandmother, still alive at the beginning of the cabin project, was joyful when each of her sons told her about the fun they were having as a threesome.

The project started in 1978 when Jerry decided he wanted a mountain retreat, perhaps to serve eventually as his and Paula's retirement home. My three uncles spent several weekends over 6 months leveling the ground, laying the foundation, and marking out the footprint of the cabin. They slept in sleeping bags outdoors or in an old, cramped trailer they moored permanently at the site and used for storage as well as sleeping; they drank beer, told stories, teased each other unmercifully, and set up a horseshoe pitch and a firing range, all the while wielding tools and hoisting lumber with ease—even Dane, a banker, and Keith, a real estate agent.

One late autumn day, while visiting my parents, my mother told me that Jerry had asked if I would be interested in joining them the next weekend in the Angeles. "I think you should go," Mom said. "You'll get to know my brothers in a whole new way."

I went. I discovered that I could not accomplish anything that men like them could. I could not move rocks fast enough to suit them. I could not hammer nails straight enough for them. Jerry brought up a cache of his firearms, and we would stop work at 4.00 p.m. to shoot handguns at the firing range until dusk. They all were better shots than I was. Starting at about 10.30 a.m., every half hour or so until quitting time in the afternoon, Dane would shout, "Michelob time," and all hands helped themselves to a cold beer from a couple of ice-filled coolers. I could not keep up with their drinking—by 2.00 in the afternoon, I alone could not walk straight.

As the mountain sun glowed on the hillside chaparral, we trudged back to the trailer and cleaned up and soon switched from beer to Cutty Sark. For dinner, we heated a casserole my mother had made. Soused and maudlin, I began weeping, drawling, "I want to be a Marcks."

"Sorry, David," said Jerry, "you can't be a Marcks." I threw up a few minutes later and passed out.

I had dinner with my parents two nights later. Forlorn, ashamed of my weakness of muscle and stomach and poor hand–eye coordination, I said to Mom, "Your brothers hate me."

"They don't hate you," my mother assured me, "but you'd better give it right back to them when they tease you. Or they'll think you're a sissy."

Next, I went to the mountains with Jerry, Keith, and Dane in midwinter. I did not let an insult go unanswered. Seldom since high school had I performed the rough male ritual of the put-down, but I dredged up and deployed sufficient skill in the art to hold my own in the badinage. I still did not drive the nails with three strokes—set, drive, finish, next—as Jerry could. But I was getting better with lifting joists and moving rocks. When an uncle would call out, "Laborer!"—my signal to report immediately to that uncle for some dreary or thankless task—it seemed as though the summons contained the edge of affection.

Snow lay on the ground all weekend. A fresh feathering occurred in mid-afternoon—which we used as an excuse to stop building and shooting and retire to the trailer to start serious drinking. After dinner (another casserole), Keith suggested that we have a "penmanship contest," so we stood on a snow-laden roadway, urinating our names into the moonlit white, complimenting one another on legibility and linearity.

I again became maudlin. "I wanna be a Marcks," I begged drunkenly. "I want it so bad!" I thought of myself as an indoor cat and wanted only to be an outdoor cat like my uncles—able, graceful, and confident in the social and professional world. If only they would recognize me as one of them, it would be some vindication, perhaps salvation.

"David," said Jerry, putting his arm around me, "forget it. But if anyone ever could become a Marcks, it would be you."

Our last visit to the Angeles was in 1987 (Jerry sold the cabin a year or two later). Dane had the idea: a reunion. I came in from Florida to participate. I had only recently returned to the United States after living several years in Asia. My uncles finished the cabin during my absence. So we had little construction work to do. For most of the weekend, therefore, we shot handguns, took leisurely walks, ate casseroles donated by my mother, drank beer and Cutty Sark, and told stories—no penmanship contests, though, because snowfall was still months away. Each of my uncles told me privately that my years abroad had matured me in his eyes. I could imagine no finer homecoming.

Too Many Shirt Buttons Left Open

In 1993, a massive stroke took the life of Paula, Jerry's wife. After a few months, Jerry made public and official his relationship with Dina, with whom he had carried on an extramarital romance for three decades. I had never known a thing about the affair, although Dane, Keith, and Beverly did. I found it disconcerting that my otherwise stalwart uncle had cheated on his wife for so long and apparently with little secrecy; I loved Paula, who always talked at length with me at family events, our conversations verging on the philosophical as both of us aged.

Jerry and Dina became inseparable. She insisted that Jerry give away his well-worn woolen shirts, jeans, khakis, and work boots and replace them with lightweight resort wear made from artificial fibers. She dictated that he must grow his hair long and wear gold necklaces and rings. After years of dressing as the carpenter and outdoorsman he was, Jerry became a caricature of the aging retiree wearing too many buttons of his shirt open.

Jerry hoped to maintain full membership in two families—Dina's and his own. Dina seldom wanted to attend the occasional parties our family might throw outside of the holiday season, and Jerry disliked leaving Dina to attend by himself. At Christmas, rushing from Dina's family party in Downey to ours in San Diego, 90 minutes away, exhausted him. Finally, in 2005, he declared he would spend Christmas only with Dina and her family. Ever thereafter, I saw Jerry only occasionally. He still regularly spent time with his brothers and sister—they called their frequent reunions "meetings"—but he was physically part of Dina's family life more than mine.

In 2003, Jerry began telephoning me every couple of months. We would have tersely affectionate conversations. At one point in most of them, he would kid me about my poor marksmanship— "You'll have to become a better shot if you want to be a Marcks" or "If you have to, throw your gun at the guy's head, maybe you'll knock him out."

Jerry passed in the summer of 2010, and his will stipulated cremation. Gary, Dina's oldest son, with whom Jerry had become extremely close, took Jerry's ashes to Alaska's Mendenhall Glacier, which Jerry, on a fishing trip to the north country with Gary, had once expressed a great love for. The ashes soaked into the snow as Gary emptied the vessel he carried them in. I sometimes wish I had acted on my impulse to invite myself to go to Alaska with Gary, to accompany Jerry there.

"You'd Look Like Bruce Willis"

Except for a brief thaw in the summer of 2010, Keith and I have became markedly estranged since 2009 or so. He flew out from California to visit me in North Carolina for a week in 2007. He did not like my house, my neighborhood, my cooking, or even my habit of wearing an undershirt ("That patch of white at the neck looks corny"). He did not tell me any of that, however; he told his older daughter, Wendolyn, when they would have cocktails a few times each week. When I remodeled my kitchen, Keith, with his experience as a builder, offered to serve from California as a long-distance counselor and coach. I welcomed his support and counsel at first, but he soon began badgering me more than facilitating my thinking or acting as a sounding board. Remodeling became all we would talk, telephone, or e-mail about after decades of hashing over movies, politics, and travel in almost any conversation, letter, phone call, or e-mail message. If I hesitated to act on his suggestions, he needled me in a pouty, dismissive manner. I did not stand up for myself; I feared losing whatever apparently dwindling affection he may have had for me. My least favorite parts of my remodeled kitchen are those that originated as his ideas.

After the kitchen project ended in 2008, Keith urged me to build a fence on my front lawn, shave my head ("You'd look like Bruce Willis!"), and give certain family heirlooms to Wendolyn. I did none of those things. In 2009, he sent me a letter sent by post that solely promoted those actions. I elected to not reply, and shortly thereafter he removed me from his e-mail list—performing what Ungar and Mahalingam (2003) refer to as a "cut-off," in which "one family member makes a choice (and acts on it) to limit or discontinue contact with . . . [another member]" (p. 170). In July 2010, Keith and I met for morning coffee to have a conversation that led to a détente. But tension (although not as much before) has nonetheless leaked back into our relationship. In 2011, at age 87, Keith married Angela, a wealthy, attractive widow 10 years his junior. They live in the California desert and have an active social life, and Angela takes up enough of his attention to dramatically limit his contact with Dane and Beverly and, of course, with me. Keith and I do exchange occasional e-mail messages, a sentence or two of discussion about a forward he has sent to his address list, which does now include me once again.

I grew up in a Jewish home. My mother converted from the Lutheran faith; my father was Jewish from birth. In my youth, Keith would occasionally make a snide remark about Jews or Judaism or declare to me that I was half Jewish. I would laugh at such comments and pretend to agree, even though it hurt to do so; I felt like I was letting down my own team. I think angrily of those comments now and marvel at how I so desperately wanted Keith's approval and goodwill that I would deny to him or, not mention, how much I cherished my identity as a Jew. I have long since ceased to think of Keith as a role model.

"How's Your Love Life?"

Dane lives in San Diego, California, as does my mother. He spends a great deal of time caring for Marlene, whose health is frail. Both of them were heavy drinkers for years. It has taken a physical toll on both of them as well as apparently having degraded Marlene's cognition. Dane still organizes the family parties that we hold during my visits to California for a few days at Christmas and in July or August. The parties have only six or eight attendees any more. Dane's younger daughter hosts them because Marlene has long been unable to do so. Now technically a guest, not a host, Dane nonetheless encourages us to help ourselves to seconds.

For several years when I would visit southern California, Dane—almost as if he were my older brother—would pick me up at the San Diego Airport and drive me to my mother's residence. During the 30-minute ride, we would catch up on what we had each been doing lately. Dane would tell me about his community volunteer activities, update me with his perspective on my mother's health and welfare, and inquire about my work at the university. He would ask for my opinion on some political issue or another and then ritualistically, usually after a segment of very serious political conversation, ask, "So, David, how's your love life?"

My mother long owned a vehicle that I would use during my sojourn. Then, in 2007, she sold her automobile because she had given up her driver's license. I began renting a car for my visits, picking one up at the airport on arrival and driving myself to her place instead of calling on Dane to chauffeur me to Mom's. I miss my conversations with Dane; squeezing in a few minutes here or there at a family party is not the same as having a concentrated half hour together. So for the past couple of visits, Dane and I now have lunch when I come to town. I always make sure to tell him that lunch with Uncle Dane has been a big deal to me since my teenage years.

Monsoon, a Shaman, and Braking with the Right Foot

My uncles have been my mentors (Milardo, 2005) and teachers. Dane taught me how to be social in the environments I inhabit—as Dane always did, I want people to like me. I believe in the importance of being sociable and the good things that follow on from being trusted. Keith taught me how sometimes, though, one does well to call on what my mother has referred to as "larceny in your heart"—Keith's adventures have demonstrated how it can be done and what may come of it. I have never, however, cultivated as much of this larceny as Keith probably would advocate. The larceny in Keith's heart has sometimes hurt me profoundly.

Jerry taught me artisanship—one way to treat a weapon, one way to treat a carpentry tool, one way to drink scotch (on the rocks, never with a mixer). Jerry always wanted to teach me something. For example, he loved introducing me to craftsmanship that I would not otherwise notice. If we were in a building, he would take me aside to point out some wonderfully executed element that caught his eye.

"Look at the grain in this wood, David," he would say, rubbing his hand along the polished mahogany of a curving banister in a grand old San Diego restaurant where several of us in the family had lunch together one day. "You don't see this kind of work any more; it's too expensive and takes too long to get right. And look here at the mitering of these joints. This is just beautiful."

Three years before he died, I stayed overnight at Jerry's house when in transit on a trip that took me through Los Angeles. We decided to eat dinner out, not cook at his place.

"You drive," said Jerry, giving me the keys to his Saturn. "I want to show you something." He then explained how he had discovered that driving was more efficient when you brake with your left foot. As I experimented with this unfamiliar and—in driver's education in the late 1960s—forbidden maneuver, we jerked along the street. "You'll get the hang of it; just practice when you get home," he assured me. I preferred to rely on the standard method of braking with right foot only and consequently did not try to make the change. But I remember that lesson fondly as the last one I had with Jerry.

My uncles have been keepers of meaning—especially Dane. He is an organizer and a ritualist and, at times, has been almost a shaman. Jerry's death profoundly saddened my mother and Dane—Keith less so, probably because Keith, I suspect due to his experiences in combat, has always had a negligent attitude about death. To celebrate Jerry's life, Dane organized an informal memorial event for about eight of us in July 2010. Dane had collected a multitude of artifacts from the shelves, walls, and storage boxes at the house where Jerry died. We passed around Jerry's hunting license, a couple of gas-rationing tickets Jerry had kept from the war years, photos, Jerry's high school diploma and contractor's license, and other ephemera, each of us briefly expressing fond memories of the man. Keith and I stood side by side, his arm around my shoulders—we had, just that morning, the conversation that ended, briefly, the estrangement—and said something that for Keith was remarkably vulnerable. "When my time comes, I don't know what they're going to say about me," he whispered, "except that I could sometimes be an asshole."

Keith always was an extraordinary intergenerational buffer for me. Starting when I was perhaps 12 or 13 and on through my mid-20s, Keith explained to me the parental mind. He nodded when I complained about my mother and father and explained how I might enhance my relationship with them. He did as much for my parents. Once, for example, my mother expressed to Keith her concern that Kay, a woman in her mid-30s whom I had recently begun seeing, was over a decade older than me. Keith arranged to meet Kay and me for drinks. He liked Kay very much (it was mutual) and reported to Mom that I was in good hands and would likely mature as a result of the relationship. During my years spent living overseas, Keith, himself an inveterate traveler, would explain to my parents what I was seeing and experiencing in the international sphere, assuring them I was capable of taking care of myself.

I now am almost exactly Jerry's age when I told him I wanted to be a Marcks—the same age as Keith when he explained to Mom that during monsoon, which had just begun in Indonesia (my home of a few weeks), people simply stay wet and that my quip in a recent letter that I needed an umbrella was a wisecrack (he was correct), not a veiled call for her to frantically procure and ship to me an umbrella and the same age as Dane when he engineered our last visit to the cabin.

More than ever before in my career as a university professor, I guide and coach students in how to respond to life beyond the confines of course content, I acquaint department newcomers (faculty, students, visitors) with the narratives that form our organizational memory, and often I explain variously to student and professor the modes of thought and action that distinguish each of those "generations" from the other.

I suppose I have become an uncle—and I like it.

Discussion Questions

1. Define the term "generativity."
2. What three roles might uncles (or aunts) play in the lives of their nieces and/or nephews?
3. In your experience, how does the uncle–aunt relationship differ from the parent–child relationship?
4. Reflect on the relationship that you experienced with an aunt, uncle, or avuncular figure growing up. What influence did his or her presence have on your life?

References

De St. Aubin, E., McAdams, D. P., & Kim, T. (Eds.). (2004). *The generative society: Caring for future generations*. Washington, DC: American Psychological Association.

Kotre, J. (2004). Generativity and culture: What meaning can do. In E. De St. Aubin, D. P. McAdams, & T. Kim (Eds.). (2004). *The generative society: Caring for future generations* (pp. 35-49). Washington, DC: American Psychological Association.

Milardo, R. M. (2005). Generative uncle and nephew relationships. *Journal of Marriage and Family, 67,* 1226-1236.

Ungar, L. R., & Mahalingam, R. (2003). "We're not speaking any more": A cross-cultural study of intergenerational cut-offs. *Journal of Cross-Cultural Gerontology, 18,* 169-183.

Chapter 34

Navigating a Mother–Daughter Relationship

K. T. Aldridge

> A mother is the truest friend we have, when trials heavy and sudden, fall upon us; when adversity takes the place of prosperity; when friends who rejoice with us in our sunshine desert us; when trouble thickens around us, still will she cling to us, and endeavor by her kind precepts and counsels to dissipate the clouds of darkness, and cause peace to return to our hearts.—Washington Irving

Since the genesis of the human race, mothers have been the most vital facet of civilization, for without their enduring dedication to be mothers, no person in the annals of the world would have ever received their first breath. However, the duties of our female progenitors far surpass any mere biological imperative; from our first steps to our adolescent misadventures, we are guided by our matriarch's words, molded by her actions, inspired by her triumphs, taught by her failures, scarred by her reprimands, encouraged by her praise, and rendered human by her love until, at long last, we join our mother as an ally on the sprawl of adulthood. Nevertheless, despite the inevitable eventuality of growing up, modifying one's perceptions, behaviors, and interactional patterns of a parent–child rapport as it matures can prove rather challenging. When will this maternal deity become mortal—when is it safe for a mother to become a friend?

Annette Seamon, who I call Mom, was born at 6:09 a.m. on December 13, 1965, in Melbourne, Florida, where she was raised as an only child by her parents Sylvia Ham Seamon and Curtis Seamon. Her birth, alone, was extremely fortunate seeing as how, at the age of 19, my grandmother was diagnosed with endometriosis and was left with only three-fourths of one ovary; she was told that conception would be virtually impossible. At 13 years old, my mother was the first student at Melbourne High School to be allowed to take college classes that counted toward both high school and college credit. In March 1986, at the age of 20, she graduated from the Florida Institute of Technology with a double degree in applied mathematics and computer science, and on May 1, 1988, she married Bruce Aldridge, who was already the father of three sons (Ben, JJ, and Scott). In September 1990, I was born, and my brother, Andy, followed in June 1992.

Regarding the nature of our relationship, I have always felt that every person has at least one true talent. Some people are born with an innate intuition or skill that, when paired with a desire to realize that potential, allows them to become expert doctors, lawyers, orators, teachers, pilots, psychologists, animal trainers, artists, or athletes. As for my mother, I solemnly believe that her divine gift is parenting. This idea is not exclusively based on the fact that she always wanted a large family but rather on observing her actions and reactions. Once, during a telephone conversation, I noted a paradox—an inconsistency between her behavior and her remarks. She was recounting what she had done that day, which included taking a loaf of pumpkin bread to my friend Josef—a waiter in my hometown—and helping him file his taxes. Next she began lamenting about how she was 44 years old and still had not discovered her true talents and gifts. I was shocked and slightly irritated at her blatant unawareness. A few of my friends have even admitted that she is more of a mother to them than their own mother is. Growing up, every kid in the neighborhood always wanted to play at our house because my mom saw the loud, unbridled lunacy of kids racing skateboards down the driveway and launching each other on the trampoline as an indispensable part of childhood. She always made lunch for my friends, rented movies for us, bought us Jiffy-Pop and let us sleep in blanket forts in the living room. In brief, my mom was cool.

Mel Lazarus said, "The secret to dealing successfully with a child is not to be a parent." The way my mother put it was, "I am raising adults not children." So many of my friends and classmates viewed their parents as authoritarian dictators whose life goal was to micromanage every aspect of their lives. As a result, they exerted a great deal of effort in hiding their lives from their parents and looked forward to getting thrown out of the house at 18. My mother, on the other hand, believed that children are not property and are not delinquents who need to be controlled. She regarded parenting as an opportunity to show another fellow human being the wonders of life and to teach them how to survive the world. I can, more or less, explain the "tone" of my mother's parenting style by invoking two phrases that I never once heard my mother say and, on many occasions, heard her criticize vehemently. The first is, "Because I said so!" My mother argues that even children and teens are logical beings and that refusing to explain a command is a manipulative, feeble, and irrational attempt to seize control by imposing legitimate power and will end only in frustration for both parties. The second term is, "I am your mother, I'm not your friend!" Today, my mother is one of my best friends because her philosophy proposed that as the age of the child increases, the "parent-to-friend" ratio style of interaction should decrease.

To begin, symbolic interaction theory—developed by George Herbert Mead (1934)—focuses on the connection between human interaction, the creation and evolution of meaning, and the development of self-concept and culture. Additionally, this theory claims that how family members react to a situation is determined by how they interpret the situation. In a family, complicated sets of meanings are transmitted through symbols that permit each member to communicate with each other and share experiences (Clark & Peterson, 1986). With regard to my and my mother's communication, several features are clearly visible and contribute greatly to the foundation of our personal and public relationship. First, whenever my mother and I entertain guests or even converse in public, people frequently comment on "how close we must be" or mention how we must "love movies." This is due to the fact that a large portion of our conversations consists of quoting movies and recounting experiences, or what scholars might term "family stories" or "narratives." These patterns are so prevalent in our interaction that my mother is currently in the process of writing a book that compiles our family stories, and on various occasions we have even been known to have complete conversations using no dialogue other than phrases from films that we have watched together.

In accordance with symbolic interaction theory, these two aspects of our daily communication play an enormous role in the creation of our "relationship culture," which is constructed and maintained by our shared cocreation of meanings. For example, others might find it odd for someone to look up a ski slope and say, "That's no moon . . . it's a space station!" (Obi-wan Kanobi), but my mother understood that what I meant by using this term was "The ski run is much more complicated, significant, and potentially dangerous than what one would assume at first glance and that it must be taken out—figuratively." As Wood (2003) claims, social life and communication between people are possible only when we understand and can use a common language. Furthermore, not only do our shared meanings and inside "quote" jokes contribute to our conversation culture, but our communication contributes to our role making as well. Clark and Peterson (1986) refer to this cultural evolution as the process of improvising, exploring, and judging what is appropriate on the basis of the situation and the response of others at the moment and to our identity as individuals and as a unit. Hecht, Jackson, and Ribeau (2003) proposed that identities fall into three divergent categories: *personal* (individual characteristics), *relational* (based on relationships), and *communal* (related to larger ideological groups). The "mother–daughter" identity is classified as relational. Interestingly, although both my mother and I agree that we have a superb mother–daughter relationship, several of my mother's friends have criticized her, saying that our interactions resemble those of two sisters and not those of a parent and child. In addition, we have, on several occasions, been mistaken for sisters in public. After the fourth or fifth time this occurred, we concluded that it was indeed a pattern and began to analyze the situation. Besides the obvious observation that my mother is short and looks young, I hypothesized that the way in which I speak to her is dissimilar to how most children address their parents. Giles, Taylor, and Bourhis (1973) have shown that people will change their accent, their rate of speech, and even the words they use to indicate a relational connection with the person to whom they are talking. The term "convergence" indicates altering your speech to show an equal relationship, whereas "divergent" speech is used to signify distance between the speaker's age or status. Regardless of venue or company, my mother always spoke to me as an adult, and I have always reciprocated by speaking to her as I would one of my college friends.

Photo courtesy of Sherilyn Marrow

Unfortunately, in spite of our open-communication standard, "stunningly brilliant" ability to recite entire scenes from movies, and our egalitarian rapport, no relationship involving human beings can perpetually evade the clash of wills that inevitably results from the combination of freedom of thought, differing experiences, warped perceptions, and the unequivocal stupidity that plagues humanity. In the words of Hocker and Wilmot (1985), conflict is the interaction of interdependent people who perceive incompatible goals and interference from each other in achieving goals. In addition, Lewis Coser (1956) distinguished "realistic" from "nonrealistic" conflicts. Realistic conflicts are those based in disagreements over the means to an end or even the ends themselves; nonrealistic conflicts are expressions of aggression in which the sole end is to defeat or hurt the other. Fortunately, arguments between my mother and myself lean more toward the former of these two conflict divisions. Tension typically arises from small personality or behavioral discrepancies. For example, I frequently become enraged during phone conversations because when I am asked a question or even when I am working my way toward a solution for my own question, I continue to talk because speaking shows that I am still engaged in the conversation and helps me to mentally process. On the other hand, my mother requires "time to think" after a question is posed, and I interpret her silence as a sign that she was distracted and did not hear me or that she did not understand that it was not a rhetorical question. After a few moments, I normally make a snarky comment asking whether the phone died, to which she responds by screaming that "she's thinking." I then reply with something to the effect of "think faster" and voila, a degenerative spiral has been born. Our phone calls generally end abruptly with the phrase "Never mind, I found it," "Call me after you've thought about it," or "Thanks, bye." Although this might seem highly dysfunctional to the casual observer, most of the time we are discussing finances, academics, recipe instructions, and so on, and this is merely the fastest way to arrive at a conclusion before the kitchen burns down; thus, it is a realistic conflict.

Another point of contention is how we negotiate the discrepancies in our love languages (words of affirmation, quality time, gifts, acts of service, and physical touch) (Chapman, 1992). My mother's top love language is, by far, acts of service, which are services done for another that require thought, planning, time, effort, and energy" (Chapman, 1992, p. 90). Conversely, my top love language is quality time, and my last, without a doubt, is acts of services. So when my mother does my laundry or makes dinner, she feels that she is performing this "great act" to show her love; I see it as a necessary everyday chore that I could have done if she had asked me. However, I feel that watching television together and pontificating over the plot, directing and acting and commenting on the aesthetic attributes of the male actors, is a wonderful shared experience that brings people closer together; she sees it as a mild form of entertainment that she could do solo at any time. Since realizing this innate personality difference between us, we have not so much changed our behaviors to align with the love language of the other person, but we do now recognize when the other is trying to show "love" using the language that would make the other feel appreciated.

To continue, similar to all relationships, my mom and I are faced with the challenge of negotiating the relational dialectics as outlined by Baxter and Montgomery. Relational dialectics is a useful theory to apply in situations when trying to explain dramatic or sudden changes in human communication behavior. The pressures that each pole (or dialectic) exerts affect how participants in the relationship perceive and act within the context of the relationship (Baxter, 1988). Relational partners are constantly fluctuating between the poles, each extreme behavior offsetting tendencies toward the other pole. Although this theory encompasses six dialectics (autonomy–connectedness, openness–closedness, novelty–predictability, favoritism–impartiality, instrumentality–affection, and equality–inequality), I will focus on the three that I feel provoke the most conflict, or "search for balance in our relationship." Number 1: Autonomy versus connectedness is the desire to have ties and connections with others versus the need to separate oneself as a unique individual. I just turned 21, I work, I have lived in Europe, and I am on the verge of graduating from college. Considering this, I feel that I have earned the right to be treated as an adult who is capable of making her own decisions and should not have to ask for parental permission; however, I am still financially dependent on my parents, which makes me want to stay geographically distant from them in order to maintain the illusion of autonomy. Number 2: Openness versus closedness is the desire to be open and divulge information versus the desire to be exclusive and private. In my family, we are extremely open with our thoughts, feelings, experiences, and opinions regarding everything from politics, finances, and religion to philosophy, relationships, and even sex. Overall, this creates a very open and accepting climate—until you want to be alone and not talk to anyone for 5 minutes, and then suddenly relatives you did not know you had are asking you what is wrong. Once I did not return my mother's phone calls for a day and a half after we had had an argument, and she knocked on my window at 7:00 a.m. the next day. Sometimes, it seems that the only way to obtain space from my mother is to infuriate her to the point where she does not want to be around you. Number 3: Novelty versus predictability is the desire for the relationship to be predictable versus the desire for it to be original and new. My mother and I have had many arguments over the fact that she claims to be spontaneous, yet she refuses to break a routine without at least a one week's notice. For instance, growing up, we went to Yellowstone National Park every year for vacation. Several years ago, after arguing and pleading to go elsewhere I stopped going on family vacations.

Despite these numerous examples of daily and annual conflicts, we get along quite well. I owe this to our compatible conflict styles. According to Thomas and Kilmann (1974), there are five principal conflict styles: (a) *competing*, a style in which one's own needs are advocated over the needs of others; (b) *accommodating*, a style in which the person yields his or her needs to those of others; (c) *avoiding,* a common response to the negative perception of conflict; (d) *compromising,*an approach to conflict in which people gain and give in a series of trade-offs; and (e) *collaborating*, the pooling of individual needs and goals toward a common goal. Depending on the demands of the situation, the style changes, but in general we typically collaborate, compromise, or accommodate. Rarely—very rarely—have we ever used competing or avoidance, which we regard as manipulative and cruel ways to coerce the other into relinquishing power in order to resolve the conflict. William James said, "Whenever you're in conflict with someone, there is one factor that can make the difference between damaging your relationship and deepening it; that factor is attitude." In other words, because my mom and I always want to resolve a conflict, we do. Our dedication to work through any disagreement is the tool that leads to resolution.

In conclusion, I firmly believe that if more people in this world had a relationship, with anyone who was as genuine and solid as the relationship that my mother and I share, the mental and emotional health of the planet would improve. I never cease to be impressed by her wisdom, energy, and commitment. She is Yoda, Jay "Flash" Garrick, and Samwise Gamgee all wrapped into one. Although our relationship does not always sail on smooth waters, it is one of the most seaworthy vessels ever crafted.

Discussion Questions

1. In this chapter, the author states that when speaking to her mother, her speech markers (i.e., rate of speech, intonation, vocabulary, and so on) shift to indicate a more equal relationship and is, thus, "convergent." Reflect on the times that you have spoken with one of your parents. How does your speech change? Do you think that your speech becomes more "convergent" or "divergent"?
2. Does this "flattened hierarchy" (where parent and child are equal) work for all evotypical families? Under what conditions may this backfire?
3. Have you ever experienced the term "Because I said so!"? What was your reaction to its use? Why do you believe this phrase is so prevalent in parenting?

4. Consider the six dialectics mentioned and choose the one that either you or your family as a whole has struggled with the most. Which dialectic did you choose? Why?
5. Competing, accommodating, avoiding, compromising, and collaborating are all general ways in which people solve their issues. Which of these styles do you believe is used the most? The most destructive? The most difficult to implement? Which one do you use the most? Are you satisfied with your decision to use this style?

References

Baxter, L. A. (1988). A dialectical perspective on communication strategies in relationship development. In S. Duck (Ed.), *Handbook of personal relationships* (pp. 257-273).

Chapman, G. (1992). *The 5 love languages: The secret to love that lasts* (4th ed.). Chicago: Northfield Publishing.

Clark, C. M., & Peterson, P. L. (1986). "Teachers' thought processes." 3rd edition. In Wittrock 1986. Interest level: academic.

Coser, L. (1956). *The functions of social conflict.* New York: Free Press.

Giles, H., Taylor, D. M., & Bourhis, R. Y. (1973). Towards a theory of interpersonal accommodation through language use. *Language in Society, 2,* 177-192.

Hecht, M. L., Jackson, R. L., II, & Ribeau, S. A. (2003) *African American communication: Exploring identity and culture* (2nd ed.). Mahwah, NJ: Lawrence Erlbaum Associates.

Hocker, J. L., & Wilmot, W. W. (1985). *Interpersonal conflict.* Dubuque, IA: Wm. C. Brown.

Mead, G. H. (1934). *Mind, self, and society: From the standpoint of a social behaviorist* . Chicago: University of Chicago Press.

Thomas, K., & Kilmann, R. (1974). *Thomas-Kilmann conflict mode instrument.* Tuxedo, NY: Xicom Publishing. http://www.kilmann.com/conflict.html

Wood, J. (2003). *Communication theories in action: An introduction* (3rd ed.). Belmont, CA: Wadsworth.

Media Depictions of Adoption Narratives

Beth M. Waggenspack

We have all seen it on talk shows: the long-lost reunion between adopted child and birth parent, with the noble birth parent "confessing" to why the adoption occurred in the first place, the tearful adoptee embracing the newly found family while sanctifying the adoptive parents, and the detective agency crowing how "anyone can do a search." We have experienced the dramatized fictionalized narrative of the surprise reveal, where the adopted adult learns that someone he has known (and usually hates) is his birth parent. Cinema has offered decades of sinister adopted children who are secret murderers; television fictionalizes international baby-selling rings. Sensational stories and fictional accounts get mixed in with real news of the legal dilemmas faced by adoptees searching for birth records, the earthquake orphans in Haiti, the Russian boys punished with hot sauce by their adoptive American parent, and adopted teens finding birth relatives on Facebook—even Oprah revealed that she had a half-sister who had been adopted at birth and whom she never knew until 2010.

Those involved in adoption (adoptees, adoptive parents and families, birth families, and adoption professionals) usually seek out accurate adoption information from a variety of sources, including popular and professional media, online resources, and informational meetings. But the vast majority of the public is not exposed to adoption except through popular press and entertainment media, which often skew coverage toward the dramatic, sensational, stigmatizing, or exploitative (Baumann, 1999; Berry & Barth, 1989; Kline, Chatterjee, & Karel, 2006; Kline, Karishma, & Karel, 2009; Marr, 2008; Trolley, Wallin, & Hansen, 1995; Waggenspack, 1998; Wegar, 1997).

It has long been accepted that mass media have the ability to shape conceptions of reality and to influence attitudes and behavior. For more than two decades, communication researchers have recognized the role that television plays in shaping social perception of what a healthy American family consists of (e.g., An & Lee, 2010; Bryant & Bryant, 2001; Callister, Robinson, & Clark, 2007; Galvin, 2003; Kim, 2006; Kromar & Vieira, 2005; Larson, 1993; Paavonen, Roine, Pennonen, & Lahikainen, 2009; Robinson & Skill, 2001). Most of this research has ignored portrayals of families formed through adoption.

Media researcher George Gerbner (1988) conducted an exploratory study of the portrayal of adoption in mass media news, information, and entertainment between 1978 and 1988. Gerbner's analysis noted that the treatment of adoption ranged from sensitive and thoughtful to the simplistic and stereotypic. He concluded that adoption is often depicted as a troublesome or troubling issue, and while he agreed that useful information is available to those who seek it, the messages most people receive are more likely to enhance the impressions of common problems of adoption that families face. Subsequent research on media coverage of adoption has described overly negative and stigmatizing exposure (e.g., Kline, Chatterjee, & Karel, 2007; Kline et al., 2006, 2009; Waggenspack, 1998; Wegar, 1997).

Although adoption is a fairly common means of family building, much of the public lacks the orientation to put a positive "face" on adoption. The realities of those who were adopted, as well as their birth and adoptive families, are at odds with a large segment of the population. Themes such as loss and abandonment, cultural differences, searching for identity, complexities of relationships, transracial adoptions, custody situations, celebrity adoptions, and the challenges of living in orphanage or foster care are glossed over or sensationalized by many media narratives. The results of this disconnect are reflected in insensitive remarks, motives questioned, and damaged self-esteems.

Narrative

The use of narratives as a primary communication form stretches to the earliest human memories. Prior to written languages, community values and rules were transmitted through narratives. Even today, we tell stories to instruct, explain, reinforce, influence, and entertain. Mass media's pervasiveness has expanded the options for experiencing narratives, providing new opportunity to tell our tales.

Walter R. Fisher (1978, 1980, 1984, 1985a, 1985b, 1987, 1989a, 1989b) argued that all forms and genres of human communication are fundamentally storytelling. Rather than considering narrative simply as a message told in story form, Fisher argued that narrative is a paradigm of human communication, suggesting that it is in our human nature to use stories to get at truth. Narratives can affirm new ideas and images by seeking acceptance for them.

Individuals begin to make sense of their lived experiences through the stories that they tell (Bergen & Braithwaite, 2009). What makes a narrative different is that it creates for the storyteller and the audience a personal involvement in the narrated world. Narratives generate involvement in a world that is particular, sharable, and personal (Foss, 2009). Narrative worlds are specific and detailed: Listeners' imaginations are called on, and they are invited to connect their experiences to those of the storyteller. The storyteller and the audience share moments of experience around the form and content of the story. Shared stories do not merely retell past events; they influence the construction of one's individual, familial, and social realities (Baxter, 2004; Bylund, 2003; Harrigan, 2010). As Foss (2009) noted, narratives have multiple motives: encouraging action; justifying or legitimizing an act; restoring order; healing from loss; teaching, instructing, or offering lessons; conveying a culture's values; challenging perceptions; making sense of the abstract or unfamiliar; constructing identity and gaining self-knowledge; entertaining; maintaining or creating community; memorializing; or managing or resolving conflict. Narratives also invite audience members to share the moral evaluation being offered of the narrated world. When listening to a story, the audience must respond in some way to the evaluation of the world as it is presented by the narrator. In hearing and telling family stories, individuals gain understanding about themselves, their families, their cultures, and the world in which they live (Fiese, Hooker, Kotary, Schwagler, & Rimmer, 1995; Galvin, 2003; Harrigan, 2009; Langellier & Peterson, 2004).

The narrative approach attempts to make connections between emotion and logic. It asks, Do stories provide new, recurring, and useful insights about society? Because it is human nature to tell stories, the narrative approach provides a way to examine how people use elements of plot, characterization, and the aesthetics of storytelling to make their messages appealing and compelling.

Critics who employ the narrative approach examine the narrative in terms of both content and how the story serves an audience as a good reason for their beliefs and behaviors.

Narratives rely on a combination of reason and emotion. The standards employed in determining the rationality of narrative ask if the narrative's tale is complete and true. It is our culture, our community of meaning, that provides a sense of the completeness and truthfulness of narrative. Two concepts from Fisher's narrative approach are especially pertinent for this chapter. First, narrative can be used to interpret human communication through the creation of narrative content, the characters, their deeds, and the setting in which those deeds are performed. Second, communication can be evaluated on the basis of narrative rationality, a judgmental standard that measures the truthfulness and completeness of a communicative act.

Understanding how media use narrative to influence belief and behavior involves looking at the structure of a story to determine what about it causes an audience to perceive it as a truth. The narrative approach enables critics to describe, analyze, and evaluate rhetorical acts in terms of the following:

- Narrative content: The tale that is told that is found in the chain of events that happen to characters in the story's settings;
- Narrative rationality: The accuracy of the story as a "truth" compared with competing narratives depends on its probability and fidelity. Narrative rationality evaluates a story's ability to serve as a reliable and desirable guide for belief and behavior.

Narrative Content

Narrative content consists of the elements of characterization, plot, and setting. For this analysis, characterization and plot play important roles in media narratives shaping the public's perception of adoption.

Characterization: Characterization is central to storytelling, and the extent to which a story is believable often depends on its characters: their motives and behavior. Characters are defined by their decisions and actions and the values reflected by their choices (Fisher, 1987). The audience adds their own real or imagined experience of what constitutes acceptable and unacceptable behavior for this type of person given the circumstances.

Because character is determined by audience perception as well as by the narrative, people expect characters who are like them to behave predictably, within their understanding of the bounds of human behavior. When a character behaves improbably, the behavior must be explained, or some feature of plot or setting must legitimize the behavior. Usually this happens by revealing or implying a motive for the behavior (Fisher, 1987).

Characterization and narrative rationality essentially is a question of trust: Can the audience develop sufficient identification with the character to trust him or her? Is it probable for a character to think or act in the way portrayed, and is that behavior consistent with human nature?

Plot: All narratives have plots. Even though all narratives might not conform to traditional plot structure, audiences view narratives on their own and consider them in terms of their common culture or life experiences. Critical analysis of the story must consider the plot in terms of whether its structure offers sufficient detail for it to be considered a good reason for belief.

Setting: Because a narrative's story can take place in any number of temporal or physical settings, the narrative approach does not offer much detail about the setting other than to advise that the mood, tone, and emotional content of a narrative are influenced by its setting. Setting may be constrained by human experience and perhaps even by imagination. At any rate, setting has the same requirements of probability and fidelity as plot and characterization.

Describing and analyzing the narrative content in terms of plot, characterization, and setting enables the audience to evaluate the tale's rationality—the basis of its ability to influence belief and behavior. What is discovered about plot, characterization, and setting, along with the details of how the tale was told, then enables the audience to consider narrative rationality.

Narrative Rationality

A narrative provides advice about how to think or what to do about something. The values that an audience accepts as good reasons to change belief or behavior are embodied in the narrative. These constitute what make that narrative persuasive. According to the narrative approach, the audience examines the story in terms of whether it offers a complete and plausible depiction of reality. Ultimately, the viewer must judge whether the narrative was a source of good reasons, that which the audience uses to authorize, sanction, or justify a belief or behavior.

Fisher (1987) describes the logic of good reasons used to test narrative rationality. One means of testing narrative rationality involves determining the completeness of a narrative and its accuracy in making assertions about social reality. When a critic attempts to perceive narrative rationality, he or she tries to determine why an audience accepts a story as true. At least a part of a narrative's success comes from telling a tale that strikes a responsive chord in the audience, providing a vision of a truth or what the audience wishes were truth in the tale being told. As a result, narratives usually compete to offer the best explanation, providing good reasons for the audience to believe in or to do something about.

Because the media offer audiences complex and varied narratives about adoption, including search and reunion tales, bad-seed legends, surprise adoption accounts, news reports about legal issues surrounding adoption, and fictionalized stories with adoption themes, viewers and readers have the opportunity to apply Fisher's concepts of narrative fidelity and narrative rationality. Koenig-Kellas and Kellas (2005) asserted that understanding the intricacies of narratives is imperative because this communicative process "can be powerfully constitutive of relationships" (p. 368). Tracy (2002) and Langellier and Peterson (2006) stated that narratives have been linked with personal identities, family satisfaction, and family culture. If a family's culture and identity is both formed and performed as part of the process of communication (Langellier & Peterson, 2006), then recognizing the narratives that media present is crucial to the adoption experience as a whole. Finally, in their discussion of what forces shape adoption conversations in families, Freeark, Rosenblum, Hus, and Root (2008) argued that scholars should move beyond the "what" and "when" of disclosure of adoption issues into the "how" and "why" of those same conversations (p. 2). This analysis will examine adoption representations presented by the media that respond to those terms of what, when, how, and why, as those narratives lead to narrative rationality, or reasons for the audience to think about adoption in a particular way.

Narrative Adoption Themes

Characterization: Bad Seeds, Uncaring Birth Parents, and Murderous Adoptive Parents

The first narrative theme involves characterization, an essential part of narrative content. Quite common are characterizations that purport to describe members of the adoption triad and/or the adoption process. Adoptive participants' behaviors or motives are differentiated as questionable, or adoptees are depicted in negative images. Cinema is rife with these characterizations (an extensive list of films until 2000 is available at http://www.adoptionhealing.com/AdoptionMovies.html). Most common is the "problem" adopted child whose flawed biological or environmental background dooms him or her to a life that is riddled with drug addiction or criminal behavior. Story lines in television movies and soap operas accentuate the dangers of adopting a child whose genetic heritage is unknown. These narratives depict adoptees who were born of rapes, black-market adoptions, and children who were lied to about their adoptions, resulting in serious adult trauma. As a result, the media perpetuate the view that there is something seamy and pitiful about adoption and its participants. The resulting message (and resulting in narrative rationality) is that adopted children are troublesome. Several examples demonstrate this characterization. In *The Bad Seed* (1956), a sweet-looking 8-year-old girl turned out to be a pathological liar and murderer. *The Omen* (1976) featured the adopted child as the Antichrist. The movie *Problem Child* (1990) depicted the adoption of a 7-year-old "devil" child whose behavior includes cruelty to animals, arson, and urinating in inappropriate places. It was followed up with *Problem Child 2* (1991) and *Problem Child 3* (1995, television movie). *Martian Child* (2007) sported a boy described as a misfit kid who believes that he is from another planet. *Orphan* (2009) offered an outwardly angelic little girl who terrorizes her adoptive parents. The television show *Arrested Development* episode "Family Ties" (2006) featured a girl who, on learning that she was adopted, attempted to seduce her brother. The made-for-television movie *Family of Strangers* (1993) is about an adult adoptee who, "facing surgery that requires her genetic history, seeks her biological parents in a desperate quest that unearths a dark mystery." (She discovers that her birth resulted from rape.) In *Twins* (1998), children who are the result of an experiment are raised differently. The handsome, athletic one is perfect, sent to an island, and raised by philosophers. The smaller, uglier one is placed in an orphanage. Perhaps the creepiest example of a "bad seed" was in *The Miracle* (1991), where a male adoptee is sexually attracted to the actress, who turns out to be his birth mother.

Biological and adoptive parents do not escape negative characterizations. As far back as 1940, the film short *Women in Hiding* focused on unwed mothers who sell their babies. *Losing Isaiah* (1995) featured the biological and adoptive mothers of a child involved in a bitter, controversial custody battle. In the drama *Secrets and Lies* (1996), a successful black woman traces her birth to a lower-class white woman who denies parentage. *The Shipping News* (2001) centered on a mother who sold her child to an illegal adoption agency. *There Will Be Blood* (2007) followed the rise to power of Daniel Plainview, who used his adopted son to project an image of a caring family man. In *A Child Lost Forever* (1995), a birth mother searches for her child, only to discover that his adoptive mother murdered him. Woody Allen's 1995 *Mighty Aphrodite* focuses on an adoptive father's search for his child's prostitute birth mother. *Second Best* (1994) chronicles the life of James, who had been in an orphanage for years since his mother committed suicide and his father was sent to prison.

The Tie That Binds (1995) is the tale of fugitives who are wanted for murder. They escape the police, but their young daughter is left behind and adopted. Even the beloved musical *Annie* (1999) features a cruel orphanage and con artists who are supposedly her biological parents. The most famous "bad adoptive mother" was surely Joan Crawford as portrayed in 1981's *Mommie Dearest*. But the ultimate "bad biological father" was Darth Vader from *Star Wars*.

On television, the long-running NBC show *Law and Order* (in its many iterations) is a primetime example of various adoption-related stories that question the character of the biological or adoptive parents. For instance, in May 2010, episodes featured a baby-selling ring and a person who adopted his gay spouse. April 2005 offered an episode where the adoptive parents and daughter are in a witness protection program. When the daughter finds her birth parents, the adoptive parents are murdered, and the birth parents conspire to murder their daughter for her inheritance. In a 2006 episode, a couple adopted a biracial child and then committed murder to try to hide the birth father's African American heritage.

Soap operas love adoption stories. *All My Children* ran a 1996 story arc about a runaway teenager who placed her child for adoption, then attempted to seduce the adoptive father but was spurned by him. Another complex story line in the same soap opera had a leading character kidnapping a child and then attempting to pass off the child as her adopted daughter. *One Life to Live* ran two long plots from 1988 to 1991 about "adoption lies." In the first story, a baby was taken from his mother to replace a child who had supposedly died in the South American jungle. *Days of Our* lives had a character whose orphanage files showed that her biological parents died 100 years earlier. Abusive adoptive parents abound in soap operas, such as Raymond Colfax in *As the World Turns* and Peter Manning in *All My Children*.

News-related coverage on television and in print likely tends toward the negative when adoption is the subject (Gerbner 1988; Kline et al., 2006, 2009; Waggenspack, 1998). Analyses of broadcast news media programming and print sources have found that while there are positive stories related to adoption policy and human interest narratives with positive outcomes for members of the adoption triad, many stories feature atypical adoption battles between birth and adoptive families, stories in which families are shown as having unwittingly adopted children who are portrayed as unsalvageable, murderous adoptees, some of whom are serial killers. News stories have featured numerous characterizations of adoptive parents (often of children from Russia) who have murdered or abused their children. Carrie Craft (2011) documented 15 cases of Russian adopted children being murdered by their American parents between 1996 and 2009. In February 2011, an adoptive mother in Alaska was charged with misdemeanor child abuse after she appeared on an episode of the *Dr. Phil* show, presenting a video where she poured hot sauce down her adopted child's throat and then forced him to take a cold shower for lying (Hopper, 2011b). Worldwide outrage occurred in 2010 when an American mother sent her adopted 7-year-old son alone on a plane back to Russia. And researcher E. M. Marr (2008) conducted a media analysis that discovered that birth parents were a subject portrayed negatively, even when adoptive parents and agencies involved were described in a positive fashion.

Given the multiple examples of bad-seed adoptees, suspect birth parents, and murderous adoptive ones, it is understandable that those not connected to adoption may reason that the truth of adoption is a seedy, dangerous, and negative one. The audience is presented with a series of descriptions that constitute an overall narrative that questions the members of the adoption triad. According to the narrative approach, those depictions cause the audience to develop a plausible depiction of reality that is based in very limited, mediated perspectives.

Adoption Plots: Illegal Adoptions and Adoption Reunions

Two plot themes characterize adoption narratives and are familiar to most viewers and readers. These include narratives about illegal adoptions and stories revealing adoption reunions. Narratives that portray adoption as immoral, with the focus on adoption as commercialism or illegal behavior, call into question the narrative's plot. If the adoption story can be advanced only as an attempt to earn money or to supplant the law, then its veracity is uncertain. The audience will likely reason that, at its core, adoption is an illegal or shady enterprise.

For example, in 2005, Fox broadcast a game show called *Who's Your Daddy* in which a woman who was placed for adoption as an infant quizzed eight men in hopes of determining which was her biological father. If correct, she would receive $100,000 and a reunion. If she was wrong, she would still get to meet the "correct" man, but the man chosen would walk away with the cash. In a commentary to the *Chicago Tribune* on December 31, 2004, Gale Sayers, board member, and Julie S. Tye, president of the adoption agency, The Cradle, discuss how this game show warps reality and taunts those involved in searching for their adoptive families. They assert that adoption is not a game and "does a disservice to all of us who strive so hard to make adoption a fulfilling experience for everyone involved" (Sayers & Tye, 2004).

Even discounting "reality television," sensational stories have fostered the belief that adopted children are often obtained illegally or under questionable circumstances. Early in 2010, extensive coverage of a group of American Baptists accused of trying to take children out of Haiti illegally captured the nation. The CBS news program *60 Minutes* profiled the Tennessee Children's Home Society, which placed hundreds of children for adoption in the 1940s. Many, it was later found, were taken illegally from their mothers. The show failed to point out, however, that incidents of illegal removal are few compared to the number of adoptions across America. Tales of adoption scams by unlicensed agencies or unethical people arise without comparison to legal adoptions (e.g., Murphy, 2009; "Utah County Families Complain of an Adoption Scam," 2010). The coverage of celebrity international adoptions (Angelina Jolie and Madonna) suggests that money and/or power are necessary ingredients for adoptions. Although most of these international adoptions are stringently managed and rigorously policed, an avalanche of stories of systematic abuse in a few places cast a shadow over the entire process and its participants. These depictions of social reality are successful in striking a chord in the audience because they appear to reflect the truth. The explanations provide "good reasons" for the audience to perceive adoption as an illegal enterprise.

Aligned to this scenario, one of the primary questions that adoptive families are asked is "How much did your child cost?" Fictional dramas also forward this image of adoption being primarily about the money, usually illegally obtained. Mary Tyler Moore starred in 1993's television movie *Stolen Babies* about a 1940s Tennessee welfare worker who learns that Georgia Tann, the charismatic head of a local adoption agency, is actually running a black-market baby ring behind the Tennessee Children's Home Society. The soap opera *General Hospital* featured a story about an adoptive mother who bought her baby from a lawyer specializing in black-market adoptions. The television movie *Border Line* (1991) focused on an attorney representing an international adoption agency who gets mixed up in an illegal operation involving Asian mothers forced to give up their babies. The documentary *Baby Business* (1995) focused on the middlemen making money off of middle-class families from more developed countries who seek to adopt in the Third World, resulting in baby trafficking. USA Network's series *White Collar* (2010) featured a story about a devious attorney who was using his adoption agency to swindle money from potential parents to support his gambling.

A second plotline, popularized in news stories, talk shows, and television or cinematic dramas, is adoption reunions. Media coverage has suggested that a large number of adopted persons search for their birth parents, reinforcing the myth that all adoptees are constantly searching. Some adoptees want to answer the big questions of who and why by finding the people who brought them into the world; others feel no need to obtain information about their birth parents. Some want to know their medical histories, and others feel an urge to discover national or ethnic identities. In many states, adoptees are battling to change laws to unseal records to give them access to health and family history (Hopper, 2011a). Most people are familiar with reunions—family, school, and workplace reconnections where shared stories, common values, and communal images maintain connections among the participants. Adoption reunions lack the basics of those collective memories. "Reunion relationships are amongst the most complicated, with no road maps or etiquette to guide the process," says Spence-Chapin postadoption expert, Ronny Diamond ("Adoption Reunion on Latest Episode of TV Show *Glee*," 2010). With the focus on the initial meeting, unrealistic expectations and fantasies are often promulgated. Rather than focusing on the development of long-term relationships or the legal rights of adoptees to their birth history, media interest has been placed on search and reunion stories, which adoption scholars point out may even perpetuate the idea that blood relatives are more important than other family ties. Examples of films portraying reunions range from *Deep in My Heart* (1991), *My Own Private Idaho* (1992), and *August Rush* (2007). *A Family Thing* (1996) told the story of a white man who found out that he was not his mother's birth child but rather the son of a black woman who died in childbirth. He traveled to meet his half brother, who did not welcome him with open arms. *Flirting with Disaster* (1995) is a farce about an adoptee's birth mother search. *The Lost Child* (2000) is a search story of a woman who discovers as an adult that she was stolen from her Navajo reservation as an infant. Fox's popular *Glee* (2010) featured a bittersweet story arc between Rachel and her biological mother Shelby, who realize that their reunion expectations were unreal and that family bonds were more than genetics. The show did not explain the search and reunion's emotional intensity (other than through a shared song), and the two parted ways.

But adoption reunions get their major play on audience participation shows and reality television, which revel in experiencing the pathos of the unexpected. Both WE's *The Locator* (2008) and ABC's *Find My Family* (2009) showed the difficulties of the search process as well as the tearjerking results. ABC's casting call for the latter show addresses the emotional difficulties affiliated with adoptive searches. Considering the "impenetrable layers of red tape that tightly secure legal documents—the simple desire to answer the question, "who is my family" can become an agonizing and frustrating undertaking" (*Find My Family*).

While the program demonstrated some noble goals (the difficulties of the search), it simplified the issues of reunion (e.g., failing to portray people who refused reunion or the aftermath of trying to blend families), and it exposed this very tenuous relationship to onlookers who were unprepared to understand the intimate, elements surrounding it.

Daytime audience participation shows such as *Oprah*, *Dr. Phil*, *Jerry Springer*, *Sally Jessy Raphael*, *Montel Williams*, *Maury Povich*, and *George Lopez* have offered numerous reunion experiences where the biologically related members meet for the first time. In 2011, Oprah herself revealed the discovery of a recently discovered (2010) half sister placed for adoption as an infant. Even the happiest of reunions can be overwhelming with the intensity of feelings and expectations, and the media simplify or ignore this overwhelming process of first encounters and gradual reconciliation (or dissolution) in favor of the instant elation and making the reunion into a spectator sport.

Reunions are the initial step in the process for those who are interested, but as Bailey and Giddens (2001) stated, before a reunion it is easy to fall prey to unrealistic expectations, and afterwards it's equally difficult to maintain those newly created relationships. Those are the realities that media do not present.

Are All Representations So Bad?

While not all media representations of adoption are negative, most do limit the public's perspective on adoption; for every *Adoption Diaries* (WE 2009) that show the matching between couples and birth mothers, there are more *Orphans* or celebrity-adoption-of-the-day exposés. But there are alternative narratives that are beginning to make inroads into the public realm. Further research into children's media with adoption themes may demonstrate a shift in characterizations, as well as plot, leading to new realities with the mass audience. PBS has run several such shows: *Dinosaur Train* (2010) includes Buddy, a T-Rex who is adopted by Mr. and Mrs. Pteranodon; the long-running *Arthur* featured events leading up to the adoption referral of a sister from China, allowing children to learn about the stages of adoption and feel the emotions along with Binky, who is about to get a sibling; and *Sesame Street* showcased two adoptions, including a single-parent adoption of Marco from Guatemala and Miles, who was adopted in 1985 by Susan and Gordon. Nick, Jr. ran *Miss Spider's Sunny Patch Friends* (2004–2008), which weaved the tale of Miss Spider, who herself was adopted, and her adopted children, consisting of a dragonfly, beetle, and bedbug who lived with five other biological siblings.

A spate of recent documentaries are allowing the broader stories of the adoption triad to be heard, particularly adoptees who are searching into their identities. These provide the audience with more potential interpretations of adoptees, their circumstances and lives, and those who gave birth to or adopted them. *The Red String* (2004) features four adopted Chinese girls and their single mothers. *5000 Miles* (2006) tells the story of a couple who want to adopt from Poland; the video diary explores the emotionally draining experience of international adoption. Hip-hop singer Darryl McDaniels chronicled his search for biological roots in *My Adoption Journey* (2006). *A Place Between: The Story of an Adoption* (2007) deals with cross-cultural adoption and the search for identity. *Off and Running* (2008) profiles Avery, who grew up with white Jewish lesbian parents and two adopted brothers, who searches for her African American roots. *Going Home* (2009) focused on Korean-born Jason, who was adopted as an infant by Jewish parents from Greenwich Village, and traced his reunion journey. *Skin Deep* (2009) developed Nisha Grayson's search for self. There are also documentaries that give a more rounded face to birth families and adoptive parents. In 1999, CBS began a holiday special showing stories of adoption of children in foster care called *A Home for the Holidays*, mixing in music and celebrity adoption testimonials along with the short narratives that portray the lives of children in foster care and the families who adopt them. The goal of the show is to increase adoptions out of foster care; it celebrated its 12th showing in 2010. In 2002, filmmaker Sheila Ganz revealed personal stories of adoptees, birthparents, and adoptive parents over a 70-year span in *Unlocking the Heart of Adoption*. Discovery Health TV's *Adoption Stories* (2003–2004) profiled different families as they considered adoption, dealt with failed adoptions, adopted large numbers of handicapped children, adopted from foster care and internationally, and other scenarios). *A Family Is Family Is a Family* (2010) is Rosie O'Donnell's documentary about family diversity, including adoptive families. While these programs do not provide the entire arc of the adoption narrative, they do present a different frame on those involved with adoption and how adoption occurs, perhaps mitigating some of the more prominent and long-running narratives that the public is familiar with.

Recent children's movies supply a more uneven narrative, some with stereotyped characterizations and inappropriate adoption language and others focusing on positive family portrayals, being different, and discovering identity. *Elf* (2003) is about an orphaned baby who winds up in Santa's toy sack, raised by elves, and 30 years later "learns who his real family is." *Snow Dogs* (2002) features a man in his 30s who suddenly discovers he was adopted. *The Country Bears* (2002) is about a young bear raised by humans who searches for his birth family. He is not told by his parents about his adoption. In *Meet the Robinsons* (2007), orphaned inventor Lewis, who was left at the doorstep of an orphanage as an infant, reveals that he has been rejected by 124 sets of prospective parents and then sets out on a time-travel journey to find his biological mother. *Hotel for Dogs* (2009) tells about two orphaned siblings in dismal foster care who spend their days on the streets. They rescue dogs, create a dog hotel, evade lots of trouble, and eventually are adopted by their social worker. But there are also *Tarzan* (1999), where an orphan raised by apes eventually discovers his human side and makes identity decisions; *Dinosaur* (2000), where an orphaned dinosaur raised by lemurs helps them to a sanctuary; and the Harry Potter series (2001–2011) whose main character is orphaned but finds strength in friends and himself.

As Fisher (1987) noted concerning narratives, they reaffirm existing ideas and images or even subvert ideas and images by discrediting them. Narratives can eviscerate ideas and images, showing them to be absurd or impossible. It may be that these new directions in media representations will lead to changing views of reality on the part of those not involved with adoption.

Conclusion

Research shows that the media play a role in forming public attitudes toward families. It also has demonstrated that biased, misleading narratives have developed a skewed public view about adoption as a means of family building. Mass media's pervasiveness has expanded the public's opportunities for experiencing narratives, providing new opportunity to tell our tales. The narrative characterizations of members of the adoption triad, circumstances of adoptions, and adoption reunions present incomplete (and often negative) pictures of the full adoption story. Narrative rationality, which measures the extent to which a story functions as an argument to believe or to do something, suggests that these representations fail to meet the tests of truth and values expected by adoptees (the need for identity), adoptive and birth parents (privacy vs. exposure as well as motives for choice and behavior), and adoption professionals (fairness in representation). Those who are involved in adoption perceive a different reality than those without adoption connections, and it is that disconnect that is problematic. Considering the characterization of adoption triad members and the plotlines of illegal, expensive adoptions and reunions, those who are already connected by adoption have expectations different from the general public. While the former may want truthful illustrations of the reality of their lives (adoption through foster care, gay adoption, the fight to unseal records, adoption of older children, and so on), the general public does not get those new, useful insights into society. Instead, these narratives are often destructive, demeaning, and biased, leading to skewed public views about adoption. At the least, the general public's view of adoption is limited through sensationalism.

Further research into contemporary media representations of adoption narratives in television, film, books, news stories, and even music or books may show a shift or evolution in the range of narratives offered, leading to new narrative rationality. For example, how are birth parents' situations and decisions being offered as a source of information in news stories or fictionalized narratives? Has language to describe the adoption experience (commonly called positive or respectful adoption language) made inroads into broadcast news as well as fictionalized accounts (eliminating the referral of children as unwanted, illegitimate, or hard to place; referring to birth parents rather than "natural" or "real"; or not mentioning the adoptive or biological status in obituaries)? Have broader representations of adoptive families been offered (transracial families, African American adoptions, gay adoptions, and single-parent adoptions)? Are adoptees characterized for their accomplishments rather than focusing only on stigmatizing presentations of criminality, fraud, behavioral problems, and mental illness? Are adoptive families portrayed as "real" families, with many of the same kinship issues as biological families? Are the legal aspects of adoption explained so that the general public has a greater understanding of concepts of closed records, adoption disputes, and difficulties of adopting? Do families know of the availability and process of adopting children through foster care adoption?

Because adoptive families often discover that their kinship truths are at odds with those of the general society, the resulting narratives often reflect a reality that is misleading and harmful. Wegar (1997) reported that popular media reinforced cultural tension between biological and social conceptions of kinship, resulting in a rendering of adoptees as unnatural and different. Kline et al. (2009) found that the discussion of adoptees' troubled backgrounds, while providing insight into social conditions leading to adoption, perpetuate stigmatizing beliefs about adoption when not followed up with contextual elaboration. They suggested that the lack of news narratives about positive adoptee experiences likely creates a misleading picture for audiences about adoption. As demonstrated, media representations of adoption narratives challenge families, whether involved in adoption or not, by failing to reflect the broad range of issues, ideas, and outcomes that adoption provides.

Discussion Questions

1. What functions or "motives" do narratives serve in society and in the family?
2. What are the three main features of "narrative content"?

3. How does "narrative content" differ from "narrative rationality"?
4. According to this chapter, which three adoption narrative themes are the most prevalent in the media?
5. How do these negative adoption narratives/stereotypes affect our views of adoption?

References

Adoption Reunion on Latest Episode of TV Show Glee. (2010, May 27). http://adoptionnews.spence-chapin.org/post-adoption/adoption-reunion-on-latest-episode-of-tv-show-glee

Bailey, J., & Giddens, L. (2001). *The adoption reunion survival guide.* Oakland, CA: New Harbinger Publications.

Baumann, C. (1999). Adoptive fathers and birthfathers: A study of attitudes. *Child and Adolescent Social Work Journal, 16,* 373–391.

Baxter, L. A. (2004). Relationships as dialogues. *Personal Relationships, 11,* 1–22.

Bergen, K. M., & Braithwaite, D. O. (2009). Identity as constituted in communication. In W. F. Eadie (Ed.), *21st century communication.* Thousand Oaks, CA: Sage.

Berry, M. B., & Barth, R. P. (1989). Behavior problems of children adopted when older. *Children and Youth Services Review, 11,* 221–238.

Bryant, J., & Bryant, J. A. (Eds.). (2001). *Television and the American family* (2nd ed.). Mahwah, NJ: Lawrence Erlbaum Associates.

Bylund, C. L. (2003). Ethnic diversity and family stories. *Journal of Family Communication, 3,* 215–236.

Callister, M. A., Robinson, T., & Clark, B. R. (2007). Media portrayals of the family in children's television programming during the 2005-2006 season in the US. *Journal of Children and Media, 1*(2), 142–161.

Craft, C. (2011) Russian adoption murders. http://adoption.about.com/od/adoptionrights/p/russiancases.htm

Fiese, B., Hooker, K., Kotary, L., Schwagler, J., & Rimmer, M. (1995). Family stories in the early stages of parenthood. *Journal of Marriage and Family, 57,* 763–770.

Fisher, W. (1978). Toward a logic of good reasons. *Quarterly Journal of Speech, 64,* 376–384.

Fisher, W. (1980). Rationality and the logic of good reasons. *Philosophy and Rhetoric, 35,* 121–130.

Fisher, W. (1984). Narration as a human communication paradigm: The case of public moral argument. *Communication Monographs, 51,* 1–22.

Fisher, W. (1985a). The narrative paradigm: In the beginning. *Journal of Communication, 35,* 74–89.

Fisher, W. (1985b). The narrative paradigm: An elaboration. *Communication Monographs, 52,* 347–367.

Fisher, W. (1987). *Human communication as narration: Toward a philosophy of reason, value and action.* Columbia: University of South Carolina Press.

Fisher, W. (1989a). Clarifying the narrative paradigm. *Communication Monographs, 56,* 55–58.

Fisher, W. (1989b). *Human communication as narration: Toward a philosophy of reason, value and action.* Columbia: University of South Carolina Press.

Foss, S. (2009). *Rhetorical criticism* (4th ed). Long Grove, IL: Waveland.

Freeark, K., Rosenblum, K. L., Hus, V. H., & Root, B. L. (2008). Fathers, mothers and marriages: What shapes adoption conversations in families with young adopted children? *Adoption Quarterly, 11*(1), 1-23.

Galvin, K. (2003). International and transracial adoption: A communication research agenda. *Journal of Family Communication, 3,* 237-253.

Gerbner, G.(1988). *Adoption in the mass media: A preliminary survey of sources of information and a pilot study.* http://encyclopedia.adoption.com/entry/media/224/1.html

Hopper, J. (2011a). The nation's adoption laws and unsealing birth certificates. *USA Today.* http://www.usatoday.com/news/nation/2008-02-12-adoption_N.htm

Hopper, J. (2011b). *Russians outraged over "hot sauce mom."* http://abcnews.go.com/Entertainment/russians-outraged-hot-sauce-mom-dr-phil-charged/story?id=12840921

Kim, Y. (2006). How TV mediates the husband-wife relationship. *Feminist Media Studies, 6*(2), 129-143.

Kline, S. L., Chatterjee, K., & Karel, A. I. (2006). Covering adoption: General depictions in broadcast news. *Family Relations, 55*(4), 487-498.

Kline, S., Chatterjee, K., & Karel, A. (2007). Depicting adoption as a family form in broadcast news: Adoption activities and their news frames. *Conference Papers—International Communication Association,* 1.

Kline, S. L., Karishma C., & Karel, A. (2009). Healthy depictions? Depicting adoption and adoption news events on broadcast news. *Journal of Health Communication, 14*(1), 56-69.

Koenig-Kellas, J., & Kellas, J. (2005). Family ties: Communicating identity through jointly told family stories. *Communication Monographs, 72,* 365-389.

Kromar, M., & Vieira, J. T. (2005). Imitating life, imitating television: The effects of family and television models on children's moral reasoning. *Communication Research, 32*(3), 267-294.

Langellier, K. M., & Peterson, E. E. (2004). *Storytelling in daily life: Performing narrative.* Philadelphia: Temple University Press.

Langellier, K. M., & Peterson, E. E. (2006). "Somebody's got to pick eggs": Family storytelling about work. *Communication Monographs, 73,* 468-473.

Larson, M. S. (1993). Family communication on prime-time television. *Journal of Broadcasting and Electronic Media, 37*(3), 349-357.

Marr, E. M. (2008, July 31). *Sweetheart stories: The portrayal of transracial adoption in newsprint.* Paper presented at the annual meeting of the American Sociological Association. http://www.allacademic.com/meta/p241089_index.html

Murphy, K. (2009, January 13). Former Wis. woman admits to adoption scam. *Capital Times.* http://www.allbusiness.com/legal/criminal-law-sentencing/12219182-1.html

Paavonen, E., Roine, M., Pennonen, M., & Lahikainen, A. (2009). Do parental co-viewing and discussions mitigate TV-induced fears in young children? *Child: Care, Health and Development, 35*(6), 773-780.

Robinson, J. D., & Skill, T. (2001). Five decades of families on television: From the 1950s through the 1990s. In J. Bryant & J. A. Bryant (Eds.), *Television and the American family* (2nd ed.). Mahwah, NJ: Lawrence Erlbaum Associates.

Sayers, G., & Tye, J. (2004, December 31). *Adoption is a profound event, not grist for TV* (letter to the editor). http://articles.chicagotribune.com/2004-12-31/news/0412310048_1_adoption-daddy-birth

Trolley, B. C., Wallin, J., & Hansen, J. (1995). International adoption: Issues of acknowledgement of adoption and birth culture. *Child and Adolescent Social Work Journal, 412*(6), 465–479.

Utah County families complain of an adoption scam.. (2010, December16). ABC 4 News. http://www.abc4.com/content/news/state/story/Utah-County-families-complain-of-an-AdoptionScam/PVmP51YauEG1EA2YZ3biaA.cspx?rss=1451

Waggenspack, B. (1998). The symbolic crises of adoption: Popular media's agenda setting. *Adoption Quarterly, 1*, 57–82.

Wegar, K. (1997). *Adoption, identity and kinship: The debate over sealed birth records.* New Haven, CT: Yale University Press.

Chapter 36

From Isolation to Connection: Former Sex Workers Conceptualize Family and Familial Interactions

Jennifer Mayer and Brian K. Richardson

Women in the sex industry[1] face a number of challenges not encountered by individuals in traditional occupations, including substance abuse issues, financial insecurity, the persistent threat of violence by "clients," and arrest and prosecution (Dalla, 2001; Farley et al., 2003). Compounding these problems is the fact that sex workers typically suffer overwhelming feelings of guilt, shame, rage, and fear from working in a stigmatized industry (Dalla, 2006; Mayer & Richardson, 2010). This confluence of negative conditions and outcomes is often manifested in strained relationships between sex workers and their family members (Dalla, 2003). Considering the plethora of problems associated with sex work, it seems reasonable to assume that this is an industry on the decline. However, the sex industry in America is pervasive, a multi-billion-dollar enterprise (Parker, 2004); further, anecdotal evidence suggests the numbers of sex workers appears to be on the increase in this economic downturn (Clark-Flory, 2009; "Sex Workers in the Recession," 2009). Thus, we can expect the number of families that include a daughter, wife, or mother in the role of sex worker to grow as well. Despite these trends, we know little about interactions and relationships in families that include a sex worker (Jackson, Bennett, & Sowinski, 2007).

Investigating the relationship between sex workers and their families is critical for understanding how and why women enter, participate in, and exit occupations such as prostitution and exotic dancing. Research suggests that a primary reason that women enter the sex industry is to provide financially for themselves and their children (Dalla, 2003; Romans, Potter, Martin, & Herbison, 2000). Many women, particularly those who are single and without advanced educations, view sex work as a profession that offers flexible work hours and potentially high pay (Philaretou, 2006). Once they are working in these positions, women face the challenge of communicating about or keeping secret their participation in these highly stigmatized professions to their family members (Jackson et al., 2003; Philaretou, 2006). Interestingly, many sex workers continue their involvement in the industry while pregnant or shortly after childbirth, putting their children at risk of domestic violence, sexual victimization, and separation from their mothers (Dalla, 2002, 2003). Furthermore, participation in the sex industry is frequently coupled with the use of drugs (Dalla, 2002), making familial interactions that much more difficult. Finally, women attempting to exit the sex industry are faced with the task of renegotiating relationships with significant others and family members, a process that is frequently complicated by drug and alcohol recovery (Dalla, 2006). The history of sex work is deeply rooted in American culture (Weitzer, 2000), and trends indicate an increase in women engaging in this type of work. Still, there is a paucity of research examining the interactions within and meanings inherent in the everyday family life of sex workers, particularly those individuals who are attempting to exit or have exited this industry. Inquiry into this area of family relations, therefore, is imperative and long overdue.

Through the present study, we seek not only to give voice to marginalized women with experience in the sex industry but also to understand how these women's notions of family are impacted and ultimately changed through transformation programs. Thus, this chapter will address a family context that is rarely studied: those families including a (former) female sex worker, typically one who is or was drug addicted. Specifically, we explore how (former) female sex workers construct meaning about family as they proceed through different stages in the exit process and how they communicatively negotiate relationships within their families.

Review of the Literature

We focus our literature review on studies illuminating the relationship between sex work and family. Despite voluminous research into the industry overall, we know little about how sex work affects the home life, family interactions, and social relations of prostitutes and exotic dancers (for exceptions, see Dalla, 2003, 2006). However, a review of the sex work literature reveals a number of empirical and narrative accounts of sex workers' lives, from which many themes surface. These include the presence of stigma associated with sex work, role conflict/tension, familial/relationship conflict, and family issues as antecedent conditions leading to both enter and exit sex work.

Familial issues related to sex work cannot be fully comprehended without first understanding the presence of stigma associated with this industry. Crocker, Major, and Steele (1998) suggest that stigmas are marks that are devalued in some social contexts and typically lead to prejudice against the person who possesses the marks. Stigmas can be brought about by many factors, including one's profession. Indeed, scholars argue that work characterized as immoral, such as exotic dancing and prostitution, is especially likely to be associated with stigma (Bergman & Chalkley, 2007; Jackson et al., 2007). Researchers have recognized stigma associated with sex work as contributing to increased drug use (Smith & Marshall, 2007), social isolation and stress (Jackson et al., 2007; Kong, 2006), acceptance of poor treatment (Ronai, 1992), and symbolic and material exclusion (Cornish, 2006). We also note a link between stigma and secrecy, specifically the literature reveals that the stigmatized nature of sex work causes women to keep these occupations secret from family members. Studies reveal that just a small percentage of sex workers tell their children about their professions (Romans et al., 2000) and that keeping this secret "creates a great deal of stress because of the possibility that their child(ren) might discover the nature of their mother's work" (Jackson et al., 2007, p. 265). This stigma–silence connection may inform why many studies reveal sex work as an isolated, lonely existence (Dalla, 2000; Jackson et al., 2007). Furthermore, stigma associated with sex work is likely associated with the role/relationship conflict reported by individuals in the sex industry.

Ronai's (1992) autoethnographic account of her experience working as an erotic dancer illuminates the role conflict present in many sex workers. She reports that her roles as dancer, wife, and researcher clashed with one another as she struggled with the guilt of balancing the dual identity of wife/stripper. Similarly, other researchers recognize the stress inherent within sex workers as they struggle to cope with the existence of tensions at the intersection of their personal and public lives (Brewis & Linstead, 2000; Jackson et al., 2007). Stress caused by role conflict and association with a stigmatized profession may be linked to interpersonal conflict between sex workers and family members, particularly their significant others. Philaretou (2006) suggests that exotic dancers face considerable challenges in "attaining/maintaining genuine, meaningful, and anxiety-free intimate interactions with their significant others" (p. 44). Her study and others reveal that boyfriends particularly dislike women's participation in the sex industry, and this displeasure is at the root of much conflict (Jackson et al., 2007; Romans et al., 2000). Finally, Jackson et al. (2007) found that sex workers often experience conflict and generally tense relationships with other family members, including their parents, children, and other women in the sex industry. This conflict can lead to sex workers distancing from their families or exiting the industry altogether; in fact, there is a great deal of research connecting family factors to a woman's decisions to both enter and exit the sex industry.

Women's decisions to enter exotic dancing have been linked to a number of familial factors, including absence of parental guidance, stability, or rules during adolescence; not having a dependable, caring male figure; negative reinforcement from parents; and becoming a single mother (Philaretou, 2006; Sweet & Tewksbury, 2000). Similarly, women's decisions to work as a prostitute include such family-related issues as becoming a single mother, literal and symbolic abandonment by adult caregivers, failure of adult caregivers to protect from sexual victimization, and being a victim of childhood sexual abuse by either family members or others (Abramovich, 2005; Dalla, 2003). Research into factors influencing women to leave sex work is sparse. Dalla's (2006) study of the exit process of street-level prostitutes, many of whom were drug addicted, is one of the few studies examining this process. She found that women who exited prostitution were buoyed by significant relationships and emotional attachments with parents, siblings, and relational partners. The desire to be a better parent to their children was another factor motivating women to exit the sex industry. Taken together, these studies support the notion that familial relationships are integral to decisions to both enter and exit the sex industry. Still, we know very little about how female (former) sex workers make sense of "family" and perceive familial interactions as they attempt to exit the industry while simultaneously ending drug and alcohol dependence. Therefore, in concert with the objectives of this volume, the present study seeks to answer the following research question: How do present and former female sex workers conceptualize family and describe familial interactions during their attempts to exit the sex industry?

Method

In order to understand the communicative practices and patterns of the families of (former) sex workers, we focused on members of a nonprofit organization in a major southwestern city, called Life Transformations[2] (LT). LT is a Christian organization, housed in a Church of Christ, that helps women leave sexually oriented occupations. Focus group interviews took place at the church during the group's weekly meetings. In the following sections, we describe LT, its members, and its processes.

LT: Organization Overview

LT supports women in their endeavors to leave sexually oriented occupations, including prostitution and exotic dancing. This nonprofit organization also guides the women through creating new lives for themselves and their children by offering practical assistance, such as educational opportunities, financial resources, and help with job procurement. LT also provides counseling services and spiritual support. As they enter LT, prospective members must complete a 3-week trial period that includes weekly meeting attendance, disclosure of financial information, and treatment for drug and alcohol abuse. Treatment typically includes joining appropriate 12-step programs. LT touts an 80% success rate.

Participants

LT was comprised of 39 active members at the time of data collection, and 20 members participated in the focus groups. Each focus group was comprised of four to six members, with five participating in the first group, four in the second, five in the third, and six in the last. Fifteen focus group participants were white, four were African American, and one was Hispanic. Their mean age was 35.5 years, with a range of 20 to 51. Focus group interviews lasted approximately 1 hour. It is important to note here two distinctions between the first three focus groups and the final focus group. Participants in the first three focus groups (newcomer groups) had been members of LT for less than 3 months; meanwhile, participants of the fourth focus group (experienced group) had been members of LT for at least 24 months. Furthermore, participants of the first three focus groups were much more likely to have been involved in prostitution and substance abuse, while members of the fourth focus group were solely former exotic dancers.

While we did not ask participants specific questions about communication with their families, many of the questions invited the women to speak about their family interactions. We asked participants questions about whom they communicated with before, during, and after their work in the sex industry, their feelings about men, whether they kept their work a secret, and what comparisons they made between themselves and women who were not in the sex industry. Data collection occurred on-site in a private conference room. Discussions were audiotaped and transcribed with the permission of LT staff and members per institutional review board requirements as well as specific releases through LT.

Analysis

We transcribed the focus group interviews, which yielded 115 double-spaced pages of data. In the first study derived from these data, we analyzed the data using social identity theory as a framework to guide our analysis (Mayer & Richardson, 2010). For the present study, we focused our coding on those statements that related to "family." Specifically, we generated themes that included statements that were similar in meaning and related to family or familial interactions (Lindlof & Taylor, 2002). Each unit of conversation, or complete statement, fell into a discrete category and was not used to support more than one theme. Finally, we sought larger patterns among the emergent themes.

Results

Data analysis revealed that female (former) sex workers conceptualized family in three distinct ways, depending on where they were in the recovery process. Each conceptualization is characterized by unique social dynamic patterns based on familial norms and expectations; furthermore, a woman's self-identification in a particular family dictates her interaction with others. The social aggregators that create familial units are sex work and/or addiction, religious faith and/or mutual support group affiliation, and biological relations. The women in this study consistently reported navigation of these three family types, with membership in the first precluding that of the second two types overall. Accounts of life events that occurred while engaged in sex work show a rejection of traditional norms in exchange for a surprising acceptance of the sex work/drug family, as we discuss next. It is important to note that we used the women's exact words when reporting results in order to accurately portray their lived experience.

Family Type 1: Family of Sex Work and/or Addiction

The first family type we will describe is one based on common engagement in sex work and/or drug and alcohol abuse. Women in this study reveal a clear distinction between other familial types and this one. They did not name this aggregation of people as family per se, but analysis of the data reveals that these groups of people became "family" to one another. This particular family was marked by the presence of well-defined roles, norms, and closeness of relationships. Additionally, there were distinct patterns of social interaction that aligned with the expectations of this family type. The following sections describe the characteristics of the sex work and addiction family type and ways in which the women enacted those characteristics.

Characteristics and Dynamics of the Sex Work/Addiction Family: The sex work/addiction family is dependent on nothing more than proximity of women in this type of lifestyle. "Family" members come and go, with no connection existing between them other than "the life." "You just got with whoever you could get with, whoever's gettin' high," said Miriam.[3] Women reported that the people they turned to "were your drug people" and "your drug dealer." The ties among individuals were therefore weak and formed in an environment of scarcity and fear. There exists in this family type extreme suspicion of one another, the need for secrecy from biological families, and backstabbing. Rita talked about keeping her drug abuse and prostitution secret from her 20-year-old daughter. She said,

> I had days . . . where I'd stay up 4 or 5 days with the same clothes on. What I would do, I would always find somewhere to clean up. . . . When my daughter would come lookin' for me when I be gone on them days, she ask them [other prostitutes and drug users] and you know they'd be so mad they'd tell my child that. . . . But still that was nothin' you would tell somebody's child.

Two LT women talked about how they were both topless dancers, both using drugs, and living together. They found out, after coming to LT, that they had both faked being asleep at night in the same room together despite the fact they were high on methamphetamine so that the other would not suspect that they were using drugs. Overall, though, women accepted and expected everyone to be "takers" and "haters." Jeanie said, "You've been used by men so many times that you become the user." The engrained belief in scarcity, because "there was never enough," caused these women to be manipulative and devious in this family dynamic.

Drug dealers, exotic dance club owners, and "tricks" filled the traditional father-figure role in the sense that power, money, and decision-making were in their control. Mother figures were often filled by strip club "moms," tending to the needs of these women as though they were children; however, these needs were fulfilled most often in order to ensure the life of the club and income of the owner. Again, the focus of this family type was on getting money and more drugs/alcohol, so the drive of each "family" was to obtain more of both at the women's expense.

Social Interactions of the Sex Work/Addiction Family: The social interactions of women in this study supported the "taker" mentality. Glenda said that she tried to steal tricks from her friend by shouting at passersby, "She's got AIDS! Don't pick her up! . . . She got bugs on her body. You want *me*." A distinct line between the sex work/addiction family and the biological and faith family existed. An individual in the former family maintained secrecy of that involvement from her biological family and was never able to overlap it with the other two family types. "Mostly everybody that I knew were drug related or sex related, so family and stuff—I never had. I haven't seen any of my family since in like 16 years."

In fact, social norms for a woman could change in an instant, depending on her perception of the family type in which she was involved. Melvonda said,

> And then sometimes we cry [other sex work/drug family members] . . . then in the next five minutes somethin' 'd come in the doors, and it changes the whole, flips the whole script, and everybody gets dirty and messy on each other. Because then it's about who's got the most, and if I can get what you've got. The same girl that will cry and will hold you and say, "We'll do it again one day. We'll get back to it [recovery]." [But] the minute the script flips . . . [long pause]

Glenda agrees:

> Same one in the script, stab you in the back. Take everything you got. Even your man. Bye bye! [singsongy] You know.

Therefore, family type could change in an instant, along with the norms for social interaction that went with it, in the same setting. Next, we discuss the family of faith and/or mutual support.

Family Type 2: Family of Faith/Mutual Support Group

The next family type described by the women of LT was one based on faith and mutual support. This study's participants are part of an established faith-based organization, so it may seem obvious that mutual support would create a new family of sorts; however, because these women come from sex work/addiction families in which competition dominated family members' behaviors, the fact that these women become sources of strength for one another is quite remarkable. The family of faith/mutual support is characterized by acceptance and shared experiences. Social dynamics prove to be inclusive, as shown by different communication devices, both verbal and nonverbal, during our focus groups sessions.

Characteristics and Dynamics of the Faith/Mutual Support Family: The family of faith/mutual support is characterized by a spirit of understanding and the connection in having shared a common stigmatized lifestyle. The women in LT empathize in a way that outsiders cannot. Additionally, because they have known such hardship, they are more accepting of others. Melvonda said, "We're the most loving and compassionate people there is as drug addicts and alcoholics." Rita added, "And people here at LT don't judge you. They look at you and they look in your eyes and they believe you and it makes you stronger."

It is important to note the difference between being connected with faith and being connected with a faith family. Some women continued a dialogue with God while immersed in sex work and addiction, but none of the women talked about being involved in both family types at the same time. Membership in the two families appeared to be mutually exclusive. Although some women have not bought into the religious aspect of LT, those who talk about faith do so in an open way. For example, Melissa said,

> If you were tellin' me to do somethin' that was gonna help me out, I'd do it. Basically that's where I'm at right now and that's all there is because I can't sit here and say that I trust God fully and I believe Jesus, you know, God and all that, I can't say that I fully believe that. But I think I'm getting to a place where I . . .

Other women followed this sentiment with comments like "It's gonna come when you're ready" and "Every church is not for you, and until you find that fit, you struggle. But when you find it, it's gonna be so easy." Ultimately, the mutual support group here moves women toward spirituality, but how fast a woman accepts religion is secondary.

Social Interactions of the Faith/Mutual Support Family: Aside from the direct statements made by LT participants, we noted communicative devices employed that speak to the inclusive dynamic of this group. These devices range from some women high-fiving each other on discovery of specific shared sex work and/or addiction experiences to finishing each other's thoughts and ending sentences together. Of specific interest were the nonverbal cues happening in conjunction with direct comments to one woman, Penny, in our last focus group. While she was expressing her feeling of being "an outsider" in LT because of her continued marijuana use and shaky religious beliefs, the other women subtly moved their chairs so that by the end of Penny's speaking her chair had moved from behind the group circle to between two more vocal members. Support of Penny was also for her role as mother, which brings us to the third family type in this study: the family of biological connection.

Family Type 3: Family of Biological Connection

Interestingly, women in LT shared little information on their biological families until the interview with the final focus group. This group is comprised of women with longer time in LT. The longer these women were out of the sex work/addiction family, the more likely they were to be focusing on their biological families. This makes sense if only because the primary dynamic of biological family expressed by LT women is that of responsibility, and for most women it is a long road from a life of trying to escape reality to one of facing it. Melvonda said that this time in recovery, she is not going to approach her mother saying, "Here Mother, put my life back together." Mel said that she is taking responsibility for her own life now. The biological family is one that these women perceive a need to be strong for and to provide for emotionally and financially.

Characteristics and Dynamics of the Biological Family: Women in LT show a progression of familial membership from drug/addiction family to faith/mutual support families and finally to biological families. The mutual support family teaches women how to have healthy relationships after coming out of sex work and drug abuse. Participants show a belief that familial support should come only when these women are choosing a healthy life, free from sex work and addiction. Once Mel stopped asking her mother to "bail her out of jail for prostitution . . . at 45 years old," her sister stepped in. The sister required responsibility on Mel's part. This woman recounted that her sister "let [her] know things are gonna be *real* different this time!" Ultimately, for most women it came down to choosing between the sex work/drug family and the biological one.

Female former sex workers, in transitioning back to biological family membership, struggle with male familial relationships. Both potential partners and sons present new situations to navigate from a completely different perspective than that of life on the street or in the clubs. Men are not seen as equal partners, and there is considerable mistrust of them. A sense of separation between these women and the males in their biological families exists. Rita describes it well:

> I was in a mentally and physically abusive relationship one time, over 10 and a half years and when I left that I went through "non-shit" is what I call it cause I didn't have to for a whole year . . . I don't care. I'm good all by myself. I just have a problem with bein' lonely. Because of the things that I did, it's hard for me to trust what [men are] telling me and take it for face value.

These women worry about being left, deceived, lonely, and not worth staying with. Interestingly, some of the best marriages in this study are between partners who do not see each other regularly. Even among the longtime members of LT, there exists a significant struggle in knowing how to relate to men.

Social Interactions of the Biological Family: Social interactions described by the LT women support the perceived imperative of responsibility and struggle in negotiating the parental role. Regarding raising her son, Jeanie noted,

> Look, he's a child and he's askin' questions. You gotta step up out of your comfort zone right now and remember that you're a mom first of all, and what you did in your past should not affect the decisions that he needs to talk about, like girls and dating and sex and—but I find myself and I catch myself all the time buildin' that wall up. What can I say to him? What I can't say to him? I just don't trust him.

Lisa talked about needing to be a good model for her daughter, noticing that "my daughter was getting older and she could walk pretty good in some heels." The LT women clearly feel the need to provide for their children, and this is one dynamic on which they are emphatic with the men in their lives. Lisa said that she would never let a man "beat on" or "disrespect [her] girls" and that any man in her life would have to hold up his end of the financial responsibility. So although those relationships with men may feel unclear, when it comes to children, there is less questioning in these women's minds about what is acceptable.

Discussion

Overall, data analysis revealed three family types as described by female former sex workers in LT. Each family type is defined by its members, accepted norms and expectations for members' behavior, and social interactions that support the dynamics within the family. The sex work/addiction family is based solely on proximity and common engagement in "the life" and is steeped in competition and scarcity. The faith/mutual support family is based on shared experiences and a spirit of inclusion. Finally, the biological family evokes a strong sense of responsibility from these women, something from which most women sought escape in the sex work/drug family. Navigating these various familial roles proves to be a struggle for most women, and this leads us to the implications of these findings.

First, results of the present study indicated a relationship between how family was conceptualized and where a woman was in her recovery. Specifically, we suspect that family saliency might be an indicator of where a sex worker/drug addict is in her recovery process. We did not ask focus group participants direct questions about their families. Instead, those stories and examples were emergent. Stories about street "families" reflected that period of time when the women were fully engrossed in their drug addiction and sex work. As they shifted away from that lifestyle, the support group surfaced as a meaningful family type for the women. Finally, a focus on biological families, particularly by the women who had been in the program the longest, seemed to indicate full recovery. This shift to "traditional" value language might mark full recovery from sex work/drug addiction (Mayer & Richardson, 2010). Future research should explore how notions of family are altered and reflected by stigmatized life situations.

Next, this study positions stigma as an important factor for some families as they manage interactions within and to outsiders. Miller (2004) suggests that stigmas are types of stressors that can lead to a number of outcomes, including feelings of anger, anxiety, hopelessness, and fear. In turn, these emotions can be reflected in dysfunctional familial interactions. Regarding stigmatized individuals, Miller stated, "Trying to cope with everything may leave stigmatized people unable to cope with anything" (p. 40). Women in the present study deal with the same stress as the rest of society, but they also have the added negative, overarching dynamic of stigma. Participants reported isolating themselves from their biological families and maintaining secrecy during their time as sex workers. Once in recovery, they struggled with how to tell their children about their pasts. Research has identified other stigmas that families must negotiate, including stepmother roles (Christian, 2005), same-sex parenting (Landau, 2009), childlessness (Miall, 1994), and family members with AIDS (Smith & Niedermyer, 2009). Families marked by stigma are likely to increase in number. This trend provides an opportunity for communication scholars to investigate how and why stigmas are constructed, the effects on families of stigmas, how families navigate communication around stigma, and how stigmas are minimized or transformed over time.

Limitations

The most obvious limitation is that we did not include family-specific questions within the interview protocol. Future studies into the family lives of sex workers, including those addicted to drugs, should include direct questions about familial interactions. Also, women speaking about a sensitive topic may not have felt comfortable discussing some issues in a focus group setting. Including one-on-one interviews would be beneficial in future research.

Conclusion

The purpose of this volume is to explore the communicative dimensions of understudied contemporary families. This chapter addressed families that included a (former) female sex worker, typically one who used or was addicted to drugs. The increasing rate of children born into single-parent families, coupled with a stagnant economy, suggests that the number of women engaging in the stigmatized sex work will likely grow. Families that include a stigma of any sort face unique communicative challenges. They are prone to secrecy, isolation, deception, and embarrassment (Burke, 2008; Smith & Niedermyer, 2009; Stockburger, 2008). The purpose of this chapter was to suggest what "family" might mean to women working in a stigmatized industry. It is further hoped that this study will demonstrate the need for continued research into families marked by stigma.

Discussion Questions

1. Researchers have found that sex work stigmas can contribute to a number of problems. What are some of these issues?
2. What "familial factors" from childhood and beyond contribute to a woman's decision to become an exotic dancer? A prostitute?
3. Present and former female sex workers conceptualize "family" into which three categories?
4. What are the defining features and "members" of each of these groups/families?

Endnotes

[1] Occupations in the sex industry include performing in pornographic movies, erotic writing, stripping, escort service prostitution, and street-level prostitution (Sweet & Tewksbury, 2000). This study focuses on stripping, or exotic dancing, and street-level prostitution.

[2] The name of this nonprofit has been changed in order to protect the anonymity of its clientele.

[3] The names of the focus group participants have been changed to protect their confidentiality.

References

Abramovich, E. (2005). Childhood sexual abuse as a risk factor for subsequent involvement in sex work: A review of empirical findings. *Journal of Psychology and Human Sexuality, 17,* 131–146.

Bergman, M. E., & Chalkley, K. M. (2007). "Ex" marks a spot: The stickiness of dirty work and other removed stigmas. *Journal of Occupational Health Psychology, 12,* 251–265.

Brewis, J., & Linstead, S. (2000). "The worst thing is the screwing": Context and career in sex work. *Gender, Work, and Organization, 7,* 168–180.

Burke, P. (2008). *Disability and impairment: Working with children and families.* London: Jessica Kingsley Publishers.

Christian, A. (2005). Contesting the myth of the "wicked stepmother": Narrative analysis of an online stepfamily support group. *Western Journal of Communication, 69,* 27–47.

Clark-Flory, T. (2009, June 22). *Going down in the downturn: More women are turning to sex in a bad economy.* http://www.salon.com/life/feature/2009/06/22/tracy_pinched

Cornish, F. (2006). Challenging the stigma of sex work in India: Material context and symbolic change. *Journal of Community and Applied Social Psychology, 16,* 462–471.

Crocker, J., Major, B., & Steele, C. (1998). Social stigma. In D. T. Gilbert, S. T. Fiske, & G. Lindzey (Eds.), *The handbook of social psychology* (Vol. 2, 4th ed., pp. 504-553). New York: McGraw-Hill.

Dalla, R. L. (2002). Night moves: A qualitative investigation of street-level sex work. *Psychology of Women Quarterly, 26,* 63-73.

Dalla, R. L. (2003). When the bough breaks. . . . : Examining intergenerational parent-child relational patterns among street-level sex workers and their parents and children. *Applied Development Science, 7,* 216-228.

Dalla, R. L. (2006). "You can't hustle all your life": An exploratory investigation of the exit process among street-level prostituted women. *Psychology of Women Quarterly, 30,* 276-290.

Farley, M., Cotton, A., Lynne, J., Zumbeck, S., Spiwak, F., Reyes, M. E., et al. (2003). Prostitution and trafficking in nine countries: An update on violence and posttraumatic stress disorder. *Journal of Trauma Practice, 2,* 33-74.

Jackson, L. A., Bennett, C. G., & Sowinski, B. A. (2007). Stress in the sex trade and beyond: Women working in the sex trade talk about the emotional stressors in their working and home lives. *Critical Public Health, 17,* 257-271.

Kong, T. S. K. (2006). What if feels like for a whore: The body politics of women performing erotic labour in Hong Kong. *Gender, Work, and Organization, 13,* 409-429.

Landau, J. (2009). Straightening out (the politics of) same-sex parenting: Representing gay families in US print news stories and photographs. *Critical Studies in Media Communication, 26,* 80-100.

Lindlof, T. R., & Taylor, B. C. (2002). *Qualitative communication research methods* (2nd ed.). Thousand Oaks, CA: Sage.

Mayer, J., & Richardson, B. K. (2010). From "living hell" to "new normal": Self-identification strategies revealed in the development of personal narratives among female former sex workers. *Journal of Communication and Religion, 33,* 56-86.

Miall, C. (1994). Community constructs of involuntary childlessness: Sympathy, stigma, and social support. *Canadian Review of Sociology and Anthropology, 31,* 392-421.

Miller, C. (2004). Social psychological perspectives on coping with stressors related to stigma. In S. Levin & C. van Laar (Eds.), *Stigma and group inequality: Social psychological perspectives* (pp. 21-44). Mahwah, NJ: Lawrence Erlbaum Associates.

Parker, J. (2004). How prostitution works. In R. Whisnant & C. Stark (Eds.), *Not for sale: Feminists resisting prostitution and pornography* (pp. 3-14). North Melbourne: Spinifex Press.

Philaretou, A. G. (2006). Female exotic dancers: Intrapersonal and interpersonal perspectives. *Sexual Addiction and Compulsivity, 13,* 41-52.

Romans, S. E., Potter, K., Martin, J., & Herbison, P. (2000). The mental and physical health of female sex workers: A comparative study. *Australian and New Zealand Journal of Psychiatry, 35,* 75-80.

Ronai, C. R. (1992). The reflexive self through narrative: A night in the life of an erotic dancer/researcher. In C. Ellis & M. G. Flaherty (Eds.), *Investigating subjectivity: Research on lived experience* (pp. 102-124). Newbury Park, CA: Sage.

Sex workers in the recession. (2009, February 6). *The Economist.* http://www.economist.com/blogs/freeexchange/2009/02/sex_workers_in_the_recession

Smith, F. M., & Marshall, L. A. (2007). Barriers to effective drug addiction treatment for women involved in street level prostitution: A qualitative investigation. *Criminal Behavior and Mental Health, 17,* 163-170.

Smith, R. A., & Niedermyer, A. J. (2009). Keepers of the secret: Desires to conceal a family member's HIV-positive status in Namibia, Africa. *Health Communication, 24,* 459-472.

Stockburger, I. (2008). Embedded stories and the life story: Retellings in a memoir and perzine. *Narrative Inquiry, 18,* 326-348.

Sweet, N., & Tewksbury, R. (2000). "What's a nice girl like you doing in a place like this?": Pathways to careers in stripping. *Sociological Spectrum, 20,* 325-343.

Weitzer, R. (2000). Why we need more research on sex work. In R. Weitzer (Ed.), *Sex for sale* (pp. 1-13). New York: Routledge.

Chapter 37

Mothering at the Boundaries: When Relative Being is More Important than Being a Relative

Deborah Eicher-Catt

I have spent over a decade researching and writing about the communicative experiences of a marginalized group of women in our society known as "noncustodial" mothers (see Eicher-Catt, 1996, 1997, 1999, 2001, 2004a, 2004b, 2005). These women (voluntarily or not) no longer provide the primary care for their dependent children. According to the Bureau of the Census in 2000 (2010 census is not yet available), there are over 2 million noncustodial mothers in the United States, with numbers rising as courts today look on fathers more favorably in contested custody cases. By the late 1980s, two-thirds of the states had rejected the "tender years" doctrine, a policy thought to discriminate against fathers since it strongly advocated the primary role that mothers have in child care and development (Comerford, 2006). Noncustodial mothers are, therefore, becoming more prevalent on the social landscape (Paskowicz, 1982) as researchers begin to investigate their demographic characteristics (Greif, 1987; Greif & Pabst, 1988), psychological health (Coysh, Johnston, Tschann, Wallerstein, & Kline, 1989; Herrerias, 1995; Stewart, 1999) and diminished social status (Glubka, 1983; West & Kissman, 1991; McMurray, 1992). Noncustodial mothers are of various racial and ethnic backgrounds, but most are 25 to 45 years old, heterosexual, lower to middle class, and educated and have more than one child.

While most of us agree that it is possible to be an acceptable noncustodial father after marital divorce or separation—after all, as long as men do not become "deadbeat dads" and abandon their financial responsibilities, their often sporadic child visitations with their children are viewed by most Americans within the parameters of social accountability. The same societal criteria, however, do not hold true for noncustodial mothers. They often experience intense scrutiny as society automatically judges them as "unfit" mothers (Wilbur & Wilbur, 1988). There is yet no model of female parenting that legitimizes this mothering style within the wider network of social relations (Eicher-Catt, 2004b). The ongoing role these mothers play in their children's lives is highly ambiguous; they both are and are not mothers—especially if we adopt the view that to be a mother means enacting everyday caretaking behaviors that reflect child care gendered norms. I realized this early on in my own experience of being a noncustodial mother of my two young sons. During that time, I lived the immensity of this precarious situation all too well. I often felt like I was "living on the edge" of social and personal norms that produced a palpable, lived-body negativity that shaped our experiences together (Eicher-Catt, 2004a). Over the last many years, I conducted numerous qualitative interviews with other noncustodial mothers and heard their stories of heartbreak and exasperation as they, too, struggled to mother at the boundaries of societal expectations for what constitutes "good enough" mothers (Thurer, 1994). There is not, after all, a social stock of knowledge about being noncustodial from which they might draw guidance (Schutz, 1970). The supposed sacrality of motherhood eludes them (Eicher-Catt, 2003).

Herein, I begin by briefly discussing the double bind (Bateson, 1972) or paradoxical situation that most of these women face as they attempt to reconcile conflicted "older and newer definitions of self" (Bartky, 1990, p. 2). This double bind, enacted through their discursive practices with their children and others, necessarily instantiates a lived oscillation between perceiving their role either through what I call a *cultural frame* or a *personal frame* of reference. The ensuing paradox activates an existential crisis for them that is extremely unsettling—physically, socially, and psychologically. This paradox is derived primarily by women desperately hanging on to the idea that they are, after all, still a blood *relative* to their children, and this thought guides their overall approach to their difficult situation.

What interests me the most, however, in attempting to understand their communicative experiences of visitation is a central theme that I found running through some of these mothers' narratives as they described their various attempts to mother at the boundaries of mother–child relations. While this theme of experience certainly feeds particular *expressions* (strategies and tactics) they use with their children during visitation, it is derived, more importantly, from their *perceptual* ability to reframe their interactions (Ruesch & Bateson, 1987) with their children in ways quite different than our traditional understanding of mothering. Rather than relying on the social position that the designation "mother" provides to legitimize (and socially constrain) their encounters with their children (exemplified in the idea of *being a relative*), I detail an alternative *perceptual scheme* that some women use that successfully brings them closer to creating meaningful, productive, and long-lasting mother–child relations. A few mothers learn that emphasizing their relations with their children from the standpoint that all concerned are "*relative beings*" (Bateson, 1979, 1991; Ruesch & Bateson, 1987) over and above "*being relatives*" actually allows for potential change, growth, and relational satisfaction.

Hanging on to "Being a Relative": A Lived Double Bind

A key to understanding mothers' experiences of visiting their children does not come from focusing on just their particular *expressions* (strategies and tactics) they use with their children during visitation. While the content of and manner by which their messages are exchanged are of importance to negotiating their difficult situation, I found in my investigations that women's *perceptions* of their relationships with their children and others played a more vital role in texturing their lived experiences and their successes and failures at being noncustodial. I label these communicative mechanisms *perceptual schemes* because they provided mothers with the metacommunicative ground by which to understand their spatial and temporal parameters from which to speak/gesture as visiting mothers (Ruesch & Bateson, 1987). I found two predominant schemes that often are in opposition, producing a lived double bind, that is, "a situation in which no matter what a person does, he 'can't win'" (Bateson, 1972, p. 201).

The first perceptual scheme I call the *cultural frame of reference*. Within this frame, mothers overidentify with the others (their absent children) to the detriment of their own well-being. There is often a longing or fascination for the child(ren)—now more absent than present, especially between visitations. The absent typicality of traditional motherhood seems to take "possession" of mothers and affects their psychological and physical well-being as they struggle to measure up to its cultural standards. "Seeing one's children" and "being a mother" again become all-consuming motivations for these women. Not unlike custodial mothers, these behaviors reflect the socially legitimized sacrificial stance that society expects women to take toward children. They want to hang on to and continue to try to fulfill these traditional codes of mothering practices that are culturally derived through a complex network of sign systems (Peirce, 1955). They attempt to overcompensate for the perceived inadequacies their current social status entails. Repeatedly during visitations, particularly when frequent disciplinary issues with their children arise by their diminishing authority, they will assert, "but *I* am your mother" in an attempt to reinstantiate their legitimacy, especially when new stepmothers or live-in girlfriends appear on the scene. Here they show the most signs of cultural accommodation.

Unfortunately, the cultural frame only accentuates their failure to live up to the traditional/typical code of motherhood. They are, after all, mothers and yet not—mothers who are no longer providing their children with *primary* care and nurturance. The cultural frame of visitation then offers mothers a hollow or barren gift (the inappropriate role of "visiting nonstranger"). It is the barren gift that leaves them grieving and wanting more.

The cultural frame is not the only metacommunicative stance that mothers employ as they struggle to find their personal/social footing. Mothers also try to foster a new personal sense of their self-worth, so they overidentify with the fledgling self. Rooted in modern individualistic thinking, within this frame, mothers are driven by a desire to escape the constraints imposed by the cultural idea of motherhood and the current negativity that entails. It is as though the "barrenness" they experienced in attempting to meet an illusory standard of motherhood is cast aside. The cultural frame serves as an index of oppression, after all, and it is a form of oppression these women can do without. Within this new *personal frame*, therefore, mothers appeal to the more personal level of interaction with their children by focusing on constituting a renewed sense of self within its parameters. Many ask, "Don't I also deserve a life?" The struggle to maintain a coherent sense of self is deeply dependent, however, on the fledgling mother–child relationship, a situation that typically thwarts their efforts.

Above all, this perceptual strategy nurtures their appeal to what they define as the more "natural" or "real" connection between mothers and children. Understandably, their abandonment of the cultural markers of motherhood is replaced by what is considered more real—the personal, the tangible. Mothers' narratives are filled with references to the "bonds," sometimes labeled as "spiritual," that *naturally* seem to exist between a mother and her child(ren). Women refer to the physicality of this bond as birth mothers, and its remembrance helps to ease the lived ambiguity their visiting status so often instantiates. By appealing to the "real," naturalized bond, mothers attempt to deny the cultural constraints of traditional motherhood while accentuating the importance of a blood connection. Mothers assume that the blood connection reinstantiates their self-worth. As a result, mothers, in this frame often assert the name "mother," especially when their continued power and legitimacy is suspect.

Unfortunately, these two perceptual frames often collide in mothers' experiences as they struggle to make sense of continuously changing social contexts. It produces a lived oscillation or double bind (Bateson, 1972) as mothers employ an either/or-motivated logic as they try to decide how to respond (expressions/perceptions) to their difficult situation both during and between visits. Simultaneously, mothers realize that they are still mothers; that is, they can lay claim to the role, and yet, in actuality, they are enacting an alternative, culturally defined "visiting nonstranger" role that accentuates their social precarity. This lived double bind activates their existential crisis. Over time, living this double bind produces what I call a radicalized space of subjectivity (Eicher-Catt, 2001). Some mothers become completely immobilized psychologically by their situation and find themselves "staring at the walls," being "numb," or even "comatose" (Eicher-Catt, 1997) for hours.

Over time, it becomes increasingly difficult for these women to understand the operative social and personal rules to follow in a given situation that would make them more competent at being noncustodial (Eicher-Catt, 2004a). Becoming "tangled in the rules," as the double bind entails (Bateson, 1972), is too often a lived reality. For example, whether they choose to frame their experience in terms of *cultural* expectations (which entails an atypical perception of the mother–child relationship) or in terms of *personal* expectations of what constitutes a mother–child bond (which entails an atypical perception of what constitutes visitation), mothers continue to vacillate between the two frames of experience. Moreover, if mothers choose to frame a particular visit according to their perceptions of it being a typical "social" visit, that is, characteristic of what most people would imagine as a visit, then they appeal to the social visit as a system of regulative rules (Searle, 1969). At the same time, they must employ constitutive rules (Searle, 1969) to negotiate their atypical situation with their children; that is, they are "visiting" (which is a strange situation) when they should be "living" with them (which is a familiar situation).

On the other hand, if mothers choose to frame a particular visit according to their perceptions of it being a typical "mother–child bond," that is, characteristic of what most people would imagine that type of interaction to be ("family"), then they appeal to the social convention of that bond as a system of regulative rules. At the same time, they must employ constitutive rules regarding how they frame the visit in order to renegotiate the visit in an atypical fashion (e.g., "distant family"/ familiar at a distance). In either case, the boundaries and social rules that normally specify appropriate interaction always seem problematic. We are reminded that "where paradox contaminates human relations, disease [system failure] appears" (Watzlawick, Beavin, & Jackson, 1967, p. 201). It is no wonder that we witness an expanse of pathological problems in the lives of these mothers as they attempt to adapt or learn new ways of dealing with their seemingly untenable position.

On closer examination, we find that underlying the double bind is an operative premise that texturizes their overall approach. Regardless of the perceptual frame they employ, the metamessage that they are still a *blood relative* to their children—whether it is culturally or physically/psychically understood—seems to pacify their fledgling egos and psychological well-being. The thought of still *being a relative*, therefore, undergirds their discursive practices, their choices of expressions and perceptions.

Unfortunately, approaching their circumstances from the premise of *being a relative* negatively shapes how they perceive themselves in relation to their children and their ensuing interactions. By adopting this communicative stance, each person (*relative*) is reduced to a "thing" for the other; for example, a "mother" is viewed as a "thing," a person who merely occupies a social role and performs particular care giving duties. Likewise, a "son" or "daughter" becomes a thing that further translates into a "possession"—an underlying assumption, we would agree, that feeds most custody disputes. For once we "name" the relationship as "mother and son," we set in motion, Bateson would say (1972, 1979), all kinds of havoc in our thinking since we make these language categories of relationships mere "things" that then dominate how we approach interactions. Above all, "things" are viewed as static entities with predetermined meanings that are "objects" we manipulate and possess. As Bateson (1991) claims, such ways of thinking distort or constrain our perceptions and cause us to think about lived experience in terms of quantities and possessions. Accordingly, mothers look at the family dynamic from the perspective of merely enacting social roles (e.g., "mother" and "sons") that operate on the basis of sedimented cultural meanings for self and other. Not surprisingly, communication becomes strategic as mothers enact what I call *posturing* interpersonal behaviors. Unfortunately, the result of *posturing* is a "leveling out," a "flattening" or symmetrization (Watzlawick et al., 1967) of interactional experiences in parenting that translates as mundane and unsatisfying personal relationships.

From a systems perspective, premising relationships on *being a relative* produces what Bateson (1979) refers to as *disintegration* of the whole organism; in this case, experience is now reduced to recognizable/nameable categorizes that are viewed as separate and distinct entities. The "pattern which connects" (Bateson, 1979, 1991) self and other is eclipsed. It is no wonder, then, that many mothers describe being noncustodial as a disciplinary "sentence" and quickly claim "victim" status as they describe their plight (Eicher-Catt, 1996). Unaware that their perceptions of their experience are guided by the value choices they make, it appears to them that they fall prey to an uncanny oppressor (both culturally and personally) no matter where they turn. Unwittingly premising their attempts to mother on *being a relative* serves only, then, to minimize their value choices for themselves and their children from within predetermined categories of experience. More important, the overall *process* of communication is presumed and not problematized. In the end, *being a relative* disciplines mothers' thoughts and actions (Foucault, 1979) at a time and within a space of social circumstance that cries out for communicative openness, flexibility, and contingency.

Taking a New Angle: Relative Being

Do any mothers, seemingly locked into an existential paradox, show signs of emancipation from the oppressiveness of their situation? A few mothers do, and these are the women who find a new operative, communicative frame by which to enact mothering. They refuse to merely adopt either pregiven frame of reference (*the cultural* or the *personal*), the double bind that induces, and the discursive competencies that each frame necessarily dictates (Eicher-Catt, 2004a). They refuse to see motherhood as an abstract "thing" that one characteristically becomes on the birth of a child. Instead, they exercise their ability to choose a different context for interaction with their children and others that produces a new style of mothering. Rather than adopting the perceptions of others as their own and sentencing themselves to an unsatisfying existence, some mothers exhibit spontaneity toward their children and situation of visitation that forecasts the importance of communicative practices.

They describe this process as taking a "new angle" toward mothering. This entails allowing children to see them as separate and distinct from the cultural prescriptions inherent with "*being a relative/mother*." This requires a presentation of themselves in relation to their children that accentuates both the fluid nature of their identities as women and their newly developing identities as noncustodial mothers. There is personal risk in this approach, however, because women have to demonstrate the very vulnerability that inheres within their difficult circumstance as noncustodial. It is precisely this vulnerability, of course, that mothers want to escape, and such efforts typically activate the detrimental logic of double-bind thinking.

For those women who do succeed in this new approach, however, they describe appearing more "human" to their children because they stand before them, complete with imperfections and a willingness to remain open to the contingent, ambiguous nature of their situation. No longer tied to traditional designations of what it means to mother or be a woman in our culture, these women relate to their children as unique "persons" rather than merely as "children," a reductive *category* of experience. They focus on the particularity and immediacy of their encounters with their children, a perceptual move that continually problematizes the experience of communication rather than taking it for granted. One mother tells how she is "a better person for leaving" her ex-husband and believes, "I am a better mom because I have been able to let go. My kids used to be my life." Making our kids "our life" reflects, of course, *being a relative* way of thinking, dictating that we look on ourselves and others as "things" and instantiating an economy of power and dominance. Another mother with whom I spoke concurs. As she states, "I feel like I am a better mother when I am with them." Ultimately, as one mother put it succinctly, "Noncustodial mothers are more 'human' than the other parent," which allows the relationships with their children to take different "angles." This perceptual stance is refreshing, many mothers admit, as they begin to honor the primacy of the *relationship* over and above the social roles each typically delegates.

Consequently, mothers give themselves "permission" to discover what mothering means to them in this new context of discourse rather than appealing to predetermined codes of understanding. When they are able to interact with their children within this new frame, the *process* of being with their children overrides the *form* typical visits should take. Because of the unusualness that inheres within this new discursive space of mothering, relationships with their children also begin to take on "mysterious" new qualities that seem to produce positive affect for all involved. As I argue elsewhere (Eicher-Catt, 1996), this mysteriousness seems to foreshadow a sacrality of motherhood that eludes typical routinized enactments of mothering.

As a result of this perceptual shift, rather than a "leveling out" or symmetrization of mothering communicative practices (as we see with the *being a relative* stance), mothers within this new context actually intensify *complementarity and differentiation* (Watzlawick et al., 1967). This perceptual maneuver requires that they not only admit that their status as mothers *is* different but also embrace that difference. This is not easy. However, they come to believe this approach brings more "quality" to their ongoing experiences of mothering and reduces, at the societal level, being held to a quantitative assessment of mothering competencies in which they always fall short (Bateson, 1979).

While on paper this perceptual shift seems simple, the lived experience of making this shift is anything but, which testifies to the lived-body constraints that such dominating cultural signs as motherhood pose for most women. As anthropologist Dorothy Lee (1986) claims, our culture does very little to help women take an alternative perspective on motherhood. As a matter of fact, "it interferes," since our "language encourages [us] to see [ourselves] as having, possessing, a baby" (p. 77). Foremost, this new shift requires mothers to step outside of their existing frames of reference (the *cultural* and the *personal*) and develop an *awareness of their situation as a double bind* and, more important, their *perceptual complicity* in its constitution. The successful mothers are those who recognize, in other words, the *power of perceptual choice* that they possess as human beings, not merely the power of *expressive* choice. Once they embody this awareness, they describe it as inhaling a "breath of fresh air," for it enables them the freedom to just "be" with their children. Privileging this "beingness" is psychologically, physically, and socially *integrating*, as they begin to experience the sacred unity that existential relatedness invokes (Bateson, 1991; Bateson & Bateson, 1987). They no longer feel as though they are living out a "sentence" under the dominating sign of motherhood.

Not surprisingly, looking closely at these new configurations of mothering, we find an alternative underlying theme that motivates their interactional logics. Instead of emphasizing *being a relative*, which, as we have seen, sediments discursive practices, these women unwittingly demonstrate how productive it is to approach mother–child relations ontologically, that is, to emphasize *the relation* between things over and above *being a relative*. By setting aside the typicality of experience provided by cultural definitions of "mother" and "child," successful mothers learn that it is, foremost, *within the relation* between them and their children that those very understandings of what it means to be a mother arise (Bakhtin, 1981). Taking the stance toward visitation as *relative beings* (Bateson, 1972, 1979; Deely, 1990; Hoffmeyer, 2008) thus affords women the opportunity to stay focused and attuned to their ongoing relationship—rather than worrying about what they ought to be doing or saying. They learned that the *process* of *being with*—where communicative choices are continuously problematized—creates the space and time with their children that possibilizes relational satisfaction and the opportunity for a true "authentic encounter." As Von Eckartsberg (1965) so eloquently states, an encounter "is a creative act and experience in that it allows and makes for a new and shared social reality to emerge which would be impossible for any one person alone. True encounter expands one's horizon and awareness, it enriches one's experience" (p. 209). These women appreciate that *the relationship* between themselves and their children is the most important sign of familial health and growth, not whether they are living up to a social standard. They begin to realize that "*relative being* seems to have a reality of its own which cannot be reduced to the individual persons that substantiates the relation" (Hoffmeyer, 2008, p. 33). And it is to this new, much-appreciated, *interdependent* reality that they slowly begin to gravitate.

The irony of this perceptual shift for noncustodial mothers should not go unnoticed, however. For, in order to find, create, or capture what it means to be a "mother," mothers must relinquish their attachment to the sedimented cultural sign (Peirce, 1955) in order to create or capture the lived potential of mothering inherent in their ongoing relations with their children. Approaching their tenuous situation from the perspective of *relative being* thus possibilizes their existence (and their children's) in new ways that actually allow for potential relational change and growth. Ultimately, they learn that "maternity *is* a relationship" (Lee, 1986, p. 77, emphasis added), not a "thing." Only when mothers successfully negotiate this perceptual shift can living on the edge of familial life take on a whole new, productive meaning.

Conclusion/Implications

The plight of noncustodial mothers testifies to the contested terrain of motherhood in general. The atypical appearance of noncustodial mothering on the social landscape ruptures and fractures the typical discursive terrain of motherhood. Yet its presence signals not only the functioning of power and cultural dominance when it comes to parenting practices but also their possible transformation (Foucault, 1971). At the very least, the decentering of the mother–child relationship induced by noncustody reveals a new discursive space, one that, if properly conceived, could transgress the rigid parameters of routinized mother–child existence. As shown, the typicality of approaching parenting as *being a relative* does not serve these women in their efforts to create *meaningful* relationships with their children. We must question if such a stance serves custodial parents as well. Seeing parent–child relations as a mere interaction of "things" or people involved commits an epistemological error because it keeps us locked into dualistic thinking that separates people from the experiences they create *through relations* (Bateson, 1979; Bateson & Bateson, 1987).

By examining the experiences of noncustodial mothers, we are led to an alternative perceptual approach—that of *relative being*, where new configurations of parenting might arise that more adequately nurture and sustain familial relationships. Bateson (1979) reminds us, after all, that *relevance* means "connectedness," and it is to the "patterns of connectedness" (not to the "things" connected) that we should remain focused if we want to understand the communicative dimensions of the living world. Above all, *relative being* certainly problematizes the communication process, which inherently enlivens parental discourse and action. While I must admit that I was not always successful during my period of being noncustodial, I did find that when I approached our situation from the perspective of *relative being*, the most important and rewarding times between us were created. Both my sons and I continue to cherish those times.

Discussion Questions

1. In your opinion, does American society look down on noncustodial mothers? Explain.
2. Describe the "cultural" and "personal" frame of references discussed in this chapter. Which one do you believe pressures women more? Why?
3. Explain the difference between "being a relative" and "relative being."
4. What are some of the pros and cons of choosing to be a "relative being" rather than a "relative"?
5. This chapter claims that "our language encourages us to see ourselves as possessing a baby." What are your thoughts regarding this statement?

References

Bakhtin, M. M. (1981). *Dialogic imagination: Four essays* (M. Holquist, Trans.). Austin: University of Texas Press.

Bartky, S. L. (1990). *Femininity and domination: Studies in the phenomenology of oppression*. New York: Routledge.

Bateson, G. (1972). *Steps to an ecology of mind*. New York: Ballantine.

Bateson, G. (1979). *Mind and nature: A necessary unity*. New York: E. P. Dutton.

Bateson, G. (1991). *A sacred unity: further steps to an ecology of mind, Gregory Bateson* (R. Donaldson, Ed.). New York: HarperCollins.

Bateson, G., & Bateson, M. C. (1987). *Angels fear: Toward an epistemology of the sacred*. New York: Bantam Books.

Comerford, L. (2006). Power and resistance in U.S. child custody mediation. *Atlantic Journal of Communication, 14*(3), 173-190.

Coysh, W. S., Johnston, J. R., Tschann, J. M., Wallerstein, J., & Kline, M. (1989). Parental post-divorce adjustment in joint and sole physical custody families. *Journal of Family Issues, 10*(1), 52-71.

Deely, J. (1990). *Basics of semiotics*. Bloomington: Indiana University Press.

Eicher-Catt, D. (1996). *Searching for the sacrality of motherhood.* Unpublished doctoral dissertation, Southern Illinois University, Carbondale.

Eicher-Catt, D. (1997). Mobilizing motherhood: Mothers' experiences of visiting their children. In L. A. M. Perry & P. Geist (Eds.), *Courage of conviction: Women's words, women's wisdom* (pp. 201-219). Mountain View, CA: Mayfield.

Eicher-Catt, D. (1999). Rhetorical reflexivity and motherhood morality: A semiotics of mothers' intuition. In *7th International Congress Proceedings of the International Association of Semiotic Studies* (pp. 11-23).

Eicher-Catt, D. (2001). A communicology of female/feminine embodiment: The case of non-custodial motherhood. *American Journal of Semiotics, 17*(4),93-130.

Eicher-Catt, D. (2003). The logic of the sacred in Bateson and Peirce. *American Journal of Semiotics, 19*(1-4),95-126.

Eicher-Catt, D. (2004a). Non-custodial mothering: A cultural paradox of competent performance-performative competence. *Journal of Contemporary Ethnography, 32*(1),72-108.

Eicher-Catt, D. (2004b). Non-custodial mothers and mental health: When absence makes the heart break, *Family Report, 49*(1), F7-F8.

Eicher-Catt, D. (2005). Advancing family communication scholarship: Toward a communicology of the family. *Journal of Family Communication, 5*(2),103-121.

Foucault, M. (1979). *Discipline and punish: The birth of the prison* (A. Sheridan, Trans.). New York: Random House.

Glubka, S. (1983). Out of the stream: An essay on unconventional motherhood. *Feminist Studies, 9*(2), 223-234.

Greif, G. L., & Pabst, M. S. (1988). *Mothers without custody.* Lexington, MA: D. C. Heath & Co.

Greif, G. L. (1987). Mothers without custody. *Social Work, 32*(1), 11-166.

Herrerias, C. (1995). Non-custodial mothers following divorce. *Marriage and Family Review, 20*(1-2), 233-243.

Hoffmeyer, J. (2008). From thing to relation. On Bateson's bioanthropology. In J. Hoffmeyer (Ed.), *A legacy for living systems: Gregory Bateson as precursor to biosemiotics* (pp. 27-44). New York: Springer.

Lee, D. (1986). *Valuing the self: What we can learn from other cultures.* Long Grove, IL: Waveland Press.

McMurray, A. (1992). Influences on parent-child relationships in non-custodial mothers. *Australian Journal of Marriage and Family, 13*(3), 138-147.

Paskowicz, P. (1982). *Absentee mothers.* New York: Allanheld, Osmun & Co.

Peirce, C. S. (1955). Logic as semiotic: The theory of signs. In J. Buchler (Ed.), *The philosophical writings of Peirce* (pp. 98-119). New York: Dover.

Ruesch, J., & Bateson, G. (1987). *Communication: The social matrix of psychiatry.* New York: Norton.

Schutz, A. (1970). *On phenomenology and social relations.* Chicago: University of Chicago Press.

Searle, J. R. (1969). *Speech acts: An essay in the philosophy of language.* New York: Cambridge University Press.

Stewart, S. (1999). Nonresident mothers' and fathers' social contact with children. *Journal of Marriage and Family, 61,* 894–907.

Thurer, S. L. (1994). *The myths of motherhood: How culture reinvents the good mother.* Boston: Houghton Mifflin.

Von Eckartsberg, R. (1965). Encounter as the basic unit of social interaction. *Humanitas, 1*(2), 195–215.

Watzlawick, P., Beavin, J., & Jackson, D. (1967). *Pragmatics of human communication: A study of interactional patterns, pathologies, and paradoxes.* New York: Norton.

West, B., & Kissman, K. (1991). Mothers without custody: Treatment issues. *Journal of Divorce and Remarriage, 16,* 229–237.

Wilbur, J. R., & Wilbur, M. (1988). The noncustodial parent: Dilemmas and interventions. *Journal of Counseling and Development, 66,* 434–437.

Tomorrow's Vision of Family

"It is not observed in history that families improve with time"—*George William Curtis*

On the surface, Curtis' (n.d.) quote seems bleak. However, we contend that, when studying the evolution of families, functional improvement is neither a fair nor appropriate consideration. The evolution and role of the family in society has typically been guided by its meaning and purpose—a lens to help us understand families of the past and speculate on families of the future. Essays in this reader and works in other modern family volumes from multiple disciplines (Albers, 1999; Arnold, 2008; Bray & Stanton, 2012; Coontz, Parson, & Raley, 2008; Turner & West, 2006; Walsh, 2003) provide evidence of the difficulty for predicting the future meaning and purposes of American families. A general understanding of the readings fortified by our own perspectives yield five interdependent axioms, or *self-evident truths*, to be considered for predicting the future of families in the United States: humans will form groups; families are unique to their times; people migrate; families are impacted by internal and external variables; and families will be perpetuated by meaningful and positive expressions.

Humans always have and will continue to form groups. In western society, these groups are referred to as families. Even travelers or single-person families have supportive persons that they treat as "family-like." R. E. Simons, (2012) clarifies what he calls the psychological, sociological, spiritual, economic, and political "substrata" of the future for families. He forwards, "The future of family resilience lies in the people, especially couples becoming more aware . . . [that the] future holds avant-garde identities for the family as they try on new behaviors and search for that which is comfortable for them" (p. 2). For everyone beyond the most isolated hermits, we are intrinsically bound, psychologically, sociologically, spiritually, economically, and politically, to create family-style environments.

Families are unique to the times. Just like families of the past: cave dwellers who relied on hunting and gathering; pre-industrialization families fixed on agriculture; or 50's families that encouraged and linked small town values to increasing electrical technology, families of today are in motion. In our rapidly changing world, fluctuations in the environment, demographics, economic conditions, religious views, social beliefs, political tendencies, technology and health care significantly influence families and make their transformations visible. All of these unpredictable elements along with emotional and psychological variations within individuals create potent subtexts in the evolutionary process of casting families. As a result, a considerable paradox arises by the motion of contemporary families. Families of the future are unpredictable; they are subject to the normal process of change and daily transitions, yet they are often perceived and treated as a stable base offering security and fulfilling individual needs.

Humans migrate for multiple reasons. According to Massey et al. (1993), "Over the past 30 years, immigration has emerged as a major force throughout the world" (p. 431). Whether voluntary or involuntary, migration has always affected kinship dynamics. As groups of people pass through environments, family members are often separated and social beliefs and norms are reformed. Migratory movements are accompanied by beliefs, values, attitudes and behaviors that shape families in new and uncommon environments. "The emergence of international migration as a basic structural feature of nearly all industrialized countries testifies to the strength and coherence of the underlying forces" (Massey et al., 1993, pp. 431–432). These forces have in the past and will always have consequences for future families.

Families are impacted by internal and external variables. With the vast array of psycho-socio-cultural variables that influence modern families, that which is typical for families of this day and age bears few resemblances to families of the ancient past. The future of families is subject to the same evolutionary processes. In Vangelisti's *Handbook of Family Communication* Kathleen Galvin (2004) asserts that families of the future will:

> (a) reflect an increasing diversity of self-conceptions, (b) live increasingly within four and five generations of familial connection, (c) function in a world of health-related genetic discoveries and fast-paced medical advances, (d) encounter rapidly changing environments due to unprecedented technological change, and (e) search for new ways to protect and enhance family life (p. 676).

Based on what is now being experienced in the U.S., Galvin's assertions are more than reasonable. As the culture becomes more complex, families and the notions about families can be expected to diversify. As humans in western society live full lives, intergenerational relationships will naturally grow accordingly. As societies are confronted with advanced health issues, both damaging (e.g., drug abuse, HIV, obesity, etc.) and exotic (e.g., laser therapy, chemotherapy, gene therapy, etc.), family life can be expected to become more complicated. The exponential growth of technology has already saturated families in both developed and developing countries and there is no end in sight. Families will ultimately be forced to adjust to the massive membrane of technology that is enveloping the planet. It is without recourse that the resiliency of families will be tested.

The life of families will be perpetuated by meaningful and positive expressions—in that dialogue and interpersonal relationships will sustain the pulses of families. The life expectancies of families, however, will be regulated by biology, off-spring and collective family memories, stories, and gatherings. Communication will serve family members well and reinforce positive potential that families need for nurturing and being safe havens for members living in a complex world. Contemporary families are faced with a daunting task as they struggle to achieve social legitimacy. Just because evotypical family structures appear in significant numbers, families are being legislated by politics, courts, and religions. The future promises the same for families as they seek to adapt to evolutionary changes. Currently, the U.S. is dealing with major structural changes within families; However, Whitchurch & Dickson (1999) advance that communicative definitions of family will be privileged over structural definitions and will necessitate new ways of talking about families. It appears that communication or structure, however, do not have to be diametrically opposed. It is likely that *both* communication and structure, along with tolerance and ingenuity, will determine the future language of families.

In conclusion, using history as a predictor of the potential for survival, families will remain a primary cornerstone of ongoing societies. Families of the future—biological or "more-than-blood," will be shaped by individual or group encounters, necessitating complex or simple actions and communication. These fluctuating dynamics, situated within familial contexts, will continue to provide a fertile environment for our personal growth. It is within the security of this growth that families will sustain their existence and give human beings, individually and collectively, a renewed sense of spirit, today, and visions of a powerful legacy, tomorrow.

References

Albers, C. (1999). *Sociology of families: Readings*. Thousand Oaks, CA: Sage.

Arnold, L. B. (2008). *Family Communication: Theory and research*. Boston: Allyn and Bacon.

Bray, J. H. & Stanton, M. (Eds.), (2012). *The Wiley-Blackwell handbook of family psychology*. Hoboken, N.J., John Wiley and Sons.

Coontz, S. (Ed.), (2008). *American Families: A multicultural reader* (2nd Ed.). New York, NY: Routledge.

Curtis, G. W. (n.d.). BrainyQuote.com. Retrieved March 3, 2013, from BrainyQuote.com Web site: http://www.brainyquote.com/quotes/quotes/g/georgewill156792.html

Galvin, K. (2004). The family of the future: What do we face? In A. L. Vangelisti (Ed.), *Handbook of Family Communication*, (pp. 675–698). Mahwah, NJ: Lawrence Erlbaum Associates.

Massey, D. S., Arango, J., Hugo, G., Kouaouci, A., Pellegrino, A., & Taylor, J. E. (Sept. 1993). Theories of international migration: A review and appraisal. *Population and Development Review, 19* (3), pp. 431–466.

Simons, R. E. (2012). The future of the family: Understanding our present to predict family resilience. Unpublished manuscript. Simons Family Institute.

Turner, L. H., & West, R. (Eds.), (2006). *The family communication sourcebook*. Thousand Oaks, CA: Sage.

Walsh, F. (Ed.), (2003). *Normal Family Processes: Growing diversity and complexity* (3rd ed.). New York, NY: Guilford.

Whitchurch, G. G., & Dickson, F. C. (1999). A communication perspective on families. In M. B. Sussman, S. K. Steinmetz, & G. Peterson (Eds.), *Handbook of marriage and the family* (2nd ed., pp. 687–704). New York: Springer/Plenum Press.